THE
FORGOTTEN
SOLDIER

THE
FORGOTTEN
SOLDIER

WAR ON THE RUSSIAN FRONT—
A TRUE STORY

GUY SAJER

CASSELL

Cassell Military Paperbacks

Cassell
Wellington House, 125 Strand
London WC2R 0BB

First published in Great Britain by Weidenfeld & Nicolson in 1971
This paperback edition published in 1999

15 17 19 20 18 16 14

A CIP catalogue record for this book is available from the British Library

ISBN-13 978-0-3043-5240-1
ISBN-10 0-3043-5240-3

Printed and bound in Great Britain by
Cox & Wyman Ltd., Reading, Berks.

The Orion Publishing group's policy is to use papers that are
natural, renewable and recyclable products and made from wood
grown in sustainable forests. The logging and manufacturing
processes are expected to conform to the environmental regulations
of the country of origin.

www.orionbooks.co.uk

CONTENTS

AUTHOR'S PREFACE

Guy Sajer ... who are you?

My parents were country people, born some hundreds of miles apart – a distance filled with difficulties, strange complexities, jumbled frontiers, and sentiments which were equivalent but untranslatable.

I was produced by this alliance, straddling this delicate combination, with only one life to deal with its manifold problems.

I was a child, but that is without significance. The problems had existed before I did, and I discovered them.

Then there was the war, and I married it because there was nothing else when I reached the age of falling in love.

I had to shoulder a brutally heavy burden. Suddenly there were two flags for me to honour, and two lines of defence – the Siegfried and the Maginot – and powerful external enemies. I entered the service, dreamed, and hoped. I also knew cold and fear in places never seen by Lilli Marlene.

A day came when I should have died, and after that nothing seemed very important.

So I have stayed as I am, without regret, separated from the normal human condition.

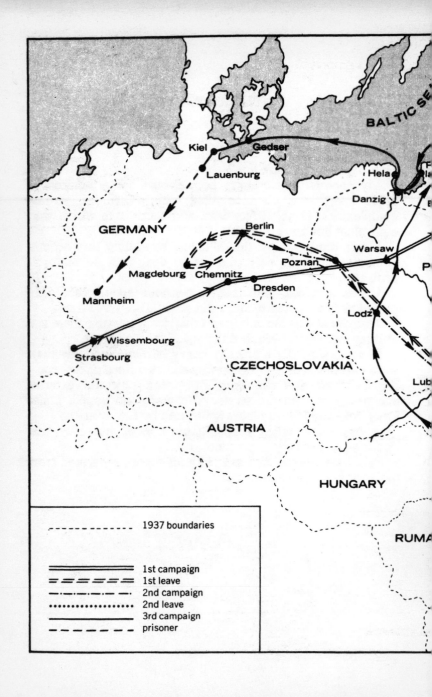

BALTIC SEA

Kiel
Gedser
Lauenburg
Hela
Danzig

GERMANY
Berlin
Warsaw
Magdeburg Chemnitz
Poznan
Mannheim
Dresden
Lodz
Wissembourg
Strasbourg
CZECHOSLOVAKIA
Lub

AUSTRIA

HUNGARY

RUMA

- - - - - - - - - - - - - 1937 boundaries

━━━━━━━━━━━━ 1st campaign
═ ═ ═ ═ ═ ═ 1st leave
─ · ─ · ─ · ─ · ─ 2nd campaign
· · · · · · · · · · · · · · · 2nd leave
━━━━━━━━━━━━ 3rd campaign
─ ─ ─ ─ ─ ─ prisoner

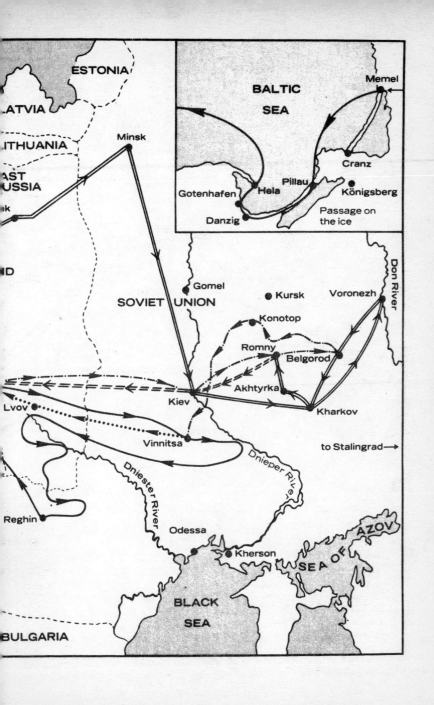

PROLOGUE

July 18, 1942. I arrive at the Chemnitz barracks, a huge oval building, entirely white. I am much impressed, with a mixture of admiration and fear. At my request, I am assigned to the 26th section of the squadron commanded by Flight Commandant Rudel. Unfortunately, I fail to pass the Luftwaffe tests, but those few moments on board the JU-87s will stay with me as a glorious memory. We live with an intensity I have never before experienced. Each day brings something new. I have a brand-new uniform, which fits me perfectly, and a pair of boots, not new but in first-class condition. I am very proud of my appearance. The food is good. I learn some military songs, which I warble with an atrocious French accent. The other soldiers laugh. They are destined to be my first comrades in this place.

Basic training in the infantry, where they send me next, is less amusing than the life of an aviator. The combat course is the most severe physical challenge I have ever experienced. I am exhausted, and several times fall asleep over my food. But I feel marvellous, filled with a sense of joy which I can't understand after so much fear and apprehension.

On the 15th of September, we leave Chemnitz, and march twenty-five miles to Dresden, where we board a train for the east.

We cross a large piece of Poland, stopping for several hours at Warsaw. Our detachment goes sightseeing in the city, including the famous ghetto – or rather, what's left of it. We return to the station in small groups. We are all smiling. The Poles smile back, especially the girls. Some of the older soldiers, more daring than myself, have arranged to return in most agreeable company. Once again we set off, to arrive finally at Bialystok.

From Bialystok we march another ten miles to a small hamlet. The weather is cool but unbelievably beautiful. Autumn is already well under way in this pretty, hilly countryside. We tramp through a forest of enormous trees.

11

Feldwebel* Laus loudly orders us to fall in, and we march in
quick-step into a clearing, where a fairy-tale castle rises up
in front of us. We proceed along an avenue of trees singing in
four parts 'Erika, We Love You.' We are met by a group of
ten or eleven soldiers, one of whom is wearing the gleaming
epaulettes of an officer.

Perfectly timed, we draw up to this group as we sing the
last notes of our song. The feldwebel shouts once again, and
we freeze. Then another order, an impeccable quarter turn,
and the air rings with the sound of three hundred pairs of
boots clicking together. After an official military welcome,
we march into the walled court of this formidable fortress.

In the courtyard roll is called. Those who have already
answered form another group which grows larger as ours
shrinks. The yard is jammed with every kind of military
vehicle and with five hundred fully equipped soldiers who
seem to be waiting for departure. We are sent off to our
quarters in groups of thirty. An old man calls to us: 'Relief
troops, this way.'

We conclude from this that the men massed by the trucks
are leaving this regal habitation, which would explain their
rather sullen faces.

Two hours later I learn that their destination is somewhere
in the immensity of Russia. Russia means the war – of
which, as yet, I know nothing.

I have just put my bundle down on the wooden bed I have
chosen for myself when we are ordered to return to the
courtyard. It is now about two o'clock in the afternoon, and
except for the biscuits we were able to pick up in Warsaw, we
haven't had anything to eat since the rye bread, white cheese,
and jam we were given the evening before as we were rolling
toward Poland. This new order must be connected with
lunch, which is already three hours late.

But not at all. A feldwebel wearing a sweater proposes
with an ironic air to share his swim with us, as an apéritif.
He makes us trot at a brisk gymnastic pace for about
three-quarters of a mile to a small sandy pool fed by a tiny
stream. The feldwebel, who has lost his smiling face, orders
us to strip. Feeling somewhat ridiculous, we are soon naked.

*Sergeant.

The feldwebel plunges into the water first, and waves us after him.

Everyone bursts out laughing, but in my case, at least, the laughter is somewhat forced. The weather is certainly beautiful – for a walk, but not for a swim. The temperature of the air can be no more than forty, and the water, when I reluctantly dip my foot into it, is really very cold. At this moment, a violent shove, accompanied by a mocking laugh, propels me into the water, where I swim vigorously to keep from fainting. When I emerge, shivering, from the plunge, convinced that by evening I shall be in the infirmary with pneumonia, I look anxiously for the towel which is indispensable after such an experience. But there isn't one! Nobody has one! Most of my comrades have nothing but the long-sleeved undershirt that also serves as a shirt in the Wehrmacht, and their fatigue jackets, which they put on next to their bare skins. I am lucky because I have a pullover, which protects my child's skin from the rough cloth.

On the double, we catch up with our leader, who is already more than halfway back to our enormous residence. We are all frantically hungry, and our avid faces look desperately for some sign of a dining hall. As it seems we are to be abandoned to our fate, a young Alsatian built like a giant accosts one of the noncoms, staring at him as if he wished to devour him.

'Are we going to have anything to eat?'

A thunderous 'Achtung!' assaults our ears. We all freeze, including our champion.

'Lunch here is at eleven,' the noncom shouts. 'You arrived three hours late. In threes, to my right. It's time for target practice.'

Gnashing our teeth, we set off after our 'foster mother.'

We take a narrow footpath through the woods. Our marching rows break up, and soon we are walking in a single column. I notice a slight disturbance about ten men in front of me, which quickly develops into a wild tumult. I press forward, as do those behind me, and there are soon about thirty of us piled up beside a thicket where three men in civilian clothes – three Poles – are standing, each carrying a basket of eggs. Everyone is asking the same question: 'Do you have any money? I don't.'

I can't understand a word the Poles are saying, but all the same I grasp that they are trying to sell us some eggs. It is our bad luck that we haven't been paid yet. Very few of us have any money of our own.

This is like the torture of Tantalus, as by now we are desperately hungry. In a sudden rush, avid hands plunge into the baskets. Eggs are broken and blows exchanged in silence: both sides fear reprisals. I don't do too badly. One of my feet is brutally trampled, but nothing worse happens, and at the end I have seven eggs.

I run to rejoin my group, and give two eggs to a fat young Austrian, who stares at me in stupefaction. I consume the five eggs that are left, together with a good part of their shells, in less than a hundred yards.

We arrive at the shooting range. There are at least a thousand men, and the firing is nonstop. We march up to a group of armed men coming to meet us, and take over their guns. I draw twenty-four cartridges, which I will fire when it's my turn – not as many as some men, but about average.

The eggs begin to work in my stomach, and I don't feel altogether easy. Night falls. We are all ravenous. We leave the shooting range with our guns on our shoulders. Other companies set off in other directions. We march down a narrow gravelled road which does not appear to be the same one we took when we came.

In fact, we shall have to tramp four miles in quick-step, singing, before we get back to that damned castle. It seems that singing while marching is an excellent respiratory exercise. As I am not dead, my lungs must have turned into bellows that evening. Between songs, I glance at my breathless companions, and notice a look of anxiety on every face. As I plainly don't understand, Peter Deleige, who is one diagonal step ahead of me, points to his wrist, where his watch gleams in the dusk, and whispers: 'The time.'

Good Lord! I catch on. It is almost night, well past five o'clock, and we've missed supper.

The whole section seems to react, and our pace accelerates. Perhaps they've saved something for us. We cling to this hope, dominating the exhaustion which threatens to overwhelm us. We outdistance the feldwebel by one and then by two paces. He stares at us in astonishment, begins to

14

shout, and then collects himself: 'So you think you can leave me behind, do you? Well, let's go then.'

On orders, we break into 'Die Wolken ziehn' for the seventh time, and, without slackening our pace, cross the massive stone bridge which straddles the moat. We peer into the shadowy courtyard, faintly illuminated by a few dim bulbs. A column of soldiers carrying mess tins and drinking cans is queuing in front of a sidecar which carries three enormous cauldrons.

At the sergeant's order we halt, and wait for his next order to break ranks and fetch our mess tins. But, alas, that moment has not yet come. This sadist obliges us to put our guns back in the gun rack, in their proper numerical order, which takes another ten minutes. We are frantic. Then, abruptly: 'Go and see if there's anything left, and in order!'

We hold ourselves in as far as the armoury door. But, once outside, nothing can stop us. We surge wildly toward our quarters. Our hobnailed boots throw off sparks as they clatter against the courtyard pavement. We rush up the monumental stone staircase like eighty madmen, driving ahead of us the few soldiers who are trying to come back down. In the dormitories the melee increases, as no one is yet entirely sure which room and bed he occupies. We run in and out of the rooms as if possessed by demons, and it seems inevitable that someone is trying to get out exactly as another man is trying to get in. We crash, swear, exchange blows. I myself receive a bash on the helmet.

Some lucky devils who have had the good luck to find their mess tins right away run back down the stairs at a triple gallop. The swine! They'll eat everything that's left! Finally, I find my pack, but as I am unhooking my mess tin someone jumps onto my bed with his dirty boots, and knocks everything to the floor. My mess tin rolls under the next bed, and when I dive to retrieve it, my hand is trampled.

I return to the courtyard, and there, under the benevolent gaze of our noncom, I take my place in line, relieved to see that there is still one cauldron with something in it.

In this momentary respite, I inspect my companions. Every face wears the same burning look of exhaustion. The thin ones, like me, have huge circles under their eyes, and the plumper ones are ashen.

I catch sight of Bruno Lensen. He has already been served, and is wolfing down his food as he walks away with careful little steps. Fahrstein, Olensheim, Lindberg, Hals: they are all doing the same thing. When my turn comes, I open my mess tin. I haven't had a chance to wash it since my last meal, and traces of food still cling to its interior.

The cook empties his ladle into my tin, and puts a large helping of yoghurt on my plate. I sit down a little way off, on one of the benches which stand against the wall of the kitchen block. Our galloping return at least had the advantage of making me get rid of the eggs I had devoured so precipitately that afternoon. I bolt my meal with ravenous hunger. The food isn't at all bad. I get up and walk over to the light of an unshaded window, and peer into the tin. It contains what looks like a mixture of semolina, prunes, and chunks of meat. It will all be gone in a few minutes.

As we haven't been given anything to drink, I go over to the horse troughs like everybody else, and swallow down three or four cups of icy water. And I take the opportunity to rinse my plate.

Evening assembly and roll call takes place in a large hall where a corporal addresses us on the subject of the German Reich. It is eight o'clock. Lights-out is sounded on a small bugle. We go back to our rooms and fall into a dead sleep.

I have just spent my first day in Poland. It is September 18, 1942.

We are out of bed at five o'clock the next morning, which is how it will be for the next two weeks. We shall also be undergoing intensive training, and shall cross that damned pond every day, no longer as bathers but with full combat equipment.

Exhausted, soaked to the skin, we fling ourselves onto our mattresses every evening, overwhelmed by a crushing sleep, without even the energy to write to our families.

As a marksman I am making rapid progress. I must have fired over five hundred cartridges, on manoeuvres and at the shooting range, during the fortnight, and hurled at least fifty practice grenades.

The days are grey. From time to time it rains, and I wonder if the rain is a foretaste of winter. But it is only the fifth of October. This morning it is clear, with a light frost. The rest of the day will probably be beautiful. We salute the flag at dawn, and take off for our daily footwork with our guns slung.

We cross the moat on the stone bridge, which resounds with the hammering of our sixty pairs of boots. Laus doesn't order us to sing, and for half an hour I hear nothing but the sound of our tramping feet – a sound which pleases me. I feel no desire to talk, and take deep lungfuls of cool forest air. A marvellous sense of life flows through my veins, and I make no effort to understand why we are all so splendidly well after such intense daily exertions. We run into a company quartered about six miles from us in a village with a name something like Cremenstövsk, and salute as we pass, we with heads left, they with heads right. Without any dispersal or change of position in the ranks we shift to the double, to ordinary marching pace, to the double again. When we get back to the castle we see a crowd of new faces.

All the sergeant-instructors have jumped on these greenhorns. We remain standing by the entrance. After an hour, as no one has done anything about us, we stack our weapons, and squat on the courtyard pavement.

I talk to a Lorrainer, half in French, half in German, and the morning goes by. The lunch bell rings, and we put away our guns before going into the dining hall.

It is now afternoon. Still no duties, no manoeuvres. We can hardly believe it. There is no question of going down to the courtyard; they would only send us off on fatigue. With one accord, we slip up to the third floor, where there are more dormitories. We see a ladder which takes us up to the attic, and then to the roof. The sun is beating down onto the massive slates. We stretch out full length, and brace our heels against the gutter so that we won't roll into the courtyard.

The day is magnificent. On the roof it is almost painfully hot, and before long we are all stripped to the waist, as if on a beach. However, after a while the heat becomes disagreeable, and like many others I abandon my roost. Up to that moment though, it is quite amusing to look down at the frenzied manoeuvres of the greenhorns under a torrent of abuse.

I find myself back in the courtyard in the company of that

damned Lorrainer, who never talks about anything but his medical studies. As I am supposed to work as a mechanic with my father, I find all his chatter quite boring. What's the point of thinking about a civilian future when you've just gone into the army?

There are still no orders for us. I walk about quite freely, and for the first time observe the details of this massive edifice. Everything about it is on a colossal scale. The smallest staircase is at least eighteen feet wide, and the whole mass is so imposing that one almost forgets its sinister character.

Beyond the entry and parallel to it rise the battlements. Another block composed of four towers like the towers of the porch completes the group of buildings. The entire mass both pleases and impresses me, and I feel in this Wagnerian décor a sense of almost invincible power. The horizon touches the vast dark-green forest on all sides.

The principal characteristic of the days which follow is a kind of robust pleasure. I learn to drive, first a big motorcycle, then a VW, and then a steiner.* I grow so confident that driving these machines seems like child's play, and I am able to manage them under any circumstances. There are fifteen of us passing around orders among ourselves without submitting to any authority, and we enjoy ourselves, like the boys we are.

October 10. The weather is still beautiful, but this morning the temperature is only twenty-five degrees. For the whole day we practise handling a small tank, driving it up some pretty steep slopes. There are fifteen of us aboard a vehicle intended for eight, which is quite uncomfortable. We manage to stay inside only by performing some extraordinary acrobatic contortions. We laugh all day, and by evening any one of us can handle the machine. We are dead tired and ache as if we'd all been given a good thrashing.

The next day, as we fling ourselves headlong into exercise, without calculating the cost of energy, and to counteract the cold, Laus calls out: 'Sajer!'

I step forward.

'Lieutenant Starfe needs a Panzer driver, and as you

*Military automobile, similar to a jeep.

18

particularly distinguished yourself yesterday ... go and get ready.'

I salute, and take myself off at a gallop. It's not possible ... I, the best driver in the platoon! I literally leap with joy, and, in less than no time, am dressed and back in the courtyard. I begin to run to the command quarters, but that proves unnecessary, as Lieutenant Starfe is already waiting for me. He is a thin, angular man, but does not look disagreeable. It seems that he was gravely wounded in Belgium and has stayed in the army as an instructor. I snap to attention.

'Do you know the way to Cremenstövsk?' he asks.

'Jawohl, Herr Leutnant.'

To tell the truth, I am only guessing that this is the road on which we sometimes run into companies who seem to be coming from that village. But I feel too pleased to hesitate. For once I am being asked for something more than a simple exercise.

'Good,' he answers, smiling. 'Let's go, then.'

Starfe points to one of the tanks we were using yesterday. Something that looks like a four-wheeled trailer is attached to it. In fact, it's an 88, covered with a camouflage net. I settle into the driver's seat and turn on the engine: the gauge shows only two and a half gallons, which isn't enough, and I ask permission to fill the tank. Permission is granted, and I am congratulated for this elementary observation. We start a few minutes later. My vehicle proceeds somewhat nervously past the porch and over the bridge. I cannot bring myself to look at Starfe, who must surely have noticed my deplorable beginner's technique. About 600 yards from the castle I turn off toward what I think must be the road to Cremenstövsk. For about ten minutes I roll along at a moderate speed, in a state of considerable anxiety about my itinerary. We pass two Polish carts loaded with hay. They take one look at my Panzer, and make for the side of the road. Starfe looks at me and smiles at their precipitate flight.

'They think you did that on purpose. They'll never believe it's because you haven't mastered the machine.'

I don't know whether I'm supposed to laugh at this observation, or take it as a warning. I feel more and more nervous, and jolt the poor lieutenant as if he were riding a camel. Finally we arrive at a decrepit group of buildings. I look desperately for a signpost, but all I can see is the gang of tow-headed boys who have rushed out to see us go by, at the risk of falling beneath our treads.

Suddenly I catch sight of about a hundred German vehicles parked in the road, and Starfe points to a building with a flag flying in front of it. I heave a sigh of relief. We were on the road to Cremenstövsk after all.

'You'll have at least an hour to wait,' Starfe tells me. 'Go to the canteen and see if they can give you something hot.'

As he speaks, he pats me on the shoulder. I feel very much moved by the friendliness of this lieutenant to whom I have just given such a frightful journey. I would never have guessed that this man whose face is somewhat frightening would be capable of a quasi-paternal gesture.

I walk over to a building which looks like a town hall. A notice board carries a white-on-black inscription: SOL-DATENSCHENKE 27ᵉ KOMPANIE. Soldiers are continuously going in and out. As there is no sentry, I walk in, and through a room where three soldiers are busy unpacking crates of food. Beyond this room is another, with a counter at the back, beside which a group of soldiers are standing and talking.

'Could I have something hot? I've just driven an officer over here, but I don't belong to the 27th.'

'So,' mutters the soldier behind the bar. 'Another one of these damned Alsatians pretending to be German.'

It's plain that I speak hideously badly.

'I'm not Alsatian, but half German, through my mother.'

They don't press me. The one behind the bar goes off into the kitchen. I stay where I am, planted in the middle of the room, wrapped in my heavy green overcoat. Five minutes later, the soldier is back with a steaming canteen half filled with goat's milk. He pours a full tumbler of alcohol into this, and hands it to me without a word.

It is burning hot, but I drink it down all the same. Every eye is fixed on me. I have never liked the taste of alcohol, but I am determined to finish this litre at any price, so that I won't look like a green girl.

I leave this bunch of louts without saluting, and find myself out in the cold once again. This time I feel certain that the Polish winter has arrived. The sky is overcast, and the thermometer has fallen to twenty degrees.

I don't really know where to go. The square is almost empty. In the surrounding houses, Poles must be warming themselves in front of their fires. I walk over to the parking lot, where some soldiers are busy with the trucks. I venture a few words, but they reply without enthusiasm. I must be too young for them: these characters are already in their thirties. I continue my aimless wandering, and catch sight of three bearded men wearing long overcoats of a strange brown colour, who are cutting a tree trunk into lengths with a large all-purpose saw. I don't recognize their uniforms.

I walk up to them, smile, and ask them if everything's all right. Their only response is to stop sawing and straighten up, and I guess that they are smiling behind their heavy beards. One of them is a tall, strapping fellow; the other two are short and stocky. I ask two or three questions, but get no reply. These characters must be laughing at me! Then I hear footsteps coming up behind me, and a voice says: 'Let them alone. You know that talking to them is forbidden, except to give them orders.'

'Those wildmen didn't answer me anyway. I was just wondering what the hell they're doing in the Wehrmacht.'

'Teufel!' says the fellow who's come to dress me down. 'I can see now that you've never been under fire. Those fellows are Russian prisoners. And if you ever do get to the front and you see one of them before he sees you, fire without hesitation, or you'll never see another.'

I am astounded, and look again at the Russians, who have resumed their sawing. So those are our enemies, who shoot at German soldiers, soldiers wearing uniforms like mine. Why did they smile at me then?

For the next two weeks, life in the castle with my companions of the 19th Company continues as usual, and I obliterate the memory of the 27th, which seemed to be composed entirely of sullen, gloomy characters. To be fair, however, I must admit that the men in the 27th have been in service since 1940.

Winter has arrived, with its snow and rain, transforming the earth into sticky glue. When we come in at dusk we are covered with mud and exhausted, but still filled with the sense

PROLOGUE

of joy that comes from youth and health. These small
fatigues are nothing compared to what awaits us. Every
evening we warm ourselves in our comfortable beds, and joke
until sleep interrupts us.

October 28. The weather, which is not very cold, is
nonetheless frightful. Grey clouds and squalls of wind and
rain fill the sky for twenty-four hours a day. Our noncoms
are tired of getting soaked to the skin, and have given up
taking us to outdoor exercises. We spend most of the time
perfecting our skills as drivers and mechanics. I don't yet
know anything more disagreeable than rummaging through
an engine under a driving rain.

The thermometer remains more or less constant at freezing.

October 30: raining and cold.

After saluting the colours, we are ordered to the supply
store, where we proceed without thinking about explanations.
At least it will be warm in there. In the store, which has been
set up in a large shed, the first two sections of our company
have just been served, and are coming out with their arms
loaded. When it's my turn, I am given four boxes of sardines,
stamped in France, two vegetable sausages wrapped in
cellophane, a package of biscuits enriched with vitamins, two
slabs of Swiss chocolate, some smoked lard, and a half pound
of lump sugar. Four steps further on, another attendant piles
onto my already encumbered arms a waterproof ground
sheet, a pair of socks, and a pair of woollen gloves. At the
door one more item is added: a cloth packet inscribed FIELD
KIT: FIRST AID. In the falling rain, I rejoin my group, which is
clustered around an officer crouched on the back of a truck.
He is well protected in his long coat of grey-green leather,
and seems to be waiting for the entire company to assemble.
When he judges that everyone has arrived, he begins to
speak. He talks so quickly that I have a hard time understanding what he says.

'You will be leaving this billet to convoy several military
trains to a more advanced post. You have just been issued
with supplies for eight days, which you will now include in
your equipment. You will assemble in twenty minutes. Now
get ready.'

Quickly, silent with anxiety, we return to our quarters and

22

gather together our possessions. As I fasten my pack to my back, my neighbour in the next bed asks: 'How long will we be gone?'

'Don't know.'

'I just wrote to my parents and asked them to send me some books.'

'The P.O. will forward your package.'

At that moment Hals, my enormous friend, hits me across the back. 'At last we'll see some Russians,' he shouts, grinning sardonically.

I sense that he is trying to build up his nerve. In reality everyone feels considerable emotion. Despite our perfect innocence, the idea of war terrifies us.

Once more we find ourselves standing in the courtyard in that damned rain. We are each given a registered Mauser and twenty-five cartridges. I don't know if it's a reaction to receiving these arms, but I notice that everyone is turning pale. Certainly we can all be excused for this: no one in the company is more than eighteen. I myself won't be seventeen for another two and a half months. The lieutenant notices our confusion, and to raise our spirits reads us the latest Wehrmacht communiqué. Von Paulus is on the Volga, von Richthofen is near Moscow, and the Anglo-Americans have suffered great losses in their attempts to bomb the cities and towns of the Reich. Our officer seems reassured by our answering cries of 'Sieg Heil.' The entire 19th Company stands at attention in front of the flag.

Laus, our feldwebel, is there, also helmeted and fully equipped. At his side he carries a long automatic in a black leather sheath, which gleams in the rain. We are all silent. The order to move out sounds like the abrupt blast of an express train's whistle: 'Achtung! Rechts um. Raus!'

In threes, we leave the place which was home during our first army experiences. We cross the stone bridge for the last time, and set off down the road which brought us here a month and a half ago. I look back several times at the imposing grey mass of the ancient Polish castle which I shall never see again, and would have succumbed to melancholy if the presence of my comrades had not raised my spirits. We arrive at Bialystok, a sea of green uniforms, and march to the station.

23

PART ONE

RUSSIA
Autumn, 1942

Chapter One

TOWARD STALINGRAD

MINSK · KIEV · BAPTISM OF FIRE · KHARKOV

We were standing beside a long railway convoy. We had been ordered to stack our guns on the tracks and take off our packs. The time was somewhere between twelve noon and one o'clock. Laus was munching on something he had taken from his pack. His face, although scarcely attractive, had grown familiar to us, even reassuring. As though his action were some kind of signal, we all took out our food, some immediately devouring the equivalent of two meals. Laus noticed this, but contented himself with a brief comment: 'All right, go ahead, gobble it all down. But there won't be another distribution before the week is over.'

Although we all felt as if we'd eaten only half of what we really needed to assuage our giant appetites, we also felt a little bit warmer.

By this time we had been waiting in the cold for more than two hours, and it was beginning to get the better of us. We tramped up and down, joking and stamping our feet. Some, who had paper, wrote letters, but my fingers were too numb, and I contented myself with observation. Trains loaded with war matériel were continuously passing through the station, which had turned into a vast bottleneck, with cars backed up for at least six hundred yards. Everything seemed very badly organized, with convoys moving out, only to be shuttled onto other sections of track, where other companies brought from God knows where were being kept waiting as we were. People were always moving out of the way to let a train go by, only to see it a few minutes later headed in the opposite direction. What a mess!

The train we were leaning against seemed to have been immobilized for eternity. Perhaps it would have been better if it had never left.

To give myself some exercise, I hoisted myself up as high

27

as the air holes in the carriages. Instead of cattle, the train was filled with munitions.

By this time we had been in the station for four hours, and felt frozen. It grew colder as it grew dark, and to kill time we plunged once more into our provisions. Although it was already quite dark, traffic continued, dimly lit. Laus was beginning to look as though he had had enough. With his cap pulled down over his ears, and his collar turned up, he was tramping up and down for warmth; he must have covered at least ten miles. We had formed a small group of friends from Chemnitz, which wasn't to break up until much later: Lensen, Olensheim, and Hals, three Germans who spoke French as badly as I spoke German; Morvan, an Alsatian; Uterbeick, an Austrian, as dark and curly as an Italian dancer, who eventually dissociated himself from our group; and me, a Franco-German. Among the six of us, we were making progress in both languages, except for that damned Uterbeick, who never stopped humming Italian love songs under his breath. These plaintive melodies sounded out of place and totally foreign to ears more accustomed to Wagner than to Italian composers, especially those lamentations of an abandoned Neapolitan swain.

Hals had a watch with a luminous dial which informed us that it was already eight-thirty. We felt sure that our departure was imminent, that they were not going to leave us on the station platform for the night. But that is how it turned out. After another hour, several men unpacked sleeping rolls and stretched out as best they could – if possible on some raised surface, for a little protection from the damp. Some even had the temerity to sleep under the train, hoping that it wouldn't start rolling.

Our sergeant had settled on a pile of railway baggage and lit a cigarette. He looked worn out. We simply couldn't accept the idea of a night out of doors. It seemed impossible that we would be left where we were. We knew that the departure whistle would blow soon, and that all the idiots who hadn't had the patience to wait would have a fine time packing up their bedrolls in a hurry. As it turned out, we would have done better to imitate them and gain two hours' sleep; two hours later we were still sitting on the cold stones of the road bed. It was growing steadily colder, and a fine rain had begun to fall. Our sergeant was busy building himself a shelter with the railway baggage – not at all a bad idea. When he covered this over with his waterproof sheet, he was completely sheltered – the old fox.

We now felt compelled to find ourselves some shelter too. We couldn't move too far from our weapons, but we left them nonetheless, with their barrels in the air, open to the rain, expecting a royal dressing-down later on. The best places, of course, were taken by this time, and the only thing we could think of was to shelter beneath the railway cars. It had certainly occurred to us to try to get inside, but the doors were held shut with wire cables.

Full of complaints, we crawled into our disquieting and altogether relative shelter. The rain blew in sideways after us, and we were furious. Later on this anger made me laugh....

As best we could, we arranged some degree of shelter from the rain. This was my first night in the open air, and needless to say I never shut my eyes for more than fifteen minutes at a time. I can remember long periods of staring at the huge axle that served as the roof of my bed. Through my exhaustion it often seemed to be shifting, as if the train were about to move; I would wake with a start to find that nothing had changed, fall back again into a half sleep, only to be startled back into wakefulness once again. At the first glimmer of daylight we left this chance resting place, stiff and numb, looking like a gang of disinterred corpses.

We fell in at eight o'clock, and marched to the embarkation platform. Hals remarked several times that we could perfectly well have spent another night at the castle. None of us as yet had any idea of the dispiriting necessities of military life in wartime. This had been our first night out of doors, but we were destined to spend many others which were far worse.

For the moment, we were train guards. Our company had been divided among three long convoys of military matériel, two or three to a car. I found myself with Hals and Lensen on a flatcar which carried airplane wings marked with a black cross, and other parts covered by canvas. These were supplies destined for the Luftwaffe; according to the inscriptions we had been able to read, they came from Ratisbonne, and were going to Minsk.

Minsk: Russia. Our mouths suddenly went dry.

We were pursued by bad luck. We were stuck on an open car; the rain had turned to snow; the unbearable cold was intensified by the motion of the train. After due consideration we ducked under the tarpaulin which covered a large DO-17 engine. This manoeuvre cut the wind, and by clinging together we managed to achieve a semblance of warmth. We stayed there a good hour, roaring with laughter over nothing. The train was rolling along and we hadn't the slightest idea what was happening outdoors. From time to time we could hear trains going in the other direction.

All of a sudden, Lensen thought he heard a voice shouting above the noise of the wheels. Carefully he stuck his head out of our shelter.

"It's Laus," he said calmly, turning back to us and pulling the canvas down again.

Ten seconds later, the canvas was ripped back to reveal the sergeant fuming with rage at the sight of our three happy faces. Laus, wearing a helmet and gloves, looked very much on the job. His face and coat were powdered with snow, like the rest of the train, whose long profile joggled and swayed behind him. The air rang with a loud 'Achtung!' but the spasmodic motion of the train prevented the order from being executed with its customary stiff precision.

The scene which followed was worthy of burlesque. I can still see that great teddy bear Hals, swaying from right to left as he tried to maintain a rigid posture. As for me, my long coat had caught on one of the numerous sections of airplane engine, which made it impossible for me to straighten up. Laus was no better than we were at maintaining a dignified attitude. Finally, beside himself with exasperation, he braced himself with one knee against the floor. We followed his example, and from a certain distance we might have been taken for a quartet of conspirators whispering secrets. In fact, I and my companions were receiving a magisterial dressing-down.

'What the hell do you think you're doing under there?' Laus shouted. 'Where in God's name do you think you are, and what do you think you're supposed to be doing on this train?'

Hals, who had a spontaneous nature, interrupted our

superior. He said that it was impossible to stay outside the canvas because the cold was so bad, and that anyway there was nothing to look at.

It would seem that by making these observations, Hals was demonstrating a total lack of objectivity. Like an enraged gorilla the sergeant seized our comrade by the collar and shook him violently, with a torrent of abuse.

'I'll make my report! At the first stop I'll have you sent to a disciplinary battalion. This is nothing less than abandoning your post. You could get the firing squad. . . . What if a car had blown up behind you? You couldn't have warned anyone from that hole of yours!'

'Why?' Lensen asked. 'Is a car going to blow up?'

'Shut up, idiot! There are terrorists all along the line, ready to risk anything. When they don't blow the trains right up they throw explosives or incendiaries. You are here precisely to prevent that sort of thing. Take your helmets and come to the front of the car, or I'll throw the whole lot of you overboard!'

We didn't wait for him to repeat himself, and despite the cold which bit into our faces, we took up the positions he appointed. Laus continued forward through the loaded cars, hanging on as he moved from one to the next. He wasn't really a bully, but a man with a clear idea of a job to be done. I never saw him try to make things easier for himself, which is probably why I felt he must have a sympathetic streak, although I hadn't yet spoken to him. None of the other feldwebels in the company were so strict; they claimed to be saving themselves for the big job; but when the moment came Laus did as much as they, if not more. He was the oldest of the sergeants; perhaps he had already been at the front. In fact, he was like every sergeant-major in the world: afraid of responsibility, and at the same time giving us a hard time.

During his tirade he had made us realize, rightly enough, that if we couldn't stand a little cold and a vague, possible danger, we would never survive at the front. It certainly would be idiotic to get killed by some anarchist before we'd seen anything.

We were rolling through a forest of squat, snow-covered pines. I had plenty of time to ponder the case of conscience the feldwebel had put to me. The north of Poland seemed to be very sparsely populated. We had passed only a few small towns. Suddenly, well ahead of the train, I caught sight of a figure running along beside the tracks. I didn't think I could be the only person who'd noticed him, but apparently no one in any of the cars ahead was doing anything about him.

Rapidly I manoeuvred my Mauser into a good position, and took aim at what could only be a terrorist.

Our train was moving very slowly: a perfect target for a bomb. In a few minutes I was level with the man. I couldn't see anything unusual about him. He was probably a Polish woodcutter who had come up out of curiosity. I felt disconcerted. I had been all ready to fire, and now nothing seemed to justify it. I aimed deliberately over his head and pulled the trigger.

The report shook the air, and the butt of my gun crashed violently into my shoulder. The poor fellow took off as fast as he could, obviously fearing the worst, and I felt certain that my ill-considered action had made another enemy for the Reich.

The train maintained its speed, and a few minutes later Laus appeared, continuing his endless patrol despite the cold. He gave me a curious look.

We had decided to take duty in shifts. While two of us watched, the third would try to warm up under the canvas. We had now been on the train for something like eight hours, and felt apprehensive about the night, which would undoubtedly be spent in these conditions. Twenty minutes ago I had taken Hals's place, and for twenty minutes had been unable to control my violent shivering. Night was drawing close; perhaps Minsk was too. The train was moving along the only track. To the north and to the south we were enclosed by dark forest. For the last quarter of an hour the train had been accelerating, which would undoubtedly result in our deaths by freezing. We had also consumed a large part of our rations to keep warm.

Suddenly the train slowed down. The brake blocks grated against the wheels, and the couplings shook violently. We were soon moving at the speed of a bicycle. I saw the front of the train turn to the right: we were diverting onto a secondary track.

The train moved forward for another five minutes, and

then stopped. Two officers had jumped down from one of the front cars and were walking back. Laus and two other noncoms went out to meet them. They conferred for a moment but didn't tell us anything. All along the train people were looking out. The forest seemed a likely haven for terrorists. Our train had been standing still for several minutes when we heard the distant sound of wheels. We were walking up and down trying to warm ourselves up when a blast from a whistle accompanied by gestures indicated that we should return to our posts at once. A locomotive appeared in the distance on the track we had just left; it was entirely blacked out.

What I saw next froze me with horror. I wish I were a writer of genius so that I could do justice to the vision which appeared before us. First we saw a car loaded with railway materials, pushed along in front of the locomotive and hiding its dim lights. Then came the smoking locomotive, its tender, and a closed car with a hole in its roof to accommodate a short length of smoking pipe – probably the train kitchen. Behind this another car with high railings carried armed German soldiers. A twin-mounted machine gun covered the rest of the train, which consisted simply of open flatcars like ours, but loaded with a very different kind of freight. The first one of these to pass my uncomprehending eyes seemed to be carrying a confused heap of objects, which only gradually became recognizable as human bodies. Directly behind this heap other people were clinging together, crouching or standing. Each car was full to the bursting point. One of us, more informed than the others, told us in two words what we were looking at: 'Russian prisoners.'

I thought I had recognized the brown coats I had seen once before, near the castle, but it was really too dark to be sure. Hals looked at me. Except for the burning red spots made by the cold, his face was as white as a sheet.

'Did you see that?' he whispered. 'They've piled up their dead to shield themselves from the wind.'

In my stupefaction I could only reply with something like a groan. Every car was carrying a shield of human bodies. I stood as if petrified by the horror of the sight rolling slowly by: faces entirely drained of blood, and bare feet stiffened by death and cold.

The tenth car had just passed us when something even more horrible happened. Four or five bodies slid from the badly balanced load and fell to the side of the track. The funereal train didn't stop. A group of officers and noncoms from our train walked over to investigate. Driven by I don't know what element of curiosity I jumped down from our car and went over to the officers. I saluted and asked in a faltering voice if the men were dead. An officer looked at me in astonishment and I realized that I had just abandoned my post. He must have noticed my confusion, as he didn't reprimand me.

'I think so,' he said sadly. 'You can help your comrades bury them.' Then he turned and walked away. Hals had come with me. We went back to our car to fetch shovels and began to dig a trench a short distance above the embankment. Laus and another fellow looked through the dead men's clothes to try to find some identification. I learned later that most of these poor devils had no civilian identity. Hals and I needed all our nerve to drag two of them over to the ditch without looking at them. We were covering them with dirt when the departure whistle blew. It was growing colder by the minute. I felt overcome by a vast sense of disgust.

An hour later our train passed through a double hedge of structures which, despite the absence of light, we could see were more or less destroyed. We passed another train, less sinister than the preceding one, but scarcely comforting. Its cars were marked with red crosses. Through some of the windows we could see stretchers, which must have been carrying badly wounded men. At other windows, soldiers swathed in bandages were waving to us.

Finally we arrived at Minsk station. Our train pulled to a stop down the whole length of a long, wide platform covered with a busy, motley crowd: armed soldiers and soldiers in fatigues, civilians, and groups of Russian prisoners cordoned in by other prisoners who wore red-and-white armbands and carried truncheons. These were the informers who had denounced the famous 'People's Commissars' and were therefore anti-Communist. They claimed the right of guarding their comrades, which suited our authorities very well, as no one would be more likely to get a decent day's work from the Russian prisoners.

We could hear orders being given, first in German, then in Russian. A crowd of men came up to our train, and the unloading began in the lights of the trucks parked along the platform. We joined in this work, which took the better part of two hours, warming ourselves a little, then plunging once more into our provisions. Hals, a greedy-guts, had consumed more than half his allotment in less than two days. We spent the night in a large building where we were able to sleep in a certain degree of comfort.

The next day we were sent to a military hospital, where we were kept for two days and given a series of shots. Minsk was very badly damaged. There were many gutted houses and walls cross-hatched by machine-gun fire. Some of the streets were totally impassable, with a continuous line of shell holes and bomb craters, often more than fifteen feet deep. Passageways of a sort had been made by planks and other solid objects thrown across this chaos. From time to time we gave way to a Russian woman loaded with provisions, and always followed by four or five children who stared at us with astonishingly round eyes. There were also many curious shops whose broken windows had been replaced by boards or sacks stuffed with straw. Hals, Lensen, Morvan, and I went into several of these out of curiosity. There was always an array of big earthenware crocks painted in various colours, which contained either a liquid and steeping plants, dried vegetables, or a curious heavy syrup which was halfway between jam and butter.

As we didn't know how to say so much as 'hello' in Russian, we always went into these places talking among ourselves. The few Russians who were inside invariably assumed an attitude half anxious, half smiling, while the shopkeeper or proprietress would approach us with a white-lipped smile and offer us large dippers of these products, in an obvious effort to placate the fierce warriors they imagined us to be.

We were often given a fine yellowish flour to mix into this syrup — whose taste was far from disagreeable, somewhat reminiscent of honey. Its only discouraging aspect was a superabundance of fat. I can still see the faces of those Russians, smiling as they held out this product and pronouncing a word which sounded rather like 'ourlka'. I never was sure whether this meant 'eat' or was simply the name of the mixture. There were days when we really gorged ourselves on 'ourlka,' which nonetheless did not prevent us from appearing at eleven o'clock for the official midday meal.

Hals accepted everything the Russians offered him with so much politeness. Sometimes I found him quite revolting, holding out his mess tin for the largess of these Soviet merchants as they poured into it mixtures resembling each other only in their loose, runny consistency. Sometimes his tin would hold a combination of the famous ourlka, cooked wheat, salt herring cut into pieces, and several other ingredients. Whatever the concoction, Hals devoured it with evident relish, like a great pig.

Except for these moments of distraction seized in the intervals between our many jobs, we scarcely had time to amuse ourselves. Minsk was an important army supply centre, where shipments were constantly loaded and unloaded.

Life for the troops in this sector was remarkably well-organized. Mail was distributed; there were films for soldiers on leave – which we were not allowed to attend – libraries, and restaurants run by Russian civilians, but reserved entirely for German soldiers. The restaurants were all too expensive for me and I never went into them, but Hals, who would sacrifice anything for a good stuffing, spent all his money in these places, and a certain amount of ours. The understanding was that he would give us a detailed account of his experiences, which he adhered to faithfully, with many embellishments. We slavered with vicarious pleasure as we listened to him.

We were much better fed than we had been in Poland, and were able to supplement our rations very cheaply – which we really needed to do. The cold in these opening days of December had become extremely sharp, dropping to more than five degrees below zero. The snow, which fell in great abundance, never melted, and in places was already over three feet deep. Evidently this slowed the movement of supplies to the front, and, according to troops returning from forward positions where the cold was even more bitter than at Minsk, the poor fellows were reduced to sharing rations which were already ridiculously small. Insufficient food

36

combined with the cold produced many cases of pneumonia, frostbite, and frozen limbs.

At this moment, the Reich was making an immense effort to protect its soldiers from the implacable hostility of the Russian winter. At Minsk, Kovno, and Kiev, there were enormous stores of blankets, special winter clothing made of sheepskin, overshoes with thick insulating soles and uppers of matted hair, gloves, hoods of double catskin, and portable heaters which operated equally well on gasoline, oil, or solidified alcohol, mountains of rations in specially conditioned boxes, and thousands of other necessities. It was our duty, as convoy troops of the Rollbahn, to deliver all of this to the front lines, where the combat troops were desperately awaiting us.

We made superhuman efforts, and yet they were not enough. The punishment we suffered, not at the hands of the Russian Army, which until that moment had done almost nothing except retreat, but from the cold, is almost beyond the powers of description. Outside the great towns there had not yet been time to repair the damaged roads — few and far between to begin with — or to open others. While our unit was doing its autumn gymnastics, the Wehrmacht, after an extraordinary advance, had marched itself and its supplies into an unbelievable quagmire. Then the first frosts had solidified the monstrous ruts leading to the east. Our machines had suffered enormously on these roads, which in fact were passable only for wagons, but the hardening of the soil had temporarily allowed the provisioning of the troops. Then winter poured down its tons of snow across the immensity of Russia, once again paralyzing traffic.

That is the point we had reached in December, 1942. We shovelled away snow so that our trucks could move forward fifteen or twenty miles in a morning, only to find our efforts covered over again the same day. The earth beneath the snow was a sinister relief of bumps and potholes, which we tamped down or blew up. In the evenings we scrambled to find shelter for the night.

Sometimes this would be a hut fitted out by the engineers, sometimes an isba,* or any house we could find. We often crowded more than fifty men into a hut intended for a couple

*A log hut.

and two children. The most desired accommodations were the big tents especially designed for Russia. They were tall and pointed, like teepees, weather-proofed, and planned for nine men. We were rarely fewer than twenty, and even at that there weren't enough tents. Luckily, we had raided our stores of food because of the cold, and with enough to eat, we were able to keep going reasonably well. Some of us began to crawl with vermin, as we were only rarely able to wash, and when we returned to Minsk, our first duty was to pass through disinfection.

I was beginning to feel that I'd had more than enough of Holy Russia and of truck driving. Like everybody else I was afraid of the idea of being under fire, but I was also beginning to long to use the Mauser which had been dragging around with me for what seemed like an eternity, without ever being the slightest use. I felt that somehow firing at something would avenge me for my sufferings from the cold, and from my blisters. My hands were badly blistered from shovelling, and my woollen gloves were already full of holes, exposing the tops of my icy fingers. My hands and feet felt the cold so sharply that it sometimes seemed as if the pain were stabbing me in the heart. The thermometer remained around five degrees below zero.

We were now billeted some fifteen miles north of Minsk, guarding a huge parking depot for military vehicles. We occupied the seven or eight houses in the hamlet, leaving only one, the largest, occupied by a Russian family. Their name was Khorsky; they had two daughters and claimed to have originally come from the Crimea, which they spoke of with nostalgia. They ran a kind of canteen where we could buy food and drink – from our own pockets – and find a few companions with whom to kill time.

The snow had stopped, but the cold was growing steadily more intense. One evening after our company had been in the hamlet for about a week, I was scheduled for two hours of guard duty. I crossed the huge parking lot, where five hundred or more vehicles of every description were half buried in snow. I had been feeling apprehensive all day at the prospect of walking across this space at night. It would be so easy for partisans to hide between the cars and shoot us as we went by. But I had gradually persuaded myself that the war, if it existed at all, was really taking place somewhere else. The only Russians I had seen were either merchants or prisoners, and it seemed highly probable that I would never see any others.

With this idea in my head, I walked to my post, about fifteen yards from the first vehicles, through a trench about a yard deep, which allowed us to advance as far as the cars, or withdraw, without being exposed. The edges of the trench had already been raised nearly another three feet by new snow, and each fresh fall obliged us to dig. I stood up on the box that allowed the sentry to see a little farther. I had wrapped a blanket over my coat, which made it very hard for me to move my arms.

I had refused my allotment of alcohol, the taste of which disgusted me, and was mentally preparing myself for another siege of uncontrollable trembling from the cold. The night was clear; I could have seen a raven a hundred yards off. In the distance the horizon was cut by a mass of stunted bushes. Three of the four telephone lines which crossed our camp were visible, stretching away in different directions. Their posts, shoved unevenly into the ground, were indifferent supports for the wire, which sometimes drooped right down to the snow.

My nose, the only part of me directly exposed, began to burn with cold. I had pulled my cap down as far as I could, so that my forehead and part of my cheeks were covered. Over this I wore the helmet required for guard duty. The turned-up collar of the pullover my parents had sent me overlapped the edge of my cap at the back of my head.

From time to time I looked at the expanse of machinery I was guarding and wondered what we would do if we had to move it all in a hurry. The engines must have reached a state of magnificent solidity!

I had been at my post for a good hour when suddenly a silhouette appeared at the edge of the parking lot. I threw myself down into the bottom of my hole. Before extracting my hands from the depths of my pockets, I risked another look over my parapet. The silhouette was advancing toward me. It must be one of our men making the rounds, but supposing it was a Bolshevik!

Grunting with the effort, I pulled my hands from their shelter and grabbed my gun. The breech, sticky with frost, bit into my fingers, as I manoeuvred my weapon into firing position and shouted out, 'Wer da?' I got back a reasonable reply, and my bullet remained in the gun.

All the same, I had been prudent to take these elementary precautions: it was an officer going his rounds. I saluted.

'Everything all right?'

'Yes, Leutnant.'

'Fine. Well, Happy Christmas.'

'What? Is it Christmas?'

'Yes. Look over there.'

He pointed to the Khorskys' house. The roof, loaded with snow, sloped down to ground level; the narrow windows were shining far more brightly than blackout regulations usually permitted, and in their light I could see the swiftly moving silhouettes of my comrades. A few moments later a tall flame burst from an enormous woodpile which must have been soaked with gasoline.

A song supported by three hundred voices ascended slowly into the stillness of the frozen night. 'O Weihnacht! O stille Nacht!' Was it possible? At that moment, everything beyond the perimeter of the camp was without meaning for me. I couldn't tear my eyes from the light of the bonfire. The faces closest to the flames were illuminated; the rest were lost in darkness, while the strong outpouring of song continued, divided now into several parts. Perhaps the circumstances of this particular Christmas night made a critical difference, but in all the time since then I haven't heard anything which moved me so much.

The memories of my earliest youth, still so close, returned to me for the first time since I had been a soldier. What was happening at home this evening? What was happening in France? We had heard bulletins which informed us that many French troops were now fighting along with us – news which made me rejoice. The thought of Frenchmen and Germans marching side by side seemed marvellous to me. Soon we would no longer have to be cold; the war would be over, and we could all recite our adventures at home. This Christmas hadn't brought me any gift I could hold in my hand, but had brought so much good news about the harmony between my two countries that I felt overwhelmed. Because I knew that I was now a man, I kept firmly at the back of my mind a foolish and embarrassing idea which kept pursuing me: I really would have liked someone to give me an ingenious mechanical toy.

My companions were still singing, and all along the front millions like them must have been singing as they were. I didn't know that, at that very hour, Soviet T-34 tanks, taking advantage of the truce which Christmas was supposed to bring, were crushing the forward posts of the Sixth Army in the Armotovsk sector. I didn't know that my comrades in the Sixth Army, in which one of my uncles was serving, were dying by the thousands in the hell of Stalingrad. I didn't know that German towns were being subjected to the horrifying bombardments of the R.A.F. and the U.S.A.F. And I would never have dared to think that the French would refuse a Franco-German entente.

This was, in its way, the most beautiful Christmas I had ever seen, made entirely of disinterested emotion and stripped of all tawdry trimmings. I was all alone beneath an enormous starred sky, and I can remember a tear running down my frozen cheek – a tear neither of pain nor of joy but of emotion created by intense experience.

By the time I got back to the billet, the officers had put an end to the celebrations, and ordered the bonfire extinguished. Hals had saved a half bottle of schnapps for me. I swallowed down a few mouthfuls, not to disappoint him.

Four more days went by. The hard cold continued, embellished by snow-filled squalls. We went out only for obligatory duties, which we reduced to the minimum, and burned tons of wood. The houses had been built to conserve heat, and we were sometimes even too hot. We felt very well, and as is usual under such circumstances, we very soon had some trouble.

Ours began one morning sometime around three o'clock. A guard noisily kicked open the door of the hut, admitting a blast of icy air and two soldiers whose stiff, bluish faces made them look remarkably alike. They rushed to our stove, and it was a few minutes before they spoke. Along with everybody else, I shouted at them to shut the door. In reply, we received a curse, and were ordered to stand at attention.

As we gaped, somewhat startled and without reaction, the fellow who had shouted kicked over the bench standing next to him, and shouting out his order a second time, hurled himself at the improvised bed of one of our men, violently ripping apart the mound of blankets, coats, and jackets in which our comrade had buried himself. In the dim light of the stove we recognized the epaulettes of a feldwebel.

'Are you bastards going to get the hell up?' he shouted pulling out everybody he could reach. 'Who's at the head of this bunch? It's a disgrace! Do you think this is how we'll stop the Russian offensive? If you're not ready in ten minutes I'll throw you out of here just the way you are.'

Stupid with sleep and stunned by our sudden awakening, we hurriedly collected our things. Leaving the door wide open, the feldwebel rushed from our hut like a madman, to inject panic into the isba across the way. We had no very clear idea of what was happening. Our sentry, who seemed quite shaken, told us that the intruders had arrived from Minsk in a sidecar. Those fifteen-odd miles must have taken them quite a long time, which would explain their furious condition.

But, despite all the demonic howling the feldwebel could muster, it was a full twenty minutes before we were standing at attention in the snow. Laus, who had been as deeply asleep as anyone else, tried to shock us into wakefulness with a pretence of rage as intense as his colleague's.

The other feldwebel, whose anger had not abated, barked out our orders: 'You will join Kommandant Ulträner's unit at Minsk before dawn.' He turned to Laus. 'You will take fifteen trucks from the depot and proceed as I've ordered.'

Why hadn't he telephoned, instead of working himself into such a state? We found out later that, while we had been sleeping peacefully, the telephone line had been cut in four places.

The difficulty of getting under way and bringing the trucks out from the depot was almost unimaginable. We had to roll out barrels of gasoline and alcohol to fill the gas tanks and radiators, crank up the engines – an exhausting labour – and shovel out cubic yards of snow, almost entirely without light. When the fifteen trucks were ready, we set out for Minsk, following the bumpy, snow-covered track the feldwebel had taken to reach us. One of the trucks skidded on the icy ground, and it took a good half hour to pull it from the ditch. We hooked it to another truck, which could only skate along the ice. In the end, almost the entire company was involved in the struggle, and we literally carried the damn machine back onto the road. Toward eight o'clock in the morning, well before the late winter dawn of those regions, we joined Ulträner and his regiment, and stood shivering, despite our exertions, in a vast city square, with two or three thousand other soldiers. Minsk seemed to be bursting with excitement and energy.

A network of loudspeakers which had been set up throughout the square disseminated a short lecture from the High Command. The lecture pointed out that even a victorious army had to accept deaths and casualties, and that our role as a convoy unit was to carry, at whatever the cost and despite all the hardships, which the High Command thoroughly recognized, the food, munitions, and matériel the combat troops required. Our convoy, by any means available, had to reach the banks of the Volga, so that von Paulus could continue to wage his victorious battle. One thousand miles separated us from our destination, and we hadn't a moment to spare.

We left after the midday meal. I found myself, separated from my closest friends, aboard a five-and-a-half-ton D.K.W. loaded with heavy automatic weapons. The road leaving the city was well ploughed, and we rolled along at a brisk pace. There must have been road gangs working around the clock. The snowbanks on either side of the road were nearly twelve feet high. We passed a signpost bristling with pointers. On the sign indicating the road we took I read NACH PRIPET, KIEV, DNIEPER, KHARKOV, DNIEPROPETROVSK.

Our troops had rounded up everyone capable of holding a shovel, and we were able to cover nearly one hundred miles in good time. We soon reached the summit of a hill from which we could see the immensity of the Ukraine stretching into the distance under a yellowish-grey sky.

The ten or twelve vehicles ahead of us had suffered a serious reduction in speed. Ahead of them, a company of soldiers were busily engaged in moving snow. A heavy truck was pushing a sled fitted with a kind of ventilator which blew out the snow in all directions. Beyond lay an infinity of immaculate snow nearly three feet deep. (Heavy snowfalls buried the road so completely after the passage of each convoy that we needed a compass to dig it out again.) Our commanding officer and his noncoms had walked a short distance out onto the unswept snow, sinking in over the tops of their boots, and were scanning the horizon, wondering how they could possibly proceed through all that soggy cotton. Inside our D.K.W., with all the windows shut, I and my travelling companion were relishing the warmth of our running engine.

But soon they were ordering us out of our machines and distributing snow shovels. As there weren't enough to go round, our noncoms told us to use anything we could lay our hands on. I saw men digging with boards, helmets, big serving platters. . . .

With two other fellows I was pushing against the tailgate of a truck which we had detached, hoping to use it as a crude sort of snow plough. The blast of a feldwebel's whistle interrupted our disorganized labour.

'What do you think you're proving over there? Come along with me; we'll go and round up some manpower. Bring your guns.'

I felt a surge of jubilation, which I kept well-hidden, as I inwardly thanked the idiots who had devised our hopeless procedure. I preferred almost anything to shovelling snow. We followed the feldwebel. I had no idea where he hoped to find more manpower. We had only passed two deserted villages since leaving Minsk. With our guns slung, our little group split off from the track the trucks had traced in the snow, and headed north. We sank in over our knees with every step, which made progress extremely difficult.

For ten minutes I did my best to follow the feldwebel, who was about fifteen feet ahead of me. I was gasping for breath, and I could feel the sweat beginning to trickle down my spine under the heavy cloth of my coat. My breath projected long streams of vapour, which vanished instantly in the icy air. I kept my eyes glued to the feldwebel's deep footprints, trying to step exactly into them, but as he was bigger than I, this meant that every step was a leap. I deliberately avoided looking at the horizon, which seemed so far away. A thin screen of birches soon hid the convoy from us.

Ludicrous in our smallness, we continued forward into the immensity of white. I was beginning to wonder where our noncom thought he would find his famous manpower. We had been exhausting ourselves in this way for nearly an hour. Suddenly, in the absolute quiet, we heard a rumbling sound which was growing steadily louder. We stopped.

Our sergeant limited himself to the observation that we hadn't much further to go, and then added that it was a pity we would miss this one.

I didn't really understand what he was talking about, but the noise was becoming increasingly clear. To our left I caught sight of a black line stretching across the snow. A train! We were approaching a railway line. I still didn't see what a train could do for us. Would they take our cargoes on board?

The train was going by very slowly about five hundred yards ahead of us. It was extremely long, a line of black broken at intervals by one of the five locomotives, spewing out impressive clouds of white vapour which vanished almost instantly, as if by magic. The train must have had a special mechanism for snow disposal.

Fifteen minutes later, we reached the tracks.

'A lot of supply trains go through here,' the feldwebel said. 'Most of the cars carry matériel, but there are usually a few passenger cars for Russian civilians. We'll stop one of them and collect some Russian labour.'

Finally I understood.

All we had to do now was wait. We tramped briskly up and down the tracks trying to keep warm. However, it felt as if the temperature had risen somewhat, as if by now it might be up to 15 degrees – which indicates the astonishing degree to which we had grown accustomed to zero temperatures. The cold, as we waited for the next train, seemed quite bearable. Soldiers wearing only pullovers were shovelling snow and streaming with sweat. I have never met anyone better able to stand punishment, whether from cold or heat or anything else, than the Germans. Each Russian I saw was more frozen than the last, but I certainly could not feel superior on that account. Life in Russia for me was a perpetual shivering fit.

The first train passed by without even slowing down. Our feldwebel, who had outdone himself in his efforts to stop it, was furious. Soldiers shouted to us from the train that their orders were not to stop for any reason whatever.

Extremely irritated, we walked on in the direction of the train which had passed us. At all events, the road must be parallel to the tracks; we would only have to make a right-angle turn to find our company again. The difficulty was that we were far from the kitchen and the hour for the distribution of food must have come and gone. I had two pieces of rye bread in my coat pocket, but I didn't want to take them out for fear of having to share them. The two soldiers with whom I had been shovelling snow must have known each other for some time. They were deep in conversation, and had stuck together ever since we'd left the convoy. Our noncom was walking ahead of us, by himself, and I tried to catch up with him. By now we had been walking for some time. The tracks were sunk between two banks which supported a thin growth of scrubby brush. They extended straight ahead into an indefinite distance. If a train came along, we would be able to see it for at least five miles. The scrub on the banks at this point was growing more thickly, and extending a greater distance from the tracks.

It was now some three hours since we had left our company. Everything stood out clearly against the snow. For some moments now I had been staring at a black shape about five hundred yards away. Ten minutes later, we could see that it was a hut. Our feldwebel was walking toward it; it must be a shelter for railway workers. The feldwebel raised his voice: 'Hurry up. We'll wait in that shelter over there.'

It didn't seem a bad idea. We had regrouped, and a young fellow covered with freckles, one of my snow-shovelling companions, was joking with his friend. We were making our way toward the hut when a violent burst of sound struck my ears. At the same moment, I saw, to the right of the hut, a light puff of white smoke.

Utterly astounded, I looked around at my companions. The feldwebel had flung himself down on the ground like a goalie onto a ball, and was loading his automatic. The fellow with the freckles was staggering toward me with enormous eyes and a curious stupefied expression. When he was about six feet from me, he fell to his knees. His mouth opened as if he wanted to shout, but no sound came, and he toppled over

46

backward. A second barrage of sound ripped the air, followed by a modulated whistle.

Without thinking, I threw myself flat on the snow. The feldwebel's automatic crackled, and I saw some snow from the roof of the hut shoot up into the air. I couldn't take my eyes off the freckled young soldier, whose motionless body lay a few yards away.

'Cover me, you idiots,' the feldwebel shouted, as he jumped up and ran forward.

I looked at the freckled soldier's friend. He seemed more surprised than frightened. Calmly, we aimed our weapons toward the woods, from which a few shots still rang out, and began to fire.

The detonation of my Mauser restored some of my confidence, but I was still very scared. Two more bullets whistled in my ears. Our sergeant, with appalling self-assurance, stood up and threw a grenade. The air rang with the noise of the explosion, and one of the worm-eaten planks of the hut disintegrated.

With incomprehensible calm, I continued to stare at the cabin. The feldwebel's automatic was still firing. Without panic, I slid another bullet into the barrel of my gun. As I was about to shoot, two black figures ran from the ruins of the hut, and headed toward the forest. It was a perfect opportunity. My gunsight stood out clearly in black against the white of the countryside, and then merged into the darkness of one of the galloping figures. I pressed the trigger ... and missed.

Our chief had run as far as the hut, firing after the fleeing men without hitting them. After a moment, he signalled us to join him, and we extricated ourselves from our holes in the snow.

The feldwebel was staring at something in the ruins of the cabin. As we drew closer we could see a man leaning against the wall. His face, half covered by a wild, shaggy beard, was turned toward us; his eyes looked damp. He gazed at us without a word; his clothes, of skin and fur, were not a military uniform. My eye was caught by his left hand. It was soaked with blood. More blood was running from his collar. I felt a twinge of unease for him. The feldwebel's voice brought me back to reality.

47

'Partisan!' he shouted. 'Hein? ... You know what you're going to get!'

He pointed his gun at the Russian, who seemed frightened and rolled farther back into the corner. I too recoiled, but our noncom was already putting his automatic back in its holster.

'You take care of him,' he ordered, waving toward the wounded man.

We carried the partisan outside. He groaned, and said something unintelligible.

The sound of an approaching train was growing steadily louder. This one, however, was returning to the rear. We managed to stop it. Three soldiers wrapped in heavy reindeer-skin coats jumped from the first carriage. One of them was a lieutenant, and we snapped to attention.

'What in God's name do you think you're doing?' he barked. 'Why did you stop us?'

Our noncom explained that we were looking for labour.

'This train is carrying only the wounded and dying,' the lieutenant said. 'If we had some troops on leave I'd help you out. As it is, I can't do anything for you.'

'We've got two wounded men,' the sergeant ventured.

The lieutenant was already walking over to the freckled soldier, who was lying motionless where he had fallen. 'You can see that this one's dead.'

'No, Mein Leutnant. He's still breathing.'

'Ah ... well, maybe ... But another fifteen minutes ...' he gestured vaguely. 'Well, all right ... we'll take him.' He whistled at two skeletal stretcherbearers, who lifted our young comrade. I thought I could see a brown stain in the middle of his back, but I wasn't sure whether it was blood mixed with the green of his coat, or something else.

'And the other one?' the lieutenant asked impatiently.

'Over there, beside the hut.'

The lieutenant looked at the bearded man, who was clearly dying. 'Who's this?'

'A Russian, Mein Leutnant, a partisan.'

'So that's it. Do you really think I'm going to saddle myself with one of those bastards who'll shoot you in the back any time – as if war at the front wasn't enough!'

He shouted an order to the two soldiers who were with

him. They walked over to the unfortunate man lying on the snow, and two shots rang out.

A short time later, we were making our way back to the road. Our noncom had abandoned the idea of an improvised labour force, and we would now rejoin our unit, which undoubtedly had not made much progress.

I had just been under fire for the first time, an experience I can no longer describe with any precision. An element of the absurd was mixed into the day's events: the feldwebel's footsteps in the snow were so enormous, and I, in my confusion, kept looking for the young freckled soldier who should have been returning with us. Everything had happened so quickly that I hadn't been able to grasp the significance of anything. Nevertheless, two human beings had suffered senseless deaths. Ours had not yet celebrated his eighteenth birthday.

It had already been dark for some time when we finally found our company. The night was clear and cold, and the thermometer was dropping with horrifying speed.

Despite our forced march of nearly four hours, we were shaking with cold, and famished. My head was swimming with exhaustion, and frost from my breath lay on the high collar which I had pulled up almost to my eyes.

For some time before we reached it, we were able to see our convoy, standing out clearly, black against white. Its progress had indeed been small. The trucks had sunk in through the icy white crust over the tops of their wheels, and great slabs of snow clung to their tyres and mudguards. Almost everyone had taken refuge inside the cabs. After chewing on their meagre rations, they had wrapped themselves in everything they could find, and were trying to sleep, despite the bitter cold. A short distance away, the two fellows who'd been chosen for guard duty were stamping on their boots, hoping to warm their feet.

Inside the cabs, through the frosted glass, I could see an occasional gleam from someone's cigarette or pipe. I climbed into my truck and felt in the darkness for my rucksack and mess tin. When the tin was propped between my icy fingers, I wolfed down a few mouthfuls of some filthy mixture that tasted like frozen soya. It was so bad that I tipped most of it onto the snow and ate something else.

Outside, I could hear somebody talking. I craned my neck to see who it was. A small fire had just been kindled in a hole in the snow, and was burning with a cheerful brilliance. I jumped down from the truck and hurried as fast as I could toward this source of light, heat, and joy. Three men were standing beside the fire, among them my feldwebel of this afternoon. He was breaking pieces of wood across his knee.

'I've had enough of this cold. I had pneumonia last winter, and if I get it again it's goodbye to me. Anyway, our trucks are visible for at least two miles, so we're not giving anything away by just lighting a few sticks.'

'You're right,' replied a fellow who must have been at least forty-five. 'The Russians, partisans or not, are all snug in their beds.'

'I certainly would be glad to be home in my bed,' said another staring into the flames.

We were all practically in the fire, except for the big feldwebel, who was busily reducing a packing case to fragments.

Suddenly someone shouted at us.

'Hey, you over there!'

A figure was approaching us between the trucks. We could see the silver trim on his cap gleaming through the darkness. Already the feldwebel and the old man were trampling on the fire. The captain came up to us, and we stood at attention.

'What do you think you're doing? You must have lost your minds! Don't you know the orders? Since you've come out to watch round the campfire, you can pick up your guns and make a nice patrol of the neighbourhood. Your festivities have undoubtedly attracted a few guests. Now it's up to you to find them. By twos until we leave. Understood?'

It was the last straw. With death in my soul, I went off to look for my damned gun. I was on the point of collapse from hunger, exhaustion, cold, and God knows what else. I would certainly never have the strength to spend the night slogging through that horrible snow, whose frozen crust covered more than two feet of white powder, into which I sank over the tops of my boots. I was filled with rage which I couldn't express. Exhaustion prevented reaction. I returned to my companions in misfortune as best I could. The feldwebel decided that the fellow who was pushing fifty and myself should take the first patrol.

'We'll relieve you in two hours, which will be easier for you.'

I have never understood why, but I had the distinct impression that the miserable cur had purposely put me with the old man. No doubt he preferred the other fellow as a companion – twenty-five years old and strongly built – to a scrawny seventeen or an old man. I started off with my fellow sufferer, convinced that we were a vulnerable combination. After the first few steps I tripped, and fell down full length onto the snow, scraping my hands against the hard, icy crust. As I was pulling myself up, I was scarcely able to contain a paroxysm of tears.

The old man was a decent sort: he too seemed to have had about enough.

'Did you hurt yourself?' he asked in a paternal tone.

'Merde,' I replied.

He said nothing. Pulling his collar a little higher against his head, he let me get in front of him. I didn't really know where we were supposed to be going, but that was unimportant. What I knew beyond a doubt was that I would double back as soon as the black mass of the convoy was out of sight, and despite my exhaustion I managed to put a considerable distance between myself and the old man. I moved forward nervously, breathing as little as possible, as the icy air burned my nose. But after a moment I couldn't go on. My knees trembled, and I dissolved in tears. I could no longer grasp anything that was happening to me. I could see clearly in my mind's eye France, and my family, and the games I used to play with my friends and my Meccano set. What was I doing here? I can remember crying out between bursts of sobs: 'I'm too young to be a soldier.'

I don't know whether or not my companion was surprised by my confusion. When he caught up with me he contented himself with saying: 'You walk too quickly, young fellow. You must forgive me if I can't keep up with you. I shouldn't even be a soldier. I was retired before the war. But six months ago they called me up anyway. They need everyone they can get, you know. Anyway, let's hope we get home again safely.'

As I didn't understand very much about the times, and needed someone to blame, I began to attack the Russians:

'And all of this on account of those bastards! The first one I meet has had it!'

However, I wasn't able to forget the events of the afternoon. The partisan and his execution had overwhelmed me. The poor old man looked at me in bewilderment. He must have wondered whether he was involved with a party fanatic or a security agent.

'Yes,' he said in a carefully veiled tone. 'They're certainly making us sweat. It would be better to let them settle it among themselves. They won't stay Bolshevik for long. And in the end, anyway, it's none of our business.'

'And Stalingrad! We certainly have to supply the Sixth Army! My uncle is there! They must be having a tough time.'

'Of course they're having a tough time. We don't know everything. Finishing off Zhukov isn't going to be easy.'

'Zhukov will quit, the way he did at Kharkov and Zhitomir. This won't be the first time General von Paulus made him run.'

He said nothing. As we lived without much information from the advanced front, the conversation came to a halt. I certainly never guessed that the doom of Stalingrad was already sealed; that the soldiers of the Sixth Army had given up hope and were fighting in horrible conditions, with heroic tenacity.

The sky was covered with stars. In the moonlight I was able to see the little student's watch strapped on my wrist, a souvenir of my *certificat d'études* in France. Time seemed to be standing still, and those two hours dragged like centuries. We walked slowly, watching the tips of our boots sink into the snow with every step. There was no wind, but the cold, which was growing increasingly severe, pierced us through and through.

For two hours at a time, throughout that accursed night, we shivered in this way. Between each tour of duty, I was able to snatch a brief sleep. The first glimmers of light, which found me shovelling snow, fell on a face creased with exhaustion.

With dawn, the cold grew even more intense. The woollen gloves we had been issued were worn through, and our frostbitten hands were wrapped in rags, or in our extra pairs of socks. But in spite of the exercise of shovelling the cold was no longer bearable. We slapped our hands against our sides and stamped our feet to keep our chilled blood moving. The captain, in a moment of compassion, ordered some ersatz coffee prepared and served to us boiling hot. This was doubly welcome because for breakfast that morning we had been given nothing but a portion each of frozen white cheese. The corporal at the canteen told us that the thermometer outside his truck read twenty-four degrees below zero.

I don't remember exactly how much longer this journey took. The days which followed have remained in my memory like a frozen nightmare. The temperature varied between fifteen and twenty-five below zero. There was a horrifying day of wind when, despite all of the orders and threats from our officers, we abandoned our shovels and took shelter behind the trucks. On that day the temperature fell to thirty-five degrees below zero, and I thought I would surely die. Nothing could warm us. We urinated into our numbed hands to warm them, and, hopefully, to cauterize the gaping cracks in our fingers.

Four of our men, who were seriously ill, suffering from pulmonary and bronchial pneumonia, lay groaning in make-shift beds set up in one of the trucks. There were only two medical orderlies for our company, and there wasn't much they could do. In addition to these serious illnesses, there were at least forty cases of frostbite. Some men had patches of skin on the ends of their noses which had been frozen and had become infected. Similar infection was common in the folds of the eyelids, around the ears, and particularly on the hands. I myself was not seriously affected, but each move-ment of my fingers opened and closed deep crevices, which oozed blood. At moments the pain was so intense that I felt sick at my stomach. At moments my despair was so intense that I broke down in tears, but as everyone was preoccupied with his own troubles, no one paid much attention.

Twice, I went to the canteen truck, which doubled as the infirmary, to have my hands washed in 90-degree alcohol. This produced paroxysms of pain which made me cry aloud, but afterward my hands felt warm for a few minutes.

Our inadequate diet contributed to our desperation. From Minsk, our point of departure, to Kiev, the first stop, was a distance of about 250 miles. With all the difficulties of the route taken into consideration, the authorities had given us food for five days. In fact, we required eight days, which obliged us to consume some of the rations intended for the front. In addition, we had to abandon three of the thirty-eight vehicles in our group because of mechanical failure, destroying them along with their cargoes, so that they wouldn't fall into the hands of the partisans. Of the four men who were seriously ill, two had died. Many others suffered from frostbite, and a few had to have frozen hands or feet amputated.

Three days before we reached Kiev, we crossed what must once have been the Russian line of defence. We drove for hours through a landscape littered with the carcasses of tanks, trucks, guns, and aircraft, gutted and burned, a scattering of junk which stretched as far as the eye could see. Here and there, crosses or stakes marked the hasty burial of the thousands of German and Russian soldiers who had fallen on this plain.

In fact, many more Russians than Germans had been killed. However, insofar as was possible, the soldiers of the Reich were given decent burials, while each orthodox emblem marked the grave of ten or twelve Soviet soldiers.

Our journey across this boneyard naturally did not make us feel any warmer. The huge shell holes, which we had to fill in as best we could, made it particularly difficult.

Finally, our convoy arrived at Kiev. This handsome city had not suffered much damage. The Red Army had tried to stop the Wehrmacht outside the town, in the zone we had passed through. When they had no longer been able to withstand German pressure, they had preferred to withdraw to the other side of the city, to spare it the kind of destruction Minsk had suffered. Kiev was our first stop, halfway between Minsk and Kharkov. Our ultimate destination, Stalingrad, was still more than six hundred miles away.

Kiev was an important strategic centre, where units coming from Poland and Rumania regrouped and made ready for the offensive which would push on to the Caucasus and the Caspian Sea. To an even greater degree than Minsk, the city swarmed with soldiers and military vehicles, with the difference that here there was a perceptible atmosphere of alert.

Our group entered the outlying zone of the city, and halted until further orders from the Kommandantur.

Once again we found ourselves walking on a snow-covered roadway as slick and firmly packed as a ski run. We thought we had reached the end of our troubles. Everyone was anticipating the arrival of orders which, we felt certain, would direct us to our new lodgings.

We were sent first of all to the hygienic centre, which was extremely welcome as the cold had made even the most cursory washing impossible. We were all disgustingly dirty and covered with vermin.

Those with serious injuries were hospitalized – a category to which only seven men were admitted. For everyone else, the journey continued; we spent only seven hours in Kiev.

As we left the remarkably well-organized sanitary service, our group was ordered to stand at attention on the snow-covered esplanade in front of the building. A hauptmann arrived at high speed in a Volkswagen. He turned toward us and delivered a short speech without getting out of the car.

'Soldiers! Germans! Convoy troops! At this hour, when the conquests of the Reich extend across a vast territory, the Fatherland depends on you to assure the victory of our arms by your devotion. It is your responsibility to hasten the pace at which essential supplies reach our fighting troops. The hour has come for you to perform your duty on the front you know so well – the road, fraught with a thousand perils and hardships, upon which you have already expended such prodigious energies. From our factories, where our workers are drawing on all their strength to forge the necessary weapons, through your exhausting journey toward our heroic combatants, no one is allowed a moment's respite so long as any German soldier might suffer from a shortage of weapons, food, or clothing. The nation is drawing on all its strength to insure that our soldiers at the front receive what they require and are thus able to retain their enthusiasm and confidence in our solidarity. Not one of us has the right to flinch or falter in the face of momentary discouragement. No one has the right to doubt the heroism daily confirmed by our fresh victories. We all have to bear the same sufferings, and dealing with them as a unified group is the best way of surmounting them. Never forget that the nation owes you everything, and that in return it expects everything of you, up to and including the supreme sacrifice. You must learn to support suffering without complaint, because you are German. Heil Hitler!'

'Heil Hitler!' we answered in unison.

The hauptmann cleared his throat and continued in a less theatrical tone: 'You will make up a full group and will rejoin the 124th and the 125th at the edge of town, on the Rollbahn to Kharkov. Your formation will be accompanied by a section of motorized combat troops belonging to Panzer-division Stülpnagel. They will protect your convoy from the terrorists who will try to impede your advance. As you will see, the Reich is making every effort to facilitate your task.'

He saluted, and his orderly immediately shifted into gear.

We joined the two other sections of our company at the selected place to form the 19th Kompanie Rollbahn, under Kommandant Ulträner. My first thought was that now I would surely run into my friends from training camp, if they hadn't been transferred or killed. I didn't know whether they'd left Minsk before or after us, but in fact our old 19th had been re-formed.

We now possessed a rolling kitchen which could serve us hot meals. This made a great difference to us. Immediately before our departure we were served a large hot meal, which produced an almost unbelievable sense of well-being, and raised our spirits to a remarkable degree. The cold seemed to have settled at about four degrees below zero, which was an improvement. But then we had just taken hot showers and changed our clothes.

I had no trouble finding Hals, whose exuberant gestures I recognized easily.

'Well, what do you think of the weather, young one? And of the restaurant, hein? It's ten days since I've swallowed anything hot. We thought we'd die of cold on that damned train.'

'You were on a train! If that's not luck . . .'

'Luck! You can talk . . . You should have been there when the locomotive blew up. It made a cloud of steam at least a hundred yards high. Four of the fellows were killed and seven wounded. Morvan was wounded while we were cleaning up the mess. It went on like that for five days. I was with a patrol that went after some terrorists. We caught two of them hiding in a kolkhoz.* One of the peasants they'd robbed put us on their trail, and afterward invited us to his place and gave us a regular feast.'

I wasted no time in telling him my adventures; talking this way made us both feel better. We had just run into Lensen and Olensheim. Our sense of happiness and relief at meeting again was so great that quite spontaneously we grabbed each other by the shoulders and mimed an exaggerated polonaise, shouting with laughter. Some of the older men stared at us in astonishment, unable to see any reason for this burst of gaiety, so inconsistent with the grey and icy atmosphere.

'Where's Fahrstein?' I asked.

'Ouf,' roared Lensen, still laughing. 'He's snug and warm in his truck. He sprained his ankle, and it's so swollen he can't take his boot off, so he's waiting for it to deflate.'

'He's making the most of it,' Hals remarked. 'If I carried on like that every time I turned my ankle . . .'

Our conversation was interrupted by the order for departure, and we returned to our posts. Knowing that my friends were there, with only a few trucks between us, made me feel a great deal better, and I almost forgot that each turn of the wheels was taking me closer to the front. It was still so far away. We were travelling on bad roads covered with snow and ice. On either side, a wall of snow thrown back by road-clearing operations hid the countryside. Through the occasional gaps we were able to see traces of the terrible fighting which had overrun this part of the country the year before. The hastily patched road was so rough that we had to crawl through several hundred miles of this ruined countryside.

The troops of von Wichs, Guderian, von Reichenau and von Stülpnagel had wrenched this territory from the Soviets after weeks of heavy fighting, and held several hundreds of thousands of prisoners between Kiev and Kharkov. The amount of Russian war matériel strewn about under the snow made me wonder how they could possibly have much left.

Rising temperatures brought fresh snowfalls which made

---

*Collective farm.

it necessary for us to bring out our shovels again. Fortunately, a section of the armoured column which was supposed to accompany us joined us two days later. We were able to attach four or five trucks to the back of a tank so that, with their engines going, the trucks were able to manage a slipping, sliding advance despite the snow and ice.

However, the low clouds soon vanished, leaving a pale blue sky. The thermometer plunged sharply, and we were caught once more by a biting cold, on that accursed Russian plain. Occasionally a group of German airplanes would pass over our column with throbbing engines. We waved wildly at the pilots, who responded by dipping their wings.

Higher up, squadrons of JU-52s passed slowly over us, flying east. Our hot meals no longer warmed us, and frostbite was eating into my hands once again. Fortunately, this time our convoy included a doctor. Each time we stopped to eat, we lined up beside his truck. He coated my hands with a greasy, curative ointment which I tried to keep on as long as possible as it reduced the pain in my cracked skin and preserved it from the cold. I kept my hands buried in the depths of my giant overcoat pockets unless absolutely forced to pull them out, and then I was very careful not to rub off the ointment against the rough cloth.

I spent long hours in the cab of a three-and-a-half-ton Renault, jolting from rut to rut. From time to time we had to remove the snow which accumulated between the mudguard and the tyre, or help another machine which had skidded and gotten stuck.

Otherwise, we avoided everything which obliged us to step outside. So far I had escaped guard duty at night. When darkness made further advance impossible, we stopped where we were. The driver had the right to the seat. I usually slept on the floor, with my legs wedged in beside the pedals and my nose on the engine, which gave off a sickening stench of hot oil. We always woke up stiff and numb with cold.

Well before daybreak we began the exhausting struggle of starting our frozen engines. Hals had come to see me several times, but my driver always protested that three was too many for our tiny cab. He advised me to go and see my friend instead, but that always came to the same thing, and there was certainly no question of standing outside for a chat.

One day, just after we had passed a large town with a Luftwaffe airfield beside it, we were joined by a reconnaissance plane, which entered into radio communication with the Kommandergruppe of the armoured section accompanying us. A moment later, the plane left the convoy and veered to the north. The tanks in our column disappeared in whirlwinds of snow thrown up by their treads. We went on as before, without feeling any special anxiety. A few hours later we heard the booming sound of distant explosions. This stopped, began again a few minutes later, then stopped, then began again. At eleven o'clock the convoy halted in a village covered with snow. The sun was shining, and its gleam on the snow made us squint. The cold, although intense, was bearable.

We walked over to the soup truck, whose two stoves were belching smoke. The first arrivals were sent by the cook to fetch the kettles. This cook was not at all a bad sort, and his skill was adequate at least to prevent insurrection. The dishes he prepared really weren't bad at all. The only oddity of his cooking style was that everything without exception was served with the same thick flour sauce. I joined Hals and Lensen, and we were walking back to our trucks, bent over our steaming mess tins. Suddenly a series of more or less distant explosions shook the icy air. We stopped for a moment and listened. Everyone else seemed to be doing the same thing. The explosions began again. Some of them were obviously far away. Instinctively we began to hurry.

'What's going on?' Lensen asked an older soldier who was climbing into his truck.

'Guns, fellows. We're getting closer,' he said.

We had all guessed this already, but we needed confirmation.

'Ha!' said Hals. 'I'm going to get my gun.'

Personally, I didn't take any of this too seriously. There were a few more explosions, some separate and distinct, others overlapping each other.

The departure whistle blew, and we climbed back into our trucks.

The convoy jolted into motion. An hour later, as we reached the top of a hill, the gunfire brought us to a complete stop. It was coming from much closer. Each explosion literally shook the air, which was a very strange sensation. Some nervous drivers had stepped on their brakes much too quickly. Their trucks had skidded on the ice, and the drivers were racing the engines, trying unsuccessfully to straighten their machines. I had opened our door, and was looking down the line of trucks. A Volkswagen was driving from the rear at top speed, and a lieutenant was shouting through its open door: 'Hurry up, get going, keep moving! You ... help that idiot out of the rut.'

I jumped down from our Renault and joined a group of soldiers trying to pull an Opel Blitz back onto the road. The firing had begun again. It seemed to be quite close and coming from the north. Slowly, and with difficulty, the convoy began to move. As we had jammed on our brakes in the middle of an ascent, my driver had a particularly hard time starting up our truck. We descended slowly into a rolling, wooded countryside. The dull sound of explosions continued. Suddenly, the trucks at the head of the column stopped again, and we heard the blast of a whistle. We quickly jumped to the ground. Soldiers were running to the head of the convoy. What was happening?

The lieutenant of a while ago was running too, collecting a group of soldiers as he went by. I was one of them. Carrying our Mausers, and running as fast as we could, we reached the front of the column. The big Kommandergruppe half-track seemed to have driven deliberately into the thick snow at the side of the road.

'Partisans up ahead,' a feldwebel shouted. 'Scatter for defence.' He pointed to our left.

Without understanding very much, I followed the sergeant who was at the head of our group of fifteen soldiers and plunged into the snowy slope. As I pulled myself up on the white barrier, I could see very clearly a swarming mass of black figures emerging from a stunted woods and proceeding at right angles to our line of march. The Russians seemed to be moving as slowly as we were. The cold and the weight of our clothes combined to deprive this spectacle of the animation of Westerns, or of American so-called 'war' films. The cold made everything sluggish: both gaiety and sadness, courage and fear.

Ducking my head like everyone else, I moved forward,

paying more attention to the position of my boots than to the movements of the enemy. The partisans were still too far away for me to see them in any detail. I imagined that, like us, they must be making huge strides to avoid disappearing in a hole in the snow.

'Dig your foxholes,' the feldwebel ordered, lowering his voice – as if the other side could hear us.

I didn't have a shovel, but scraped away some snow with the butt of my rifle. Once I was crouched in this relative shelter, I was able to observe the scene at leisure. I was astounded by the number of men coming out of the woods opposite; there were so many of them! And I could see still others in the forest itself, through the branches of the leafless trees. They looked like ants swarming through tall grass. They were obviously moving from north to south. As we were moving east to west, I couldn't grasp their intention. Perhaps they were going to try to encircle us.

Our troops had just set up a heavy machine-gun battery on the slope nearest us, about twenty yards away. I didn't understand why there had not yet been any exchange of fire. The enemy had begun to cross the road, about two hundred yards from us. The sound of big guns from the north was louder than ever, and there seemed to be some answering fire directly opposite us. My hands and feet were beginning to feel the cold. I didn't understand our situation, and felt entirely calm.

The band of Russians crossed the road without bothering us. They appeared to outnumber us by three or four to one. Our convoy consisted of a hundred trucks with a hundred armed drivers, and sixty accompanying troops whose sole function was defence. In addition, there were ten officers and noncoms, a doctor, and two medical orderlies.

Each explosion created clouds of powdered snow. From the wooded hill in the near distance, plumes of smoke synchronized with the increasingly frequent sounds of explosion rose into the air. The heavy machine gun to my right burst into sound for a moment, and then fell silent.

Stupidly, instead of crouching down in my hole, I lifted my head. I could see little white clouds puffing out among the numerous silhouettes of the partisans. There was a sound of dry detonation, with an answer in kind from the Russians.

My eardrums had begun to feel as though they would burst from the noise of the machine gun, which was joined by another on the slope opposite. Everywhere, soldiers were firing their Mausers. Over in the Russian sector, the black silhouettes were running in all directions, faster and faster, through the puffs of white smoke. Some of them fell and lay motionless. The sun went on shining. None of it seemed really serious. Here and there, Russian bullets whistled through the air. The noise was deafening. With my slow reflexes, I hadn't yet fired.

To my right, someone cried out. The sound of firing was almost continuous. The Bolsheviks were running as fast as they could toward the shelter of the snowy thickets. Our tanks were rolling toward them with sharp bursts of gunfire.

Three or four Russian bullets landed in the snow in front of me, and I began to fire blindly, like everyone else. Seven or eight other tanks had arrived and were harassing the partisans. The whole episode lasted about twenty minutes, and when it was over, I had fired about a dozen cartridges.

A short time later, our tanks and armoured cars returned. Three of them were driving prisoners ahead of them, in groups of about fifteen men, who all looked deeply humiliated. Three German soldiers supported by their comrades climbed down from one of the cars. One of them seemed almost unconscious, and the other two were grimacing with pain. Three wounded Russians and two Germans were lying inert on the back of one of the tanks, one of them moaning. A short distance off a German soldier, leaning against a snowbank, was gesturing to us and holding his head, which was red with blood.

'The road is clear,' announced the commanding officer of the Mark-4 nearest us. 'You can go ahead.'

We helped carry the wounded to the hospital truck. I went back to my Renault. Lensen passed by close to me, and shook his head in perplexity.

'Did you see that?' he asked.

'Yes. Do you know if anyone was killed?'

'Of course.'

The convoy started off again. The idea of death troubled me, and suddenly I felt afraid. The sunshine of a moment ago had been pale, and the cold had become more intense. Bodies in long brown coats were lying along the sides of the road. One of them gestured as we passed.

'Hey,' I nudged my driver. 'There's a wounded man waving at us.'

'Poor fellow. Let's hope his side takes care of him. War is hard that way. Tomorrow it may be our turn.'

'Yes, but we've got a doctor. He could do something for him.'

'You can talk. We've got two truckloads of wounded already, and the doctor has more than enough to keep him busy. You mustn't be upset by all this, you know. You'll see plenty more of it.'

'I already have.'

'I have too,' he said, without believing me. 'Especially, I've seen my own knee. The whole kneecap was taken out by a shell in Poland. I thought they were going to send me home again. But they stuck me into the drivers' corps instead, along with the old men, the boys, and the infirm. It's no joke you know; a wound like that really hurts, especially if you have to wait for hours before they give you any morphine.'

He launched into the history of the Polish campaign as he had experienced it. At that time, he had belonged to the Sixth Army, which now was fighting in Stalingrad.

It was growing dark. Our long convoy stopped in a small hamlet. The armoured column was there too. The captain had ordered this halt so that the wounded could be cared for. The crust of snow and the roughness of the road made the hospital truck rock and jolt. The surgeon couldn't operate under such conditions. Two Russians had already died of haemorrhage, and the rest of the men had already been waiting for several hours.

Our truck had just stopped beside a large building where the peasants stored the harvest. I was about to open the door and run to the kitchen truck when my driver held me back: 'Don't be in such a hurry, unless you want to be on guard duty tonight. The sergeant doesn't keep records here, you know, the way he does at the barracks. He just grabs the first people he sees, assigns them, and then takes it easy.'

It was true. A short time later I was listening to the complaints of the eternally hungry Hals: 'Scheisse! They've stuck me for guard duty again. God knows what'll happen to us all.

It's getting colder and colder. We won't be able to stand it.'

It was another clear night, and the thermometer fell to twenty-two degrees below freezing.

I thanked my driver for saving me from another night in the open air. However, the fate that befell me instead almost made me regret my luck. We were walking toward the kitchen truck feeling somewhat anxious about dinner, wondering if there would be enough left to fill our mess tins. When the cook saw us coming, he couldn't resist a little sarcasm: 'So, you're not feeling hungry tonight?'

He had already taken the tureens off the fire and replaced them with the big serving dishes, which were filled with hissing water coming to the boil.

'Hurry up and eat,' he said, plunging his gloved hand armed with a big spoon into the depths of one of the tureens. 'I have to boil this water for the surgeon. He's busy carving up the wounded.'

We were bolting our tepid meal, still wearing our ragged gloves, when a lieutenant arrived.

'Is the water nearly ready?'

'Just now, Leutnant. It's just boiling.'

'Good.' The lieutenant's eye fell on us. 'You two: take the water to the doctor.' He pointed to the lighted doorway of one of the houses.

We closed our mess tins, still half full of food, and hooked them onto our belts. I grabbed one of the steaming basins, taking care not to empty its contents onto my feet, and walked toward the improvised operating room.

The sole advantage of being inside this house was its temperature. It had been a long time since any of us had experienced indoor warmth. The doctor had requisitioned the large common room of a Soviet farmer, and was busy with the leg of a poor fellow stretched out on the central table. Two other soldiers were holding the patient, who was jerking spasmodically and moaning with pain. Everywhere – on benches, on the floor, on the big storage chests – wounded soldiers were lying or sitting, groaning as they waited. Two orderlies were tending to them. The floor was littered with bloody bandages.

Two Russian women were washing the surgical instruments in basins of hot water. The room was extremely badly lit. The doctor had put the farmer's big gas lamp beside the operating table. The farmer himself was holding another lamp over the surgeon's head. A lieutenant and a sergeant were each holding another lamp.

In an angle of the room made by the big corner chimney, a young Russian was crying. He looked about seventeen, like me. I put my basin down beside the doctor, who plunged a thick wad of dressing into it. I stayed where I was, transfixed by the terrible sight in front of me. I couldn't lift my eyes from that naked thigh inside which the surgeon was working. The skin around the wound seemed to have been crushed, and everything was soaked with blood. New streams of blood, of a brighter, clearer red, kept running from the enormous hole in which the doctor was working, with what looked like a pair of flat-bladed scissors. My head began to swim, and I felt sick at my stomach, but I couldn't look away. The patient was tossing his head from one side to the other. He was being held down firmly by two other soldiers. His face was completely drained of colour, and streaming with sweat. They had stuffed a bandage into his mouth, perhaps to keep him from crying out. It was one of the soldiers from the armoured column. I couldn't move.

'Hold his leg,' the doctor said softly to me.

I hesitated, and he looked at me again. My trembling hands took hold of the mangled leg. As they touched the skin, I could feel myself shaking.

'Gently,' murmured the doctor.

I saw the scalpel cut even more deeply into the wound, and I could feel the muscles of the leg tensing and relaxing. Then I closed my eyes. I could hear the sounds made by the surgical instruments, and the heavy, panting breath of the patient, who kept moving in agony, despite the partial anaesthetic.

Then, although I could hardly bear to recognize it, I heard the sound of a saw. A moment later, the leg was heavier in my hand – unbelievably heavy – and I saw that it was supported five inches above the table only by my anguished hands. The surgeon had just detached it from the body.

I remained for a moment in a ludicrous and tragic attitude, holding my hideous burden. I thought I was going to faint. Finally, I put it down on a pile of bandages beside the table. I shall never forget that leg, even if I live a hundred years.

65

My driver had managed to leave, and I waited for a moment of general inattention to do the same thing. Unfortunately, such a moment did not arrive until very late that night. I had to do a great many other things almost as troubling as the amputation. It was nearly one o'clock in the morning when I finally opened the double doors of the house.

As the cold struck me, it seemed more violent than ever. I hesitated, but the thought of returning to those dying men and those streams of blood turned me resolutely back into the night. The sky was clear and light, and the air seemed absolutely still. The shadows of the houses and the trucks were stamped with precise outlines on the hard, gleaming snow. I couldn't see a living soul.

I walked through the village looking for my Renault; the whole convoy could have been destroyed before anyone gave the alarm. The door of an isba flew open and a bundle of blankets with a Mauser slung across it ventured a few faltering steps onto the snow. When the man inside the blankets caught sight of me he mumbled a few words.

'You go in now. It's my turn.'

'Go where?'

'To warm up. Unless you feel like taking another round.'

'But I'm not on guard. I've just been helping the surgeon, and now I'm going to get some sleep.'

'I see. I thought you were . . .' He mumbled a name.

'Did you say there was somewhere to get warm?'

'Yes. You go on in there. They've made it headquarters for the guard. We take shifts every fifteen or twenty minutes. Of course, you don't get any sleep that way, but it's better than freezing for two hours.'

'Yes. Thank you. I'll go in.'

I pushed open the heavy door and went inside. A big fire was blazing in the fireplace. Four soldiers, one of whom was Hals, were roasting potatoes and other vegetables under the ashes. The light from the fire was the only light in the room. Another fellow came in right after me, probably the guard I had been mistaken for. I warmed up the rest of the food in my mess tin, ate without appetite, and stretched out on the floor in front of the fireplace to sleep as best I could. Every fifteen or twenty minutes, one of the guards would shake awake some poor fellow flattened by sleep. From time to time the voice of someone protesting his fate would waken me. It was still dark when the reveille whistle shrilled in my ears.

Slowly we stood up on the floor which had served as our bed. We were rather stiff, but it had been a long time since any of us had slept without feeling cold. A young Russian woman was coming toward us from the shadows in the corner of the room. She was carrying a steaming pot which she held out to us, smiling. It was hot milk. For a moment I wondered if the milk might not be poisoned, but Hals, who preferred to die with a full stomach, had already grabbed the pot and helped himself to a generous swig. We passed the milk around among the four of us, then Hals laughed and returned it to the Russian woman. Neither of them could understand a word the other said. Hals went up to her and kissed her on both cheeks. She blushed a deep red. We bowed, and left.

Immediately, the cold fell on us like an icy shower. There was roll call, and distribution of lukewarm ersatz coffee. As on every other morning, we needed a good half hour to warm up the engines and get them started. Well before daybreak, the 19th Kompanie Rollbahn was jolting along the glare ice of that damned Soviet highway, the 'Third International.'

Several times, we had to make way for convoys driving to the rear. We stopped for lunch in a squalid hamlet where the column of tanks which preceded us had also stopped, and we learned that we were only fifty miles from Kharkov.

We were all jubilant to hear that we were so close to our destination. Our convoy should arrive in two or three hours. We tried to imagine our quarters in Kharkov.

'What do you think it will be like?' Lensen asked.

The fellow who'd been with me for this interminable trip, the one without a kneecap, was not one to jump for joy.

'I hope we won't be spending too much time there,' he said. 'It would be just like them to send us on to the Volga. I'd rather start back the other way than keep on going east.'

'If no one wants to go east, we'll never be through with the Russians,' someone said.

'That's true,' another voice remarked.

'Some people would do better to shut up instead of always talking about how afraid they are.'

We were back on the road about half an hour later. The

sun had disappeared into a fog which veiled the horizon. The cold seemed less sharp, but damp and penetrating. We drove for about an hour. My eyes were half closed, and I had nearly fallen asleep, staring at an illuminated spot on the dashboard. My head was jolting from side to side with the motion of the truck. I decided I might as well sleep, and propped myself against the door. Before closing my eyes, I looked out once more at the snowy countryside. The sky had turned grey, and seemed heavier than the earth. Two tiny black spots were coming toward us over the top of the nearest hill. Probably a couple of patrol planes. I closed my eyes.

A few seconds later, my eyes flew open again. The roar of an engine passed right over our heads, and was immediately followed by a series of crackling detonations.

Then something unimaginable hurled me against the windshield, and I felt as if my chest and eardrums were going to explode. There was an intensity of noise which sounded like the end of the world, and we were engulfed in a shower of ice, stones, boxes, helmets, and mess tins. Our Renault nearly crashed into the car in front of us, which had come to a dead stop.

Stupefied and bewildered, I opened the door and jumped down to the ground, looking back toward the source of the noise. The truck behind had almost run into us, and behind it a third truck had rolled over. Its wheels were still turning in the air. Beyond it there was nothing but flames and smoke.

'Quick! Get over the bank!'

Soldiers were scattering across the snow as far as I could see.

'They're shooting at the trucks!' someone shouted.

I dug myself into three feet of snow behind the bank.

'Anti-aircraft defence!' yelled a sergeant, who was running, doubled over, along the side of the bank.

The soldiers floundering in the snow beside me aimed their guns at the sky.

Good Lord! My gun was still in the Renault. I was already running back to the truck when I heard the noise of airplane engines once again. I pushed my head into the snow. A hurricane passed over me, followed by explosions, both nearby and far away.

I lifted my snowy face and looked at the two bimotors

diving down behind distant birch woods. The captain's Volkswagen was bouncing from rut to rut, driving down the length of the convoy in reverse. Soldiers were running in every direction.

I got up and ran toward a pillar of black smoke. A truck loaded with explosives had been hit by Soviet planes. The truck had exploded, destroying the vehicles immediately in front of it and behind it. The snow was strewn with smoking debris for a distance of nearly sixty yards. What was left of the trucks was burning, giving off a black, acrid smoke. I saw the feldwebel emerging from this cloud with another soldier. They were carrying a bloody, blackened body.

Instinctively, I and some others ran into the black fog to see what we could do. Through the smoke which stung my eyes I tried to see if I could recognize any human beings. A silhouette crossed my path, coughing.

'Don't stay here; it's too dangerous. The munitions cases are about to blow up.'

I heard the sound of a racing engine, and then two headlights pierced the curtain of smoke. A truck was coming along the bank, and behind it another, and two others . . . The convoy was continuing its journey.

Despite the flames, I was beginning to freeze. I decided to return to the relatively warm cab of my Renault. As the road was becoming visible once more, through the veil of thinning smoke, I noticed a group of soldiers, wrapped in their long overcoats, lined up in front of an officer.

'Come over here, you two,' shouted the lieutenant.

We ran over to the line.

'You,' he said, pointing at me. 'Where's your gun?'

'Over there, Leutnant . . . behind you . . . in the Renault.'

My voice was trembling with anxiety. The lieutenant looked furious. He must have thought I'd lost my gun, and that I was just telling him a story to cover up. He walked over to me like an enraged sheep dog.

'Break ranks!' he shouted. 'Attention.'

I stepped out, and had only just snapped to attention when I was rocked by a thunderous slap. Although I had pulled it down as far as I could, my cap rolled onto the snow, exposing my dirty uncombed hair. I thought the lieutenant was going to shower me with kicks.

'Guard duty until further orders,' he muttered, shifting his furious grey eyes from me to the sergeant, who saluted. 'At ease,' he added, staring at me with a petrifying expression.

'You scum,' he went on. 'While your comrades in arms are getting themselves killed to protect you, you are incapable of spotting two stinking Bolshevik aircraft firing at us. You should have seen them. You must have been asleep. I'm going to get all of you sent to the front in a disciplinary battalion. Three trucks destroyed, seven men killed, two wounded. They must have been asleep too. There's your result. You are unworthy of the arms you bear. I am going to report your attitude.'

He walked off without saluting.

'To your posts,' the sergeant shouted, trying to maintain the tone of his superior.

We all ran off our separate ways. I darted for my cap, but the sergeant caught me by the shoulder.

'Back to your post!'

'My cap, Sergeant.'

A soldier who was standing right beside my hat gave it back to me. In a daze I climbed into my truck, which was just starting up.

'Wipe your nose,' said my driver.

'Yes ... It seems as if I'm getting it in the neck for everybody.'

'Oh, don't worry. Tonight we'll be at Kharkov. Maybe there won't even be anything to guard.'

After the shock of a moment ago, I was beginning to feel angry.

'He could have seen those planes himself. After all, he's part of the convoy too!'

'Why don't you go tell him that?'

I thought of the two little black dots I had noticed in my half sleep. There was some truth in what the lieutenant had said, but we hadn't been prepared for anything like that. In fact, we hadn't yet encountered any of the real dangers of war, and we were all exhausted by the lack of sleep, the cold, this endless journey, and by our revolting condition of almost unbelievable filth. We were too cold to wash during the few minutes of our daytime halts, and in any case it was almost impossible to find water. We had to ask the peasants for it, and as they didn't understand a word we said we had to proceed without their permission, in front of their stupefied faces and their enormous eyes. All of that took time, and we had time only in the evening, after dark, when all we could think of was sleep.

But all these excuses wouldn't bring my comrades back to life. I was appalled by the thought that a difference of three trucks would have meant our life. I had never been wounded, but I already had an idea of how painful that could be.... I glued myself to the window.

'If any others come back, I certainly won't miss them.'

My driver looked at me with his habitual mocking expression. 'You'd better look in the rear-view mirror too. They might come up from behind.' He was almost sneering.

'You think I'm an idiot. What should we do?'

He shrugged his shoulders. His expression didn't change. 'Well, you know, there really isn't too much you can do. When I broke my knee, I was thinking about my head. The best thing would be to go in the other direction.'

'That's it! And quit on our comrades at the front!'

He looked at me, and for a moment stopped smiling. Then his face relaxed again, and he added in the same offhand tone as before: 'All they have to do is what I just said: half-turn, right face.' He imitated the tone of a feldwebel.

'You're not really thinking about what you're saying,' I said. 'The Bolsheviks would certainly take advantage of anything like that. It's impossible. The war isn't over. You have no right to talk that way.'

He looked me full in the face. 'You're too young. You thought I was serious. No. We've got to go as fast as we can, and faster.' As if to emphasize his remarks, he stepped on the gas.

'I'm too young! You all drive me crazy saying that. As if only fellows your age were any good. Don't I wear the same uniform you do?'

I didn't really believe what I was saying with such passion, or even that I was really there, among all those soldiers.

'If you're not satisfied, get another taxi.' He was openly laughing at me.

As he plainly wasn't going to take me seriously, I was silent. I was both furious and sad. First they beat me up for

71

lack of vigilance, then they bawl me out. Our line of trucks was continuing its sliding advance across the ice and snow. Night was falling, and with the darkness the cold was increasing. The thought that we were nearly at the end of our journey was in some way encouraging. We would be approaching the outskirts of Kharkov within a half hour. What condition would the town be in? It was the last big city before the front, before the Don, and beyond that, the Volga, and Stalingrad. Stalingrad was still four hundred miles from Kharkov. Secretly, despite my feeling of revulsion toward the Soviet countryside, I felt almost disappointed that we weren't yet at the front. Then came the crushing blow.

I remember that we were going down a hill. The trucks ahead of us slowed down, and then stopped.

'What now?' I had already opened the door.

'Shut that door. It's too cold.'

I slammed the door in his face, and walked across the icy crust that covered the narrow 'Third International' highway. A sidecar had just come to a stop ahead of me, and was still skidding on the ice. A courier from Kharkov was bringing us an order. In the grey light I could see some officers talking rapidly to each other. They seemed to be trying to make a plan, to be discussing some serious news. One of them, our captain, was reading a paper.

Another moment went by, and then a sergeant ran down the length of the convoy, blowing the whistle for assembly. While everyone was collecting, the sidecar, which had started up again, drove by in front of me. There were two soldiers in it, wearing what looked like diving suits. The captain came over to us, followed by his two lieutenants and three feldwebels. He didn't lift his eyes from the ground, and his expression was one of despair.

A shiver of anxiety ran across our shaggy and exhausted faces.

'Achtung! Stillgestanden!' shouted a feldwebel.

We stood at attention. The captain gave us a long look. Then slowly, in his gloved hand, he lifted a paper to the level of his eyes.

'Soldiers,' he said. 'I have some very serious news for you; serious for you, for all the fighting men of the Axis, for our people, and for everything our faith and sacrifice represents.

Wherever this news will be heard this evening, it will be received with emotion and profound grief. Everywhere along our vast front, and in the heart of our fatherland, we will find it difficult to contain our emotion.'

'Stillgestanden!' insisted the feldwebel.

'Stalingrad has fallen!' the captain continued. 'Marshal von Paulus and his Sixth Army, driven to the ultimate sacrifice, have been obliged to lay down their arms unconditionally.'

We felt stunned and profoundly anxious. The captain continued after a moment of silence.

'Marshal von Paulus, in the next to last message he sent, informed the Führer that he was awarding the Cross for bravery with exceptional merit to every one of his soldiers. The Marshal added that the calvary of these unfortunate combatants had reached a peak, and that after the hell of this battle, which lasted for months, the halo of glory has never been more truly deserved. I have here the last message picked up by short wave from the ruins of the tractor factory Red October. The High Command requests that I read it to you.

'It was sent by one of the last fighting soldiers of the Sixth Army, Heinrich Stoda. Heinrich states in this message that in the southwest district of Stalingrad he could still hear the sound of fighting. Here is the message:

' "We are the last seven survivors in this place. Four of us are wounded. We have been entrenched in the wreckage of the tractor factory for four days. We have not had any food for four days. I have just opened the last magazine for my automatic. In ten minutes the Bolsheviks will overrun us. Tell my father that I have done my duty, and that I shall know how to die. Long live Germany! Heil! Hitler!" '

Heinrich Stoda was the son of Doctor of Medicine Adolph Stoda of Munich. There was an impressive silence, broken only by a few blasts of wind. I thought of my uncle there, whom I had never met because of the rupture between our two families. I had only seen his photograph, and they had told me he was a poet. I felt very keenly that I had lost a friend. A man in the ranks began to whimper. His white temples made him look like an old man. Then he quit his rigid posture and began to walk toward the officers, crying and shouting at the same time.

'My two sons are dead. It was bound to happen. It's all your fault – you officers. It's fatal. We'll never be able to stand up to the Russian winter.' He bowed almost double, and burst into tears. 'My two children have died there . . . my poor children . . .'

'At ease,' ordered the feldwebel.

'No. Kill me if you like. It doesn't matter. Nothing matters. . . .'

Two soldiers stepped forward and took the poor man by the arms, trying to lead him back to his place before anything worse happened. Hadn't he just insulted the officers? Unfortunately he struggled, like someone possessed by demons.

'Take him to the infirmary,' the captain said. 'Give him a sedative.'

I thought he was going to add something else, but his expression remained fixed. Perhaps he too had lost a relative.

'At ease.'

We returned to our trucks in small, silent groups. By now it was full night. The rolling white horizon was tinged with a cold bluish grey. I shivered.

'It's getting colder and colder,' I said to the fellow walking beside me.

'Yes. Colder and colder,' he answered, staring into the distance.

For the first time I was strongly impressed by the dismal vastness of Russia. I felt quite distinctly that the huge, heavy grey horizon was closing in around us, and shivered more violently than ever. Three-quarters of an hour later, we were rolling through the ravaged outskirts of Kharkov. We couldn't see very much by our dim headlights but everything that appeared in the path of the light was damaged.

The next day, after one more night on the floor of the Renault, I was able to look at the chaos which was all that remained of Kharkov, a city of considerable importance, despite the devastation of war.

During the years 1941, 1942, and 1943 it was taken by our army, retaken by the Russians, taken back by the Germans, and then finally retaken by the Russians. At this particular moment, our troops were holding it for the first time. But the town looked like a jumble of burnt-out wreckage. Acres of total destruction had been used as dumps for the piles of wrecked machinery of every kind which the occupying troops had collected in their efforts to clear the roads. This mass of twisted, torn metal reflected the ferocious violence of the battle. It was all too easy to imagine the fate of the combatants. Now, motionless beneath the shroud of snow which only partially covered them, these steel cadavers marked a stage of the war: the battles of Kharkov.

The Wehrmacht had organized itself in the few sections of the city which were more or less standing. The sanitary service, ingeniously installed in a large building, was a bath of rejuvenation for us. When we were clean we were taken to a series of cellar rooms which made up a large basement filled with every conceivable kind of bed. We were advised to try to sleep, and despite the hour – it was the middle of the afternoon – we almost all fell into leaden unconsciousness. We were wakened by a sergeant, who led us to the canteen. There I found Hals, Lensen, and Olensheim. We talked about everything; particularly about the fall of Stalingrad.

Hals maintained that it wasn't possible: 'The Sixth Army! My God! They *couldn't* be beaten by the Soviets!'

'But since the communiqué said they were surrounded, that they didn't have anything more to fight with, what else could they do? They were *forced* to surrender.'

'Well, then we'll have to try and rescue them,' someone else said.

'It's too late,' remarked one of the older men. 'It's all over. . . .'

'Shit, shit, shit!' Hals clenched his fists. 'I just can't believe it!'

If for some the fall of Stalingrad was a staggering blow, for others it provoked a spirit of revenge which rekindled faltering spirits. In our group, given the wide range of ages, opinion was divided. The older men were, generally speaking, defeatist, while the younger ones were determined to liberate their comrades. We were walking back to our dormitory when a fight broke out for which I was mainly responsible.

The fellow with the broken knee, my companion in that damned Renault, had just fallen into step with me.

'Well, you must be pleased,' he said. 'It sounds as if we'll be going back tomorrow.'

I could see a certain irony on his face, and felt myself turning red with anger.

'That's enough from you,' I shouted. 'I hope you're satisfied. We're going back, and it's at least partly your fault if my uncle is dead in Stalingrad.'

He turned pale. 'Who told you he's dead?'

'If he's not dead that's even worse,' I went on shouting. 'You're nothing but a coward. It's you who told me we ought to leave them to their fate.'

My companion was astonished, and looked around for reactions. Then he grabbed my collar. 'Shut up!' he ordered, lifting his fist.

I kicked him in the shin. He was going to hit me when Hals grabbed his arm.

'That's enough,' he said calmly. 'Stop it, or you'll get yourselves thrown in jail.'

'So. You're another young fellow who wants what's coming to him?' My antagonist was now carried away with rage. 'I'm going to give it to all of you, you . . .'

'Drop it,' Hals insisted.

'Shit.'

He didn't say anything more. A blow from Hals's fist caught him on the chin. He spun round and fell onto his backside in the snow. By now Lensen had come up too.

'You bunch of kid shits,' shouted my driver. He tried to get up to return to the attack.

Lensen, short and thick-set, kicked him in the face with his metalled boot before he'd regained his balance. He fell onto his knees with a cry of pain, lifting his hands to his bloody face.

'Savage,' somebody shouted.

We didn't persist further, and rejoined the group, swearing under our breath. The others looked at us blackly, and two of them helped my driver to his feet. He was still groaning.

'We'll have to look out for that one,' Hals warned. 'He might very well shoot one of us in the back the next time we're attacked.'

Reveille the next day was later than usual. We went out for company roll call and were greeted by a whirlwind of snow. With our heads muffled in our upturned collars to escape the stinging ice fragments in the wind, we heard some good

76

news. Feldwebel Laus, whom we hadn't seen in an eternity, was standing in front of us holding a piece of paper with both hands. He too was having trouble with the wind.

'Soldiers!' he read, in the lull between two gusts. 'The High Command, aware of your condition, grants you a leave of twenty-four hours. Nevertheless, given the present situation, a counter order could come at any time. You will, therefore, present yourselves at your billets every two hours. Needless to say, this will not give you time to call on lady friends or visit your families,' he added, laughing. 'But at least you'll be able to write to them.'

Laus sent two men to fetch the mail, which was then distributed. There were four letters and a package for me. We would have liked to look at Kharkov, but the appalling weather kept us indoors. We spent a restful day, preparing for the return journey. We were therefore astonished to be told next day that we would resupply with food and weapons a unit stationed in the combat zone. We were even given more or less precisely the location of our new destination. We were to proceed to a sector somewhere to the south of Voronezh. We received this news without enthusiasm.

'Bah!' said Hals. 'Whether we tramp through the snow to Kiev or to Voronezh, it's all the same thing.'

'Yes,' said Olensheim somewhat cautiously. 'But Voronezh is at the front.'

'I know,' said Hals. 'But we'll have to see it sometime.'

As for me, I didn't know what to think. What really happened on a battlefield? I felt torn by curiosity and fear.

Chapter Two

THE FRONT

SOUTH OF VORONEZH · THE DON

Winter seemed endless. It snowed every day, almost without a break. At the end of February or beginning of March – I no longer remember which – we were taken by rail to a town used as a major supply centre, some fifty miles from Kharkov. Food, blankets, medicines, and other supplies were stored in big sheds, and every cellar and hole in the ground was jammed with munitions. There were also repair shops – some indoors, others in the open air. Soldiers perching on tanks blew on their fingers when they grew too numb to hold a wrench. A system of trenches and strongpoints had been organized on the outskirts of the town. This part of the country suffered from frequent partisan attacks, often by large groups of men. Whenever this happened, every mechanic and warehouseman abandoned his tools and inventories for a machine gun, to protect the supplies and himself.

'The only advantage we have here,' one of the soldiers said to me, 'is that we're very well fed. There's an awful lot of work. We have to organize our own defence – we take turns standing guard – and things can get pretty tough with the partisans. They've given us some hard times, even with all of us fighting, and they've already destroyed a lot. Several times the C.O. has asked for an infantry unit to help him out – but it's only happened once. An S.S. company came, but three days later they were sent on to the Sixth Army. We've already had forty killed, which is a lot for one company.'

That afternoon, we organized an odd-looking convoy using four-wheeled Russian carts to which runners could be attached, transforming them into sleighs. There were also some real sleighs – a few eidekas and even two or three troikas covered with decorations – all requisitioned from Russian civilians. As we started off, I remember wondering

where we were taking this convoy, which looked so like
Christmas, but whose load of shells and grenades was of such
a different character.

We set off towards the northwest, and a sector somewhere
near Voronezh. We had been given special rations for the
cold, new first-aid kits, and a two-day supply of precooked
dinners. We took a track – more or less blocked with snow –
which crossed the line of defences that cut off the steppe. A
bulky, hooded soldier, who was the only sentry in sight,
waved to us as we slowly went by him. His round shape
looked enormously vulnerable as he stood there, puffing on a
huge covered pipe, with his feet planted in the snow.

After an hour or so on the trail, which grew increasingly
snowy, we fastened the runners to the wheels. Our leather
boots, although they were remarkably waterproof, were not
the ideal foot gear for tramping through nearly two feet of
snow. We tired quickly, and hung on to the horses' harnesses
or the edges of the sleighs with the desperation of cripples
clinging to their canes. I myself twisted my fingers into the
long hair of one of those shaggy ponies whose pelts are thick
and tufted, like sheep's wool. However, the horses' pace was
too quick, and forced us into an exhausting rhythm which
made us pour with sweat despite the cold. From time to time
one of the leaders of a column would stop and watch the long
convoy going by, catching his breath under the pretext of
checking the line of march. When they rejoined the column,
it was always at the end of the line: I never saw anyone run
back to the front.

Hals, who had become a real friend, was holding on to the
other side of my horse. Although he was much bigger and
stronger than I, he also looked as though he were nearly
through. His face was almost hidden between his upturned
collar and his cap, which had been pulled down as far as it
could go. His red nose, like everyone else's, was producing a
plume of white vapour.

We hardly spoke. I had learned to be as silent as Germans
usually are. But, even without words, I knew that Hals was a
friend who felt as warmly toward me as I did toward him.
We gave each other occasional smiles of encouragement, as
if to say: 'Hang on! We'll make it!'

We halted at dusk. Feeling that I had been pushed beyond

the limits of my strength, I collapsed onto a cart shaft. My legs ached with stiffness, and I could feel exhaustion pulling down my face.

Hals let himself fall onto the snow.

'Aie, my poor feet.' All along the convoy, men were sitting or lying on the snow.

'We're not spending the night here, are we?' asked a young soldier who was sitting next to me. We looked at each other uneasily.

'I don't give a damn what anyone else does,' said Hals, opening his mess tin. 'I'm not taking another step.'

'You say that because you're still sweating. Wait until you're a little colder. Then you'll have to move if you don't want to freeze.'

'Shit,' said Hals without looking up. 'This food stinks.'

I opened my mess tin too. The cooked dinners they had given us early in the afternoon had long since cooled, and then frozen in the metal containers. It looked like tripe.

All around us, other soldiers were making the same discovery.

'God damn it!' said Hals. 'But there's no point in just throwing it out.'

'What do *you* think?' someone asked a feld, who was looking at the stuff in his own tin.

'Those bastards must have given us rotten meat.'

'Or a week of leftovers. It's unbelievable. There's enough food in that town for a whole division.'

'It's not edible. . . . It stinks!'

'We'll have to get out some cans.'

'No you won't,' the feldwebel flared out at us. 'We still have a long way to go, and none too much food as it is. Throw away the meat if you don't like it, and eat the cereal.'

Hals, who was never too particular, crunched something vaguely like a lamb cutlet between his teeth. Two seconds later, he spat it out on the snow.

'Pah! It's rotten. The shits must have cooked a Bolshevik.'

In spite of our dismal situation, we couldn't help laughing. Faced with the ruins of the meal he had been anticipating with such eagerness, Hals was on the brink of one of his rare fits of rage. Given his giant size, these were always impressive. With a stream of oaths, he gave his mess tin a magisterial kick, which sent it flying across the snow. There was a silence, and then a few laughs.

'You've made things a lot better for yourself,' said the young soldier standing beside me.

Hals spun round, but said nothing. Then he slowly went off to pick up his tin. I began to wolf down the mess which had been flavoured by the rotten meat. Hals, who looked crushed, collected his battered tin, whose contents had been scattered across the snow. A few minutes later, cursing a cruel fate, we were both digging into my ration.

The noncoms appointed guards, and we were faced with the problem of where to sleep. Already clenched with cold, we wondered where and how to spread out our ground sheets. Some men dug themselves hollows in the snow, others constructed rough huts, using the sacks of dried grass which hung from each side of the horses' collars. Others tried to insure a supply of warmth by making the horses lie down. We had already spent several nights out of doors, but always under more or less sheltered conditions. The fact of sleeping absolutely in the open in such appalling cold terrified us. Here and there, clusters of men discussed what we might do. Some thought we should keep on walking until we came to a village, or at least to some sort of building, on the grounds that it was better to die of exhaustion than of cold. According to this faction, if we stayed where we were, at least half of us would be dead by morning.

'We won't be coming to any village for at least three days,' the noncoms told us. 'We'll have to make out the best we can.'

'If only we could light a fire!' one man exclaimed. His teeth were chattering, and his voice was almost a whimper. Appalled by the prospect, we prepared ourselves for the night as best we could. Hals and I reorganized the load on a sleigh so that there was a space between the cases of explosives big enough to hold us both. Despite the obvious danger of such a resting place, we preferred disintegration in a hot flash to death by freezing.

Hals had the spirit to crack a few obscene jokes, and they made me laugh in spite of my misery. We managed to doze intermittently, huddled together, haunted by the fear of freezing in our sleep.

We spent a fortnight in these bitter conditions, and it

proved fatal for many of our group. On the third day we had two cases of pneumonia. On subsequent days we had frozen limbs and *hergezogener Brand*, a kind of gangrene from cold, which first attacks the exposed portion of the face, and then other parts of the body, even if they are covered. Those affected by this condition had to apply a thick yellow pomade, which made them look both comic and pitiable. Two soldiers, driven mad by despair, left the convoy one night, and lost themselves in the featureless immensity of snow. Another very young soldier called for his mother, and cried for hours. We tried alternately comforting and cursing him for disturbing our rest. Toward morning, after he had been quiet for a while, a shot jolted us all awake. We found him a short way off, where he had tried to put an end to his nightmare. But he had bungled his effort and didn't die until the afternoon.

My feet, tortured by so much walking and by the cold, caused me agonizing pain at first, but soon became so numb that I felt almost nothing. Later, when a doctor checked us, I saw that three of my toes had turned an ashen grey. Their nails remained stuck to the double pair of pestilential socks which I took off for the examination. A painful injection saved my toes from amputation. It still seems astonishing to me that any of us should have survived such an ordeal; especially I, who have never been particularly strong.

Now, 'at last,' I was going to experience war at the front – and ordeals far worse than anything I had yet known.

We used the huts and bunkers of a temporary Luftwaffe airfield for a rest that was indispensable. Most of the field had been abandoned by the Luftwaffe, which had been forced to withdraw farther to the west. Some fighter planes were still there, in various states of disrepair and covered with ice, but a rump ground staff had moved out most of the equipment on big sleighs pulled by tractors.

We were allowed several days to restore ourselves in these more or less comfortable circumstances. However, the moment we began to look better, the authorities plunged us back into the thick of things. For the fighting troops of that sector, our company represented a considerable and unexpected supply of manpower. We were divided into fatigue parties and assigned various jobs. Three-quarters of our men were put to work preparing positions for 77s and even for light machine guns. This meant shovelling masses of snow, and then attacking the earth, which was as hard as rock, with picks and explosives.

Hals, Lensen, and I had managed to stay together. We were in a group that was ordered to supply an infantry section about ten miles away with food and ammunition. We were given two sleighs, each with a troika of shaggy steppe ponies. The distance was not great, our equipment was better than we'd had on our last tragic expedition, and thinking that we could easily manage the round trip in a day, we accepted the job as an easy one.

There were eight of us altogether, counting the sergeant. I was on the second sleigh, which was carrying grenades and magazines for spandaus.* Sitting on the back of the sleigh, I had plenty of time to observe the dreary, empty landscape. At rare intervals, small stands of spindly trees thrust up from the immaculate white ground. They seemed to be engaged in an unequal struggle with the overpowering whiteness; it seemed to be gaining on them, slowly but surely. There was nothing else to be seen in this countryside, which must surely be inhabited by wolves – nothing except for the opaque, greyish-yellow sky. We seemed to have reached the far end of the world.

After a short time, we were following a depression in the snow which we took as an indication of a path. As we came to the edge of a thick forest, a soldier jumped up from behind a pile of wood, and stood in front of our first sleigh, which came to a dead stop. After a few words with our sergeant, he stepped aside, and we entered the forest, where we saw a spandau in action, manned by two soldiers, and further on an antlike swarm of soldiers and innumerable grey tents. There were a great many big guns, light tanks of the Alpenberg type, Paks,† and mortars set up on sleighs. A slaughtered horse had been pulled up into a tree, and was gradually being transformed into steaks by soldiers whose coats were spattered with blood. We were besieged by soldiers who asked us for mail, and cursed us when we said we didn't have any.

*Machine gun from the Spandau works.
†Anti-tank guns.

An officer checked our orders. The company we were to resupply was farther to the east. He sent an orderly to guide us. We continued through the woods, which concealed some three or four thousand men, and then crossed a series of small, partly cleared hills; I can still see them with absolute clarity. The white snow was crossed by three telephone lines which had been more or less covered over.

'Here we are,' said the orderly, who was on horseback. 'Beyond this crest you will be under enemy fire, so go as quickly as you can. Follow the telephone line. The company you're looking for is about a mile and a quarter from here.'

He saluted in the prescribed fashion and went off at a trot. We looked at each other.

'Well, here I go again,' said our sergeant, who undoubtedly was a long-time Rollbahn veteran.

He waved us forward, then stopped us.

'We're going to try and get there really fast. Don't be afraid to beat the horses. If the Russians see us, they'll open fire, but it usually takes them a while. If things get too hot we'll leave the sleigh with ammunition, because if that goes anyone closer than thirty yards will never see his mother again.'

I thought of the attack on the convoy near Kharkov.

'Let's go,' someone shouted, to prove he wasn't afraid.

The sergeant jumped onto the first sleigh and waved us forward. We soon reached the top of the hill. The horses, panting from the climb, stopped for a moment before dashing down the other side.

'Get going!' shouted the sergeant. 'We can't stay here!'

'Use the whip!' Hals shouted to the fellow who was driving.

Our sleigh was the first to start down. I can still see our three plucky ponies jumping through the snow like rabbits, from one depression to the next, churning up a white cloud which undoubtedly was visible a long way off. The three of us huddled behind the driver, in the centre of the sleigh, perched on dark green boxes which carried a disquieting inscription in white stencilled letters. We were all feeling nervous, and had forgotten the cold.

I tried to watch the horizon through veils of white dust, despite our jolting progress. I thought that I could dimly see a group of isbas in front of us. All around us, shell holes of a remarkable symmetry mutilated the immaculate whiteness of the slope. Despite our precipitate speed, I noticed the curious borders of these excavations, which the earth thrown up by the explosions had tinged a light yellow. They looked like enormous, stylized flowers, with dark brown centres and yellow petals which turned very pale, almost white, at their outer edges. The holes which had already been there for long enough to be partly filled by new snow made a subtle variation in this curiously decorative pattern.

We reached the bottom of the slope without incident. There were a few heavily damaged isbas, and several large guns almost buried in the snow.

We stopped beside an isba whose roof sloped right down to the ground. The wall nearest us was of open lattice, and we could see some engineers working inside. They seemed to be taking the building apart. A few men came out carrying pieces of wood. Then a plump sergeant with a white garment pulled over his coat came up to us.

'Unload right here,' he said. 'The engineers are preparing a shelter. It'll be finished in an hour.'

A loud explosion made us jump. To our right, we saw a yellow flash, and then a geyser of stones and dirt, which spouted almost thirty feet into the air.

The sergeant turned calmly toward the noise.

'Goddamned dirt,' he said. 'Harder than a rock.'

We concluded that these fellows were engineers playing with dynamite. The corpulent noncom looked at our orders.

'Ah,' he said, tapping a box of cans with a gloved finger. 'These aren't for us. But our supplies are already three days late, and we're living on our reserves which we're not supposed to touch. If this goes on ... You truck drivers certainly take your own sweet time! That's why fellows up front die of the cold. When you haven't got anything inside, you know, you can't keep going.' He slapped his belly.

Judging by his waistline, it was hard to imagine that he'd fasted for long. He must have had a private store of food hidden away somewhere, because it was clear that, despite our best efforts, the front lines were extremely short of supplies.

'You'll have to get over that way,' he pointed down the

track. 'That section is holding a piece of the Don bank ...
and you'll go there on your hands and knees, if you know
what's good for you.'

We set off across the snow-covered chaos, following a trail
marked by trucks half buried in snow. Beyond an embankment, some big guns and heavy howitzers were hidden by a
heap of piled-up snow. Once we had passed them, they
simply vanished from sight: their camouflage was perfect.

We came to a big trench in which a group of thin,
shivering horses were pawing the hard ground. Some sacks
of hay – so dry it was practically dust – had been ripped
open and put down for them. The poor animals were sniffing
at the hay with their rimy nostrils, but didn't seem too
tempted. A few frozen horse cadavers lay on the ground
among the animals that were still standing. A handful of
soldiers in long coats were watching the horses. We passed
through a string of rough dugouts, and heard machine-gun
fire coming from quite nearby.

'Machine guns!' our driver remarked, smiling strangely.
'That means we're here.' Trenches, foxholes, and dugouts
stretched away as far as we could see in all directions. We
were stopped by a patrol.

'Ninth Infantry Regiment, — company,' said the
lieutenant. 'Is it for us?'

'No, Mein Leutnant. We're looking for the — section.'

'Ah,' said the officer. 'You'll have to leave your sleighs
here. The section you want is over there on the river bank,
and on that little island. You'll have to stick to the trenches,
and be careful, because you'll be in range of the Russian
forward positions, and they wake up from time to time.'

'Thank you, Mein Leutnant.' The sergeant's voice was
trembling.

The lieutenant called over one of the men who was with
him: 'Show them the way, and then come back.'

The man saluted and joined us. Like everybody else, I had
grabbed a box that was too heavy for me, and was going to
carry it on my back. The sound of machine-gun fire began
again, only louder.

'There it goes again. Is it serious or not?'

The gunfire grew louder, stopped, and began again,
passionate and violent.

'That's us,' our guide replied. 'But wait a few minutes. You can't tell right away whether they're doing it just for laughs, or whether it's the beginning of a push onto the ice.'

We listened to him without a word. He seemed almost relaxed in this disquieting atmosphere. We were perfect novices: our few scrapes on the 'Third International' seemed liked nothing compared to what might happen here. The firing kept stopping and starting, sometimes very close. At other moments we could hear guns that were plainly further off.

Hals suggested that we lay our two boxes across our Mausers, to make a kind of carrying litter. We had just reorganized ourselves to put this plan into effect when we heard some heavy detonations which followed each other in rapid succession.

'That's the Russians,' grinned the veteran, who was walking just ahead of us.

The air shook with the rhythm of the explosions. They seemed to be about three or four hundred yards ahead of us, to our left.

'That's their assault artillery. . . . It might be an attack.'

Suddenly, about thirty yards to the left, there was a sharp and violent burst of sound, followed by a curious, catlike whine, followed by a series of similar sounds. We hastily put down our burdens, and ducked, looking anxiously in all directions. The air was still for a moment.

'Don't panic, boys,' said our guide, who had also ducked. 'We've got a battery of 107s behind that pile of stuff over there, and we're answering the Russians.'

The infernal noise began again. Even though our guide had told us what it was, I could feel my stomach contracting.

'Put on your helmets,' said the sergeant. 'If the Russians spot that battery, they'll fire on it.'

'And let's keep going,' our guide added. 'There isn't a quiet corner within sixty miles. We're no safer here than anywhere else.'

We began to move forward, bent double. The air around us shook for the third time, and we could hear gunfire all around us. The German battery was firing nonstop, and ahead the noise of the spandau was getting closer. We passed three soldiers who were unrolling a telephone wire along a footpath which crossed our route. The sound of explosions now seemed to have a regular rhythm.

'This might be an attack,' said the soldier who had come with us. 'I'll leave you here. I've got to get back to my section.'

'Which way do we go?' asked our sergeant, who was clearly terrified.

'Follow the path as far as the geschnauz* over there on the right. They'll be able to tell you. But eat something first. It's lunchtime.'

He took a few steps in the other direction, doubled over, as before. So, that is how one moves on a battlefield! A few days later I was used to it, and paid no more attention.

We opened our mess tins, and ate huddled in the snow. I didn't feel particularly hungry. The explosions, which made my head ring inside my icy helmet, seemed far more interesting than food.

Hals, who was not entirely in control of his feelings, rolled his eyes like a hunted animal, and looked at me, shaking his head. 'Maybe we shouldn't stop to eat ... If an officer came along ...'

A deafening salvo which seemed to be passing right over our heads interrupted us, and we instinctively hunched our shoulders and shut our eyes. Hals was about to speak again when another explosion, different in kind, but no less brutal, shook the earth, followed by a loud whistle and another explosion. This time we felt as if we were being lifted from the ground. We were shaken by a displacement of the air of an astonishing violence. Then an avalanche of stones and chunks of ice poured down on us.

We made ourselves as small as we could, not daring to move or speak. We had dropped our guns and our mess tins.

'They'll kill me!' shouted a young fellow who had hurled himself into my lap in the general confusion. 'They're going to kill me!'

There was another loud boom, and then a deafening German salvo passed over our heads.

'Let's go on; we can't stay here!' yelled our sergeant, shoving his helmet further down onto his head.

*Assault gun.

We picked up our boxes like automatons. The trench was wide enough for four men to walk abreast, but we proceeded single file, keeping close to one of the walls. I was with Hals, directly behind the sergeant, who kept exhorting us to move.

'Hurry up! Quick! The Russians have spotted our battery! They can see it, and we're right beside it! This damned trench is heading right into their fire. We've got to get to that communication trench down there.'

Every other minute we had to throw ourselves into the bottom of the trench. The heavy cases kept slipping from our icy fingers no matter how tightly we tried to hold them: it still seems astonishing that they didn't explode in our faces.

'Hurry up,' said the sergeant, disregarding our troubles. 'It's down there.'

'Tell me,' said Hals. 'There's still twice as much as this on the sleighs. Do we have to bring all that too?'

'Yes, of course ... I don't know.... Hurry up, for God's sake!'

While the Russians were reloading, our battery had fired twice. The next Russian salvo fell about forty yards behind us, followed by two others at an indefinable distance, which nonetheless made us double over a little lower. Suddenly there was a deafening hooting sound, followed by an overwhelming noise which shook the earth and the air. One side of the trench collapsed. It all happened so quickly I had no time to duck. I remember seeing what looked like a disintegrating scarecrow flying through the rubble in a cone of flame, and falling in several pieces onto the edge of the trench, before rolling to the bottom. We were all thrown to the ground without the strength or courage to get up again.

'Quick! Up! We've got to get to the other trench!' shouted the sergeant, whose face was contorted by fear. 'If a shell lands here, it will be a volcano.'

There were two more explosions. Our guns were firing steadily. Dragging the cases, we climbed across the debris and the body of the poor wretch who had been blown into the air. I glanced at him quickly as we went by. It was a horrible sight. His helmet had fallen down over his face, and its visor was half-buried in his chin, or neck. His heavy winter clothes were like a sack holding together something which no longer bore any resemblance to the human form. He was missing a leg – or perhaps it was doubled under him. Another body was mixed into the rubble a short way off. The Russian shell must have landed right on some poor fellows who had ducked their heads and were waiting for the storm to pass.

I can remember very distinctly the first deaths I encountered in the war. The thousands upon thousands which followed are blurred and faceless: a vast, cumulative nightmare which still haunts me, in which atrocious mutilations appear side by side with figures who seem to be peacefully sleeping, or with others whose eyes are opened astonishingly wide, stamped by death with an uncommunicable terror. I thought I had already experienced the limits of horror and of endurance, that I was a tough fighting man who would return home in due course to recount my heroic exploits. I have used the words and expressions which my experiences from Minsk to Kharkov to the Don suggested to me. But I should have reserved those words and expressions for what came later, even though they are not strong enough.

It is a mistake to use intense words without carefully weighing and measuring them, or they will have already been used when one needs them later. It's a mistake, for instance, to use the word 'frightful' to describe a few broken-up companions mixed into the ground: but it's a mistake which might be forgiven.

I should perhaps end my account here, because my powers are inadequate for what I have to tell. Those who haven't lived through the experience may sympathize as they read, the way one sympathizes with the hero of a novel or a play, but they certainly will never understand, as one cannot understand the unexplainable. This stammering outpouring may be without interest to the sector of the world to which I now belong. However, I shall try to let my memory speak as clearly as possible. I dedicate the remainder of this account to my friends Marius and Jean-Marie Kaiser, who are in a position to understand me, as they lived through the same general events in the same part of the world. I shall try to reach and translate the deepest level of human aberration, which I never could have imagined, which I never would have thought possible, if I hadn't known it firsthand.

We reached the communications trench, which had seemed like safety to our sergeant, and literally dived into it as a brutal burst of fire scattered the soil beyond the parapet. The two men in white overalls who were already there jumped up in astonishment.

One of them had been standing beside the gun surveying the scene through field glasses. The other, hunched down at the bottom of the hole, had been fiddling with the knobs of a radio apparatus.

'The — section?' asked our sergeant, puffing for breath. 'We've got some supplies for them.'

'It's not very far,' said the soldier with the field glasses, 'but you won't be able to get there right now; you'd only be blown up. Put your explosives down — but not right here — and use the bunker.' He smiled.

Without waiting for him to repeat the invitation, we slid down into a tomblike structure of boards and hard earth, which was almost without light. Inside, there were four soldiers dressed in white. One of them had somehow managed to go to sleep. The others were writing beside a flickering candle.

The bunker wasn't high enough for us to stand, and everyone had to move over so we could get in, but we were, at any rate, something new.

'Is it solid?' Hals asked, pointing his tattered finger at the roof of the rathole.

'Well ... if something lands a little closer, it might collapse,' one of the soldiers answered mockingly.

'And if something lands square on us, our pals won't have to bury us,' added another.

How could they joke? Habit, probably. The fellow who had been asleep woke up and yawned.

'I thought they'd sent us some women.'

'No ... just a bunch of kids. Where did you find this brood, sergeant?'

We all laughed.

As if to rub our noses in our situation, the ground shook again. From here the noise was less violent.

'These boys are new recruits, part of the supply train, and they've crossed the whole of Russia so you can fill your stomachs.'

'That's nothing,' said the fellow who'd just waked up. 'We've been sweating it out here for three months already, while you were taking your own sweet time. I know they've got pretty girls in the Ukraine, but you shouldn't have stayed there so long. We've been dying of hunger.'

I ventured a few words in my atrocious German: 'Girls! We didn't see any girls! All we saw was snow.'

'Alsatian?' somebody asked.

'No, he's French,' Hals answered, joking.

Everyone burst out laughing. Hals was taken aback, and didn't know what to say.

'Merci,' the questioner added with a good accent, holding out his hand to me.

'Ma mère est allemande,' I replied.

'Ach, gut. Votre mutter ist Deutsche? Sehr gut.'

The ground shook again. Some pieces from the ceiling rattled down onto our helmets.

'Things don't seem to be going very well here,' said our sergeant, whose mind was absorbed by his terror, and who plainly didn't give a damn whether my mother was German or Chinese.

'Oh, they're just having fun,' the other one said. 'The beating they took three days ago really calmed them down.'

'Ah?'

'Yes. Those bastards made us recross the Don about a month ago. We had to give up at least forty miles. Now our front is on the west bank. They've tried to cross on the ice at least four times already. The last time was five days ago. Then you would really have seen something. They attacked for two days, especially at night. It was really pretty rough. You see how I am today. I'm trying to catch up on my sleep. We haven't had much lately. We're supposed to counter-attack too, but nothing's happened yet. Take a look through the glasses. The ice is still covered with Russians. The pigs don't even pick up their wounded. I'll bet some of them down there are still groaning.'

'We're supposed to resupply the — section,' our wretched sergeant explained anxiously.

'You'll find them a little further on – right down on the river bank – real daredevils. I think they've got the little island too. They lost it one night when they had to fight hand to hand, but in the morning they took it back. It's a pretty tight spot down there, I can tell you. I'd rather be where I am.'

Our battery had been silent for a few minutes, but the Russian shells were still coming over at a slow but regular pace. The soldier with the field glasses came in, hunched up and blowing on his fingers.

'Your turn,' he said to one of the soldiers. 'I'm shaking so hard I'm afraid my teeth will fall out.'

The man he called got up with a groan, and pushed his way through to the exit.

'Our guns aren't firing any more. Have they been destroyed?' our sergeant asked the newcomer.

'You've got some funny ideas,' the soldier replied, still rubbing his fingers. 'We'd be in a fine fix without them. A few days ago, we'd have just been overrun without those guns. I sincerely hope that all our comrades of the 107th are still among the living.'

'I do too,' our sergeant agreed emphatically, realizing that he'd said the wrong thing. 'But why have they stopped firing?'

'You should know how tight supplies are. We have to fire drop by drop, so to speak, or when we know we can't miss. The infantry and the artillery both have to economize on munitions to the maximum. But we can't let the Soviets know that, so from time to time we give them a heavy dose . . . you see?'

'I see.'

'They're not shooting any more,' said someone in our group.

'Yes. It's quieted down. You'd better make the most of it,' said one of the soldiers from the geschnauz.

'Let's go, children,' said our sergeant, who seemed to have regained some confidence.

Children . . . he wasn't far wrong: we seemed like children beside these Don veterans. A few rounds from the big guns had seemed to us like the end of the world. There was a great difference between the proud soldiers we'd been in Poland, marching smartly through the villages with our guns slung, and what we were now. How many times in the past I had thought myself invulnerable, filled with the pride we all felt, admiring our shoulder straps and helmets and magnificent uniforms – and the sound of our footsteps, which I loved, and love still, despite everything. But here, by the banks of the Don, we seemed like nothing, like bundles of rags which each sheltered a small, trembling creature. We were underfed and unbelievably filthy. The immensity of Russia seemed to have absorbed us, and as truck drivers we were not dashing figures, but more like the junior maidservants of the army. We were dying of cold like everybody else, only our plight was never mentioned.

We left the shelter timidly, glancing toward the nearby parapet which screened off the war, and picked up our dangerous burdens. Everything seemed to have calmed down. There was no more noise, and the light in the sky had become less brilliant. We took a zigzag line of trenches, which ran parallel to the point we had to reach. Everywhere there were shelters filled with half-frozen soldiers trying to warm themselves beside those miraculous gasoline lamp-heaters, and everywhere we were greeted by the same question: 'Any mail?' Three Messerschmitts passed over-head, and were greeted by a loud cheer. The confidence which the infantry placed in the Luftwaffe was absolute, and on innumerable occasions the familiar shapes of the planes with the black crosses restored faltering courage and frustrated a Russian attack.

Several times, as we moved forward, we had to press ourselves against the side of the trench so that stretcher-bearers carrying wounded could get through. We were drawing close to the outermost limit of the German lines. The trenches grew progressively narrower and shallower, so that eventually we became a kind of human chain, bent nearly double in order to remain unseen. Several times, I sneaked a look over the parapet. Some sixty yards ahead, I could see the tall grass on the river bank, stiff with frost; and some-where in that space was the section we were supposed to supply.

Now we were advancing half exposed, setting off slides of earth and snow as we jumped from one hole to the next. We clattered down into a huge crater, where an orderly in heavy winter clothes was bandaging two fellows who were clenching their teeth to keep themselves from crying out. He told us we had reached our destination. We wasted no time inspecting the situation of this cursed section, but put our cases in the hole we were shown, and turned back for another trip.

By nightfall we had completed what we later learned to call the 'priority' supply of this front-line section. Nothing had happened since the bombardment of the afternoon, and the unfortunate soldiers on the Don were preparing themselves for another icy night. Although the temperature had risen a little, it was still very cold.

We were waiting for two of our men who were collecting the scattering of letters these soldiers had managed to write. Hals, another soldier, and I were sitting on a mound of frost-hardened earth, hidden from enemy eyes.

'I wonder where we'll be sleeping tonight,' said Hals, staring at his boots.

'Outdoors, I guess,' our companion answered. 'I don't see any hotels around here.'

'Come over this way,' called someone else from our group. 'You can see the river very well from here.'

We got up from the ground to look through a heap of frosty branches that camouflaged a spandau aimed and ready to fire.

'Look,' Hals said. 'Bodies lying on the ice.'

There were numbers of motionless bodies, victims of the fighting of a few days earlier. The soldiers at the geschnauz had not been exaggerating: the Russians had not removed their dead.

I tried to see further into the distance, to what must be the island we had heard so much about, but this was difficult, as it was growing dark. I could recognize only vaguely what looked like snow-covered trees. Our soldiers must be crouched among them, watching in the silence, with every sense alert. Beyond, in the heavy, unbreathable mist falling across this mournful landscape, the far bank was almost invisible. On this bank, the German advance had been halted, and Russian soldiers were watching for us.

I had reached the front line, the line I had thought about with such dread and had been so curious to see. For the moment, nothing was happening. The silence was almost complete, broken only by occasional voices. I thought I could see a few thin streams of smoke rising through the mist on the Russian side. Then some other soldiers pushed me aside.

'If it interests you so much,' said one of the grenadiers standing at the foot of the spandau, 'I'll gladly give you my place. I've had enough of this cold.'

We didn't know what to say. His place was certainly not very enviable.

A lieutenant in a long hooded coat jumped into our hole. Before we had time to salute, he lifted a pair of field glasses, and stared into the distance. A few seconds later, we heard the sound of heavy detonations coming from behind us.

Almost at once, there were explosions on the ice, immediately reproduced by a long, repetitive echo, and then a sharp whistling sound which rang through the air very close to us. The entire German front responded immediately. The noise of the guns became indistinguishable from the explosion of their projectiles. We all dropped to the bottom of the hole. We felt lost, and stared at each other with anguished, questioning eyes.

'They're attacking,' someone said.

The two machine gunners didn't fire right away, but stayed beside the lieutenant, staring at the Don. Some of the explosions were loud and strident; others sounded heavy, and as if they were coming from underground. Finally, the grenadier who had so generously offered his place decided to speak to us: 'The ice is breaking more easily tonight; it's not so cold. Pretty soon they'll have to swim over.'

We all hung on his words, as none of us understood what was happening.

'We'll send out the lightest one here,' he said. 'If the ice holds his weight, we'll have to blow it up.'

'He's the lightest,' said Hals with a constricted laugh, pointing to a cringing, very young soldier.

'What will I have to do?' the boy asked, white with anxiety.

'Nothing just yet,' the gunner said jokingly.

The bombardment stopped as suddenly as it had begun. The lieutenant looked out through his glasses for a few more minutes, then climbed over the parapet and vanished. We

stayed where we were, without moving or speaking. To break
the anxious silence, our sergeant ordered us to open our mess
tins and eat dinner, while we waited for the fellows with the
mail.

We swallowed down our tasteless, frozen portions without
much appetite. As I chewed I went over to the spandau to
look down once more at the river.

What I saw explained the German bombardment of a few
moments ago. Great blocks of ice, some of them two feet
thick, were standing up at right angles to the surface of the
river. These ice blocks, partly broken and crushed, formed
steep hills of ice, whose crests oscillated with the rhythm of
the current beneath the frozen surface. The German gunners
fired on the ice every night to deny access to the incessant
Soviet patrols, who nonetheless exposed themselves to great
danger on these moving blocks. Now the broken ice was
rearing up and crashing into other pieces with a strange,
heavy sound. New fissures were opening, and the night was
filled with the noises of cracking, breaking ice.

I stood for a long time, transfixed by the unreal vision,
gradually noticing that hundreds of lights were springing up
on the east bank. With my eye glued to the loophole, I stared
at these lights, which seemed to be growing stronger.

'Hey,' I shouted at the two regulars, 'something's happening!'

They rushed over to me, pushing me aside so they could
see. I stayed where I was, shoving my head between theirs.

'Hell, you really scared us,' one of them said. 'That's
nothing; they do it every night. The Popovs like to make us
think they're warming up. Not at all a bad idea, either. Those
lights are a damned nuisance. Look how hard it is to see the
river now. Even flares make it hard.'

I couldn't tear myself away from this disquieting vision.
All along the vast horizon, the Russians had lit hundreds of
braziers, not to warm themselves, because they must
certainly have kept their distance from them, but to dazzle
our observers. And in fact, when the eye travelled to the east
bank, it remained fixed on those fires. Everything else, by
contrast, was plunged into darkness, and this enabled the
enemy to effect numerous changes which we could deduce
only with difficulty. We were able to see a little with flares,

but their radiance, although intense, was reduced at least to half strength by the enemy's arrangement of alternating light and darkness.

I would have stood and stared much longer if our sergeant hadn't given the signal for departure. We had no trouble returning to the rear. The night, undisturbed by the noises of war, hid our movements perfectly.

Everywhere, soldiers were curled up in their holes. Those who were asleep had covered themselves with everything they could find, leaving no fraction of themselves exposed – not a nose, or the tip of an ear. One needed to be accustomed to this strange mode of existence to know that beneath these mounds of cloth subtle human mechanisms were managing to survive and garner their strength.

Others were playing cards in the depths of their lairs, or writing letters in the flickering light of a candle, or of a lamp-heater. These marvellous objects – and I call them 'marvellous' deliberately – were about two feet high, and would operate on gasoline or kerosene: one simply had to regulate the nozzle and the intake of air. A reflector behind a glass projected the light. A story had it that the army was working on an improved model which would also dispense beer.

Those who were neither asleep, on guard, playing cards, nor writing letters were absorbing the alcohol which was freely distributed along with our ammunition. 'There's as much vodka, schnapps and Terek liquor on the front as there are Paks,' I was told later by a wounded infantryman who was waiting for evacuation on the hospital train. 'It's the easiest way to make heroes. Vodka purges the brain and expands the strength. I've been doing nothing but drink for two days now. It's the best way to forget that I've got seven pieces of metal in my gut, if you can believe the doctor.'

We got back to our two sleighs without incident.

'Am I dreaming,' Hals said, 'or has it grown warmer? I'm sweating like an ox in these clothes. Maybe I've got a fever: that's all I need.'

'Then I've got one too,' I said. 'I'm soaking wet.'

'That's because you had the balls scared off you today,' said the fellow who earlier in the afternoon had shouted, 'They'll kill me!'

'Listen to who's talking,' Hals said. 'You're still as green as your clothes, and you think you can judge us.'

Our sleighs were now carrying six wounded as well as ourselves. Although they were less heavily loaded than they had been, they ran less smoothly. The little horses were clearly having a hard time: we could almost see the snow growing softer as we looked at it. The wind was carrying large flakes of melting snow, which soon changed to rain. This milder air, after such terrible cold, seemed to us like the Côte d'Azur.

It took us two hours to reach our huts in the rear lines, and we needed no urging to fling ourselves onto our rough pallets. However, despite the physical and emotional exhaustion of that wearing day, I wasn't able to sleep immediately. I kept seeing the banks of the Don, and hearing the whine of enemy projectiles, and the explosions, whose violence I would never have been able to imagine. For me, whose eardrums were shattered by the firing of a Mauser, our Polish exercises now seemed like the most trifling of games.

The infantry on the west bank had to fight as well as survive: that was the difference between them and us. We had been promised that we would be as honoured as the infantry, as combat troops, if we distinguished ourselves on our supply missions. This promise, which had been made to us on behalf of our commander at the Wagenlager near Minsk, was clearly addressed to young recruits like Hals, Lensen, Olensheim, and me. We had taken it as an honour, and were proud of the confidence which had been placed in us.

Yet the reports in the front-line journal blamed us squarely, almost making us responsible for the German retreat from the Caucasus, and back beyond Rostov. For lack of supplies these troops had been forced to abandon territories won with great sacrifices, so that they would not suffer the same fate as the defenders of Stalingrad. In their exhortations to us, our officers often asked us to achieve a certain goal despite adverse conditions, at whatever the cost, to do more than was humanly possible, to face the prospect of the worst, including death. We had thought that we had accomplished more than the bare minimum. In fact, despite our unstinted efforts, and all our bitter moments, we had achieved somewhat less than half of what had been expected. Maybe we should have given our lives too.

'Absolute sacrifice' was what the High Command called it. These words made my head spin, as I stared with wide eyes into the impenetrable darkness, sinking gradually into sleep, as into a large black pit.

Chapter Three

THE MARCH TO THE REAR

For three or four more days, we were involved in occupations of more or less the same kind. The snow was melting everywhere, and the cold was lessening as rapidly as it had increased – which seemed to be the way of Russian seasons. From implacable winter one was shifted into torrid summer, with no spring in between. The thaw did not improve our military situation, but made it worse. The temperature rose from five degrees below zero to forty degrees above, melting the unimaginable ocean of snow which had accumulated all winter.

Enormous pools of water and swampy patches appeared everywhere in the partly melted snow. For the Wehrmacht, which had endured the horrors of five winter months, this softening of the temperature fell like a blessing from heaven. With or without orders, we took off our filthy overcoats and began a general cleanup. Men plunged naked into the icy waters of these temporary ponds for the sake of a wash. No gunfire disturbed the tranquil air, which was sometimes even sunny.

The war itself, whose indefinable presence we still felt, seemed to have grown less savage. I had made the acquaintance of a sympathetic fellow, a noncom in the engineers, whose section was temporarily billeted in the hut opposite ours. He came from Kehl, right across the Rhine from Strasbourg, and knew France better than his own country. He spoke perfect French. My conversations with him, which were always in French, were like rest periods after the painstaking gibberish I was forced into with my other companions. Hals often joined us to improve his French in the same way I tried to improve my German.

101

Ernst Neubach – my new friend – seemed to be a born engineer. He had no equal in his ability to knock a few old boards into a shelter as weatherproof as one a fully-equipped mason might build. He made a shower from the gas tank of a large tractor, and it functioned miraculously, with a lamp-heater continuously warming its forty gallons of water. The first men to use this shower unfortunately received a tepid downpour of water flavoured with gasoline. Although we rinsed the tank repeatedly, the water remained tainted for a long time.

In the evenings waiting to use the shower there was always a crowd of shouting, pushing men which often included our superiors. Priority was awarded to whoever produced the largest number of cigarettes, or a portion of the bread ration. Our feldwebel, Laus, once paid three hundred cigarettes. The showers always began after the five-o'clock meal and continued late into the night in an atmosphere of rowdy horseplay. Those who got through the showers first often found themselves tossed onto their backsides in the liquid mud which flooded the outskirts of the camp. Here we had no curfew or other barracks regulations. Once all the day's work was done, we were free to joke and drink for the whole night, if we wanted to.

We spent about a week in this way, with quiet, uneventful days. Each fatigue party obliged us to flounder through a sea of increasingly sticky mud. We made three trips back to the front; each time it was unbelievably quiet. On horseback or in carts, we took supplies to our troops, whose laundry was spread out to dry on all the parapets. Across the Don, the Russians appeared to be similarly engaged.

We spoke to a bearded soldier and asked him if everything was going well. He laughed. 'The war must be over. Hitler and Stalin have made it up. I've never seen it so calm for so long. The Popovs do nothing but drink all day and sing all night. They have terrific nerve, too, walking around in the open air, right under our guns. Werk saw three of them going to get water from the river, just like that. Didn't you, Werk?' He turned to a sly-faced soldier who was washing his feet in a puddle.

'Yes,' Werk said. 'We just couldn't shoot them. For once, let's all stick our noses out without getting a bullet between the eyes.'

A feeling of joy and hope had begun to take hold. Could the war be over?

'It really might be,' Hals said. 'The fellows on the front are always the last to be told anything like that. If it's true, we'll know in a few days. You'll see, Sajer. Maybe we'll all be going home soon. We'll have a terrific celebration. It's almost too good to be true!'

'Don't count your chickens before they're hatched,' said one of the older men from the Rollbahn. His realism damped us down a little.

As usual, we set off down the track — more accurately, canal — of liquid mud which led to our camp. We stopped a moment to talk to Ernst, whose section was trying to restore the track to a usable condition.

'If it goes on this way,' he said, 'we'll have to take to boats. Two trucks came through here, and the stones we broke our backs shoving into the mud completely disappeared. It must be nice down in the trenches.'

'They're in a mess,' Hals said. 'And their morale is really terrible, too. I wouldn't be at all surprised if they broke up their guns for kindling. Our fellows and the Popovs are having a real spree down there.'

'Well let them make the most of it,' Ernst said. 'There's something funny going on. That radio truck over there is taking messages nonstop. And messengers all the time, too. The last one had to leave his scooter and wade in here to bring the Kommandant his message.'

'Maybe it was congratulations for your showers,' said Hals.

'That would be fine by me, but I doubt it. When those fellows run around like that, everybody else will too, before you know it.'

'Defeatist,' Hals shouted as we left.

When we got back to the camp, nothing seemed to have changed. We devoured the steaming mess the cook served up and prepared for another evening of larking. Then Laus blew the whistle for assembly.

'Lord,' I thought. 'Neubach was right. Here we go again.'

'I'm not going to say anything about the way you look,' Laus said. 'Just pack up. We could be moving out of here any time now. Got it?'

'Fuck,' someone said. 'It was too good to last.'

'You don't think you could just sit here and fart, did you? There's a war on.'

'Packing up' meant that we had to be ready for inspection, with our uniforms in impeccable order, and all our straps and buckles polished and fastened in the prescribed manner. At least, that is what it had meant at Chemnitz and Bialystok. Here, of course, that kind of discipline was somewhat relaxed, but it all still depended on the humour of the inspecting officer, who could quibble at anything from the inside of a gun barrel to the state of our toes, and impose heavy details, or endless guard duty.

I could still remember only too well the four hours of punishment handed out to me a few days after I had arrived at Chemnitz. The lieutenant had drawn a circle on the cement of the courtyard, which was fully exposed to the sun. Then I had to put on the 'punishment pack' – knapsack filled with sand, which weighed nearly eighty pounds. I weighed one hundred and thirty. After two hours, my helmet was burning hot from the sun, and by the end I needed all my will power to keep my knees from buckling. I had nearly fainted several times. That is how I learned that a good soldier does not cross the barracks yard with his hands in his pockets.

So we rushed to get our gear in order, and frantically polished our sodden leather boots.

'And before we've walked ten yards, all this will be for nothing!'

It took us a good hour to make our kit more or less respectable. Then we had another twenty-four before our country holiday on the Don was transformed into a nightmare.

The day after our sprucing-up, I was put on guard duty and given the period from midnight until 2:30 A.M. I had summoned up all my patience, and was standing on the platform of empty munitions cases which had been put there so the sentry wouldn't sink into the mud. Beside the platform, a foxhole half filled with water was ready to receive the guard responsible for the stocks of gasoline – in this case, myself.

The night was mild. A rainy wind blew fat white clouds rapidly across the sky, occasionally revealing a large white moon. To my right, the outlines of our vehicles and the camp buildings stood out sharply. Ahead of me, the enormous dark, hilly horizon melted into the sky. As the crow flies, the Don lay about five miles from our first line of German reserves. Between us and the river, some thousands of men were sleeping in conditions of almost unimaginable squalor. The sound of engines came to us on the wind. Both sides used the dark for moving supplies and troops. Two of the sentries patrolling our perimeter came by, and we exchanged the usual formalities. One of the men told a joke. I was about to reply when the whole horizon, from north to south, was suddenly lit by a series of brilliant flashes.

Then there was a second series of flickering intensity, and I thought I felt the earth shake, as the air filled with a sound like thunder.

'Lord! It's an attack!' shouted one of the men on patrol. 'I think it's them!'

We could already hear whistles in the camp and voices shouting orders through the still-distant noise of explosions. Groups of men went by on the run. Artillerymen who had been asleep were running to their guns on the edge of the abandoned airfield. As no one had told me to leave my post, I stayed where I was, wondering what would be asked of my comrades. A supply expedition through such a heavy bombardment would be an operation of an entirely different kind from the ones we had recently grown used to. The bursts of distant fire continued, mixed with the sound of our guns. Flashes of light, closer and more brilliant than before, turned the groups of men running through pools of water into shadow puppets.

It was as if a giant, in a fit of terrible fury, were shaking the universe, reducing each man to a ludicrous fragment which the colossus of war could trample without even noticing. Despite the relative distance of danger, I bent double, ready to plunge into my water-filled hole at a moment's notice. Two big crawler tractors came toward me, with all their lights out. Their wheels and treads had churned the mud into a kind of liquid sludge. Two men jumped down, and almost disappeared in it.

'Give us a hand, guard,' one of them called. They were splattered with mud right up to their helmets.

The bombardment continued to enflame the earth and sky, as we loaded some drums of gasoline onto their machine.

'There's always something to fart in your face,' one of them said to me.

'Good luck,' I answered.

Further off, the soldiers in my unit were rounding up the nervous, jostling horses, which kept falling in the mud and whinnying frantically. Several times, trucks came to collect drums of gasoline, so that by daybreak, when my relief hadn't appeared, I wondered how much there was left for me to guard. The bombardment was almost as strong as ever. I felt exhausted and confused. A group of boys from my company came by, led by a sergeant who waved me over to join them. At that moment precisely, one of the first Soviet long-range shells landed about a hundred yards behind us. The explosion shook us, and we all started to run as hard as we could. I didn't ask any questions, but looked in vain for the broad shoulders of Hals.

Other projectiles were now falling on the camp, which was lit up everywhere. We had thrown ourselves onto the ground, and stood up again covered with mud.

'Don't dive like that,' said the sergeant. 'You're always late. Keep your eye on me, and do what I do.'

A significant howl filled our ears, and all twelve of us, the sergeant included, plunged into the liquid mess. An enormous explosion sucked all the air from our lungs, and a simultaneous wave of mud washed over us.

We stood up again, soaked with filth, and wearing the pinched smiles of civilians who climb unscathed from a bad wreck. Three or four more bursts quite nearby forced us down again. Behind us, something was burning. As soon as we could, we ran to the nearest munitions dump.

The sight of this mountain of canvas-covered boxes made our stomachs turn over. If anything hit it, no one within a hundred yards would have a chance.

'Good God,' said the sergeant. 'There's nobody here. It's incredible.'

With no apparent thought of danger, he climbed onto the hill of dynamite, and began to check the numbers on the boxes, which indicated their next destination. We stood and watched him, petrified, like condemned prisoners, with our

feet apart, and our heads empty, waiting for orders. Two
fellows soaked through, like us, came running up. The
sergeant began to shout at them from his eminence. They
snapped to attention despite the thunder of the guns.

'Are you supposed to be on duty here?'

'Yes, Herr Sergeant,' they answered in unison.

'Then where were you?'

'The call of nature,' one of them said.

'You went off to crap like that, both of you at once?
Idiots! We've got too much trouble here for fun and games.
Your names and units.' The sergeant had not climbed down.

Silently, I cursed this animal with his niggling discipline,
who stood there preparing a report, as if nothing unusual
were happening. Fresh explosions which sounded very close
threw us all onto the ground except the sergeant, who
continued to provoke Providence.

'They're cleaning up our rear,' he said. 'They must have let
loose their goddamned infantry. Get your fat tails up here
and help me!'

Half paralyzed by fear, we climbed onto the volcano. The
flashes of light all around us lit our bodies in a tragic glare. A
few moments later, we were running as hard as we could,
oblivious of the weight of the cases, in our anxiety to get
away.

Daylight had now begun to rob the spectacle of some of its
brilliance. The flashes of light were scarcely visible, and the
horizon was shrouded by a dense cloud of smoke, irregularly
punctuated by darker plumes. Toward noon, our artillery
began to fire. We were still running from job to job, although
we were nearly dropping with exhaustion. I can remember
sitting in a huge crater which had been dried out by an
explosion, staring at the long barrel of a 155 spitting fire with
rhythmic regularity. I had found Hals and Lensen, and we
were sitting together, with our hands over our ears. Hals was
smiling, and nodding at each explosion.

For two days we had practically no sleep. The dance of
death continued. We were carrying the growing number of
wounded to shelters half filled with water, and laying them on
hastily improvised stretchers made of branches. The orderlies
administered first aid. Soon these rough infirmaries, filled
with the groans of the wounded, were overflowing, and we

had to put fresh casualties outside, on the mud. The surgeons operated on the dying men then and there. I saw horrifying things at these collection points – vaguely human trunks which seemed to be made of blood and mud.

On the morning of the third day, the battle intensified. We were all grey with fatigue. The shelling went on until dusk, and then, inside of an hour, stopped. Clouds of smoke were rising all along the battered front. We felt as if we could smell the presence of death – and by this I don't mean the process of decomposition, but the smell that emanates from death when its proportions have reached a certain magnitude. Anyone who has been on a battlefield will know what I mean.

Two of the eight huts that made up our camp had been reduced to ashes. The ones that remained standing were overflowing with wounded. Laus – who had a good heart when the chips were down – saw that we were foundering, and allowed us each an hour or two of sleep, as he could. We dropped to the ground wherever we were, as if felled by sleep. When our time was up, and we were shaken awake, we felt as though we'd only been asleep for a few minutes.

With exhaustion threatening to overwhelm us again, we returned to the nightmare of carrying agonized, mutilated men, or laying out rows of horribly burned bodies, which we had to search for their identity tags. These were then sent to the families of the deceased with the citation 'Fallen like a hero on the field of honour for Germany and for the Führer.'

Despite the thousands of dead and wounded, the last battle fought by the German army on the Don was celebrated the day after the shooting stopped. The mouths of dying men were pried open so that they could toast this Pyrrhic victory with vodka. On a front approximately forty miles long, General Zhukov, with the help of the accursed 'Siberia' Army, which had just contributed to the German defeat at Stalingrad, had been trying to break the Don line south of Voronezh. Instead, the furious Russian assaults had broken against our solidly held lines. Thousands of Soviet soldiers had paid with their lives for this abortive effort – which had also cost us very dear.

Three-quarters of my company left that evening. The trucks were jammed with wounded, who were lying almost in piles. I was separated from Hals and Lensen for the moment:

a separation I never liked. Friendships counted for a great deal during the war, their value perhaps increased by the generalized hate, consolidating men on the same side in friendships which never would have broken through the barriers of ordinary peacetime life. I found myself alone with a couple of men who may have been more or less interesting, but with whom I never had the chance to talk. As soon as I could, I abandoned them for a truck seat on which I attempted to regain some of my strength.

The assembly whistle rang in my ears very early the next morning. I opened my eyes. The truck cab had made an excellent bed, more or less the right size, and I felt at last as though I'd had some sleep. But exhaustion had stiffened my muscles, and despite my sleep, I had a terrible time pulling myself onto my feet. Lining up outside, I saw the same exhausted, dishevelled look on almost every face.

Even Laus wasn't feeling particularly energetic: he had slept with his equipment like all the rest of us. He told us that we were going to leave this area for a point farther west. As a preliminary, we should stand by to help the engineers load up, or destroy what we weren't taking with us. We filed past a big kettle from which we were served a hot liquid that made no pretence to being coffee, and went to join the engineers.

We were sent out with donkeys, under orders to range widely, picking up all the ammunition we could find, so that it wouldn't fall into the hands of the enemy. The departure seemed to be general. Long lines of infantry caked with filth were marching away from this sea of mud, to the west. At first we thought we were being replaced, but this proved to be untrue. The entire Wehrmacht along the western bank of the Don had been ordered to withdraw. We couldn't grasp the logic of following a heroic three-day resistance with retreat.

Most of us were unaware that the Eastern Front had entirely changed since January. After the fall of Stalingrad, a strong Soviet push had reached the outskirts of Kharkov, recrossed the Donets, and moved on to Rostov, almost cutting the German retreat from the Caucasus. Troops there had been forced to return to the Crimea by way of the Sea of Azov, with heavy losses. Our periodical *Ost Front und Panzer Wolfram* reported that there had been heavy fighting at Kharkov, Kuban, and even Anapa.

We never heard a frank admission of retreat, and as most soldiers had never studied Russian geography we had very little idea of what was happening. Nevertheless, a glance at any map was enough to inform us that the west bank of the Don was the easternmost German line in Russian territory. Luckily for us, the High Command ordered our retreat before an encirclement from the north and south could cut us off from our bases at Belgorod and Kharkov. The Don was no longer one of our defences; it had been crossed both in the north and in the south. The thought that we might have been trapped, like the defenders of Stalingrad, still makes my blood run cold.

For two days, the landser* had been pulling out – either on foot or loaded in trucks. Soon only a small section of the Panzergruppe was left at the nearly empty camp. The passage of vehicles and men had turned the Luftwaffe field into an extraordinary quagmire: thousands of trucks, tanks, tractors, and men rolled and tramped for two days and two nights through terrain running with streams of mud.

We were in the middle of this syrup, trying to reorganize the matériel we had to abandon. The engineers were working with us, preparing to dynamite the ammunition we had heaped against the huts, over the carcasses of eight dismantled trucks. Toward noon, we organized a fireworks display which any municipality might have envied. Carts, sleighs, and buildings were all dynamited and burned. Two heavy howitzers which the tractors hadn't been able to pull from the mire were loaded with shells of any calibre. Then we poured any explosive that came to hand into their tubes, and shut the breech as best we could. The howitzers were split in two by the explosions, scattering showers of lethal shrapnel. We felt exhilarated, filled with the spirit of destructive delight. In the evening, the spandaus stopped a few Soviet patrols, who had undoubtedly come to see what was happening. During our last hour, we were under light artillery fire, which caused us a certain emotion. Then we left.

After the period of light artillery fire, the troops covering the Panzergruppe signalled several enemy penetrations into our former positions. A hasty departure order was given. We

*Infantry.

were no longer organized to hold off the Russians for any length of time. I was carrying my belongings, looking for a vehicle, when our feld assigned me to a truck we had captured from the enemy which was now carrying our wounded.

'Step on the gas!' he shouted. 'We're getting out!'

Every soldier in the Wehrmacht was supposed to know how to drive. I had been given some idea of how to handle military vehicles during my training in Poland, but on machines of a very different kind. However, as one never discussed orders, I jumped into the driver's seat of the Tatra. In front of me, the dashboard presented an array of dials whose needles uniformly pointed down, a few buttons, and a series of words in indecipherable characters. The engineers had just attached the heavy truck to the back of a Mark-4. We would be leaving instantly; it was essential that I get the wretched machine to start. I considered climbing out and confessing my incapacity, but repressed the idea on reflection that they might assign me to something more difficult, or even leave me behind, to get out on my own feet as best I could.

If I couldn't move, I would be captured by the Bolsheviks – a thought which terrified me. I pawed frantically at the dashboard, and was blessed by a miracle. My desperate eye fell on Ernst, who was clearly looking for a lift. I felt saved.

'Ernst!' I shouted. 'Over here! I've got room!'

My friend joyfully jumped aboard.

'I was ready to hang on to the back of a tank,' he said. 'Thanks for the seat.'

'Ernst,' I asked in a voice of supplication. 'Do you know how these damned things work?'

'You're a fine fellow, sitting here when you don't know the first thing about it!'

I had no time to explain. The powerful engine of the tank to which we were attached was already roaring. Hurriedly, we pulled at the controls. From the turret, one of the tank men signalled to me to put the truck in gear at the same time as the tank, to reduce the jolt for the wounded. Neubach pulled a lever under the dashboard, and we felt a responding throb from under the hood. I pressed down hard on the accelerator, and the engine made a series of loud bangs.

'Gently,' the feld shouted at me. I smiled, nodded, and let up on the pedal. The chain stretched taut, and we increased our speed. How fast were we going? I had no idea. I knew with certainty only that we were not in reverse. The heavy truck took off with a brusque jolt, producing a chorus of groans and curses behind me.

Later on, in France, a pretentious bastard undertook to instruct me on a wretched Renault 4 CV, with all the airs of a commander of an ocean liner. I had to sit through a course of ludicrous demonstrations to receive a scrap of pink paper declaring me competent to drive an automobile. I didn't waste any time explaining that I had driven through Russia on a track which was more like a river than a road, fastened to a huge tank whose jolts were a constant threat to the front of my machine, which I felt certain would be wrenched off.

He would never have believed me. By that time I belonged to the Victorious Allies, who were all heroes, like every French soldier I met after the war. Only victors have stories to tell. We, the vanquished, were all cowards and weaklings by then, whose memories, fears, and enthusiasms should not be remembered.

The first night of retreat was complicated by a fine rain, which required of Ernst and me the agility and balance of acrobats simply to keep our Tatra in the wake of the Mark-4. Without the tank, we would never have been able to escape from that swamp. The driver stepped on the accelerator in fits of irritation, dragging the Tatra, which threatened to disintegrate. The tank treads churned the ground into a heavy syrup, which the rain thinned into soup. The windshield became completely caked with mud, and Ernst waded through the liquid ground to scrape it away with his hands.

The blacked-out headlight had been left with only a narrow strip uncovered. Within a few minutes this strip was sealed by mud, so that we had no light at all. I couldn't even see the back of the tank, although it was no more than five yards ahead of us. Our truck, more often than not at an oblique angle to the tank, was constantly being pulled back into line by the tightly stretched chain. Each time this happened, I wondered if we still had our front wheels.

Behind us, the wounded had stopped moaning. Maybe they were all dead – what difference did it make! The convoy moved ahead, and daylight dawned on faces haggard with exhaustion. During the night, the convoy had spread out. It no longer seemed to matter whether we were ahead of schedule or behind. The driver of our Panzer suddenly turned off to the right, leaving the track, which had become impassable even for a tank, and drove straight up the scrub-covered bank, crushing the sodden birches under his treads.

Our truck, whose wheels by this time were balls of mud, was pulled forward, while its engine rattled helplessly. Then everything came to a complete halt. This was the second stop since our departure. We had stopped once in the night to gas up. The poor bastards on the back of the tank jumped down among the broken branches. Their backsides had been burning all night on the hot metal over the engine, while the rest of their bodies froze in the cold rain. An exchange of shouted abuse which was nearly a fight broke out at once between a noncom in the engineers and the Panzerführer. Everyone else took advantage of this opportunity to crap and eat.

'One hour's rest!' shouted the noncom, who had taken on himself the leadership of the group. 'Make the most of it!'

'Fuck you,' shouted the Panzerführer, who had no intention of being pushed around by some half-baked engineer. 'We'll leave when I've had enough sleep.'

'We have to get to Belgorod this morning,' the noncom said in a steely voice. He undoubtedly nourished dreams of being an officer. Then, putting his hand on the Mauser which hung at his side, he added: 'We'll leave when I give the order. I've got the highest rank here, and you'll obey me.'

'Shoot me if you like, and drive the tank yourself. I haven't slept in two days, and you're going to leave me the hell alone.'

The other flushed crimson, but said nothing. Then he turned to us. 'You two! Instead of standing there asleep on your feet, get into the truck and help the wounded. They have their needs, too.'

'That's it,' added the tank driver, who was clearly looking for trouble. 'And, when they're finished, the Herr Sergeant will wipe their asses.'

'You watch it, or I'll report you,' snorted the sergeant. He was now white with rage.

Inside the truck, the wounded had not died, despite the jolting of the journey. They were no longer making any noise, and we could see that some of their bandages were soaked with fresh blood. Fighting the exhaustion which made our hearts race, we helped them down and back as best we could – omitting only one man, who was missing both legs. They all asked us for something to drink, and in our ignorance we gave them as much water or brandy as they wanted. We certainly shouldn't have done this: two men died a short time later.

We buried them in the mud, with sticks and their helmets to mark their graves. Then Ernst and I curled up in the cab, to try to snatch a little sleep. But sleep wouldn't come, and we lay instead, with throbbing temples, talking of peace. Two hours later, it was the tank driver who gave the order to depart, as he had predicted. It was now midmorning. The day was clear and bright, and large chunks of snow fell slowly from the trees.

'Hah!' he said. 'Our general left us all while we were asleep. Maybe he felt like taking a walk!'

It seemed that the noncom really was gone. He must have managed a ride in one of the trucks that had passed us during our rest.

'That shit has gone to make his report!' shouted the tank driver. 'If I catch up with him, I'll drive right over him, flatten him out like a goddamned Bolshevik!'

It took us a while to extricate ourselves from the bank we had driven into. However, two hours later we arrived at a hamlet whose name I no longer remember, some five miles from Belgorod. It was filled with soldiers from every branch of the army. The few streets were perfectly straight, and lined with low houses; the way the roofs sat on the walls reminded me of heads with no foreheads, whose hair grows right into the eyebrows. There were swarms of soldiers, and a multitude of rolling equipment covered with mud, pushing through the shouting mob of soldiers, most of whom were looking for their regiments. The road at this point had been roughly resurfaced, and was much more negotiable.

We unhooked ourselves from the tank, and took on eight or ten of the engineers who had been riding on its back. Somewhat bewildered by this flood of soldiers, I had stopped the truck, and was looking for my company. Two M.P.s told me they thought it had gone on toward Kharkov, but as they weren't sure, they sent me to the redirection centre which had been organized in a trailer and was staffed by three officers, who were tearing their hair. When I was finally able to catch their attention through the thousands of shouts and gesticulations besieging them, I was harshly reprimanded for straggling. They probably would have sent me to be court-martialled, if they'd had time. The disorder was incredible, and the landser, half furious, half joking, flooded into the Russian huts.

'We might as well sleep while we wait for all this to settle down.'

All they wanted was a dry corner where they could lie down, but there were so many men crammed into each isba that there was almost no room left for the Russians who lived in them.

Not knowing what to do with myself, I went to find Ernst, who had gone to look for information. However, he had run into a truck hospital, and had returned to the Tatra with an orderly, who was checking over our wounded.

'They can go on as they are,' he said.

'What?' Ernst asked. 'But we've already buried two of them. At least we should give them fresh dressings.'

'Don't be stubborn and stupid. If I label them "urgent," they'll have to wait their turn, lying in the street. You'll get to Belgorod quicker than that — and escape the trap that's closing on us.'

'Is the situation serious?' Ernst asked.

'Yes.'

So Ernst and I found ourselves responsible for twenty wounded men, some of them in critical condition, who had already been waiting several days for essential medical attention. We didn't know what to say when a man grimacing with pain asked us if he would soon be at the hospital.

'Let's get going,' Ernst said, frowning anxiously. 'Maybe he's right. If I'd ever thought it would be like this . . .'

I had been at the wheel for only a few minutes when Ernst tapped me on the shoulder. 'Come on, little one, stop. You'll finish somebody off if it goes on like this. Hand over.'

'But I'm supposed to drive, Ernst. I'm the one who's in the drivers' corps.'

'Never mind. Let me do it. You'll never get us out of here.'

It was true. Despite my best efforts, the truck was jolting and sliding from one side of the road to the other.

We arrived at the village exit point, where there was an interminable line of vehicles waiting for gas. Thousands of soldiers were walking up and down on either side of the road. An M.P. ran over to us.

'Why aren't you waiting like everybody else?'

'We've got to leave right away, Herr Gendarm. We're carrying wounded, and that's what the infirmary told us.'

'Wounded? Serious cases?' He spoke in the doubting, disbelieving tone of every policeman in the world.

'Of course,' said Ernst, who certainly wasn't exaggerating.

The policeman had to peer under the canvas anyway: 'They don't look so bad to me.'

There was a furious outburst of swearing. From time to time, wounded men availed themselves of their special position to abuse the police.

'You sonofabitch,' groaned one man, who was missing a piece of his shoulder. 'It's shits like you who should be sent to the front. Let us through, or I'll strangle you with the one good hand I have left.'

The feverish landser was sitting up in spite of his pain, which made him frighteningly white. He seemed quite capable of putting this threat into action.

The policeman flushed, and his nerve faltered at the sight of these twenty battered wrecks. The position of a big-city policeman roaring at some pathetic bourgeois for going through a red light is a far cry from that of an M.P. behind the lines dealing with a gang of combat veterans who are holding their guts in with their hands, or have just bayonetted the guts out of somebody else. His display of bad temper turned into a set little smile.

'Get out of here,' he said, with the air of someone who doesn't give a damn. When the wheels of the truck began to turn, he vented the last of his spleen: 'Go and die somewhere else!'

It was hard to get even eight gallons of gas, and when we managed it our tank swallowed them in an instant. But we were glad to take what we could and get out. A feeble attempt had been made at surfacing the road, but there were still long stretches of bare ground which had become deep quagmires, to be avoided at all costs. We proceeded on the highway, or beside it, as circumstances required.

Far to the right, we could see another convoy struggling forward in a line parallel to ours. The men were dressed for battle, and seemed to be prepared for an encounter with the Soviets. We were stopped by a new set of police, who combed our papers to see if they could find any mistakes. They checked the truck, verified our I.D. cards and our destination . . . but when it came to the destination, they had to give us directions. One of them looked through the directory hanging around his neck, and told us, in a voice like a barking dog's, that we had to turn off the road a hundred yards ahead and proceed to Kharkov. We followed these instructions with regret, because the new road rapidly deteriorated into a ribbon of mire.

At our speed, we would soon have exhausted our supply of gas. We kept passing vehicles abandoned in the mud because of mechanical failure, or because they had run out of gas. A short distance along the new road, we were stopped by a group of about fifty landser, on foot, and in a state of unbelievable filth. They took our truck by storm. There were several wounded men among them. Some of them had ripped off their filthy dressings, and were walking with their wounds open to the air.

'Make room for us, fellows,' they said, hanging on as hard as they could.

'You can see that we haven't got any room,' Ernst answered. 'Let go.'

But we couldn't get rid of them. They swarmed over the tailgate, trampling on our wounded to try to make them move over. Ernst and I shouted at them, but it didn't do any good: they piled on everywhere.

'Take me,' whimpered a poor devil scratching at my door with bloody hands. Another waved a pass which was already almost expired. The arrival of a steiner followed by two trucks restored order. An S.S. captain climbed out of the steiner.

'What's this ant heap? No wonder you've broken down! It's impossible! There must be at least a hundred men here.'

117

The men scattered immediately, without asking for anything more. Ernst saluted, and explained the situation.

'Very good,' said the captain. 'You take five more along with your wounded. We'll take another five, and the rest will have to walk until the convoy comes by. Let's get going.'

Ernst explained that we would be out of gas in a few minutes. The captain signalled to some soldiers on the steiner, who gave us six gallons. A few minutes later we were on our way again.

We kept passing groups of men wading through the mud who begged us to pick them up, but we didn't stop. Toward noon, with our last drop of gas, we reached a town where a unit was being assembled for the front. I escaped becoming an infantryman before my time by a hair's breadth.

We had to wait until the following day before we could use the reserve of five gallons of gas which Ernst was able to draw. We were about to leave, when an unexpected and unpleasant sound struck our ears. In the distance – still quite far away – we heard the booming of big guns. As we thought we were by now far from the front, we were both astonished and alarmed. We didn't know – and I didn't know until much later – that our course had been taking us parallel to the Belgorod-Kharkov line.

Nonetheless, after unloading two dying men to make room for three more wounded, we set off without delay. In the middle of that afternoon, everything went wrong again.

Our truck was more or less in the middle of a column of ten. We had just passed an armoured unit whose tanks looked like a giant version of the slimy creatures that emerge on mud flats at low tide. They must have been on their way to meet the enemy, who seemed to be very close. We could hear artillery on our left, despite the loud labouring noises of the trucks. Ernst and I exchanged anxious looks. We were stopped by some soldiers who were setting up an anti-tank gun.

'Dig in, fellows,' shouted an officer as we slowed down. 'Ivan's getting pretty close.'

This time, at least, they were telling us something. But I wondered how the Russians, who had been left some ninety miles behind, could already be in this district. Ernst, who was driving, stepped on the gas. Two other trucks did the same.

Suddenly, five planes appeared in the sky, at a moderate altitude. I pointed them out to Ernst.

'They're Yaks,' he shouted. 'Take cover!'

We were surrounded by bare mud, with occasional clumps of stunted brush. There was a sound of machine-gun fire from the sky. The column drove more quickly, toward a shallow fold in the ground which might give some protection. I was leaning out the window, trying to see through the flying mud spun by our wheels. Two Focke-Wulfs had appeared, and had shot down two of the Yaks, which crashed far to the west.

Until the final stages of the war, Russian aircraft were no match for the Luftwaffe. Even in Prussia, where Russian airpower was its most active, the appearance of one Messerschmitt-109, or one Focke-Wulf would make a dozen armoured Ilyushin bombers turn and run. At this period, when German airpower still possessed important reserves, the lot of the Russian pilots was not enviable.

Two of the three remaining Yaks had taken flight, pursued by our planes, when the last dived straight at the convoy. One of the Focke-Wulfs was chasing him, and was plainly trying to get him in his sights.

We reached the dip in the road. The Soviet plane had come down very low, to use its machine guns. The trucks ahead of us had stopped short, and the able-bodied were jumping down into the mud. I was already holding the door open, and I jumped, with my feet together, plunging face downward, when I heard the machine guns.

With my nose in the mud, my hands on my head, and my eyes instinctively shut, I heard the machine gun and the two planes through a hellish intensity of noise. The sound of racing engines was followed by a loud explosion. I looked up, to watch the plane with the black crosses on its wings regain altitude. Three or four hundred yards away, where the Yak had crashed, there was a plume of black smoke. Everybody was getting up again.

'One more who won't give any trouble,' shouted a fat corporal who was clearly delighted to be still alive.

Several voices joined in a cheer for the Luftwaffe.

'Anybody hit?' one of the noncoms called out. 'Let's get going, then.'

I walked over to the Tatra, trying to brush off the worst of
the mud that clung to my uniform. I noticed two holes in the
door I had opened to get out which appeared to have swung
shut on its own momentum: two round holes, each outlined
by a ring of metal from which the paint had been scraped
away. Nervously, I pulled open the door. Inside, I saw a man
I shall never forget – a man sitting normally on the seat,
whose lower face had been reduced to a bloody pulp.

'Ernst?' I asked in a choking voice. 'Ernst!' I threw myself
at him. 'Ernst! What ... ? Say something! Ernst!' I looked
frantically for some features on that horrible face. 'Ernst!' I
was nearly crying.

Outside, the column was getting ready to leave. The two
trucks behind me were impatiently blowing their horns.

'Hey.' I ran toward the first of the trucks. 'Stop. Come
with me. I've got a wounded man.'

I was frantic. The doors of the truck behind me swung
open and two soldiers stuck out their heads.

'Well, young fellow, are you going to move, or aren't you?'

'Stop!' I shouted louder than ever. 'I've got a wounded
man.'

'We have thirty,' one of the soldiers shouted back. 'Get
going. The hospital isn't too far from here.'

Their voices rose over mine, and the noise of their trucks,
which had pulled out, and were passing me, drowned my
cries of desperation. Now I was alone, with a Russian truck
loaded with wounded men, and Ernst Neubach, who was
dead, or dying.

'You shits! Wait for me! Don't go without us!'

I burst into tears, and gave way to a mad impulse. I
grabbed my Mauser, which I'd left in the truck. My eyes were
swimming, and I could barely see. I felt for the trigger, and
pointing the gun at the sky, fired all five cartridges in the
magazine, hoping that to someone in the trucks this would
sound like a cry for help. But no one stopped. The trucks
continued to roll away from me, sending out a spray of mud
on each side. In despair, I returned to the cabin, and ripped
open my kit to look for a package of dressings.

'Ernst,' I said. 'I'm going to bandage you. Don't cry.'

I was insane. Ernst wasn't crying: I was. His coat was
covered with blood. With the dressings in my hand, I stared

at my friend. He must have been hit in the lower jaw. His teeth were mixed with fragments of bone, and through the gore I could see the muscles of his face contracting, moving what was left of his features.

In a state of near shock, I tried to put the dressing somewhere on that cavernous wound. When this proved impossible, I pushed a needle into the tube of morphine, and jabbed ineffectually through the thicknesses of cloth. Crying like a small boy, I pushed my friend to the other end of the seat, holding him in my arms, and soaking in his blood. Two eyes opened, brilliant with anguish, and looked at me from his ruined face.

'Ernst!' I laughed through my tears. 'Ernst!'

He slowly lifted his hand and put it on my forearm. Half choked with emotion, I started the truck, and managed to begin moving without too great a jolt.

For a quarter of an hour, I drove through a web of ruts with one eye on my friend. His grip on my arm tightened and eased in proportion to his pain, and his death rattle rose and fell, sometimes louder than the noise of the truck.

Choking back my tears, I prayed, without reason or thought, saying anything that came into my head.

'Save him. Save Ernst, God. He believed in you. Save him. Show yourself.'

But God did not answer my appeals. In the cab of a grey Russian truck, somewhere in the vastness of the Russian hinterland, a man and an adolescent were caught in a desperate struggle. The man struggled with death, and the adolescent struggled with despair, which is close to death. And God, who watches everything, did nothing. The breath of the dying man passed with difficulty through that horrible wound, making huge bubbles of blood and saliva. I considered every possibility. I could turn back and look for help, or force the men I was carrying to tend Ernst, at gunpoint if necessary, or even kill Ernst, to cut short his sufferings. But I knew very well I couldn't kill him. I had not yet been obliged to fire directly at anyone.

My tears had dried, leaving the trace of their passage on my filthy face, to betray my weakness to the world. I was no longer crying, and my feverish eyes stared at the knob on the radiator two metres in front of me, which cut hypnotically into the interminable horizon. For long moments, Ernst's hand would tighten on my arm, and each time I was overwhelmed by fresh panic. I couldn't look at that horrifying face. Several German planes passed overhead, through the cloudy sky, and in a desperate attempt at telepathy every fibre in my body appealed to them for help. But maybe they were Russian planes. It didn't matter; I had no time to spare. No time to spare: the expression assumed its full significance, as so many expressions do in wartime.

Ernst's hand gripped my arm convulsively. The pressure continued for so long that I slid my foot off the accelerator, and stopped, afraid of the worst. I turned and looked at the mutilated face, whose eyes seemed to be fixed on something the living can't see. Those eyes were veiled by a curious film. My heart was pumping so hard that I felt actual physical pain. I refused to believe what I could guess without difficulty.

'Ernst!' I shouted.

From the back of the truck my shout was answered by several others.

I pushed my companion down on the seat, imploring heaven to let him live. But his body fell heavily against the other side of the cabin.

Death! He was dead! Ernst! Mama! Help me!

In a delirium of terror, I leaned against the truck door, and then let myself drop, trembling, onto the runningboard. I tried to persuade myself that none of this was happening, that it was all a nightmare from which I would wake to see another horizon.

As I sat and thought, I still had no idea of the extent of irremediable evil. I dreamed of what life would be like when I shook off this horrible nightmare in which my friend had just died. But my eyes could see only mud, sucking at my boots.

Two heads looked out from the back of the truck. They were saying something but I didn't hear them. I stood up, and turning my back on them, walked off a short distance. That small physical effort reawakened some sense of life and hope, and I tried to tell myself that all of this wasn't really serious, that it was only a bad dream I had to forget. I tried to impose an expression of smiling derision on my features. Two of the wounded men jumped down from the truck to relieve themselves. I stared at them unseeing, while the vitality of being alive beat back the darkness. I began to think with hope that surely all the German soldiers in Russia would be sent to help us, that something must be coming to help us. Suddenly I thought of the French. They were already on their way: all our newspapers said so. The first legionnaires had already set out. I had seen the photographs.

I felt a hot flush run through me. Ernst would be avenged: that poor fool who had never hurt a fly, who had spent his time making life more endurable for wretched soldiers shaking with cold. And his marvellous hot showers! The French would come, and I would run to embrace them. Ernst had loved them like his own compatriots. This surge of hope and joy could not be damped by facts I didn't know – like the fact that the French had decided on quite another course.

'What's happened?' asked one of the men, whose grey bandage was falling over his eyes. 'Are we out of gas?'

'No. My friend has just been killed.'

They looked into the cabin.

'Fuck ... that's not so bad. At least he didn't have to suffer.'

I knew that Ernst's agony had lasted for nearly half an hour.

'We ought to bury him,' one of them said.

The three of us lifted out the body, which was already stiffening. I moved like an automaton, and my face was without expression. I saw a small rise of ground which was less trampled than everywhere else, and we took Ernst there.

We had no shovels, so we dug the grave with our helmets, rifle butts, and bare hands. I myself collected Ernst's identity tags and papers. The other two were already pushing back the dirt, and trampling it down with their boots when I looked my last on that mutilated face. I felt that something had hardened in my spirit forever. Nothing could be worse than this. We pushed in a stick at the head of the grave, and hung Ernst's helmet on it. I slit the stick with the point of my bayonet, and slid in a piece of paper torn from the notebook Ernst always carried with him, inscribed naïvely in French: 'Ici j'ai enterré mon ami, Ernst Neubach.'

Then, to forestall another emotional crisis, I turned and ran back to the truck.

We started off again. One of the wounded had come to the front and taken Ernst's place: a stupid-looking man, who fell asleep almost at once. Ten minutes later, the motor coughed, and then died. The jolt woke my sleeping companion.

'Something wrong with the engine?'

'No,' I said in an offhand voice. 'We're out of gas.'

'Shit. So what'll we do?'

'We'll walk. On this nice sunny day it should be grand. The strongest will have to help the others.'

My friend's death had abruptly turned me into a cynic, and I felt almost glad that the others would have to suffer with me. My companion looked me up and down.

'You don't mean that. We can't walk. We're all burning up with fever.'

His stupid assurance made me furious. He was clearly a half-wit who never questioned anything, and had gone to war because he'd been sent. Then a Russian shell had gone off too close, and he'd been pierced, and that is all he felt or knew. Since then, he'd been dozing and stuffing himself with sulfanilamide.

'Well, you can stay here, and wait for help, or for Ivan. I'm clearing out.'

I ran to the back door, kicked it open, and explained the situation. Inside, it stank. The men were lying in a revolting mess. Some of them didn't even hear me, and I felt ashamed and brutal. But what else was there to do? Seven or eight haggard men pulled themselves up. Their faces were amazingly drawn. Shaggy beards sprouted from their lined cheeks, and their eyes burned with fever. I felt sickened, and unwilling to insist that they walk. When they had climbed down, they discussed the fate of the others.

'It's impossible to get them up. Let's just leave without telling them. Maybe someone will be along to help them. They're still coming behind us.'

Our wretched group set off, haunted by the dying men we had abandoned in the Tatra. But what else could we have done?

I was the only man without an injury, and the only man with a gun. I had offered Neubach's gun, but no one wanted to carry it. A short time later, a muddy sidecar caught up with us, and stopped, although we hadn't flagged them. It carried two soldiers who belonged to an armoured unit: two generous men. One of them decided to give his place to a wounded man, and, collecting his belongings, got out and walked with us. Somehow, the sidecar managed to take on three wounded.

And so once more I had a strong young man to keep me company, whose humane gesture, if nothing else, made him a sympathetic human being. I no longer remember his name, but I do remember that we talked long and deeply about many things. He told me that the Russian offensive had been mounted very suddenly, and that throughout this vast region we might be stopped at any moment by a Russian motorized unit. My throat went dry, but my companion seemed sure of himself, and of our army.

'We'll resume the offensive now that it's spring. We'll throw the Popovs back across the Don, and then the Volga.'

It's astonishing how agreeable it is to meet confidence and enthusiasm when one is feeling lost. It was as if heaven had sent me this healthy animal to revive my morale. I would have liked things more if Neubach had still been alive, but one must remain humble and resigned in the face of Providence. After all, it was I who should have been driving instead of Neubach.

Toward evening, we came to an isolated country farmhouse. We approached cautiously. The partisans often used places like this: they had the same choices we did, and for anyone a roof is a roof.

The tall young man who had joined us walked out ahead, slowly and deliberately, with his hand on his gun. For a moment he disappeared behind the farmyard buildings, and we felt a twinge of anxiety. But he reappeared and waved us on. The farm was inhabited by a group of Russians who did everything they could to make the wounded men comfortable. The women cooked us a hot meal. They told us that they hated Communism. They had been deported from a small farm they had owned in the neighbourhood of Vitebsk to work on the big kolkhoz we were now walking through. They said they had often given shelter to German soldiers. They had an amphibious V.W. in one of their sheds, which had broken down and been abandoned by one of our sections. They said that the partisans never bothered them because they knew that the Wehrmacht often used their

125

buildings. Our tall newcomer felt somewhat uneasy about the V.W.; the Russians might be lying. They could have stolen it. We tried to start it, but although the engine turned over, the vehicle wouldn't move.

'We'll fix it tomorrow,' the big man said. 'We ought to rest now. I'll take the first watch, and you can relieve me at midnight.'

'We're going to stand watch?' I asked in surprise.

'We have to. You can't trust these people. All Russians are liars.'

This meant another night of anxiety. I walked to the back of the shed, which was dark. There was a jumble of sacks, sheaves of dried sunflower stalks, ropes, and boards, which I arranged as a rough bed. I was about to take off my boots when my companion stopped me.

'Don't do that. You'll never be able to stand them tomorrow. You have to let them dry on your feet.'

I was on the point of replying that the sodden leather would prevent my feet from drying ... but I didn't. What difference did it make if my feet were wet or my boots were wet? I myself was soaked through and filthy and so tired. . . .

'You should wash your feet though. That will make you feel fresher, and better tomorrow, too.'

What sort of a fellow was this? He was as dirty as I, but he seemed to be full of will and ardour and spirit, as if nothing fundamental to his being had been damaged.

'I'm too tired,' I said.

He laughed.

I threw myself down on my back, overcome by the exhaustion which ached in the muscles of my shoulders and neck. I stared into the shadows, caught by an indefinable fear. Above me, the dusty beams were lost in the darkness. My sleep was leaden and dreamless. Only happy people have nightmares, from overeating. For those who live a nightmare reality, sleep is a black hole, lost in time, like death.

A movement of air shook my heavy head. I sat up slowly. It was already broad daylight, and the sky was shining through the wide door of the shed. Beside the door, next to a large chest, my companion of yesterday sat slumped in sleep. I jumped up like a shot. The idea crossed my mind that he might already be dead. I had learned that life and death can

126

be so close that one can pass from one to the other without attracting any attention. The fresh morning air was shaken by the sound of explosions.

I went over to the other soldier and shook him vigorously.

He groaned like a drunk who is being questioned.

'Wake up!'

This time he stood up in a single movement. His sleep had exploded like a bomb. Instinctively he reached for his gun. I felt almost afraid.

'Yes? ... What is it?' he asked. '*Teufel*, it's daylight. I fell asleep on guard, Goddamnit!'

He looked so furious that I kept myself from laughing. His inadequate vigilance had given us both a good night's sleep. Suddenly he pointed his gun at the open door. Before I could turn around, I heard a foreign voice, and one of the Russians who had received us the day before came and stood in the doorway.

'Kamerad,' he repeated in German. 'This morning no good. Boom boom pretty close.'

We went out of the shed. On the roof of the little building in front of us, some Russians from the kolkhoz were inspecting the horizon. We heard some more long-drawn-out explosions.

'Bolsheviks very close,' said one of the Ukrainians, turning to us. 'We'll leave with kamerad soldat German.'

'Where are the wounded?' my companion asked, irritated at having been caught off balance.

'Where you put yesterday,' answered the Popov. 'Two kamerad German dead.'

We looked at him in confusion.

'Come and help us,' my companion said.

Two of the more seriously wounded men had died. There were now four, all in poor condition. One of them was groaning and holding his right arm, whose hand was missing. His purulent dressing glistened with the gangrene which was already devouring him.

'Dig two graves over there,' ordered the tall soldier. 'We must bury these men.'

'We not soldiers,' answered the Popov, still smiling.

'You ... dig grave ... two graves,' insisted the German, aiming his gun at the Russians. 'Two graves, and quick!'

The Russian's eye gleamed wildly as he stared at the black hollow of the gun barrel. He said a few words in Russian, and the others busied themselves with the job.

We had begun to change the dressings of the wounded when we heard the sound of a motor in the courtyard. Without thinking, we ran out. Several armoured vehicles had just driven in, and a gang of German soldiers were running toward the big drinking trough. They were followed by four or five Mark-4s. An officer climbed from a steiner, and we ran to meet him, telling him who we were.

'Alles gut,' said the officer. 'Help us load up, and leave with us.'

We tried to get the amphibious V.W. to start, but that proved impossible. We dragged it from the hut, and one of the landser threw a grenade into the engine. A moment later, it blew to pieces. More vehicles arrived. Others left in the direction from which we'd come. We couldn't understand what was happening. The sound of explosions from the southeast was continuous. The road that ran through the kolkhoz was a stream of traffic of every description. Whenever anyone stopped I asked for news of my unit, but no one knew anything. It seemed likely that my companions of the 19th Rollbahn were far to the west by now — far from the front, to which it seemed I was being sent.

A little while later, I turned west again, in a company of soldiers drawn from many infantry units. The fact that I was involved with this group caused me considerable difficulty a few days later. We appeared to be taking a line parallel to the front, at right angles to the Russian thrust. Far to the north, the Russians were pushing toward the south, hoping to surround the German forces still in the Voronezh-Kursk-Kharkov triangle. For a day and a half, we followed a muddy rut, on which our only troubles were mechanical. The machines we were using had been in Russia since the German advance of 1941, and had been pushed hard. Our forces were obliged to abandon large numbers of trucks and tractors and tanks.

The tanks in particular had taken a beating, often having been used for work their designers had never imagined. They were almost the only vehicles able to move normally during the winter months, and a tank pulling five trucks along a

snowy mule track was not an unusual sight. When they had
to face the Russian counter-offensive, this rough usage,
coupled with their lightness, which had served us so well until
then, made them no match for the famous T-34s, incon-
testably superior to the Mark-2s and -3s. Later, our Tigers
and Panthers stood up to Soviet armour, and played with
their T-34s and KW-85s.

Unfortunately, as in the air, our inadequate numbers had
to yield to an enemy multitude fighting on two fronts. We
were obliged, in effect, to defend a fortress with a circum-
ference of two thousand miles. To cite a single example: the
fighting on the Vistula, north of Cracow, pitted twenty-eight
thousand Germans supported by thirty-six Tiger tanks and
twenty Panthers against two strong Soviet armies of six
hundred thousand men and seven armoured regiments disposing of eleven hundred tanks of various kinds.

Toward noon the next day, we arrived at a small village
about fifteen miles northeast of Kharkov, with a name like
Outcheni. I can no longer remember precisely. The place was
filled with smoke, and to judge by the noise fighting was still
going on quite nearby.

The steiner of the officer who had picked us up at the
kolkhoz drew ahead, while the rest of us jumped down from
our machines. Flickering light a mile or so to the south
marked the line of fire. The soldiers who had come with me
peed into a hedge or chewed some food, with blank faces. I
myself have never been able to achieve a resigned, indifferent
attitude in the face of pressing danger; nevertheless, I tried to
hide my desperate anxiety. Perhaps the others were doing the
same thing. The steiner came back, and two noncoms wrote
down our names. Then we were organized into groups of
fifteen, led either by a sergeant or an obergefreiter.* The
officer climbed onto the seat of the steiner and spoke to us
briefly, mincing no words.

'The enemy has cut us off from our line of retreat. To get
around them, we would have to turn north, onto the plain,
where there are no roads. This could be fatal. Therefore, we
will have to break through their barrage to reach our new
positions, which are quite close.

*Senior lance corporal, or acting corporal.

'As further elements of the Don army arrive, they will be used to maintain the passage already opened, which will allow all our soldiers to escape the Bolshevik noose. Thereafter, you will proceed to positions which will be announced, and which you will maintain until further orders. Good luck! Heil Hitler!'

I was about to say that I belonged to the transport service, when I suddenly felt ashamed. Munitions boxes were opened, and their contents distributed. My pockets and cartridge pouches were full, and I was given two defensive grenades, which I didn't know how to operate. We moved single file to the edge of the village past houses burning from enemy incendiaries. Groups of men were walking about in the debris; others were tending to the wounded. Some burnt-out German vehicles were still smoking. We were taken over by a lieutenant, who asked five or six of us to follow him down a long street which was still more or less intact. A salvo whistled past us, and we threw ourselves to the ground. It fell somewhere in the centre of the village, about seven or eight hundred yards behind us. Enemy shells had dug several holes in the packed earth which lay between two rows of buildings, and occasional mutilated bodies lay sprawled on the streets.

We walked for about fifteen minutes, sticking close to the buildings, until we heard the sound of automatic weapons. About a hundred yards ahead of us, the street was swept by mortar fire. We hesitated for a moment. Then we saw some running figures emerging from the wall of dust stirred up by the enemy salvo.

'Achtung!' shouted the lieutenant.

Instantly, we dropped to our knees, or even onto our stomachs, ready to open fire, but stood up again when we saw German uniforms. The other soldiers ran over to us, and threw themselves down by our sides. We could see that still more were coming through the flying dust. Several of them were howling at the tops of their lungs, a sound which combined fear, anger, and pain.

I watched a soldier without a gun, who was trying to run holding his right thigh with both hands. He fell, stood up, and fell again. Two others were staggering slowly after him. I heard someone shout, 'A moi!' and was trying to see which of them had used my language, when a fresh salvo struck the group, scattering about ten of them in search of shelter.

Two of the men continued toward us, despite the danger. They ran to a door, which they were able to kick in without much trouble, and stood in its opening, shouting curses in French.

Amazed, and without a thought of danger, I ran across the street, bursting in on them like a whirlwind. They paid no attention to me.

'Hey,' I said, shaking one of them by his straps. 'Are you French?'

They turned toward me and looked at me for a fraction of a second. Then their eyes returned to a cloud of dust and smoke pouring from a house which had just burst into flames.

'No. The Walloon Division,' one of them said, without looking back a second time.

A series of explosions made us blink and hunch our shoulders.

'Those shits shoot us just like rabbits. They never take prisoners, the bastards.'

'I'm French,' I said, with an uncertain smile.

'Well then, look out. Volunteers are never prisoners.'

'But I'm not a volunteer!'

The street was raked by a new salvo of mortar fire, somewhat closer than before. Twenty yards away, a roof disintegrated, and the retreat whistle broke off our conversation. We ran as hard as we could back the way we had just come, followed by a burst of machine-gun fire. Two or three men spun round and doubled up, screaming with pain. We almost ran over two men with a heavy machine gun, which they hadn't been able to fire, because we'd been in the way.

Several groups of men had reached a street at right angles to ours, and had scattered among the ruins. The lieutenant was blowing his whistle again, to regroup us, when two Mark-3s suddenly came into sight. They rolled up to the lieutenant, who stood in the middle of the street waving them forward. After a brief consultation, they moved obliquely into the street we had just left, advancing toward the Bolsheviks. The lieutenant tried to reorganize us again, and we set off in the wake of the tanks, which made an infernal din in the rubble-filled streets. I jumped from the corners of buildings to piles of rubble, in a state of terror, unable to grasp why I was there, or to distinguish anything to fire at.

For seconds at a time, our tanks would disappear from view in the turmoil of dust and smoke and flames, but they always re-emerged, with their guns firing. Soon we had run past the point where our retreat had begun, and into an open space surrounded by wooden peasant houses grouped around a pond. The tanks were driving around the pond, crushing every obstacle. On the far side of the pond we could easily see men running in several directions. We stood on the bank, and opened a concentrated fire. Another German company arrived on our right, and threw grenades at a house in which some of the enemy had taken shelter.

Our tanks were now on the other side of the pond, and were flattening the position just taken from the enemy. At last I had the opportunity to fire at some Russians. They were no more than thirty yards away, running from the house our soldiers had attacked with grenades. At least ten Mausers fired, and not one of the Russians stood up again. The fact that we were advancing, and that we felt ourselves suddenly in control of the situation, stimulated us in spite of everything. We had just dislodged an enemy numerically stronger than we – as was always the case in Russia – and we felt as if we'd been given wings.

The sound of firing and the groans of the wounded incited us to massacre the Russians, who had inflicted us with so many horrifying wounds. An attacking army is always more enthusiastic than an army on the defensive, and more likely to accomplish prodigies. This was particularly true of the German Army, which was organized to attack, and whose defence consisted of slowing the enemy by counter-attack. A few of our men took over a Russian cannon, and immediately put it into action. A rapid liaison was established between our two tanks and this newly improvised artillery, which poured all the shells just captured from the Russians onto precisely selected targets.

Then the tanks turned back, leaving the defence of the area to us. Directed by the lieutenant, we placed ourselves as best we could, in readiness for any new surprises. We could hear the sound of continuous firing all around us. A fine rain began to fall.

At dusk, we were still exchanging fire with the enemy, who had grown bolder, and were trying to come back. With darkness, our terror returned, and the firing almost stopped. The lieutenant sent someone to fetch some flares. To the southwest, the horizon lit up in time with sporadic heavy artillery fire. Without knowing it, we had become part of the third battle of Kharkov, whose front extended for some two hundred miles around the city. With darkness and rain, the fighting, for our group, was almost over. Behind us, we could still hear the sound of automatics, which penetrated the noise of engines. Our vehicles were using the darkness to try to get through the Russian barrage. We thought that at any moment we might see the Popovs running toward us through the night. A Volkswagen came up from behind with all its lights out. The driver spoke for a moment with the leader of our group, and then handed some flat mines to four of our men.

With white faces, they went off into the darkness, to place the mines on either side of the pond. Five minutes later, we heard a rough cry from the left, and a short time after that, two of the four came back from the right. After another half hour, we concluded that the two who had gone to the left had run into a Russian knife.

Much later that night, when we were all feeling overwhelmed by sleep, we witnessed a tragedy that froze my blood. We had just thrown about a dozen grenades at random, to forestall some suspected danger, when a prolonged and penetrating cry rose from the hole on my left. It lasted for several minutes, as if it were coming from the throat of someone who was fighting desperately. Then there was a cry for help, which brought us all from our holes and shelters. About ten of us ran toward the sound. The darkness was torn by the white lights of several shots. Fortunately, no one was hit.

We arrived at the edge of a foxhole, where a Russian, who had just thrown down his revolver, was holding his hands in the air. At the bottom of the hole, two men were fighting. One of them, a Russian, was waving a large cutlass, holding a man from our group pinned beneath him. Two of us covered the Russian who had raised his hands, while a young obergefreiter jumped into the hole and struck the other

133

Russian a blow on the back of his neck with a trenching tool.
The Russian let go at once, and the German who had been
under him, who had just missed having his throat cut, ran up
to ground level. He was covered with blood, brandishing the
Russian knife with one hand, like a madman, while with the
other he tried to stop the flow of blood pouring from his
wound.

'Where is he?' he shouted in a fury. 'Where's the other
one?' In a few bounding steps he reached the two men and
their prisoner. Before anyone could do anything, he had run
his knife into the belly of the petrified Russian.

'Cutthroat,' he yelled, looking with wild eyes for another
belly to open.

We had to hold him so he wouldn't run past our lines.

'Let me go!' he shrieked. 'I want to show these savages
how to use a knife.'

'Shut up!' shouted the lieutenant, exasperated by having to
deal with such a motley crew. 'Get back into your foxholes
before Ivan machine guns the lot of you.'

The lunatic, who was losing a lot of blood, was dragged to
the rear by two men. I went back to the hole I was sharing
with four others. I would gladly have fallen asleep, but
nervous exhaustion kept me awake. I had not yet absorbed
all the emotions of the day, and was suffering a belated
reaction.

The intermittent rain began to soak into our clothes and
weight them down. The pond gave off a faint smell. Two men
began to snore. Throughout the night, which seemed
interminable, I kept up a dull conversation with my companions, to prevent a nervous collapse. In the distance, we
could hear the continuous rumble of our retreating trucks.
Enemy action began again well before dawn. Flares above
our position blinded us with their unexpected white lights.
We looked at each other in wordless confusion. The intensity
of this diabolical light threw a sinister, almost indecent glare
on our ghostly faces.

At daybreak, enemy artillery poured a hail of projectiles of
every calibre onto the road about a quarter of a mile behind
us. Beyond my hole, when I dared look outside, I could see
other helmets poking up here and there from below the
ground. Under their visors, eyes gleaming with fatigue were

trying to discern our immediate future on the dim bank. across the pond.

I scraped up some crumbs of vitamin biscuit, which was the last food in my possession. Insomnia and exhaustion made us incapable of grasping the situation with any precision. We were simply there, shivering and wet, and if even a small group of Russians had appeared, we wouldn't have been able to stop them.

Fortunately, the Soviets didn't attack, and we were only subjected to one round of mortar fire, which nevertheless wounded nine of us. At last the sun rose, and we felt somewhat better. When it reached its zenith, we were still waiting in our holes, which the spring warmth had not been able to dry out. We had not been given any more food, but then a soldier of the Reich was supposed to be able to withstand cold, heat, rain, suffering, hunger, and fear. Our stomachs growled, and the blood beat in our temples and at our smallest joints. But the air and the earth and the universe were growling too. From habit, we were almost able to persuade ourselves that this was a possible way to live. I know of many who actually managed it.

Toward six o'clock that evening, we were ordered to abandon our positions. This step required many precautions. We had to cover a considerable distance with all our equipment, while two men stayed behind to lay mines for the enemy. When we reached the ruins of the first house, we were finally able to straighten up. We went into the battered buildings, whenever we could, to look for food. I can remember devouring three raw potatoes, and finding them delicious.

We arrived at the crossroads from which our group had set out twenty-four hours earlier. The two mutilated but recognizable roads we had taken the day before had been turned into a jumble of churned earth. As far as I could see, the disabled carcasses of Wehrmacht vehicles lay scattered in a haze of whirling smoke, across the ruins of what must once have been houses. There were several muddy German bodies, too, lying in rigid attitudes beside wrecked machines, waiting for the burial squad.

Some men from the engineers were setting fire to the vehicles that blocked the road. We walked through this chaos for a while, supporting our wounded. A hundred yards away, another group, larger than ours, was also withdrawing, with arms and equipment.

We followed the lieutenant as far as the regroupment centre, abandoned by the officers two hours before we received the order to withdraw. Not a soul was left in the battered building which had housed the officers responsible for the defence of the town. A sergeant on a motorcycle was waiting alone in front of the building to instruct stragglers. The lieutenant seemed disgusted by the available options, and continued to lead us westward.

We covered another twelve miles on foot, constantly threatened by Soviet patrols, who would open fire without hesitation on even a single famished landser. After diving down some thirty times or more to avoid Russian salvos, we arrived at a Luftwaffe airfield, which had already been abandoned. We thought that the wooden buildings – which were like the ones we had occupied on the Don – might still contain some scraps of food. Carrying our four wounded men on improvised stretchers, we walked toward one of the huts, stumbling with exhaustion. But we never reached it: a scene of intense horror stopped six or seven of us.

We had just passed a bunker in which we noticed a body lying at the bottom. Two emaciated cats were eating one of its hands. I felt sick.

'Get out, you damned cats!' shouted my companion.

Everyone came over to look. The lieutenant, as sickened as I had been, threw a grenade. The two ghostly cats ran off into the countryside, while the explosion sent a column of more or less human debris straight up into the air, like a chimney.

'If the cats are eating stiffs,' somebody said, 'there couldn't be much left in the pantry.'

There were still two bimotors with Maltese crosses on their wings standing on the empty field – probably inoperable in some way. From the sky, we heard a disquieting sound, which was growing louder. We all turned our white faces the same way, suddenly realizing that we were standing beside two planes in the centre of a vast, flat space, and could hardly fail to attract attention.

We scattered without waiting for any orders, flinging

ourselves onto the ground, trying to escape those six black
dots, which were already falling toward us like lightning. I
thought immediately of the bunker where the cats had been
feasting. Six others had the same idea, and although I ran as
fast as I could, I arrived next to last beside the hole where
four soldiers were already trampling on what was left of a
human being.

I looked desperately into that crowded space, hoping that
some miracle would make it larger. Two others were doing
the same thing. Maybe we'd made a mistake; maybe the
planes were really ours.... But that was impossible; the
sound was unmistakable.

The noise grew louder and louder. We threw ourselves
down, painfully aware of our absolute exposure. I held my
head between my hands, and closed my eyes, trying to
obliterate the muffled explosions which reached my partially
blocked ears. I felt the fury of hell pass over me like a
hurricane. The blows striking the earth shook every organ in
my body, and I knew that I was going to die. Then the storm
passed as quickly as it had come. I lifted my head to see the
enemy formation break apart as it climbed higher into the
pale blue sky. Here and there across the field, men were
getting up and running for better cover. The Russian planes
had regrouped and were turning as tightly as they could.
Then they swooped down at us again. I felt a bitter presenti-
ment freeze my blood. I began to run like a madman, with
my legs flying, trying to force myself to go faster. But I knew
that exhaustion had the upper hand, that I would never reach
the road, with its ditch, which might shelter me. I kept
stumbling over my heavy boots.

In desperation, and despite myself, I fell onto the wet
grass, instinctively aware that the planes were on top of us
again. The first explosions shook the ground, filling me with a
frantic fear. I scratched at the ground like a rabbit whose last
hope of escape is to bury itself. I could hear the earth being
torn, and horrifying human shrieks. White flashes burned
into my eyes through my clenched fists and eyelids. I lay
there for two or three minutes, which seemed like an eternity.

When I finally looked up, the two bimotors were burning
like torches. The Russian planes were far off, turning back
into formation for another attack. They had pulled up after

this one in all directions. Once again I called on all my reserves of strength to get up and run, the other way this time, to the wooden buildings, which suddenly seemed to offer refuge. I had covered about a third of the distance when the Russian planes attacked, shooting rockets into the buildings, which disintegrated like matchwood. After a few moments of further terror, we could hear the engines of the planes fading into the distance. Everyone who was able stood up again. No one spoke. We stared at the flames, at the sky, at the reddening heaps of human remains. Our lieutenant, who seemed to have lost his sanity, although he was unhurt, was running from one wounded man to another.

'Shit,' someone shouted. 'Another attack like that, and there won't be anyone left. They've just left us here. We'll never get out. . . .'

'Shut up!' shouted the lieutenant, who was supporting a wounded man. 'War is never a picnic.'

Who did he think he was telling? We gathered around him. He lifted the shoulders of a poor fellow covered with mud and blood, who was laughing to split his sides. For a moment, I thought he was crying with pain, but he was in fact howling with laughter.

'Das ist der Philosoph,' someone said.

I had never noticed the man before. His friend added that he had always believed he would return home unscathed. Three of us tried to lift him to his feet, but soon realized this was impossible. His bursts of laughter were interrupted by words which I understood perfectly, and thought about for a long time afterward, and which still trouble me. As I remember his laugh, there was nothing mad about it, it was more like the laugh of someone who has been the victim of a practical joke, a farce in which he had believed until suddenly he realized his folly. No one questioned the philosopher, but he himself, through his hilarity and his agony, tried to explain: 'Now I know why. . . . I know why. . . . It's too simple. . . . It's idiotic. . . .'

Perhaps we would have learned what he meant, but a sudden surge of blood poured from his mouth, and ended his life. We dug graves for the new victims, and then stretched out, exhausted, on the bed of warm ashes that marked the site of the destroyed buildings.

At nightfall, we were wakened by the sound of guns, which seemed to be following us. By now we all felt desperately hungry and thirsty. Despite our rest, we had not recovered our strength, and we looked appalling. We stared at each other suspiciously, wondering if the next fellow didn't have a couple of biscuits hidden somewhere, forgetting the lessons of comradeship we had been taught in Poland. But apparently we were all cleaned out. If anyone had been hiding something, we could scarcely have reproached him, as we all might easily have done the same thing.

In the darkness, as we fled the curtain of flares which had pursued us since our retreat from the Don, we heard once again the sound of a moving column, and were once again filled with panic. The night was as black as pitch. A fine rain was falling. We followed the lieutenant: God knows where he was taking us. No one spoke. Our strength seemed barely adequate to move our legs, weighted by exhaustion and mud.

Finally the lieutenant spoke: 'Maybe they'll go by without seeing us. Are any of you anti-tank gunners?'

Quickly, our solitary spandau was set up for a final effort of defence. Luckily, the exhaustion which made my temples throb under my leaden helmet prevented me from clearly grasping the seriousness of our situation. The simple fact that we had stopped walking presented my foundering body with a moment of relief which had to be used to the utmost. I knew that my fear would return with my breath, and that I would again be aware of everything that was happening.

The first black mass which came into view, with all its lights out, seemed to be some kind of light vehicle. We tried to see what it was, but the darkness was too thick. Then we heard tank treads, unmistakable and frightening, as those who have heard the sound on the front at night will appreciate.

As the noise grew louder, our panic increased. While some were trying to see where the tanks would come from, others – including myself – lay with their faces pressed into the ground. Two black shapes loomed against the sky some thirty metres away. Another, less than ten metres from us, made the earth shake, and every hair stand on end. Someone called out: 'Die Maltkreuze, mein Gott! ... Kameraden! Hilfe! Hilfe!'

For me, who spoke German so badly, and understood it even worse, this was a signal for everyone to save his skin. I jumped up and started to run. This, evidently, is what one should not do. Through the noise of the tanks, I could hear shouts and curses. The group had taken my action as a signal for general flight. Everyone had jumped up, and was running, shouting at the tanks – with the exception of the lieutenant and one or two more reflective, prudent soldiers. Later it occurred to me that even German tanks might have machine-gunned us, taking us for Russians. Also, they might have been Russian tanks.

However, we managed to make ourselves recognized, and were taken in by a detachment of the 25th Panzerdivision, commanded by General Guderian.

These men were extremely well-equipped, and had not been involved in our retreat. They put us wherever there was room on the backs of the tanks, where the heat of the engine burned our buttocks. No one asked if we'd eaten, and it wasn't until hours later, under the rolling fire of the Russian artillery which was raking Kharkov, that we were served a hot, greasy soup, which we received like a benediction.

It was here that I first saw one of the enormous Tiger tanks and two or three Panthers. I also saw, a few hours later, the appalling avalanche of the famous Katoushas, which poured hours of devastating fire on the German infantry advancing with appalling losses through the outlying district of Slaviansk-Kiniskov. Guderian's tanks took us right into Kharkov, where the Donets battles had already been in progress for more than a week. Once again, the Wehrmacht took the battered city, before losing it finally in September, after the failure of the Belgorod counter-offensive.

Dawn found us in the sand pits to the northwest of the city, where our group was gone over with a fine-toothed comb by the Kommandos responsible for sending men back to their original units. As they didn't know where most of these units were, the best they could do was to form the strays into new groups, which everyone wished to avoid. These new units, with no official affiliation or assignments, simply sapped the actual strength of the army as recorded by military registration and on the maps at headquarters. The men assigned to these varied and unmeasurable groups could not be fitted into any logical organization. Already classified as missing or dead by their original units, they were officially considered dead, and used as unexpected reinforcements whom there was no reason to spare. Long lines of soldiers, sitting, lying down, asleep and awake, were waiting for orders which would somehow fit them into the battle.

I can still remember the look of the Donets Valley, and the river, with its wide sand banks stretching some eight or ten miles back from the water. The thunder of guns reached us from the front, which was about twenty miles to the south. The German attack was moving from the north and west. With their left wing protected by the Donets, the Panzer assault was driving into the Russian artillery, which had rapidly crossed the river in an attempt to follow up their counter-offensive. Now these batteries had been driven back to the river, and were unable to recross it, as all the bridges were out. In effect, the Russians had just made the same mistake as the Germans at Stalingrad, although not on the same scale. In their haste to drive us out, they had over-extended their supply lines and underestimated the forces pitted against them. A hundred thousand Russians, of whom fifty thousand were killed, were caught for over a week in the Slaviansk-Kiniskov pocket.

Of course, I didn't know what had happened around Kharkov until months later. For me, the Donets battle, like the battles of the Don and of Outcheni, was a smoking chaos, a wellspring of continuous fear, alarm and rumour, and thousands of explosions.

I had just been reassigned, and was waiting for further instructions with a handful of other filthy, shaggy men, when a policeman handed me a scrap of paper. The police, like the Kommandos, were authorized to organize strays, and the scrap of paper purported to give us the route we must take to return to our company. It seemed that the 19th Rollbahn was operating in the neighbourhood, and the three other fellows also belonged to it.

We cleared out as quickly as we could. The fear of being incorporated into an impromptu battalion lent wings to our feet. I have never had a very strong sense of direction, but here in this chaos of mud and ruin even a migratory bird would have lost the north. Our scrawled note only gave us the principal points to look for, which might have been recognizable to regiments camped on the spot. To us, however, in an entirely new landscape, it was almost impossible to distinguish one point from another. The rare signposts that remained on the battered streets had been twisted in the fighting, and had to be disregarded.

After a thousand false leads and a thousand delays, we finally found our company two days later. In the meantime, we had been pressed into service unrolling telephone wire for an S.S. regiment which was mounting an attack. I still remember a railway embankment which some very young S.S. were charging under heavy machine-gun fire.

We huddled in a drainage pipe which had been uncovered in a bombardment, waiting for the S.S. to take the area — which they did, with heavy losses. Beyond the two cement walls, the flash of mortar fire and red-hot metal fragments streaked through the air. Then the same regiment used us to supply a Haubitz battery, which had been engaged for several days in an artillery duel with the Soviet guns on the east bank of the Donets. We were moving the heavy projectiles from their distant depot when we ran into some men from our company, repairing a collapsed bunker.

The first familiar face I saw belonged to Olensheim.

'Hey!' I shouted, running to my friend, followed by the three others. 'It's us!' Olensheim stared, as if he'd been struck by lightning.

'Another four!' he shouted. 'God must be with us! Laus scratched you off the list long ago. There are still thirty who haven't showed up. We thought you must have been put in one of the scrap units.'

'Don't mention bad luck,' I said. 'Where's Hals?'

'That fellow has *all* the luck. Right now, he's in Trevda, being taken care of, while we dig up this damn dirt.'

'Was he wounded?'

'A fragment in the neck. Absolutely nothing. But he was collected along with the seriously wounded. He said he was unconscious for two hours. But he always exaggerates.'

'And Lensen?'

'He's fine. He's changing a tread over there.'

Laus arrived, and we instinctively saluted.

142

'Glad to see you, boys. Really glad.' He shook each of us by the hand, his old soldier's face filled with emotion. Then he took a few steps backward. 'Announce yourselves clearly and intelligibly, the way I taught you.'

We conformed to the prescribed pattern with a good will that came from a deep sense of comradeship. But, apart from this encounter, everything looked dark. The sky was filled with lowering clouds which threatened rain, and at the four cardinal points white flashes preceded geysers of damp earth and rubble by fractions of seconds.

A short time later, Lensen, who was heavier and stronger than I, lifted me bodily from the ground in his delight at seeing me again. Despite the heavy labour we had to perform, the day was coloured by the joy of this reunion.

Two days later, I managed to get to Trevda, which was some twenty-five miles from the front. Another fellow gave me his place in the D.K.W. he was supposed to drive, and I was able to visit Hals. I found him in a swarm of wounded men, singing at the top of his lungs. Spring had arrived at last, and the heavily wounded were cavorting between two avenues of wild pear trees.

Hals was unable to curb his delight at seeing me. I was carried in triumph by men who had lost arms, who were powdered with sulfanilamides and smeared with unguents. I was made to finish the remains of all the bottles they had opened, and accordingly was not able to keep the appointment I had made with the fellow who had brought me out. After waiting for a while, he grew bored, and left without me. I was taken back much later by a driver attached to my camp. Hals made me promise to visit him again, but I never had the chance: a few days later, the doctor found him fit, and he rejoined us.

Hals detested the squalid cellar where we were established, and following his lead, I volunteered for service in the motorized infantry. We were fed up with digging and acting as maidservants to the rest of the army. This decision almost cost us our lives many times, but even now, looking back on everything that happened, I cannot regret having belonged to a combat unit. We discovered a sense of comradeship which I have never found again, inexplicable and steady, through thick and thin.

PART TWO

'THE GROSS DEUTSCHLAND'
Spring, 1943 – Summer, 1943

Chapter Four

LEAVE

BERLIN   PAULA

On a beautiful spring morning, we were assembled at Trevda, where Hals had spent such an enjoyable time. Two other companies joined us on a hillside covered with short, velvety grass – the kind which thrusts up so thickly that each blade seems to be fighting for space, and which becomes a tall savannah within a month. There were about nine hundred of us. A group of officers standing on the platform of a half-destroyed truck addressed us from the top of the hill. About twenty flags and regimental pennants had been propped around the base of the truck. The speeches were very courteous. We were even congratulated for our attitude in the past – an attitude which made us feel ashamed whenever we heard any bulletins from the front. We stared at the officers with enormous eyes. They said that because of our attitude they were prepared to honour any one of us who might wish it by transferring him to a combat unit. About twenty men volunteered at once. The officers, recognizing our 'timidity,' tried to put us at our ease, and went on talking in the same style. Certain heroic actions were described in detail. Fifteen more volunteers stepped out of the ranks, among them Lensen, who was clearly born for trouble. Next, the officers mentioned a fortnight's leave, which produced at least three hundred volunteers. Then several lieutenants stepped down from the platform. They threaded their way through our ranks, selecting individual men and inviting them to take the three fateful steps forward, while a captain maintained the tone of eloquent pressure.

The men chosen were always among the largest, healthiest, and strongest. Suddenly, an index finger sheathed in black leather was pointing, like the barrel of a Mauser, into the ribs of my best friend, my war brother. As if hypnotized, Hals

147

large steps, and the sound of his heels as he
rapped them together was like a door slamming shut, a door
which threatened to separate me – perhaps forever – from the
only real friend I had ever made and from the friendship
which was my only incentive for life in the midst of despair.

After a moment's hesitation, I joined the group of
volunteers without any further pressure. I looked confusedly
at Hals, whose face was glowing like the face of a child who
has just been given a delightful surprise, and who doesn't
know what to say. Henceforth, my identification would be
Gefreiter Sajer, G. 100/1010 G4. Siebzehntes Bataillon,
Leichtinfanterie Gross Deutschland Division, Süd, G.

In the evening, we went back to the squalid shelters we had
already occupied. Nothing seemed to have changed. The fact
that our names had been added to the infantry recruitment
lists was the only difference between the life we had led
yesterday as truck drivers and our new life as combat troops.
We felt somewhat confused as to the attitude we should
adopt, but our noncoms allowed us very little time for
meditation. They kept us busy cleaning up, and restoring to
good condition the weapons which had taken a beating
during the last battle – a job which took several days.
Everything seemed to have quieted down, although strong
Soviet counter-thrusts had started several fires to the northeast, at Slaviansk. We were also used for the revolting chore
of burying the thousands of men who had died in the battle
for Kharkov.

We were officially designated 'burial squad' one morning
at dawn. The light was so faint it was still almost as dark as
the middle of the night. Laus informed us that our new job
would take the place of the fortnight's leave we had been
promised, and were so much looking forward to. As a rule,
the Russian prisoners were used to bury the dead, but it
seemed they had taken to robbing the bodies, stealing
wedding rings and other pieces of jewellery. In fact, I think
the poor fellows – many of them wounded but designated fit
for work – were probably going over the bodies for something to eat. The rations we gave them were absurd – for
example, one three-quart mess tin of weak soup for every
four prisoners every twenty-four hours. On some days, they
were given nothing but water.

Every prisoner caught robbing a German body was immediately shot. There were no official firing squads for these executions. An officer would simply shoot the offender on the spot, or hand him over to a couple of toughs who were regularly given this sort of job. Once, to my horror, I saw one of these thugs tying the hands of three prisoners to the bars of a gate. When his victims had been secured, he stuck a grenade into the pocket of one of their coats, pulled the pin, and ran for shelter. The three Russians, whose guts were blown out, screamed for mercy until the last moment.

Although we had already met birds of every colour, these proceedings revolted us so much that violent arguments broke out between us and these criminals every time. They invariably became furious and abusive, shouting insults at us. They said they had escaped from the camp at Tomvos, where the Russians dumped German prisoners, and they told us how our countrymen were being slaughtered. According to them, the infamous Tomvos camp, sixty miles east of Moscow, was an extermination camp. Rations as ludicrous as those we handed out to Russian prisoners at Kharkov were served once a day to men reporting for labour. Men who did not work received nothing. One bowl of millet was provided for every four men. There was never enough, even for the prisoners who could work. The daily surplus were simply killed: a favourite method of execution was to hammer an empty cartridge case into the nape of the prisoner's neck. It seemed that the Russians often distracted themselves with this type of sport.

I myself can well believe that the Russians were capable of this kind of cruelty, after seeing them at work among the pitiful columns of refugees in East Prussia. But Russian excesses did not in any way excuse us for the excesses by our own side. War always reaches the depths of horror because of idiots who perpetuate terror from generation to generation under the pretext of vengeance.

We spent hours digging out a long tunnel which had been turned into an emergency hospital during the fighting. The surgeons had been so overloaded that the wounded had almost certainly been abandoned. A line of rough triple-decker beds extended some hundreds of yards down the corridor, each containing three blackened, stiff, and muti-

lated bodies. From time to time, an empty space marked the
final flight of a dying man.

There was no light in this charnel house, except from the
electric torches which some of us had fastened to our tunics.
These threw beams of horrifying illumination on the thin,
swollen faces of the cadavers, which we had to pull out with
hooks.

Finally, one delicious spring morning, incongruous in that
sad, ruined landscape, a muddy truck drove down the track
to the new barracks we had moved into the day before. After
a brisk half turn, it stopped about ten yards from the first
building, where a group of men which included myself were
busy removing a heap of gravel and small stones. The back
flap of the truck was kicked open, and a plump little corporal
jumped down and clicked his heels. Without saluting or
saying a word, he rummaged in his right breast pocket,
where all military instructions were supposed to be kept. He
pulled out a sheet of paper which had been carefully folded
four times, and read out a long list of names. As he read, he
indicated with a wave of his hand that the men named should
step to the right. There were about one hundred names on the
list, among them Olensheim, Lensen, Hals, and Sajer. Feeling
somewhat anxious, I joined the group on the right. The
corporal told us we had three minutes to climb aboard the
truck with our weapons and packs. Then he clicked his heels
again, saluting this time, and turned his back without another
word, striding off as if he were suddenly going for a walk.

We ran frantically to collect our things. There was no time
for conversation. Three minutes later, a hundred breathless
soldiers were packed into the truck, whose bulging sides
threatened to collapse. The corporal was also on time. He
threw a withering glance at the eccentrically bulging packs
some of us were carrying, but said nothing. Then he bent
down to look at something under the truck.

'No more than forty-five on board,' he barked. 'Departure
in thirty seconds.'

He took another hundred paces.

We all groaned silently. No one wanted to get down;
everyone had the best of reasons for staying put. Two or
three men were shoved off the back. As I was right in the
middle, packed in like a sardine, there was no question of

moving. Laus finally took matters in hand. He made half the
men on the truck get down. The remainder came to exactly
forty-five. The corporal, who was already climbing into the
front seat, told the driver to start. Laus gave us a friendly
wave. We had received our final orders from him. His last
smile more than made up in our eyes for all the duties he had
imposed on us. Beside him, the other half of the group called
out by the corporal watched with dazed faces as we vanished
in a whirl of dust.

This half of the group joined us four days later, one
hundred miles behind the front lines, at the rest camp of
the famous Gross Deutschland Division. A large part of the
division, especially the convalescing wounded, occupied the
rustic Akhtyrka camp. The division itself held a mobile
sector in the vast Kursk-Belgorod region. Everything at the
camp was clean and neatly organized, as in the Boy Scouts,
only far more lavishly supplied. Akhtyrka reminded us of an
oasis, surrounded by the trackless steppe.

We jumped down at the corporal's order, and lined up in a
double file. A captain, a first lieutenant, and a feldwebel
walked toward us. Our plump little corporal snapped to
attention. These officers were all dressed with astonishing
style. The hauptmann looked like a figure from a costume
party, in a jacket of fine grey-green cloth with the red facings
of a combat unit, dark-green riding breeches, and gleaming
cavalry boots. He waved at us, and then said something we
couldn't quite hear to the feldwebel, who was every bit his
equal in elegance. After a short conversation with the
hauptmann, the feld walked over to us, clicked his heels, and
addressed us in a tone which at least was more agreeable
than that of the corporal who had come to fetch us.

'Welcome to the Gross Deutschland Division!' he shouted.
'With us, you will experience a genuine soldier's life, the only
life which brings men close to each other on terms of
absolute sincerity. Here, a sense of comradeship exists
between each and every one of us, which might be put to the
test at any moment. Any black sheep, anyone unsuited for
comradeship, does not stay in this division. Everyone must
be able to count on everyone else, without any qualification
whatever. The slightest error on anyone's part affects the
whole section. We want no slackers and no strays: everyone

must be prepared either to obey without question, or to give orders. Your officers will think for you. Your duty is to show yourselves worthy of them. You will now get yourselves some new clothes and throw away your stinking rags. Absolute cleanliness is the essential foundation for a decent frame of mind. We do not tolerate any sloppiness of appearance.' He took a deep breath, and then continued. 'When these preliminaries have been accomplished, this group of volunteers will receive their passes for the fortnight's leave which has been promised them. If there is no counter-order, these passes will become effective in five days, when the convoy leaves for Nedrigailov. You may now proceed. Heil Hitler!'

It was a beautiful day. Everything in the camp seemed to be efficiently organized. According to what we'd just heard, one did not trifle with orders, but that seemed a reasonable change, after the universe of shit and horror and suffering and panic we had just come from. And then there were our passes! Hals was jumping with delight, like a young goat. Everyone felt overjoyed.

Our plump corporal had one more nasty surprise in store for us, but we were all in such a good humour nothing could ruffle us. He ordered us to wash our filthy clothes before turning them in to the supply store where we would draw new ones. We found ourselves transformed into washerwomen, standing stripped to the skin in front of long troughs. Our underclothes were caked with filth, beyond hope of recovery. I kicked my shorts into the air, and tore my undershirt into shreds. My last pair of socks, which I'd been wearing since the beginning of the retreat, were nothing but holes and joined my shorts. Then, stark naked, we walked across the grass to the store, to hand in our old clothes, which were soaking wet but neatly folded – and receive new ones. Two women soldiers nearly choked with laughter when they saw us coming.

'Hang on to your boots!' shouted the sergeant, who was not particularly amused by the sight of naked boys. 'No new boots here!'

We were given a fresh issue of everything from caps to first-aid kits. However, certain indispensable items were missing – among these, underpants and socks – which in the long run proved to be serious omissions. But our spirits were too high to be disturbed at the time.

When we were dressed, we were directed to a wooden army barrack. A notice in large, legible characters was tacked beside the door to remind us of the cleanliness which was officially obligatory: 'Eine Laus, der Tod!'* The plump little corporal who had accompanied us from Kharkov waved us inside. We looked curiously around our new room, which was rough but impeccably clean.

'Ruhe, Mensch!' shouted the corporal. We instantly fell silent. 'Since there isn't a noncom here, I am going to put one of you in charge.'

He worked his way through our ranks, with his eyes half closed, as if he wished to surprise his choice — who of course would not want the responsibility — or as if the decision were somehow significant. Finally, with a sharp cry, he selected a fellow who didn't seem to have anything special about him:

'Du!'

The man he pointed to stepped forward.

'Your name?'

'Wiederbeck!'

'Wiederbeck, until further notice, you will be responsible for the order of this room. You will go to the Warenlager to pick up the divisional patches which everyone must sew on his left sleeve. You will also ...' He enumerated a list of duties, each of which made poor Wiederbeck's head droop a little lower.

A few minutes later, we each received the famous insignia of the Gross Deutschland division, with its divisional title in silver Gothic letters on a black ground. This band remained on my sleeve until 1945, when the rumour ran through our scattered ranks that the Americans were shooting any man wearing a divisional name instead of a number. And at that moment of hasty judgment, they might very well have shot a nobody from the Gross Deutschland or the Brandenburg as easily as a hero from the Leibstandarte, or the Totenkopf. But that time was still far in the future. We were then in the spring of 1943, on the territory of a conquered country. The weather was marvellous, and as a finishing touch we all had two-week passes in our pockets. After everything we had been through, this new life seemed like a dream.

*"A louse means death!'

153

Except for morning and evening roll call, we were free to wander about and entertain ourselves as we pleased. Akhtyrka was a curious place. Between the houses or groups of houses, which were built in an agreeable Russian peasant style, the grasses and wild flowers of the steppe grew with vigorous abundance, making a kind of thick lawn, which was often nearly three feet high. These plants and grasses, which all turned brown at the end of summer, were scattered with enormous daisies and a variety of aromatic plants which the Russians collected for seasoning their food and preparing drinks. Fields of rough, light-green gherkins were set off by enormous sunflowers. The groups of houses were inhabited either by members of a family, or by friends, who built in clusters to reduce the effort of paying visits.

The Russians – especially the Ukrainians – are very gay and hospitable, and ready to celebrate almost any occasion. I remember several pleasant gatherings at the homes of these enthusiastic people, during which everyone managed to forget the rivalries of the war. And I remember the girls, shouting with laughter when they had every reason to hate us – on another human scale altogether from the affected Parisian beauty, obsessed by her appearance and her cosmetics.

Each group of houses also had its own burial ground, which was never a sad place, but always a beautiful flowery plot, with wooden tables where people often sat and drank, and an ornamental signpost with an affectionate variation of the place name: Beautiful Akhtyrka, Our Town, Akhtyrka, Sweet Akhtyrka.

Four days after our arrival, the second section of our group of volunteers joined us. It seemed they really had to sweat to make it: almost the whole journey had been on foot.

At last, on the fifth day, we took our places in the convoy for Nedrigailov. Our passes would not become operative until we reached Poznań, which was another thousand miles to the west. After· that, there would be six hundred miles to my parents at Wissembourg. I would therefore be travelling for several days. We drove across a huge expanse of country which was absolutely flat – without the slightest trace of hillock or hollow. Here and there, we could see military tractors being used for agricultural work. We were able to maintain a decent speed as far as Nedrigailov, on a road which had been rebuilt by the army engineers, and which, every three or four miles, was littered with the wreckage of hastily abandoned Soviet matériel. We had driven for about 150 miles when our attention was attracted by some tiny shapes outlined against the distant sky. Their silhouettes were marked by little white clouds, and the sound of explosions.

The two trucks ahead of us slowed down, and then stopped. As usual, the feld responsible for the convoy jumped down from the first truck and stared through his field glasses. As usual, we waited for an order before plunging to the ground. Everyone was quiet, watching the feld attentively, trying to fathom his reactions. Only the sound of the idling engine broke the stillness. The joy which had transformed our faces these last few days slowly faded as our anxiety grew. A few voices cursed our bad luck.

'I thought that by now we were good and far from any trouble.'

'Goddamnit!'

'What do you think it could be?'

'Partisans,' muttered Hals, who had already taken part in a 'man hunt.' There were several other conjectures as well.

'Whoever they are, I'm not going to let the bastards wreck my leave.'

'I wonder what we're waiting for. Why don't they just tell us to go ahead and shoot them?'

Each of us had already picked up the Mauser which soldiers on leave in an occupied country were required to carry at all times. The idea that somebody or something might prevent us from going home made us feel savage. We were ready to shoot anyone at a moment's notice if that's what was needed to keep moving west. But the order to fire never came. The feld climbed back onto his truck, and the convoy started off again. We stared at each other in confusion. When, some five hundred yards further on, we ran into a group of twenty German officers carrying shotguns, we felt so surprised and delighted that our assumption had been mistaken that we cheered them as if we were driving past the Führer himself.

At last, we reached Nedrigailov, where we left the convoy,

which turned south. We went on to Romny, the gypsy paradise, where we were supposed to be picked up by another convoy moving west. At Nedrigailov, our ranks were swelled by other men on leave from various parts of Russia, until there were nearly a thousand of us. However, the supply of available trucks had to be used for many purposes other than simply transporting men on leave. The few trucks for Romny took on about twenty fortunate souls; the rest of us were left to mill about in front of a field kitchen equipped to feed barely a quarter of our number. Although we were famished, we decided to walk the thirty miles to Romny, and set off despite the lateness of the hour, in the best of spirits. About twenty fellows who were considerably older than the rest of us and belonged to the Gross Deutschland Division came along. There were also seven or eight fellows from the S.S., who sang at the tops of their lungs. The others took swigs from bottles which they passed from hand to hand. They must have emptied several cellars: every one of them seemed to be carrying a generous collection.

We had instinctively arranged ourselves in threes, as if we were going up to the line, and were proceeding on the double, consciously reducing the distance which separated us from Romny. Evening was slowly falling across the endless green, rolling landscape. Our uniforms, so perfectly matched to outdoor colours, seemed to take on the tone of the surrounding landscape, like chameleon skins. After the first ten miles, our high spirits faded somewhat, leaving us more inclined to contemplate the immense panorama of the Ukraine. The earth, engaged in the processes of spring germination, exhaled a subtle but nonetheless powerful odour, as the horizon faded into the boundless emptiness of the darkening sky. Our uniforms grew darker as the earth darkened, almost as if by magic, and our footsteps seemed to be setting the rhythm of the whole mysterious universe. The blackness of night was spreading behind us, and we fell silent, hushed by the respect which immensity imposes on simple men. Our group of soldiers, members of an army hated throughout the world, was seized by an indefinable emotion. As one sometimes jokes to hide sadness, we began to sing to avoid thought. The favourite song of the S.S. rose up like a hymn to the earth, offered to men:

So weit die braune Heide geht
Gehört das alles wir ...

Then darkness engulfed us — a darkness which, for the first
time in months, seemed made for nothing more than watching over us. Although we had begun to feel our exhaustion,
no one suggested a halt. The road home was long, and we
didn't want to lose any time. For me, hoping to reach my
other country, the road was even longer. Although our leave
did not officially begin until Poznań, the idea of getting home
overrode every other consideration, and enabled me to
endure the painful condition of my bare feet, rubbed raw by
my boots.

Hals, who was having the same sort of trouble, cursed the
storekeeper at Akhtyrka for failing to supply us with socks.
After about twenty miles, we were forced to reduce our
speed. Naturally, the veterans who had joined us, and whose
feet must have been made of iron, treated us like crybabies.
But they gave us their own socks, so that we could go on. For
a few of us, however, this was not enough. Our feet were too
lacerated, and the three additional miles we were able to
manage cost us too much pain. As the rest of the group kept
on despite our cries pleading for a halt, we decided to try
walking barefoot on the dewy grass. At first, this seemed like
an improvement — but not for long. Some even thought of
wrapping their feet in the new undershirts we had been
issued, but the possibility of an inspection made them
hesitate. The last few miles, as we hobbled through the
growing daylight, were torture — a torture refined by the first
military police we met on the outskirts of Romny, who made
us put back our boots. They said they wouldn't allow us into
town looking like a bunch of tramps. We could have
murdered them. Further on, we asked some gypsies to take
the worst cases as far as the Kommandantur in their carts.
They were prudent enough not to argue.

The infirmary was in the same building as the Kommandantur. We even spoke with the Kommandant, who was
outraged that soldiers from the Gross Deutschland should
have to go without socks. He sent an official statement of
indignation to the Akhtyrka camp for failing to provide

properly for new troops. Those who wished medical attention were sent to the infirmary, where their feet were washed in basins of warm water to which chloroform had been added. This had an extraordinary effect, easing our pain almost at once. We were each given a small red metal box of cream for coating our feet before setting out on a march. But we still had no socks.

Those of our group who had not gone to the infirmary were looking into the prospects for the rest of our journey. The Kharkov-Kiev line ran through Romny, with daily trains in both directions. Our disappointment therefore was great when our two feldwebels announced that we wouldn't be leaving for at least two days. All available space on trains moving toward the front was reserved for essentials, and on returning trains emergencies were given priority over soldiers on leave. Rumours multiplied among our group of five hundred anxious men for whom each hour counted. People spoke of leaving for Kiev on their own – thumbing a ride on one of the convoys, or sneaking onto a train on the quiet, or stealing some Russian horses. Some even spoke of doing the journey on foot – 150 miles, which would take at least five days, even with forced marches. As all of these were really out of the question, we decided it would be better simply to stay where we were.

Old hands groaned: 'I can tell you, we'll just sit here and watch our passes expire. We've got to get out of here. Who says we'll leave in two days? We'll probably be right where we are a week from now; so fuck the whole damn mess – I'm clearing out!'

My feet were still feeling too sensitive even to think about a march – no matter how pressing it might be. Hals and Lensen were in the same state. So, for better or for worse, we had to wait in Romny without any idea of what to do, or even where to sleep. The police were always after us, telling us to move on: it was useless to try to explain to them – the bastards weren't interested. In the Ukraine – that paradise for troops on leave – they had rediscovered all the exasperating authority they exercised in peacetime. Anyone rash enough to argue with them risked having his pass torn up in front of his eyes. We saw this happen to one poor devil about forty years old. The gendarmes kicked his pack like some kind of football, and the fellow remarked in an angry voice that he had just spent six months fighting in the Caucasus, and felt entitled to a certain amount of common courtesy.

'Traitors!' shouted one of the horrible cops. 'Traitors who ran away from the Russians and lost Rostov! They should send the whole lot of you back to the front, which you never should have left in the first place!' And he ripped the poor man's pass into shreds before his horrified eyes. We thought he would break down and howl. Instead, he threw himself on the two cops, knocking both of them flat. He was gone before we could recover from our stupefaction. The furious cops picked themselves up, swearing to have the man shot. We took ourselves off in a hurry, before they had the chance to turn their guns on us.

Two days later, we left for Kiev after all, crammed into a train which was also loaded with cattle. But we didn't care about travelling in comfort. We were interested only in getting to Kiev, which – several months before its destruction – was still a beautiful city.

In Kiev, we felt that we had been saved, that the war no longer existed. The city looked beautiful, and was full of flowers. People were going quietly about their ordinary, everyday occupations. White street-cars edged in red moved through the brightly dressed civilian crowds of the pleasant town. Everywhere, troops in trim, brushed uniforms were walking with Ukrainian girls. I had already liked the look of the town in the winter. Now all my agreeable impressions were confirmed. I would gladly have ended the war right there.

From Kiev, we had no trouble finding a train leaving for Poland. Our journey was vivid and colourful. We left in a crowded civilian train and, mixed in this way with ordinary Russian people, had more of a chance to become acquainted with them than at any time during the war. Our train of oddly assorted carriages rolled for hours along a track that crossed the empty expanse of the Pripet marshes. The Russians, who drank and sang nonstop, offered drinks to all the soldiers too, and the noise throughout the journey was almost beyond belief. At the occasional station stops, people got on and off, and the most outrageous jokes were cracked amid shouts of laughter. The women made even more noise than the men. Hals put on a *gourbaritchka* for a short time. We passed in this way from the Ukraine into Poland, arriving after two and a half days in Lublin, where we had to change trains. At Lublin there was also a meticulous police inspection, and we were ordered to go to the camp barber for haircuts before departure. However, our anxiety about missing the train was so great that we decided to take what seemed like an enormous risk – which succeeded. Hals, Lensen, and I managed to walk out past the military police with our hair untouched by any shears. This proved to have been a risk well worth taking, as without it we would surely have missed the train.

We arrived at Poznań in the middle of the night, and were received by a very efficient centre. We were given tickets for the canteen and the dormitory, and told to be at the office in the morning to have our passes validated. The office was open from seven to eleven, but we were warned to be there no later than six, as there was usually a queue. This struck us as somewhat strange. In effect it meant that troops arriving in Poznań at 11:05 in the morning had to wait until the following day before they could continue their journey. I think this arrangement was probably motivated by a desire to keep men under army control even when they were theoretically on leave. In this way, a cancellation order could be sent east while the troops were waiting. By contrast, the office which processed returning troops was open twenty-four hours a day.

We spent what was left of the night in a comfortable dormitory which reminded me of the barracks at Chemnitz, and were at the office for passes by six the next morning. There were already some twenty men ahead of us, who must have spent the night on the spot, and by seven there must have been at least three hundred. The self-important bureaucrats who ran the place took their own time verifying our documents, while we stood in agitated silence. The police standing by the door were ready to cancel the leave of anyone foolish enough to lose his temper.

When our papers had been stamped, we were sent across the courtyard into a large hall where our uniforms were inspected. We were given the opportunity to polish our boots and brush our clothes beforehand, and one might almost

160

have believed that there was no mud in Russia! Then, a final, charming detail: women soldiers distributed packages of choice foods wrapped in paper covered with eagles and swastikas, and inscribed: 'A Happy Holiday to Our Brave Soldiers.' Sweet, sensitive Germany!

Hals, who would have been capable of killing himself for a cup of beef broth, rolled enormous eyes. 'If we'd only had something like this at Kharkov!'

We felt profoundly moved by these attentions. A package of sausages, jam, and cigarettes seemed generous repayment for our endless nights in the stone-cracking cold, and our wanderings through the mud of the Don Valley. Hals and I set off for Berlin, bearing our gifts. Lensen left us to travel to his native Prussia.

In Berlin, we were once again reminded of the war's existence. Around the Silesian station, and in the Weissensee and Pankov districts, many buildings had been reduced to rubble, in the first stages of the city's destruction. But otherwise the active, busy life of a capital metropolis went on as usual.

In Berlin, which I was seeing for the first time, I was reminded of a promise I had made. I had promised myself to go see Enrst Neubach's wife. She lived with his parents in the southern part of the city. I explained this to Hals, who advised me to postpone the obligation until my return trip. But I knew very well that I would never be able to bring myself to leave home a day early, and that my parents would try to hang on to me until the last moment. Hals understood this, even though he tried to persuade me to do something else. He didn't want to lose any time either, and left for Dortmund as soon as he could, making me promise to come to see him.

I would have done better to listen to the voice of wisdom, speaking through my friend. My journey came to an end the next day, in the flames of Magdeburg, and I had to stay in Berlin, a city entirely unknown to me, where I had to work hard to make myself understood.

Still carrying my pack and gun, which were beginning to feel very heavy, I set out to try to find the Neubachs' house. Fortunately, I was still able to read the scribbled address I had found among my poor friend's papers. But should I try to get there by subway, or by bus? As I really didn't know where I was going, I decided to proceed on foot, which would at least give me the chance to look around; the idea of walking across the city still seemed normal at that time. However, I didn't want to stray too far afield, to walk west when I should have been walking south. I had noticed a sign, BERLIN SÜD, which must be roughly correct. I passed two cops who gave me a long, cold stare when they noticed the spectacular package of a soldier on leave. I saluted them as required – one had to salute those bastards as if they were army officers – and went on my way.

The city seemed beautiful, but serious and well organized. The bombing had only recently begun, and in Berlin affected only the districts immediately around the railway stations. In this large, imposing town, with its austere houses set off by sumptuous, intricate railings, everything seemed to be regulated by a precise, organized rhythm: no raucous crowds or parents pulling down their children's pants to let them pee. Men, women, children, bicycles, cars, and trucks – all seemed to be moving at an even, regular pace toward a precise destination, with a rhythm that seemed conscious and assertive, and designed to avoid any dissipation of energy. It was all very different from Paris, for example. Undue haste seemed out of place, and my legs seemed to fall instinctively into the accepted tempo of the city. To stop moving without good reason would have seemed strange. The huge machine which the regime had set in motion for the cause was turning, and this was evident even in the gestures of the little old lady who was walking just ahead of me, and whom I stopped to ask for directions. Her neat white hair was impeccable, like the streets and the railings and the edges of the sidewalks. The sound of my voice seemed to call her back from some distant daydream.

'Excuse me, gnädige Frau,' I said, feeling somewhat embarrassed, as if I were speaking in a theatre where the play had already begun. 'Could you give me some directions? I am going to this address.' I showed her my scrap of paper, which really looked like something pulled out of a waste-paper basket.

The old lady smiled, as if she had seen an angel.

'It's very far, young man,' she said in a gentle voice

162

which suddenly reminded me of my childhood. 'It's very far. You must go to the Tempelhof autobahn. But it's really very far.'

'That doesn't matter.' I couldn't think of anything else to say.

'You really ought to take a bus. It would be much easier for you.'

'That doesn't matter,' I repeated, like someone in a dream. In fact, I couldn't think of the German words for anything else. This woman's obvious goodness, after so much loud-mouthed bullying and malignity, moved me even more deeply than the exhausted men at Outcheni.

'I don't mind walking. I'm in the infantry,' I finally said, smiling.

'I know,' she said, smiling even more tenderly than a moment before. 'You must be used to walking. I'll go with you as far as the Schloss von Kaiser Wilhelm. From there, I'll be able to explain to you.'

She walked along beside me. As I didn't know what to say, the burden of the conversation fell on her.

'Where have you come from, young man?'

'From Russia.'

'Russia's a big country. What part were you in?'

'Russia's very big, yes. I was in the South, around Kharkov.'

'Kharkov!' she said, giving the name a very German sound. 'I see. Is it a big town?'

'Yes. It's big.'

For my kindly companion, Kharkov was clearly nothing more than a name which there was no particular need to remember. For me, Kharkov meant a city which had lost its life. If it had ever been a big town, it was now only a heap of rubble, crowned by a cloud of dust, smoke, and fire. It was also the sound of cries and moaning one shouldn't hear in towns. It was a long corridor of stiffened corpses we had to drag out into the air, and three Bolsheviks tied to a fence, with their guts spilling from their bellies.

'My son is in Briansk,' the old lady remarked, clearly hoping for news of the front.

'Briansk,' I repeated in a thoughtful tone. 'I believe that's in the central sector. I've never been there.'

163

'He tells me that everything's going quite well. He's a first lieutenant in an armoured division.'

'A lieutenant!' I thought. 'An officer!' The opinions of a private soldier must have sounded ridiculous.

'Were things difficult in your sector?'

'Things were pretty hard, but they're better now. I'm on leave,' I added, smiling.

'I'm really happy for you, young man,' she said, and her voice sounded as if she meant it. 'Are you in Berlin to see your family?'

'No, gnädige Frau. I'm going to see the parents of a friend.'

A friend! Ernst: a corpse. What friend was I tramping along like this for? The old woman was beginning to get on my nerves.

'A friend from your regiment,' she said, sharing my pleasure at being on leave. I felt like knocking her onto one of those intricate railings full of spikes.

'Where do your parents come from?' she asked.

'From Wissembourg, in Alsace.'

She looked at me with surprise.

'So you're Alsatian. I know Alsace very well.'

I almost told her that she knew it better than I did.

'Yes, I'm Alsatian,' I said, hoping to get a little peace.

She began to tell me about a trip she'd taken to Strasbourg, but I wasn't listening any more. By forcing me to remember Ernst, she had irritated me. I had better things to do than listen to this old bird reminisce about her travels. It was a beautiful day, I was on leave, and I needed to see something gay. This desire made me wonder what attitude to take when I got to the Neubachs'. These people had just lost their son, and were probably overwhelmed by grief. . . . Maybe they didn't even know he was dead. If that's how it was, what on earth could I say to them? It would be better to visit them on my way back. By then, they would surely have been told. Hals was right. I should have listened to him. He, at least, was still alive.

We came to a crossroad opposite a bridge over a stream — or even perhaps a large river. I knew that the Seine flowed through Paris, but couldn't have said whether Berlin was on the Elbe or the Oder. To the right, there was a massive block of buildings – the Schloss von Kaiser Wilhelm – and directly across the avenue an impressive memorial to the heroes of 1914-18: twelve hundred helmets of that time set round a forecourt, to give some idea of the sacrifice. Two sentries from Hitler's guard walked slowly back and forth along a cement apron at the base of the monument; their slow, even pace seemed to me strangely symbolic of a human being's slow progress toward eternity. With a regularity which a master watchmaker might well have envied, the two men executed impeccably synchronized half turns, faced each other at a distance of about thirty metres, resumed their march, crossed, turned, and began again. I found this spectacle somehow oppressive.

'Here we are, young man,' the old woman said. 'You cross the bridge and follow that avenue.'

She pointed toward the vast, stony backdrop of the city, in which I would have to find my address. But I had already stopped listening. I knew that I wasn't going to the Neubachs', and that these explanations were superfluous. Nevertheless, I outdid myself in expressions of gratitude, and pressed the old lady's hand. She withdrew, repeating her protestations of good will. I couldn't help smiling. As soon as she had disappeared, I rushed back in the direction from which we'd come, trying to make up for lost time, and find the station for the West as quickly as possible.

I walked along the river bank with the obsessive speed of a maniac. Suddenly, the air filled with martial music, and an elegantly dressed military band marched out through a tall gateway, and turned into the street. I remembered what we were taught at Bialystok, and snapped to attention, presenting arms to the indifferent troupe. After an hour and a half, with innumerable stops to ask my way, I arrived at the station from which trains left for the West, and France. I looked desperately for Hals amid the throngs on the platform: he would surely be on this train too – but I couldn't find him in the few minutes before departure. As I caught my breath on the train, the slow regular progress of our acceleration seemed to merge with the measured tempo of the German capital. Everything here was so entirely different from Russia. Even the soldiers had an air of seriousness which matched the civilized, organized life of all large

European countries. The contrast with Russia was so great that I wondered if what I'd seen there wasn't part of a bad dream.

Night fell, and the train rolled on. We had been moving for at least three hours, during which it seemed that we had never left the city. There was no countryside, only buildings. Suddenly, the train came to a stop, although we were not in a station. Everyone leaned out the windows to see what was happening. Although it was dark, the distant sky glowed with red light. We could hear a muffled rumbling, mingled with the boom of guns. The throbbing of a mass of airplanes overhead rattled the windows of the train.

'That must be Magdeburg, getting it in the neck,' said a soldier who had shoved in beside me to look out too.

'Who's giving it to them?' I asked.

He looked at me curiously. 'Those Yankee bastards, of course,' he said, as if he were talking to a simpleton. 'Things are just as hot here as they are at the front.'

I couldn't tear my eyes away from the glow of the burning city. I had thought that we'd left the war far behind us. The train began to move again, only to come to a fresh halt fifteen minutes later. Soldiers ran up the track, calling everybody off. Somebody said that the line had been cut, and that all military personnel, whether on active duty or on leave, had to put themselves at the disposal of the local authorities. Thus I found myself, in my clean uniform and carrying my holiday package, falling into step with about a hundred resigned soldiers.

We walked for about half an hour into the blinding, acrid smoke of countless fires, and began shifting fallen timbers and massive masonry blocks, while delayed-action bombs pulverized what was left of a terrified bourgeois population. Groups of whimpering civilians were impressed into cleanup squads by foul-mouthed officials shouting at the tops of their lungs. Everyone was put to work. Although it was pitch dark, we were able to see: broken gas pipes thrown up into the torn earth blazed like blow torches, amid the heaps of stones, broken wood, window glass, furniture, arms, and legs.

A gang of territorials handed out picks, and we piled the rest of our equipment beside a fire truck. We had to dig into the ruins with the greatest possible speed: we could hear the groans and cries of people trapped in the cellars. Women and children weeping with terror were carting away bricks and stones to clear some space. Shouted orders overlapped: 'Quick! This way!' 'We need help over here!' Of course, the military were chosen to deal with the most dangerous situations, and sent into places threatened with immediate collapse.

We reached the cellars through the deep airshafts. We attacked a brick wall which seemed to be blocking the entrance to a basement where people were calling for help. My pick sank into something soft: probably the stomach of some poor soul crushed by the debris. And damn it! I was on leave, and all of this was holding me up! An explosion shifted the ground we were standing on: another one of those American bombs which blow up some time after they've landed. Nonetheless, our efforts were finally successful. The last brick wall fell beneath our blows, and a bunch of haggard, blackened people surged through the jagged opening, engulfed in a swirling cloud of dust. Several people embraced us, sobbing with relief and recognition. Others were in a state of literal madness. Everyone was somehow hurt or wounded. We had to climb down ourselves to bring out terrified women clutching their children so tightly they were nearly suffocating them.

I pulled out the first child I saw. A kid of about five was tugging at one of my trouser legs so hard that it came right out of my boot. He was trying to drag me to a particular spot, and he was crying so hard that his gasps for breath between each sob were extraordinarily long. He pulled me over to a recess where a crushed wine bin was holding up the base of a vault on the brink of collapse. An inert human form was lying in the jumble of rubble at my feet. The kid was still howling, in a passion of grief that couldn't be helped.

I shouted as loud as I could: 'Licht aus! Schnell!'

Someone came over with a torch, and we saw the body of a woman crushed by the metal of the bottle rack, which had collapsed under the weight of thirty or forty tons of disintegrating masonry. The body of a child was wedged in beside her. Pulling against the stiff, dusty clothes of the corpse, I dragged out the child's body as if it were just another stone. But maybe the kid was still alive: it seemed to move a little. Dragging the two kids with me, I made for the exit hole, and handed over the child in my arms to some rescue workers. The one who was howling trailed along with me for a short distance, until I abandoned him. He could shift for himself, for God's sake. In Germany, everyone had to be ready for that — the younger the better. We were already needed for another job.

The sirens were howling again: the Anglo-Americans were faithfully adhering to their practice of coming back with a second dose before we had time to help the victims of the first. The gang chiefs blew their whistles for retreat. Voices were shouting: 'Everyone take cover.'

But where? For four hundred yards around us we could see nothing but heaps of rubble. People who knew the district ran in what they hoped were likely directions. Bewildered children were crying. Above us, we could hear the roar of four-engined planes. I was running too, and I knew what I was looking for. The fire truck had disappeared, but our heap of packs remained where we'd left them. Soldiers were turning them over, grabbing the right one, and running off. I recognized mine by the metal eidelweiss I had sewed onto the piece of calfskin which served as a pillow. I pulled it out, along with my gun. . . . But my gift package . . . God damn it!

'Hey . . . you . . . my package!'

Someone threw me a package across the maelstrom. Everyone was hurrying off.

'Hey . . . This isn't it! Wait a minute! God damn it!'

Bombs were beginning to fall at the other end of the city. God damn it to hell!

I ran as fast as I could across an empty space where I narrowly escaped a car in as great a hurry as I. The surface of the road seemed to be rising and falling in ripples, and the sound of thousands of panes shattering simultaneously added a crystalline note to the huge shock produced by bombs of four and five thousand kilos.

The number of people on the street was shrinking rapidly. Only a few fools like myself were still running about looking for shelter. My eyes, stinging from the clouds of acrid dust, could see, in the intermittent flashes of white light, the outline of the houses bordering the street. On one of the buildings I could make out a white poster with black letters: SHELTER: THIRTY PERSONS. Never mind if there were already a hundred! I ran down a spiral staircase between the only two walls left intact in the building. A dim lamp which some thoughtful soul had hooked to the wall lit the turns in the stair. But after two spirals the way was blocked by a large grey cylinder, which was even taller than I. I tried to squeeze through the narrow gap next to the stair wall, but a closer look at the object made my blood freeze. I was pressing myself against an enormous bomb, whose broken wings indicated that it had crashed through every floor of the building from the roof down. It must have weighed at least four tons, and might explode any minute. I streaked back up the stairs and out the door into the darkness, which flickered unevenly into brilliant light like a huge neon sign. Finally, gasping for breath, I collapsed beside a bench in a square, and lay there for about twenty minutes, until the sirens sounded the all clear. When everything was quiet again, I went back to the job of cleaning up, from which I was released at the end of the morning. Then I was given the most depressing news of all.

I was ready to continue my journey westward. Two days of my leave had already been wasted, and I couldn't spare another minute. I asked a territorial where I would find the train for Kassel and Frankfurt. He asked for my pass, looked it over, and told me to follow him. He took me to a military police station. I watched through the little window as my pass travelled from hand to hand, keeping my eyes firmly fixed on it. I saw several stamps being added to the scrap of paper I had brought from Akhtyrka. Then it was handed back to me, and I was informed, in an indifferent, administrative tone, that I could not proceed beyond the Magdeburg sector. Given the location of my army corps, I had come to the extreme western limit of permissible travel.

I was absolutely stunned, and stood staring at the cops. The shock of disappointment was so great that for a few moments I felt numb.

'We can understand that you are upset,' one of them said, officially taking note of my condition. 'You will be well taken care of at the reception centre here in town.'

Without a word, I took my pass from the counter, where

169

the cop had put it down when he got tired of holding it out to me, and walked through the door. My throat felt as if it would burst from the effort of holding back my tears.

In the street, where the sun continued to shine, I stumbled on in a daze. I could see that people were staring at me as if I were drunk. Suddenly I felt ashamed, and looked for someplace where I could withdraw for a few minutes to compose myself. A little farther on, I took shelter in the ruins of a large building, collapsing onto a stone in the darkest corner I could find. Clutching my stamp-covered document, I burst into tears like a child. The sound of footsteps made me look up. Someone had followed me into the building, thinking, perhaps, that I was a thief. When he saw that I was only crying, he turned back to the street. Luckily, people cared more about ration cards than about tears in those days, so at least I was allowed to remain alone with my sorrow.

That evening, I caught a train back to Berlin, letting Fate dictate that I should call on the Neubachs after all. I didn't know where any of my German relatives lived – although at that time they were quite near Berlin – so I was reduced to either the reception centre or the Neubachs'. I felt obsessed by my disappointment: I had been looking forward to this leave so much! And I had earned it, too: I had joined the infantry expressly to get it. And now, here I was with nothing but a ludicrous scrap of paper. I didn't even have my gift package any more: it had vanished at Magdeburg, which I had left with a box of some soldier's dirty laundry. Now I would have to show up with empty hands at the house of people I had never met. I certainly didn't have enough money to buy them anything.

That evening, I counted myself lucky to get a bed at the reception centre in Berlin. One of the older soldiers there listened to the story of my pass, and advised me to speak to a noncom at the registration desk. The noncom turned out to be quite sympathetic, noted down all the details, and told me to come back in twenty-four hours.

Early the next morning, I set out to find the Neubachs' house. After several hours of hesitant, groping progress, I finally found myself in front of number 112, Killeringstrasse, a simple, three-storey house with a gravelled walk beside it, which could be shut off from the street by a low gate. A

young girl who seemed to be about my age was leaning on
the bottom half of the front door, looking out into the street.
After a moment's hesitation, I went over to ask a final
direction.

'Yes, sir,' she said, smiling. 'This is the right house: they
live on the second floor. But at this time of day they're all out
at work.'

'Thank you, miss. Do you know when they'll be back?'

'They'll be here this evening, after seven.'

'Thank you,' I said, thinking of the long day ahead of me.
What could I do with all that time? As I shut the gate, I
thanked the girl once again. She smiled faintly, and nodded
her head. Who was she waiting for? Certainly not the
Neubachs.

I had already walked a short way down Killeringstrasse
when it occurred to me that I could, at any rate, have talked
to the girl a little longer. After several moments of hesitation,
I turned back, hoping that she would still be there. Every
minute I could subtract from the interminable day ahead
seemed like a minute gained. As long as she didn't laugh at
me right to my face, I was ready to take almost any amount
of sarcasm. I was soon back at number 112. She was exactly
where I'd left her.

'You think they're already home?' she said, laughing.

'Of course not. But I feel so lost in this town that I'd rather
sit here on the steps and wait than have to hunt for the house
all over again.'

'You want to wait here all day?' She seemed astonished.

'I'm afraid so.'

'But you ought to look around Berlin. It's an interesting
place.'

'I agree with you. I should. But really, I feel so lost I'm
afraid I wouldn't see anything.'

And I still felt so disappointed that I had no wish to flirt.

'Are you on leave?'

'Yes. I've still got twelve days. But I'm not allowed to leave
the Berlin sector.'

'Are you from the Eastern front?'

'Yes.'

'It must have been very hard. I can see it on your face.'

I glanced up at her in surprise. I suspected that I did look

171

like the undertaker's assistant, but for a pretty girl to remark on it after the first few minutes!

Then she said something about the people on the third floor, but I wasn't really listening. If she thought I looked as bad as all that, this minuscule conversation that was bringing me somewhat closer to normal life might end at any moment. The idea terrified me. I would have done almost anything to keep this encounter going.

I tried to change my expression, to force my mouth to smile, to make myself agreeable. Heavily and clumsily I asked her if she knew the city.

'Oh yes,' she said, apparently unaware of the trap I was arranging. 'I've lived in Berlin since before the war.'

Then she told me about herself: how she studied for part of the day and was a first-aid assistant for an eight-hour shift. She was studying for a teacher's licence. I listened, but with only half my attention. The simple sound of her voice seemed to wrap me in tenderness; I only wanted it to continue. I tried to look agreeable. When she fell silent, I thrust home with my question: the technique of a feldwebel.

'Since you don't have to be at the first-aid station until five, couldn't you show me some of the sights? That is to say, if you don't have anything else to do . . .'

She blushed a little.

'I'd like to,' she said, looking down at the ground. 'But I can't say until I've spoken to Frau X. . . .' (I no longer remember the woman's name.)

'Oh. Well, I've got lots of time. . . . Twelve days . . .'

She laughed. 'Good sign,' I thought.

We talked for about an hour, until the good lady arrived. We couldn't avoid the war, of course — although I certainly wanted to — but I did my best to embroider what I said. I described heroic deeds the like of which I'd never seen. I couldn't believe that the filth of the steppe was what this girl wanted to hear about, and I was afraid of speaking too frankly. I didn't want her to understand what our experiences had really been like. I didn't want her to catch the stench of mud and blood through anything I said, or to see the huge grey horizon still stamped across my vision. I was afraid of infecting her with my terror and disgust, and afraid that if I did she'd resent it. My descriptions of heroism came straight from Hollywood, but at least we were able to laugh, and I could go on talking to her.

Finally, Frau X arrived. At first, she looked at us disapprovingly. Then Paula — she had told me her name — introduced me as a friend of the Neubachs.

'To tell you the truth, gnädige Frau, I was a friend of Ernst's. I wanted to visit his family.'

'I understand, young man. Come in and wait in my place — you'll be more comfortable there. Those poor Neubachs. Their courage is almost unbelievable. To think of losing two sons in ten days: it's too awful! My God, I hope this war ends before one of mine is killed!'

So the Neubachs already knew.... They knew not only that Ernst was dead, but another son as well. I hadn't even known that Ernst had a brother. Suddenly, Ernst's death came back to me in all its detail: Ernst, the Don, the Tatra ... 'Ernst, I'll save you! Don't cry, Ernst!' These things were blotted out only when I looked at Paula; and they had to be blotted out; I had to forget them. Paula was beside me, smiling ... to forget: how hard it was!

'You may wait here, dear sir, or at the Neubachs' — whichever you wish,' said the older woman, addressing the boy of seventeen like a grownup gentleman. 'How was Ernst killed?'

'Forgive me if I don't speak of it,' I said, looking down.

But looking down was no help. My eyes fell on my boots: the boots which had trampled the earth on Ernst's grave. Everything here kept reminding me, except Paula's smile.

'You must invent something, then,' said the kind-hearted woman, guessing at the horror behind my silence. 'You must spare those poor people.'

'You can depend on that, gnädige Frau,' I said. 'I've already had some practice.'

Frau X changed the subject, which was clearly too painful. She brought out a large bowl of cocoa and milk, and then began talking to Paula, who worked for her as a dressmaker's assistant.

'I hope, Paula, that you will entertain our friend Sajer here. You should show him Unter den Linden, and the Siegesallee. This young man needs some distraction, and that will be your job today.'

173

I could have kissed her!

'But Frau X, there's all that work I should finish, and . . .'

'Ta, ta, ta . . . You take him on a tour of the capital. There's nothing more urgent.'

I thanked the kindly woman effusively. Was Paula glad to have a holiday? I didn't really care. I was too pleased with my circumstances to analyze them.

We set out, promising to be back for lunch. I walked along beside Paula, struck dumb with pleasure. She tried to fall into step with me, miming my military stride to tease me, but I only laughed. We passed a little booth painted red, where a woman was selling fried fish, and I thought of buying some for Paula. She followed me, smiling her delicious smile. The woman behind the counter prepared two helpings of fish on two slices of thick bread spread with some kind of ersatz butter. Then she asked for our ration cards.

'But I don't have any ration card. I'm here on leave.' I smiled, hoping to gain the woman's sympathy.

This did no good at all. Paula laughed as though she would burst. I felt ridiculous.

'J'aurai ta peau, vermine,' I added in French.

The fish woman naturally didn't understand me, and went on raking out her ashes. We walked off without our fish.

Our lunch with Paula's employer crowned my happiness. Despite rationing and shortages, the good-hearted woman had managed to prepare some delicious dishes. She also produced some liqueur, which went straight to my head. I left the table aware of an unusual state of excitement, and began to bellow out a marching song, which my two companions absolutely could not sing with me. Belatedly coming to my senses, I begged their pardon, and then began another song which was just as objectionable.

My hostess seemed amused, but somewhat apprehensive. Paula writhed in her seat, and stared at me as if I were some kind of grotesque Punch. Her employer, weighing my drunkenness against her concern for her china, suggested to Paula that she take me out for some air. Paula obediently dragged me off, plainly displeased by the company of a drunken soldier, who might do something stupid at any moment.

On the staircase, my timidity was suddenly overcome by a ludicrous surge of confidence. I grabbed Paula by the waist and spun her into a dance in time to my stamping boots. She frowned, and pulled herself away so abruptly that I almost lost my balance.

'Stop it, or I won't come with you,' she said.

This brought me crashing to my senses. The simple fact that she was no longer smiling filled me with anxiety. A fog seemed to have risen between her suddenly hardened eyes and mine, momentarily clouded by a good meal. I felt as if I were back in a foxhole seeing in a dream a glowing fragment from what had been my youth. I felt chilled to the bone. Perhaps by my stupidity I'd lost Paula already.

'Paula!' I cried in desperation.

I stood frozen in my tracks. Paula had already reached the bottom of the stairs, and was standing in the doorway, framed in sunlight.

'All right,' she said. 'Come along, but pull yourself together.'

Still somewhat numb, I clutched at my imperilled happiness.

'What would you like to see?'

'I don't know, Paula. Whatever you like.'

I felt panic-stricken. Clearly Paula was exasperated by the company of a drunken enlisted man. I would have to become an officer. Paula was trying to make me decide something I knew nothing about. Inside my head, her irritated voice seemed to blend with the remembered voices of sergeants shouting orders, exhorting me to actions which I had no hope of accomplishing. 'You there! Jump into that Tatra! Well, have you decided? What would you like to do? Put your foot on the gas! Watch out for that chain! Your uniform is spotted; you have to be more careful. Well, have you decided?'

Yes, Herr Leutnant, jawohl! Yes, Paula. Of course.

Suddenly, she took hold of my sleeve and dragged me from my lethargy. I looked at her. My eyes must have been full of sadness. She seemed astonished.

'Let's go to the square, anyway,' she said. 'Then we'll decide something. Come on.'

She pulled me after her. I let her do it, knowing that, if we ran into an officer or one of the military police, my leave would swiftly come to an end in a labour camp. Holding a girl's arm in the street was strictly forbidden, but when I mentioned this to Paula, she only laughed.

'Don't worry,' she said. 'I'm not drunk. I'll be able to see them coming.'

Finally, as I remained more or less incapable of speech, she took the initiative herself, and showed me a round of sights. I stared at them with unseeing eyes. I couldn't shake off the feeling that she was simply doing her duty, that my company was no pleasure for her – and I wanted her to enjoy me as much as I enjoyed her. But that was impossible. There was no reason for her to concede me that happiness. There was no reason, either, for me to be walking along that clean, well-organized street in a state of disarray, and no reason for anyone to be patient with a poor, befuddled soldier, just because he'd spent months wallowing in snow and mud and horror. People at peace with themselves have no idea that anyone unaccustomed to happiness shouts himself breathless in the face of joy. I was the one who had to try to understand, to adapt myself to this mood of tranquillity, to avoid shocking anyone, to smile a correct smile, neither too wide nor too tense. At the risk of seeming wild or apathetic, I had to make the effort, to invent, and avoid the impression I often felt I was making in France, after the war, of telling boring war stories. I often felt like killing the people who then accused me of lying. It is so easy to kill – especially when one no longer feels any particular link with existence. I – a poor bastard soldier in the wrong army – I had to learn how to live, because I hadn't been able to die. Why, Paula, did you make a point of the stain on my jacket? Why was a stain enough to erase your smile? Why? And why do I still like to smile – I, who have seen an infinity of horrifying stains? This evening, perhaps, the Neubachs will laugh, Paula, and I will try to laugh too, like you.

Paula left me near the Oder bruke, at five o'clock, with detailed instructions on how to return to the Killeringstrasse. She held my hand as she spoke, and smiled, as if in pity. I smiled as if I were happy.

'I'll come by the Neubachs' for a moment this evening,' she said. 'Anyway, we'll see each other tomorrow. Good night.'

'Gute Nacht, Paula.'

176

That evening I met the Neubachs. I could easily recognize my friend Ernst in his mother's face. These poor people did not dwell on the double catastrophe which had obliterated all their hopes. The idea of Europe after the war no longer had any meaning for them, because those who should have inherited it no longer existed. But they made heroic efforts to celebrate my passage. The kindly woman from upstairs who had so generously wet my throat that afternoon joined us, and Paula came in for a moment about eleven. Our eyes met, and Paula saw fit to make a joke about our earlier falling-out.

'I had to preach him a sermon about decent deportment this afternoon. He was singing and dancing right in the middle of the street.'

I looked carefully at all the faces. Were they going to scold me, or would they laugh? Luckily, all I had to do was laugh with the others.

'That wasn't nice of you, Paula,' said the good, kind, generous lady from the third floor. 'You must ask him to forgive you.'

Paula, blushing and smiling, made her way round the table through a circle of laughter, and put a kiss on my forehead. I received the touch of her lips like a man condemned to the electric chair, and sat blushing, unable to move. Everyone recognized my emotion, and called out: 'Forgiven!'

Paula herself waved a cheerful goodbye to us all, and vanished through the door.

Paula! Paula! I would have liked . . . I didn't know what. I sat motionless, turned to stone, deaf to the conversation.

They asked me about my parents, my former life . . . thank God, not about the war. I answered evasively. Paula's kiss burned against my forehead like a hot cartridge case. I would gladly have done a daily patrol with her, instead of with the war, and five or six other soldiers . . . God damn it!

It was late, and I would have liked an excuse to leave the table. But I had to sit patiently with these people for another hour, until everyone was ready for bed. The Neubachs offered me Ernst's room. I thanked them effusively, and explained that for military reasons I was required to return to the centre. In fact, I couldn't bear the thought of sleeping in my friend's bed. Also, I felt like walking through the streets. I might run into Paula.

177

The Neubachs understood about military regulations, and didn't insist. In the street, I was suddenly seized by a wild sense of gaiety, and began to whistle. I asked for a few directions, and found my way back to the centre without too much trouble. But I didn't run into Paula. I walked past the reception desk, where two civilians were playing cards with two soldiers, one of them the feld who had taken my deposition.

'Hey, you there!' he called.

Instinctively, I spun round and saluted.

'Aren't you Gefreiter Sajer?'

'Ja, Herr Feldwebel.'

'Good. I have good news for you. One of your relatives will be coming to see you in a couple of days. I managed to get a special authorization for a member of your family.'

'I don't know how to thank you, Herr Feldwebel. I am really very grateful.'

'I can see that, boy. You certainly took your time coming back.'

I clicked my heels and spun round, while the four of them joked about me.

'Put in a little time at the Fantasio Hotel, eh?' They must have been talking about a bordello. I spent an agitated night, unable to think of anything but Paula.

Two days went by, filled with pleasures and delights. I never left Paula's side. We always had lunch with Frau X, and dinner at the Neubachs'. Frau X, who noticed everything, was aware of the growing feeling between Paula and me, and was horrified. She tried several times to make me realize that the war wasn't over, that it was idiotic to fall in love. After the war, it would be a fine thing for me to unleash my emotions, but for the moment anything like that was premature.

To my adolescent mind, the war had no power over my love for this girl, and holding back any emotion was out of the question. The only limits would be set by my leave, whose duration, unfortunately, I was powerless to affect.

One of my family was coming to see me, so I couldn't move too far from the centre, where I spent my nights. This restriction irritated me, because I lost precious time which I could have spent with Paula. On the day of my visitor's expected arrival, I must have made five or six trips to the centre. Finally, in the middle of the afternoon, the kind-hearted sergeant answered my question even before I asked it.

'Someone's waiting for you in the dormitory, Sajer.'

'Ah!' I said, as if this was the last thing I'd expected. 'Thank you, Herr Feldwebel.'

I ran up the stairs, and pushed open the door of the large room where I'd already spent several nights. My eye travelled past the double-row of beds to a man in a blue-grey overcoat: my father.

'Hello, Papa,' I said.

'You've turned into a man,' he said, with the air of timidity which was always one of his characteristics. 'How are you? We haven't heard much from you, you know. Your mother's been very worried.'

I listened, as I always did when my father spoke to me. I sensed that he felt ill at ease in the heart of Germany, in this dormitory, where everything reflected implacable military discipline.

'Shall we go out, Papa?'

'If you like. Ah! By the way, I brought along a small package for you. Your mother and I had a hard time getting all these things. The Germans kept it downstairs.' He lowered his voice when he said 'Germans,' as though he were speaking of a bunch of savages.

Although he had married a German woman, my father did not feel particularly friendly toward Germany. He had never shaken off the hatreds of the 1914-18 war, although he himself had been well treated when he was a prisoner. However, the fact that one of his sons had been stuck into the German army prevented him from listening to Radio London with any sense of relief.

Downstairs, I asked the feldwebel for my package. He handed it to me, while speaking to my father in almost perfect French:

'I'm sorry about this, sir, but all food is strictly forbidden in the dormitories. Here is your package.'

'Thank you, sir,' my father said, clearly abashed.

I checked over the contents of the box while we walked through the streets, talking: a chocolate bar, some biscuits, and – joy! a pair of socks, knitted by my paternal grandmother.

'These are just what I need,' I said.

'I thought you'd be most pleased by the cigarettes, or the chocolate. But of course, there's no shortage for you.' My father was convinced that we feasted from morning to night. 'With us, it's different. The Germans take everything.'

'We do all right.' I had learned to make the most of present pleasures, to forget the miseries of another day. But this answer was a mistake.

'Well, that's fine for you. For us it's another story. Your mother really has a hard time scraping our meals together. Life is far from easy.'

I didn't know what to say to this. I thought of giving him back the package.

'Well,' my father said. 'Let's hope it's all over quickly. Things are going badly for the Germans. On London Radio all we hear is the Americans here, the Americans there ... Italy ... the Allies ...'

This was all news to me. A group of men from the Kreigsmarine passed by, singing. I saluted, as required. My father stared at me with dismay. France was in such a state of chaos, and talking about it filled him with such despair that it was very hard to cheer him up.

For the next twenty-four hours, he told me about the suffering in France, explaining things to me as if I were Canadian or English. All of this put me in a very difficult position, and I didn't know quite what attitude to adopt. I held myself in check, contenting myself with 'Yes, Papa. Exactly, Papa.' I would have loved to talk about something else, to have forgotten the war, to have told him that I loved Paula. But I was afraid he wouldn't understand, that he might even be angry.

The next day I took my sorrowing father to the station. I was fool enough to snap to attention as the train pulled out – a gesture which I'm sure gave him no pleasure. I watched his anxious face pull away from me, into the hot June evening. I wouldn't see him again for two years – two years so full of experience they might as well have been a century.

As soon as my father was gone, I ran to the Neubachs'. I excused myself for not having introduced him, explaining that we had only been together for a very short time. They understood perfectly, and were not in the least offended. As I was clearly bursting with impatience, Frau Neubach gave me news of Paula. I was extremely disappointed to learn that she would be away until the afternoon of the following day. This was hard to bear. We had already lost twenty-four hours plus a day and a night: in the seven or eight days I had left, this counted for a great deal. I ate with the Neubachs, maintaining a gloomy silence which they understood and respected. Then I left them, to walk the streets, in the hope of meeting my love. I walked for about an hour, until the air-raid sirens drowned out the clocks, which were just striking eleven. The city filled with the sound of their long-drawn-out howling, and the few lights which had remained in the blacked-out streets disappeared. Our fighters were already climbing into the black sky above Tempelhof. The roar of their engines swept over the roof tops, and their trailing exhaust left occasional pink traces in the darkness. The sidecars of the territorial defence were ploughing through the streets, urging the few pedestrians to take shelter. I was still on the street, obsessed by a single idea, when we were suddenly enveloped in the heavy throb of enemy bombers.

I knew that the first-aid teams would turn out as the first bombs began to fall, and that perhaps then I would see Paula. I slid into a doorway opposite the entrance to a shelter under a low building beside a canal. I could see quite far down the canal to a large horizon washed in light fog. The sky to the northwest glowed in the light of an improbable-looking curtain of fire, which was probably concentrated on the big Spandau factories. Everywhere, little points of light crackled like fireworks. The numerous anti-aircraft guns defending the capital — some of them firing from the terraces of houses — were erecting a lethal barricade against the approaching rain of death. Each brilliant light flaming suddenly in the sky and then falling to earth marked the death of an enemy plane. A thudding and hammering of incredible violence shook the wall of the stone porch against which I had pressed myself. Forcing my eyes to accept the brutal contrast between the darkness and flashes of light, I stared down the street and along the quay, where a few laggards were still running for shelter. Then a cacophony of breaking glass marked the blanket of bombs falling across a section of the city about a mile ahead of me. A hurricane of displaced air ran over the surface of the canal, whose water responded in a pattern of sinister waves.

I could hear thousands of objects falling all around me. In spite of my intense desire to stay in the street, an irresistible fear made me run to the shelter. The pavement trembled under my feet like a piece of badly attached plating on the hood of a moving truck. In no time, I was in the midst of a crowd of desperate, anxious people. The atmosphere was suffocating. A loud roaring which seemed to emanate with equal strength from above and below shook loose pieces of plaster from the ceiling. People looked for some reassurance on faces as tense with fear as their own. Children asked questions of childish innocence: 'What's making that noise, Mama?' – while the mothers caressed the small blond heads with trembling fingers. The lucky ones, who believed in some God, prayed. I was leaning against a pipe which transmitted every sound and vibration from the street. The roaring noise grew suddenly louder, crushing the air in our lungs. The room filled with cries of pain, and then with an intensified din, like the sound of a thousand locomotives. Horrifying screams of terror, like screams from hell, rang through the darkness. The electric lights came on. Then the entire shelter filled with thick black dust, which poured in from the outside and engulfed us. We could hear some men shouting: 'Shut that door!'

The door slammed. We felt trapped in a communal grave. Some of the women broke down from nervous tension and began to howl and wave their arms wildly. We felt the floor shake five or six times, as if in the grip of some overpowering force. We were all terrified, and clung together, despite a hideous sense of suffocation. An hour later, when the storm seemed to have died down, we left that ghastly hole. We were confronted by a scene worthy of Dante. The dark waters of the canal reflected the numerous fires ravaging its banks and destroying the structures which had given it some point. What was left of the tidy street and its white-edged sidewalks lay strewn with rubble between two giant crevasses. A constellation of sparks ascended into the summer sky in a rising column of acrid, suffocating smoke. People were running everywhere, and as at Magdeburg I was immediately impressed into a cleanup squad.

182

After an exhausting night, and most of the next morning, I finally found Paula, who was just as done in as I. The happiness I felt when she told me she had worried about me during the bombing erased the miseries of the night in a single stroke.

'I was thinking of you too, Paula. I looked for you all night long.'

'Really?' she asked, in a tone which told me that her sentiment was as strong as mine.

I felt giddy with emotion. My eyes remained fixed on the young girl before me. I wanted passionately to take her in my arms, and knew that I was blushing. She broke the silence.

'I feel like a limp rag,' she said. 'Why don't we go out to the country, somewhere around Tempelhof? It might make us feel better.'

'That's a good idea, Paula. Let's go.'

I rode out with my first love in a little motorcycle taxi to the sandy countryside near the civil and military airfield at Tempelhof. We left the autobahn and climbed onto a small hillock covered with a kind of spongy lichen onto which we collapsed with delight. We both felt crushed by exhaustion. It was a marvellous day. Less than a mile away the ground was cut up and crisscrossed by the network of airport runways from which Focke-Wulf trainers leaped into the sky with astonishing speed. Paula lay on her back with her eyes closed, as if she were nearly asleep. I leaned on my elbow and stared at her, as if the rest of the world didn't exist.

My head was filled with things to say to her — a thousand amorous communications — but my mouth remained ludicrously shut. I felt that I should and must say everything to her right away, that they could wait no longer, that I must take advantage of this ideal moment and make her understand, that it was idiotic to be so timid. . . . Perhaps Paula was being deliberately silent, so that I would have a chance to speak. Time was passing — especially the time still left in my leave: but, despite all these considerations, my love for Paula imposed silence. She murmured: 'The sun is so hot.'

I stammered a few stupidities. Finally, in a surge of courage, I slid my hand toward hers. The ends of our fingers touched, and I lingered for a moment at this delicious contact. Then I screwed up my courage so that my breath almost stopped, and Paula's hand was entirely mine. I grasped it fervently, and she didn't try to withdraw it.

My shyness had presented me with a problem more taxing than finding a safe passage through a mined field. I lay stretched on my back for a moment longer, recovering my strength. I stared at the sky, overwhelmed with happiness, lost to the rest of the world.

Paula turned her face toward me. Her eyes were still closed, and her hand gripped mine. I felt that I might faint. In a fever of emotion, I think I told her I loved her. Then I pulled myself together. I didn't know whether I had spoken or not. Paula hadn't moved. I must have been dreaming.

Suddenly, we turned our heads. The air was filled once again with the sinister sound of sirens howling in unison from the airport to the edge of the city. We stared at each other, astounded.

'Can it be another raid?'

This seemed unlikely. At that time, daytime raids near the capital were still extremely rare. However, the sirens were impossible to mistake: they were signalling the start of a raid, and we quickly believed them. Planes were rolling down all the runways, gathering speed.

'The fighters are taking off, Paula! It really is a raid!'

'You're right! Look down there – all those people running to the shelter!'

'We should get into a shelter too, Paula.'

'But we're perfectly safe here – it's the country. They're going to bomb Berlin again.'

'I guess you're right. We're as well off here as in one of those airless holes.'

The German fighters roared over our heads.

'Ten ... twelve ... thirteen ... fourteen,' cried Paula, waving at the Focke-Wulfs boring through the air over our heads. 'Good luck to our pilots! Three cheers for them!'

'Go on, boys!' I shouted, to fall in with her mood.

'Go on,' Paula repeated. 'It's not night-time now – they'll be able to see. Twenty-two, twenty-three, twenty-four – how many there are! Hooray!'

Thirty fighters had taken off, and were soaring into the sky. Their tactic was to climb as high as possible, so that they could swoop down on the bombers from above and sting them in the back. The Luftwaffe had perfected the formidable Focke-Wulf 190s and 195s, which could soar up quickly, for precisely this purpose. We could hear the distant firing of anti-aircraft guns.

'If we catch them that far away, they'll never even get to Berlin,' Paula said.

'I hope not, Paula.'

I had already forgotten about the damned raid, which had made me drop my girl's hand. Leaving the fighters to look out for themselves, I was preparing a second attack. I was already quite close to Paula, when the roar of enemy bombers drowned out the sounds of the nearby city, and overwhelmed us.

'Oh, look, Guille,' she said, as always mispronouncing my name. 'They're coming from over there — look!'

With her delicate hand, she pointed to a huge mass of black dots which were steadily growing larger against the pale blue sky.

'How high they are,' she said. 'And look — there are others over there.'

I stared at the double apparition bearing down on the city and on us.

'My God, how many there are!'

The noise grew louder and louder.

'There must be hundreds of them!'

'It's impossible to count,' Paula said. 'They're still too far away.'

I began to feel afraid — for us, for her, for my happiness.

'We've got to get away from here, Paula. It could get very dangerous.'

'Oh no,' she said, unconcerned. 'What would happen to us here?'

'We could be strafed, Paula. We've got to find a shelter.'

I tried to drag her after me.

'Look,' she said, fascinated by the spectacle of danger growing visibly larger. 'They're coming straight at us. And look at the white trails they make. Isn't it strange!'

Now our flak went into action. On all sides, thousands of guns were spitting steel at the attackers.

'Come quick,' I said to Paula, tugging her hand. 'We've got to get to a shelter.'

185

The shelters at the airfield were too far away for us now, so I pulled her toward a hollow in the ground, beside a large tree.

'Where are our fighters?' cried Paula, gasping for breath.

'Perhaps they've run away – there are so many enemy planes.'

'You mustn't say that! German soldiers never run away!'

'But what can they do, Paula? There must be at least a thousand bombers.'

'You have no right to say that about our heroic pilots!'

'Forgive me, Paula – you're right. I would be astonished if they ran away.'

The thunder of bombs once again filled the air of the martyred city. German soldiers never run away. I, who had run from the Don to Kharkov, knew that perfectly well – although it must be admitted that German soldiers could fight against odds as great as thirty to one – as in Russia, for instance. From the hole into which Paula and I had dived, we were able to watch the avalanche which flattened a third of the airfield and ninety per cent of Tempelhof.

The daytime raids were always stronger than the ones at night. On that particular day, eleven hundred British and American planes attacked the Berlin region, opposed by roughly sixty fighters. The heavy American losses were caused largely by flak: at least a hundred planes were shot down. The German fighters had not run away: not a single German plane came through undamaged.

I can still see very clearly the whistling clusters of bombs falling seven or eight thousand feet onto Tempelhof and the airfield, and feel the earth trembling under their giant blows. I can see the ground cracking, and houses bursting into flame, and the oil depots near the field spreading the flames over hundreds of yards.... I can see a suburb of 150,000 people blotted out in a blanket of smoke. And with my eyes involuntarily wide from the shock, I can see trees tearing upward from the ground in groups of ten or twelve, and hear them ripping open the earth. I can hear doomed planes roaring their engines, and see them spinning, exploding, falling. And I can see the terror in Paula's eyes, as she pressed herself against me. Flaming debris was falling all around us, so we made ourselves as small as we could at the

bottom of our hole. Paula hid her face between my shoulder
and my cheek, and I could feel her trembling, quite apart
from the trembling of the earth.

Pressed together like two lost children, we watched helplessly. Long after the planes had gone, delayed-action bombs
were exploding in Tempelhof, where the raid had taken
twenty-two thousand lives. Berlin had received a battering
too, and its rescue services were completely overwhelmed.
The streets were still strewn with wreckage from the night
raid, Spandau was still burning, and in the southwest quarter
of the city delayed-action bombs were still exploding fifteen
hours later. Tempelhof was shrieking with pain.

When we stumbled from our hole, haggard with exhaustion, Paula clung to my arm. Her nerves were strained to
their utmost, and she couldn't stop trembling.

'Guille,' she said. 'I feel terrible. And look at me — I'm
filthy.'

She seemed to have lost control of her reason. Her head
fell back on my shoulder. Without even thinking, I kissed her
on the forehead. She made no effort to stop me.

I was unable to reassemble the thoughts which had
obsessed me at the beginning of our walk. I no longer felt any
hesitation about kissing my friend: we seemed to have passed
beyond the stage of infantile flirting. I kissed her hair as if I
were consoling an anxious child, and saw, through her tears,
the tears of the child in Magdeburg, shaking with sobs. I
thought of Ernst, of all the tears in this war, and all the
anguish. I tried to feel pity, and to show it. My happiness was
mixed with too much suffering. I couldn't simply accept it,
and forget all the rest. My love for Paula seemed somehow
impossible, in this setting of permanent chaos. As long as
children were crying in the dust of their crumbled homes, I
would never be able to live with my love. Nothing seemed
certain. Perhaps nothing would survive this marvellous
spring day except my love for Paula — and I didn't know how
to declare it.

Three-quarters of the sky was darkened by smoke from
the thousands of fires which were burning at Tempelhof,
along the autobahns, and in Berlin. I looked from Paula's
blonde hair to the ravaged landscape.

Once more, we fell down on the grass. I didn't know what

to say to comfort her. When we had regained some of our strength, we walked slowly down the autobahn. There, truckloads of rescue workers were driving toward Tempelhof. Without any signal, a truck stopped beside us. 'Come on, you young ones. They need you down there.'

We looked at each other.

'Yes. We're just coming.'

'Paula, I'll help you climb up.'

The trucks were picking up everyone they met. One section of the city was abandoned so that another, at least, might be saved. We worked for hours, pulling out the wounded. The Hitlerjugend from a nearby hostel volunteered for the most dangerous jobs, in search of heroism. Many of them were killed, disappearing in the torrential collapse of burning timber frames.

We managed to find a refuge late that night, in an apartment that had been three-quarters destroyed. Dizzy with fatigue, we collapsed onto a bed, and lay there, too tired to speak, staring into the darkness with wide-open eyes. Thousands of luminous butterflies seemed to be dancing in front of us. They looked as solid and tangible as living creatures. My retina, stamped with the lights of the fires, continued to light my inner vision. One of Paula's hands twisted a button on my dusty tunic.

'Do you think we can sleep here?' she said.

'I don't know, but anyway . . .'

'If anyone found us here, we might get into trouble.'

What could she be thinking of?

'I don't care. I'm too tired.'

Paula, who was sucking one of her skinned fingers, said nothing. I slid my hand under her head, and fully prepared to affront God or the Devil, pulled her to me, kissing her passionately, as her torn hands stroked my hair. We were trying to catch up with what life had denied us that afternoon, but quickly succumbed to sleep, overcome by exhaustion.

We spent all next day cleaning up. It took about a week to restore some kind of functional order. However, in the evening, we were relieved by fresh volunteers, who had been rounded up so that the first group could return to their usual occupations. Luckily for me, I was not impressed into any obligatory duties, although as a soldier on leave I was not involved in any essential activities.

Two more days went by, during which I hardly left Paula's side. Every morning I brought a fresh supply of chocolates and cigarettes from my father's package for us to consume together. The capital was binding up its wounds and burying its dead. Long funeral processions twisted through the streets. The heroic city was returning to its usual productive rhythm.

I only had five days left, and felt oppressed and anguished by the prospect of departure. Paula, who dreaded it as much as I did, tried to fill my mind with other thoughts. Luckily, there were no further raids. The Neubachs had lost all their windows, and had to repair a section of their roof. Three bombs had fallen only 150 yards away, on the square, which now looked like a street in Minsk.

Paula's mother, whom I had met, began to think it rather strange that her daughter never left my side — we met every evening, as well as every day — but she took the times into account, and raised no objection. Paula, who had more money than I did, took me to the movies one evening. We saw a film called *Immen See*, based on a poem about water lilies.

We lived this way until the day of my departure. I was due at the Silesian station at seven in the evening. The Neubachs were touching in their expressions of good will when I said goodbye to them. They understood that I wished to spend my last hours with the girl they considered my fiancée. Frau Neubach insisted on giving me a heavy pullover which had belonged to Ernst. Her husband gave me cigars, soap, and two boxes of tinned food. They both embraced me, and made me promise to come and see them on my next leave. I assured them I would, and that I'd send them my news from time to time. I asked them to look out for Paula.

'You love her, don't you?' Frau Neubach asked me gently.

'Oh yes, Frau Neubach.' Despite an attempt at calm, my voice rang with emotion.

I kissed them both, and left. At the reception centre, the feld gave Paula permission to go up to the dormitory with me and help me pack.

I could feel my throat knotting with sorrow. How long would it be before I saw Paula again? We repeated over and over again how much we loved each other, and began to feel somewhat calmer. I would certainly have another leave in three or four months, and Paula, of course, would wait for me. She swore that she would write to me every day, that soon we would belong to each other, that we would marry. Her warm lips murmured this to me a thousand times as we kissed. The war must end soon ... it can't go on like this. We can't have another horrible winter like the one last year. Everyone had suffered more than enough, and the fighting would have to stop: we felt sure of it.

We arrived at the Silesian station, to find that the departure platform had been moved to another position half a mile away because of bomb damage. Paula walked beside me, smiling despite her emotion. She was carrying a package which she wanted to give me at the last minute. The platform was decorated with pennants and flags to salute the long line of men returning to the East. We stopped beside the first carriage of the Poznań train. I shoved my bulging sack inside, and turned back to catch a moment of unguarded sadness on Paula's face.

'Don't be sad, beloved. I love you so much.'

I stood for a long time, holding her hands, unable to think of anything else to say. I longed to hold her in my arms, but this was forbidden in public. People walked by, talking. The cement platform rang with the sound of the metalled boots of fellows in the same position as myself. But my eyes were glued to Paula: I was oblivious of everyone and everything else.

The hour of departure had almost arrived. A shiver ran through my body, and made my hands tremble. A station-master in a red cap was walking down the platform calling out the stops ahead: Poznań, Warsaw, Lublin, Lvov, Russia. These words crushed my sense of happiness. I braced myself for the whistle which would interrupt our last moment.

'Paula ...'

The stationmaster continued his list of distant destinations.

'Paula ... What would it have been without you?'

'Auf Wiedersehen, mein Lieber,' Paula whispered, in tears.

'Paula, I beg you . . . don't cry . . . please . . . You know I'll be back soon.'

'Ich weiss, mein Lieber, auf Morgen Guille.'

A section was tramping by on the other side of the tracks singing gaily:

> *Erika, we love you,*
> *Erika, we love you,*
> *And that's why we'll come back,*
> *That's why we'll come back.*

'You see, Paula . . . even the song says so. Listen . . .'

I felt overwhelmed by the words. I would come back only for Paula . . . that's what the song meant to say. Then the whistle demolished my sense of joy. I pulled Paula to me and embraced her wildly.

'Einsteigen! Los! Los! Reisende einsteigen! Achtung! Passagiere einsteigen! Achtung! Achtung!'

'I love you, Paula. We'll see each other soon. Don't be sad. See how beautiful it is today. We can't be sad.'

Paula was inconsolable, and I felt that I was going to burst into tears myself. I kissed her for the last time. The couplings of the carriages clashed; the train was beginning to move. I jumped onto the step of the carriage. Paula clung to my hand. The train slowly gathered speed. Many of the people standing on the platform were crying, and soldiers leaning halfway out the windows were still hanging on to someone's hand, or kissing a child. Paula ran beside us as long as she could. Then she had to let go.

'See you soon, my love.'

The day was so beautiful we should have been leaving for a day in the country. I stood on the step for a long time, watching the outline of my beloved growing smaller and smaller, and finally disappearing forever. I will soon come back, Paula. But I never went back. I never saw Paula again, or Berlin, or Killeringstrasse, or the Neubachs. . . .

Paula, we'll be married, I swear it. But the war prevented me from keeping my word, and the peace made it lose all its value. France reminded me of that severely enough. So please forgive me, Paula. It wasn't all my fault. You knew the misery of war too, and fear, and anguish. Perhaps — and I wish it with all my heart – perhaps you also were spared. That at least would allow us both to remember. The war destroyed Berlin, and Germany, and Killeringstrasse, and perhaps the Neubachs too, but not you, Paula ... that would be too horrible. I have forgotten nothing. Whenever I close my eyes, I relive our marvellous moments, and hear once again the sound of your voice, and smell your skin, and feel your hand in mine. . . .

Chapter Five

TRAINING FOR AN ELITE DIVISION

AUF, MARSCH! MARSCH!

I remained in the corridor of the crowded train, and quickly opened the little box Paula had given me as we parted. It contained two packs of cigarettes which I had given her from my father's parcel. My father wasn't a smoker, and must have collected those cigarettes on odd occasions, for years. Paula had added a short note, and her photograph. In her note, she said that she hoped the cigarettes would help me through some of the hard moments ahead. I must have read her words over at least ten times before tucking her letter and photograph into my pass book.

The train lurched forward. Everyone was wrapped in his private melancholy. I tried to find a relatively stable spot where I could press a piece of paper against the window frame and begin a lettter to Paula, but some bastard from the Alpine Corps had to try and talk to me.

'So, leave's over. Always too short, isn't it? Mine's over too. Now, back to the guns!'

I looked at him without answering. He was a pain in the neck.

'And with good weather like this things must be really rough out there. I can remember that very well from last summer. One day we . . .'

'Excuse me, Kamerad, but I'm writing a letter.'

'Ah. A girl, eh? Always girls. Well, don't worry about it.'

I felt like sticking my bayonet into his stomach.

'There are such marvellous girls everywhere! I can remember in Austria once . . .'

Enraged, I turned my back on him, and tried to begin my letter, but the general uproar was too distracting, and I had to give up till later. I stood for a long time with my forehead pressed against the glass, staring with unseeing eyes at the countryside sliding past us. The carriage was full of raucous talk and laughter. Some of the men were trying to joke, to help themselves forget the hideous reality of a front which stretched from Murmansk to the Sea of Azov – a reality in which two million of them would lose their lives. The train moved slowly, making frequent stops. At every station, both soldiers and civilians got on and off, although most of the passengers were military, and bound for the East. We arrived at Poznań during the night, and I ran to the regroupment centre, where my pass had to be stamped before midnight. I thought that I would then go to the dormitory where I had slept for a few hours passing through the other way. The crush of the crowd at the military police office kept me from thinking of Paula. All the formalities were handled far more rapidly than on the way out, as if the double line of soldiers was moving forward to be devoured by a diabolic machine with the appetite of a giant. Inside of ten minutes, my expired pass had been initialled, stamped, and registered, and I was told to proceed to train number 50 for Korosten.

'Oh?' I was surprised. 'When does it leave?'

'In an hour and a half. You've got time.'

We would be travelling that night, then. I followed a group of soldiers who were walking along the wooden gallery toward train 50 – an interminable string of passenger and freight cars which would be crammed to the bursting point with soldiers.

I walked through the frantic din, looking for a more or less comfortable corner where I could settle myself and write my letter. Following the advice of my father, who considered the rear cars safest in case of derailment, I was thinking of one of the carriages with straw-covered floors at the back of the train. I pushed my way inside one of the cars, past five pairs of boots dangling from an open door.

'Welcome aboard, young fellow,' cried the landser already there. 'Get set for Paradise.'

'Well, kid, coming with us to shoot some Russians?'

'Going back to shoot Russians, you mean.'

'Hell. The first time around, you must have still been in your diapers.'

Despite everything, we were able to laugh. Suddenly, in that sea of green cloth, I saw Lensen.

'Hey, Lensen! Over here!'

'I'll be damned,' Lensen said, climbing over the fellows in the doorway. 'So you didn't desert!'

'And you didn't either!'

'It's not the same for me, though. I'm Prussian. I've got nothing in common with you black-haired bastards from the other side of Berlin.'

'Good answer!' shouted one of the boys in the doorway.

Lensen was laughing, but I knew that he had meant every word.

'Look,' he said. 'There's another of our gang.'

'Where?'

'Over there — the big fellow who thinks he's so tough.'

'Hals!'

I jumped down from the carriage. 'Whoever quits the nest loses his nook,' someone shouted.

'Hey, Hals!' I was already running to meet him. I could see his face lighting up.

'Sajer! I was wondering how I'd ever find you in this mob.'

'Lensen saw you.'

'Is he here too?'

We turned back to the train.

'Too late, boys. Full up.'

'That's what you think!' shouted Hals, grabbing the legs of one of the kibitzers, and pulling him down onto the platform on his backside. Everybody laughed, and, with a jump, we were on board.

'Well, that's fine,' said the fellow Hals had dislodged, rubbbing his backside. 'If this goes on, we'll be jammed in here like frankfurters in a box, and there won't be any room to sleep.'

'So it's you, you bastard,' said Hals, giving me a long stare. 'I've been waiting to hear from you for two solid weeks.'

'I'm really sorry ... but when I tell you what happened ...'

'You'd better make it good. It got so that I really didn't know what to say to my parents.'

I gave my friend an account of my misadventures.

'Goddamn it,' Hals said. 'They certainly fucked you up, didn't they? If you'd only listened to me. We could have gone to Dortmund together. Plenty of alerts there too, of course, but the planes only passed over. You got it right in the neck.'

'Well, that's life,' I answered, in a mock-melancholy tone.

In reality, of course, the experiences of my leave left no regrets. If I had gone straight home with Hals I would never have met Paula. And Paula had been able to obliterate for me all the sights and sounds of Tempelhof's blazing fires.

'You certainly have a long face,' Hals said, commiserating with me.

But I didn't feel like talking. Hals quickly understood, and left me to myself. We were sprawled on the straw like animals, trying to sleep. Each piercing jolt of the wheels passing over the joints in the rails seemed to be adding to the barrier separating Paula from me. We passed through villages and towns and forests, all as dark as the night, and distances which stretched into infinity. The train seemed indefatigable, unending. At daybreak we were still rolling, and three hours later we were in lower Poland, crossing the Pinsk marshes, parallel to the rough, rutted roads pock-marked by war, and washed with sadness, and with the sweat of the armies that had tramped along them. The sky seemed inordinately large, and filled with the summer which the earth was denied. I fell asleep several times. Each time I woke the jolting wheels were still striking the same two notes: CLANG glang, CLANG, glang, CLANG, glang.

Finally, the train slowed down and stopped. The loco-motive was resupplied with coal and water at a pitiful hovel which passed for a station. We all jumped down onto the ballast, which was made of God knows what, to relieve ourselves. There was no question of official nourishment. German troop transports at that period were officially con-sidered to be without that category of need, and no food would be distributed before Korosten. Luckily, nearly every-one had brought supplies from home – which is what the quartermaster general was counting on.

The train resumed its eastward journey. Hals tried to engage me in conversation several times, but always without success. I would have liked to tell him about Paula, but was afraid he'd treat it as a joke. We reached Korosten at nightfall, and were ordered to disembark, and line up beside a mess truck, which produced a revolting gruel. I felt very far from the excellent cooking of Frau X. When we had eaten, we all went to rinse our tins and drink at the tank which held water for the locomotives.

Then we set out again on a Russian train, which was no more comfortable than the one we'd just left, and into another eternity eastward. Trains were moving non-stop toward the front, both day and night. We had nearly reached our sector in less than three days. The Southern Front, where fierce fighting was under way at Kremenchug, had shifted, but our sector seemed almost unchanged. Our exhausting railway journey came to an end at Romny, where we had met with so many difficulties on the way out. From the train we were herded straight to the canteen, where we were given food and drink to quiet us as if we were frantic sheep on the way to the slaughterhouse. Then, with a haste which gave us no time to think, the military police called us out for our various units. It was very hot, and we would have been glad of a chance to sleep. A great many idle Russians stood and watched us, as though they were watching a fairground being prepared for a fair. When our group for the Gross Deutschland was called out, we were told to follow a sidecar, which led us to the edge of town. Instead of staying in first, or slowing down his machine, the bastard forced us onto the double. Heavily loaded, in that heat, we were nearly choking when we arrived at our designated position.

The stabsfeldwebel climbed down from his sidecar, called the other noncoms, to whom he distributed our marching orders, and divided up our grroup. In sections of forty or fifty at a time we marched off to our new camp. As we were commanded by fellows who were also just back from leave, and none too anxious to return to the firing line, we made numerous stops before arriving at Camp F of the Gross Deutschland Division, about twenty miles from Romny and over a hundred from Belgorod — out in the country, like Akhtyrka.

In this training camp for an élite division — all divisions with names instead of numbers were considered élite — one sweated blood and water. One was either hospitalized after a week of almost insane effort or incorporated into the division and marched off to the war, which was even worse.

We entered the camp through a large symbolic gateway

197

cut into the trees of the forest which stretched away thickly to the northeast. Although we were marching in step, as we'd been ordered to do, and singing 'Die Wolken Ziehn' at the tops of our lungs, we were still able to read the slogan which decorated the impressive entrance in large black letters, against à white ground: WE ARE BORN TO DIE.

I don't think anyone could pass through that gate without a swallow of fear. A little further on another sign bore the words ICH DIENE (I serve).

Our noncoms marched us in impeccable order to the right-hand side of the rough courtyard, and ordered us to halt. A huge hauptmann walked over to us, flanked by two feldwebels.

'Stillgestanden!' shouted our group leader.

The giant captain saluted us with a slow but definitive gesture. Then he walked up and down our ranks, giving each of us a long stare. He was at least a head taller than anybody else. Even Hals seemed small beside this impressive personage. When he had petrified each of us with his astonishingly hard stare, he stepped back and rejoined the two felds, who were standing as still as the cedars of Jussieu.

'GOOD MORNING GENTLEMEN.' His words sounded like stakes being driven into the earth. 'I CAN SEE ON YOUR FACES THAT YOU'VE ALL BEEN ENJOYING YOUR LEAVES, AND I'M VERY GLAD TO SEE IT.' Even the birds seemed to have been stilled by the sound of that voice. 'HOWEVER, TOMORROW YOU SHALL HAVE TO THINK OF THE WORK WHICH MUST ABSORB ALL OF US.'

A dust-covered company had marched up to the gateway, but had stopped short, in order not to interrupt the captain's speech.

'TOMORROW A PERIOD OF TRAINING BEGINS FOR YOU, WHICH WILL TURN YOU INTO THE BEST FIGHTING MEN IN THE WORLD. FELDWEBEL,' he shouted in a voice which was even louder, "REVEILLE AT SUNRISE FOR THE NEW SECTION.'

'Jawohl, Herr Hauptmann.'

'GOOD EVENING, GENTLEMEN.'

He turned on his heel, then changed his mind, gesturing with one finger for the group of men at the gate to come in. When the fellows, stripped to the waist, and grey with dust, drew even with us, he stopped them, with a similar tiny gesture.

'Here are some new friends,' he said, addressing himself to both groups. 'Salute each other, please.'

Three hundred men, their faces drawn with exhaustion, made a quarter turn to the right and saluted, shouting, 'Thank you, comrades, for joining us.'

We presented arms, and the captain walked off, looking very pleased with himself. As soon as he was gone, the two feldwebels who'd come with him chased us off to the barracks as if they'd suddenly gone mad.

'You've got four minutes to settle in!' they shouted.

Forgetting our tiredness, we were presently standing at attention at the feet of our double-decker beds. Our non-coms, who were clearly terrified, called the roll under the baleful eyes of the two camp felds, who then explained what they expected of us in the way of order, cleanliness, and discipline. They also advised us to sleep, although it was still early, as we would need all our strength tomorrow. We knew that in the German army words of that sort often had a significance far greater than their literal meaning. The word 'exhaustion,' for instance, had nothing to do with the 'exhaustion' I've encountered since the war. At that time and place, it meant a power which could strip a strong man of fifteen pounds of weight in a few days. When the felds had gone, slamming the door behind them, we stared at each other in perplexity.

'It seems that life here won't be a joke,' Hals said, from his bed beneath mine.

'God, no! Did you see that captain?'

'He's all I saw, and I dread the day I get his foot in my backside.'

Outside, a section was leaving in camouflaged combat uniform — probably on some night exercise.

'Excuse me, Hals. I've got to write a letter, and I want to do it while there's still daylight.'

The feld had told us we weren't supposed to use candles after lights out except for emergencies.

'Go ahead,' Hals said. 'I'll leave you alone.'

I hurriedly pulled out the scrap of paper I hadn't yet been able to turn into a letter.

'My dearest love . . .'

I described our journey and arrival at the camp.

'I am all right, Paula, and think of nothing but you. Everything here is quiet. I remember every minute of our time together, and long to get back to you.

'I love you passionately.'

The sun had barely touched the tops of the trees with pink light when the door flew back against the dormitory wall as if the Soviets themselves were bursting in. A feldwebel produced some piercing blasts on a whistle, and made us jump.

'Thirty seconds to get to the troughs,' he shouted. 'Then everybody stripped and outside in front of the barracks for P.T.'

One hundred and fifty of us, stripped to the skin, ran for the troughs on the other side of the buildings. A short distance away, in the dim half-light, we could see another group of soldiers jumping to the bark of another watchdog.

In no time, we had washed and were lined up in front of our barracks. Luckily we had reached the first days of July, so we didn't have to worry about the cold. Then the feld chose one of us to put the rest through a gymnastic routine until he came back. We had to stretch our arms in various directions, touch first the tips of our toes and then the ground to the right and to the left, at the greatest possible extension, and begin again.

'Get going,' he said as he went off. 'And no stopping.'

We turned and stretched in this way for nearly fifteen minutes.

When the feldwebel came back and ordered us to stop, our heads were spinning.

'You have forty-five seconds to get back here in battle order. Raus!'

Forty-five seconds later, 150 steel helmets topping 150 men whose pulses were racing to the explosion point lined up facing the flag. It was then that we made the acquaintance of Herr Hauptmann Fink and his formidable training methods. He arrived wearing riding breeches, and carrying a whip under his arm.

'*Stillgestanden!*' ordered the feld.

The captain stopped at the appropriate distance, made a slow half-turn, and saluted the flag. We were ordered to present arms.

'At ease,' he said in a calm voice, turning back to us.

'Feldwebel, you will simply accompany us today. In honour of the new section, I myself am going to drill them.'

He shifted his weight, and stared down at the ground, which was already lit by the sun. Then he jerked up his head again.

'Attention!'

In a hundredth of a second, we were standing at attention.

'Very good,' he said in a honeyed voice. He walked toward the first row of men. 'Gentlemen, I have the impression that you perhaps entered the infantry a trifle hastily, without sufficient reflection. You probably do not realize that the specialized infantry, such as we are here, has nothing in common with what you knew in the auxiliary service, which you voluntarily quit. Not one of you seems adequate to the job we have to do. I hope that I am wrong, that you will prove the contrary to me, that you will not oblige me to send you to a disciplinary unit to teach you that you have made a mistake.' We listened to him transfixed, with empty heads and rapt attention.

'The task which you will all have to assume sooner or later will certainly require more of you than you supposed. Simply maintaining a decent level of morale and knowing how to handle a weapon will no longer be enough. You will also require a very great deal of courage, of perseverence and endurance, and of resistance in any situation. We, of the Gross Deutschland, have merited mention in the official commiqués which are published throughout the Reich, and this is an honour not lightly bestowed. To deserve this honour we need men, and not pitiful specimens like you. I must warn you that everything here is hard, nothing is forgiven, and that everyone in consequence must have quick reflexes.'

We didn't know how we ought to receive this tirade.

'Attention!' he shouted. 'Down on the ground, and full length!'

Without a moment's hesitation, we were all stretched out on the sandy soil. Then Captain Fink stepped forward and, like someone strolling down a beach, walked across the human ground, continuing his speech as his boots, loaded with at least two hundred pounds, trampled the paralyzed bodies of our section. His heels calmly crushed down on a back, a hip, a head, or a hand – but no one moved.

201

'Today,' he said, 'I am going to take you for a little outing, so I can judge your abilities for myself.'

He divided us into two groups: one of a hundred, the other of fifty.

'Today, gentlemen,' he said, addressing himself to the group of fifty, to which neither Hals nor I belonged, 'it will be your privilege to assume the role of the supposed wounded. Tomorrow, it will be your turn to look out for your comrades. WOUNDED SECTION ON THE GROUND!' Then he turned to us: 'In twos! Pick up the wounded!'

Hals and I made a seat of our hands for a wincing fellow who must have weighed at least 170 pounds. Then Captain Fink led us to the camp exit. We walked as far as a low hill which seemed to be about three-quarters of a mile away. Our arms felt as though they would break under the weight of our comrade, who gradually grew used to the situation. When we reached the top of the hillock, we had to climb down the other side. Our boots cracked as we stumbled down the steep slope. By now the day had turned hot, and we began to run with sweat. Every so often an exhausted man let his grip slip for an instant, and the supposed victim slid to the ground. Whenever this occurred, Fink, with the help of his feld, would separate the enfeebled trio from the main body of men and assign them an even heavier load: each man would have to carry another on his back. At the bottom of the slope, I sensed that it was going to be my turn.

'I can't go on, Hals. My wrists are giving way. I've got to let go.'

'You're crazy. You can't. Would you rather lug him all by yourself?'

'I know, Hals. But I really can't help it.'

'Keep going,' said the captain. 'Los, los.'

Hals tightened his grip on my hands to keep me from letting go. We could hear the men behind us gasping for breath, and stumbling on the rocky ground under the weight of a comrade and full equipment. The feld was trying to keep them going, urging them on with a torrent of abuse. Hals, who was a great deal stronger than I, clenched his teeth. Each crease in his face was pouring with sweat.

'I'm sorry boys,' said the fellow we were carrying. 'I'd gladly walk this, if they'd only let me.'

We somehow managed to stagger to the next wooded hill, which we climbed with almost unbearable effort. By now the wretched fellows with their separate burdens had dropped far behind us, still relentlessly pursued by the feld. The captain never took his eyes off us. With every yard, we were expecting the order to halt, but every yard was followed by another, which was still more difficult. My numbed hands were now entirely without circulation.

'I can't stand it any more, Hals. Let go.'

Hals clenched his teeth and didn't answer. The pain and pressure had become so great that I'd lost my grip altogether, and Hals was hanging on alone. The groups of men who had broken apart were straggling over a wide distance. Captain Fink reorganized them into couples. Then it was our turn.

I shook my bloodless hands, and heaved a long sigh. The giant shadow of the captain loomed over me, and I was ordered to lift a man heavier than myself onto my trembling shoulders. But the shift in position was a relief. Although my head was swimming, I was able to keep going.

This torture went on for nearly an hour, until we were all on the point of losing consciousness and at the extreme limit of our capacities, which Captain Fink seemed to be deliberately overestimating. Finally, he decided to shift us to a new exercise.

'Since you all seem to be tired, I shall now assign you a lying-down exercise, which may revive you. Picture to yourselves that over there behind that hill there is a nest of Bolshevik resistance.' He gestured toward a hillock about a half mile away. 'Furthermore,' he went on in a jovial tone, 'imagine that you have the best of reasons for taking that hill, but that if you walk over there on your feet, the Bolsheviks will make it their business to lay you flat. Therefore, you will make yourselves even flatter than the ground, and proceed toward your objective on your bellies. I shall precede you, and shall fire on anyone I see. Understood?'

We gaped at him, astounded. He was already walking away from us, pulling his Mauser from the holster on his belt. The few minutes he needed to reach the hill gave us a chance to breathe – almost the only chance we were to have during our three weeks of training. We kept our eyes glued to the

hauptmann, who had gone to take up his position, wondering
if we had heard him correctly.

On the feld's orders, we threw ourselves down on our
stomachs, and began to squirm forward. The feld ran to join
the captain, and we drew slowly closer to the rocky outcrop.
Hals was struggling along on my left. We had covered about
four fifths of the distance when the tiny silhouette of the
captain appeared against the sky. He began firing almost at
once. We hesitated for a moment, wondering what was
happening, but the feld's whistle was still summoning us
forward. The captain must have been under orders to avoid
undue damage to his trainees, otherwise I am sure he
wouldn't have hesitated to aim true.

His bullets whistled down among us until we had reached
our objective. The game was not entirely without danger.
During our three weeks of training, we buried four companions to the strains of 'Ich hat ein Kamerad' – victims of
so-called 'training accidents.' There were also some twenty
wounded, with injuries ranging from a long infected scratch
received during a crawl through a barbed-wire entanglement,
to a wound from a bullet or a fragment of shrapnel, to a limb
crushed by the track of a training tank. We also pulled out
two fellows who had nearly drowned crossing a piece of
water on waterlogged wooden crosses made of old railway
ties.

We were sent on interminable marches. One day, we spent
hours following the edge of a swamp, on the water side, while
another section fired at us, forcing us to remain submerged
up to our chins. During that particular game, everyone's
head was down in earnest. We were trained to hurl grenades,
both offensive and defensive, on a carefully prepared piece of
ground. We were given bayonet practice, and exercises to
develop balance, in which one in five cracked his head, and
tests of endurance which seemed to last forever. One of these,
for instance, took place in an old conduit, which must have
been used to supply several towns with gas. It was made of
two elbows, and the fellows in the middle learned all about
the horrors of claustrophobia. There were many thousands of
similar tests. In addition there was the famous 'härteübung,'
which was almost continuous. We were put on thirty-
six-hour shifts, which were broken by only three half-hour

periods, during which we devoured the contents of our mess tins, before returning to the ranks in an obligatory clean and orderly condition. At the end of these thirty-six hours, we were allowed eight hours of rest. Then there was another thirty-six-hour period, after which everything began all over again. There were also false alarms, which tore us from our leaden sleep and forced us into the courtyard fully dressed and equipped, in record time, before we could return to our uncomfortable beds. Our first days were a time of martyrdom. No one had the right to talk. Sometimes a fellow would drop from exhaustion, which would place an extra charge on the section, obliging them to get the fellow onto his feet again, slapping him and spraying him with water.

Sometimes one of our comrades would return to camp so exhausted he could only stagger with the support of two other men. In principle, within five-hundred yards of the camp we were supposed to line up in order, fall into marching step, and sing, as if we were returning from a healthy and enjoyable hike. On some evenings, however, despite every curse in the book, and the threat of the disciplinary hut, we were so exhausted it was impossible for us to assume the attitude the feld required. To his chagrin and fury, he was obliged to drag a long line of sleepwalkers past the flag, before chasing us into our barracks, where we dropped onto our beds with all our clothes and equipment, our mouths bone dry and our heads aching. Nothing ever affected the routine at Camp F; Captain Fink simply carried on, in total disregard of our bleeding gums and pinched faces, until the stabbing pains in our heads made us forget the bleeding blisters on our feet. A cry for mercy would have brought no relief: any appeal was guaranteed an identical reception: 'Auf marsch! Marsch!'

For us there was the heat of the Russian summer, which followed the winter with practically no spring in between. There were the storms, with their torrents of rain. There were our tender-skinned shoulders rubbed raw by our straps, particularly at the point which bore the weight of the gun. There were kicks and scuffs, and for many of us, the whip. There were mess tins half-filled with tasteless pap. There was the fear of failure and of the disciplinary battalion, and the fear of ultimate success as a dead hero. There were our heads, emptied of every thought, and the fixed, staring eyes of comrades who no longer saw anything but the earth on which we had to crawl. There were also two letters from Paula, which my heavy, exhausted eyes could no longer make any sense of, and my remorse at being unable to reply during my eight hours of rest.

Two thousand miles to the west, people were complaining because at certain hours it was impossible to find anything to drink at the Paris bistros. It still makes me laugh to hear how bitterly this abstinence made them suffer.

Throughout the war, one of the biggest German mistakes was to treat German soldiers even worse than prisoners, instead of allowing us to rape and steal – crimes which we were condemned for in the end, anyway.

One day we were given anti-tank exercises – defensive and counterattack. As we had already been taught to dig foxholes in record time, we had no trouble opening a trench 150 yards long, 20 inches wide, and a yard deep. We were ordered into the trench in close ranks, and forbidden to leave it, no matter what happened. Then four or five Mark-3s rolled forward at right angles to us, and crossed the trench at different speeds. The weight of these machines alone made them sink four or five inches into the crumbling ground. When their monstrous treads ploughed into the rim of the trench only a few inches from our heads, cries of terror broke from almost all of us. Even today, I am fascinated by the sight of a bulldozer at work: its treads remind me of those terrifying moments. We were also taught how to handle the dangerous Panzerfaust, and how to attack tanks with magnetic mines. One had to hide in a hole and wait until the tank came close enough. Then one ran, and dropped an explosive device – unprimed during practice – between the body and the turret of the machine. We weren't allowed to leave our holes until the tank was within five yards of us. Then, with the speed of desperation, we had to run straight at the terrifying monster, grab the tow hook and pull ourselves onto the hood, place the mine at the joint of the body and turret, and drop off the tank to the right, with a decisive rolling motion. Thank God, I myself never had to mine a tank coming straight at me. Lensen, who was promoted to ober, and then sergeant, partly because of his prowess in this exercise, gave us a demonstration which no suspense film could ever hope to equal. His assurance was partly responsible for his horrible end a year and a half later.

There was a hut in the courtyard – a roof supported by four stakes – for those who retained some trace of individualism or disobedience. Under the roof there were some empty boxes which served as benches. This structure was familiarly known as 'Die Hundehütte.' I never saw anyone there, but heard enough about the treatment dished out to men who were being punished to realize that this was in an entirely different category from the punishment huts in France, where the fellows spent their time lying on a mattress. At Camp F, soldiers being disciplined spent their thirty-six hours of active training like everyone else. However, at the end of this period they were led to the Hundehütte and chained, with their wrists behind their backs, to a heavy horizontal beam. Their eight-hour rest period would be spent in this position, their backsides supported by an empty box. Soup was brought to them in one of the big tureens for eight, from which they had to lap like dogs, as their hands were immobilized behind their backs. Suffice it to say that after two or three sessions in this chalet, the wretched victim, denied a rest which was absolutely essential, lapsed into a coma, which would put a merciful end to his sufferings. He would then be sent to the hospital. There was a horrible story about a fellow named Knutke, who had been to the hut six times but who still refused, despite kicks and beatings, to follow the section out for training. One day, they took the dying man to the foot of a tree and shot him. 'That's what the hut leads to,' everyone said. 'You've got to avoid it.' So, despite groans of pain, everyone marched.

It surprises me most of all that at that time we thought we were useless, impossibly inferior, and that we would never make decent soldiers. Despite our desperate life, we really tried, with the best of wills, to do better and better. But Herr Hauptmann Fink had his own ideas about 'better,' which could lead to the brink of death.

Toward the middle of July, only a few days before the battle of Belgorod, the captain Kommandant of Camp F swore us into the infantry at an open-air ceremony. We dedicated ourselves to the Führer in front of a stand, made of branches and decorated with flags, which held the officers of

207

the camp. One by one, we marched alone, in parade step, to the level of the stand, made a quarter-turn, and marched toward it. When we had reached the stipulated distance – about seven or eight yards – we snapped to attention, and declared in a loud, clear voice: 'I swear to serve Germany and the Führer until victory or death.'

Then we executed another quarter-turn to the left, and joined the ranks of those who had already completed the ceremony, in a high state of emotion, ready to convert the Bolsheviks, like so many Christian knights by the walls of Jerusalem.

For me, only half German, this ceremony may have had even more significance than for the others. Despite all the hardship we had been through, my vanity was flattered by my acceptance as a German among Germans, and as a warrior worthy of bearing arms.

Then – a miracle. Fink produced a glass of excellent wine for each of us, and lifted his own glass along with ours, to a chorus of 'Sieg Heils.' Then he walked through our ranks, shaking each of us by the hand, thanking us, and declaring himself equally pleased with us and with himself. He said that he felt well satisfied that he was sending a good group of soldiers to the division. I really don't know whether we were good soldiers or not, but we had assuredly been through the mill. We had all lost pounds, which was evident in our sunken eyes and lined faces. But all that had been foreseen. Before we left the camp, we were given two days of complete rest, which we used to maximum advantage. It seems scarcely credible that by the time we left we all nourished a certain admiration for the Herr Hauptmann. Everyone, in fact, dreamed of someday becoming an officer of the same stripe.

Chapter Six

BELGOROD

On a hot evening in the summer of 1943, we found ourselves once again in the immediate vicinity of the front. Belgorod had recently been retaken by the Russians, who had set up their advance positions just beyond the town, inside our own lines. The front, which ran through Belgorod, from Kharkov to Kursk, was more or less quiet. The campaign, which had continued almost without a break since our withdrawal from the Belgorod-Voronezh-Kursk triangle, had been exhausting. The Russians were now catching their breath and collecting their innumerable dead, before launching an even stronger attack against our positions in September. Kharkov had remained in our hands after the slaughter at Slaviansk, and the Russian breakthrough on our Southern Front had finally been stopped somewhere near Kremenchug.

The Soviets had regained some of their strength, and had forced the German and Rumanian troops to withdraw from the Caucasus and the Kalmuck plain. They had also pushed us back from the Donets. However, the situation was not yet entirely in their hands, and strong counter-attacks from our side often broke their frantic thrust. Belgorod, Kharkov, and Stalino all figure prominently in any account of German counter-attacks. Sixty thousand troops took part in the battle of Belgorod. I was one of them. Eighteen thousand Hitler-jugend had also arrived from Silesian camps to receive their baptism of fire in this unequal combat, in which a third of them lost their lives. I can remember their arrival very well, in brisk columns, ready for anything. Some units carried flags with inscriptions embroidered in gold letters: JUNGE LÖWEN, or THE WORLD BELONGS TO US. Platoons of machine gunners arrived, and infantry regiments loaded with bandoliers stuffed with grenades, and motorized regiments with all their heavy equipment. The plain was covered with soldiers, and for the next three or four days more and more came . . .

Then everything quieted down. By regiment, section, and group we were all directed to precise locations, where we settled down to an armed watch. Once again, I speak as though we knew of the impending attack. In fact, we engaged in these preparations as part of the normal routine.

As in the past, I and my comrades were used for a thousand and one chores, which reminded us of the old days in the Rollbahn. It was suffocatingly hot, and the dried yellow grasses of the steppe did not hold down the dust, which was stirred up in clouds by the slightest movement.

In the evenings we sat beside enormous campfires and talked or sang. The front was some fifteen miles away, so fires were permitted. There was plenty of time for an abundant correspondence with Paula, and I thought about her constantly.

Then, one afternoon, we were assembled for distribution of ammunition. Each man was given 120 cartridges and four grenades. Ten of us – nine men and a noncom – were organized as an assault group. Hals was a machine gunner, one of two men with F. M. spandaus, each with a number-two man. There were three men with rifles, one of them me, two grenadiers armed with automatics and heavy bags of grenades, and a noncom. In total silence, and with every possible precaution, we were led to a shelter near a large farm, right behind the front line. An armoured section of the Gross Deutschland was next to us, with Tiger tanks and heavy howitzers pulled by tractors and camouflaged by real and artificial leaves. We walked past a table set up near one of the buildings, and a fat clerk took down our identification numbers. At another table, a lieutenant in the cavalry was studying a map, surrounded by other Panzer officers and a couple of noncoms. With painstaking precision we were taken from the farm to the place marked for us on the map. Suddenly, at the edge of some woods, I recognized the wide communication trenches which led to the front line, and I think we all had the same thought: now we're in for it. All around us, other groups were taking up their positions.

We formed part of Company 5, which was sent down a communications trench cutting in at right angles and leading to the brush where the trees stopped. The engineers must have really sweated, cutting through all those roots. Every-where, sections were settling in, improving and deepening their shelters. It was about six o'clock in the evening, and the heat of the day was beginning to slacken off.

We followed the trench out of the woods and across a range of low hills with wooded crests. An officer with his eyes glued to a map showed us the way. We turned off to the right, which brought us back under the trees, where the heat was trapped and much more oppressive than out in the open. Everywhere, men pouring with sweat were jostling each other, looking for their positions. Finally, we came to a large half-covered shelter packed with young soldiers from the Hitlerjugend.

'Halt!' shouted the noncom who'd been leading us. 'You'll split up here, and take your positions when the order's given. Your feldwebel will explain what's expected of you.'

He saluted, and left us with the Hitlerjugend, who were sitting on the ground or squatting on their haunches, talking gaily. I went over to Hals, who had just put down his MG-42, and was wiping the sweat from his face.

'Hell,' he said. 'I was better off with my Mauser. This damn thing weighs a ton.'

'I'll be with you, Hals. It seems we're part of the same group.'

We compared left hands, which had both been stamped 5 K. 8.

'What does that mean?' asked Olensheim, who had just come up.

'Our group number, gefreiter,' said Hals. 'If you're not in the 8th, we don't know you.'

Olensheim looked anxiously at his hand.

'Damn – I'm eleven. Do you know what that means?'

'Not I,' said Hals. 'But ask Corporal Lensen. He must have an inside tip.'

'We're going on a picnic,' Lensen said, laughing, secretly displeased that his rank did not let him in on the secrets of the gods.

One of the Hitlerjugend came over to us, as pretty as a ripe young girl.

'Do the Soviets hang together in combat?' he asked, as though he were inquiring about an opposing football team.

'Extremely well,' said Hals, sounding like an old lady in a tea-room.

'I was only asking because I thought you looked experienced,' he said. We were all about the same age.

'Let me give you a piece of advice, young man,' said Lensen, whose tiny promotion was after all worth a little something. 'Fire on anything Russian without the least hesitation. The Russians are the worst sons of bitches the world has ever seen.'

'Are the Russians going to attack?' Olensheim looked very white.

'We'll surely attack first,' said the beautiful young man, whose Madonna face was incapable of a ferocious expression. He walked back to his gang of boy companions.

'Do you think someone will tell us what all this is about?' Lensen said, in a voice loud enough to be overheard by the feldwebel.

'Shut up,' shouted a real veteran, sprawled full length on the ground. 'You'll know soon enough where they're going to do you in.'

'Hey,' one of the Hitlerjugend took him up. 'Who's the shit talking like that?'

'You shut up too, you crap heads,' said the veteran, an old man in his thirties, who must have been taking it for several years now. 'We'll have enough of listening to you when you get your first scratch.'

One of the Junge Löwen got up and walked over to the veteran.

'Sir,' he said in the assured voice of a law or medical student, 'will you please explain your defeatist attitude, which is sapping the morale of everyone here?'

'You just let me whistle my own tune,' said the other, who appeared unimpressed by a flowery turn of speech.

'But I'm afraid I must insist on a reply,' said the young man.

'And I say you're a bunch of fatheads, who won't begin to think until you've been cracked on your nice little skulls.'

Another of the young Hitler boys jumped up, as if he'd been shot. His features were regular and firm, and his steel-grey eyes reflected an unshakable determination. I thought he was going to rush the older fellow, who wasn't looking at anyone.

'Do you think we're still tied to our mothers' apron strings?' he asked, in a voice as steady as his look. 'We've been through months of training too, and we're just as tough as you. We've all been in endurance squads. Rümmer,' he said, turning to a friend. 'Hit me in the face.'

Rümmer jumped to his feet, and his strong, nervous fist struck his friend in the mouth. The latter staggered for a moment under the impact of the blow, and then walked over to the veteran, who decided to look up. Two streams of bright red blood were pouring from thé mouth of the Junge Löwe and running down his chin.

'Fatheads like me can take it just as well as bourgeois shits like you.'

'All right,' said the veteran, who had decided against coming to blows ahead of H-hour. 'You're all heroes.'

He turned away, and tried to whistle.

'How about writing to your families, instead of squabbling like this?' said our feld. 'Mail will be collected in a little while.'

'That's a good idea,' Hals said. 'I'm going to write to my parents.'

I had a letter to Paula in my pocket which I'd been carrying around for a couple of days, waiting for a chance to finish it. I added a few tender sentiments, and sealed it. Then I wrote to my family. When anyone is afraid, he thinks of his family, especially of his mother, and as the moment of attack drew closer, my terror was rising. I wanted to confide something of my anguish to my mother, and felt that somehow I could do it in a letter. I had always found it difficult to confide in my parents face to face – even the slightest of crimes – and had often criticized them for failing to help me. But on that occasion I was able to express myself.

Dear parents, especially Maman:

I know you must be quite angry with me for writing to you so little. I have already explained to Papa that the life we lead here leaves almost no time for letters. [This was not strictly speaking true: I had written to Paula at least twenty times, and only once to my family.]

At last, I want to ask your pardon, and describe something of my life here. I could have written to you in

213

German, Maman, because I'm getting much better at it, but it is still easier for me to write in French. Everything here is all right. I've finished my training, and I'm a real soldier now. I wish you could see Russia. You can't imagine how huge it is. The wheatfields near Paris seem like tiny gardens compared to what we have here. Now it's as hot as the winter is cold. I hope we won't have to spend another winter here. You wouldn't believe what we went through. Today, we've moved up to the front line. Everything is quiet, and it seems as if we've just come here to relieve our comrades. Hals is still my best friend, and I have a good time with him. I think you'll like him when you meet him on my next leave – unless the war is over before then, and we're home for good. Everyone thinks it must be going to end soon – that we can't have another winter like last one. I hope that my brothers and sisters are well, and that my youngest brother doesn't broadcast my affairs too much. I look forward more than I can say to seeing them again. Papa told me that life was hard for you. I hope it's easier now, and that you don't have to do without too much. Don't go short yourselves to make a package for me – I'm more or less all right. Dear Maman, soon I want to tell you about something wonderful that happened to me in Berlin. For now, I send all of you my love.

I sealed my letter and, together with the one to Paula, handed it to the postman. Hals, Olensheim, Kraus, and Lensen all had letters too. . . .

Everything was quiet on that summer evening in 1943. After dark, of course, there would be a few clashes between patrols – nothing more. But that's war.

Some of us were rounded up to distribute supper, which we ate late. We were forbidden to touch the few cans we had, for they constituted our total reserve.

Dusk was falling when the feld responsible for our section waved us over to him. We were soon listening intently, as he told us what we would be expected to do. He had a large map of the district, on which he showed us the points we should attain, taking every precaution. When the order was given, we should be prepared to protect the infantry, who would quickly join and then pass us. We were given a list of rallying points and other details which I only partly understood, and advised to rest, as we would not be called before the middle of the night.

We stood and stared at each other for a long time. Now we knew. We were going to be part of a full-scale attack. A heavy sense of foreboding settled over us, and the knowledge that soon some of us would be dead was stamped on every face. Even a victorious army suffers dead and wounded: the Führer himself had said it. In fact, none of us could imagine his own death. Some would be killed — we all knew that — but each one imagined himself doing the burying. No one, despite the obvious danger, could think of himself lying mortally wounded. That was something which happened to other people — thousands of them — but never to oneself. Everyone clung to this idea, despite fear and doubt. Even the Hitlerjugend, who spent years cultivating the idea of sacrifice, couldn't consciously envisage their own ends occurring within a few hours. One might be exalted by a grand idea based on a structure of logic, and even be prepared to run large risks, but to believe in the worst is impossible.

Finally, night came: a soft summer night, which brought with it a breath of freshness after the torrid day. Everywhere free of the war, people must have been stretched out on the grass beside their houses, enjoying the season with their friends. Sometimes, when I was small, I used to take a walk with my parents before going to bed. My father believed one should enjoy these summer evenings to the maximum, and kept me out until my eyelids drooped with sleep. Hals pulled me back from my thoughts.

'My dear Sajer, be sure to look out for yourself when we get going. It would be too stupid to get killed just before the war's over.'

'Yes,' I said. 'That would be stupid.'

All of us were haunted by so many thoughts that conversation was impossible. And each of us was obsessed by the particular question: 'How shall I come through this time?'

In the depths of the covered shelter, one of the Jungen Löwen was playing quietly on his harmonica, and the voices of his companions joined softly in the melody. Then the sound of gunfire made us jump.

215

'Here we go!' we thought.

But everything quieted down again.

Lensen came up to us.

'The first Soviet line is less than four hundred yards from here,' he said. 'The feld just told me. That's really not very far.'

'But it's not too bad, either,' said the veteran of a little while ago. 'At least we can sleep in peace. At Smolensk the Popovs' holes were less than a grenade's throw from ours.'

No one answered him.

'I'm commanding Group 6,' said Lensen, 'and I have to get right under Ivan's nose, to keep him from moving when the assault troops begin their attack. You can imagine . . .'

'We'll have it about the same,' said the sergeant who would lead us. 'According to what I've heard, we'll be right in line with one of their positions.'

We listened attentively, hoping that our part of the enter-prise was not going to be too dangerous.

'But the Russian scouts are sure to see us!' cried Lindberg, horrified. 'That's crazy!'

'That will be the hardest part of it, but let's hope the night is dark. Also, we've been advised not to fire before the attack – to get into position without any noise.'

'Don't forget mines,' said the veteran, who in fact had not gone to sleep.

'The ground was checked for mines by details from the disciplinary battalion – insofar as possible,' the noncom retorted.

'Insofar as possible,' sneered the veteran. 'I like that! All the same, you'd better be careful if you see any wires. Don't go tugging them.'

'If you keep on like this,' Lensen shouted in a threatening voice, 'I'll put you to sleep until the attack.' He shook his stubby-fingered fist under the older man's nose. The veteran only smiled, but didn't say anything.

'What if we run right into Ivan?' asked grenadier Kraus. 'Then we'll have to use our guns, won't we?'

'Only as a last resort,' the noncom answered. 'In principle, we're supposed to take them by surprise, and knock them out without any noise.'

Without any noise! What did he mean?

'With the butts of our guns, or spades?' asked Hals anxiously.

'Spades, bayonets, anything. We've got to get rid of them – that's all. And without raising any alarm.'

'We'll take them prisoner,' murmured young Lindberg.

'Are you off your rocker?' said the noncom. 'An assault group can't take prisoners during a mission. What would we do with them?'

'Hell,' said Hals. 'You mean we'll have to skewer them?'

'Lost your guts?' asked Lensen.

'Hell, no,' said Hals, to show that he was a man. But his face was white.

I glanced at the spade-pick hooked to my big friend's waist. Then we had to stand up so a hauptmann and his group could get through.

'Where are we, exactly?' young Lindberg asked naïvely.

'In Russia,' said the veteran.

No one smiled at this feeble joke, and the noncom tried to give us a rough idea of our position – some three miles northwest of Belgorod.

'I'm going to try and sleep,' stammered Hals, who was clearly shaken by all these preparations.

We lay down side by side, without bothering to undo our bedrolls. The steel of the spandau which Hals had set up pointing down the length of the trench gleamed with a dull lustre. Sleep was impossible – not because of the discomfort of a night out of doors, strapped into all our gear – we'd done that often before – but because of our anxiety about what lay ahead.

'Hell – I'll have plenty of time to sleep when I'm dead,' said Grenadier Kraus in a loud voice. He stood up and pissed against the wall of the trench.

I lay awake for a long time, thinking and thinking. . . . Finally, I did sleep, for about three hours, until I was wakened by the distant sound of a motor. My movement woke Hals and Grumpers, the other grenadier, who was lying beside me with his head on my shoulder.

'What's the matter?' he groaned sleepily.

'I don't know. I thought maybe they'd called us.'

'What time is it?' Hals asked.

I looked at my school watch. 'Two-twenty.'

217

'What time is dawn?' asked young Lindberg, who hadn't been able to sleep at all.

'Probably very early this time of year,' someone said.

The sound of engines continued.

'If those fucking drivers keep it up, they'll wake every one of the goddamn Russkis.'

We tried to go back to sleep, but couldn't. About half an hour later we heard a muted noise of bustle and commotion just beyond the walls of the covered shelter. In the darkness, we guessed that we were listening to some fellows collecting their gear. We all turned toward the sound, trying to grasp what was happening, when a feld appeared, wearing camouflage.

'Groups 8 and 9?' he asked in a low voice.

'Present!' answered the two group leaders.

'You'll be leaving in five minutes, by way of access C, and will proceed to your respective positions. Good luck!'

He pointed to a small sign, scarcely visible in the darkness, marked with the letter C. All our reflections came to a dead stop, and our brains emptied, as if we had been anaesthetized. Everyone grabbed his gun, and checked the critical points of his harness and straps, as Hauptmann Fink had taught us – especially the chin straps of our helmets. Hals lifted the big F.M. onto his shoulders, and Lindberg, who was his number-two man, slipped his slender silhouette in beside the man he was supposed to serve. Only the veteran – our second machine gunner – behaved as if he'd forgotten the object of all these preparations. His movements were not marked by the febrile haste which characterized the actions of all the rest of us. He knew all this from before. He propped the heavy F.M. against his leg, and waited for the order to move out.

'I hope you're in good shape,' he said to the gun, grinning sardonically.

'Group 8!' called the sergeant, sounding as if he'd been struck by a sudden electric shock. 'After me, and silence!'

We took exit C and, sticking close together, followed the trench to the forward positions. Our noncom was at the head of the column. Behind him came Grumpers, the grenadier, who was about twenty-two years old; then Hals, just past eighteen, and Lindberg, not quite seventeen; then our three

218

gunners: a Czech of indefinable age with an unpronounceable name, a Sudeten of nineteen, whose name ended with an 'a,' and me. Right behind me was the veteran with his number-two man, another terrified boy, and finally Grenadier Kraus, who must have been well into his twenties. We moved out in good order, exactly as we'd been taught at Camp F, where we'd sweated so hard.

Indefinable noises reached us, coming from either the Russian or the German lines. We crossed several trenches jammed with troops who were still half asleep in the warm summer air, before climbing out of our own trench in the middle of the woods. Young Lindberg, who was loaded down like a donkey, slipped on the earth embankment, and the magazines of the spandau he was carrying clashed together. The noncom grabbed him by his straps and helped him climb up. Then he glared at him furiously, and kicked him in the shin. We walked to the edge of the wood in single file. The noncom stopped short very suddenly, and we all more or less piled into each other.

'It's darker than Hades here,' the veteran muttered in my ear.

It seemed to me that our guide, having signed us to stop, was now going on ahead. We stayed where we were, bent double, waiting for an order to proceed. Despite our best efforts to keep quiet, we couldn't avoid a certain amount of metallic clatter from all the weapons we were carrying.

The noncom came back, and we set out again, walking forward another short distance to the foxholes at the edge of the wood, where our scouts were waiting, as quiet as snakes. We threw ourselves down into their short trench.

'As flat as you can,' whispered the Sudeten, who in principle walked just ahead of me. 'Pass it on.'

One by one, we left the last German positions, and crawled out onto the warm earth of no man's land. I kept my eyes glued to the hob-nailed soles of the Sudeten's boots, trying nervously to keep in sight all that could be seen of my closest companion. From time to time the air ahead of me would darken with the looming shape of a comrade who had to climb over some obstacle. At other moments, the soles of the boots ahead of me would suddenly stop inches from the end of my nose. Then I would be gripped by a horrible

219

anxiety: maybe the Sudeten had lost sight of the fellow in front of him. A moment later he would begin to move again, and the instinctive confidence I felt as part of the group would unknot my throat.

During such moments, even naturally reflective characters suddenly feel their heads emptying, and nothing seems to matter except the dry, cracking stick pressing into one's stomach, which one must somehow crush and pass over without making any noise. A new, hitherto unsuspected acuteness sharpens every sense, and the tension seems pressing enough to subdue one's wildly racing heart.

We inched slowly forward across that damnable Russian soil, which all of us had already trampled more than enough.

We had to crawl around a short stretch of light sand against which we would show up too easily, crushing under our bodies a mat of thorny creepers which we took at first for Russian barbed wire. Then we came to a mossy hollow where we stopped for a moment. Our sergeant, who had a very good sense of direction, was going over our route in his head, trying to fix our position. The hollow reeked with a pestilential smell. When we began to move again, I was startled to see two motionless figures lying on the sand some two yards to our right. I pointed at them, nudging the veteran, who looked and grabbed his nose. With a shock of horror, I understood that we had just passed two corpses, which were quietly rotting as they waited for burial in a common grave.

We seemed to have crawled as far as China. About half an hour after we had started, we came to the first Russian wire. We waited with beating hearts while our first men opened a precarious passage. Every time we heard the cutters snap we expected to see a spray of dirt shooting up from an exploding mine. Our faces, blackened with soot from the canteen kettles, were pouring with sweat, and the tension was so great we certainly must have aged several years during the few minutes we needed to crawl under the Soviet wire, at a speed of about fifteen yards an hour.

When we had all made it through, we stopped for several moments and huddled together. Every one of us was trembling. We could hear faint sounds from the Russian forward positions. We rolled our eyes at each other and understood without words that we all felt the same way. We

crept forward another twenty yards to a stand of low scrub
or tall grass. We could hear the sound of voices and knew
beyond any doubt that we had reached the first Russian line.

Suddenly, we were staring incredulously at an almost
invisible figure – a Soviet reconnaissance man, who was
bending over a hole which undoubtedly contained some of
his comrades. We almost stopped breathing, and slowly lifted
our guns, looking at our leader, who seemed to have frozen,
and then at each other, with a look beyond expression, as the
Russian walked slowly toward us. Then he turned back. Our
sergeant pulled a knife from his belt. Its blade flashed white
for a moment, before he thrust it slowly into the ground in
front of Grumpers, pointing to the Russian with one finger.

The grenadier opened his eyes enormously wide, and
looked with horror from the Russian to the knife to the
sergeant. The latter gestured him on, as Grumpers' quivering
hand clenched round the knife handle. With a final mute look
of supplication, the grenadier began to creep forward. We
followed the progress of his dark shape with an anxiety
which made us clench our teeth to keep from crying out.
Then he was lost in the darkness.

The Russian was still talking to his friends, as if the war
were thousands of miles away. He took a few more steps. We
could hear more voices a little farther off. For a few long
moments, each of us forgot his own existence. The Russian
walked toward the spot where Grumpers must have hidden,
and turned back. As he turned, a second silhouette rose up
behind him. Grumpers covered the four or five yards that
separated him from his quarry in one jump. The Russian
whirled around. We heard a rough cry and the sound of a
struggle. From a hole a short way off, we heard Russian
voices. Then we were able to distinguish the silhouette of our
grenadier rolling on the ground, and hear the sound of his
voice.

'Hilfe, kameraden!'

The Russian jumped to one side, and the sound of his
machine gun tore into the quiet of the night, as its white
flashes striped the darkness. To my left another machine gun
opened fire, and its bullets followed the howling Russian as
far as the earth embankment in front of the foxhole, into
which he finally plunged.

221

From the hole, we could hear voices shouting: 'Germanski! Germanski!'

With a leap which looked beyond his capacities, the veteran propelled himself forward, hurling a grenade from his right fist. The object vanished into the darkness for two or three seconds. Then the hole was lit by a brilliant white light, and we heard the outcry of several voices, before a moment of silence.

We withdrew as fast as we could, keeping parallel to the barbed wire. Behind us, we could hear a rising tumult. Risking mines and bullets, we ran for a small hillock, and, gasping for breath, hastily attempted to organize a defensible position in a thicket.

'Idiots!' the sergeant exploded, meaning Kraus and the veteran. 'I didn't give an order to fire. We'll never get out of this now.' He was as scared as anybody else.

'But Grumpers asked for help, sergeant,' Kraus answered. 'He was in bad trouble.'

An instant later a dozen flares lit our surroundings as brightly as day, and a Russian fusillade shook the air all around us. The Russians were also heaving grenades at random, the way we would have done.

'We're finished,' whimpered young Lindberg.

'Quick, a shovel,' shouted the Sudeten. 'We've got to dig in, or they'll slaughter us.'

'Nobody move!' the veteran commanded authoritatively. In our terror, we obeyed him. His voice sounded more confident than the sergeant's. We tried to freeze absolutely, even down to the fluttering of our eyelids. A flare burst into brilliant white light directly overhead, and anyone whose face wasn't buried in the ground could see every detail of our circumstances. Just beyond us lay the bodies of Grumpers and the Russian, and five or six foxholes preceding a V-shaped infantry position. Other flares lit the edge of the wood from which our adventures had begun. Luckily, the Russians nearest us hadn't noticed the rise of ground which was giving us cover. However, their soldiers in the more distant positions which we had seen in the light of the flares could see us. They began to throw grenades too, and they were using the superb Russian grenade throwers.

'God,' said the veteran. 'If they've got those damned things, we've had it.'

'We ought to dig,' snivelled Lindberg.

'Shut up. Dig with your belly if you like, but don't move anything else. If we play dead, maybe they'll think we are.'

Something fell with a dull thud on the other side of the hillock. Its crest disintegrated, and we were spattered by a rain of earth. There were no new flares coming over, and the ones still falling were fading. As usual, the Russians were shouting curses at us. Another grenade landed somewhere to our left, and we could hear the whistling fall of its fragments through the noise of the explosion. Someone lying beside the veteran groaned.

'Shut up! Hold it back!' muttered the veteran between clenched teeth. 'If they hear anything, that's it.'

He was talking to his number-two man. The boy was clawing at his face, which was twisted with pain. His hands were trembling.

'Don't make a sound,' said the veteran, putting his hand on the boy's forearm. 'Be strong.'

Grenades were still falling all around us. The boy clenched his fists, and his eyes flooded with tears. He sniffed.

'Quiet,' insisted the veteran.

The flares died out, and everything around us became pitch black. The Russians must have spotted another group of our men somewhat to the north of us: it was their turn to get the lights and the noise. Then we heard other sounds directly ahead of us. By deliberately dilating our pupils as wide as we could, we were able to distinguish several men creeping forward parallel to our position. A cold sweat trickled down our backs. The veteran was holding a large grenade about four inches from my nose. Once again, we froze. The hunched figures came toward us as far as the barbed wire, and then turned back.

We all breathed again. The wounded boy buried his face in the ground, to try to stifle his groans.

'They're just as scared as we are,' said the veteran. 'Somebody orders them up here to see what's going on, so they take a few steps and then run back as fast as they can and say they don't see anything.'

'It's almost dawn,' whispered our noncom. 'I think we could stay here. It seems a pretty good spot.'

'I don't, sergeant. I think we should get out.'

'Maybe you're right. You,' he said, pointing to Hals. 'There's a hole about twenty yards from here, level with the barbed wire. You get over there.'

Hals and Lindberg slid off like snakes.

'Where are you hurt?' the veteran asked the wounded boy, touching him on the shoulder.

The young man lifted his face, which was smeared with dirt and tears.

'I can't move,' he said. 'Something hurts here.' He touched his hip.

'A splinter. Don't move. We'll send someone to help you.'

'Yes,' said the boy, thrusting his face back into the dirt.

'Our assault troops should be here in ten or fifteen minutes, if everything goes well,' said the noncom, looking at his watch. The horizon was beginning to turn pink. Soon the sun would be up. We waited feverishly.

'Isn't there going to be a bombardment first?' asked Kraus.

'Lucky there's not,' said the veteran. 'We'd get it just as badly as the Popovs.'

'There won't be,' said the sergeant. 'The first waves are supposed to take the enemy by surprise. We're here to neutralize enemy defence.'

'But our fellows might mistake us for Russians, and do us in.'

'Exactly,' said the veteran, laughing.

Russian voices came to us in bursts as clearly as if we were in the trench with them.

'At least they don't seem worried,' the Czech remarked.

'What's the use of worrying? We'll all be dead in an hour anyway,' said the veteran, as if he were thinking aloud.

The light was increasing rapidly. Everything was still grey, but we could distinguish a portion of the Russian V position in line with the veteran's spandau, and lower down to the left, a motionless grey mass: Hals, Lindberg, and the F.M.

'You, young fellow,' said the veteran, looking at me. 'You'll replace my number-two man. Get over here on my left.'

'Right,' I said, worming my way toward him. A minute

224

later, my nose was pressed against the metal of the F.M.'s magazine.

We could see most of the details of the Russian position a hundred yards ahead of us. From our hillock overlooking the enemy, we glimpsed momentary snatches of pale faces, like faces in a dream. It now seems to me astonishing that the Russians hadn't occupied our little hill. However, there were similar rises in the ground all around us, and they couldn't have occupied all of it. We were staring straight ahead when our leader's hand pointed to our rear left.

'Look!' he said, in almost full voice.

We carefully turned our heads the way he was pointing, and saw the bodies of many men slithering along the ground, breaking through the network of Russian protection. As far as we could see, the ground was covered with creeping figures.

'They're ours!' said the veteran, and a faint smile crossed his face.

'Get ready to fire, if anyone moves in Ivan's hole,' our leader added.

Suddenly, I began to shake uncontrollably — not precisely because of fear, but because at that moment, when our mission was about to be accomplished, all the nervousness and anxiety which I had been able to master until then burst out in violent spasms. I tried shifting my weight, but nothing did any good. I managed to open the magazine and nervously slip the first belt into the breech of the gun, which the veteran held open for me, and left partly open, to prevent the sound of its clicking shut.

Far to our left, the dance had already begun: a dance which would surely have inspired Saint-Saëns, and which lasted for days. A moment later, among the German troops we were watching, someone must have pulled a wire attached to a string of mines. Our immediate surroundings — the Russian position, the bodies of Grumpers and his adversary, our little hill, and all our hearts — were shaken by a series of thunderous explosions. For a moment we thought that the whole mass of creeping soldiers we had seen just the minute before had been blown to pieces. Everywhere among the Hitlerjugend — for it was they who had been crawling toward us — young men were jumping up and trying to rush through

225

the tangles of barbed wire. Hals had just opened fire. The veteran slammed our gun shut and fitted it into the hollow of his shoulder.

'Fire!' shouted the noncom. 'Wipe them out!'

The Russians ran to take their places. The string of 7.7 cartridges slid through my hands with brutal rapidity, while the noise of the gun burst against my eardrums.

I could see what was happening only with the greatest difficulty. The spandau was shuddering and jumping on its legs, and shaking the veteran, who kept trying to steady himself. Its percussive bark put a final touch on the vast din which had broken out. Through the vibrations and smoke, we were able to observe the horrible impact of our projectiles on the lost mass of Red soldiers in the trench in front of us. Day broke over the frenzied scene, and the sky slowly lightened. From far behind us, German artillery was roaring through every tube, pounding the enemy's secondary positions. The Russians, taken by surprise, were attempting a desperate defence, but from every side the Junge Löwen were surging out of the darkness, breaking like waves over their entrenchments and pulverizing both men and matériel. An overwhelming din engulfed the plain, which rang with the sound of thousands of explosions.

Ahead of us, and far to the right, we were bombarding a town of considerable size. Slow spirals of smoke some fifty yards across rolled along the ground from enormous fires. I was feeding a second magazine into our infernal machine, and the veteran continued to pour his projectiles onto the dead and living who were jammed into the advanced Soviet position. Then, through all the noise, we heard the unmistakable rumble of tanks.

'Our Panzers!' shouted the Czech with a demoniac laugh.

Hals left his position and rushed toward us with a leap which made us think he'd been hit. He and Lindberg had run just in time. A second later, a huge tank rolled over the ground they had occupied, crushing the barbed wire beneath its treads. The churned-up earth continued to shake with the explosion of mines, which here and there immobilized a heavy armoured vehicle, or tossed a landser some fifteen yards. The tank, followed by two others, passed very close to us, thrusting toward the enemy position we had already been peppering for several minutes. In no time, it had crossed the trench, which was overflowing with the bodies of Russian soldiers. Then a second and a third tank plunged through the bloody paste, and rolled on, their treads stuck with horrible human remnants. Our noncom gave an involuntary cry of horror at the sight. Soon the young soldiers fresh from the sportive pleasures of the barracks would arrive at this foul reality. We heard a cry of horror, followed by one of victory, as the first assault wave continued its advance. More tanks were pouring out of the woods behind us, crushing the saplings and brush, and driving, almost rearing up on their treads, toward companies of infantry who had to hurry out of the way. If there were any wounded lying on the ground, that was their bad luck.

The first phase of the attack was supposed to occur like a flash of lightning, with nothing permitted to hinder the progress of the tanks. An infantry group had just joined us, and their leader was talking with ours when a tank bore down exactly on our position. Everyone jumped aside. A young soldier ran toward the tank, trying to wave it off with large gestures. But the monster continued unswervingly, like a blind animal, churning up the ground a bare two yards from our hillock. In my haste, my foot caught on the spandau, and I fell full length down the other side of the rise. The huge machine flattened the edge of our protection, and the steel sections of its treads rolled past, horribly close to my haggard eyes.

What happened next? I retain nothing from those terrible minutes except indistinct memories which flash into my mind with sudden brutality, like apparitions, among bursts and scenes and visions that are scarcely imaginable. It is difficult even to try to remember moments during which nothing is considered, foreseen, or understood, when there is nothing under a steel helmet but an astonishingly empty head and a pair of eyes which translate nothing more than would the eyes of an animal facing mortal danger. There is nothing but the rhythm of explosions, more or less distant, more or less violent, and the cries of madmen, to be classified later, according to the outcome of the battle, as the cries of heroes or of murderers. And there are the cries of the wounded, of the agonizingly dying, shrieking as they stare at a part of their body reduced to pulp, the cries of men touched by the shock of battle before everybody else, who run in any and every direction, howling like banshees. There are the tragic, unbelievable visions, which carry from one moment of nausea to another: guts splattered across the rubble and sprayed from one dying man onto another; tightly riveted machines ripped like the belly of a cow which has just been sliced open, flaming and groaning; trees broken into tiny fragments; gaping windows pouring out torrents of billowing dust, dispersing into oblivion all that remains of a comfortable parlour. . . .

And then there are the cries of officers and noncoms, trying to shout across the cataclysm to regroup their sections and companies. That is how we took part in the German advance, being called through the noise and dust, following the clouds churned up by our tanks to the northern outskirts of Belgorod. All resistance was overwhelmed, and once again everything was either German or dead, and a sea of Russian soldiers had drawn back into the limitless confines of their country.

There were thousands of prisoners – including the pro-Germans, who immediately placed in the hands of our indifferent soldiers lists of those we should shoot. There was the park of Russian vehicles hiding two or three thousand enemy soldiers determined to slow our advance, and the spandau, into which the veteran and I continued to feed cartridges, and Hals's spandau, and the one attached to Group 10, decimated and re-formed, firing and laughing as they fired, in vengeance for their fallen comrades. We sent a rain of anti-tank shells onto the park, and listened to the howls of the Russians, who no longer dared to move or surrender or attack, before flames devoured the area, and forced us to retire from their unbearable heat.

Toward noon, the Soviets began to retaliate, and rained a devastating fire on the rising waves of Jungen Löwen. But nothing stopped the young lions, even for a moment, and the burnt-out ruin of Belgorod fell into the hands of their survivors on the second evening.

In a heady state, near delirium, we went on, with almost no rest, to enlarge the wedge our troops had driven into the mass of the Soviet central front: a front of 150,000 men, according to our so-called information services. In fact, closer to 400,000 or 500,000 Russians were jostled back by 60,000 Germans.

By the evening of the third day of continuous battle, during which we had only been able to snatch an occasional half hour of sleep, we were seized by the furious strength of madmen. Our group had lost both the Czech and the sergeant, and as they lay either dead or wounded among the ruins, two grenadiers who had lost their units joined us. We were now split into three groups – including the 11th, in which Olensheim was still alive, and the 17th, which had rejoined us – jointly commanded by a lieutenant. We had been ordered to reduce the pockets of resistance in the ashes of a suburb called Deptréoka, if I remember correctly – enclaves which continued to defend themselves, although they had been left behind by the retreating Soviet forces.

Our faces streaked with dust and filth and sweat stared across the ruined, apocalyptic landscape through which we were advancing, more interested in quiet corners for a few moments of sleep than in Russian strays. Explosions from the forefront of our advance were continuously shaking the air around us, and compressing our weakened lungs. No one spoke, except for an occasional 'Halt!' or 'Achtung!' which threw us down onto the burning ground. We were so exhausted that we stood up only when our fire had subdued the isolated and hopeless resistance from some entrenched hole. Sometimes one or two prisoners might emerge from their hideout with their hands in the air, and each time the same tragedy repeated itself. Kraus killed four of them on the lieutenant's orders; the Sudeten, two; Group 17, nine. Young Lindberg, who had been in a state of panic ever since the beginning of the offensive, and who had been either weeping in terror or laughing in hope, took Kraus's machine gun and shoved two Bolsheviks into a shell hole. The two wretched victims were both a good deal older than the boy, and kept imploring his mercy. We could hear their desperate shouts for a long time. But Lindberg, in a paroxysm of uncontrollable rage, kept firing until they were quiet.

Then there was the bread house, so called because after the massacre we found a few wretched biscuits there, which we devoured, hoping to extract some return for the horrors which the war forced upon us. We were mad with harassment and exhaustion, running on our nerves, which were stretched to the utmost, and which alone made it possible to respond to the endless succession of crises and alerts. We were forbidden to take prisoners until our return trip. We knew that the Russians didn't take any, and although we longed for sleep we knew that we had to stay awake as long as there were any Bolsheviks in our sector. It was either them or us – which is why my friend Hals and I threw grenades into the bread house, at some Russians who were trying to wave a white flag.

When we reached the end of our sweep, we collapsed at the bottom of a large crater, and stared at each other for a long time in dazed silence. None of us could speak. Our uniforms were unbuttoned, torn, and so permeated with dust they were the colour of the ground. The air still roared and shook and smelled of burning. Four more of our men had been killed, and we were dragging along five or six wounded, one of them Olensheim. There were about twenty of us huddled in that huge hole, trying to put our thoughts into some kind of order. But our stupefied eyes continued to wander vacantly over the burned landscape, and our heads remained empty.

The radio announced that our Belgorod offensive had been crowned with success, and marked the beginning of our further progress eastward.

By the fourth or fifth evening, we had gone through Belgorod without even knowing it. Our assault troops were catching their breath, and numberless ranks of infantry were sleeping on the great battered plain. We were soon loaded onto a truck and driven to a key position. I didn't understand why the ruined hamlet where we were put down was considered strategic, but grasped that this was one of the places from which the next phase of our offensive would be launched. The gently rolling landscape of fat-bellied orchards and willow-bordered streams and irrigation canals reminded me somehow of Normandy; it was occupied either by lines of defence or by rallying points for our assault troops.

We began to organize our position among the poor, half-ruined houses of the hamlet. Our first job was to get rid of some thirty Bolshevik corpses scattered through the rubble. We dumped them into a small garden, which must once have ьeen cultivated. The day was hot and heavy. A greasy sun threw sharp shadows, and made us squint in the harsh light, which emphasized every hollow in our exhausted faces. The same light poured down onto the faces of the dead Russians, whose fixed eyes were opened inordinately wide. Looking at them, and thinking about us all, made my stomach turn over.

'Isn't it funny,' the Sudeten remarked calmly, 'how quickly a fellow's beard grows when he's dead? Look at this one.' He turned over a body with his foot. The man's tunic was torn by seven or eight bloody holes. 'He probably shaved yesterday, just before he was killed. And look at him now. He's got a beard on him that would have taken him at least a week otherwise.'

'See this one,' laughed another fellow, who was clearing out a building which had been hit by a heavy mortar shell. He was dragging a Russian soldier whose head had been blown off.

'You'd do better to go and shave yourself, if you want anyone to recognize you when it's your turn tomorrow. You give me a pain with your idiotic remarks. Anyone would think that's the first stiff you've ever seen.' The veteran sat down on a heap of rubble, and opened his mess tin.

We found a cellar which made a perfect defence point and moved into it with our two machine guns. We dug out the air vent which had been blocked by the collapse of the house, and even enlarged it, stopping work for a moment to watch a flight of Stukas pass overhead. Somewhere, not too far away, Ivan must have been drenched by a rain of bombs.

Hals had made a hole in the masonry walls, and was estimating the firing possibilities. Lindberg was almost jubilant to be setting up this precarious shelter. Everything which now seemed to be working to our advantage stirred him to a strange excitement, in contrast to the helpless fear in the flaming alleys of Belgorod, which had reduced him to whining and pissing in his pants. Three yards away, the veteran and I were shoving in supports to brace the enlarged air vent, which, at best, seemed a shaky proposition. Whenever we moved, our helmets scraped against the low ceiling. Behind us, Kraus and two other grenadiers were removing

231

the fallen stones and rubble which littered the floor. One of them picked up an empty bottle, and with a civilian reflex, stood it against the wall to wait for the harvest.

As I've said, we had lost our noncom, and the veteran, who was an obergefreiter, was now commanding our group. However, we were still under the orders of a fat stabsfeldwebel, who directed all three groups, and who was killed two days later. The bastard checked our work with all the airs of a superior officer, forcing us to check this detail or that, unaware that he had only forty-eight hours left. We spent the day waiting and watching companies of sweating troops march by, against a continuous background of heavy explosions, and a variety of other noises.

It was in precisely these moments that everything became intensely painful. As we slowly regained our spirits, we began to grasp what had happened to us. It suddenly struck us that our noncom, and Grumpers, and the Czech, and the wounded boy abandoned to his fate were in fact no longer with us. We tried to blot out the memory of the Russian trench we had machine gunned, and the tanks driving heavily over that moving mass of human flesh, and Deptréoka, with its piles of Bolshevik corpses, and the hammering of enemy artillery in the narrow streets crammed with Hitlerjugend – all the appalling, inexplicable details. We suddenly felt gripped by something horrible, which made our skins crawl and our hair stand on end. For me, these memories produced a loss of physical sensation, almost as if my personality had split. I knew that I was actually incapable of such experiences – not because I was superior to other people, but because I knew that such things don't happen to young men who have led normal lives more or less like other people's.

The three grenadiers stood talking beside the staircase. The veteran, alone by the air vent, through which floods of sunlight poured into the room, was going through his pockets, spreading out their wretched contents on a flat stone. Hals had curled his big body onto a rough bench and was lying silent, while Lindberg and the Sudeten were staring through holes in the wall, with their minds clearly far away. I went over to Hals and lay down beside him. We stared at each other for a moment, unable to speak.

'What the hell are we doing here?' Hals said finally. His face had grown noticeably harder since Bialystok.

I limited myself to a gesture of ignorance.

'I'd like to sleep, but I can't,' he said.

'Yes. It's just as hot in here as outside.'

'Let's go out anyway.'

We went out and took a few steps. The light was blinding.

'Maybe there's some cold water over there,' I said, pointing to an orchard divided by a thin stream.

'I'm not thirsty — not hungry either,' Hals answered to my great surprise. I was used to his enormous appetite.

'Are you sick?'

'No. I just feel like vomiting. I'm so tired — and those fellows over there don't help either.' He nodded at the thirty putrefying corpses in the little garden.

'That's always how it is, with fellows who won't make any more trouble,' I answered, in a tone which still surprises me.

'Ours were picked up before we got here,' Hals continued. 'There's some freshly turned ground just inside the village. I don't know how many they were able to stuff in there. Do you know how many we've had killed already?'

We were silent for a moment.

'We'll probably be relieved soon, Hals.'

'Yes,' he said. 'I hope so. We really were shits to kill those Popovs at the bread house.'

He was clearly desperately troubled by the same things that troubled me.

'The bread house is how it is, and all there is,' I answered.

I could still feel the cartridges running through my hands, see them entering the spandau, and see the bluish smoking metal of the barrel and the sparks that flew out each time the gun fired, painfully striking my hands and face, and hear the shrieks penetrating the infernal din, and the cries for help: 'Pomoshch! Pomoshch!' Something hideous had entered our spirits, to remain and haunt us forever.

It was broad daylight, but we had no idea what time it was. Was it still morning? Was it afternoon? It didn't matter: everyone ate and drank when he could, slept when he could, and tried to think whenever he could take off his helmet. It's strange how much a helmet interferes with thought. . . .

It was still daylight when an enemy barrage ripped into the

orchards and the advancing troops, who had stopped only a short distance from us. We dived into our cellar shelter, and stared anxiously at the ceiling, which rained down plaster with each explosion.

'We'll have to shore it up too,' said the veteran. 'If anything lands too close, the whole thing will come down on our heads.'

The bombardment lasted for at least two hours. A few Soviet shells fell right beside us, but they were clearly intended for the assault troops. Our big guns answered theirs, and all other sounds were drowned in the noise of artillery. Shells from our howitzer were shooting right over our ruin, contributing as much to the collapse of our ceiling as the Russian shells which sometimes burst less than thirty yards away.

During the bombardment, we were all gripped by an extreme and exhausting tension. Some of us attempted predictions, only to be contradicted by events a few moments later. The veteran smoked nervously, continuously begging us to shut up. Kraus had drawn apart and sat muttering in a corner. Perhaps he was praying.

In the evening, one of the counter-attack units visited us, and installed an anti-tank gun nearby. A colonel came by a little later and tested the new supports we had put in to prevent any further collapse of the roof.

'Well done,' he said. He made the rounds of our little group, offering each man a cigarette. Then he rejoined his unit, which was part of the Gross Deutschland, a little closer to the front.

It grew dark. Through the tattered silhouettes of the remaining orchard trees, the horizon glowed red with fire. The battle was not yet over, and the extreme tension it generated was almost unbearable. We had to take turns standing guard outside, and no one had a good night's sleep. We were rounded up well before dawn and forced to abandon our well-organized hole and proceed further into Soviet territory. The German advance had not been stopped.

During our advance, we crossed a frightful slaughtering ground of Hitlerjugend, mixed into the dirt by the bombardment of the day before. Each step made us realize with fresh horror what could become of our miserable flesh.

'Somebody should have buried all this mincemeat so we

wouldn't have to look at it,' Hals grumbled. Everyone laughed, as if he'd just said something funny.

We crossed a piece of ground so heavily pitted with shell holes it was hard to imagine that anyone who'd been on it could have survived, and an open-air hospital behind an embankment from which the shrieks and groans came so thick and fast it sounded like a scalding room for pigs. We were staggered by what we saw. I thought I would faint. Lindberg was crying with terror. We crossed the enclosure with our eyes fixed on the sky, seeing as if in a dream young men howling with pain, with crushed forearms or gaping abdominal wounds, staring with incomprehension at their own guts puffing out the piece of cloth which had been hastily flung over them.

Immediately beyond the hospital, we had to wade across a canal. The cool water which rose over our waists made us feel much better. On the far bank, the springing turf was strewn with Russian bodies. A Soviet tank, twisted and blackened by fire, stood beside a big gun and the shattered bodies of its operators. To our left, in the northeast, the battle continued more fiercely than ever. We thought we heard a groan from one of the Russian gunners, and went over to a man smeared with blood, who was leaning, gasping, against one of the wheels of the gun carriage. One of our men uncorked his drinking bottle, and lifted the head of the dying man. The Russian stared at us through enormous eyes, widened by terror or shock. He cried out, and then his head fell back, thudding against the metal of the wheel. He was dead.

We continued across a series of rolling wooded hills, where our front-line troops were regrouping and catching a moment's rest in the shade of the trees. Many men wore bandages, whose whiteness stood out sharply against their grey, dusty faces. We were rapidly regrouped, called out, and sent to precise locations.

The two grenadiers who had joined us were sent some-where else, while our 8th group was completed by a new pair of strays. Unfortunately, the stabsfeldwebel whom I've mentioned before, and who had only one more day of life, was made the leader of our group. We were swiftly attached to an armoured section which transported us on the backs of their machines to the edge of an enormous plateau, which seemed to stretch into infinity. . . .

We jumped off the backs of the moving Panzers to join a group of soldiers lying flat at the bottom of a shallow trench. Already, several 50-mm. rounds fired directly at us by enemy artillery had brought it home to us that we were in the front line. The tanks turned back, and vanished under the trees some fifty yards behind us.

We plunged down beside the fellows who were already there, who seemed none too cheerful. The Russian fire followed the tanks, and was lost in the brush. Our idiot stabsfeldwebel was already feeling uneasy about the distractions of the neighbourhood, and was discussing them with a very young lieutenant. Then the young officer waved to his men, who followed him toward the woods, running, and bent nearly double. The Popovs, who must have been watching, sent over five or six rounds aimed directly at them. Some of their bullets landed very close to us.

Once again we were alone – nine of us in a hole, facing the Soviet lines. The sun was directly above us.

'Get cracking on that hole, now,' shouted the stabs in a perfect parade-ground voice.

We began to turn over the dusty Ukrainian soil with our short pick-spades. We barely had time to speak. The heat of the sun was crushing, and increased our lassitude.

'We'll probably die of exhaustion before anything else has a chance to get us,' Hals said. 'I give up.'

'My head is killing me,' I answered with a sigh.

But our bastard stabs kept after us, staring anxiously out over the grassless plain, which stretched into the distance as far as the eye could see.

We had just finished setting up our two spandaus when the noise of tanks rolling over the brush behind us made us shudder. On that magnificent summer afternoon, German tanks were once again leaving the shade and driving toward the east. From behind them, entire regiments, bent double, passed us and vanished into a wall of dust, which hid them from view. About five minutes later, the Russians began a bombardment of unprecedented ferocity. Everything became opaque, and the sun vanished from our eyes, which had become enormous with fright. The storm cloud of dust was relieved only by continuous red flashes shooting up against the darker masses of trees eighty or a hundred yards away. The earth shook harder than I'd yet felt it do, and the brush behind us burst into flame. Screams of fear froze in our constricted throats. Everything seemed displaced. The air all around us was filled with flying clods, mixed with fragments of metal and fire. Kraus and one of the newcomers were buried in a landslide before they even knew what had happened to them. I threw myself into the deepest corner of our hole, and stared uncomprehendingly at the stream of earth flooding towards our shelter. I began to howl like a madman. Hals pressed his filthy head against mine, and our helmets clattered together like two mess tins. Hals's face was transfigured by terror.

'It's ... the ... end,' he gasped, his words broken up by the explosions, which took away our breath. Overwhelmed by horror, I could only agree.

Suddenly, a human figure crashed into our hole. We both trembled with desperation and fright. Then a second human shape joined the first, in a great leap. This time our huge eyes took in that these were two of our own men. One of the newcomers shouted to us through his frantic gasps for breath: 'My whole company was wiped out! It's terrible!'

He carefully lifted his head just over the edge of the embankment as a series of explosions began to rip through the air beside us. His helmet and a piece of his head were sent flying, and he fell backward, with a horrifying cry. His shattered skull crashed into Hals's hands, and we were splattered with blood and fragments of flesh. Hals threw the revolting cadaver as far as he could, and buried his face in the dirt. The explosions had become so violent that we felt the ground all around us must be shifting. Outside our hole, on the torn and ravaged plain, we could hear an engine roaring out of control. Then there was another explosion, more violent than all the others, and an enormous flash of light swept the edge of our trench. Our two spandaus fell back on top of us in a wave of loose earth. Those who weren't struck dumb with fright howled like madmen:

'We're finished!'

'Mama! It's me!'

'No, no!'

'We'll be buried alive!'

'Help!'

But nothing we said could put an end to this hell, which seemed to go on forever. . . .

About thirty soldiers on the run plunged in with us. We were kicked and shoved without mercy, as everyone tried to burrow down as deeply as possible. Whoever was left on top was finished. The earth all around us was pocked with thousands of shell holes, and from each of these we could hear the sounds of fleeing soldiers looking for refuge. But the cruel Russian soil was torn by fresh salvoes, and those who thought they'd been saved continued to die.

We heard the roar of airplane engines, and cheers for the Luftwaffe rose from thousands of desperate men. The bombardment continued for a few more seconds, and then decreased dramatically. The officers who were still alive blew their whistles for retreat, and the men packed into our hole poured out like rabbits chased by a ferret. We were about to follow when our stabsfeldwebel, who hadn't yet been killed, shouted loudly after us: 'Not you! We're here to stop a Russian counter-offensive. Get your guns ready to fire.'

Six Hitlerjugend cadavers were lying on the bottom of the trench, which had completely changed shape. To the left, one end was caved in, and Kraus's boots were sticking out of two cubic yards of grey dirt. The other grenadier had been completely buried.

With the help of the veteran, whose face was streaming with blood, we were able to get the F.M. back into place. The plain, which had been altered beyond recognition, was scarred with holes and lumps, as if giant moles had been at work. Wherever one looked, there were smoke and flame and a scattering of motionless bodies. In the distance, through spirals of dust and smoke, we could see geysers of fire from the bombs which our ME-110's were dropping on the Russian artillery. It looked as though we'd hit a couple of their ammunition dumps. The shock waves from those explosions engulfed the earth and sky in an extraordinary intensity of light and displacement of air.

'Those bastards!' shouted the ober. 'Now they're getting what they deserve.'

Our ME-110's turned back to the west, and the Russian

artillery opened up again. They were concentrating particularly on the Panzers, which were retreating in disorder, with at least half their number destroyed.

Although my left arm had almost been broken when the gang of panic-stricken soldiers jumped into the trench on top of us, I had felt nothing at the time. Now, it was beginning to cause me violent pain, which hovered beside me like a supplementary presence; but I was too busy to pay much attention to it. The bombardment was continuing to the north and to the south, and then passed over us once again, intensifying and spreading its complement of pain and terror. Our group of stupefied men could breathe only with difficulty, like an invalid who gets up after a long illness to find he has lost both strength and wind. We were all unable to speak: there was nothing to say then about the hours we had just lived through, and there is no way of describing them now with the vehemence and force they require. Nothing remains for those who have survived such an experience but a sense of uncontrollable imbalance, and a sharp, sordid anguish which reaches across the years unblunted and undiminished, even for someone like me, who is attempting to translate it into words, although a precise and appropriate vocabulary remains elusive.

Abandoned by a God in whom many of us believed, we lay prostrate and dazed in our demi-tomb. From time to time, one of us would look over the parapet to stare across the dusty plain into the east, from which death might bear down on us at any moment. We felt like lost souls, who had forgotten that men are made for something else, that time exists, and hope, and sentiments other than anguish; that friendship can be more than ephemeral, that love can sometimes occur, that the earth can be productive, and used for something other than burying the dead.

We were madmen, gesturing and moving without thought or hope. Our legs and arms were numbed by hours of crowding and shoving against neighbours, living or dead, who were taking up too much room. The stabsfeldwebel repeated mechanically that we must maintain our position, but each new series of explosions sent us plunging to the bottom of our hole.

Night fell before we realized day had ended, and with darkness our terror returned. Lindberg, whose nervous condition was alarming, had collapsed into a kind of stupor which, for the moment, made him oblivious of hell. The Sudeten was almost as badly affected. He had begun to tremble, like someone in a fit, and to vomit uncontrollably. Madness had invaded our group, and was gaining ground rapidly. In a state of semi-delirium, I saw a giant, whom I had known in another time as Hals, leap to his machine gun and fire at the sky, which continued to pour down its rain of flame and metal. I also saw the stabs, seized by a kind of dementia, beat the ground with his clenched fist, and then deliberately turn on the surviving grenadier, and pound him. The grenadier, who had seemed to be functioning normally until that moment, simply stared at the stabs, like someone in a trance, and then burst into tears. I could hear the millions of echoes ringing through the ground with an almost infernal precision, and I felt that I was going to faint. I stood up, totally unaware of what I was doing, shouting curses and obscenities at the sky. I had reached the edge of the abyss, like all my companions, and like them I was nearly finished. My rage burned like a straw fire, consuming my last reserves of strength, my head began to swim, and I fell forward against the edge of the trench. My mouth, which was wide open, filled with dirt. I began to vomit, and knew I wouldn't be able to stop until I had emptied myself completely. I waded through my vomit with my trembling hands stretched out in front of me, reaching for the support of the crumbling parapet. A white flash, like an element of a nightmare, lit the darkness which had enveloped us, and kept me from losing consciousness. I slowly raised my eyes above the level of the trench wall, to follow the Russian flare as it fell to the ground. During those moments I felt strangely certain that I was at home, that none of my surroundings existed, and that the descending flare was really a falling star.

I remained in my stupor for a long time, while the explosions continued to compress my lungs. Some men stood in one position for hours, asleep on their feet with their eyes wide open. Finally, toward midnight, everything fell silent. However, no one moved. We all felt so weakened that movement was beyond the limit of possibility. Finally the veteran was able to make us pay attention: 'Don't go to sleep, boys – this is when Ivan will attack.'

The stabs stared at him with troubled eyes. He stood up and leaned against the trench wall. A few minutes later, his head fell forward, and he was lost in paralytic sleep.

The veteran continued to exhort us, but the six of us who were left received his pleas with a silence as absolute as the silence of our eight corpses. Sleep was crushing us, as the guns had not quite managed to do. If the Russians had chosen that moment to attack, they would undoubtedly have saved a great many lives on their side. Our advance interception positions were manned only by sleepers and dead men. Although there must have been more noise from the big guns, and more flares, our ears picked up nothing for the next four hours.

The stabsfeldwebel was the first to wake. When we opened our eyes, we found him leaning over the Sudeten, who was sleeping beside him. The Sudeten had just cried out, which must have waked the stabs. We felt so ground down by exhaustion that every gesture made us grimace with pain. The sky once again was turning pink, and we could already see the chaos scattered across the plain. Everything was calm, and we couldn't hear a sound. We stared out at the enormous space surrounding us. The horizon was almost a perfect circle, losing its line only in the hedge of woods to the north and to the south. We got out some tins of food, and tried to eat and talk a little.

'That's right — you should build up your strength,' joked the stabs, who was living through his last moments. 'I'd be surprised if this quiet lasted.'

'Maybe it will, though,' someone else said. 'That show yesterday must have done in quite a few fellows. We might even get two or three days like this.'

'I doubt it,' said the stabs. 'The Führer has given the order to march east, and nothing can stop our troops now. The offensive will begin as soon as the sun is up.'

'Do you really think so?' asked Lindberg, excited as usual when something seemed to be going our way. 'Will our troops be able to knock out those damned Russian guns?'

'If it starts up again,' Hals muttered to me, 'I'll go right off my rocker.'

'Or be killed,' I answered. 'We can't expect the same luck we had yesterday.'

241

Hals stared at me as he chewed. The stabs, Lindberg, and the surviving grenadier were still talking, while Hals and I traded pessimistic predictions. Only the veteran went on eating in silence, his eyes, red from sleeplessness, fixed on the morning star.

'You two,' said the stabs pointing to Hals and me, 'you keep your eyes open for another couple of hours, while the rest of us try to get some sleep. But first we have to get rid of these stiffs.' He waved at the eight mutilated corpses which were already beginning to swarm with big blue flies.

We watched the dead being stripped of their tags: for once we were not playing undertaker's assistant, and guard duty seemed like a stroke of luck. The same curses and exclamations seemed to occur to survivors every time they had to deal with the remains of their slaughtered comrades.

'Fuck it . . . this fellow weighs a ton.'

'My God . . . he would have been better off if they'd finished him right away. Look at that!'

And then the metallic click as the identity tags slid off.

'Pach . . . he's swimming in shit!'

We looked away with indifference; death had lost any dramatic importance for us; we were used to it. While the others were shifting the carrion, Hals and I continued to discuss our chances of survival.

'Hands and feet hurt more than other places, but aren't really serious.'

'I wonder what happened to Olensheim.'

'Broken arm, I heard.'

'How's your arm?'

'My shoulder hurts like hell.'

Behind our backs the others were hard at their filthy work.

'Heinz Veller, 1925, unmarried . . . poor fellow.'

'Let's see your shoulder,' Hals said. 'Maybe you're badly hurt.'

'I don't think so . . . just a bruise,' I said, unfastening my harness.

I was about to pull the cloth away from my shoulder when a roll of thunder shook the pure morning air. A second later, a hail of Russian shells fell all around us, and once again we collapsed in terror at the bottom of our hole.

'My God,' someone shouted. 'It's starting again.'

Hals was moving closer to me, through a shower of flying clods. He had just opened his mouth to say something when a violent explosion very near us drowned the sound of his voice.

'We'll never be able to hold on,' he said. 'We'd better get out.'

A shell fell so close to us that the grey earth wall of the trench glowed red in the light of its flames. A thick cloud of smoke enveloped us, and cubic yards of earth fell into our holes. We could hear cries of fright, and then the voice of the stabs: 'Anyone hit?'

'God!' shouted the veteran through a spasm of coughing. 'Where the hell's our artillery?'

Lindberg had begun to tremble again. Then the Russian fire stopped. The veteran peered carefully out, and after him our seven heads rose above the rampart. We stared at the plain, which was still scattered with trailing clouds of dust. In the distance, besides the wood, someone was howling.

'They must be running short of shells,' said the stabs, grinning. 'Otherwise, they wouldn't have stopped so quickly.'

The veteran looked at him with his habitual resigned expression. 'I was just thinking the same thing about our artillery, stabsfeldwebel. I was wondering why they weren't firing.'

'We're preparing an offensive — that's why our side is quiet. Soon we'll see our tanks. . . .'

The veteran stared at the horizon.

'I'm sure,' the stabs went on, 'that our offensive will begin again, any minute now. . . .'

But we were watching the veteran: his eyes were growing wider and wider, and so was his mouth, which seemed ready to howl. The stabs had shut up too; we all followed the direction of our gunner's eyes.

In the remote distance, a thin black line stretched from one end of the horizon to the other, and was moving toward us like a wave rolling toward the shore. We stood watching for a moment: the line was dense, and somehow unreal. Then the veteran shouted in a voice which paralyzed us with fear: 'It's the Siberians! They're here! There must be at least a million of them!'

He gripped the butt of his F.M., and a demented laugh

243

burst through his clenched teeth. In the distance, a confused tumult of thousands of roaring voices swelled like a hurricane wind.

'Every man to his post,' shouted the stabs, whose eyes remained fixed, as if hypnotized, on the irresistible Soviet tide.

We had all picked up our guns like automatons, and braced our elbows against the parapet. Hals was trembling like a leaf, and Lindberg, his number-two man, seemed unable to handle the belt of 7.7s.

'Get closer to me,' Hals shouted. 'Get closer or I'll kill you!'

Lindberg's face was quivering, as if he were about to burst into tears. The veteran wasn't shouting any more. His gun was on the crook of his shoulder, his finger was on the trigger, and his teeth were clenched tightly enough to break. The Soviet war cry was growing continuously louder and more distinct. It was like a long shout, muffled by its great volume.

We remained frozen by the danger, unable to judge its magnitude. Our stupor was too great; we were like paralyzed mice facing a snake. Then Lindberg broke down. He began to cry and shout, and left his post, throwing himself down on the trench floor. 'They'll kill us! They'll kill us! We'll all be killed!'

'Get up!' shouted the stabs. 'Get back to your post or I'll shoot you right now!'

He dragged him to his feet, but Lindberg had gone as limp as a rag, and was streaming with tears.

'You bastard!' shouted Hals. 'Get killed then. I'll take care of this damned thing myself.'

By now we could hear the Russian cries distinctly – a huge, continuous Ourrah!

'Maman!' I thought to myself. 'Maman!'

'Ourrah! Ourrah pobieda!' muttered the veteran. 'Just get a little closer.'

The human wave was now about four hundred yards from us. We could also hear the throb of engines, and see three planes, high in the brightening sky.

'Planes,' said the Sudeten. But we'd all noticed them already.

244

Our anxious eyes left the Russian horde for a moment. The airplane engines were screaming, as the planes dived down at top speed.

'Messerschmitts!' shouted the stabs. 'What guts!'

'Hurrah!' we all shouted. 'Hurrah for the Luftwaffe!'

The three planes were strung out over the huge Russian thrust, spraying it with death. This seemed to be a signal for our mortars to open fire. They were hidden in the brush, and had lengthened their range. The spandaus which had survived the bombardment began to fire too, while the planes dived down, stimulating our troops to a feverish pitch of courage. I could feel the F.M. cartridges running through my hand at a dizzying speed. One clip was emptied, and we started another. Some of the big Wehrmacht guns had also opened fire, which must have had a lethal effect on the ranks of Bolsheviks, who were charging as in the days of Napoleon.

However, the human tide continued to roll toward us, making our scalps crawl. Only the weight of our helmets kept our filthy hair from standing straight up on our heads, although the idea of death itself no longer terrified us. My eyes remained fixed on the smoking metal of the F.M. in the steady hands of the veteran. The trembling belt of cartridges moved forward into the machine, shaken as if by a titanic frenzy.

'Prepare the grenades!' shouted the stabs, who was firing with his Luger braced on his left arm.

'It's useless!' shouted the veteran even louder. 'We haven't got enough ammunition. We can't stop them. Order the retreat, stabsfeldwebel, while there's still time.'

Our frantic eyes moved from the lips of one man to the other. The Russian war cry, 'Ourrah pobieda!' roared closer and closer. The men were firing from their hips as they ran, and the air shook with the rushing flight of their bullets.

'You're crazy,' answered the stabs. 'No one can get away from here, and our boys should be coming any minute now — so keep firing, for the love of God.'

But the veteran had already loaded his F.M. and picked up the last magazine.

'You're the one who's crazy. "Any minute now" is too late. But you go ahead and die right here, if that's what you want.'

'No! No!' shouted the stabs.

The veteran had just jumped from the trench and was galloping toward the woods, bent over as far as he could, and calling to us as he ran. We grabbed our guns in frantic haste.

'Run!' shouted the Sudeten.

We all followed him. For a moment we were almost mad with terror, racing toward the shattered trees with our lungs on fire, while Russian bullets whistled through the air all around us. There were still seven of us, which seemed astonishing. The stabs had finally followed everyone else, but was still protesting and shouting: 'Cowards! Shoot back! You'll all be killed! Put up a fight!'

But we continued to run for the trees.

'Halt!' the stabs shouted. 'Halt, you cowards!'

We had just caught up with the veteran, who had stopped for a minute behind what was left of a tree. I was right beside him.

'You bastard!' the stabs yelled. 'I'll report you for this!'

'I know,' the veteran said gasping, almost laughing. 'But I'd take one of our firing squads over Ivan's bayonet any day.'

We began to run again, climbing a pock-marked hillside stripped of its brush.

'Ai-ee,' howled the veteran, as Russian bullets struck the earth bank with hollow thuds.

'Hurry, stabs! Quick!' he shouted to our leader, who was still climbing the bank and would never complete his ascent. 'You'll see. We'll stop them when we get to our lines.'

The veteran had barely finished speaking when our noncom suddenly cried out and stood up, flapping his arms in an almost comical way. Then he ran back down the little hill and collapsed, with his face pressed into the ground.

'Damned stabs,' said the veteran. 'I told him to hurry up.'

Stripped of a leader for the second time, our 8th group continued its flight through the brush, staggering under our load of weapons.

'Let's stop for a second,' I said. 'I can't breathe.'

Hals had dropped to the ground, and was trying to regain control of his breath. Behind us we could hear guns popping, and an occasional German projectile falling toward the east.

'As if that would stop Ivan!' said the veteran. 'Hasn't

anybody told them, for the love of God? Keep moving boys. This is no time to take it easy.'

'Thank God you were there,' Hals said to the veteran, 'or we'd all be dead by now.'

'Damn right. Now beat it.'

We began to run again, despite the exhaustion which prevented us from grasping the critical importance of every step. Three other landser joined us.

'You really scared us,' one of them said. 'We thought you were Bolsheviks.'

We came to a small clearing, which we could see at a glance was not a natural glade but the site of one of our munitions dumps which must have been hit the day before by a Russian shell. We found a few fragments of a Pak, but everything else had been burned. A blackened corpse was still tangled in the branches of a fallen tree, some four yards above the ground. Suddenly we were surrounded by a full company of soldiers, ready to attack. A tall lieutenant ran to meet us.

'Sergeant?' he said, without wasting a moment.

'Killed,' answered the veteran, pulling himself approximately to attention.

'Damn!' said the officer. 'Where've you come from? What company do you belong to?'

'Eighth Group, 5th Company: interception group of the Gross Deutschland Division, Herr Leutnant.'

'Twenty-first Group, 3rd Company,' added the three fellows who'd just joined us. 'We're the only survivors.'

The officer looked at us, but said nothing. There was a continuous rumble of guns, and from time to time the shouts of the Siberians.

'Where's the enemy?' asked the lieutenant.

'In front of you, Herr Leutnant, everywhere. They just poured onto the plain; there must be several hundred thousand, anyway.'

'Keep going back. We're not part of the Gross Deutschland. Reattach when you run into one of your own regiments.'

We didn't wait for him to repeat himself, but plunged into the brush once again, while the officer turned back to his troops, shouting his orders. We passed many other groups

ready for the slaughter, finally arriving at the hamlet where
we had organized the defence post in the cellar a short time
before. We stopped because a unit from our division had
settled in there, but no one knew anything about the 5th
Company. We were bombarded with questions, first by
officers and then by anxious soldiers, but we were also
allowed a few minutes' rest in the shadow of a ruined house,
and were brought something to drink. Everywhere, harassed
soldiers were digging in, constructing defensive fortifications,
camouflaging, checking over what had already been done.
Toward noon, we could hear the battle approaching. A salvo
from the Russian artillery made us run for the cellar we
already knew, where we saw a fat soldier, a Gross Deutschland veteran, dancing and singing as the earth and air shook
with explosions. His companions paid no attention to him.

'He's off his rocker,' Hals said.

'He was that way already when we got here,' someone else
explained.

Pretty soon, we too paid no more attention to the fat
lunatic who was trying to execute a French cancan.

'He's too much,' Hals muttered.

But the madman went right on waving his arms.

In the afternoon, five or six tanks went to meet the
Russians, with several groups of grenadiers right behind
them. In the distance we could hear fighting, which seemed to
go on for about an hour. Then we saw the grenadiers coming
back, surrounded by a thick swarm of fleeing soldiers. The
woods beyond the orchards were red with fire. Scattered
shots were falling all around the gasping soldiers, who were
dragging their wounded comrades with them.

We realized that in a short time we would again be on the
front line. The battle was drawing continuously closer, with
its rumbling explosions and loud bursts of sound, and we felt
ourselves gripped once again by the essential, inescapable
anguish of the front. The counter-attacks of the regiments
whose positions we had crossed had been swamped, like our
tanks, by the irresistible Soviet flood, for whom the most
enormous losses seemed immaterial.

The hamlet had become an important strategic point,
jammed with machine guns, mortars, and even an anti-tank
gun – which no doubt was the reason for the hell we suffered

during the next thirty-six hours. Some sixty yards ahead of us, two holes had been fitted out to hide two spandaus, just in front of the ones manned by the veteran and Hals, which we had re-installed in our position of the day before. To our right, protected by the ruins, a big geschnauz had been set up and was ready to fire, surrounded by some fifty other infantry weapons — rifles, machine guns, and grenade throwers — hidden in the ruins of four or five wooden sheds, or behind piles of wood, or half-collapsed garden fences. A little further along, behind a low wall, some of the soldiers who had fled were being regrouped and set to digging new trenches. To our left, in a trench beside the only structure left more or less intact, a mortar section had set up its position, swelled by numbers of retreating infantry troops, who were reattaching themselves wherever they could. Further to the left and somewhat behind us, above the road which cut through the hamlet, a 50-mm. anti-tank gun protected by earth built up into something like a bunker was aimed toward the orchards, and behind it, somewhat lower down, a radio truck had parked beside the tractor for the gun. We had watched the truck arrive while we were resting.

An endless stream of orders was pouring from our basement shelter. Officers were regrouping all the fugitives, forming emergency units, and lengthening the line of defence above the hamlet, where there must have been a command post under the authority of a superior officer. From time to time, a bullet fired at random obliged one or another of our groups to dive for the ground. But, compared to what we'd been through the day before, nothing seemed particularly alarming. Only in the distance, about a mile away, violent contact persisted between the last of our retreating troops and advance Russian forces.

The veteran nodded as he listened to the rush above and beyond us.

'Well,' he kept saying, 'they're trying to make another Siegfried line up there. Do they really think that's how they'll stop the Russkis? You, preacher,' he turned to a chaplain, 'ask your kind God to send us some lightning to help us out. We could use it, since there doesn't seem to be any artillery.'

Everyone laughed, including the chaplain, who was less sure of his arguments now that he'd seen God's creatures

249

tearing each other to pieces without the slightest trace of remorse.

A feld looked into the shelter.

'What the hell's a crowd like this doing in here?'

'Interception Group 8, 5th Company, feldwebel,' shouted the veteran, gesturing at the six of us. 'The rest invited themselves in a little while ago.'

'O.K.,' said the sergeant. 'Your group stay put, but everybody else out. There are still plenty of holes outside that need to be filled.'

The other men groaned and got up.

'Feldwebel,' said the veteran. 'Leave us a couple of extra men to help out, in case some of us are killed. We've got to be able to hold this place.'

'O.K.' But, before he was able to point to anyone, the fat lunatic who'd been dancing when we arrived proposed himself.

'I was a machine gunner outside Moscow, Herr Feldwebel, and nobody criticized my performance.'

'You stay then, and that fellow over there. The rest come with me.'

So our group was enlarged by the fat man, whom we'd nicknamed 'French Cancan,' and a thin, gloomy-looking character.

'I beg your pardon,' French Cancan said to us. 'I hope you'll forgive me for encumbering you with my voluminous presence. You must see that digging a foxhole big enough to take me would be an awful lot of work.'

He began to talk, enlarging on anything that came into his head. From time to time, an explosion made him fall silent, blinking his little pig eyes, but as soon as the danger was past he would start talking again, more voluble than ever.

'You can set your mind at ease about the hole we'll dig for you,' said the veteran without a smile. 'A few stones on your beer sack, and that'll be it.'

'I don't drink much beer,' said French Cancan. But Hals interrupted him.

'Things must be pretty rough outside,' he said. 'Look — there are two of our tanks coming back.'

'The hell they're ours,' said the veteran. 'Those are T-34s, and our anti-tank boys had better notice them.'

250

We stared at the two monsters roaring toward us.

'God help us,' said Hals. 'We'll never be able to reach them with these pop guns.' He began to fire the heavy machine gun, and a moment later, the tanks were surrounded by flying clods. We also saw luminous impacts on their turrets, which otherwise seemed to be undamaged. Their long tubes, waving and balancing like elephants' trunks, kept moving forward. An explosion sent us down to the floor, and a Russian shell screamed over us, before exploding somewhere beyond the hamlet. The tanks had just slowed down, and the second one was already shifting into reverse. Our geschnauz was still firing at the two monsters, which were now lurching slowly backward. A second Russian shell hit the left-hand wall of our building, and made the whole cellar shake.

There were several other explosions, but we no longer dared look out. Then an exultant shout from outside gave us a moment of courage, and we saw that the first tank, which had been knocked askew by one of our anti-tank guns, was drawing back, zigzagging on a single tread. It bumped the other tank, which wobbled from the impact, and turned, offering its flank to our geschnauz. A few minutes later, enveloped in a thick cloud of smoke, it joined the other tank, which had completed a half turn, and withdrew. One of them was spouting a thick stream of black smoke, and would certainly not get very far. We could hear all our men cheering.

'You see that, boys!' exclaimed the veteran. 'That's how to make Ivan run!'

We all laughed nervously, except the thin, dark boy.

'Why are you looking so grim?' Hals asked him.

'I'm sick,' the other replied.

'You mean scared,' the Sudeten said. 'But that's something we've all got.'

'Sure I'm scared. But I'm sick too. Every time I have to crap, blood pours out of my ass.'

'You ought to go to the hospital,' said the veteran.

'I've tried, but the major doesn't believe me. What I've got he can't see.'

'Yes. I guess a fellow's better off without an arm, or with a big hole somewhere. That's more spectacular.'

'Try and sleep,' the veteran said. 'For the moment, we can do without you.'

A mess truck had arrived at the hamlet, and anyone who had the nerve to go out could get his mess tin filled. The simple fact that we were being supplied restored some of our confidence. We felt that we hadn't lost all contact with the outside world. However, our panic returned at nightfall.

The fighting flared up again with renewed violence, and in short order the rest of the German troops were retreating from the Russians, who arrived before the last of the landser were able to get through. We could see the oncoming muzhiks everywhere, outlined against the shattered orchards. They were running toward us shouting, but the noise of our guns covered their voices. A horrible massacre had begun.

In the cellar, filled with smoke from our two spandaus, the air was almost unbreathable. The noise of the anti-tank gun, which must have been red-hot, had enlarged and multiplied the cracks in the ceiling, whose plaster fell onto our helmets like rain.

'Let's take turns firing,' the veteran shouted to Hals. 'Otherwise, the guns will melt.'

Lindberg, whose face had turned the colour of his tunic, stuffed some dirt into his ears so that he wouldn't hear any more. A fifth belt of cartridges was running through my torn hands into the red-hot machine, which the veteran kept on firing.

One of the two machine guns in front of us had been knocked out by a grenade. The other was still firing, sweeping across the ranks of Soviet troops, who were piling up in a horrible bottleneck. In spite of their desperate efforts to break through, waves of howling men were dying under our mortar and machine-gun fire. We had no idea what was happening beyond our range of vision. Directly in front of us, however, the enemy was taking a terrible beating.

Two or three fragments of shrapnel had come through the holes in the wall, but miraculously no one had been hit.

Then we heard a heavy rumbling sound, and two or three thousand soldiers ducked their heads a little lower. In front of us, among the living and the dead, hundreds of flares lit the darkness. For a moment, we were terrified. Then someone shouted: 'It's our artillery!'

'Thank God,' said the veteran. 'I'd given up on them. O.K., boys, we'll be able to stick it out — this means the Popovs can't get through.'

The Wehrmacht artillery had finally regrouped, and was pouring down its deadly rain onto the enemy. In the darkness of our smoke-filled hole, our faces lit up with relief.

'That's more like it,' shouted Cancan. 'Look at the pounding those Russkis are taking! That's how it ought to be. Bravo!'

In front of us, we could see the earth flying into the air. Lindberg, who seemed almost mad with excitement, was yelling 'Sieg Heil!' at the top of his lungs. Evidently the Russians were no better at standing up to our guns than we had been to their waves of assault the day before.

The German artillery lengthened its range, and pursued the terrified Russians into the trees beyond the orchards. The 'Ourrah, pobieda!' of the Russians had been replaced by the death rattle of thousands of dying men, which filled the air with a horrible sound. We thought the hamlet had been saved.

'Let's have a drink,' the veteran said. 'We really ought to celebrate. I haven't seen such slaughter the whole time I've been in Russia. We should be able to breathe a little easier now. You,' he said to Lindberg, pulling him from his corner. 'Go find us something, instead of sitting there snivelling.'

It was easy to see that Lindberg had gone mad. He was alternately laughing and crying uncontrollably.

'Get going,' said Hals, who was fed up with him. 'Run and find us something to drink.' He gave him a kick in the seat of his pants.

Lindberg went off, holding his head in his hands. 'Where will I find anything?' he asked.

'That's your worry. At the radio truck — those fellows usually have something hidden — or anywhere else. Just don't come back with empty hands.'

Outside, other soldiers were celebrating the rout of so many Popovs. In our cellar, the level of gaiety rose too. Cancan began to dance again, and we imitated him.

'For a while there I thought we were finished. Thank God the artillery stood by us.'

'"Thank God" is right!' laughed the grenadier who'd been with us for three days.

Tears of joy and relief were streaming from our reddened eyes and running down our blackened faces. The veteran was singing and calling for drink, and we trusted him. He had saved us that morning, and if he was rejoicing, so could we. He knew how the Russians operated, and had already done a lot of fighting. He told us we would have a lull – but he was wrong. The Russian units had grown enormously, and were no longer the crippled divisions which had been shoved out of Poland by the Wehrmacht, and on into Russia for hundreds of miles. Times had changed. Beyond the cellar, beyond the hamlet and its trenches, beyond the thousands of muzhik cadavers and the flaming woods, the Soviet mass was moving into action again, trampling on its own dead and on ours, more powerful than ever, with hundreds upon hundreds of guns wheel to wheel. Soon their cries of victory would drown our laughter.

We had become five pairs of terrified eyes staring into the murky brilliance of the orchard, which was lit by thousands of dazzling, quick-burning fires. The German lines had already been attacked three times by Soviet troops, and three times had repulsed them with extraordinary effort and bravery. Between the assaults the big Russian guns pounded our troops and our artillery, which kept on shelling the enemy as long as it could. For five hours already, our laughter had been stilled, as 'Stalin's organs' hammered at our positions, killing many of our defending troops. The rest were either killed or driven mad by bombs. A few, like our group, who had been lucky enough to dig in solidly, went on firing haphazardly with what they had left. Our ceiling had finally caved in, and the hole in the roof acted like a chimney to let the smoke escape. The tall, thin boy with dysentery had taken Hals's place at the spandau for a few moments. A bullet or fragment of shrapnel had grazed Hal's forehead just below the visor of his helmet, and he was lying down beside three dying men who had been brought into our shelter to spend their last moments in relative tranquillity. Then Hals's gun jammed, and only the veteran was left firing, stiff with exhaustion, helped by Cancan, the Sudeten, and me.

We felt a crushing sense of despair when Russian rockets erected a wall of white fire over our mortar trench. The geschnauz had been dismantled, and the anti-tank gunners had given up long since. Only a few spandaus supported by light infantry guns prevented the howling mob from taking the village. We were threatened with being overrun or surrounded any minute.

'I guess we'll have to die now,' said the veteran. 'Too bad for us, but I don't see any other solution.'

From time to time, in the light of the flares, we could see the nest of machine gunners in front of us, heroically fighting on.

The Russians pressed their attack, bringing on their tanks as soon as it began to grow light, and death to anyone who remained upright. A shell destroyed what was left of our shelter, and sent us all rolling along the floor. Our cries of distress were mingled with the screams of the two machine gunners and then the shouts of revenge from the Russian tank crew as it drove over the hole, grinding the remains of the two gunners into that hateful soil.

Hals stood for a moment, fascinated by the spectacle. He was the only one of us who had remained on his feet, and the only one who could see what was happening. He told us later that the treads worked over the hole for a long time, and that as they manipulated their machine the Russian crew kept shouting, 'Kaputt, soldat Germanski! Kaputt!'

We managed to get out about ten minutes before the Russians arrived. There was no longer any question in our minds: the rest of our forces had abandoned us. God knows how we managed to drag ourselves through the dead and the chaos and the lights of the flares. Our heads were filled with the sound of continuous explosions; it was impossible even to imagine silence. Hals was walking behind me, his hands red with blood from a wound in his neck. Lindberg, who had finally fallen silent, was staggering just ahead of us. The veteran was a short way back, shouting imprecations against the war, our artillery, and the Russians. The fat lunatic was beside me, letting off an endless stream of incomprehensible muttering. As the noise of battle grew louder, and the sky brighter, we forced ourselves into a run.

'We're finished, Sajer,' Hals shouted. 'We're not going to make it.'

I began to tremble and to cry with fright. My head hurt almost beyond bearing, aching with the noise of explosions and fusillades. We kept falling, standing up again, and running on, like automatons. Suddenly, Cancan cried out. I turned my head to look at him through my exhausted eyes, and it seemed as if I were dreaming. I looked at him without feeling, as I moved one foot in front of the other mechanically and with difficulty.

'Don't let me fall,' said Cancan imploringly.

His hands were clutching his belly, holding in something foul, like the offal on the floors of slaughterhouses.

'How can you go on like that?' I asked him, only half aware of what I was saying.

Suddenly he cried out again, and doubled over onto himself.

'Come on,' said the Sudeten in a thick voice like a drunkard's. 'There's nothing we can do for him.'

We staggered on like sleepwalkers. We heard the sound of an engine behind us, and turned to see what new danger might be threatening. A dark shape was jolting rapidly toward us with all its lights extinguished. We summoned up what was left of our energy, and tried to scatter. The half-track, which was almost on top of us, gleamed with dull reflections of the blazing explosions all around it.

'Climb aboard, friends,' shouted a kindly soul.

We stumbled toward the vehicle, which turned out to be the one that had moved the geschnauz into position above our cellar in the hamlet. Three fellows who had also been in the hamlet had managed to get it started. We pulled ourselves onto the narrow platform, which was almost totally occupied by the heavy, dismantled gun, and the engine started up again, carrying us across a heavily rutted piece of ground which must have been the site of several gun emplacements. The soldiers standing beside piles of empty ammunition boxes waved to us as we passed, their faces drawn with exhaustion.

'Clear out!' our driver shouted to them. 'Ivan is almost here!'

One of the artillery tractors was blazing brightly. Perhaps its flames dazzled our driver. In any case, we plunged nose first into a deep crater, and everyone was thrown out. I think

I went through the windshield. I felt a stabbing pain in my shoulder, which was already sore, and found myself doubled over against one of the front wheels of the machine.

'God damn!' someone said. 'What are you doing to us?'

'Shut up!' shouted the driver. 'I think I've broken my knee.'

I stood up, gripping my shoulder. My left arm seemed to be paralyzed.

'Your face is covered with blood,' said the Sudeten, looking at me.

'Only my shoulder hurts, though.'

I saw Hals lying on the ground. Already wounded, he had been thrown a considerable distance, and was either unconscious or dead.

I shook him and called him, and he lifted one of his hands to his neck. Thank God he wasn't dead. Somebody tried to drive our machine out of the hole, but its wheels only dug into the ground and spun helplessly. We walked on to the next artillery position, where the fellows were just pulling up stakes. They loaded us onto trucks along with their gear, and we left in search of a quieter spot.

In the distance, the horizon glowed red.

'You've come from that inferno?' one of the artillerymen asked. He was talking to the veteran, who didn't answer because he'd dropped into a deep, anaesthetic sleep. Within a few minutes, almost everyone had done the same, despite the rough jolts of our progress. Only Hals and I remained half awake. My shoulder prevented me from moving, and caused me great pain. Someone was leaning over me: my face was covered with blood. The shattered glass of the windshield had cut me in hundreds of places, so that I looked as if my blood were pouring from a deep wound.

'This one must be dying,' said the fellow looking down at me.

'I'm not!' I shouted back.

Sometime later, we were all helped down. Every movement hurt my shoulder, and the pain, intensified by fatigue, made me feel sick at my stomach. I began to retch and vomit violently. Two soldiers helped me to a building where the wounded were stretched out on the floor. Hals joined me with his bloody neck, and our driver, who was hopping on one leg.

'You in a bad way?' Hals asked. 'You're not dying, are you, Sajer?'

His words reached me through a loud buzzing noise, across an immense distance.

'I want to go home,' I said, between two spasms of retching.

'So do I,' Hals said. He stretched out on his back and fell asleep.

Sometime later, we were wakened by men from the sanitary service, who had come to sort out the dead and wounded. I felt a set of cold fingers lifting my eyelids, as someone peered into my eyes.

'It's all right, boy,' he said. 'Where are you hurt?'

'My shoulder. I can't move it.'

The orderly unbuckled my straps, which made me howl with pain.

'No visible wounds, Herr Major,' he said to a tall man wearing a cap.

'What about his head?'

'Nothing there,' the other said. 'His face is bloody, that's all. And there's something wrong with his shoulder.'

The orderly moved my left arm back and forth, and I screamed. The major nodded, and the orderly pinned a white slip of paper to my tunic. He did the same to Hals and to the driver, and then helped the driver into an ambulance which was already nearly full. Hals and I remained on the ground. Toward noon, two more orderlies came back to deal with the men like us, who'd been left to wait. They tried to help me to my feet.

'That's all right,' I said. 'I can walk. It's my shoulder that hurts.'

The orderlies lined up everybody who could walk, and sent us to the canteen.

'Everyone strip!' shouted a feld.

The pain of undressing nearly made me faint. Two fellows helped me, and my swollen, battered shoulder was bared. We were each given an injection in the thigh. Then the orderlies washed our wounds with ether, and stuck plaster on anyone who needed it. Beside the door they were sewing up a fellow who had a huge rip down his back, and who screamed as the instruments bit into his flesh. Two of them came over and grabbed hold of my shoulder. I howled and cursed, but they paid no attention. With a cracking sound which sent spasms of pain right down to my toes, they pulled my dislocated arm back into place, and moved on to the next case.

I found Hals outside. They had just stuck a gauze bandage onto his neck with a long strip of tape. My friend had been wounded by a metal fragment three inches below the first wound he had received at Kharkov.

'Next time, they'll get me in the head,' he said.

A short distance along, we found the veteran, the Sudeten, Lindberg, and the grenadier asleep and snoring on the grass. We lay down beside them, and were very quickly asleep too.

And that was the end of the battle for Belgorod. The German offensive had lost all the ground it had taken at such cost during those ten days, and even more. A third of the forces engaged in the fighting had been killed, including many of the Hitlerjugend.

What happened to the beautiful young man with the Madonna face and his friend with clear, loyal eyes, and the student who spoke so well? Probably they were left lying on the mutilated soil of Russia, like the melancholy harmonica player who sang of his desire to return to his peaceful, green valley, if only to die there.

There is no sepulchre for the Germans killed in Russia. One day some muzhik will turn over their remains and plough them under with his fertilizer, and sow his furrow with sunflower seeds.

PART THREE

THE RETREAT
Autumn, 1943

Chapter Seven

THE NEW FRONT

In September, Kharkov was retaken by the Soviets. The entire south and central front was seriously shaken, with several major breaks through which the enemy poured their tanks, jeopardizing our whole system of defence. A general withdrawal began, during which the Russians often managed to surround entire divisions. Our unit had been re-equipped with new weapons and rapid motor vehicles, and was used to check enemy penetration behind our lines, often achieving prodigies which were cited in the orders of the day. Wherever the Gross Deutschland appeared, our troops took heart and routed the enemy – or so it seemed. Of course, the general difficulties of our situation – our encirclement, and the despair of troops forced to abandon their weapons in a sea of mud – were never mentioned. Nor were such things as the adjutant and his section taken prisoner, and liberated too late, or the profound sense of hopelessness and misery which settled over the adult children we were, facing another winter of war – more human bridges across icy rivers, like the one over the Dnieper; more frozen, abandoned regiments and scorched earth and weeks of terror, like our week at Chernigov; more hands cracked open by chilblains; and more fatal acceptance of the idea of death. Generals have since written accounts of these events, locating particular catastrophes, and summarizing in a sentence, or a few lines, the losses from sickness or freezing. But they never, to my knowledge, give sufficient expression to the wretchedness of soldiers abandoned to a fate one would wish to spare even the most miserable cur. They never evoke the hours upon hours of agony, or the obvious resentment of individuals swamped by the herd, in which each man is lost in his own misery, and oblivious of the sufferings of others. They never mention the common soldier, sometimes covered with glory, sometimes beaten and defeated, burdened by the angry remonstrances of the noncoms and by the hatred of another herd of human beings whom it is officially permissible to hate, confounded by murder and degradation, and later by disillusion, when he realizes that victory will not return him his liberty. In the end, there was only the physical crime of war, and the hypocritical and intellectual crime of peace.

'That's why you're fighting,' Hauptmann Wesreidau, our captain, said to us one day. 'You're nothing more than animals on the defensive, even when you're obligated to take the offensive. So be brave: life is war, and war is life. Liberty doesn't exist.'

Captain Wesreidau often helped us to endure the worst. He was always on good terms with his men, and was never one of those officers who are so impressed by their own rank that they treat ordinary soldiers like valueless pawns to be used without scruple. He stood beside us during countless grey watches, and came into our bunkers to talk with us, and make us forget the howling storm outside. I can still see his thin face, faintly lit by a wavering lamp, leaning over, beside one of ours.

'Germany is a great country,' he used to tell us. 'Today, our difficulties are immense. The system in which we more or less believe is every bit as good as the slogans on the other side. Even if we don't always approve of what we have to do, we must carry out orders for the sake of our country, our comrades, and our families, against whom the other half of the world is fighting in the name of truth and justice. All of you are old enough to understand that. I have done a good deal of travelling – to South America, and even to New Zealand. Since Spain, I have fought in Poland and France, and now Russia – and I can tell you that everywhere there are the same dominating hypocrisies. Life, my father, the example of former times – all of these taught me to sustain my existence with rectitude and loyalty. And I have clung to these principles in spite of all the hardships and follies which have been my lot. Many times, when I could have responded with a thrust of the sword, I only smiled, and blamed myself, assuming that I myself was the cause of all my troubles.

'When I had my first taste of war, in Spain, I thought of suicide – it all seemed so vile. But then I saw the ferocity of others, who also believed in the justice of their cause, and

offered themselves up to acts of murder, as to a purification. I
watched the soft, effete French shift from terror to toughness,
and take up the arms they couldn't use when they needed
them, once we had restored their confidence, and offered
them the hand of friendship. In general, human beings don't
accept the unaccustomed. Change frightens and upsets them,
and they will fight even to preserve situations they have
always detested. But a slick armchair philosopher can easily
arouse a rabble to support an abstract proposition – for
instance, "all men are equal" – even when the differences
between men are obviously as great as the differences
between cows and roosters. Then those exhausted societies,
drained by their "liberty," begin to bellow about their
"convictions" and become a threat to us and to peace. It's
basic wisdom to keep people like that well fed and content, if
one wishes to extract even a tenth of the possible return.

'Something of this kind is happening on the other side. As
a people, we are fortunate in being somewhat less indolent
than they. If someone tells us to examine ourselves, we at
least have the courage to do it. Our condition is not
absolutely perfect, but at least we agree to look at other
things, and take chances. We are now embarked on a risky
enterprise, with no assurance of safety. We are advancing an
idea of unity which is neither rich nor easily digestible, but
the vast majority of the German people accept it and adhere
to it, forging and forming it in an admirable collective effort.
This is where we are now risking everything. We are trying,
taking due account of the attitudes of society, to change the
face of the world, hoping to revive the ancient virtues buried
under the layers of filth bequeathed to us by our forebears.
We can expect no reward for this effort. We are loathed
everywhere: if we should lose tomorrow those of us still alive
after so much suffering will be judged without justice. We
shall be accused of an infinity of murder, as if everywhere,
and at all times, men at war did not behave in the same way.
Those who have an interest in putting an end to our ideals
will ridicule everything we believe in. We shall be spared
nothing. Even the tombs of our heroes will be destroyed, only
preserving – as a gesture of respect toward the dead – a few
which contain figures of doubtful heroism, who were never
fully committed to our cause. With our deaths, all the

prodigies of heroism which our daily circumstances require of us, and the memory of our comrades, dead and alive, and our communion of spirits, our fears and our hopes, will vanish, and our history will never be told. Future generations will speak only of an idiotic, unqualified sacrifice. Whether you wanted it or not, you are now part of this undertaking, and nothing which follows can equal the efforts you have made, if you must sleep tomorrow under the quieter skies of the opposite camp. In that case, you will never be forgiven for having survived. You will either be rejected or preserved like a rare animal which has escaped a cataclysm. With other men, you will be as cats are to dogs and you will never have any real friends. Do you wish such an end for yourselves?

'Anyone who wishes to go but is hesitating from fear of our authority should speak to me; I will take as many nights as it needs to reassure you. I repeat: those who wish to leave should do so. We cannot count on men who feel that way, and our efforts cannot gain from their presence. Please believe that I understand your sufferings. I feel the cold and fear as you do, and I fire at the enemy as you do, because I feel that my duty as an officer requires at least as much from me as your duty does of you. I wish to stay alive, even if it's only to continue the struggle somewhere else. I wish my company to be united in thought and in deed. Once the fighting begins, I will not tolerate doubt and defeatism. We shall be suffering not only in the interests of ultimate victory, but in the interests of daily victory against those who hurl themselves at us without respite, and whose only thought is to exterminate us, without any understanding of what is at stake. You can feel certain of me, in return, and certain that I will not expose you to any unnecessary dangers.

'I would burn and destroy entire villages if by so doing I could prevent even one of us from dying of hunger. Here, deep in the wilds of the steppe, we shall be all the more aware of our unity. We are surrounded by hatred and death, and in these circumstances we shall daily oppose our perfect cohesion to the indiscipline and disorder of our enemies. Our group must be as one, and our thoughts must be identical. Your duty lies in your efforts to achieve that goal, and if we do achieve it, and maintain it, we shall be victors even in death.'

266

Our conversations with Captain Wesreidau made a deep impression on us. His obvious and passionate sincerity affected even the most hesitant, and seemed of another order than the standard appeals to our sense of sacrifice, which left us stupefied and incredulous. He invited questions, which he answered with intelligence and clarity. He spent his time with us, whenever he was free from other duties. We all loved him, and felt we had a true leader, as well as a friend on whom we could count. Herr Hauptmann Wesreidau was a terror to the enemy, and a father to his men. Every time we moved, or were sent out on an operation, his steiner preceded our vehicles.

The veteran, who had a good sense of men, had pointed him out to us the day after the battle for Belgorod, while we were resting in the rear, nursing our wounds.

'I've seen our captain,' he said. 'He looks intelligent and wise.'

We fought two more battles before recrossing the Dnieper in the beginning of the autumn. Several of us had to be re-equipped before these engagements, and the most serious accusations were levelled against anyone who returned without his weapons.

Lindberg, the Sudeten, and Hals, however, were officially recognized as wounded, when they came back the evening of the rout, in rags, without weapons or equipment. It can easily be imagined that equipment has to be abandoned when one is on the run, but in Russia our soldiers were never supposed to abandon their arms. They were supposed to die with them – or live, hanging on to them at all times. I myself had kept my gun without thinking of the consequences, like a blind man who never lets go of his white cane, and the veteran had dragged along his heavy spandau, out of habit or discipline; but I had lost my helmet, my ground sheet, the gas mask we never used, and what remained of the ammunition for the veteran's spandau.

We met Lensen, who had come out alive too, although he had left behind most of his gear. He was tearing his hair at the thought that this oversight might cost him his rank.

The veteran, who was also an obergefreiter, suggested that next time Lensen think of putting in for a posthumous promotion. Lensen's anxiety and our laughter were simul-

267

taneously drowned a short time later in the samahonka*
someone found in the cellar of an abandoned house.

It was almost surely because of Wesreidau that we all
escaped a court martial, which filled us with just as much
terror as Soviet rockets.

We had three good weeks of rest behind our lines, in a
village of dreary, identical shacks. Luckily, the weather was
magnificent. I took advantage of the lull to write often to
Paula, but I could never bring myself to tell her of my terror
at Belgorod. Hals had made the acquaintance of a Russian
girl, with whom he was able to arrange a mutually profitable
relationship. It turned out he was not the only one to enjoy
the good woman's favours. One evening he arrived to find
himself part of a troika. The other masculine member was the
Catholic chaplain, who had survived hell and was indulging a
few sins of the flesh as his consciousness of life returned,
hoping they would be pardoned because they were so rare.
From that moment on, he was never able to intone a psalm
without an accompanying chorus of laughter, at which he
would blush furiously, and laugh as loudly as the rest of us.

All went well until one morning toward the end of
September, when the distant rumble of guns reminded us that
we had not come to Russia to play. In fact, the Russians had
just broken through the front which our troops had managed
to re-establish west of Belgorod, and our grand debacle was
beginning.

Our generals, who believed that our troops could, if not
attack, at least hold the reconstituted front, noticed somewhat
belatedly that our regiments were being decimated simply to
slow down the irresistible momentum of the strong Russian
forces which were attacking all along the central sector.

What we should have done, before even thinking of
turning back to the east, now seems like a simple act of
realism which should have been recognized while it was still
possible. At the time, however, the order to withdraw to the
west bank of the Dnieper was given very late. The line of the
Dnieper meant Kiev on the central axis, Cherkassy on the
south, and Chernigov to the north, on the Desna: a distance
of hundreds of miles. We were continuously pursued by an

*Home-brewed alcoholic drink.

enemy who was fast becoming far more mobile than we, and threatening to overtake us at any moment, filling our ranks with panic and confusion. What might have been possible before Belgorod was no longer so, except at an inordinate price in blood and sweat, with incessant rearguard fighting. The Wehrmacht, adhering strictly to orders, sacrificed many more men on this belated retreat than they had during their advance. We died by the thousands that autumn on the Ukrainian plain, and our battles, unheralded by any fanfare, consumed many heroes. The front-line troops, in constant contact with an ever more pressing enemy, had already made up their minds about the future. Even the most hermetically sealed of our men understood that no matter how many hundreds of Russians he killed, or how bravely he fought, the next day hundreds more would appear, and so on for the next day and the day after that. And even the blindest saw that the Russian soldiers were moved by a blind heroism and boldness, so that even a mountain of dead compatriots wouldn't stop them.

We knew that under such circumstances combat often favours simple numerical superiority, and much of the time we felt desperate. Can anyone blame us? We knew that we would almost surely be killed, buying time for a large-scale redeployment of troops. We knew that our sacrifice was in a good cause, and if our courage incited us to hours of resignation, the hours and days which followed would find us with dry eyes which were filled with an immense sadness. Then we would fire in a lunatic frenzy, without mercy. We didn't wish to die, and would kill and massacre as if to avenge ourselves in advance for what we knew was going to happen. When we died, it was with fury, because we hadn't been able to exact enough retribution. And, if we survived, it was as madmen, never able to readapt to the peacetime world. Sometimes, we would try to run away; but orders, adroitly worded and spaced, soothed us like shots of morphine. 'On the Dnieper,' we were told, 'everything will be easier. Ivan won't be able to force the barrage. So courage, and do your best to hold him off, if you want everyone to get through. The Russian counter-offensive will be crushed on the Dnieper, and then we'll resume our push to the east.'

Through our panic and despair, an order became a duty.

Our adversaries were astonished by the courage of ordinary German soldiers. A hundred yards at a time, we withdrew to the Dnieper and safety, slowing down the enemy as much as we could, watching our comrades fall all around us. Our desperate efforts sometimes continued for days at a time, across hundreds of miles. When men who had escaped from rearguard units finally reached the river, they were faced with a vast human swarm. Entire armies were waiting beside the few bridges which our engineers had managed to restore, tramping up and down the sandy bank, climbing onto anything that could float. The Russians were right on our heels, pressing against our perimeter of defence, which shrank alarmingly. The Luftwaffe was always somewhere overhead, and partly saved the situation, but our planes were soon outnumbered by Migs, and Yabos. Those of our planes which escaped the long-range anti-aircraft fire had to face a constantly growing swarm of fighters. The men who had not crossed the river were pressed into counter-attacks at odds of a hundred to one. We performed deeds of astonishing heroism, which demonstrated once again the extraordinary resourcefulness of our soldiers. The weather was still good, and we fought many successful battles. However, these are victories which can never be celebrated. An army fighting for its life cannot speak of victory.

Nonetheless, they were victories, which cost us far more than those we had fought as conquerors. This time, on the banks of the river, we were fighting not simply to take this or that town or district, but to avoid catastrophe. Everyone felt it and knew it. We had hours and even days of calm, but our anguish and anxiety always increased to a point of unbearable pressure, and we would throw ourselves back into battle to try to drive off the red monster about to devour us. This time, we managed to avert a total catastrophe: Army Group Centre passed through, and the regiments still fighting were ordered to disengage. During the night, we destroyed almost everything, leaving only men and light arms to be transported in the ferries which had been provided to embark the last of our troops to the west.

At dawn, our exhausted men arrived at the river, which was heavily shrouded in autumn fog. Expecting friendly faces, they called out, only to be answered by Ivan's machine guns. In many places, the Russians had arrived ahead of us, sunk the boats, and killed the ferrymen. Our men threw themselves into the river, and tried to swim, abandoning everything. The Russians, of course, opened fire, shooting at the heads bobbing in the water as if they were clay pigeons at a fair. Perhaps a few Germans managed to reach the western bank. Elsewhere, our men crowded onto the precarious ferries which were fired at from both the shore and the sky. Others were surrounded, and fought to the last. Most of these men were killed, as the Russians were in no mood to take prisoners.

Thus we established a new front, hoping to find safety on the western bank of the Dnieper. We dug ourselves in, preparing for a long stay. This time, Ivan would not break through. It had begun to snow, and we set about arranging our bunkers, calming ourselves, reorganizing, and waiting. But news was spreading with the rapidity of the flash which followed a Russian rocket. The staff officers had done everything they could to keep the true nature of the situation from the troops. But reality was too strong, and too important, and broke down all the barriers of discretion, smashing the fragile hopes of the soldiers, and sweeping them away in a tumultuous flood.

The Red Army was moving toward us from Cherkassy in the east, and the Dnieper in the west. To the north, they had crossed the Desna, and a large number of our troops were trapped at the confluence of the Desna and the Dnieper. Winter had begun, and with the falling snow a deep feeling of despair settled over us. We were exhausted, and had no hope of future respite. Where could we find it? How far would we have to withdraw? To the Pripet? The Bug?

'The Oder?' The veteran grinned sardonically. That seemed impossible, unimaginable.

One can only draw a very general view of our situation from the lines I've just written, without any of the details. I am not trying to recreate precise geographic chronologies of the Russo-German War, but to give an account of the almost inconceivable difficulties we faced. I have never had more than a very approximate idea of our movements and centres of operation, and would certainly be incapable of drawing an accurate diagram of the front at any point in the war. That is the province of the various disbanded staffs. I, on the other hand, can describe certain moments down to the last detail. A simple smell can revive a whole tragic past for me, and leave me, for long stretches of time, wrapped in memory, and lost to the present.

I know in my bones what our watchword 'Courage' means – from days and nights of resigned desperation, and from the insurmountable fear which one continues to accept, even though one's brain has ceased to function normally. I know what it means, remembering deliberate immobility against frozen soil, whose coldness penetrates to the marrow of the bones, and the howling of a stranger in the next hole. I know that one can call on all the saints in heaven for help without believing in any God: and it is this that I must describe, even if it means plunging back into a nightmare for nights at a time. For that is the substance of my task: to reanimate, with all the intensity I can summon, those distant cries from the slaughterhouse.

Too many people learn about war with no inconvenience to themselves. They read about Verdun or Stalingrad without comprehension, sitting in a comfortable armchair, with their feet beside the fire, preparing to go about their business the next day, as usual. One should really read such accounts under compulsion, in discomfort, considering oneself fortunate not to be describing the events in a letter home, writing from a hole in the mud. One should read about war in the worst circumstances, when everything is going badly, remembering that the torments of peace are trivial, and not worth any white hairs. Nothing is really serious in the tranquillity of peace; only an idiot could be really disturbed by a question of salary. One should read about war standing up, late at night, when one is tired, as I am writing about it now, at dawn, while my asthma attack wears off. And even now, in my sleepless exhaustion, how gentle and easy peace seems!

Those who read about Verdun or Stalingrad, and expound theories later to friends, over a cup of coffee, haven't understood anything. Those who can read such accounts with a silent smile, smile as they walk, and feel lucky to be alive.

I shall now resume my account of our life and how we

272

began to regain our health and spirits, despite the distant thunder of guns.

'It was too good to last,' muttered the Sudeten, as we watched the stream of troop carriers and other vehicles which had been flooding back for the past twenty-four hours.

Each house in the small hamlet had become temporary headquarters for groups of officers deliberating the immediate fate of the men they were leading. The men themselves waited patiently beside their equipment – whose total mass must have been at least ten times as great as the mass of the buildings. We had just been chased from our billets, and were waiting under the trees at the edge of the village. Our entire company was there, grouped in order, with our equipment loaded into civilian vehicles. A rough wind swept across the dried steppe, raising clouds of dust that veiled the empty horizon.

'They've thrown us out!' said the veteran to a heavy drinker named Woortenbeck. 'But we've left them nothing but empty bottles.'

They waved toward the newly-arrived troops who had pushed us from the isbas where we'd been taking it easy.

'I packed all the samahonka that was left under the seats of the car.'

'Good for you, Woortenbeck,' shouted a thin sergeant. 'Samahonka's for an élite unit like us. The rest can get water from the troughs.'

I had made a new friend my own age, who spoke French well. Holen Grauer had spent some time studying in France in '41. Then the army had collared him, promising him that he would be able to continue his studies as well as provide the indispensable value of his presence in the service. Like me, he had been overwhelmed by military enthusiasm at the age of sixteen, and had volunteered, marching in step, and singing 'Wölken ziehn dahin, daher,' in the impeccable ranks of the Wehrmacht. Then he had experienced the war through Poland and across a huge expanse of Russia, in Belgorod, and on the sack where we were sitting, contemplating the world and the war.

Like me, he had dreamed of becoming a famous aviator, piloting JU-87s, and like me, all he retained of this dream was a vision of huge birds screaming as they swooped down

273

from the sky. As we couldn't speak of the ordinary life we had never shared, the shattered dream we had so much desired often illuminated our misfortune.

Hals had made himself scarce for the last few days: his girl, who helped him forget the war, had absorbed him almost entirely. He had just reappeared with one of his comrades in sin. His forehead was creased by an anxious frown, and he couldn't stop fretting. He unburdened himself to Grauer and me: 'If Captain Wesreidau won't let Emi come with us, the Reds will kill her. We can't let that happen.'

'I understand how you feel,' I said to Hals.

Woortenbeck and the veteran, who were amused by our innocence, roared with laughter.

'If everyone in the company brought along the girl he's sleeping with, there wouldn't be enough transportation in the whole division.'

'But there's no question of that, you bastards.'

'Don't cry over it. You'll have plenty of time to do the same thing somewhere else.'

'You're too thick to understand what I'm talking about.'

There were many jokes on this subject, which Hals did not find funny.

'Are you in love with her, Hals?' I asked, quite by chance, understanding, because of Paula, what 'being in love' meant.

Hals continued to bristle.

'Because it would certainly be possible to fall in love with a whore.'

'Sure. Why not?' said Grauer, who undoubtedly was about as experienced in these matters as I.

Hals calmed down somewhat.

'Let's go for a walk,' he said, taking us each by the shoulder. 'With you two, at least, it's possible to talk.'

When we had drawn apart, he unburdened himself. He had fallen head over heels in love and was certain he could never love anyone else. On that point he was absolutely beyond any reason or argument. As for me, despite my earlier certainty that I could never mention Paula to anyone, I found myself pouring out the whole story to Hals and Grauer.

'So that's why you had such a long face at the end of leave,' said Hals. 'Why didn't you say anything? I would have understood, you know.'

We talked over our amorous difficulties for a long time, and Hals decided I was lucky.

'You, at least, are sure to see her again,' he said, opening his mess tin. Through eyes misty with youthful passion, we watched the sky grow dark and the stars come out.

Our company moved out at dawn, heading west. During the day we watched an aerial combat which revived — for Grauer and me — all our old feelings about the Luftwaffe. Our ME-109s had the upper hand, and seven or eight Yabos fell from the sky in whirling flames, like enlarged fireworks.

Toward noon, we reached an important divisional base. Thirty companies, including ours, were regrouped to form a large motorized armoured section.

For the first time, we were given overgarments of reversible cloth: white on one side and ordinary camouflage on the other. We were also given medical checkups, which we hadn't expected, and drew a large quantity of supplies. A Panzer colonel commanded our group, which was classified as 'autonomous.'

We were surprised by the quantity of new supplies for our armoured section. Everywhere, drivers and mechanics were giving their machines a final lookover, and revving the enormous tank engines.

Tiger tanks on Porsche bodies roared as their engines began to turn over. From the sound of it, we could have been at the start of a giant motor race. We waited about two hours for the order to leave.

Hals, Grauer, several other friends, and I were loaded onto a brand-new truck, which had tyres in front and treads at the back. We drove as far as some woods on the edge of an airfield. Everything was perfect, except for the whirlwind of dust raised by our passage. The new vehicles had all been fitted with huge filters against this hazard; some of the filters were so big it was impossible to shut the hoods of the trucks or put back all of the heavy metal plating which protected the tank engines.

In the welcome shade, we shook our clothes, which were grey with dust. Although we had only gone a short distance, dust had penetrated everything, especially our parched throats.

'Damned country!' someone grumbled. 'Even the autumn's unlivable here!'

A second group as large as ours joined us. We were now spread over several acres of brush. A short distance away, Wesreidau had just joined a cluster of officers, who were conferring beside a large radio truck entirely covered with camouflage netting, and all but indistinguishable from the leaves of the woods. Thin scraps of cloth in the whole range of woodland colours fluttered and rustled in the wind, like the leaves themselves.

We were a powerful, well-organized unit. Our two groups together included six or seven thousand men, about a hundred tanks, an equal number of machine-gun carriers, and several mobile machine shops. There were also three companies of light cavalry, equipped with sidecars, who were supposed to seek out the enemy and guide the unit to him. During this period, which was already very critical for the army, matériel was concentrated in motorized units, which in turn were supposed to support selected underequipped infantry divisions. It is certain that the abundance of impeccable, well-conceived new matériel showered upon us at this time gave our morale, which had been faltering seriously since Belgorod, a much needed lift. Soldiers once more walked about with the assured air of men who feel that everything is going well. Only Hals was miserable, because he had been forced to abandon his Emi to a fate which was almost certainly predictable. He was inconsolable.

'They should cut the balls off soldiers in wartime. That would stop fellows like Hals from making things so hard for themselves,' murmured Woortenbeck.

'Have you ever heard of eunuchs making war?'

'Well,' our chaplain put in, 'geldings are just as strong as other horses.'

Luckily, the padre had already proved that he was as much inclined that way as any of us, otherwise we would have imagined the worst and refused to listen to him.

When it was dark, our formidable armoured column took off. As I watched, I began to understand the powerful impression our long columns of Panzers must have made at the beginning of the war, when they invaded the countries we still occupied. The roaring masses of tanks, their exhausts bursting into intermittent flame, gathered speed, and passed our heavy trucks, spreading out fanwise across the large and favourable terrain. We felt curiously moved and stirred by the sight.

We drove through the deepening darkness, enveloped by a terrible uproar and din, which must have been audible for a great distance. As usual, the common soldiers knew very little about their situation, and for us this movement seemed to mean that everything was going better. We felt very strong, and in fact, as a group, we were strong. We didn't realize that a general and laborious retreat was under way throughout the central sector, approximately from Smolensk to Kharkov, involving whole divisions and several hundred thousand men. In our case, our rate of progress was determined by the speed of our engines, but this was not generally so. Hundreds of regiments stripped of even the basic necessities were withdrawing on foot, while fighting constantly against an enemy who enjoyed an almost unbelievable numerical superiority. This time, our armies were even without the horses we had used the year before for dragging heavy machinery through the snow, as most of them had died during that winter. We were also seriously short of fuel. Everywhere, columns of vehicles in perfect condition were burned to keep them from falling into enemy hands, while the infantry plodded slowly westward in tattered boots. The Russians were well aware of our disarray and worked overtime, hoping to weaken the centre army.

All our available resources were placed at the disposition of certain units which were then reorganized from top to bottom and sent out to deal with particular desperate situations. This is what happened to our group, giving us the impression, for a couple of weeks, that we once again controlled the steppe. Our principal difficulty, which was clear to us even then, was the question of supply, as we always reached the prearranged sectors too late.

At dawn, when our Panzergruppe stopped, both men and machines were grey with dust. As planned, we had reached a vast forest, which stretched right across the eastern horizon. We were allowed two hours to rest and put them to immediate use, as the jolting of the trucks had been exhausting; but we were wakened again before we had really slept. The weather was perfect, with a soft, almost cool breeze rustling the autumn leaves, and this perfection made everything seem

277

easier. We jumped on board again, wreathed in smiles. Toward noon the dispatch riders, who were always quite far ahead of us, rejoined the front of the column. Brief orders were issued, and shortly afterward a large part of our group turned off for a village which was soon in sight. We could hear the sound of automatic weapons, and before we quite realized what was happening, about fifteen Tiger tanks were firing at a small cluster of houses.

Our heavy tractor was pulling a couple of sixteen-barrel rocket launchers. We were told to prepare for action, and everyone flung himself down on the ground, regretting that the tranquillity of such a beautiful day was going to be disturbed.

There seemed to be nothing for us to do. The tanks and one mortar unit whirled like Sioux around the village, which was soon blazing. In the distance, some Russian artillery, whose presence we hadn't suspected, opened a restrained fire. Several groups were detached and sent to deal with it. They returned twenty minutes later with two or three hundred Russian prisoners. Then the tanks drove through the burnt-out village, knocking down everything which was still standing. The whole operation took less than three-quarters of an hour. Then the whistle blew, calling us back to our places, and we went on our way. During the afternoon we also flattened two advanced Soviet positions. The Russians were so surprised to see us that they offered almost no resistance.

On the second day we reached Konotop, in a dense swarm of troops looking for transport. Our group moved to the southwest to meet a strong Russian army. We had been supplied in town under the horrified eyes of the Commissariat officers, who had to give us the gas they had been saving for their own personal use. Twenty minutes later, we were in contact with advanced Russian elements, which surprised us. In town, our soldiers were busy with odd jobs, like repairing bicycles. Our tanks were briefly engaged, and then withdrew on orders.

We drove for the rest of the day to reach a point where, according to plan, we should have been supplied. We arrived at the dump just a few minutes before the engineers blew it up. An enormous silo filled with tin cans, drinks, and foods of all kinds was about to be burned. We stuffed our pockets and every cranny in our trucks with everything we could grab, but we had to leave behind enough to feed the whole division for several days, and the flames consumed precious provisions which would have made a great difference somewhere else.

Hals watched the silo collapse with tears in his eyes, cramming as much food into his mouth as his stomach could possibly hold. The whole company witnessed the scene with regret, puffing on the cigars we'd been able to save. Then we had about six hours' rest before returning to business. During this time, the Red Army entered Konotop, and the German forces withdrew, fighting hard as they went.

Our group thrust violently into the south wing of the Russian offensive, and once again our tanks opened a passage for us through the enemy reserves, which scattered before our guns were ready to fire. However, that evening, the Russians turned away from the town, and concentrated their efforts on us. Our tanks made a half turn, and left six of theirs in flames. All the guns we'd brought with us were prepared to fire, and I saw our famous rocket launchers go into action for the first time.

Commanded by Captain Wesreidau, our company and two others were used to protect the left wing of an armoured detachment. Some of our fellows squeezed onto the platforms of the motorized geschnauz. The rest tramped along behind the machines, which proceeded at more or less a normal walking pace. It is strange how often the sense of having the initiative can lead men to confront an enemy far stronger than they. The progress of our Panzers had seemed so irresistible during the last couple of days that everything seemed possible to us. Our three companies, in groups of thirty, tramped through the relatively cool night among the ragged stands of brush scattered across this part of the plain. From the near distance, the roar of our engines filled the air, giving us a sense of reassurance, and, we hoped, a proportionate sense of alarm to the Soviets who were trying to intercept us. From time to time we could hear shots, which were undoubtedly intended for the shadowy figures fleeing through the brush. We went on in this way for about two miles, until suddenly we were surrounded by flares, shooting upward and throwing their light onto the ground all around us. Everyone – that is to say, every one of our eight hundred souls – plunged down in a single movement. Our steel helmets, which in theory had a dull finish, glinted in the flashes of brilliant light. In no time, the armoured cars had turned back into the brush, their formidable barrels swinging silently in search of a moving silhouette. We braced ourselves for a shower of missiles from the Russian bomb throwers, instantly aware of the shrinking sensation which comes with bad moments.

Two violet German flares shot into the sky. We knew that this was the signal to advance. After a moment of surprise and hesitation, we began to crawl forward, taking every precaution. A few men stood up, and advanced bent double. Most of the Russian rockets had already landed, and we took advantage of the lull to make a leap forward. I reached a small hollow edged with low scrub. A moment later, two companions caught up with me, and the sound of their quick, loud breathing betrayed the nervous tension knotting their throats. There is nothing more terrifying than moving at night through a piece of wooded or bushy country, in which every shrub might release a sudden flash of white light to dazzle and blind a moment before the intense pain which could mean the end of life. There was no way of keeping our progress silent, and for an invisible Russian waiting with his finger on the trigger any moment might present an ideal opportunity.

However, everything remained more or less quiet. The enemy, who must have been very close to us, decided to stay hidden, and kept us in a state of prolonged tension. We continued to advance, slowly and cautiously. My temples throbbed, and my body was taut, ready for the plunge which might be necessary any minute.

We heard a voice some twenty or thirty yards to our left, and the three of us shoved our noses into the dry grass. For a moment, we thought we were finished. I fitted my Mauser into the hollow of my shoulder with my eyes screwed up, anticipating the first shot. However, nothing more happened. On the left, where we'd heard the noise, two Russians had just surrendered to some of our men. A short distance in the other direction, the same thing happened. We couldn't understand it. What could have been happening inside the heads of these men who'd been ordered to intercept us? It's anybody's guess. Maybe they thought they were cut off from their main body of men and were afraid. For at that time, when the spirit of vengeance was the rule, the Russians were just as afraid of us as we were of them. We even thought we might have fallen into some kind of trap.

An hour went by before we were ordered to regroup. During that time, our tanks went back into action, and as we silently withdrew, the flashes of their guns lit our faces with glimmers of pink light. We climbed into our trucks and started off again, apparently in the same direction as before. Dispatch riders whirled busily around our group of heavy transports. About two miles ahead, the tanks were apparently pushing back an enemy who was putting up only a feeble show of resistance. In these circumstances, the first light of dawn fell over our column – or rather columns – for we were out of line by as much as five hundred yards, both to the left and to the right.

During the night our forward troops had been firing continuously. Ahead of us, through a veil of fog, we could see a town whose name I no longer remember. The motorized troops of the Gross Deutschland were fighting through streets lined with houses with tightly closed shutters. Our vehicles moved slowly forward, with soldiers walking on either side, holding their guns, and ready for anything. We came to a small square where a group of vehicles which included two ambulances had stopped. About thirty Russian civilians were standing under guard beside one of the houses. We kept straight on. At the edge of town we passed several tank crews patching up minor damage. The miserable shacks all around them were on fire. We stopped for a moment and stared at what was left of these wood-and-straw hovels. There was no sidewalk, no orientation or alignment of the buildings; this place, like the outlying districts of innumerable Russian towns, looked like an oversized barnyard. Watering troughs or preikas obstructed without any rhyme or reason passageways which might eventually be turned into streets. Villages buried in the wilds of the steppe seemed more attractive, with their clusters of isbas turning their backs to the north. The outlying districts and even most of the town

281

centres I saw – with the exception of Kiev – were of an incredible dreariness.

We had stopped above all to wash and get water, and we knew we had only a very short time. Some men beat their clothes against trees or the sides of buildings, as if they were ambulatory doormats; others drenched themselves with water from the preikas or wash troughs, although the day was cool and a damp wind boded no good. Nonetheless, we were frantic with thirst from the dust stirred up by our machines. German water bottles are small, so we took along extra water in anything we could find. Next, joined and encouraged by the veteran, we climbed over a low wall surrounding a small orchard. The branches of the nearest tree were weighed down with masses of skimpy, unripe pears, which refreshed our parched mouths even though they were hard and sour. We were busily picking them when a Russian popped up, like a jack-in-the-box. He had summoned up the nerve to come out of his house, carrying a kind of bowl of braided straw full of pears like the ones we were nibbling. He jabbered a few words to the veteran, who had gone over to him. His white face was trying to smile, but was only able to manage a stiff and desperate grin. His eyes were glued to the straps of the veteran's gun belt, which crossed his chest, and especially to his spandau. 'Davai,' said the veteran, reaching out a hand. The Russian held up the basket, from which our friend took a pear. He threw it away and took another, which he also rejected. This was repeated some five or six times. Then the veteran began to shout at the Popov, who backed away, with nervous little steps.

'They're all half rotten,' roared the veteran as he came back to us.

The Russian, hoping to save his orchard, had offered us the putrefying fruit he kept for his pig. As soon as we realized this, we shook the tree, which filled a tent cloth. The Popov disappeared into his lair.

We could hear guns to the northwest; our advance troops must have made contact with the enemy. We were ordered to move out. Half an hour later, we climbed down from the trucks again. The feld's whistle was blowing for combat readiness. Fighting was in progress about half a mile away, in a small village built round a factory.

Wesreidau quickly explained that we had to neutralize a large enemy force which was holding the place. Two companies had been detached for the job; the rest of the group would keep moving.

With our guns slung, we walked toward the village, while our tractors pulled our rocket launchers and anti-tank guns into firing position. Almost immediately, the Russians, who were watching from their trenches, showered us with a rain of shells. If their aim had been more precise, it would have been the end of us. As it was, their only effect was to make everyone run for cover. Our two companies spread out and partly surrounded the fortified point. Then we had about ten minutes of quiet while our captain, sheltered behind a pile of stones, discussed the forthcoming action with his subordinates.

The noncoms rejoined us and told us what positions we should try to reach. We scanned our surroundings as they talked, observing with our combat sense, which by now was quite well developed, every fold and hollow which might offer some shelter. Everything was quiet, and the instructions seemed ludicrously easy.

Nothing was moving, and the silence would have been total, if it had not been for the vehicles of our armoured group bumping along the rocky road below us, filling the air with exhaust and deafening noise. The Russians kept quiet, and many of us thought they had already been knocked out. The immediate presence of our main body of troops reassured us, and it seemed likely that the approaching fight would be no more than a skirmish.

We were ordered to move out, and from every nook and cranny troops proceeded toward the village, bent double. Here and there we could hear someone laughing, and wondered if it was innocence or bravado.

Our men reached the first houses. The Russians remained silent and invisible. I had just joined my group, which included Hals, the dear friend who so often saved me from feeling completely lost. His innocent, good-natured face smiled at me from the crowd, and I smiled back. We exchanged a look which said a great deal more than many long conversations do.

The war seemed quite different to us now that we had an aerial escort. Our terrible memories of the Don, and the retreat from Belgorod belonged to the past, and to bad times which wouldn't come back. Of course, we knew that the war wasn't over, but for the last week we had been making the enemy run.

We were watching the progress of about thirty of our men who were leaping through the ruins of a brickworks. Five or six Panzer grenadiers were running along beside the principal building. One of them had just thrown a grenade through a gaping window. A moment later the air was shaken by its explosion, which was immediately followed by a heart-rending scream of a kind we had often heard before. We knew that nothing must distract us from our objective; however, we saw a human figure dressed in white fall from the window and roll down to the feet of our soldiers. It was a Russian civilian, a woman, who had been cowering beside the window, probably praying to all the saints. In spite of her fall, she seemed to be unhurt, and ran toward us, screaming. One of our soldiers lifted his gun, and we thought we heard it fire, but nothing happened. The Russian woman in her white shirt ran screaming through the ranks of petrified men.

No one said a word, and for a half minute, the war seemed to be standing still. Our grenadiers had already kicked in the door, and were in the house. Three other civilians came out, two men and a child. Once again we watched as they ran through our astounded ranks. The Russians had not evacuated the village, and we would have to take the civilian population into account. Wesreidau, who had just realized this, installed a loudspeaker on a half-track, which drove between the rows of houses waving a white rag fastened to a pole. The loudspeaker crackled out some nasal Russian words, while the four men on the half-track looked desperately at their comrades, who had remained in shelter.

The loudspeaker must have been giving the Russians a chance to evacuate civilians or to lay down their arms. But the half-track had gone less than a hundred yards when the irreparable occurred. It suddenly seemed to fly upward, as a series of deafening explosions rang out, and five or six huts disintegrated. The truck had driven over a minefield.

A heavy cloud of dust and smoke hid the village from our eyes. We could see two black silhouettes gesticulating in the flaming half-track, and hear them screaming.

'Look out for mines!' someone shouted.

But his voice was drowned by the roaring of mortars and Paks, as the ground in front of us burst into geysers of flame and earth. Thatched roofs flew off in one piece, leaving the houses exposed, like bald men who've lost their wigs.

The Russians reacted, using at least two batteries of heavy howitzers. Every shell landing within 150 yards of us made the ground shake under our feet, and sucked the air from our lungs. Despite the almost certain presence of mines, the assault whistles blew. Everyone left shelter and ran for the nearest embankment. Our mortars pounded the ground some thirty yards ahead of us, to disrupt the arrangement of mines, and if possible explode some of them. The Russians, with multi-barrelled machine guns set up on trucks, poured a devastating fire on everything they could see.

What had seemed so simple only fifteen minutes earlier now looked impossibly difficult, and suddenly no one felt confident. There were five of us hiding in the rubble of the brickworks, and our faces, pressed into the ground, knocked against the dirt with every explosion. From another heap of shattered bricks, a noncom was shouting at the top of his lungs to fire at anything we could see. One at a time we risked looking out, but the whine of shells made even the boldest duck down immediately.

Only our mortars and rocket launchers kept on firing steadily and profusely at an enemy who, for the moment, had the upper hand. In the distance, the metallic factory tower we had noticed when we arrived was proving curiously resistant to our Pak shells, which must have passed right through it at several points. Once again, we had to jump to a more advanced position. Some men were shouting to give themselves courage. Others, like me, ground their teeth, and clenched their sweaty hands on their guns, less from emotion than from a reflex akin to that of a drowning man hanging on to a rope.

Accompanied by deep or shrill sounds, and brilliant or fading light, the earth flew up all around us, sometimes engulfing pathetic human figures dressed as soldiers. About thirty yards away, on our left, five of our men who had hidden behind a small wooden building, like a blacksmith's shed, fell, one after the other. The last two had no idea where

285

to run, and looked frantically for the enemy who would presently knock them off too. Finally, they threw themselves down among the bodies of their companions. A thick stream of blood ran out from the tangled mass of limbs and trunks and sank into the grey dust, which absorbed it like blotting paper.

Suddenly, to our left, a raging fire broke out in a cluster of four or five sheds. Its smoke and heat climbed into the sky, and a huge sheet of flame quivered and grew with astounding speed, giving off giant wreaths of black smoke and intense heat, which we could feel even where we were.

Our men surged back rapidly from that quarter. The metal roofs of the sheds buckled in the heat, and the isbas closest to the fire burst into flame. A horde of Russians – both civilian and military – ran from the burning buildings; our soldiers shot them down like rabbits.

One of our shells must have hit a gasoline dump. The resulting inferno routed the panic-stricken enemy, who paid dearly for having concentrated so many men beside such a volcano. Their men rushed through the confusion with their hands in the air, occasionally remembering the way to other Russian entrenchments.

Our Paks were now concentrating their fire on the area immediately surrounding the factory, and the job of cleaning up the people running from the gasoline dump was left to us. The fore-sight of my gun often disappeared in a swiftly moving Russian silhouette. A light pressure on the trigger, a puff of smoke, which for an instant veiled the end of my weapon, and my Mauser looked for another victim. Will I be forgiven? Was I responsible? That young muzhik, already wounded several times, more bewildered than anything else by the lethal uproar whose purpose was as obscure to him as it was to me, who stayed in my sights a moment too long and then turned ashen and clutched his breast with both hands before making a half turn and falling face down onto the ground – shall I ever deserve pardon for that? Can I ever forget?

But the almost drunken exhilaration which follows fear induces the most innocent youths on whatever side to commit inconceivable atrocities. Suddenly, for us, as it had been for Ivan a moment before, everything that moved

through the din and the smoke became hateful, and overwhelmed us with a desire for destruction, a desire which led
many soldiers to their deaths as they pursued the panic-
stricken enemy.

Our big guns pulverized the top end of the village, where
the Russian artillery had dug in. In the general flight, the few
wretched hovels which had not been burned fell, one by one,
into our young, criminal hands. We ran full speed over
ground which might have been mined; nothing could stop us.
Nothing stopped my good friend Hals from jumping across a
stable threshold and shooting the Russian gunners who were
desperately trying to fire their jammed weapon. Nothing
could stop the glorious 8th and 14th companies of German
infantry. As the communiqués later observed: 'With an
irresistible thrust, our valiant troops retook the town of X
this morning....' Nothing could stop our demoniac assault,
not even the rending cries of obergefreiter Woortenbeck, who
clenched his trembling hands on an iron grille and stiffened
himself against the death which flooded from the bloody pulp
which had once held his entrails.

A few more of our comrades were destroyed before we
reached the factory. At that point, the Paks stopped firing to
spare our own troops, who were right beside the Soviet
defenders. The Russians clung stubbornly to what they still
had, particularly to the sector immediately around the
factory.

I no longer remember exactly what happened. My group
joined the veteran and his men, who were snatching a few
moments of rest in a large cement settling tank. We all
emptied our water bottles without quenching our thirst.
Everyone was covered with dust. A telephone operator
settled down beside us, and spoke with Group Commandant
Wesreidau. The fighting had died down somewhat, and the
German troops were regrouping for the final assault. The
veteran's section had a mortar as well as its two F.M.s. Ours
consisted of grenadiers armed with machine guns and rifles.
Our sergeant placed us down the length of the cistern,
specifying the points we should try to reach once the attack
had started. We agreed to do as he asked before there was
time for our terror to grow uncontrollable. These moments of
waiting were often the hardest of all.

A group of Russians suddenly appeared, climbing through some dismantled scaffolding near the factory, waving a white cloth. There must have been at least sixty of them – all civilians – probably factory workers. Maybe they were partisans, and afraid of execution. They walked up to the veteran's men, and turned themselves in; the anxiety stamped across every man's face lent great pathos to the moment.

The veteran, who was fluent in Russian, talked to them. Protected by the white cloth, four of our men took the prisoners to the rear. It was one of those odd moments of calm, when it almost seemed as if a few friendly words between the adversaries might produce a settlement which would have allowed all of us to sit down and have a drink.

But in the madness of our existence the most simple things eluded us. Everyone was absorbed by immediate necessities; most of us never even thought of the symbolic value of the steps those men had just taken – first steps back to the essentials of life. Even the exceptions to this general insensibility kept their wild eyes glued to the metallic wreckage of the factory, which we would soon be obliged to attack and enter. Animals, which have a stronger instinctive sense than human beings, turn and run from a fire. But we, the elect among living creatures, press forward, like moths to a candle. That is what we call courage – a quality I lack. Fear knotted my throat, and I felt like a sheep at the threshold of the slaughterhouse.

I'm sure I wasn't the only one who had this feeling. The fellow beside me stared at me for a moment from his blackened face and murmured: 'If only those bastards would give up!'

But our feelings, of course, were unimportant. The trench telephone rang and crackled out an order: 'One-third of the men forward. Count off by threes.'

One, two, three . . . One, two, three . . . Like a miracle from heaven, I drew a 'one,' and could stay in that splendid cement hole, which at that moment seemed to me as magnificent as any palace. It was a secure refuge in which I would have spent my days in gratitude so long as death was stalking outside. I cut off a smile, in case the sergeant should notice and send me onto the field, but inwardly thanked God, and Allah, and Buddha, and heaven, earth, water, fire, trees, anything I could think of, that I was in that cement depression, which had held God knows what kind of filth before it sheltered me.

The fellow beside me had number three. He was looking at me, with a long, desperate face, but I kept my eyes turned front, so he wouldn't notice my joy and relief, and stared at the factory as if it were I who was going to leap forward, as if I were number three. But, in fact, everything was normal. 'Drei' was my neighbour; he was going to inspect the factory. Then the sergeant made his fatal gesture, and the brave German soldier beside me sprang from his shelter with a hundred others.

Immediately, we heard the sound of Russian automatic weapons. Before vanishing to the bottom of my hole I saw the impact of the bullets raising little fountains of dust all along the route of my recent companion, who would never again contemplate the implications of number three. The noise of guns and grenades was deafening and almost drowned the cries of the fellows who'd been hit.

'Achtung! Nummer zwei, voraus!'

The veteran and his spandau ran up in turn.

Next, it was going to be me, along with everybody else who'd counted 'one.' While everything outside was flashing and exploding, I thought for a moment about numbers. Usually, people begin counting with 'one.' Why had they started with 'three' this time? But I could only pose the question. Before there was time to consider it, my turn had come.

'Nummer eins, nachgehen, los!'

After a moment of hesitation, I sprang from my shelter like a jack-in-the-box, into madness. Everything looked grey, through a thick fog of whirling, choking dust, except for the glimmering flashes of light. In a few jumps I had reached the foundation of a shattered hut where a German soldier had died staring at the open breech of his machine gun.

It's strange how often human beings die without any kind of style. Two years before I had seen a woman run over by a milk truck, and had nearly fainted at the sight of her mangled body. Now, after two years in Russia, visible death meant nothing at all, and the tragic element of even the best murder novels seemed petty and frivolous.

With my watering eyes, I stared through the smoke, trying to see the enemy and do my duty.

About twenty-five yards away some trucks exploded into little fragments, one after the other, engulfing four or five running soldiers. Were the men German or Russian? I couldn't tell.

I was with two companions in an open shelter made of logs packed with dirt, which the Russians had built to take a machine gun. We were more or less sitting on the mangled bodies of the four Popovs who'd been killed by grenades.

'I did that bunch in, with one shot,' shouted a strong young soldier from the Gross Deutschland.

A burst of mortar fire forced us down into the heap of enemy corpses. A shell hit the edge of the bunker, and the earth and logs blew apart, falling back onto our heads. The fellow huddled between me and a dead Russian was hit. As his body jerked up from the impact, I tensed myself to run. Another shell struck the shelter, disintegrating it. The debris poured down onto my legs and sent me reeling back against the opposite wall. I howled for help, sure that my legs were broken, and afraid to move. My trousers were ripped down the leg, but the bruised skin underneath was unbroken, although I could trace the red-violet passage of the blow I'd taken.

I plunged back into the heap of Russian corpses, falling onto the fellow who'd been hit a moment before. He let out a howl. We lay side by side, with our heads touching, as an avalanche of rubble poured down all around us.

'I'm wounded,' he groaned. 'Something is burning in my back. Call for a stretcher.'

I looked at him, and dazedly shouted: 'Sänftenträger!'

But my ludicrous cries were lost in the deafening uproar of two spandaus firing quite near us. The big fellow from the Gross Deutschland was shouting at us to advance, as loud as he could: 'Come on, fellows! Some of our boys are already at the water tank.'

I looked at the wounded man, who was staring at me with desperate, imploring eyes and clutching my sleeve. I didn't know how to tell him that there was nothing I could do for him just then. The big soldier had jumped out of the shelter. I pulled myself brutally away, and turned my head. The wounded man called again, but I had already jumped from the shelter and was running like a madman after the other fellow, who was nearly fifteen yards ahead of me.

I joined another group who were hurriedly setting up two trench mortars, and helped them manoeuvre the tubes into position. Instantly our mortar bombs were shooting almost straight up. A landser, whose face was pouring blood, shouted that the Russians had withdrawn to the central tower.

The veteran, whom I hadn't noticed before, let out a savage howl: 'Got 'em!'

As he shouted, a white flash lit his face, which was covered with an incredible layer of dust, and a geyser of flame enveloped the tower.

The Russian defence crumbled and fell under the impact of our concentrated fire. Our assault groups moved in and cleaned up the last resistance. Another German soldier fell, clutching his face, and then it was all over, except for a few widely scattered shots.

I and my companions ran into the ruins of what had once been a factory but was now reduced to rubble beyond classification. Once again, we were victorious; but the victory gave us no joy. Stupefied by the noise and the nervous tension, we wandered among the twisted, collapsed metal roofs. A landser with a face drawn by exhaustion mechanically picked up an enamelled plaque which had something written on it in Cyrillic characters, perhaps a direction, or the word for 'toilet.'

The town had fallen to us. There were about three hundred prisoners, in addition to two hundred enemy dead or wounded. The noncoms regrouped us, and led us back through the smoking devastation of the village. Herr Hauptmann Wesreidau reviewed his two companies, and called roll. About sixty men were missing. We collected the wounded, and regrouped them to wait for our three orderlies to give them first aid. There were about fifteen wounded men, including Holen Grauer, whose right eye was gone.

Finding water was difficult. The preikas had been smashed, and we finally had to lower soup kettles down a well in the ashes of one of the isbas. The water was black with soot. The wounded were screaming with pain; most of them were delirious.

There were also about seventy-five Russian wounded, who presented a dilemma to our Kommandant. In principle, we should have helped them too, as best we could. But we were under orders to rejoin our division as soon as the operation was completed. So we abandoned the Russian wounded, and piled ours into and onto the vehicles we had, which bore no resemblance to ambulances, or even to ordinary trucks – a few gun carriages and a couple of light artillery tractors. We felt exhausted, disgusted, and numb.

There was also the question of how to move the prisoners. There was no room in our collection of already overloaded vehicles. Finally, a sidecar fitted with an F.M. slowly drove some fifty of the prisoners along ahead of it. We turned them loose two days later, for lack of anything better to do with them.

As an autonomous group, we were faced with extremely difficult problems of supply. In theory, the vehicles carrying munitions and gasoline picked up the flotsam of war as their loads grew lighter. But the division already had some eleven hundred prisoners, and we didn't know what to do with them. We set off with clusters of men – German and Russian – hanging on to everything that could roll.

We all looked back at the town, from which a thick cloud of smoke was climbing, and spreading out to the horizon. The dark grey sky was threatening rain, which would soon fall on the graves of forty German soldiers sacrificed to neutralize a single point of enemy resistance, which we weren't even interested in holding. We moved on to another operation, not as part of any design to conquer, but simply as part of an attempt to protect our vast withdrawal of troops to the west bank of the Dnieper.

No one smiled. We knew that our victory couldn't make any difference to the outcome of the war, and only hoped that it might have some strategic interest. The experience of the battle itself had been as always – more fear and, for some, like my friend Grauer, irreparable mutilation.

A young blond soldier, huddled beside the driver of the machine which was carrying about thirty of us, began to play on his harmonica. The melody rang softly in our nearly

insensible ears: '... mit dir, Lilli Marlene, mit dir, Lilli
Marlene ...' The music was slow and filled with a nostalgia
which weighed heavily on our exhaustion. Hals was listening,
his mouth hanging half open, making no sound, and staring
at nothing.

Chapter Eight

THE BREAKTHROUGH AT KONOTOP

We drove for an hour – which meant about thirty miles – before it grew dark. We were all anxious to stop so that we could get rid of the thick, choking dust which coated us from head to foot. We were also exhausted and longing for sleep. Although a good bed in a warm barracks would have been paradise, any place where we could have stretched out and lost consciousness would have done, and we knew that when we did stop we would collapse onto the ground, and sink immediately into blackness.

The dark sky was filled with heavy black clouds lit up on their outer fringes. Large drops of rain began to fall as the storm broke. The rain – so often a curse – seemed like a blessing this time, washing off the filthy faces we turned up to meet it. It soon became a downpour, running down our collars and over our bodies, like a gift from Providence to friend and foe alike, making us all smile with a sense, however partial, of returning well-being. The soaking cloth of the uniforms on our tightly packed bodies clung to all of us – grey-green for the Germans, violet-brown for the Russians. We all grinned at each other without distinction, like players from two teams in the showers after a match. There was no longer any feeling of hatred or vengeance, only a sense of life preserved and overwhelming exhaustion. The rain became so heavy that we had to improvise shelter, and covered our heads and shoulders with our ground sheets. Although hardly anyone understood more than a few words of the other language, we were all laughing and trading cigarettes – Hannover cigarettes for machorka tobacco from the Tartar plain. We smoked and joked over nothing – a 'nothing' which in fact represented the most absolute human joy I had ever known. The exchange of tobacco, the smoke under the ground sheets, which made us choke and cough, and the simple fact of laughter without reserve – all of this made a small island of joy in a sea of tragedy, which affected us like a shot of morphine. We were able to forget the hate which divided us, as our stupefied senses reawakened to an awareness of life. Understanding nothing, I laughed uncontrollably, as a curious sensation took hold of me and filled my veins. Suddenly I was covered with gooseflesh, as one is during a particularly moving piece of music. The rain was beating on the metal hood. Would we have to shoot our Russian fellow passengers tomorrow? That seemed impossible; it was impossible that such things could continue.

We had just caught up with a regiment of motorized cavalry, stopped in the middle of nowhere. Streams of water were running down every exposed surface; the dull finish of the sidecars sheltering under the dripping leaves of the trees at the edge of the woods glistened with raindrops.

Wesreidau climbed down from his sidecar to talk to the cavalry commander. The fellows in the sidecars had long oilskins which pretty well covered them, and kept them more or less dry. However, all their camping equipment was in the trucks of the supply column, so instead of sleeping they had to spend their rest period tramping up and down through the puddles.

Two fellows distributed food: a stale sausage for each German soldier and loaves of bread to be divided among eight. There was no food for the prisoners, whose rations, in theory, would be provided by the division. We thought of walking off a short way to devour our meagre portions, but we were bunched around our dripping communal plates. The Russians, who had nothing but their lives, kept their feverish eyes fixed on the food, which was impossible to hide. Finally, our torn and filthy hands broke the hard bread and held it out to the men who had been trying to kill us only a few hours before.

Our stomachs were still rumbling with hunger five minutes later, as we swallowed down the last mouthfuls of our rations. Everyone was thirsty, and our water bottles had been emptied after the fighting. Like feverish sheep, we needed water. We had obtained permission to leave the trucks to relieve ourselves, but for no other reason. We were in the middle of wild, uninhabited country, and there were no preikas or drinking troughs. However, the rain was still pouring down, and we collected the run-off from the backs of the trucks, and the leaves, and the puddles in the oilcloths. When we had quenched our thirst, we left with the cavalry regiment.

Finally, the rain stopped, leaving us chilled and bone-tired, to the misery of our throbbing machines. Lightning was still streaking through the sky behind us and over our heads, and the thunder was still rumbling. Ahead, there were other flashes too, which unfortunately had nothing to do with the storm. These were produced by Stalin's organs, firing at the division blocked behind Konotop. As we drew nearer, we were able to gauge the size of the battle by the intensity of the fire flashing across the horizon. Soon we also could hear the loud and continuous sound of guns.

We had been hoping for a refuge where we could spend the night. Instead, we were faced with the anguish of a fresh hell, and a fresh uncertainty of survival, as war tightened its vicelike grip once again around our throbbing temples. The young face of the blond boy who had played the harmonica a short time before hardened suddenly into the face of a man. Was it exhaustion, or did he simply want to get it over with? In the space of a few moments, he suddenly aged twenty years.

We arrived at the town, which was black and deserted. Intermittent flashes from the battle being fought somewhere to the west of us, through the outer fringes of the town, lit the darkness. The thunder of explosions filled the air, shattering window panes and breaking off the gutters of the houses all around us.

The rain had begun again, falling in small, delicate drops. We were ordered to leave the trucks, and jumped down like sleepwalkers. The shock of contact with the ground reverberated through our numbed bodies, and we felt sickness rising in undulating waves, along the entire length of our spinal columns. In a herd, we followed our leaders, while the trucks drove off to a nearby street. I could feel the sleep weighting down my eyelids, and, only half awake, staggered like an automaton after the sound of the boots of the fellow in front of me, without grasping that I was going back into battle.

What happened that night at Konotop? I only know that there were explosions and fire and houses collapsing down the length of dark, indefinable back streets. There was a gutter full of running water, and there were my hard, heavy boots, which I scarcely had the strength to lift, and my big bony feet inside them, which felt as if they were growing smaller and smaller, and the heat of my throbbing temples, which had begun to burn with fever, and the crushing fatigue which had settled around my thin shoulders, trapped in the filth of my undershirt and waterlogged tunic, and the tangle of leather straps and cartridge belts, heavy with ammunition, and the incomprehensible, hostile world, whose weight we still had to bear, where we still had to march and crawl and tremble. . . .

Toward morning, which dawned as pale as the last morning of a condemned man, I was overwhelmed by a crushing sleep, and briefly lost my waking nightmare. We collapsed in the shelter of an entranceway, which protected us from most of the rain, except when the wind blew a particularly strong gust. We spent a few hours there – then we were wakened, to stare at a hundred other faces as white and drawn as our own. Our closest relatives would probably have hesitated before identifying us. My eyes, which felt as if they had sunk into my aching head, instinctively looked around to see what the new day would bring.

Directly in front of the gate where we had slept was a building of several stories. Its grey walls were stained with long streaks which dribbled down from its gaping windows. A short distance to one side stood a cluster of miserable shacks which now offered shelter only to a few wandering cats, and troops looking for refuge. These buildings, which at their best could never have looked like much, now seemed soiled by the passage of something monstrous. Further along, the street was entirely blocked by the houses which had collapsed when the Russians had shelled the town the evening before.

I looked for something which might produce an instant of pleasure, and distract me for a moment from the effort of trying to control the spasmodic shivers which shook my whole body.

A sound behind me made me turn my head. The veteran was coming back with two canteens of hot soup, which he had found God knows where. I watched him blankly as he limped through the puddles and the scattered rubble. His uniform was as grey and filthy as the setting, and his thin, shaggy face beneath his heavy steel helmet seemed to fit perfectly with everything else. Above our heads, the sky flowed slowly toward the horizon, trailing grey clouds, like dirty rags, as far as the eye could see.

'Anyone who wants to eat better open his eyes,' the veteran called, putting down the canteens.

I quickly shook Hals, whose sleep, as always, seemed impenetrable. He jumped, but when he realized it wasn't a new bombardment or attack he pulled himself together, muttering a few incomprehensible words, and finally stood up, rubbing his stiff and aching body.

'God, I'm sick of this,' he said, in a disgusted, weary voice. 'Where are we, and what the hell are we doing here?'

'Come and eat,' said the veteran.

In silence, we devoured the millet and soup, which was already beginning to cool. Some of the fellows preferred to sleep a little longer. Then we were ordered out again, and began to walk slowly through the devastated sector of Konotop. We were too exhausted to notice much, and walked without thinking or looking. When we were forced to recognize an explosion or an airplane, we slid to the ground without haste. Then we got up again ... and so on. I was certainly ill. My head and back ached, probably from exhaustion, and I was shaking with the cold shivers of fever. But there was nothing to do about it. If I felt any worse later, I would try to get sent to a hospital – but, for that, I would have to faint.

We reached a section of the town that had suffered particularly heavy damage. In the ruins, we could see an enormous Tiger tank, which had ploughed a large furrow through the heaps of rubble and appeared to have been stopped by a mine, which had blown off its right tread. Despite this it was otherwise intact, and its gun was still spitting occasional shells at the enemy formations, which were very close.

Groups of soldiers hiding in the ruins seemed to be waiting for Ivan, who must have been digging in near by. We moved carefully through the rubble to a hole where Hals and I settled down. For at least a half mile ahead of us, and five hundred yards behind us, we could see nothing but wreckage. Groaning with the effort, we piled up all the solid pieces of rubble we could move, to keep ourselves off the bottom of the hole, which was covered with blackish water. We stared at each other in a kind of stupefied silence: we had already said everything there was to say under the circumstances. Our lives at that moment were reduced to waiting. The force of events had already inflicted enough horror to drive us mad.

'You really look filthy,' Hals said finally.

'I'm sick,' I said.

'We're all sick,' Hals answered, his eyes fixed on our universe of destruction. Our exhausted eyes met for a moment, and I saw on my friend's face an almost limitless depth of weariness and despair.

I was also haunted by the thought of what might happen to us. It seemed literally impossible that this existence could go on much longer. We had been living in this way for over a year now, like gypsies – except that that is far too mild a comparison. Even the poorest, most wretched gypsies lived better than we did. For over a year I had been watching my comrades die. Suddenly, all the memories of that year came flooding back: the Don, the 'Third International,' Outcheni, the battalions of stragglers, Ernst, Tempelhof, Berlin, Magdeburg, the horrors of Belgorod, the retreat, and only yesterday Wootenbeck, his belly striped by a dozen streams of red blood, which ran down to his boots. What stroke of fortune had saved me from those giant explosions? So many men had already been consumed right in front of my horrified eyes that I wondered if what I had seen could possibly have been true. What miracle had preserved Hals, Lensen, the veteran, and the other survivors of our ill-fated unit? Although our luck had been almost incredible, and had spared us so far, it must almost surely run out, if this went on much longer. Tomorrow, perhaps the veteran, or Hals, or maybe even I would be buried. I suddenly felt terribly afraid. I looked out as far as I could see, in all directions. It would probably be my turn soon. I would be killed, just like that, and no one would even notice. We had all grown used to just about everything, and I would be missed only until the next fellow got it, wiping out the memory of preceding tragedies. As my panic rose, my hands began to tremble. I knew how terrible people looked when they were dead. I'd seen plenty of fellows fall face down in a sea of mud, and stay like that. The idea made me cold with horror. And my parents: I really should see them again; I couldn't just die like that. And Paula? My eyes filled with tears.... Hals was looking at me, as still as that horrible landscape, indifferent to suffering, death, everything. There was nothing we could do about it – the screams of fear, the groans of the dying, the torrents of blood soaking into the ground like a vile sacrilege – nothing. Millions of men could suffer and weep and scream, and the war would go on, implacable and indifferent. We could only wait and hope; but hope for what? To escape dying face down in the mud? And the war? All it needed was an order from the authorities, and it would end – an order, which the men would respect like a sacrament. And why? Because, after all, the men were only human.... I went on crying, and muttering incoherently to my impassive companion.

'Hals,' I said. 'We've got to get out of here. I'm afraid.'

Hals looked at me, and then at the horizon.

'Get out? Where to? Go to sleep; you're sick.'

I looked back at him with sudden hate. He too was part of this indifference and inertia.

The tank near us fired a shell, and the Russians sent back about half a dozen, scattering the piles of rubble a little further. Maybe they knocked off a few more of our fellows too: the veteran, perhaps. Suddenly it all seemed unbearable. My trembling hands clutched my head as if they were trying to crush it, and I sank into total despair. My sobs attracted Hals's attention. He looked at me, almost in irritation.

'Go to sleep, for God's sake. You can't go on like that.'

'What difference does it make to you whether I sleep or die? You don't give a damn, and nobody gives a damn. Nobody gives a damn about anything. And nobody will give a damn when you're killed, either.'

'You're right. So what?'

'So what? We've got to do something, for the love of God, and not just sit here in a stupor, the way you're doing now.'

Hals's listless eyes were without expression. His feeling of misery was probably as great as mine, but for the moment it was dulled, and his listlessness had overcome his outrage.

'Go to sleep, I tell you. You're sick.'

'No!' I was shouting now. 'I'd rather be killed and get it over with, right now.'

I jumped up, and left our hole. But before I had taken more than two steps Hals had grabbed me by the belt and pulled me back.

'Let go, Hals,' I shouted, louder than ever. 'Let go, do you hear?'

'You're going to shut up, for God's sake! And calm down! And be quick about it!'

Hals clenched his teeth, and clasped his two big hands around my neck.

'You know as well as I do we're all going to get it, one after the other. So let the hell go of me. What business is it of yours anyway? What difference does it make?'

'The difference is that I need to see your face from time to time, the way I need to see the veteran, or that bastard Lindberg. Do you hear? If you go on like this, I'll smash you on the head, just to keep you quiet.'

'But if Ivan gets me, I'll be dead anyway, and you won't be able to do a thing about it.'

'If that happens, I'll cry, the way I did when my little brother Ludovik died. But he died because he was sick; he didn't do it on purpose. And if Ivan gets you, you won't have done it on purpose.'

A violent shiver engulfed my whole body. Tears continued to pour down my cheeks, and I felt like kissing my poor friend's filthy face. Hals loosened his grip, and then let go. A burst of fire forced him to duck. He looked at me, and we both smiled.

At the end of the day, our third attempt to move failed like the others. By this time, the piles of rubble which stretched out to the dark horizon seemed to have been levelled absolutely flat, with no protruding shapes – although a few chimneys were in fact still standing.

Once again, the darkness was streaked with white lights, which glimmered back at me from the insensible retinas of my companion, and we began another interminable night of fear, in a dark hole, with a pool of cold water under the stones, and an exhaustion so heavy one wished to die; a night in which nothing – or everything – could happen. There were fires, and explosions, and short or long flashes of light, which

301

killed the sleep pressing at the backs of our eyeballs. We listened to the cries of our fellow combatants, and the lethal rain of rockets crashing into the ground behind us. A thousand memories of my other life passed through my head – France, and my youth, still so close, and so remote – an act of childish naughtiness, a toy, a scolding, which now seemed so gentle, my mother, and the new focus in my life, Paula. . . .

We hardly spoke during that night, but I knew that I should try to live for the sake of my friend. . . .

Long before daylight, a violent fit of shivering destroyed what was left of my resolution. In the grey daylight, Hals wrapped me in my cover, which I no longer had the will to unfasten.

'Take this,' he said, handing me a half-eaten can of food. 'Eat it. You'll feel better.'

I looked despairingly at the jam mixed with lint and dust from the inside of the pack.

'What is it?'

'Eat it. It's good. You'll see.'

I did as I was told, and scooped out the jam with two fingers. But, before I'd swallowed even half of it, I was overwhelmed by nausea, and my vomit increased the filth of our refuge.

'Damn it,' Hals said. 'You're much sicker than I thought. Try to sleep.'

Shaking with fever, I let myself fall into the mire, which I pushed back with my elbows and feet to try to make a flat place where I could stretch out and perhaps really sleep. Several hours passed before I regained consciousness.

Later that morning, we were sent some reinforcements, and Hals was able to help me to another hole a little farther back, where two fellows put me on a makeshift bed laid across the shattered remnants of a ladder. Two other fellows were lying on boards which had been put directly onto the stones.

Behind my head and my ears, ringing with fever, the war went on. I lay where I was, listening to its roar for an indefinable time, shaking with feverish chills, despite the pile of covers and coats which several well-meaning companions had thrown down on top of me. Once, somebody woke me up and made me swallow a pill.

302

How much time went by? Perhaps a day. I fought my fever while Russians and Germans fought each other through the outskirts of the town. After turning the end of the enemy lines to the east of Konotop, we withdrew to the west, only to find a defensive wall which cut us off from our rear. Several attempts to move out to the west failed, and our autonomous group, already weakened, was faced with the prospect of entrapment in a Bolshevik noose, which was drawing tight, from the north, west, and south.

While I lay shivering on my ladder, our situation grew extremely critical. Our staff officers were doing everything they could to kill the terrible rumour that we were encircled.

The next night I was ordered to leave my ladder in a hurry, and tottered on my unsteady legs to a more secure shelter in a cellar, where about fifty sick or wounded men had been collected. I was almost turned away from this improvised infirmary, but as I looked pretty sick, an orderly stuck a thermometer in my mouth. When this registered nearly 104°, I was told to sit in a corner, where I waited for morning and someone to look further into my case.

Outside, the town was undergoing heavy bombardment simultaneously from the ground and from the air, and the orderlies were run off their feet by a flood of freshly wounded men. My comrades had gone back into the line, to face the increasingly ferocious enemy assaults. Toward noon, the orderlies filled me with quinine, and made me give my place to a fellow who was dripping with blood, and no longer able to stand on his feet.

With stars dancing in front of my eyes, I staggered from the dark cellar into brilliant sunshine. A final burst of summery sun lit a landscape of total devastation. Everywhere, columns of smoke were climbing into the sky. Groups of slightly wounded men stood staring and talking, visibly stricken with desperation and horror. One of them told me we were surrounded.

This terrible news was almost as destructive as the bombardment. A sense of every man for himself had begun to spread, and our officers needed all the severity they could muster to prevent a hopeless rout.

Still another day passed, and I slowly began to recover, but my head swam, like the head of a convalescent who has gotten up too quickly. I stayed huddled in a corner as long as I could, gleaning fragments of news from the rest of the city.

Surrounded ... dangerous situation ... the Russians have already reached ... we're trapped ... the Luftwaffe is coming. ... But, instead of our planes, we heard Yaks and Ils throbbing overhead in the pale blue sky, and torrents of Russian bombs shaking what was left of the town.

What, exactly, was happening? Almost no one really knew. I can still remember a roll call, and then the noncoms coming to comb the infirmary. A fellow had to be missing a foot, at least, to be able to stay behind. I was among those who could still be used, and was led back with several bandaged companions to a zone near the front of the fighting.

In a vast space bordered by roofless houses, a new group was hastily organized. Among the five or six officers present, I immediately recognized Herr Hauptmann Wesreidau. From nearby, to the northeast, the thunder of Stalin's organs drowned our voices, and provoked a wave of panic which was difficult to control. I was still very sick. My mouth tasted sour, and I felt as if my thin, faltering body was supported only by my boots and my filthy clothes.

Wesreidau began to speak, raising his voice to make himself heard above the noise of the guns. He would probably have preferred to give us a more detailed explanation, but the continuous uproar, the pressure of time, and the risk of Russian planes suddenly diving at our three companies drawn up in the square forced him to be brief.

'Kameraden! We're surrounded! ... The entire division has ... been ... surrounded!'

We already knew it, but hearing it officially made us horribly afraid. A situation officially acknowledged to be dangerous by the staff must be very serious indeed. In the near distance, through the sound of explosions, we could hear the howl of Russian rockets. Both the earth and sky were filled with roaring noise, as if to emphasize the desperation of Captain Wesreidau's announcement.

'We still have one hope,' he went on, 'a swift and brutal breakthrough by all our forces pressing at a single point. This point must be to the west, and we shall engage all our units at once. The success of this attempt depends on the courage of every one of us. There will only be one attempt, and it must be successful. There are some strong infantry units which will be going into action to help us, on the other side of the Russian ring. If each one of us performs his duty, I feel confident that we shall break out of the Bolshevik noose. I know the qualities of the German soldier.'

Wesreidau saluted and requested us to get ready.

Our companies were directed to the points from which they were to press our final assault. There were many wounded men among us, more deserving of a warm bed than of further battles, and fellows like me, who were sick. The vast majority were utterly exhausted, staring with infinite weariness from glittering feverish eyes. These were the troops Wesreidau had been exhorting to an excess of courage: valiant German soldiers who looked more like worn-out stock ready for the slaughterhouse.

And yet we had to attack, or die. At that time, there was no question of captivity. As always, after a hard knock, we rediscovered a kind of unity, and seemed to be held together by tighter bonds. What provoked the sentiments of generosity which brought out the last cigarettes, or the chocolates so rare they were usually devoured in secret, a fraction at a time, inciting all the scum to fake friendship, leading the noncoms, who had probably been mixed up with every kind of dirt in civilian life, to pat a suspected possessor on the shoulder and talk of trust and faith, when they were really hinting for a bite, just like everyone else? Where did they come from, precisely when no one could use them?

I was sick of the whole thing. My stomach was turning over and I felt cold. I looked for Hals or some other friend, but couldn't see any familiar faces. They must all have been sent to a different position. For me, they had become almost like relatives, and their absence weighed on me. I felt very much alone among these mutilated men with their raging fevers, trying to find some excuse for hope and encouragement. I myself began to daydream about a soft bed with silk covers, imitating the veteran, who liked to dream aloud about beds like that, which he himself had never known. Even before the war, he'd been an unfortunate and unhappy man, but he knew how to dream. Sometimes, as his bony body lay stretched out on the hard ground, he smiled in a way which suggested such a powerful sense of well-being that I am sure,

305

in those moments at least, he was unaware of the harshness of his situation, and that his dream was more powerful than reality. I myself was not yet that well trained, and my dreams could not obliterate the feverish vice which gripped my temples.

Straight ahead, to the west, the smoke had climbed so high it blotted out the sky, and the distant horizon was ringed with fire. What substance could be feeding such a huge conflagration?

Companies of men black with dust and soot were pouring back, on the run. It seemed that our first contact with the Russians had not been in our favour. The retreating troops left a certain number of wounded with us, but no one knew what to do with them. The medical teams, which at best were inadequate, had already packed up and gone, or were about to leave. The wounded men were left lying in the street where they had been put down, trying to stanch the flood of their own blood, which was often pouring from several wounds at once. Everyone tried to help as much as possible, but we were capable only of ludicrous gestures. The most extraordinary scenes unfolded in front of our incredulous eyes. As we were sponging off a fellow who'd passed out, a fat gefreiter came to help us, explaining that he'd just dropped a fellow with a smashed knee. 'He was making too much noise, and I couldn't stand it. Give me someone who's knocked out, any time.'

For the moment, our stretch of cleared street was not under bombardment. The battle was raging directly ahead, as well as to the northwest and southwest. Directly to the north, the Russian artillery was raking over the ruins like a monstrous plough. However, as a few of the retreating men huddled beside us trying to catch their breaths, the Russian fire shifted, and began to sweep through our position like a giant scythe. Our officers' orders were drowned by the shouts of the men, and the uproar of a frantic stampede for shelter.

Our jostling and cries for help and screams of panic were finally obliterated by explosions. Everyone who was able to had run off the street. The slightest protuberance offered some hope of survival, as a wall of fire passed over the two thousand troops concentrated on that spot. The wounded, abandoned in the open, lay writhing in the dust. Through the uproar, we could hear the sound of disarticulated bodies falling back to the ground in broken pieces. As at Belgorod, the earth shook, and everything trembled and grew dim, as the whole landscape suddenly became mobile. The filthy hands of ill and wounded men resigned to death scratched the ground for one last time, and the lined faces of veterans who believed they had already seen everything were transformed by desperate, imploring panic. Quite near us, behind a heap of tiles, a Russian shell scored a bull's eye, exploding in the midst of eleven men who had huddled together like children caught in a sudden rain. The Russian shell landed in the precise centre of their trembling group, mixing flesh and bones and tiles in a torrent of blood.

Chance, which continued to favour me, had driven me along with three companions to the shelter of a staircase in a roofless house. The building was hit on all sides during the bombardment, and the cellar filled with broken beams and other debris. However, thanks to our extraordinary helmets, our heads survived intact. When the thunder stopped for a moment and we heard the screams of the newly wounded, we looked outside. The horror of what we saw was so overwhelming that we fell back, as if paralyzed, onto the shaky stairs.

'God help us,' someone shouted. 'There's nothing but blood.'

'We've got to get away from here,' screamed another voice, in a tone close to madness.

He ran outside, and we followed him. The air was filled with bestial cries. Everyone who'd been lucky enough to survive was falling back to the west, where, as always, safety lay, and now the front, and the gap through which we would try to escape. Anyone who could still stand was helped. The wounded grabbed at the men running past. Two haggard soldiers in front of me were dragging a third man through the dust, probably a friend who was nearly dead. How long had they pulled him along like that, and how long would it take them to dump him?

I can no longer tell how long our stampede lasted, through the anonymous ruins and thick smoke and roaring guns. The Russians were firing at us from all sides, at close range, with

50-mm. guns. We staggered on carrying the wounded as best we could.

In complete disorder, we came to a railroad track strewn with the burnt-out wreckage of a train, and a few Russian corpses. We trampled over them with a kind of fierce delight, taking our revenge for their artillery and their 50-mm. fire. The tracks ran through a kind of trench. We galloped down it, passing a second train as still and broken as the first. Some of our vehicles seemed to be parked there too, surrounded by a crowd of soldiers and several Panzermänner. We ran right into a group of officers. Wesreidau, who had stayed with us throughout, was one of them. We were given a few minutes' rest, and everyone dropped where he stood. To the southwest, the din seemed to have increased tenfold, and made my head swim.

Then we received a fresh blow. Wesreidau and two of his aides ran through the groups of exhausted men.

'Get up! Get moving! We've got to push on now! The division has broken through. If you don't hurry, we'll be caught in the trap, so get the hell up! We're the last ones left.'

Already, men half dead with exhaustion were staggering to their feet. The noncoms tapped on the shoulders of the stronger men, who were trying to help the wounded comrades they had carried out of town, and told them not to bother any more.

'Don't load yourself with anyone who can't walk. You'll need all the strength you've got just to make it yourself.'

And so we were forced to abandon a great many men to an almost inconceivably horrible fate, despite their desperate pleas for help. Half paralyzed by terror and fear, men who had lost almost all their blood managed to get up and even hide their pain so that they would be allowed to walk beside the healthy. The heroism, pathos, and determination of our breakout exceeds by far my powers of description. Men who had always been cowards became heroes despite themselves. A great many managed to cover barely half the distance.

We fought our way through the fires of hell, losing almost half of our remaining men, as we pushed for more than nine hours, from shell hole to shell hole, along the famous and tragic Konotop-Kiev road, past burnt-out tanks and piles of hundreds of shrivelled corpses.

You who perhaps will some day read these lines may also remember that one evening in the autumn of 1943 the bulletins announced that German troops caught in Konotop had managed to break out of a Russian trap. This was true. Of course, the price was never mentioned, because it didn't matter. For you, the day of deliverance was coming.

Chapter Nine

CROSSING THE DNIEPER

The rain blew in from the horizon in waves. Occasionally a brief moment of light enabled us to spot the next undulating curtain of water sweeping across the streaming steppe. It had rained steadily for two days, and despite the discomfort and inconvenience we hoped the rain would last for at least that long again. In another two days, if we could maintain our rate of thirty miles a day, and had any luck at all, we should reach the Dnieper.

No planes could fly through such a torrential downpour, so there had been no Yaks – and every day without Yaks was a reprieve from death for hundreds of men. The extraordinary mobility of the Wehrmacht – one of its principal sources of strength up to that moment – had entirely disappeared in that part of Russia, and the men from Army Group Centre were plodding toward the river in interminable columns at the rate of three miles an hour. Our mobility, which had always given us an advantage over the vast but slow Soviet formations, was now only a memory, and the disproportion of numbers made even flight a doubtful prospect. Moreover, the equipment of the Red Army was constantly improving, and we often found ourselves pitted against extremely mobile motorized regiments of fresh troops. To complete our disarray, the Soviet troops which had been tied up in the attempt to trap us at Konotop were now free to pursue our slow withdrawal.

German aviation, which was entirely occupied south of Cherkassy, had abandoned our part of the sky to the Yaks, which took advantage of this freedom to harass us unmercifully. So, despite our heavy, waterlogged clothes, worn-out boots, fever, and the impossibility of lying down except on the soaking ground, we blessed fortune for sending us grey skies and rain.

During the morning, five Bolshevik planes had appeared

despite the weather. Our harassed men reacted with an automatic impulse of self-defence and self-preservation, staring desperately at the flat plain for somewhere to hide. But, like animals caught in a trap, we understood there was no way out. The companies in a direct line of fire dropped to one knee, in the regulation position for anti-aircraft defence. These companies received the Yaks' fire, and saw several men torn to pieces by Russian bullets, but nevertheless managed to bring down one of the planes. It was our bad luck that the plane went into a spin, and fell directly onto our convoy, crushing a truck full of wounded men, and opening a crater twenty yards wide filled with shattered flesh. No one cried out: in fact, almost no one looked. We simply picked up our burdens and went on.

We were all too exhausted to react, and almost nothing stirred our emotions. We had all seen too much. In my sick and aching brain, life had lost its importance and meaning, and seemed of no more consequence than the power of motion one lends to a marionette, so that it can agitate for a few seconds. Of course, there was friendship – there were Hals and Paula – but immediately behind them was that hole full of guts, red, yellow, and foul smelling; piles of guts, almost as large as the earth itself. Life could be snuffed out like that, in an instant, but the guts remained for a long time, stamped on the memory.

We walked without stopping. The interminable line of men ahead curved in a semicircle which seemed to be standing still. The Dnieper was not yet in sight. We had planned to reach it in five days, but we were now in the sixth, ploughing through the mud at an average speed of two or two and a half miles an hour. I had never seen a countryside so huge and so empty. The trucks and other vehicles which had gas had all passed us long ago. The rest were pulled by the few half-starved nags we had not already killed and eaten. From time to time, someone gave up his place on a crowded steiner, pulled by two horses, to continue on foot. We were under orders not to abandon matériel for any reason whatever. We were supposed to receive more gasoline – God knows how – probably by air – so that we could continue to drive our machines. In fact, one morning we did receive a delivery from aircraft. Two JU-52s threw down eight large packages

311

of rope, which we retrieved with derision. We were supposed
to use them for tying our vehicles to the tanks which had
been destroyed at Konotop the week before. In default of gas,
our gaunt horses stubbornly pulled our vehicles through the
gluey muck which had been freshly trampled by thirty
retreating regiments. Our steiner, on which I had hung all my
gear, was pulled by two Rhenish horses, probably taken from
their peacetime labour about a year before. One of them was
covered with sores, and his eyes glittered with fever.

Two days later, on the bank of the Dnieper, our brave
horse received his reward. A noncom from the cavalry shot
him in the head, along with some ten others. Very few horses
were allowed onto the pontoons, whose capacity was inadequate even for the men, and nothing could be left behind
which might be useful to the Russians. In a way, this was the
beginning of our 'scorched earth' policy.

The proportion of sick men to healthy rose at an alarming
rate. 'A healthy mind in a healthy body' was the slogan our
leaders had held up to us. Under the conditions of our retreat,
it was often hard to tell which was affected first – mind or
body. It seemed that well over half our men had nothing
healthy about them.

Luckily, the weather remained frightful. This was particularly hard on the sick and feverish – undernourished, de-
hydrated men with filthy, suppurating wounds and bodies
barely covered by torn, ragged uniforms. But anything the
weather could produce – wind, rain, heavy clouds trailing
down to the ground – was preferable to clear skies, which
invariably meant the humming planes, diving down at us like
carrion crows attacking a moribund animal. Indifferent to
everything, we continued our slow march.

Two or three times a day, covering troops were organized
and left behind to slow down the enemy, who were following
at a leisurely pace. The men chosen for this task dug shallow
holes which protected less than a quarter of their bodies, and
waited, resigned, for the juggernaut to crush them.

We knew that we would never see them again. In other
districts, entire regiments had been wiped out by Russian
armoured troops which had caught up with them. The retreat
was costly, and reached its climax on the east bank of the
river, in an incredible crush of men and materiel, spread out

over acres of flat sand, so that each Russian missile was assured a maximum destructive effect. A healthy mind in a healthy body would have done everything possible to escape those circumstances.

Our eyes, which had grown used to accepting everything without surprise, gaped at the most astonishing sights.

Everyone reached the river, the outer boundary of safety, in a state of indescribable panic, only to find it was necessary to trample on the men already there, even drown them, to have any hope of getting onto the wretchedly inadequate vessels, which often foundered before they reached the other side.

On the eighth day, after skirting a broad hill, we reached the bank of the river, or, more precisely, the swarm of landser who covered the bank, hiding it completely. Through the noise and confusion we could hear the sound of engines, which we found curiously reassuring: working engines must mean there was gasoline somewhere. We knew that motorized transport was essential for such a huge country, and that even with motors we could only move very slowly because of the terrible roads. However, if we heard engines, it must at least mean that some reorganization had begun. Among the crowd of men there were many vehicles which had been dragged as far as the river despite almost insuperable obstacles, and were waiting in the long grass, which looked like dune grass. In fact, the engines we heard did not belong to refuelled trucks, but to the boats – inadequate in size and number – which the engineers were using to move across as many men and machines as they could. Whenever matériel could be moved, it was given priority. Loading trucks and guns and light tanks onto vessels built to carry hay carts was not easy, but fortunately we had plenty of manpower to replace the cranes and derricks of a port – at least a hundred thousand at our point of arrival alone. I saw men standing up to their necks in water, supporting makeshift landing stages until the water rose over their chins – rickety, hastily improvised piers which collapsed as soon as their human props moved away. Half drowned, these men worked frantically against time, with extraordinary persistence and patience. The urgent task of transporting five divisions was not begun until two days after our arrival, when all materiel

313

that could be moved was across the river. We had ten boats at our disposal, each with a maximum capacity of twenty men, four barges which had run out of gas and were towed in turn by two small boats equipped with B.M.W. portable engines, and four precarious pontoons, each with a capacity of 150 men.

At this point, south of Kiev, the Dnieper is about eight hundred yards wide. Had we chosen a section to the north of the city, we would have been in rich, densely populated country, where we would undoubtedly have been able to acquire plenty of boats for crossing, and where, in addition, the river often narrows to less than a hundred yards. There were also bridges in Kiev itself; some had undoubtedly been destroyed, but others must have been standing.... By the evening of the third day after our arrival at the river, at least ten thousand men had crossed to the west bank. First of all, the sick and wounded were taken, and I witnessed many instances of lightly wounded or sick men giving up their places to the more seriously injured. Although the rain was remorseless and savage, and we all were sickened by our diet of horsemeat – often raw – we nonetheless made use of this forced delay to rest as much as we could.

During the night of our third or fourth day, everything turned hellish again. As we had feared, we heard the roar of war again as soon as the rain stopped – dull and unclear at first, and then unmistakable: the rumble of tanks moving slowly through the mud.

To begin with, there was only the noise, which in itself was enough to send a wave of terror through the eighty-five thousand men trapped beside the water. On the slopes littered with exhausted soldiers, thousands of men lifted their heads to verify the terrifying sound.

We stared through the darkness, trying to see the unseeable, frozen, for a minute, with our heads lifted to listen. Then, everywhere, shadowy figures began to move, with frantic, intensifying speed.

'Tanks!'

Every man grabbed his things and began to run toward what we knew was an insuperable barrier, hoping that the boats were still moving, and that somehow they would be able to take all of us at once.

314

We were packed in a dense crowd onto a narrow strip of ground beside the river, and the sound of our shouting voices rose above the heavy rumble of tanks which now filled the night. Frantic men were abandoning everything on the bank and plunging into the water to try to swim to the opposite shore; thousands of voices were shouting toward the grey water and the opposite bank, where they hoped they would at last be able to rest. Men waded out into the icy water until they lost their footing, and the sound of voices pleading and calling for help rose to such a pitch that the boats still operating hesitated to draw into shore for fear of being swamped. Madness seemed to be spreading like wildfire. Almost unconscious with exhaustion, I sat through about twenty minutes of panic with five or six other soldiers, collapsed onto a heap of packs which had been abandoned on the wet grass, letting the howling mob and the rush of events pass us by. Here and there, we could see other small groups like ours, moving only when the frantic stampede swept them along.

The officers, who had managed to keep some self-control, organized a few more or less conscious men, and ran to meet the mob, trying to stop them, like shepherds trying to control a herd of crazed sheep. They were able to reorganize a few groups, which they posted on the slopes of the hills to attempt interception of the Soviet tanks, if they should come that way. Our dense crowd of men stretched down the river bank as thinly as possible, to offer fewer opportunities for mass destruction by the T-34s which appeared about an hour and a half later. Fortunately, there were not many tanks, and they didn't linger, as their real objective was Kiev, where heavy fighting was in progress.

I stayed where I was, sitting on the heap of packs with a few strays, when we heard that a raft made of tyres taken from the trucks parked nearby would be able to carry a certain number of landser across to the west bank. We ran several hundred yards upstream, and saw a tight cluster of men beside the dark water. We quickly went over to them. There must have been about a hundred men wading in the mud. In the centre of the group, about a dozen fellows were busily taking out the inner tubes of a heap of tyres, and tying them together to make a raft – which would clearly never be

315

large enough to hold everyone. We were greeted with un-welcoming stares, and given no encouragement to stay. Finally, a big fellow who was standing watching the work spoke to us: 'You can see that this thing won't even take half the men here. Go on a little further – you'll be sure to find something.'

He must have said more or less the same thing several times over to the fellows who'd arrived ahead of us, but most of them had stayed, hoping to get onto the raft somehow – even to fight their way on, if necessary. I had neither the build nor the strength to force my way onto a contraption that would probably sink anyway. So, despite the distant rumble which came to us in spurts on the wind, I went on up the river, accompanied by two stray artillerymen.

We walked through a damp, heavy fog, between clumps of dripping furze, past groups of frantic, terrified men pacing up and down that interminable bank. The fog grew steadily thicker, until at last it blotted out the countryside completely, and turned us into Chinese shadow puppets. We could no longer tell which way we were going, and were gripped by continual anxiety that we were walking in the wrong direction. Luckily, from time to time someone would check on the position of the river, and shout out into the darkness: 'Ach gut! das Wasser ist da.'

We went on without thinking, unaware that if we followed the river long enough we would arrive at Kiev, which was the heart of the fighting. No one seemed capable of any logical, connected thought, but the constant fear, exhaustion, and threat of tanks kept us moving, trying to get away. It didn't really matter where we might get to, or how – just away.

The darkness of the night was continually broken by flares, and by the noise of guns. A group of men passed by, invisible, but quite close to judge by the sound of their voices.

'Achtung! Ivans! Achtung!'

I looked imploringly at the man from the artillery who had been stumbling along beside me for more than half an hour, but received nothing except the fixed stare of a hunted animal. We no longer understood anything. We had thought the Russians were on our right, behind the hills – but the firing was coming from the river bank, which was on our left.

Expecting the Russians to begin shooting at us at any

minute, we began to run, to look for some hole or hollow where we could hide. Once we had flattened ourselves down into what seemed to be a shallow frog pond, we tried to grasp the facts of our situation.

A noncom in our group thought the Popovs must be patrolling in boats, knocking off Germans whenever they could. To judge by the lights of the explosions, which were sometimes hundreds of yards apart, there must have been several Russian boats. The darkness which hid our trapped men rang with the sounds of our frantic disorder.

Shells were coming in from the west, and landing somewhere to the east of us, beyond the hills. This comforted us somewhat; since the shells were falling beyond the hills, they must be landing on the Russians, and our men must be firing them. The artilleryman remarked in a pleased and knowing voice: 'Those are ours all right. I'd know that yap anywhere.'

'I never thought we'd get any help,' said a soldier who had just joined us.

In the end, the shelling lasted only ten minutes, and probably had very little effect, as there was no effort to aim it with any precision. The fog had grown so thick that the glow of the discharges of the 77s was almost invisible, emerging from the darkness and vanishing again, as if we were watching through a thin, semi-transparent cloth. But, although the fog was thicker, the air had also grown astonishingly cold, stabbing our lungs every time we took a breath.

'My God, it's cold,' someone said.

The temperature of the water, which came to the middle of our boots, must have been close to freezing. Despite their remarkable resistance to water, our boots had at last become waterlogged, and our feet felt frozen.

'We can't keep on like this,' said the artilleryman, almost laughing. 'We've got to get out of here, or we'll catch our deaths. Anyway, why should we be afraid of our own guns?'

My boots each seemed to weigh a ton: a ton of dense, solid matter which was, in fact something like 95 per cent water.

The exhaustion we had been dragging about with us for days increased the fear we could no longer control. Fear intensified our exhaustion, as it required constant vigilance. We had learned to see in the dark, like cats, but on that particular night no look, however penetrating, could pierce the fog, which was as thick as a London pea souper. I could no longer breathe through my clogged nose, and only drew in through my pursed lips the bare minimum necessary to sustain life. We seemed to be moving through a mixture of water and sulphur, and each icy breath stabbed me with hundreds of sharp points, all the way down to my empty stomach.

I remembered the veteran's advice, but couldn't think of anything convincingly warm or dry, so I began deliberately to recollect pleasant things that had happened to me, that I might have experienced a long time ago. But this proved almost impossibly difficult; my mind filled only with unpleasant memories. The hunched back of the soldier in front of me could not be transformed into the back of my mother busy with some household task on a long winter evening, or my brother's back, or the back of anyone I had ever known in peacetime. All I saw was a silhouette of the history of the war, and Russia, which memories of youth could not blot out. It seemed as if the war would mark men for life. They might forget women, or money, or how to be happy, but they would never forget the war, which spoiled everything – even the joy which was bound to come, like the victory ahead. The laughter of men who lived through the war has something forced and desperate about it. It does them no good to say that they must now make use of the experience; their mechanisms have been run too hard, and something has gone out of balance. Laughter no longer has any more value for them than tears.

The back of the soldier in front of me filled me with pity and respect and even exasperation. I felt like hitting him until he fell, so that he would be on a level with the war. But, if that man fell, there would be another right after him, and then thousands more after that – thousands of hunched backs swollen by acid fog. Russia is still full of backs like that, the hunched backs of men who have forgotten how to dream, and it will take more toil and war, too, before they all have been toppled.

The roar of the guns was growing louder, like the noise of an oncoming train, and there was the sound of machine guns too, although we still couldn't see anything. We could also hear a vast din of human voices which rose above the thunder of guns and machinery. We stopped where we were, a light trace of breath escaping from each half-open mouth. I looked for some explanation on the filthy faces of my companions, but their expressions were as bewildered as my own, which had probably not changed much since I had begun to try to lose myself in memories. Since surprises in wartime can only be dangerous, we immediately looked for a hole. All I could find was the river bank. I slid over the edge until I was up to my thighs in the invisible water, which seemed almost warm after the icy air.

I immediately lost hold of my attempted daydream, and stared feverishly through the black and impenetrable wall which hid the action from us, like a curtain in the theatre. The roar of the tanks grew louder, and made the surface of the water tremble, with a motion I was just able to perceive.

When danger finally comes, after hours of harassing fear, it is almost like a liberation. At least one knows what the confrontation will be, and if the danger is terrible, one knows that at least it will soon be over. But, when danger continues indefinitely, it becomes unbearable. Then even an outburst of tears is no release. After hours and then days of danger, as at Belgorod, one collapses into unbearable madness, and a crisis of nerves and tears is only the beginning. Finally, one vomits and collapses, entirely brutalized and inert, as if death had already won.

For the moment, I remained calm. The river blocked our escape but, at the same time, offered a prospect of safety. I was already over my knees in water. The fog hid the terrifying breadth of the river from me, and I thought that, if the worst came to the worst, I could always try that way out, skimming over the surface like a will-o'-the-wisp. I felt almost convinced that I could do it. Then we saw lights, and heard explosions like grenades, and crackling sounds accompanied by little points of light. Five or six gasping soldiers splashed into the water beside me.

'It's those dumb bastards in the artillery who brought Ivan here.'

Terrifying screams drowned the sound of engines, screams so prolonged and horrible that my blood froze, and the water around my legs seemed even colder than before.

319

'Mein Gott!' someone murmured in the darkness beside me.

We heard the sounds of gunfire and explosions coming closer, punctuated by bloodcurdling screams. Men suddenly plunged out of the pale, enveloping cotton, and disappeared like ghosts into the black water. From the sounds of splashing, we guessed they were trying to swim. We felt petrified by fear, and stayed where we were. A terrible, growling mass of machines passed by close to us, shaking the earth and water, and a penetrating headlight pierced the fog. We couldn't see where it was going, only that it was moving. During those moments of terror, we clung to each other like children. A piece of the bank broke away under our weight, and our heap of belongings slid into the mud. My head went under for a few seconds, and when I surfaced the river bank and the long grasses hid what was happening. We could hear the sound of machine guns ripping into the air very close to us, over the grinding roar of tank treads. And always, terrifying screams, as the tanks drove a bloody furrow through the tightly packed crowd paralyzed by terror and darkness. A little higher up, two other lights, barely visible in the gloom, were seeking out other victims.

With daylight, we saw that there must have been about ten tanks, passing through without stopping, on their way to Kiev.

However, our tension was so great that we stayed in the water for a long time, without moving, in spite of the stinking mud which had seeped into our helmets, and through our hair, which was standing on end with terror.

With absolute accuracy, the German guns, firing from the other side of the river, had drawn the Bolshevik tanks onto us, and contributed to the horrible deaths of many of our men.

Cries for help drew us from our slimy refuge, and we ran to do what we could to help the dying – which was very little. We saw sights so horrible they were beyond any imagining. We shot a great many men to put them out of their misery, although mercy killings were strictly forbidden. At dawn the fog lifted, and an almost springlike sun ushered in a new day of difficulties and disappointments.

Burial squads were forcibly organized and began their grisly work, grimacing with horror. Everyone who managed to escape this duty went off as far as he could, to try to sleep or warm up. My partly dried clothes had gone stiff, and I felt uncomfortable and ill. But my exhaustion, which weighed on my eyes and made the sunlight unbearable, prevented me from grasping that I should have stripped and washed in the river, allowing the sun to nourish my exhausted body. I stayed as I was, immobilized by my need for sleep, staring through half-closed eyes at the damp grey-green of my uniform, turning slowly yellow as it dried. When I finally did sleep, I was awakened almost immediately by shouts of terror.

I opened my eyes, and stared up into an infinite, pale blue sky, in which there was a familiar noise: planes. My bones creaked as I propped myself up on one elbow. I couldn't see anything unusual – only the piles of sleeping bodies among the gorse. Everywhere, faces drowning in sleep were turning to the sky. A fellow in a fatigue cap ran by, shouting like a deaf man.

A heavy machine gun behind me opened fire. It took us a while to shake off our torpor. Four Russian planes were circling like hornets about three thousand feet above us. Everyone was shouting – both men and officers.

'Do you all want to be killed?' a ragged lieutenant was yelling at us. 'You should at least try to defend yourselves.'

We feverishly grabbed our guns, and waited with one knee on the ground for the enemy, who was about to drop from the clouds. However, the Yaks went away. It was inconceivable that they should have been afraid of us, so we concluded they were running out of gas. We rubbed our eyes and sighed with relief, as our partially revived sense of vigilance died down. Everyone was thinking of stretching out again and catching up with his lost sleep. Then the heavy machine gun pivoted rapidly on its mount and began to fire toward the north. Everyone turned that way too, before throwing himself flat. The four planes roared over us almost at ground level, firing rapidly with all their guns. We could just hear the lieutenant, who was very near us, shouting as loud as he could to make himself heard above the noise of the planes: 'Fire, you bastards!'

The planes passed overhead. I saw the lieutenant roll onto the ground, stand up again, and with one hand clutching his stomach fire his revolver at the roaring planes. Then he grimaced, fell to his knees, and rolled over onto himself. Of all the men around us, he was the only one who had been hit. The planes had reserved most of their fire for the overloaded, almost motionless rafts, which made perfect targets.

'Give us some help!' shouted a fellow with a long thin face, who'd gone with a companion to see what he could do for the lieutenant. 'Why in God's name did he stand up?'

'He was acting like a hero,' answered one of the felds, 'and he was the only one. We should all be ashamed.'

The thin-faced fellow was helping to carry the dying man down to the river's edge. I was behind him with some of the lieutenant's things.

'Shame has nothing to do with it,' he said, sighing heavily.

We had not been abandoned. From the west bank, our anti-aircraft guns were firing on the Russian vultures overhead, and the two ramshackle rafts on the river were continuing their dangerous journey. There must have been many dead and wounded men on board, to judge by the agitation we could all see.

The planes dived down toward the swarming strip of ground which rang with screams of pain and cries for help, and toward the rafts, and achieved a hideous massacre. Every time the danger withdrew for a moment, so that we could lift our heads and look out over the reeds, we saw scenes of tragedy. Almost everyone on the rafts who hadn't been killed or immobilized by wounds had jumped into the water and was trying to swim. The planes made a fourth pass, and were met this time by all our guns and spandaus, which finally drove them away. We heard a loud sound of shooting. One of the Russian planes had been hit, and was spiralling upward, trying to gain height, leaving a thick plume of black smoke behind it. Suddenly it lurched into an irrevocable dive toward the water. We saw a smaller shape detach from the mass of the plane – probably the pilot, trying to jump to safety. But his parachute, if he had one, failed to open. Man and machine hit the water at the same speed, and disintegrated. For a moment, our cheers drowned the groans of the wounded on the rafts. However, toward noon the Russian planes were back again – about a dozen fighter-bombers this time.

In the interval, we had deepened our holes so that we were better protected; but we couldn't reach the planes with our fire. The Russians, as before, attacked the heavily loaded rafts on the river, which had almost reached the west bank. Our flak tried unsuccessfully to keep the planes away, and we watched, pale with helpless rage, as the bombs fell toward the water. A raft and all its human cargo were blown to pieces. Our fleet was being liquidated, and the attacks were just beginning. The Ilyushins were gaining height, to dive down again. A soldier beside me was weeping and shouting over and over: 'The bastards, the bastards.' Our damp hands scraped nervously against the ground as we manoeuvred our guns.

'We'll never get out of this,' shouted my companion. 'They'll wipe us out, the shits.'

Then a miracle occurred, which completely changed the tone of our cries.

'Sieg! Sieg! Der Luftwaffe!'

Nine Messerschmitt 109-Fs had appeared and were diving down onto the Russian planes, which had just completed an attack formation. The Russian pilots, aware of the technical inferiority of their planes, were trying to get away as fast as they could. We could hear bursts of fire, and felt a surge of intense, savage, and vengeful joy when we saw two of the Ilyushins spinning through the air like partridges hit by hunters' bullets. Then our cries grew even louder. Five Russian planes passed right overhead before we realized they meant danger. We shook our fists at them.

The fellow beside me, who'd been trembling with fury a moment before, was now trembling with joy, as uncontrolled as a madman. Our fighters were chasing the Ilyushins, which fled, skimming low over the ground. Then the pack disappeared behind the hills, which blocked our view. We heard guns, and a loud explosion. After that we had nothing to do but tend the wounded.

The next day we felt almost happy to wake in the rain. Traffic across the river had continued all night, carrying over as many men as possible; nevertheless, a vast number were still waiting on the east bank. We no longer knew how many days we'd been there, but, despite all our difficulties, we'd been able to reorganize somewhat. Men belonging to the same units had sorted each other out, and waited in distinct groups. Our officers had posted armed men on the hills to warn against a sudden attack. We knew that the Russians were very close, and felt rather surprised that they hadn't attacked already. Probably the battle for Kiev had absorbed almost all of them.

I had joined a large group of men made up for the most part of members of the Gross Deutschland, and men who had escaped from the infantry regiment which had come to our aid when we broke through at Konotop. The officers present – among whom I was delighted to see Herr Haupt-mann Wesreidau – told us that as members of an élite division, and as specialized offensive troops, we should have been among the first to embark for the west. They also said that we would be the next to go. Naturally, we were glad to hear it, as everyone wished to reach the west bank as quickly as possible. Some fellows suggested a technique that had occurred to many of us as soon as we arrived at the river. This was to tie together bunches of reeds with our belts, and use them as floats. This had been proved successful many times, but it was not possible for moving the equipment indispensable to any soldier who did not wish to be considered a deserter.

The reception of these unequipped men on the other bank must have been sufficiently poor for our officers to forbid escape by reed float. But it was difficult for them to impose discipline on men simultaneously paralyzed by fear and prepared to affront the devil. Many men, in fact, drowned, or died of pneumonia, and many, after risking everything, were court-martialled.

I no longer had any clear idea of our situation, and set about trying to discover from the soldiers in my unit what had happened to my friends. Perhaps someone among these three thousand men waiting in the mud had run into Hals or Lensen or the veteran, stretched out on an armful of long, soaking stalks, dreaming of a distant utopia, indifferent to the rain running down his resigned features.

But my researches were in vain, and my questions remained unanswered. Once I thought I recognized a couple of faces from our disbanded company. I talked to the fellows, who answered evasively that they no longer remembered anything that had happened. They were absolutely exhausted, and my questions only seemed to annoy them. Their stunned minds seemed capable of only one idea: they had to cross the river.

There was only one person who might know a little more than the others – Herr Kapitän Wesreidau. But the respect and fear which officers required of us made it almost impossible to speak to them. A few of the older soldiers were bold enough to approach them, but for a boy like myself it was entirely different. However, I was so consumed by desire to speak to the captain that it must have showed on my face. Also, I was always lingering somewhere near him or his group. I was sitting on my bundle a short distance away from Wesreidau and two or three other officers, including a major, when Wesreidau began to walk toward me. I stared in confusion at the tall figure in the long leather coat shining with rain, ready to leap to my feet and snap to attention. But the captain gestured to me to stay as I was, so I remained on the ground, with my eyes glued to his face. He seemed even taller than usual, because I was so low down.

'What regiment do you belong to, young fellow?' he asked.

I stammered out my regimental number, as well as the number of the scratch company I was taken into for the retreat from Konotop. He took me for a Czech, so I explained my origins to him.

'Hm,' was all he said about that. 'Those scratch companies were the last ones out. I led several of them myself.'

'I know, Herr Hauptmann,' I said, blushing. 'I saw you.'

I couldn't get used to the idea that the captain really was talking to me.

'Ah,' said Wesreidau. 'Then we have memories in common, of a difficult time.'

'Ja, Herr Hauptmann.'

He reached for a cigarette, but the packet was empty. Had he perhaps been going to offer me one?

'We'll be crossing tomorrow, young fellow, and I expect you'll be getting a long leave.'

The word 'leave' was like a sudden sip of champagne.

'Leave!'

'I think so. We won't have stolen it from you.'

Sensations which I had thought I would never feel again

325

immediately revived – all the emotions I had buried with so much difficulty. Could it be possible ...? But it had always been possible; how could I doubt it? I suddenly realized the full weight of my despair, how absolutely I had given up hope. Now I began to think again, timidly and gently, of Paula. Since we had been organized into the special assault group, there had been no mail. Although we had been moving continuously, this lack of news had weighed on me terribly. And then, in the face of such intense misery and disgust, words describing love and tenderness lost their meaning. Everything I had felt seemed to have been swept away in the dust and noise of crumbling houses, and in misery far more intense than the miseries of love. I had often thought that if I managed to live through the war I wouldn't expect too much of life. How could one resent disappointment in love if life itself was constantly in doubt? Since Belgorod, terror had overturned all my preconceptions, and the pace of life had been so intense one no longer knew what elements of ordinary life to abandon in order to maintain some semblance of balance. I was still unresigned to the idea of death, but I had already sworn to myself during moments of intense fear that I would exchange anything – fortune, love, even a limb – if I could simply survive.

I sensed that Captain Wesreidau was about to leave, so I asked him if he knew anything of my usual companions. He was only able to remember the veteran, calling him by his proper name.

'August Wiener's company was supporting a howitzer battery at the beginning of the offensive. The first troops had a hard time. It was very difficult. In any case, the men who got through were probably sent to Kiev. That's where we would have regrouped if we'd had the trucks.'

I listened to him in silence. He nodded, and walked away.

'We'll be crossing tomorrow.'

My head was spinning with the thought of a leave, and with the anguish of the possible loss of my special comrades. Perhaps I had already walked past their burnt bodies on the shattered pavement of the Konotop-Kiev road. Would I also have to renounce the friendships which had seen me through so much? I knew that they also were so close to being stripped of everything that the sentiment I had for them seemed permissible, it was so gratuitous and disinterested. Must I also obliterate, without remorse — for remorse is a dangerous luxury in battle — the memories of Hals, and Lensen, and even that bastard Lindberg?

However, if my friends had disappeared, the veteran had left me an inheritance, a special faculty. I would relive all my good memories, even in the worst moments, and lie on the ground, inert and almost insensible, oblivious of the rain which my saturated cap was no longer able to soak up, and which ran over my face and collar and down my neck. The rain streaming across my cheeks would take the place of the tears I should have shed.

The rain continued for a long time, through the night and the next day, until the end of the afternoon. The soil on which we waited had become a giant sponge. Each fresh bundle of rushes soaked up as much water from the ground as it received from the sky. We were so thoroughly soaked through that some of us stripped altogether, to wait naked. Most of the time, we stayed on our feet, with tent cloths over our shoulders, watching the endless back-and-forth of the rafts.

Toward noon, despite the terrible weather, a squadron of Ilyushins appeared. Once again, we cursed those birds of ill-omen, which forced us to lie with our noses in the gluey Dnieper mud. The planes made three passes, scattering bombs and bullets wherever they could see anything. Once again, we were filled with a panic which ended only when the list of killed and wounded had grown a little longer.

Finally, toward six in the evening, as the light was fading, our group was taken in charge by the transit services. We were ordered to collect our things and proceed in good order to the three embarkation points which the incessant trampling had transformed into an astonishing quagmire.

Carrying our arms and baggage, covered with slimy mire, we set off down the road despite the mud which threatened to engulf us.

With heroic patience and discipline, each man waited his turn, enduring the torrential rain without complaint. With our feet in the muddy water our boots could no longer resist, we kept our assigned places. The last men to embark had to wait for several hours.

Vague, momentary smiles lit our almost unrecognizable faces. At last we were going to cross, and all of this would be over. We would be able to dry ourselves, and sleep, perhaps even in comfort, and stop feeling afraid. We clung to our more hopeful thoughts, although we were haunted by one last fear: what would happen on the trip across? Would the overused, overloaded boats make it? Or would they sink, carrying a hundred desperate souls to the bottom? And then there were the Yabos ... If any Russian planes appeared ... We could all remember in clear detail the horrible massacre of the day before.

Then it grew dark. Russian planes rarely flew at night, so perhaps we were at least safe from them.

When it was my turn, I climbed with a hundred other men onto a raft whose planks had been splintered by the passage of thousands of hobnailed boots. I watched anxiously as the water rose to within a foot of swamping us.

'That's enough, cap'n,' shouted a noncom who looked about forty years old. 'Do you want us to sink?'

'As many as possible, Herr Spiess,' an engineer said, laughing. 'That's orders, and we're used to it. Come on – let's have another ten.'

When we were on the point of foundering, the boatmen let go of the ropes and, with the agility of young goats, jumped onto the few inches they had reserved for themselves.

So slowly we were almost unaware of it, the raft began to move out onto the water, which was barely creased by our momentum. Our balance seemed so precarious that no one dared move. The cursed bank, veiled in fog, disappeared from sight. I was huddled in the centre of the raft between two fellows I didn't know: a young lieutenant from an infantry regiment which had come to help us at Konotop, and a fellow from my own company, who seemed to be asleep on his feet. He was the only one who seemed so indifferent. Everyone else was listening and looking intently, especially toward the rainy sky, which we mistrusted absolutely. A boat half the size of ours, but with the same engine, slowly pulled level with us. Its deck was as jammed as ours.

How long was the crossing? Perhaps a quarter of an hour. It seemed interminable. The water slid past us with an easy, regular motion, whose slowness made us frantic. Some of the fellows were counting aloud, marking off the seconds perhaps, or using them as one uses imaginary sheep, to force sleep.

Then voices announced the approach of the west bank and safety and release from our torments. The men at the front of the raft could see it, enveloped in fog. Our blood ran faster in our veins, as we tried, by willpower, to increase the speed of the engine. We were about to land, to be safe – quick, while the sky was still quiet.

An empty raft crossed our path, heading back for the east bank. We looked at it coldly. Any movement toward the east made us shiver. Then the west bank was only twenty yards away. We no longer dared to move for fear of foundering, despite an intense joy which we would have expressed in other circumstances by jumping and shouting. After so many days and hours of waiting and despair, we had been saved.

Then there were only ten yards . . . then five. The engines went into reverse, to slow us down. We drew up beside a pier made of tied branches, and we heard voices telling us to move slowly and carefully. With a sense of enormous privilege, we stepped, one after the other, onto the solid earth – which is to say, onto a quagmire exactly like the east bank. But the mud no longer mattered; we had crossed to the other side. The west bank meant security and safety, a barrier between us and the Russians. We had dreamed of this safety for so long, and so intensely, that we almost felt as if there were a barrier between us and the war itself. The bulletins had been official: we would hold on to the Dnieper. The enemy would not pass beyond that line, and in the spring we would push them back beyond the Volga. During our long and painful retreat to the river and our endless wait, our thoughts had crystallized around this idea, and actually stepping onto the west bank seemed like the end of our misfortune: reorganization, clean clothes, leave, and the assurance that we had not been beaten. Of course, the west bank was still Russia, but it was the part of Russia which had welcomed us a few years earlier, the part of Russia which really favoured us. Our exhausted brains clung to this fantasy: the west bank was almost the motherland.

PART FOUR

TO THE WEST
Winter, 1943 – Summer, 1944

Chapter Ten

'GOTT MIT UNS'

The officers and soldiers waiting to direct us were not particularly agreeable, and the military police, with their badges glistening damply in the fog, were downright unpleasant. All organizations have police, and some of them must be fine fellows. However, we wanted to forget the police at Romny, and on the retreat from the Don, to preserve some of the joy we felt at being back in the West.

We tramped along, herded by a couple of fellows in a sidecar covered with mud. They didn't bother to line us up in threes, but let us walk any way we liked, almost as if we were out for a stroll — which was a pleasant variation of usual practice. Maybe they knew what a hard time we'd had, and had decided to give us a break. Now that we were out of it, maybe everything was going to be all right. The sidecar forced us to increase our pace. We went on for about a mile and a half, stumbling through the mud and splattering our companions, to arrive finally at a big camp, where the men who'd crossed ahead of us were already waiting. It was dark and a fine rain was falling. We could see the barbed wire gleaming with wetness. Two soldiers with machine guns under their arms waved us through a makeshift entrance. Then we stopped, and the sidecar drove rapidly away. We stood where we'd been left, surrounded by barbed wire, not knowing what to think.

We tried to tell ourselves that this was just how things happened in the army, and that this welcome seemed excessively cold because we were fresh from the hell of Konotop. They were probably making us wait so that they could take us straight to clean, comfortable barracks, where we would sleep and regain our strength. Or perhaps they were getting our passes ready. This last idea filled us with joy, and annihilated the liquid mud, and the rain, and the barbed wire, which in reality held us prisoner.

We waited for about two hours. A second group of new arrivals joined us. The rain had become heavier, and we were all streaming with water. Quite nearby, we could see a row of huts with firm roofs and weather-tight windows, to which men were being sent in groups of twenty. We waited expectantly, certain that we were living through the last of our miseries. The fellows who went into the huts weren't coming out again. They must already be sleeping on soft beds, the lucky bastards.

An hour later, it was my turn, along with nineteen others. There were two noncoms and a lieutenant in our group. We went into the building, which had its own generator and was brightly lit. Our state of extreme filth suddenly made us feel awkward. Military men of all ranks and military police were sitting facing us behind a row of long tables. An obergefreiter came up to us, yelling as in the old days at training camp. He told us to get over to the tables to be screened. We should be ready to produce on demand the papers and equipment entrusted to us by the army. This reception only increased our sense of astonished unease.

'First, your documents,' an M.P. shouted across the table.

The lieutenant, who was directly ahead of me in the line, was being interrogated.

'Where is your unit, lieutenant?'

'Annihilated, Herr Gendarme. Missing or dead. We had a hard time.'

The M.P. said nothing to this, but went on leafing through the lieutenant's papers.

'Did you leave your men, or were they killed?'

The lieutenant hesitated for a moment. We were all watching in frozen silence.

'Is this a court-martial?' The lieutenant's voice was exasperated.

'You must answer my questions, Herr Leutnant. Where is your unit?'

The lieutenant clearly felt caught in a trap, as did we all. Very few of us could have answered that question with any precision. He tried to explain. But there is never any point in explaining to an M.P.: their powers of comprehension are always limited to the form they wish to fill.

Further, it appeared that the lieutenant was missing a great many things. This fact obsessed his interrogator. It didn't matter that the man in front of him was effecting a miracle simply by staying on his feet, and had lost at least thirty pounds since entering the army. The M.P. only noted that the Zeiss fieldglasses, which are part of an officer's equipment, were missing. Also missing were a map case, and the section telephone, for which the lieutenant was responsible. In fact, the lieutenant, who had managed to save only his life, was missing far too many things. The army did not distribute its papers and equipment only to have them scattered and lost. A German soldier is expected to die rather than indulge in carelessness with army property.

The careless lieutenant was assigned to a penal battalion, and three grades were stripped from his rank. At that, he could think himself lucky.

The lieutenant's eyes were wild, and he seemed to be fighting for breath. He was a pitiful and terrifying sight. Two soldiers dragged him off to the right, toward a group of broken men, who'd been dealt with in the same way.

Then it was my turn. I felt stiff with fright. I pulled my crumpled documents from an inside pocket. The M.P. rifled through them, throwing me a reproving look. His bad temper seemed to soften somewhat at the sight of my apprehensive, mortified face, and he continued his inventory in silence.

Fortunately, I had been able to reintegrate with my unit, and had saved the scrap of white cardboard which stated that I had left the infirmary to take part in an attack. My head was swimming, and I thought I was going to faint. Then the M.P. read off a list of articles which ordinary soldiers like myself were supposed to carry at all times. The words rolled off his tongue, but I didn't catch them quickly enough, and didn't immediately produce the items still in my possession. The M.P. then treated me to a certain German word, which I was hearing for the first time. It appeared I was missing four items, including that fucking gas mask I had deliberately abandoned.

My pay book was passed from hand to hand to be inspected and stamped. In my panic, I made an idiotic move. Hoping to gain favour, I produced nine unused cartridges from my cartridge belt. The M.P.'s eyes lit on these like the eyes of an alpinist who spots a good foothold.

'You were retreating?'

'Ja, Herr Unteroffizier.'

'Why didn't you try to defend yourself? Why didn't you fight?' he shouted.

'Ja, Herr Unteroffizier.'

'What do you mean – ja?'

'We were ordered to retreat, Herr Unteroffizier.'

'God damn it to hell!' he roared. 'What kind of an army runs without shooting?'

My pay book came down the line. My interrogator grabbed it, and rifled the pages for a moment. His eyes travelled from the filthy, tattered page to my face.

I followed the movement of his lips, which might be about to assign me a penal battalion – to the life of a prisoner, to forward positions, mine clearing, infrequent leaves always confined to camp, so that the word 'liberty' lost all meaning, and the cancellation of mail. . . .

I held back my tears with difficulty. Finally the M.P.'s rigid fingers handed back my liberty. I had not been assigned to a penal battalion, but my emotion overwhelmed me anyway. As I picked up my pack, I sobbed convulsively, unable to stop. A fellow beside me was doing the same.

The crowd of men still waiting stared at me in astonishment. Like a miserable tramp, I ran past the line of tables and left by a door opposite the one we'd entered by. I felt that I had disgraced myself.

I rejoined my comrades, who were standing in the rain in the other part of the camp. They weren't resting on the soft beds we'd dreamed of before coming to this place, and the rain streaming down their shoulders and backs was another hope disappointed.

However, despite the slap in the face we had just received from our grateful country, we could still count ourselves lucky. Three days later, we learned that the day after our crossing, with six or seven thousand of our men still waiting on the east bank, the Russians had attacked. They were probably discouraged by their failure to retake Kiev, where the heavily outnumbered German Army was fighting desperately, and had decided to clean up the pockets still occupied by the Wehrmacht. Twenty-four hours after our group left, our comrades on the east bank were suddenly dazzled by the flares that flooded their temporary encampments with brilliant light.

The lookouts in the shallow trenches scratched into the hills overlooking the river, who were supposed to provide an illusion of protection, watched the shouting hordes of Russian infantry flood down to the river. These soldiers quickly realized they would never be able to stop that irresistible tide, and succumbed to a moment of absolute panic. Some ran, through the deafening explosions of Soviet rockets which drowned out our spandaus and light mortars. The Russians, driven by expectations of victory and by the exhortations of the people's commissars, pushed forward regardless of the cost.

The cost was enormous. Each German projectile seemed to hit home. But Ivan continued his inexorable advance. On the mud landing stage from which I had embarked, panic gave way to madness. One of the rafts, which was loading up as usual, was swamped by a human flood. The few who managed to keep cool heads shouted for calm, and sometimes even used their guns. In the grotesque, trampling rush, mooring ropes gave way, and the raft drifted out a few yards, shuddering under the weight of the mob which had overrun it. Hands trying to grip the edges of the raft were trampled and crushed by heavy boots. On the landing stage, friends were fighting each other. Some of the officers committed suicide. The raft moved out another couple of yards, and then suddenly tipped away from the bank like a child's toy. A loud cry mingled with the sound of the approaching battle, and two hundred terrified men floundered in the water, clinging together or trying to swim. A great many sank and drowned instantly.

At that moment, Ivan appeared at the crest of the hills, having swept the defenders aside. Drunk with excitement, the Russian soldiers dropped to the ground on one knee, and picked off Germans as if they were clay pigeons at a fair. A few Germans, white as ghosts, fired back with their F.M.s, but their numbers were so small the Russians scarcely noticed them. Several thousand others were running, screaming, trying to get away, and dying as they ran. The Russians also fired at the men in the water who were trying to swim, using flares to light the darkness.

An hour after they had appeared on the skyline, the Russians reached the river. There were a few more scattered shots, but their victory was complete. A third of the remaining German troops were taken prisoner, and for the rest every-

337

thing was over. Their military responsibilities had come to an end, and they would never again be victimized by military police.

At the reception camp, we stood in the rain a little longer, and then three blacked-out trucks appeared to collect us. Despite the appalling road and the overload which threatened to burst the slatted sides, fifty soldiers wrapped in sacking were piled onto each truck with all their equipment. I was stuffed into one of these human ant heaps: that is to say, one leg was buried in the swarm, while the other dangled out. I was astride the back flap, but there were other fellows hanging on for dear life who were almost entirely outside the truck. We rolled off through the quiet night. I felt completely disoriented, and hadn't the faintest sense of our direction.

An hour later, we drew up to a group of buildings, which first appeared as a vague, blurred mass in the dim, bluish light. We realized that an unusual rush of activity was taking place all around, and then gradually perceived that we were looking at a row of structures bordered on both sides by tree-lined roads jammed with innumerable vehicles. There were troops everywhere, on foot or arriving and leaving on high-speed motorcycles, and many officers and M.P.s. The trucks jerked to a sudden halt, and we were told to get off. Although we still understood that we'd been saved, we were beginning to feel that we'd had enough. We were famished and dropping with sleep.

We had to wait for another half hour before someone came to take charge of us. The rain fell steadily. Was it raining anywhere else? Was it raining in France? I tried to think of my house and my bed. Where were they now? In which direction? But I could only summon up confused and fragmented memories of the life I had left behind. My only world was the vast anonymity of Russia, which seemed to be engulfing all of us, absorbing entire regiments, so that even their names vanished.

Finally, a noncom came over to us. Our group leader handed him our papers, which he examined with a dimmed flashlight. Then he ordered us to collect our gear and follow him. At last, we entered the shelter of a roof, an amenity to which we'd grown so unaccustomed that we stared at it as if it were the ceiling of the Sistine Chapel.

338

'You'll be sent to your units later,' shouted the noncom, who, like the rest of us, seemed to have had just about enough. 'While you're waiting, try to get a little rest.'

He didn't have to repeat himself. We explored the darkness of the hut with our pocket flashlights, and discovered that it contained a couple of benches and four or five large tables. Everyone stretched out where he could, making pillows of the nearest leg, or buttocks, or boot. The discomfort seemed unimportant beside the fact that at last we were out of the rain. Some fellows began to snore immediately. Others tried to pretend they were somewhere else. Despite our harsh reception, we all had a sense that from now on everything would go better, and that once again life was offering its possibilities. We all thought of the leave we would surely be getting, which was now only a question of patience.

However, soldiers fresh from the front cannot indulge the luxury of daydreams. The accumulated lack of sleep gripped our temples like an iron band. Like people suffering a serious illness, we dropped swiftly from consciousness into deep sleep.

We probably slept for a long time. It was broad daylight when a burst of noise suddenly woke us. Then a long blast of a whistle ordered us to our feet. We were all filthy and horribly crumpled. If the Führer had seen us, he would either have sent us all home or had us shot. The noncom who had waked us looked at us with an expression of surprise. Perhaps he too had never imagined that the German Army could be reduced to such a state. He spoke to us, but I no longer remember what he said. I was still only half awake, and understood that he was talking, without really listening to him. We gathered that we were to prepare for departure. We were going to be returned to our units.

One of the huts had been fitted with showers, but so many men were waiting that we clearly had no chance of getting inside. Instead, we were given some empty gasoline vats full of hot water. However, we all felt too exhausted to want to wash. Our days of training, when we were appalled by the smallest spot on our tunics, seemed very far away. Our concern had shifted from hygiene to something far more urgent. Furthermore, it was bitterly cold, and no one wanted to take anything off – not even the sacking draped over our shoulders.

I was so cold I was shivering, and I wondered if I was getting sick again. We had to go outside for food, and lined up like a column of tramps beside the field kitchen. A cold east wind was blowing damp patches of fog in from the river. Two cooks emptied large ladles of hot soup into our chipped and filthy mess tins. We had been expecting the usual ersatz, but it seemed that the time for that had long gone by. As a special gesture, they were serving us eleven-o'clock soup early. The burning-hot mixture made us feel much better.

A hauptmann stared at us as he walked by, and then turned back, obviously looking for our unit leader. The lieutenant who filled this position got up and walked over to him.

'Kamerad,' the captain said, 'you and your men have been given this opportunity to clean up. I think you should make the most of it.'

'Jawohl, Herr Hauptmann.'

The lieutenant ordered us over to the vats, which were standing under the eaves of one of the huts. We looked enviously across at the fellows who were going to get into hot showers. At least three hundred men were waiting for an experience which seemed like a blessing from heaven, so close to the front.

Those at the front of the line had more or less undressed, and were scratching the lice which had settled in a ring at the belt line, when we were suddenly ordered to prepare for immediate departure. For me, at least, this was a reprieve. Stripping in that icy air had begun to seem impossibly difficult. I much preferred to keep my lice relatively warm between my grey undervest and my stomach, which was rumbling with hunger. I was certainly ill again – I no longer had any doubts. I couldn't stop shivering, and felt cold right down to the soles of my feet. We piled into the open trucks, overloading them as usual. But no one complained. No matter how squashed we were, it was better than walking. However, I was soon caught in a grotesque predicament.

The trucks rolled off down a road which the rains had transformed into a swamp. The truck behind us gave off two sprays of liquid mud as steady and uniform as the sprays of a municipal fountain. I was strangely reminded of the retreat from the Don. Was Russia nothing but a vast sea of mud? As always, we were driving toward a northern horizon marked by dark forests. The echoes of occasional explosions drifted to us on the wind, but they didn't sound serious. The sky was overcast and threatened rain.

Huddled between two companions, I swayed to the slow rhythm of the trucks struggling through the mire. I felt more and more uncomfortable and ill. My lips and face seemed to be burning, and the slightest motion of the air felt like ice against my skin. My stomach was griped by a brutal pain, which travelled outward through my body, in waves of violent shivers. At first I thought this must be an after-effect of the hard times we'd been through, especially as I had never entirely recovered from my illness at Konotop. I knew that I must look more cadaverous than ever. My intestines were twisting themselves in knots. Naturally, no one gave a damn, and besides I was certainly not the only one with a pain in my gut. Then my pain became so imperative that I tried to double over, despite the crowding and all my gear.

The fellow beside me noticed my restlessness, and leaned his hairy face toward me: 'Take it easy, friend. . . . We'll soon be there.' But he clearly had no more idea where we were going than I did.

'I've got a hell of a pain in the gut.'

'And this is a hell of a time to crap.'

Suddenly, I realized what was the matter with me. My stomach was churning with increasing violence and threatened to explode. I certainly couldn't stop a military convoy because my guts were about to turn inside out. I had to laugh at my predicament despite my shivers and cramps and salivating mouth. But I also had to try to think of a solution. The convoy was now in the middle of a forest, where there was no reason to stop. And, even if we came to a camp, I couldn't just leave my group the moment we arrived, without any apparent motive. If I did that, they might even shoot me as a deserter.

But could I hold out much longer? I tried desperately to think of something else, but failed. My pains increased, and I broke out in gooseflesh. Finally, my gut simply opened.

'Move over a little, fellow,' I said, grimacing. 'I've got terrible diarrhoea, and I can't wait any more.'

The truck was making a lot of noise, and no one seemed to hear me. I shoved with my elbows, and shouted louder. The fellows on either side of me moved back about four inches, but paid no further attention. I could feel myself blushing with embarrassment. I tried to undo my clothes, jostling one of my neighbours.

'What's the hurry?' he said. 'You'll be able to crap when we get there.'

'But I'm sick, damn it.'

He muttered something and moved one of his feet, although there was really nowhere to put it. No one laughed; in fact, everybody seemed entirely indifferent to my plight. I struggled desperately with my clothes, but in the cramped space, encumbered with all my equipment, I was unable to free the lower half of my body. Finally, I realized there was nothing I could do. My bowels emptied, pouring a stream of vile liquid down my legs. No one seemed even to notice my condition, which left me in a state of indescribable misery. My stomach was knotted with pain, and I collapsed into a stupefied torpor which prevented me from appreciating the ridiculous aspects of my situation. In fact, the situation was not particularly funny. I was really seriously ill, and my head was spinning and burning with fever. This was the first attack of a chronic dysentery which has plagued me ever since.

Our journey continued for a considerable time, during which I suffered two further attacks of uncontrollable diarrhoea. Although my state of filth was scarcely aggravated by these eruptions, I would gladly have exchanged ten years of my life for a chance to clean off and fall asleep in a warm bed. I was shaken by alternate fits of shivers and burning heat, and the pain in my intestines grew more and more intense.

After what seemed like an eternity, we arrived at our new camp, and I was dragged from the truck for roll call. My head was swimming, but, although fainting would have guaranteed the quickest route to the infirmary, I struggled to remain conscious. Somehow, I managed to stay upright among my comrades, each preoccupied with his own fate. However, my ghastly appearance did not escape the attention of the inspecting officer, and my gasping replies to his questions interrupted the regular rhythm of roll call.

'What's the matter with you?' he asked.

'I'm sick ... I ... I ...' I was barely able to stammer a reply, and saw him only as a blurred and shifting silhouette.

'What's bothering you?'

'My stomach ... I have a fever ... Could I please go and wash, Herr...'

'Take him to the medical service as an urgent case,' continued the officer, speaking to a subordinate.

The latter stepped forward and took me by the arm. Someone was actually trying to help me! I could hardly believe it.

'I've got acute diarrhoea, and I have to clean off,' I groaned as we tottered off.

'You'll find everything you need in the sanitary block, Kamerad.'

At the infirmary, I stood in line behind some thirty other men. The pains in my abdomen tore at my entrails with an intensity which made me scream. I knew that my gut was about to pour out some more filth. I staggered from the line, trying to make my step firm, and followed the signs to the latrine. When that series of intestinal explosions was finished, I hesitated before pulling up my revolting trousers. Although I was in an incredible state of filth, I noticed that my excrement was streaked with blood. I went back to the infirmary to stand in line for another half hour. Then my turn came. One after the other, I peeled off my nauseating rags.

'My God, what a stink,' exclaimed one of the orderlies, whose outlook was probably identical with that of the motto over the gate of our training camp: EIN LAUS, DER TOD!

I looked at the long table where members of the sanitary service were sitting like judges. The only plea I could possibly make was guilty.

'Dysenteric diarrhoea,' muttered one of the judges, obviously shocked by the shit which ran down below my knees.

'Get to the showers, you pig,' the other said. 'We'll look at you when you're clean.'

'There's nothing I'd like better. You don't know how long I've been dreaming of a shower.'

'Right over that way,' said the first fellow, who was clearly anxious to be rid of me.

I threw my coat over my bony shoulders, and went across to the showers. Luckily, no one was there but a bewildered-looking boy who was scrubbing the floor.

'Any hot water in the showers?'

'Do you want hot water?' His voice was gentle and friendly.

'Do you have any?'

'Yes. Two big vats for 16th Company laundry. I could let you have some, though. The showers only run cold.'

Through my fever, I saw him as another bastard who'd do a favour for cigarettes or something else.

'I don't have any cigarettes.'

'That doesn't matter. I don't smoke.'

I stood where I was, considerably surprised.

'Well, then, could you do it right away?'

But the fellow was already hurrying off. 'Go in there,' he said, pointing over his shoulder to an open cubicle. 'You'll be more comfortable.' Two minutes later he was back, carrying two buckets of steaming water.

'Were you at the front?' he asked.

I looked at him, wondering what he was trying to find out. He was still smiling his foolish smile.

'Yes. And I've had enough of it, too, if you want to know. I'm sick and disgusted.'

'It must be terrible . . . Feldwebel Hulf says that pretty soon now he'll be sending me off to get killed.'

I went on with the extraordinary relief of washing off my backside, but looked up at him with some surprise.

'There are always fellows like that, who enjoy sending other fellows out to get it in the neck. What do you do?'

'I was called up three months ago. I left Herr Feshter, and after basic training in Poland was enrolled in the Gross Deutschland.'

'That's a familiar story,' I thought to myself.

'Who's Herr Feshter?'

'My boss. A little strict, but nice anyway. I've worked for him since I was a kid.'

'Your parents sent you out so young?'

'I don't have any parents. Herr Feshter took me straight from the orphanage. There's a lot of work on his farm.'

I stared at him: someone else whose luck had been a little thin. He was still smiling. I clutched my stomach, which once again felt as if it might explode.

'What's your name?'

'Frösch. Helmut Frösch.'

344

'Thank you, Frösch. Now I must try to get into the infirmary.'

I was preparing to leave when I noticed a short, thickset figure standing in the doorway watching us. Before I could say a word, the man shouted: 'Frösch!'

Frösch spun around, and ran back to the wet rag he'd left on the floor. I went out slowly, trying to pass by unnoticed. But the feldwebel in any case was concentrating on Frösch.

'Frösch! You left your work. Why?'

'I was only asking him about the war, sergeant.'

'You were forbidden to talk during punishment fatigue, Frösch, except to answer my questions.'

Frösch was about to reply when a sonorous whack cut him short. I looked back. The feld's hand, which had just given it to Frösch full in the face, was still raised. I took myself off as fast as I could, as a torrent of abuse poured over my unfortunate companion.

'Bastard!' I shouted silently at the feld.

At the sanitary service, the aide looked at me without enthusiasm. I understood immediately that he was one of these fastidious fellows for whom a day of filthy scarecrows like myself was less than a pleasure, especially as he received no fees to encourage civility. He fingered all my parts, poking me a little all over, and concluded his examination by sticking his finger into my mouth to check the condition of my teeth. Then he added a string of numbers and letters to a card clipped to my papers, and I was sent down the line of tables to the surgical service. Five or six fellows there checked my documents and asked me to remove some of the clothes I'd thrown over my shoulders. A brute who must have been a wild man of the woods in civilian life gave me a shot in the left pectoral muscle, and I was taken to the hospital hut, where there were beds for the officially disabled. My papers were checked once again, and then, like a miracle, I was shown to a bed – which in fact was only a simple pallet covered with grey cloth. There were no sheets or blankets, but it was nonetheless a genuine bed on a wooden frame, in a dry room protected by a roof.

I collapsed onto the bed, to relish its comforts. My head was ringing with fever, and filled with a host of half-realized impressions. I had grown so used to sleeping on the ground

345

that the degree of well-being a soft, clean mattress can induce struck me with astonishment. The room was full of cots like mine on which fellows were lying, whimpering and groaning. But I paid no more attention to them than one does to a hotel carpet which is not entirely to one's liking. I felt almost light-headed with well-being, despite the pain which tore at my entrails. I took off some of my clothes and spread my filthy coat and ground sheet over my body instead of blankets, burying myself in them and in the sense that I had been saved. I lay like that for a long time, trying to control the cramps which knotted my guts.

After a while, two orderlies arrived, carrying a cumbersome piece of equipment. Without a word of warning, they pulled off my covers.

'Turn over, kamerad, and let us have a look at your ass. We want to clean out your gut.'

Before I understood what was happening, they had administered a copious enema, and moved on to the next patient, leaving me with some five quarts of medicated liquid gurgling painfully in my distended abdomen.

I don't know anything about medicine, but an enema has always struck me as a strange treatment for someone who is suffering from excessively frequent evacuations. The fact is that two repetitions of this operation enormously increased the misery of the next day and night, which I spent tottering to and from the latrine. This was situated some distance from the infirmary, which meant fighting the strong, icy wind which blew continuously. Any benefits I might have received from this amount of time ostensibly resting in bed were thus reduced to almost nothing.

Two days later, I was pronounced cured, and sent back to my company on rubber legs. My company – the one which had been organized as an assault group – was stationed in the immediate vicinity, only five or six miles from divisional headquarters, in a tiny hamlet which had been half abandoned by the Russian civilian population. Despite my intense joy at reuniting with my friends – all of whom were present, including Olensheim – my condition remained as precarious as it had been the day before I went to the infirmary.

My close friends, Hals, Lensen, and the veteran, made a special effort over me, and did everything they could to help me get well. Above all, they insisted on pouring large quantities of vodka down my throat – which, according to them, was the only reliable remedy for my complaint. However, my precipitate visits to the latrine continued despite these excellent attentions, and the sight of my bloody excrement worried even the veteran, who went with me on these trips in case I fainted. Twice, on the urging of my friends, I tried to re-enter the hospital, which was inundated with wounded from the battle of Kiev. But my papers, stating that I had been cured, presented an insuperable barrier.

I began to look like a tragic protagonist, made of some curious, white diaphanous substance, instead of flesh and blood. I no longer left the pallet which had been given to me in one of the isbas. Fortunately, a reduced service requirement allowed me to stay where I was. Several times, my friends took guard duty for me and did the other jobs which would ordinarily have been required of me. Everything was going well in the company, which was still commanded by Wesreidau. Unfortunately, we were still in a combat zone, which meant that at any minute we might be sent to some exposed position. Wesreidau knew that I would not be able to function in combat conditions as well as I knew it myself.

One evening, about a week after I'd left the infirmary, I became delirious, and was completely unaware of a fierce aerial battle which took place directly overhead.

'From some points of view, you're really the lucky one,' Hals joked.

Hals even went to speak to Wesreidau about me. But, before he was able to explain himself, Wesreidau stood up and smiled.

'My boy, we'll be pulling out almost immediately. They're sending us to an occupied zone at least sixty miles farther west. We'll have a certain amount to do there, but even so it will seem like a holiday after this. Tell your sick friend to hang on for another twenty-four hours – and spread the news that we're moving. We'll all be better off.'

Hals clicked his heels hard enough to shatter his shins, and burst out of Wesreidau's quarters like a hurricane. He looked into every hut he passed, shouting out the good news. When he reached us, he shook me from my torpor.

'You're saved, Sajer! You're saved!' he shouted. 'We'll be leaving soon for a real rest.' He turned to a couple of fellows

347

who shared the hut with us. 'We've got to get all the quinine we can for him. He has to hang on another twenty-four hours.'

Despite my overwhelming weakness, Hals's intense joy communicated itself to me, and ran through me like a restorative balm.

'You're saved!' he said again. 'And just think: with a fever like yours, they're bound to take you in a hospital – and they won't cut it off your leave either. You are a lucky dog!'

Every time I moved I felt it in my stomach, which seemed to be rapidly liquefying. Nonetheless, I began to collect my things. Everyone around me was doing the same. I put my packet of letters within easy reach. A voluminous backlog of correspondence had been kept for me by the divisional postal service. There were at least a dozen letters from Paula, which greatly eased my illness, as well as three from my parents, full of questions, anxiety, and reproaches about my long silence. There was even one from Frau Neubach. Somehow I found the strength to write everyone, although my fever undoubtedly interfered with the coherence of my messages.

Finally, we left. I was given a place in a small Auto-Union truck, and we drove to Vinnitsa on roads which belonged to the Carolingian era. Our faltering machines almost drowned in incredible quagmires, whose condition was aggravated by the rain. For a while I thought we had reached the notorious Pripet marshes, which were in fact not very far away. We avoided them by driving around them, on extraordinary wooden pavements which seemed to be floating on mud. These uneven roads made of split logs, on which one could obviously not drive very fast, were surprisingly effective in wet weather. However, it took us at least eight hours to travel ninety miles. The weather was cold and bad – snow flurries alternating with violent bursts of rain – but at least this protected us from Soviet aircraft, which were very active at that time.

When we arrived, I was sent immediately to a hospital, along with some six others from my company. Diarrhoea was a common complaint at that time, and a group of specialists were able to stop mine very quickly. My friends were stationed some fifteen miles away, and I knew I would rejoin them once I was well.

The doctors had some trouble getting me on my feet again. I was told that because my complaint had not been attacked until late in the day my 'intestinal flora' had been severely damaged.

In fact, it was a good two weeks before I was able to eat normally again. Every day I offered my backside to the orderly, who stabbed me as full of holes as a dressmaker's pincushion. Twice a day, the thermometer recorded my fever, which remained obstinately at 100°.

Winter had arrived, and I rejoiced as I watched the snow falling from behind the panes of a heated dormitory. I knew that for the moment my friends were out of danger, and, in a state of blissful ignorance, was unaware that over the whole front things were going from bad to worse.

Our paper's coverage of news from the front was limited to photographs of smiling artillerymen installing themselves in a new position, or organizing their winter quarters, and articles which said nothing at all. Hals came to see me twice, bringing mail. He had managed to get himself made a postal assistant, which allowed him to visit me quite easily. He rejoiced at the slightest occasion for rejoicing, roaring with laughter whenever he missed me in a snowball fight. He was just as ignorant as I of the realities of our situation, which would soon involve us in an agonizing retreat, and acquaint us with the depths of horror.

When I had been in the hospital for about three weeks, I was given some marvellous news. I was told to go to the office to be checked for discharge. There an orderly inspected me, and told me that, since I was making a good recovery, he was going to authorize a leave for me.

'It occurs to me,' he said, 'that you would rather complete your convalescence at home than here in the hospital.'

I replied that I would, restricting myself to mild assent, lest I offend that kindly angel with excessive exuberance. As a result, I found myself with a ten-day pass – a little shorter than the first one – which would go into effect as soon as it had been stamped. I thought immediately of Berlin and Paula. I would try to get permission for her to go with me to France. And, if that was impossible, I would stay in Berlin with her.

Despite the weakness, which still limited me severely, I was overjoyed. I got ready in record time, and left the hospital grinning broadly. I also wrote a note to my friends, excusing myself for not having visited them before I left. I thought they would surely understand.

My polished boots moved noiselessly across the snow as I walked to the station. I was so overflowing with happiness that I even nodded and spoke to the Russians I passed on the way. My linen and uniform had been cleaned and mended, and I myself felt neat and new. I forgot my bygone sufferings, and felt only gratitude to the German army and to the Führer for having made me into a man who knew the value of clean sheets and a watertight roof, and of friends who had nothing to offer but devotion, and offered that without reserve. I felt happy once again, and ashamed to have been despairing and afraid. I thought back, from a great distance, to some of the hard times I had experienced during my youth in France, which had sometimes made me think sourly of life. But was there anything that could sour me now? What disappointment could possibly darken things for me? Perhaps if Paula suddenly told me she no longer cared for me? . . . Yes, perhaps that.

But I felt as though I were now cured of a great many things. During some of my worst moments, I had imagined certain personal disasters – the death of my mother, for instance – and told myself that I could accept even that, if only the firing would stop. I had asked the pardon of every supernatural power for harbouring such thoughts, but was prepared to pay that price if it would cut short the carnage by even a little.

The war seemed to have turned me into a monster of indifference, a man without feelings. I was still three months short of eighteen, but felt at least thirty-five. Now that I have reached that age, I know better.

Peace has brought me many pleasures, but nothing as powerful as that passion for survival in wartime, that faith in love, and that sense of absolutes. It often strikes me with horror that peace is really extremely monotonous. During the terrible moments of war one longs for peace with a passion that is painful to bear. But in peacetime one should never, even for an instant, long for war!

The station was at the end of a cul-de-sac. In front of the esplanade, which took the place of a platform, three wide-gauge Russian tracks ran for a short distance, and then were regrouped into two switchings. A third section of the track vanished after five hundred yards, without any apparent reason. The soft snow deadened all noise and made everything still uncovered look cold and black.

A few wagons and a few empty boxes lay scattered across this peculiarly empty place. Beside the principal station building stood a neat pile of boxes marked WH. Inside, next to a hot stove, four or five Russian railwaymen sat absolutely motionless, as if they had died of boredom. There was no sign of a train in any direction, except for a large stationary locomotive, which appeared to be near death after a century of hard use. I no longer remember the name of the place. Perhaps it didn't have one, or perhaps the signboard had been stuck off in some odd corner so that we Europeans shouldn't catch sight of its unreadable characters. The prospect of a train passing through seemed as remote and uncertain as the first day of spring.

Despite the slip of paper in my pocket entitling me to a leave and warming my whole being like a glowing stove, I suddenly felt extremely lost in this huge, heavy country. Instinctively, I went to the main station building, where the Russian railwaymen had seemed more profoundly sunk in inertia than any postal worker in France. I knew that it would be almost impossible for me to make myself understood because, even if one of them knew some German, I still spoke it so badly that my fellow soldiers were often hard put to it to make me out. I walked past the door several times, hoping that someone would see me through the pane of glass set in the heavy wood, and give me some information. As no one moved, I pressed my nose against the glass. Inside, I could see four railwaymen identifiable only by the filthy armbands they wore on their sleeves. Otherwise, they were just civilians, and seemed paralysed by inertia. Not one so much as looked in my direction. I was astonished to see a grey-haired soldier sitting beside them, apparently infected by the same immobility. I looked again, to make sure I wasn't dreaming, but there it was – a soldier of the Reich fast asleep beside four citizens of occupied Russia. Outraged, I shoved violently against the door, and entered the room, where a heartwarming heat instantly inflamed my cheeks. I clicked my heels as loudly as I could, and the noise resounded like a gunshot through the calm heat of this remarkable place.

The Russians started, and slowly stood up. My half-countryman and fellow soldier only shifted one of his legs. He looked about fifty.

351

'What can I do for you, Kamerad?' he asked, like a shopkeeper greeting a potential customer.

I stood there for a moment, astounded by such casualness.

'Well,' I said finally, becoming more German than the Germans, 'I'd like to know when the train to the Fatherland will be coming through. I'm going home on leave.'

The other soldier smiled and slowly stood up. Then he walked toward me, bracing himself against the table, like a rheumatic.

'So you're going home on leave, young fellow?' His voice sounded as though it might break into laughter at any movement, which irritated me. 'A fine time to take a vacation!'

'When will there be a train?'

I was hoping to cut short the conversation I knew was coming.

'You have a strange accent. Where are you from?'

Unmasked again! I felt sure that I was blushing.

'I have French relatives,' I said, almost angry. 'My father ... in any case, I grew up in France. But I've been in the German army for nearly two years now.'

'Are you French?'

'No. My mother is German.'

'In cases of that kind it's the father who counts, though.'

He was getting angry, too.

'Look at that,' he said to the Popovs, who apparently hadn't understood a word. 'They're even taking French kids now.'

'What time will there be a train?'

'Don't worry about trains. Hereabouts, they come when they can.'

'What do you mean?'

'There's no timetable, you know. What do you expect? This is no Reichsbahndienst.'

'But after all . . .'

'Trains come through from time to time, naturally – but you can never predict them.'

He smiled and gestured vaguely.

'Have a seat here with us. You've got plenty of time.'

'No. I haven't got plenty of time. I've got to get out of here. I'm not going to sit here gassing with you.'

'Suit yourself. If you'd rather walk around outside and get

cold . . . Or you could hike over to Vinnitsa. Trains go through there more regularly. Only I warn you – it's forty miles through thick woods, infested with the friends of these fellows here,' he nodded toward the railwaymen, 'who aren't exactly in agreement with Adolf, and who might very well put an end to your leave.'

He looked at the Russians and grinned. They smiled back, without any idea why.

'What do you mean?' I asked.

'Partisans, for God's sake!'

'You mean those bastards are around here, too?'

This time, it was his turn to be astonished. 'Of course . . . and in Rumania too, and in Hungary, and Poland. Maybe even in Germany.'

I was flabbergasted.

'So sit down, young fellow. It's a big mess that really has nothing to do with you, and you shouldn't be mixed up in it at all. It would be crazy to get killed just for the sake of a few hours. I managed to get hold of some real coffee, and it's here in this kitchen, nice and hot. There's a fellow at the commissary with a good heart, who's just about fed up with this war himself.'

He came back carrying a big army coffeepot.

'We drink enough coffee here to send us right up the walls,' he said, looking at the Popovs, who were still smiling.

I felt somewhat disconcerted. 'Would you mind telling me what your job is?'

'Hell!' he said in irritation. 'I'm supposed to be guarding that pile of boxes' – he nodded at the neatly stacked crates outside – 'and these poor fellows here. Who the hell do they think I am? Nearly sixty years old, and they bring me here to play sentry. I spent thirty years of my life working for the railways in Prussia and Germany – and this is the thanks I get. Specialisation – that's what it is. No useless efforts. Everyone in his place. An efficient force. Sieg Heil! I can tell you – I'm fed up!' By the time he was finished, he was shouting. He slammed the coffeepot down on the table. We might have been in a Paris bistro. I felt as if the world had suddenly turned upside down.

'That coffeepot is army property, and you just took it,' I said, clinging to the thread of my first idea.

The fellow looked at me, and slowly put down a cup, which he filled with steaming liquid. Then he held it out to me.

'Here, young fellow. Drink this.'

There was a moment of silence, and then he began talking again in a calm, serious tone which one could interrupt only with difficulty.

'Now, you listen to me, my boy. I am fifty-seven years old. I fought in the cavalry in '14-'18, and was a prisoner in Holland for two years. Now it's been three and a half years since they put me back in the army again. I have three sons fighting on three of the fronts which our beloved country has decided to defend. I am an old man, and even if I once felt fiery about political principles which have long since been altered by time, the politics of today leave me cold, and I don't give any more of a damn for them than I do for this coffeepot. So drink in a little of the heat it offers you, and take this chance to forget for a few minutes that you're mixed up in all this mess.'

I looked at him, astounded.

'I'm not a spiess, or an officer, or the Führer, but only an old railway worker who was forced to change uniforms. Sit down and relax and drink your coffee.'

'But what you just said is outrageous. After all, every minute of the day soldiers are dying for our country, and . . .'

'If our country needs something from me, I'll postpone my retirement for a couple of years.'

'But . . . but . . .'

I felt as if I were choking. I couldn't find the words to express the intensity of emotion which German idealism created in me. I had already suffered a great deal from the war, but couldn't conceive a life other than the one assigned to me. I felt that this man was somehow missing the point, and that I was unable to express it adequately. Perhaps I was too young to understand it.

'I don't agree with you at all!' I shouted, beside myself with rage. 'If everyone thought the way you did, nothing would be worth anything! Your way of thinking strips life of all its meaning!'

His gun was lying in the corner of the room.

'Your friends might pick that up,' I said, nodding at the gun, and then at the Popovs. 'Did that ever occur to you?'

I thought he was going to throw me out. But his attitude was inconsistent. Perhaps he was a little afraid of me.

'I'll take the coffeepot back when we're through with it,' he said with a bitter laugh. 'Would you like a little more?'

I held out my cup, feeling pleased with myself for putting a fellow soldier back on the right track.

I waited for more than nine hours, and had almost given up hope, when at last a train arrived and took me away.

Chapter Eleven

CANCELLED LEAVE

PARTISANS

On the train from Vinnitsa toward Lvov and Lublin, I was travelling with soldiers who'd been at Cherkassy and Kremenchug. They told me about the hellish fighting which had taken place near those towns, now lost to us or slipping from our grasp. Everywhere, the crushing numerical superiority of the enemy was finally overwhelming our positions, which we defended with desperate determination, paying an appalling price in casualties. All the fellows on the train were going on leave too, but despite their joy, they seemed crushed by the experiences they had just lived through.

The train came into Lublin station at dawn on a winter morning. The ground was covered with snow, and the Polish cold felt much sharper than the cold in Russia. Even though we were used to sleeping outdoors, no one had been able to rest on the train, and we greeted the morning with turned-up collars and grey faces. Despite the early hour, the station platforms were crowded with soldiers walking up and down to keep warm, dressed and equipped for the front. There were many new recruits, easily distinguishable by their boyish, rosy faces. Military police had been stationed at intervals of ten yards down the length of the platform for incoming trains. I had overestimated my strength. As I obeyed the orders barked over the P.A. system, and jumped down onto the platform, I was shaking with sleeplessness and cold, and my legs were buckling under me.

We lined up parallel to the train, and marched into the big hall which stood at one end of the station. As we tramped toward the hall, the gasping locomotive pulled the empty train onto a secondary track.

In the hall, we were each given a cup of steaming ersatz and two spoonfuls of a curious jam. As we ate, several officers

356

climbed onto a wheeled platform equipped with a loudspeaker. Military policemen were standing watchfully on either side of them, and at the foot of the platform.

First, the amplifier crackled and buzzed for a moment, and then a nasal voice roared unintelligibly until someone adjusted the mechanism. The principal thrust of the officer's speech struck all of us like a slap in the face: '... leaves must be cancelled.' We thought we must have misunderstood him, but then the familiar series — 'necessity ... difficulty ... duty ... supplementary effort ... victory' brought it home to us that this was no dream. The crowd buzzed angrily, and a few fellows even shouted their outrage. But the loudspeakers were already blaring the 'Deutsche Marsche,' drowning our fury in martial music. As the hopes and plans of several thousand men crumbled, the music grew louder. The jam we were swallowing suddenly seemed tasteless, and the ersatz bitter. Before we had time to feel sorry for ourselves, the M.P.s were herding us toward a train which was ready to leave for the East.

Three cars were loaded with supplies for the troops, and we were ordered to line up beside them. Because our nervous exhaustion and disappointment were so evident, and the desire to desert was so clearly stamped on so many faces, we were closely hemmed in by police. We were issued fur hats, like the hats worn by Russian troops, crudely made overvests of reversed sheepskin, cotton gloves with woollen linings, and enormous overshoes with reinforced cork soles and felt uppers. A few boxes of tinned food were added to this voluminous issue, and we no longer entertained any doubts as to our fate: we were obviously being shipped back for another winter in Russia. Most of us were ready to cry with disappointment.

The train was crammed to the bursting point. Some of the passengers were young boys about to go into combat for the first time. Others were veterans returning from leave, who were scarcely any happier than we were, and others, like myself, had been suddenly obliged to replace their plans for leave with the sinking apprehension which all men, no matter how brave, feel as they are about to confront a highly problematical fate.

We rolled east for a considerable time, before we finally grasped what had happened to us. I was dumb with disappointment, remembering Magdeburg and my despair when

357

the scope of that leave was abruptly limited. This time Berlin
wasn't even on my route, and there was no chance of encountering Paula. There had been no period of grace at all – not even
twenty-four hours. As I thought about it, the weight of what had
just occurred seemed to increase, dragging me down into a
black depression. However, I still had one hope. As soon as I
had returned to my unit, I would have my status as a convalescent officially verified. Why hadn't I thought of explaining
that to the police at the station? But, of course, no one in his right
mind should ever expect anything decent from a military policeman. My last chance was that once I got back to the company
Wesreidau would be able to arrange things for me.

As always, the trains for the front were moving at top speed,
unlike westbound trains, which often made long, inexplicable
stops. Ours was no exception to this rule. Nevertheless, an
important incident broke our momentum. The locomotive had
just refuelled and resumed the speed which was to carry us
through to Vinnitsa. The station where we had stopped had
bristled with signs bearing the names of towns no longer
accessible to us: Konotop, Kursk, Kharkov – names which
evoked unbearably painful memories.

About fifteen minutes out of the station the train braked so
violently that all the carriages shuddered, and we nearly left
the rails. Inside, men and boxes were flung to the floor, and
the air rang with angry curses. We all thought we had in fact
been derailed. Soldiers in long coats were running down the
length of the tracks, answering our shouted questions by
waving ahead.

'You were lucky we could stop you,' one of them yelled.

About five hundred yards to the east, the track, which ran
between two walls of sparse woodland, was blocked by a chaos
of overturned cars. We jumped down to the ground to find out
what had happened. Partisans ... dynamite on the track ...
train loaded with munitions ... 150 soldiers killed ... reprisals
... patrols ... pursuit.

The immediate work had already been divided among three
hundred unhurt soldiers. One group remained on the spot to
help the wounded and another left in pursuit of the partisans,
who had not been content simply to derail the train, but had
opened fire as our men struggled to get free of the wreckage.
Officers were blowing their whistles, and at least three

WINTER, 1943 – SUMMER, 1944

thousand men from our train climbed down. We were divided into three groups. The largest of these, about two thousand strong, was sent out in pursuit of the enemy. I was included in this section. The second was sent to help our wounded comrades, while the third was deployed in the immediate area, to ensure the protection of the train. The bulk of my belongings, like everyone else's, remained on the train, and at the blast of the whistle we dogtrotted off into the countryside, which lay under a foot of snow.

Running through snow isn't easy. In less than two minutes one is lathered with sweat, and after twenty it is almost impossible to breathe. Within an hour one's lungs feel bruised by the pressure of one's ribs, and everything is dancing with coloured lights. The weather wasn't very cold, and the effects of our gymnastic efforts nearly suffocated us. The noncoms and officers who had followed us eventually grew tired of sustaining a zealous performance and resumed a walking pace. An hour and a half after leaving the train, we slogged into a large peasant village, our heads drooping with fatigue. Almost all the houses had thatched roofs, and attached sheds made of woven sunflower stalks, for storing winter supplies.

When we arrived, the place was already full of German soldiers, and the snow-covered central square was tightly packed with civilians – men, women, and children – gesturing excitedly and talking loudly. Soldiers – some of them with spandaus ready to fire – were stationed all around the square, and toward the centre other soldiers were shoving their way through the mass of civilians, roughly driving some of them off to one side. To the right, beside a building which probably served as the village hall, a third group of soldiers were standing with drawn guns over a dozen Russians lying on their stomachs in the snow. At first I thought they were dead.

'Partisans we caught here,' explained one of the soldiers standing beside me.

Were they really guilty, or were they only suspects? None of the questioning was up to me. The interrogations lasted for at least an hour. The Popovs lying on their stomachs must have had frozen guts – but that was true for our machine gunners too.

An S.S. section had been included in the pursuit group. I had the honour of being assigned by them to a smaller group of a hundred men who, like me, were returning to duty. Their attention was undoubtedly drawn to me by the edge of my left sleeve with its Gross Deutschland inscription. The S.S. preferred to use men belonging to élite divisions. Without explanation, we were loaded onto S.S. trucks, ignorant of the fate of the civilians lying on the ground. We drove for about twenty minutes over very hilly country. Then we were ordered to leave the trucks. An S.S. hauptmann in a long, dark leather coat addressed us briefly.

'You will fan out to the right, and move into those woods, taking every precaution. A factory which you can't see from here is situated about three-quarters of a mile to the west. The Russian informants who are accompanying us have indicated that this is an important centre of terrorist operations. We must take them by surprise and wipe them out.'

He appointed squad leaders, and we moved off. What a splendid convalescence! I would have done better to stay in the hospital at Vinnitsa.

After a short time, we saw a series of metal roofs, which must have been part of the factory. But, before we had a chance to give them a second look, a burst of machine-gun fire broke the silence. One of the S.S. men shouted: 'We've got you, you bastards! You might as well give up!'

It looked as though the Russian partisans we'd caught in the village had given this place away under pressure. There were some more shots, and then the familiar clatter of Russian machine guns coming from the edge of the buildings. Another fellow and I threw ourselves down under a small tree, whose snow-laden branches touched the ground. We heard whistles ordering us to advance, but for the moment I stayed where I was. It would be too stupid to get knocked off by a handful of terrorists. The other fellow muttered in my ear: 'The bastards! We've really got them this time! Now we'll teach them to blow up trains!'

After five minutes of hard fighting, German soldiers began to stand up all around us. We had taken about ten more Russian prisoners. Some were singing a Russian song of vengeance, but most were begging for mercy. About thirty S.S. men were herding them toward the truck, already beating them and shouting questions. We thought everything was over, when the S.S. captain blew his whistle to fall in.

'Those bastards,' he said, gesturing at the sobbing prisoners, 'claim they're the only ones here. Maybe they think they can fool us and protect their friends who are still hiding inside, but I want you to clear the place.' He pointed at the factory buildings. 'We've got to take the whole bunch, and all the weapons they're hiding there.'

Of course, there was no question of argument. With dry mouths, we moved forward into the factory buildings, which were littered with hundreds of large objects — ideal for snipers and as bad as possible for us. The relatively large size of our force was in no way reassuring. Even if we overwhelmed the partisans in the end, each bullet they fired was bound to hit someone, and if I should happen to be the only casualty in a victorious army of a million men, the victory would be without interest for me. The percentage of corpses, in which generals sometimes take pride, doesn't alter the fate of the men who've been killed. The only leader I know of who finally made a sensible remark on this point, Adolf Hitler, once said to his troops: 'Even a victorious army must count its victims.'

What was made in this factory lost in the wilderness? Perhaps they processed timber. The first shed housed a large band saw, and farther on we passed several others, as well as a kind of dredging machine with a string of rusty scoops. The first two sheds were empty. Perhaps the prisoners had been telling the truth. But our orders were to check the whole place. Our group surrounded the entire factory complex, and then began to move toward the centre. We passed through a series of enormous barnlike buildings which seemed to be on the point of collapse. They had never been painted, and every iron fixture was half eaten away by rust, like the old anchor chains at a port.

The wind was blowing hard, and the buildings echoed with sinister creaking sounds. Otherwise, everything was quiet, except for an occasional clatter made by one of our men deliberately shoving aside some metal object, or overturning a pile of crates.

About eight of us had moved into the darkness of a building littered with a jumble of miscellaneous clutter. There were no windows, and consequently there was almost no light. Then we all heard a series of clicking sounds. But the wind blowing through the building filled the air with the bangings and clickings of loose boards and tiles. Although everyone understood that theoretically each moment might be our last, no one really accepted that idea, and no one took any special precautions. Outside, the S.S. must have cornered several Russians. We heard a series of shots and cries, and sounds of running and shouting. Suddenly, our shed was filled with the noise of explosions. Five or six flares thrown from a room or closet in an upper story lit the darkness, and almost simultaneously four of our companions screamed with pain. A moment later, two of them had collapsed onto the dusty floor, while the other two staggered toward the open door. The rest of us looked hastily for shelter, stumbling through the darkness, uncertain off where we might find cover. There were several more shots, and somewhere to my right two more soldiers howled with pain. My gun shuddered violently in my hands. A bullet had struck it in the butt, taking a piece with it, and missing me by inches. The two fellows trying to get to the door were both hit again, but neither of them fell until they had reached a drift of white snow which the wind had blown over the threshold. Outside, more soldiers had run up, but they stopped at the door and fired a few shots which were far more likely to hit one of us than any partisan. There were two of us still unhurt, and we began to shout as if we were fifty. Some idiot might think of tossing in a grenade, which would finish us off along with all the Russians. Luckily, someone heard us in time to think of another tactic. While our comrades outside tried to break through the corrugated iron walls, the Russians inside were firing at every detectable movement. The bullets, which pierced the flimsy walls, were as dangerous to our men outside as they were to us. I was half dead with fright.

Was I going to be the last German soldier left in that damned shack? I knew that at least one other comrade was hiding somewhere. I felt even more caught in a vice of terror and danger than I had at Belgorod. I bit my lips to keep from screaming. Our men outside were pressing in, about to blow the building apart, while inside the Russians were perched in the rafters as silent as spiders. From where I lay, I could see nothing. Suddenly I heard a scratching noise behind me, somewhere between a haphazard pile of objects and an upright support. I froze as still as the large glazed pipe behind which I was hiding. The uproar outside prevented me from distinguishing anything clearly. I tried deliberately to extend my hearing beyond the limit of its capacity, and caught a series of scratching sounds, some very faint, some a little louder. I held my breath until my lungs were on the point of bursting, and tried to stop the pounding of my heart. My brain was teeming with horrible possibilities. I saw myself dead or a prisoner of the partisans, who would use me in an attempt to escape from our noose. I was overwhelmed with an intensity of panic greater than anything I had ever felt before, which was suddenly replaced by a savage passion of self-preservation. Trembling with terror and rage, I abruptly stopped thinking. Some supplementary sense informed me that danger had drawn very close. Had I been a millionaire, I would have staked my entire fortune on the certainty that someone was moving on the other side of the barrier which concealed me. I felt very much alone and desperate and determined to defend myself at any price. Suddenly I saw a man no more than five yards from me. I felt my skin crawl. Then a second man appeared behind him, crawling toward a pile of sacks. Although they had both been in shadow, I had seen enough to recognize civilian clothes. The one nearest me was wearing a large cap. His silhouette remains indelibly stamped on my memory. He was tall and looked strong. He froze for a moment and appeared to be inspecting the shadows. Then he moved a few steps away from me. As slowly and silently as sand running through an hour glass, I raised my gun until it was pointing at him. I knew that there was still one bullet left in the barrel, so I didn't have to move the bolt. Tightening every nerve, I tried to suppress the trembling which made my gestures uncertain. I knew that at the slightest sound the other fellow would let me have it. Luckily, there was plenty of noise outside, which divided his attention. My gun was now level, and my finger lay nervously against the trigger. Then I hesitated for a moment. It isn't easy to kill a man in cold blood, unless one is entirely heartless or, as I was, numb with fear. The man changed his course a little, and began to move slowly toward my hiding place. His companion was scarcely visible now, and must have been some twenty yards away from us.

I could hear the man breathing as he approached. For a moment, perhaps, he distinguished a figure crouching in the shadows, or glimpsed a dull metallic gleam. For a tenth of a second, perhaps, he hesitated. Then a sudden glow of brilliant light blinded him, and he collapsed in the dust, his belly torn open by the shot fired from the weapon which still quivered in my sweat-drenched hands. The other Russian had run off, leaving his companion dead at my feet. I felt as if my skull enclosed a black void, and that a nightmare enclosed me, like a fever. As the noise outside grew louder, I felt myself sinking into a pit of unimaginable depth. I was torn between the desire to flee and my paralyzing fear. I stared at the corpse lying face down on the ground in front of me. I couldn't really believe I had killed him, and waited for the tide of blood which would soon begin to seep from beneath his body. Nothing else mattered to me. The weight of the drama which had just occurred was so overwhelming that I could only stare at the motionless body.

Suddenly a piece of the wall collapsed. The soldiers outside had managed to pull off a section of corrugated sheeting, and the glare of full daylight somehow diminished the importance of what had happened. The sight of other German soldiers entering the building snapped me from my lethargy. I even distinguished the S.S. captain, who had just joined them, ducking down behind a piece of crumpled metal. He was facing me, at a distance of about twenty yards.

'Anyone still alive in here?' he shouted. I waved a hand, and he saw me. I knew that there was still at least one Russian in the building, and I didn't want to attract too much attention to myself. Another German, who must have been as terrified as I was, shouted from somewhere deeper in the ruins: 'Over here, Kameraden. I've got a wounded man, too.'

'Don't move yet,' the captain shouted back. 'We're going to clear out the rest of the Popovs.'

He had just spotted the dead man, lying almost at my feet. We heard the sound of an engine, which was rapidly growing louder. From my hiding place, I could see a black machine-gun carrier rolling across the snow. A moment later, it was thrusting through the hole in the wall, with an S.M.G. pointing from its turret. A powerful headlight lit up the shed, and soldiers crouched beside the vehicle were aiming their guns at the interior. The beam of light passed over me for a moment, and a shiver ran down my spine. I could almost imagine the faces of the waiting Russians, contorted with terror. In the doorway, beside the two German bodies, I could see other German soldiers regrouping.

The hauptmann shouted: 'Surrender, or we'll shoot you down like rats!'

There was no answer. Then a cry of terror rang out from the dimly lit rafters, like the cry I had fought back in myself a few moments before. The heavy machine gun began its slaughter. Each explosion echoed through the shed as if it would blow it apart. The bullets themselves were explosive and ripped open the roof, letting in new streams of daylight. All the German soldiers outside were firing into the rafters, where some fifteen Russian terrorists were still hiding. I doubled over onto the floor, and pressed my hands against my ears, trying to deaden the sound. Directly overhead, I could hear Russian machine guns. Once again, there were bloodcurdling screams, and a body fell to the floor with the heavy thud of a quarter carcass thrown down onto the butcher's block. The S.M.G. demolished the rest of the roof, and full daylight flooded in, destroying the partisans' last hope of invisibility and escape. Another fell to the floor as the rest began a frantic attempt to scramble away through the twisted metal supports overhead. Some dropped to the floor, others clung to the rafters. In the end, all were killed, and our deaths on the train were avenged. The place filled with German soldiers, and I was able to leave my hideout. I was covered with dust, and even found pieces of debris between my belt and my coat.

We marched back to the village singing:

> *Märkische Heide,*
> *Märkische Sand,*
> *Sind des Märkers Freude,*
> *Sind mein Heimatland.* . . .

We were still the masters, and no one under heaven could judge us.

The S.S. took over the few prisoners who had surrendered before the massacre and loaded them into their trucks, which then drove off down the road that had brought us here. We were ordered to fall in by threes. By the time we reached the village, the crowd that had watched us leave was gone, which was a relief.

The S.S. task force gave each of us a slip of paper to explain

365

the delay in our return to our units. We were advised to rejoin the wrecked train immediately. No one regretted leaving that place, with its miserable memories. Unfortunately, a final spectacle, as depressing as anything we'd seen in the shed, was unfolding just as we marched by. A firing squad was performing its duties. Four consecutive salvos rang out, each one disposing of four partisans. Their bodies were left on the snow, and the squad marched back to the village. Not one of us said a word. At least a hundred of our soldiers had been summarily killed in the derailment and the disintegration of some of the cars. An officer spoke to us briefly about the tragedy we'd just witnessed. The partisans were held responsible for everything that had happened. Also, partisans were not eligible for the consideration due to a man in uniform. The laws of war condemned them to death automatically, without trial.

We spent the night on the motionless train. I was able to sleep only fitfully and with difficulty. Each time I closed my eyes, I was caught in a hideous nightmare. A huge stone rose up in front of me, and from beneath it a flood of dark, blackish blood flowed toward my feet, burning them as it touched.

The next day was piercingly cold. We joined another train which came to our rescue farther down the line, and settled down to listen to the penetrating clang of the wheels on the rails. We stared out at the tundra, buried under deep snow. From time to time the monotony was broken by a distant horizon marked by pine-covered hills. Once again, the vastness of this countryside, untouched by any human life, filled us with a sense of constraint. The idea of space, the conception of immensity, could not be more perfectly expressed than by this scenery designed for giants. Could anyone possibly control this country? Could we? Could the N.K.V.D.?

We arrived at Vinnitsa that evening. An air-raid alert had disorganized the traffic, and the station was overflowing with soldiers in long winter coats. At that time, the Gross Deutschland division was partly based in the town, and the military police were able to direct me to its command post. I was surprised by the efficiency of divisional organization. With only the name and number of my company, they were able to give me its precise location. I was horrified to learn that we had returned to the front, and, along with twenty other companies, were occupying a zone some three hundred miles from Vinnitsa. I was given a precise district and the number of the sector. I had mentally prepared myself for a reunion with my friends, huddled around some blazing Russian hearth, discussing my cancelled leave and the possibilities of getting it revalidated. Instead, we were destined to meet in some frozen trench, in conditions of misery and danger. This misfortune overwhelmed me with the force of a stupefying blow. I stood, motionless and stunned, in front of the stabsfeldwebel who had just checked my name on the list. He would have paid me no other attention, but was suddenly struck by something about my appearance.

'What's the matter?' he said. 'Are you sick?'

I was too numb to think of a suitable answer, so I told him the truth.

'I was just beginning a convalescence leave, Herr Stabsfeld-webel, and it was cancelled at Lublin.'

'The fatherland is living through a time of serious trial, young man,' he answered after a short pause. 'You are not the only one to be deprived of a well-earned rest. The men who have gone through here before you and those coming after you are all in your situation.'

I was about to remark that this was in fact my official convalescence when he came on the paper from the S.S. hauptmann.

'I see that you recently distinguished yourself in an encounter with partisans,' he said. 'My congratulations. I shall include that information in your dossier, and your company commander will undoubtedly promote you.'

Despite my nervous exhaustion, I smiled for a moment.

'I am very pleased, Herr Stabsfeldwebel,' I said in a semi-sincere, semi-official tone.

'And I am equally pleased for you,' he answered, holding out his hand.

I left with some thirty others in the same plight as myself, my mind torn by conflicting thoughts and feelings.

However, we were sent to spend the night in a warm and comfortable house which had been turned into a military dormitory. There weren't enough beds, but every room was heated, and the floors were thickly carpeted. We all slept well, despite our anxiety about the immediate future.

We had all learned to use waiting periods for sleep whenever we could, simply to stop thinking and lapse into unconsciousness. Reflection added nothing to such times except increased awareness of the misery that weighed on the world. Sleep, on the other hand helped in many ways: it blotted out the present, and revived one's strength. It seemed most unfortunate that one couldn't store up a surplus of its benefits to use in future emergencies when sleep would be impossible.

We spent most of that night and the next twenty-four hours asleep or dozing, interrupting our rest only for meals. During the second night, we were finally dragged from our torpor by a noncom who led us to the trucks which were to take us to our positions. The brutal winter cold fell onto our backs with the shock of a poorly regulated shower. Winter had arrived in full strength, coating everything with a bluish glitter. Roll was called, and we boarded the trucks.

Before daybreak, we arrived at a village of huts which had been built by the engineers. We were ordered out of the trucks and offered an ersatz drink which was kept hot through the day in three large kettles. The cold was piercing, and revived all our memories of the previous winter: the shivering mornings, the cold, which became an almost unbearable torture, the impossibility of washing, the lice, and the thousand other elements which made life insupportable. Everything smelled of the war, and every face was stamped with urgent anxiety. Large holes, which suggested air raids, also implied that matters were not entirely under control in this sector.

About fifty of us were rejoining units in sectors separated by as much as forty or fifty miles. We were divided into four groups, each of which was given mail and the supplies requested by particular companies. Then we were shown our approximate routes, and a noncom informed us in a tone of triumph that we would have to cover at least twenty miles.

We began our march, through a chain of long snowy valleys. A network of heavy defences extended for about a half mile around the centre we had just left: anti-tank guns, minefields, which we were careful to avoid, and innumerable nests of machine guns. Beyond us, wild, empty country stretched out into infinity, hardened by winter, and favourable to any kind of hostile surprise. As soon as we left the last line of defences, we knew we were on ground which belonged to whoever was walking across it at any moment, and which could change hands from day to day. The front in this sector was never precisely drawn, but was more like a piece of lace embroidery, with a multitude of recesses which sheltered ambushes, and encounters more or less foreseen, and unpredictable clashes.

One of the men in our group was a new recruit, very young and tall and stringy, like a weed that has grown too fast in a spell of damp weather. His enormous gazelle-like eyes stared at the anonymous vastness of the landscape, which he was clearly incapable of absorbing. He was visibly affected by the loss of his native dimensions: the short vistas of the Rhineland had never led him to suspect that such a huge scale was possible.

A year ago, I had felt the same way.

The cold, which had turned dry after ten days of snow and cloudy skies, made the landscape into a white screen against which darker objects were startlingly visible. The wind of the preceding days had swept across the snow, piling it up against every barrier, filling in hollows, and leaving brown patches of bare soil in other places, like great stains. As long as we didn't have to make any excessive detours, we preferred to follow the bare patches. Every hour, we stopped for a short rest.

Five or six planes flew by to the south. We froze for a minute, trying to discern their purpose, but they vanished over the horizon before we were able to distinguish whether they were Yaks or ME-109s.

By lunchtime, we were still unsure of our bearings. The noncom responsible for getting us to our destinations claimed that we were moving in the right direction, but his face and voice betrayed his panic. Country on such a vast scale cannot be trifled with. One can play explorer in the forest of Fontainebleau, but not on the tundra, where one feels too small and trivial for games. The hostile indifference of nature seems so overwhelming it is almost necessary to believe in God.

We walked for a long time, and finally came to a line of telegraph poles stuck unevenly into the ground. They were following the edge of a road which we could see was in use, as it was deeply marked by fresh ruts.

The noncom decided we should take the road to the south, as the quickest way of finding our units. This seemed odd, as it was clear that we would be proceeding perpendicular to our previous direction. However, no one hesitated. We had long ago learned that it was useless to argue points which had lost all meaning. We also felt heavily oppressed by the prospect of a night in the open – the first of a long series which would require all the patience and endurance we could muster. For a fraction of a second the thought of my wrecked leave flared through my consciousness like a shooting star in the night sky. I swallowed hard, and everything sank back into uniform grey.

The weedy young recruit remained speechless. His astonished eyes moved from the snowy steppe to the faces of the experienced veterans we seemed to be. Trusting us as a shepherd trusts the stars, he plodded dutifully on.

We suddenly caught sight of a massive object buried in the snow about five hundred yards ahead of us. A long gun barrel poked through the white crust, and we realized we were facing a camouflaged tank. Of course, it was one of ours, otherwise we would all have been dead. The Panther was buried up to its turret, and behind it two or three bulges indicated bunkers. Suddenly a fellow appeared on top of the tank, wearing a sheepskin vest over his black tank-corps uniform. He jumped down and walked out to meet us, shouting his name. We did the same, according to the custom of the times. He told us that when his tank had broken down he had been ordered to half bury it and turn it into a blockhouse. With considerable difficulty, he and the eight other men with him had carried out the order. Separated from their armoured unit by the force of circumstances, they had been standing guard over this vast, empty panorama for three weeks now. Once in that time some Russians had come by, but the tank's two S.M.G.s had forced them to pass far to one side. This accident had transformed them into an official surveillance post, and they were due to be relieved in two weeks' time. They had been there for three weeks already, and admitted that it was difficult to sleep really soundly at night.

'Where is the front?' our noncom asked.

'More or less everywhere,' the other said. 'And mostly mobile units. In the evenings, convoys come through on the track. They never have their lights on, and every time it scares us to death. A plane knocked our radio out, so we're completely cut off. It's enough to drive a fellow mad.'

'We're supposed to be rejoining our units,' the noncom explained. 'Do you think we've still got far to go?'

'Well, the front is certainly five or ten miles east of here. But it's very fluid. It's impossible to be exact.'

We all felt extremely perplexed.

'Let's go along that way,' our guide said finally. 'We're bound to find something.'

The tank crew watched us go with regret. With darkness, which fell earlier than we had expected, accompanied by a heavy fog, we arrived at the precarious approximation of a front which existed in that sector. A few arbitrarily disposed Paks emerged from the darkness, and a sentry, green with terror, shouted, 'Wer da?' in a trembling voice. The same terror made our noncom squeak an incomprehensible reply. Our preservation from the guns of our own men could only be laid to a simple collapse of vigilance. A frozen, ill-tempered soldier led us to the company commander.

'The Russians come through this way from any direction,' he said as we walked along. 'It's pretty demoralizing, and unless the front is stabilized again, it'll go on this way, as far as I can see. Anyway, the regiment you're looking for isn't around here.'

We ran into the company commander, a captain, coming up from a candle-lit hole. He looked old and ill. His long overcoat was thrown carelessly over his shoulders, and his chest was covered by a thick, pale scarf which stood out against the grey green of his uniform. He wore a forage cap instead of a helmet. We snapped to attention out of habit.

The officer studied our map, trying to find some helpful directions he might give us. He seemed bewildered. The map included very few details, which made it almost as easy to get lost on paper as it was on the ground. He made some deductions in the light of a pocket flashlight, and decided to send us to the northeast. As the regiments were disposed, ours must be in that direction. This seemed a long way from the orderly procedures of the Gross Deutschland office in Vinnitsa.

Despite the exhaustion of the long, painful march on which we had been engaged since dawn, we set off again, into the icy, foggy darkness. Three-quarters of an hour later, some fellows in a company buried in that white desert huddled a little closer in their shelter to make room for us. We had to stop, or we might have been lost for good. The acid, almost palpable fog burned out throats and made every effort excessively painful. We managed to fall asleep despite the cold, which, as always, was much harder to bear at the beginning of the season, before our bodies were used to it. Outside, in the trenches, the sentries were stamping up and down to keep from freezing on their feet. The veil of fog wrapped them round completely, cutting them off from everything that lay beyond their parapets.

We spent a harassed night of half sleep. Despite the lamp-heaters and the canvas stretched across the mouth of our shelter, the cold, still only relative at the beginning of the season, was severe enough to make us feel half frozen. The thermometer must have fallen to as low as fifteen degrees, and the fog poured in, almost as thick as outdoors.

The troops passed the time as best they could, either sunk in sleep despite the discomfort, or playing Skat, or writing home with a pen precariously balanced between numbed fingers. The candles, on which they had been ordered to economize as much as possible, were stuck into empty tins which caught the melting wax, prolonging their lives by as much as four or five times. The memory of those bunkers buried in the wildness of the steppe still haunts my memory, like a legendary tale heard in childhood.

The demoralizing dawn cold greeted us as we left the hole. Silently, we resumed our march and our search. Everything was quiet, as if paralyzed by the cold, as dangerous an enemy as the Red Army. For a long time, we walked parallel to a frieze of barbed wire, coated with frost. The fog, which had not yet lifted, clung to the wire in minute drops which froze instantly.

Toward the end of the morning, two-thirds of our group at last found their regiment, whose officers were able to tell us the approximate positions of the other two regiments we still had to find. More precisely, for the sixteen of us still at loose ends, we were looking for two regiments and three companies – the young recruit and I, for example, belonged to separate companies – and the weather was no help. The inescapable necessity of trial and error added a considerable number of miles to our progress. We grew increasingly angry. How could our instructions have been so vague? Organizational failure of this kind were particularly hard on German troops, who were accustomed to the utmost efficiency. In fact, the centres of responsibility had practically ceased to exist. The extraordinarily tight army organization, which had functioned so superbly in Poland and France and all the smaller countries invaded by the Wehrmacht, was lost in the immensity of Russia, where the front was nearly fifteen hundred miles long. Our rapidly dwindling transport capability further complicated the situation during the terrible winter, which was to be followed by only one more.

Our group of sixteen men was made up of fourteen fellows belonging to one unit; myself, attached to another; and the tall young recruit, who was looking for still a third. To be exact, he and I belonged to two separate companies in the same regiment.

Just before dark, the main group of fourteen ran into their unit unexpectedly, as had the others. The young fellow and I were left to fend for ourselves on the icy track already packed hard by endless comings and goings. Feverish with anxiety, we pursued our tentative route, passing through a half-deserted hamlet. The few soldiers occupying it, dressed as they pleased, or as they could, stared at us in silence. We felt embarrassed and frightened.

According to our instructions, we were to keep on to the northeast. As long as there was any light, we tried to fix reference points on the slightest hollow or hump in the ground, on features more imaginary than real which we projected onto the infinite monotony. We kept the earthworks and trenches of the front on our right. However, the fog soon reduced the possibilities of navigation to nil.

Despite my youth, it seemed that circumstances required me to assert myself. The other fellow was looking at me with wild, questioning eyes. I suggested digging a hole deep enough to cover with our two canvases to make a shelter for the night. This idea terrified my companion, who wanted to keep going.

'Our regiment must be quite close now,' he said.

'You're crazy,' I said. 'We can't keep on like this. We'll only get completely lost, and then the wolves will eat us.'

'Wolves?'

'Yes, wolves. And there are plenty of other things about Russia even worse than that.'

'But they could come after us right here, too.'

'Of course – if we're in the open. But once we're under canvas they'll leave us alone. And then if they do come, we'll shoot them.'

'Well, then it comes to the same thing. And by tomorrow, we won't remember any of the directions.'

'We're following a sort of track, aren't we? We'll keep on with it tomorrow, and that's that. Believe me, it's the best thing to do.'

I finally persuaded him to do as I said. We had just begun to attack the rock-hard ground with our picks when we heard the sound of an engine.

'A truck!' the young fellow shouted.

'A truck? You're crazy! Don't you hear the treads?'

He stared at me. 'A tank? Is it a German tank?'

'How the hell would I know?'

'But we're behind our lines, aren't we?'

'Oh, for God's sake . . . of course . . . I hope so.'

People who need long explanations at moments when everything depends on instinct have always irritated me.

'What are we going to do?' he asked.

'Get the hell off the track, and try to hide in the snow.'

I was already moving back. The noise had grown terrible. The tank was nearly on top of us, and was still totally invisible. I know of no other experience which twists the guts harder than that. We waited for what seemed an eternity before we perceived a squat silhouette sliding smoothly over the ground. The noise was overwhelming. I stared through the darkness, trying to catch some distinguishing details. Finally, drawn by an inexplicable force, I got up, and moved forward cautiously, leaving my astonished companion to his own devices. After a moment, he joined me, staring at me with anguished, questioning eyes.

'It's a Tiger – one of ours. We've got to try and catch it.'

'Let's run after it!'

'We have to be careful, though. They might think we're Russians.'

'But if we catch up with them they could take us along.'

'Exactly.'

We began to shout like madmen, running after the tank with some anxiety, but as hard as we could. The noise of its engines drowned our voices, and it passed us by.

'Grab your things,' I yelled at the recruit. 'We've got to gallop behind them. We've got to catch them.'

We began to run along the ruts left by the treads. Although the tank was moving slowly, it was still going faster than we could run. We were already gasping for breath. I quickly realized that we were never going to catch it, and that we would have to take a chance. I grabbed my Mauser and fired into the fog, into which the tank had almost disappeared. This, of course, was extremely dangerous. The tank crew might think they were being attacked and let us have it with their machine guns.

The tank stopped. They must have heard the shot. We shouted, 'Kamerad!' as loudly as we could. The engine was idling, and was making much less noise. We heard someone from the turret: 'Was ist da?'

We rushed forward, drawing on all our strength. We were now very close. The fellow in the turret must surely have had his finger on the trigger.

'Only two of you?' he yelled when he could see us. 'What the hell are you doing here?'

'We're trying to find our unit, Kamerad. We're lost.'

'I'm not surprised. We're lost too.'

We noticed with relief that he was wearing a white helmet stencilled with tiger stripes – which meant that he belonged to the Gross Deutschland. We explained our situation, and they pulled us into the tank.

'You're both Gross Deutschland?'

'Yes.'

The interior of the tank, which seemed to be painted with orange lead, was filled with the dim, yellowish light of a metal mechanic's lamp which hung from the ceiling. There were two fellows in the turret, and probably a couple more up front. The engine made so much noise that it was almost impossible to talk, but it warmed the air agreeably, and filled it with the smell of hot oil and exhaust.

Despite the ample dimensions of the turret, the steering gear and ammunition cases took up so much room it was a squeeze to fit us in. The tank commander was keeping his eyes and ears open, thrusting his head from the turret at closely spaced intervals. He wore a thick winter hat which looked quite Russian.

The tank crew told us that they too were looking for their unit. Some engine trouble had held them up for nearly two days. Now they were trying to orient themselves by the batteries and companies they passed – a dangerous business, because a solitary tank is like a blinded animal. They didn't have a radio, and their group leader seemed to be doing nothing about them. Maybe he had already classified them as missing.

They also told us that the new Panzers were coated with a magnetic anti-mine paste, and exterior fire extinguishers. The most dangerous weapon for them was still the rocket launchers which the Russians had perfected after encountering our Panzerfaust.

They said that none of the Russian tanks could stand up to our Tigers. In the spring, on the Rumanian frontier, we would see the Tigers in action for ourselves. The T-37s and KW-85s discovered the Tiger's superiority for themselves, the hard way.

An hour later, the tank stopped.

'A signpost!' shouted the commander. 'There must be a camp near here!'

It had begun to snow – large, feathery flakes which clung to every surface. A post bristling with signs loomed unexpectedly out of the darkness. One of the crew brushed the snow off the signs with his gloved hand, and read out the directions. It seemed that the company the young recruit was looking for, along with three or four others, was somewhere to the east. The rest of the regiment was to the northeast, which was the way the tank was headed.

The young soldier who was arriving at the front for the first time had to say goodbye, and walk off alone into the darkness. I can still see the expression of terror on his white face.

Twenty minutes later, we ran into my unit, and the tank crew decided to stop for the night. I jumped down, and went over to a cluster of wretched isbas to ask directions. The long, peaked roofs rose from the ground like large tents. In the command hut, a noncom was sitting at a rough desk made of a couple of boards propped up on boxes, and lit by three candles. As there was no heat, he had thrown a blanket over his coat. He was able to tell me roughly where I could find my company.

I found myself moving through a succession of bunkers,

foxholes, and trenches, as on my first visit to the front, only these were far more precarious and much shallower than the ones on the Don. The engineers, who were spread very thin on the ground in this sector, had done what they could, but most of the work had been left to the picks of the exhausted infantry. Winter had begun in earnest. The ground was frozen hard, and from now on things could only get worse.

I kept asking questions, and finally a fellow from liaison took me to our officers' bunker. The sentry at the entrance inspected me narrowly before pulling back the canvas, astonished to see an ordinary soldier escorted like an officer.

Wesreidau was not asleep. A short pipe which had gone out jutted from the high collar which hid most of his face. He was bare-headed, and seemed to be studying a map. Two lamp-heaters lit the hole, but didn't have much of an effect on the cold. At the back of the dugout, a man was lying on the ground, dead asleep. A lieutenant, sitting on a pack, was also sleeping, with his head in his hands. Captain Wesreidau looked up, to see who had come in. I was about to announce myself when the telephone rang – probably some unimportant report.

A moment later, I began again: 'Gefreiter Sajer, Herr Hauptmann.'

'Back from leave, my boy?'

'Not exactly, Herr Hauptmann. My leave was cancelled.'

'Ah. But you're well now? How do you feel?'

I wanted to tell him how disappointed I was, and how much I still hoped to have at least a few days off, but the words stuck in my throat. I suddenly felt the full strength of my attachment to all the friends who must have been very nearby, an emotion which struck me as both idiotic and profound.

'I'm all right, Herr Hauptmann. I can wait until my next leave.'

Wesreidau stood up. Although I couldn't really see his face, I thought he was smiling. He put one hand on my shoulder, and I felt myself tremble at his touch.

'I'll take you to your friends. I know that being with friends can make up for the lack of a comfortable bed, even for the lack of food.'

I felt stunned. Herr Hauptmann led the way out, and I followed him.

'I always try to group my men as friends,' he explained. 'Wiener, Hals, Lensen, and Lindberg are covering a Pak position. They'll be glad to see you again.'

Wesreidau's tall figure strode through the ghostly fog, which drifted against the darkness in white patches. As we passed, fellows stupefied by sleep stumbled to their feet, and noncoms signalled that everything was calm.

We came to a hole which was somewhat deeper than the others, and which seemed to be occupied by three hunched-up sacks, and two figures leaning against the parapet. I recognized the veteran's voice immediately.

'Welcome to our hole, Herr Hauptmann. We'll be able to talk tonight. Everything's quiet.'

The familiarity of that voice astonished me.

Wesreidau said: 'Here's Sajer, who's just come back.'

'Sajer! I don't believe it! I thought he was living it up in Berlin.'

'I felt lonesome for you fellows,' I said.

'That's a good boy,' the veteran answered. 'You're quite right, too. Here we sometimes even have fireworks, and in Berlin it's total blackout. I remember that from the last time I was there, over a year and a half ago.'

I could hear Hals grumbling sleepily: 'What the hell's going on up there?'

'Wake up, steppe boy,' Wiener shouted even louder than before. 'Herr Hauptmann is here with our dear friend Sajer.'

Hals jumped up as if he'd been shot.

'Sajer!' he said. 'But he's crazy to come back here!'

Wesreidau felt obliged to make a formal intervention. 'If I wasn't aware of your courage in combat, I should be forced to assign you to a penal battalion, Gefreiter Hals.'

Hals was suddenly fully awake.

'Please excuse me, Herr Hauptmann. I was half asleep.'

'Your sleep is pessimistic, Gefreiter Hals.'

The veteran answered for him. 'The day before yesterday, the Don; yesterday, the Donets; this morning, the Dnieper . . . You must admit, Herr Hauptmann, that even an elephant hide would find that somewhat discouraging.'

'I know,' Wesreidau answered. 'It's just what I've been afraid of ever since we came to Russia. But if we lose our confidence everything will be much harder.'

'It's territory and men that we're losing, Herr Hauptmann, much faster than confidence.'

'The Russians will not be able to cross the Pripet, for absolute geographical reasons. Believe me.'

'Where could we retreat to after that?' Lindberg asked stupidly.

'To the Oder,' the veteran said.

The cold seemed to strike all of us in the vitals.

'God keep us from such a catastrophe,' murmured Herr Hauptmann. 'I would rather be dead than see that day.'

Probably Wesreidau believed in God. In any case, his prayer was granted.

Chapter Twelve

RED TANKS

THE SECOND FRONT ON THE DNIEPER

It was now ten days since my return, which we had celebrated according to the circumstances. In the windowless isba we were assigned for rest periods, we had emptied a five-quart container of ersatz – no vodka, no biscuits, but then, that's war.

In any case, we had reserved the ersatz for me and my friends. The rest of the company might as well have been in limbo. Beyond the boundary of our friendship, and indifferent to it, they washed their dirty feet in large dishes of faintly warmed water or attacked their lice or organized lice races to pass the time. For a brief moment, we felt a sense of occasion, but that quickly faded. One can tell the same stories only a certain number of times. We very soon sank back into the torpor characteristic of soldiers at the front. Nothing was new to us; we had been through it all before – and even on days when our morale was relatively high, we felt constrained by the inevitable anxieties of the front.

For ten days we shuttled back and forth between our hole in the ground and the isba where we rested. Every twelve hours, we tramped the half mile which lay between our outpost and the shattered remnants of a village overrun by war. During the day, we stared vacantly at the empty, frozen country beyond our hole. At night, the fog limited our vision to ten or fifteen yards at most. We weren't yet trying to stop the enemy; their front was still extremely fluid.

From time to time, a few attempts at penetration, always motorized, forced us to open fire. And once, since my return, enemy tanks had appeared and fired at our frozen batteries. Otherwise, we had all the time in the world to observe the crystal structure of snowflakes against our infantry half boots, which became as hard as wood during our twelve hours of duty, and softened again in the stable-like warmth of sixty bodies huddled together in the isba during our twelve hours off. Fires, of course, were *streng verboten*, as smoke would give away our position.

Wesreidau often visited us. I think he felt especially warm toward our group, and with the veteran, able to speak directly, as man to man. We young ones listened to them talking, the way boys listen to their elders, and what we heard was always alarming. Our exhausted troops had abandoned Kiev, which, in spite of everything, remained a centre of combat. We were still trying to hold the Dnieper — but even that famous barrage seemed to be doing us very little good. From Cherkassy to Kremenchug, the Russians were on both banks of the river. They also held both banks of the Desna. At Nedrigailov, victory was no longer a possibility for us, and our men were faced with a choice of captivity or death.

Fortunately, as our front was extremely precarious and shallow, we were only supposed to be covering the southern wing of the fighting. The area we were holding was as flat as a billiard table, and a strong defence would have been difficult even with adequate supplies. On the twelfth day after my return, we were attacked by Russian planes, which cost us many casualties. Later that day, a column of German soldiers straggled over the horizon, partially made up of troops pushed from Cherkassy. Seven or eight ragged, famished regiments, overloaded with wounded, descended on us like a plague of locusts, ravaging and plundering our reserves. The intensity of the battle they had just survived could easily be read on their shaggy, exhausted faces. This fragment of the Wehrmacht, with wornout boots, empty packs, and eyes glittering with fever, preceded by four days the Russian thrust which began at Kherson and pushed through to the west bank of the Dnieper. At precisely this moment, winter also began to attack in earnest. The thermometer suddenly plunged to five degrees below zero.

On an evening of savage cold, the enemy reached our lines. The noise of their arrival preceded them, carried on the wind to the shivering bundles of rugs and blankets waiting behind frozen parapets. We listened, as animals at bay listen to the pack closing in. For at least two hours, we lay with straining ears, our enormous eyes staring fixedly through frozen films of protective tears. Although we could see nothing, voices kept announcing: 'Here they are!'

Our tense imaginations invested the visible edge of our defences with a thousand imaginary movements, and a thousand thoughts and visions whirled through our heads: our distant homelands, our families and friends, and our desperate, passionate loves. We imagined every possible outcome to the imminent fighting: surrender, captivity, flight ... flight, or death ... a quick death, to be done with it all. Some grasped their weapons all the more firmly, dreaming of a heroic defence which would push the Russians back, and hold the line. But most of us were resigned to death – a resignation which often created the most glorious heroes of the war. Simple cowards or pacifists, who had been opposed to Hitler from the start, often saved their lives and the lives of many others in a delirium of terror provoked by the accident of an overwhelming situation.

Faced with the Russian hurricane, we ran whenever we could. But often we had no choice, and became heroes without glory, who were somehow able to conjure up a strength superior to the enemy's. We no longer fought for Hitler, or for National Socialism, or for the Third Reich – or even for our fiancées or mothers or families trapped in bomb-ravaged towns. We fought from simple fear, which was our motivating power. The idea of death, even when we accepted it, made us howl with powerless rage. We fought for reasons which are perhaps shameful, but are, in the end, stronger than any doctrine. We fought for ourselves, so that we wouldn't die in holes filled with mud and snow; we fought like rats, which do not hesitate to spring with all their teeth bared when they are cornered by a man infinitely larger than they are.

Although we were already beaten ten times over, our terror became a fortress of despair, which the Russians found difficult to breach. We lay huddled against the frozen soil, and listened to the growing tumult of their approach.

We began to hear distinct, separable sounds. The black potato sack which was Hals changed shape and moved toward me.

'Do you hear that?' he whispered. 'They've got tanks.'

At first I heard nothing but tanks. Then there was the sound of singing too: a Russian victory song. It was their turn now to feel the infectious enthusiasm of advancing troops.

'A year and a half ago, we were marching on Moscow, and I was singing just like that,' muttered the veteran.

The night wore on. The noise of the Russian advance changed in quality and intensity, but never stopped. The men who had been resting in the isbas came back to their forward positions. Everyone was now in the line. Even the auxiliary services had been organized to defend the village. The front was long and thin; our division alone held some sixty miles, with the regiments standing elbow to elbow. There were a great many of us, but at least thirty times as many of them.

Our anxiety hovered over us like a pessimistic exhalation trapped by our heavy steel helmets. Our breath condensed on our nostrils and lips, and on the upturned collars of our coats. For a long time now, our hands and feet had been hurting us. For the moment, stiffened by cold, they seemed detached and separate from our general nervous tension. On other evenings, the fellows moved about in their holes to keep from freezing. This evening, however, our cumbersome overshoes had been tossed aside, and everyone was still. The biting cold passed over us like a silent dream, depositing a film of frost on the earth and on us. Periodically, we had to clear our weapons, and every time the touch of the icy metal struck us like an electric shock. To the east, the Russian troops were silent. All we heard from their side was the disquieting roar of their engines.

Occasionally, we heard a horse whinnying: one of our starving beasts protesting the onset of death. The desire for sleep weighed on us as heavily and oppressively as our fear and the cold, and kept overwhelming us for five and even ten minutes at a time, despite our wide-open eyes. Then we would jolt back to reality, to wait for the first hours of morning – a time when men and animals often die of cold.

The Russians were taking their time. Since we had caught the first sounds of their new front, a full day had gone by, but nothing more had happened. Had we possessed sufficient strength and equipment, a counter-attack would almost surely have been successful. But our orders were simply to resist and hang on. We were operating on a system of four hours on and four hours off, organized so that a maximum number of men was in the line at any given moment. Many men fell asleep beside their guns, to wake suddenly, badly frozen. We were steadily losing sick and wounded men, who withdrew on foot or on horseback – and no reinforcements were arriving to fill the gaps.

'It's a racket,' grumbled the veteran.

At dusk, we found Lindberg naked from the waist down. He had gone off a short distance, supposedly to crap, and had stayed that way for nearly three-quarters of an hour. By the time we found him, he was crying like a baby, and he wouldn't have lasted much longer. Hals blew up at him, and let him have it on the backside and thighs with the strap of his gas mask.

By the next morning, the Russians had still not attacked. We had grown steadily colder and more nervous, and it was difficult to seem calm.

One of our planes flew over, and dropped four sacks of mail. I had four letters: two from my family, and two from Paula. All were very out of date – particularly one of the letters from France, which was more than a month old. I devoured Paula's letters, which seemed filled with sadness. She had been sent to a small factory out in the country some forty miles from Berlin. She said that life in the capital was no longer possible.

What was I supposed to think? What could I imagine?

My parents' letter, with the standard two-line refrain from my father, irritated me by its tone of unjustified complaint. I mentioned this to Wiener, who replied: 'That's all the French know how to do – complain.'

My mother's last letter astounded me by its lack of realism. The poor woman begged me to take care of myself, to avoid showing off, to do my duty, but nothing more – to protect myself from meaningless risks. This sort of advice seemed so irrelevant that for the moment I was staggered. I looked up from the letter, yellow against the snow, to the whiteness which veiled the appalling danger threatening us from the east. The pathetic futility of my mother's attitude made my eyes fill with tears.

Everyone seemed to be reading a letter whose contents were so unexpected that fellows far older than I were overcome by tears. Others jumped to their feet, screaming like madmen: a close relative or friend had been killed in an air raid.

'This mail is only upsetting everyone,' said a tall fellow next to me, as he looked at a friend who was weeping like a child.

It seemed we were to be spared nothing.

In the afternoon, some patrols were sent out into the whirling snow. Our command had grown tired of waiting and had decided to test the enemy. We heard a few shots, and then the patrols came back, reporting that they'd seen a heavy concentration of Russian matériel.

I and my comrades were wakened just before nightfall. With pounding hearts, we ran to our forward positions. The Russian tanks were rolling through the storm, and we could feel the vibration of their treads against the frozen ground.

Our anti-tank gunners and men with Panzerfausts kept their eyes glued to their telescopic sights, which they had to wipe continually. A few anti-tank trenches had been dug, but these were ludicrously inadequate both in number and size. We knew that if our anti-tank defences gave way, we were lost, and we nervously clenched our fingers around the anti-tank grenades and magnetic mines which had been distributed.

At the Pak we were protecting, Olensheim, Ballers, Freivitch and others were ready to work the gun. Our visibility had been seriously reduced by falling snow. To the north of us, an S.M.G. had just opened fire. The rumbling of tanks was louder than ever, but the tanks themselves were still invisible. To the north, fighting had already begun, and we could see flashes of light despite the thickly whirling snow and the rapidly growing darkness. Short bursts of anti-tank fire lashed the plain, producing a curious muffled echo. As the roar of tanks grew louder, we felt our lungs lift. Long flames ran the length of the horizon, while others rose vertically, illuminating at different levels the whirling masses of falling snow. Then the sound of tank engines in full acceleration shattered the night and our eardrums. Five vaguely defined monsters loomed out of the darkness, rolling parallel to our line of defence. Our anti-tank crew was already firing. Wiener calmly steadied the butt of his F.M. against his shoulder, and I felt myself stiffen with a thousand indescribable terrors. Flashes of yellow light burst against the lead tank in the group of T-34s, whose turrets were pointed toward our line. Five shells had already left white traces on the huge machine, which otherwise appeared to be unaffected by the efforts of our anti-tank gunners.

A tank was roaring past us, at a distance of about ten yards. We heard a howling sound, and a shell from a Panzerfaust burst against its side. The monster immediately reduced its speed, and thick black smoke began to seep from every joint, to be lashed to the ground by the wind. The hatches opened, clanging back against the heavy metal plates. We could hear shouts and cries, which were quickly drowned by a powerful explosion. The turret disintegrated, leaving fragments of human beings suspended from the shattered metal in colours ranging from purple to gold. But there were no cries of triumph from our position – only the barking voice of our Pak. One of our shells hit a joint on the back of a second tank, and it too began to pour smoke. Then the cartridges were running through my fingers. Everyone who escaped from the immobilized tank was shot down without mercy. For a moment, we breathed more easily. By now, our surroundings were lit by flames and we were able to see the Russian tanks before they got so close. One of them had actually crossed our lines, and as it drew near us, we could feel our hair stiffening with terror. The anti-tank crew were working as fast as they could. Within three seconds, their gun was facing this new threat, and a shell, fired at the earliest possible instant, was bursting against the enemy's front apron. At the moment of impact, the engine stopped, and then began to scream, as if it had been thrown out of gear. Simultaneously, somewhere to our right, we were aware of two brilliant flashes, and heard a long-drawn-out explosion. Another tank began to fire at us, and large pieces of frozen earth hurtled into the air.

I no longer knew what was happening. The tank to our right burst into flames, groaning at all its seams.

'Für den Panzerfaust: Sieg Heil! Heil!' someone shouted.

Our gunners were now firing at the second tank which had penetrated to our rear, and which seemed to be having mechanical difficulties. Then its left side disintegrated in a prolonged explosion. But our attention was drawn to a hallucinating spectacle farther to the rear. A T-34 had driven over one of our positions, crushing our men under its treads. One of our half-tracks, armed with an anti-tank machine gun was chasing it from behind, firing as rapidly as it could. Our anti-tank crew were in trouble. Freivitch was wounded, perhaps even dead. We fired our machine guns at the Russian monster, which never slackened its speed but continued to make for its lines as fast as possible. Two shells fired by other tanks exploded beside our half-track, and a third disintegrated it right in front of us. But the enemy tank, believing it was still pursued, vanished into the whirling snow.

The Russian armoured assault was over. It had lasted for about half an hour, and had clearly been testing our defences. A certain number of tanks had been disabled or destroyed; their losses were visibly greater than ours. Unfortunately, these losses counted for nothing compared to the vast armada regrouping opposite us. For us, although quantitively our losses were smaller, the destruction of four anti-tank positions in our sector was extremely serious.

For the moment, the tension dropped somewhat. Trench telephones rang, asking for reports, and voices shouted for the stretcherbearers who were running and sliding across the icy ground. The veteran slid to the bottom of our hole and lit a cigarette, despite the ban. Hals jumped down and joined us.

'I just heard that Wesreidau's bunker was crushed by a T-34,' he said, gasping.

We gaped at him, waiting for more information.

'Stay here,' the veteran said finally. 'I'll go and see.'

'Achtung! Zigaretten!' warned Hals.

'Danke.'

The veteran extinguished his butt, and tucked it into the cuff of his sleeve. He reappeared half an hour later.

'We had to dig for ten minutes before we could get Wesreidau out,' he told us. 'He's all right, and so are the two other officers – just a few scratches. But the fellow from liaison outside was killed. He must have panicked and tried to get inside. We found his body in the rubble.'

We quickly suppressed that mangled vision to rejoice that our hauptmann was safe. We all felt very attached to him, and dependent on his survival.

By next morning, the snow had stopped. The plain was strewn with the carcasses of wrecked tanks, which the storm had not entirely covered – at least twenty in the immediate vicinity of our position. Parts of these huge black cadavers, still warm from the fires which had burned over and through them, had turned red in the intensity of the flames. It seemed that the Russians had attacked our line at four points, separated by intervals of fifteen miles. One of those had been centred directly on our position, which was held by six companies. The other three were farther to the north.

We went back into the line at eight o'clock. Everything was motionless and muffled, under a low, dark sky, as opaque and heavy as a lead roof. Nowhere else have I seen skies quite like the skies of Russian winter. We used to stare up, amazed by the oppressive solidity. The diffused light seeping slowly downward made everything look unreal. Our reversible winter overalls stood out against the immaculate new snow a dingy piss yellow. A great many men were already wearing all the winter clothes we'd been issued: coat, vest, sheepskin, etc., which made their movements slow and clumsy. As the overalls had not been cut to cover so much bulk, they often tore. We looked like a collection of filthy, tattered pillows.

Despite our sense of inferiority, we all felt much less tense. The carcasses of the Russian tanks looked to our otherwise pessimistic eyes like the slaughtered beasts of a triumphant hunting scene. We all knew that it had not been a serious attack; nonetheless, we had managed to hold off the enemy's most dangerous machines. The possibility that the Russian tanks had been ordered not to advance any further occurred only to the veterans among us. All the younger men preferred to believe that we had stopped them. A few bottles of alcohol theoretically reserved for wounded men were opened by the captain himself, and that evening we celebrated in the isbas. In our hut we particularly honoured our Panzerfaust team.

In the dim, wavering light of seven or eight candles, we drank to the healths of Obergefreiters Lensen, Kellermann, and Dunde. Grenadiers Smellens and Prinz touched glasses with Herr Hauptmann Wesreidau, who wore a large dressing on his left hand, and two others on his face. There were also two wounded men lying on stretchers, to whom we gave as many cigarettes as they wished.

Hals, exuberant as always, was describing the battle, miming certain scenes with sweeping gestures of his left arm and hand, which held his glass, while with his right he vigorously scratched his armpits, which swarmed with lice. Lindberg, as always when things were going well for us, was in a state of high excitement. Cowardice had affected him more than anybody else, and his face, although it looked as young as ever, bore the traces.

Several men had fallen asleep, despite the noise. Everyone who stayed awake was soon quite drunk. As always at a

German celebration, several fellows began to sing – marching songs, because we knew hardly any others. In the shadowy light of the isba, the scene looked fantastic and unreal.

The veteran began a Russian song. None of the rest of us understood him. We didn't know whether we were listening to a Revolutionary song or a song from the friendly Ukraine – although the distinction no longer mattered, as our Ukrainian days were over.

Everyone was singing whatever he liked, as part of a continuously increasing uproar. Hals had been twisting my arm to sing something in French, and I obliged, despite a growing desire to vomit, adding the 'Sambre et Meuse' and a series of more or less obscene songs to the general discord.

Hals, who was as tight as a drum, burst out laughing and shouted: 'Here come the Franzosen to the rescue: Ourrah pobieda!'

Then something disagreeable happened. Lensen stood up, stiff with drunkenness. 'Who the hell is talking about the Franzosen? What can anyone expect from a bunch of lousy milquetoasts like that?'

He was shouting at Hals, who was dancing heavily, like a bear. Hals grabbed him by the arm, and tried to pull him into a waltz.

'Shut up, you idiot!' Lensen yelled. 'Go stick your head in the snow instead of belching out such crap.'

Hals, who was almost a head taller, went right on dancing. Then Lensen let him have it with his fists, shouting at him louder than his minuscule superiority of rank gave him any right to do. 'Stillgestanden, gefreiter!' he yelled.

'Who the hell do you think you are? Are you telling me to shut up?' Hals was trying to stare at Lensen through eyes clouded by drink.

'Stillgestanden!' Lensen repeated. 'Or I'll give you something you won't like.'

'But you're forgetting Sajer!' Hals shouted, waving at me. By now he was purple-faced too. 'He's half French, and he's lived in France all his life. And anyway the French are with us now.' He'd obviously been reading the same stories I had.

'You damned fool. Where the hell did you get that?'

'But it's true!' someone else shouted. 'I read it in *Ost Front*.'

I no longer knew which way to look.

'Wake up, you dummkopf. So what if a handful of those milksops have come over to us? It doesn't mean a damn thing. And anyone who thinks anything different is no better than they are – goddamned black-haired guitarists whining over their goddamned love songs.'

I knew that Lensen was talking about the fundamental discord which has always existed between South Germany and Prussia.

'You're forgetting, Lensen, that my mother grew up just outside Berlin,' I said.

'Well, then, you've got to choose. Either you're German like us, or you're one of those worthless, feckless Frogs.'

I was on the point of saying that after all I didn't really have much choice.

'And you were asked to make just that choice in Poland, even at Chemnitz. I remember. I was there.'

'But he did choose!' Hals shouted. 'And here he is, in the same boat as you and me and all the rest of us.'

'So – he doesn't have any more goddamn connection with the French.' Lensen, who was unquestionably brave, had been awarded the Iron Cross after destroying his seventh tank.

I suddenly felt overwhelmingly depressed and vulnerable, and incapable of ever attaining anything like Lensen's record. As always, I found the war almost totally paralyzing – probably because of my soft French blood, which Lensen despised so much. I was really almost as bad as Lindberg. He wasn't a true German either, but came from somewhere near Lake Constance – one of Lensen's typical 'black-hairs.'

A joyous group had begun to sing 'Marienka,' and general drunken revelry took over again. This time, though, I stayed on the sidelines, sunk in thought. All the pride I had felt when I had sworn my oath at Camp F, all my joy in feeling that at last I was the equal of my companions, for whom I felt an unquestioning respect, all the struggles and miseries undertaken and endured with the burning faith of a true believer – all of these had been once again cast into doubt by Lensen's drunken outburst. I had always sensed a certain scorn on his part. However, once in Poland he had come to my defence, and I had jumped to the conclusion that he held nothing against me on account of my origins. Now I knew the truth. Despite all my efforts, and all the suffering we had been through together, my comrades rejected me. Would they ever think me worthy of bearing German arms? Inwardly, I cursed my parents for having brought me into the world at their particular crossroads.

I felt angry and sad and incredibly alone. I knew that I could count on Hals and Wiener and maybe a few others; but even they had started drinking and singing again, beside their blood brothers. I would never again be able to sing with a light, casual spirit those German songs I enjoyed so much. And someday, maybe very soon, I might die, in a position not much better than that of an adoring black slave at his master's side. This vision of things was unbearable, and increased the nausea brought on by alcohol. I went outside to vomit and take a few breaths of icy air. My drunkenness prevented any further thought, and when I returned to the hut, I collapsed onto a heap of packs, to scratch at the lice biting me under my belt.

The next morning, the Russian front began to move again. First they sent over a few rounds of artillery. They had been keeping us in a state of expectation for several days now, undoubtedly preparing a definitive offensive with the slowness characteristic of their organization. During the day, we were reinforced by an artillery column – which meant digging new trenches, and blistered hands for all of us. All along the front, our troops were ordered to break up the Russian positions.

That afternoon, we pounded the enemy with our big guns. They remained obstinately quiet. As soon as it was dark, certain sections loaded with ammunition left our trenches and advanced across the snowy ground. We had resumed our push to the east. Scheisse! In a state of considerable apprehension, these groups fell on a motorized Soviet regiment, whose mass of vehicles seemed immobilized for all eternity. The night stillness was broken by the sound of our F.M.s and grenades, the cries of the Russians, surprised by this sudden and unexpected display of aggressiveness, and the roar of incendiary bombs, which must have consumed a costly quantity of matériel.

Then our men made a half turn, before the Russians were able to muster an organized reaction, and ran back to our trenches, bathed in transistory glory.

We had, in fact, aroused the anger of the Russians, who decided to retaliate as soon as it was light.

As at Belgorod, the whole horizon burst into flame, with the sudden, total involvement of the opening bars of a Wagner opera. Our frantic dash to our positions assumed a tragic quality, as the rain of fire was so dense that a quarter of our men fell before they'd reached the line. Then, we relived scenes and experiences very like what we'd known before. The sight of comrades screaming and writhing through final moments of agony had become no more bearable with familiarity, and I, despite my longing to live or die a worthy hero of the Wehrmacht, was no less of an animal stiff with uncontrollable terror.

Fortunately for us, the Luftwaffe, on which we could no longer rely, made an unexpected appearance, and somewhat reduced the force of the Russian blow. But the next day this intervention was answered in kind, and Russian planes did what they could to knock out our artillery. As a result, our artillery was withdrawn during the night, leaving us to do the honours unsupported.

We held our positions for four more terrible days, in spite of continuous infantry attacks supported by armour. Whenever possible, we buried our dead in the holes where they fell. Eighty-three names were scratched off the company list – among these, Olensheim, who had recovered from a serious wound at Belgorod, to receive his coup-de-grâce here, on the west bank of the Dnieper, where tranquillity was to have been assured.

The Russians had finally regrouped for their supreme effort, and were delaying only to complete last-minute preparations. Their artillery, which seemed to be growing stronger by the hour, pounded our positions and the countryside for a long way back. The veteran had just been wounded, and was waiting, along with some hundred other men, for evacuation to a hospital, or at least to a quieter zone in the rear. A brusque sergeant had taken Wiener's place, and I continued to feed ammunition into the spandau, operated by someone considerably less expert than my friend.

The night which followed was so horrible that I retain only a confused and fragmented memory of it. Fresh supplies of ammunition were often slung into a length of canvas and carried across the trenches by two or four fellows. The 'night' of which I speak was, of course, total by five in the evening.

Time in Russia is like that: in the summer there is almost no night, and in the winter, no day.

We had just withstood two or three major assaults. From the screams of anguish to our left, we concluded that a great many of our men had been killed. We had emptied five magazines, and were warming our fingers on the hot metal of the machine gun. Our sixth and last magazine had been attached, and we were anxiously waiting for fresh supplies. The night was continuously lit by the explosions of thousands of Russian shells, which made movement extremely difficult. Our trenches, which in any case were not deep enough, extended only to certain positions. The others had to be reached by leaps and bounds, alternating with plunges to the ground, and writhing on our stomachs across dozens of yards of snow mixed with chunks of frozen earth.

From time to time, we could see four figures moving toward us, jumping from crater to crater, carrying shells for our 50-mm. mortar, and magazines for the spandau. They were still about forty yards away, when their shadowy mass was surrounded by a flash of white light. We never heard any cries. A few minutes later, I was sent out to crawl to the point of impact. The sergeant ordered me to bring back at least two magazines. I had just arrived at my destination when I heard the Russian assault cry, followed by a shower of grenades and mortar shells. The ground shook beneath me in a manner which defied all prediction. I felt like a pea inside a ferociously beaten drum. I was lying flat on the ground among the bodies of comrades killed only a few minutes before, unable to see any of the supplies I'd been sent to fetch. Then I heard the sound of a tank. The darkness all around me was broken by streaks of light and large pink and yellow explosions. In a momentary beam from some head-light, I could see a small sign marked S. 157. I opened my mouth wide, as prescribed, because I could hardly breathe, and lay where I was, frantically groping for something to hang on to in that diabolical setting, where horizontal and vertical alternated to the rhythm of the lights which slashed the darkness. I thought that I could recognize through the uproar the crackle of the weapon I had operated with Wiener and had left only a moment before, and felt that my sanity might be close to collapse. I could see no escape from my situation, and lay glued to the ground with my head down, like a trussed animal, waiting for the butcher's axe.

A hundred yards to my left, the Pak, with its barrel marked for eleven kills, was fleeing into the striped darkness with its ammunition and gun crew. I heard the terrifying roar of a tank rising above the general tumult, and a headlight wavered and leaped through the undulating darkness. It had obviously driven through our defences and was now passing within twenty yards of where I lay. I saw it suddenly burst into flame, and despite the intense cold a wave of hot air almost asphyxiated me. Half unconscious, I could hear the trample of running feet all around me, and, despite the noise of guns and explosions, cries which sounded more like curses than anything else, and were certainly neither French nor German.

I thought I could distinguish three or four pairs of boots thumping past me. Everything happened so quickly at that moment that I am no longer sure of what in fact I did see. I could still hear the sound of a machine gun, and then there were hundreds of shouting voices. The tank exploded a second time, showering steel fragments all around me. Some of our soldiers must still have been firing.

Then there was a period of relative calm, which lasted for about three-quarters of an hour. Exhausted by nervous tension, I managed to pull myself out of my torpor enough to take a few steps toward the position I had left twenty minutes earlier. But nothing remained of it except smoke and motionless bodies. Furthermore, the entire sector, as far as I could see, was veiled in smoke. I turned back again, heading for our rear lines, and, too late to stop myself, tripped over a corpse. I realized that I had no weapon, and grabbed the dead man's gun, which was lying beside him. Then I began to run.

I heard four or five shots. The whistling flight of the balls made me think of hell. I knew that I might faint at any moment, and between two spasms of nausea fell into a hole where three fellows in roughly the same state as myself were staring fixidly at the dark, sombre east. Literally crumpled into the bottom of the hole, I attempted to order my thoughts. My retina still bore the imprint of a thousand darting, luminous points, which prolonged my sense of vertigo.

For a long moment, I stayed where I was, wondering where to head for next. Then I heard the other fellows in the hole exclaiming with astonishment. Far to the south, the earth seemed to have caught on fire, and the sky rang with the sound of thunder.

Twenty miles to the south, the second Dnieper front had given way in the face of irresistible Russian pressure, and thousands of German and Rumanian soldiers met an apocalyptic end. Some twenty regiments had been unable to disengage in time, and had laid down their arms, to be rewarded for their bravery by captivity and degradation.

For the rest of us, the war continued. In a rush, I decided to leave the hole which had received me a few moments before. Doubled over, I ran like a madman to another defensive position, where a group of soldiers were clustered around a motionless figure who was being bandaged. A fellow I didn't recognize hailed me by name: 'Where've you come from, Sajer?'

My head was still pounding to the rhythm of the bombardment. I stared at him. 'I don't know. . . . I don't know any more. . . . Everyone back there is dead. . . . I ran away, through all the Russians.'

Behind us, we could hear the roar of an engine. A tractor was pulling a heavy anti-tank gun into position. Then we heard the burst of the exhaust a moment before each shell exploded. Our overwhelming weariness was now affecting us like a drug. Russian shells were coming over in profusion. For a moment, we watched the storm closing in. Then, with a cry of despair and a prayer for mercy, we dived to the bottom of our hole, trembling as the earth shook and the intensity of our fear grew. The shocks, whose centre seemed closer each time, were of an extraordinary violence. Torrents of snow and frozen earth poured down on us. A white flash, accompanied by an extraordinary displacement of air, and an intensity of noise which deafened us, lifted the edge of the trench. None of us immediately grasped what had happened. We were thrown in a heap against the far wall of the hole, wounded and intact together. Then, with a roar, the earth poured in and covered us.

In that moment, so close to death, I was seized by a rush of terror so powerful that I felt my mind was cracking. Trapped by the weight of earth, I began to howl like a madman. The memory of that moment terrifies me still. The sense that one has been buried alive is horrible beyond the powers of ordinary language. Dirt had run down my neck and into my mouth and eyes, and my whole body was gripped by a heavy and astonishingly inert substance which only held me more tightly the harder I struggled. Under my thigh I felt a leg kicking with the desperation of a horse between the shafts of a heavy cart. Something else was rubbing against my shoulder. With a sudden jerk, I pulled my head free of the dirt and of my helmet, whose strap was cutting into my windpipe, nearly strangling me. Some two feet from my face a horrible mask pouring blood was howling like a demon. My body was still entirely trapped. I knew that I was either going to die or lose my reason.

My throat burst with screams of rage and despair. No nightmare could possibly reach such a pitch of horror. At that moment, I suddenly understood the meaning of all the cries and shrieks I had heard on every battlefield. And I also understood the marching songs, which so often begin with a ringing description of a soldier dying in glory and then suddenly turn sombre:

> *We marched together like brothers,*
> *And now he lies in the dust.*
> *My heart is torn with despair,*
> *My heart is torn with despair. . . .*

Once again I learned how hard it is to watch a comrade die: almost as hard as dying oneself.

During the night, the Russians made nine attempts to break through our lines, and failed. If they had persevered once, or maybe twice more, they would surely have been successful. I watched, three-quarters buried, for about twenty minutes, while a hurricane of fire broke over our rear, destroying what was left of the village, and killing something like 700 men in our regiment alone, which, at the beginning of the offensive had numbered about 2,800 men. I scratched at the ground with my hands, and somehow managed to free myself. Two men were lying beside me in pools of blood. The dying man had been buried under more than a yard of earth, and could no longer hope for anything but the mercy of heaven. A fellow beside me, who had been wounded, was groaning with pain. He was buried almost as deeply as I had been. I dug him out as fast as I could, and helped him to crawl through the explosions toward the rear. On the way, I saw a gun lying on the ground and picked it up.

The rest of the night was consumed by a series of almost insuperably difficult problems, as if we were caught in a terrible game with all the odds against us and our lives at stake.

At dawn, in the first faint light of a dark winter day, the front grew quiet. The scattered remnants of our regiments collected as they met among the craters and shell holes. A cloud of stale smoke hung over the snowy ground, which was littered with Russian and German dead. The wounded who had not yet succumbed to the bitter cold were still groaning, filling the air with a chorus of misery which our exhausted ears heard as they might have heard a winter wind howling over the roof of an isba in an isolated hamlet on the steppe. Sections were organized to help the stretcherbearers with a job of impossible magnitude.

As always, the Russians left all rescue efforts to us. Their wounded were left lying where they fell, with a possibility of either dying on the spot or of being picked up by one of our first-aid teams. Their supplies of matériel seemed to be increasing daily in quantity and quality, but their medical services barely functioned. As our army grew more and more disorganized by retreat, we became increasingly unable to care for the thousands of wounded soldiers, whose number was continuously growing. The Russian wounded could hope for very little from us.

While the medical service tried to deal with the wounded, some twelve of us settled into a half-covered bunker back of our former sleeping quarters, which had been entirely destroyed. Herr Hauptmann Wesreidau, who had just arrived, was one of the group. Despite a general sense of foreboding in the face of disaster, we all felt a surge of joy whenever a particular friend appeared. Hals, Lensen, and Lindberg were all there. I was helping a wounded corporal bandage his severely burned right hand when the captain announced that we would retreat. He sent us out to help the noncoms count off and regroup our decimated company before moving camp at dawn. I went with Lensen, to help him find what was left of his section. The Russians, who had also taken a beating, were catching a moment's rest before demolishing what remained of our front. For the moment, everything was quiet in the eerie half light of December.

Lensen couldn't quite grasp what had happened to me. For him, the simple fact that I had survived the Soviet thrust was extraordinary. My explanations that at the time I had understood nothing made no difference to him; he simply supplied his own scenario.

My winter overalls had entirely disappeared, leaving me with nothing but my singed overcoat. During my flight, I had picked up a gun which proved to be Russian. For Lensen, it was all clear. The Russians had overrun my position, and had either failed to notice me or had taken me for dead. In a desperate man-to-man struggle, I had managed to wrest a weapon from one of them and, with his gun, had fought my way to our lines.

'You're still stunned,' he insisted. 'But I'm sure you'll remember later. I don't see any other explanation.'

Lensen's version certainly had its advantages. I myself retained nothing but a chaotic impression of flashing lights and thunderous noises over a sense of such total disorientation that I had no longer been capable of distinguishing east from west or up from down. Perhaps Lensen was only trying to compensate for his attitude during our evening of celebration.

At dusk, which fell in the middle of the afternoon, the German Army abandoned the second Dnieper front. While the immense Russian thrust whose fringe had swept over us was pressing with its principal strength against German and Rumanian units further to the south, our depleted columns withdrew from their positions, abandoning all matériel which was no longer usable or transportable. Our Gross Deutschland regiments, half of us on foot, left in relative silence, our backs bent by the weight of our burdens, hoping that the grey skies would hold back for a while longer the rain of metal and fire which the pursuing enemy was bound to send after us.

Chapter Thirteen

THE THIRD RETREAT

PARTISANS · CHRISTMAS, 1943 · THE SIEGE OF
BOPOROEIVSKA

Our prayers were granted and we were able to march for thirty
miles undisturbed. We were unpleasantly surprised to find no
reserve positions in that distance. Except for a few surveillance
posts, where the fellows to their astonishment were told to
pack up and leave with us, we encountered no serious
defensive efforts. The Russians could easily have continued
their advance without firing a shot.

On the second day of this third retreat, the most mobile
portion of our battalion stopped and settled in to act as a
covering force while the rest continued westward. Some two
thousand men, among them myself, were stationed near a
village which was not marked on any of the staff maps. As we
arrived, the inhabitants fled into the thick forest. We established ourselves with light but motorized weapons. We had
four minuscule tanks, which had been effective in Poland but
were like toys compared to the T-34s. Their armament
consisted of a double-barrelled machine gun and a grenade
thrower, and we used them principally as tractors, to pull the
twelve sleighs which made up our train. Four half-tracks
doubled as anti-tank machine-gun posts, and as a source of
emergency power for our six trucks when they stuck in the
deep snowdrifts. Three enormous Zundapp-Russland sidecars
skated through the powdery snow, which often plugged the
space between the front mudguard and tyre, preventing that
wheel from turning. Their engines were powerful enough to
free the back wheel and the wheel of the sidecar, which was
also motorized, and send the whole machine zigzagging
forward, roaring from its twin exhausts, while the blocked
driving wheel skated over the surface like the runner of a
sleigh. Three Paks completed our defence. With these wea-

399

pons, which were suitable for chasing partisans, and the classic infantry weapons – P.M.s, mortars, F.M.s and grenades – we had been ordered to stop three Russian divisions, including several armoured regiments, for at least twenty-four hours. Lastly, our orders were to withdraw, even if our efforts should be triumphantly successful.

Throughout our sector, whose front was roughly sixty miles long, groups analogous to ours were left behind, while the main body of troops withdrew to the west in a series of forced marches.

The Russians, who had broken through further south, neglected our sector. There was no need for them to take any more losses pursuing an enemy who was withdrawing anyway. The Red Army left our harassment to the partisans, whose numbers were continuously increasing, and which soon reached proportions astonishing in a country nominally under our control. On Stalin's orders, they intensified the desperation of our retreat with sudden ambushes; shells with delayed-action fuses; booby-trapped and mutilated bodies of men from interior positions; attacks on supply trains, isolated groups, and rallying points; hideous mutilation of prisoners; and a constant refusal of contact with units capable of fighting. The partisans – or terrorists, a name they richly deserved – always took on easy victims, and greatly intensified the usual cruelties of wartime. By these means, they achieved an effect which the regular army was never able to equal.

The Wehrmacht bent before the power of an incomparably greater enemy. The unbearable harassment by partisans was added to the overwhelming and heroic rigours of the front, while our territories in the rear no longer guaranteed any repose to our exhausted troops. The Ukraine, which had shown some sympathy for us, was itself pillaged by partisan bands – on orders from Moscow. The Ukrainian population had to choose, and be actively for one side or another. The partisans either killed or enlisted the young Ukrainians who had until then been so respectful to us. The invisible war triumphed: war which no longer offered any retreat, or calm, or pity. Wars of subversion have no face, and like revolutions create their own martyrs, innocent victims, and hostages, and provoke confused judgments of ill-considered actions. Men kill for revenge, in reprisal for what has happened or might happen. The partisans were pouring oil onto a huge conflagration.

In the name of Marxist liberty, the Ukraine was forced to alter its attitude. German and Ukrainian alike grew bitter and full of hate. The war became a total war, a war of scorched earth, offering the towns and villages in its path no more relief than we would eventually receive when we became the vanquished. In this period, as the war attained the most violent paroxysms of an already unbearable conflict, our unit sat out its sentence of round-the-clock guard duty in the murderous cold.

Over the snow-covered ground silence hung, unbroken except for the occasional howl of a grey taiga wolf deep in the forests, which were still largely unexplored. A quarter of our men were always on guard, watching from the shelter of ludicrously inadequate fortifications or frost-covered tank turrets, or mounting hurried patrols at the edge of the forest. The rest waited in the abandoned isbas.

The stoves in these huts had been systematically destroyed before we arrived – no doubt by partisans, who hoped that without shelter we would die of cold. Some of the isbas were open to the sky, with their roofs burned or pulled off. Probably the partisans had not had time to destroy the village completely before we arrived. There were far too many of us for the number of buildings still standing, and hundreds of men were reduced to finding what shelter they could, huddled behind gutted walls whose only roof was the heavy, opaque fog. Inside the walls, these men burned everything they could find. In the better isbas, the intense flames threatened to set fire at any moment to the structures themselves. Our exhausted troops no longer bothered to collect deadwood from the forest, and burned every combustible fitting left in the huts. Cursing at the smoke which blinded them, and which in the roofed isbas escaped only through the open doors, our soldiers packed closely together for warmth, tried to sleep on their feet, despite the coughs which shook their bodies. In the isbas without roofs smoke was never a difficulty, but the men were never warm. Those closest to the fires rapidly grew so hot they had to move, while others, only four or five yards away, felt only the faintest warming of the air, whose temperature rose to fifteen or sixteen degrees above zero.

Every two hours another quarter of the men went back to

the dugouts to make room in our precarious sleeping quarters for those who would return white with cold. The winter was now serious: fifteen degrees below zero, according to the thermometer of our radio group. As before, our general state of filth aggravated the situation. Any desire to piss was announced to all present, so that hands swollen by chilblains could be held out under the warm urine, which often infected our cracked fingers.

I was taking my first tour of guard duty in the early-morning hours of polar darkness, and my second began at one o'clock, in the diffused light of midday, which was veiled by a sky as dark as the sky over Tempelhof the day it was destroyed. Toward the end of my patrol, the day would turn an unusual pink. By three o'clock, when I returned to the smokehouse, there was nothing further to report.

My eyes hurt me, and my nose was so inflamed by frostbite I could no longer bear to leave it uncovered. We hid our faces like Chicago gangsters, with our collars raised and tied around our faces with scarves or strings. An hour later, the pink light turned violet, and then grey. The snow turned grey too, and then it was dark – from midafternoon until nine the next morning. With darkness, the temperature always plunged sharply – often to thirty-five or forty degrees below zero. Our matériel was paralysed: gasoline froze, and oil became first a paste and then a glue, which entirely blocked the mechanism. The forest rang with strange sounds: the bark of trees bursting under the pressure of the freezing. Stones cracked only when the temperature fell to sixty degrees below zero. For us, the horror we had been dreading for so long had arrived.

Winter at war – a reality we had almost forgotten – fell on us like the die of a gigantic press ready to crush us. Everything combustible was burned. A lieutenant defended two of our sleighs with a gun against some forty landser, whose breath rattled through their congested lungs. The nose of every face cover developed a block of ice which grew larger as each fresh breath condensed and froze.

'We want the sleighs for wood!' the men shouted.

'Get back!' the lieutenant screamed in reply. 'The forest is full of wood.'

The landser stared at him, wondering what good the sleighs would do them if they all froze.

A party sent out to fetch wood from the forest ran to the shelter of the trees. Faceless spectres returned with bundles which they threw down onto the dying fires. The fires had to be kept alive, which made rest impossible. We prayed that the Russians wouldn't attack: all attempts at defence had been abandoned.

Guard duty was the hardest of all. To stand still one seriously risked being frozen alive. At nine o'clock it was my turn again. Fifteen of us were standing watch in the ruins of a building crusted with hard snow which cracked like glass. We got through the first half hour beating each other to keep our blood moving. The second half hour was torture. Two men fainted. We thrust our stiffened hands from our sleeves and clumsily tried to help them. Our gloves, part wool and part leather, were already full of holes and good for nothing. The pain in our hands and feet seemed to travel through our bodies and clutch at our hearts. Four men carried the unconscious soldiers to the fires which gleamed in the darkness. If the Russians had come, they could easily have wiped us out. One man was running round and round in small circles, crying like a baby. The pain in my feet made me scream aloud. Despite orders, I abandoned my post and ran to the nearest isba. Shoving my way through a compact mass of soldiers, I stopped just short of the fire, and fell grimacing to my knees. Then I thrust my boots right into the coals. They immediately began to crackle and hiss, and at the pain of contact between hot and cold I burst into loud sobs. I was not the only one to cry, and there were others whose screams and moans were far louder than mine.

The hour of release finally came, and we prepared to leave. The Russians had not swarmed down on us, and the steel of our frosted weapons, which had not been heated by explosions, glimmered bluer than ever in the horrible cold, and looked as brittle as glass. Our men assembled listlessly, torn by a conflict of disloyalties which brought them close to madness. Although no one had covered himself with glory fighting against the Russians, another fight, which was equally formidable, had been fought against the cold and our exhaustion and filth and the lice we scarcely felt, they had become so much a part of our everyday condition. The cold had also claimed its victims. Three times, detachments of the last group on guard had returned to the fires carrying inert bodies Pneumonia, generalized frostbite, and physical weakness had been unable to resist the overwhelming cold. For three men, their return to the fire came too late. Five others were revived by flagellation and alcohol.

In the motionless cold of the polar night, we covered the rigid corpses with snow, marking each improvised grave with a stick and a helmet. There was no time for sentiment or reflection. Those who were still – to their astonishment – among the living were trying to shake off the general numbness enough to start our solidly frozen engines. The situation seemed desperate. Not one of the engines turned over.

Feldwebel Sperlovski stamped down on the pedals of his Zundapp, which resisted the pressure his 190 pounds of flesh and bone could still bring to bear and then cracked like a piece of dead wood. The metal itself seemed to be affected. We lit fires under the Panzers, to try to thaw them slowly before making any attempt to start them. For the cursing, gasping landser, the effort was immense, straining our congested lungs, which whistled and rattled. Wesreidau himself was impatient. He had wrapped his boots in rags picked up during the retreat.

'We should have kept at least one engine running all night,' he exclaimed. 'It's elementary. This sort of carelessness could ruin all of us.'

We listened to him with expressionless faces. Undoubtedly several among us would have regarded death as a deliverance.

An hour or so later, we heard the asthmatic backfire of an engine. Someone had managed to start one of the half-tracks. The driver let it warm up for a while, and set to work on the gear box, which had not yet thawed. After two hours of intense effort, our column set out, under orders to maintain the lowest possible speed. Until the machines had reached a certain minimum temperature, we had to limp after them on foot.

At midday, there were several breakdowns, and the convoy had to stop. The radiator hoses of several vehicles had been damaged by the pure alcohol in the radiators, and we had to repair them, using spare parts if we were fortunate enough to have them. Otherwise, we patched them up as best we could. While the work was in progress, we opened some cans of solidly frozen food: meat which could be chopped with an axe, a purée of peas and soya with the consistency of cement, and a solid brick of wine. Our enforced stop cost us an hour. According to radio instructions, we had one more hour to rejoin the main body of troops.

We were crossing the territory of one of our interior defence posts: two round blockhouses and three or four huts built into the ground. No one came out to meet us, and the place seemed deserted. However, a plume of smoke was rising from one of the blockhouses. No doubt the men inside were asleep beside a warm fire. We sent a small group over to investigate. Five minutes later, one of them ran back to the column, his breath spreading around his face in white clouds. When he reached us, he stopped, gasping.

'Everything in there has been destroyed, Herr Hauptmann, and everyone is dead. It's terrible!'

Every grey face filled with anxiety. Looking more closely, we saw that the doors of the isbas had all been knocked in, and that four or five bodies lay beside one of the huts.

'Partisans!' someone shouted. 'Six men recently killed!'

'There's been fighting here recently, Herr Hauptmann. Those bandits must still be holding their guns.'

Another detachment went into the second blockhouse. There was a long, echoing explosion, and a geyser of earth and snow and fragments of wood shot into the air over the building. Wesreidau cursed aloud, and ran toward the smoking bunker. We followed him. Three men had just been torn to pieces. Two were unrecognizable, while the third was gasping his last breath, rattling as the blood spurted from his body. Mixed into the rubble lay the bodies of four German soldiers who had been killed before we arrived.

'Watch out for mines!' Wesreidau shouted.

The word passed from mouth to mouth. Soldiers stopped at the door of the second blockhouse and looked in without daring to enter.

Six men, who had been stripped almost naked and hideously mutilated, were lying in pools of black, congealed blood. Some of the mutilations were so horrible that we couldn't look at them. Two soldiers – men who had fought outside of Moscow, at Kursk, Briansk, and Belgorod, and seen appalling horrors – hid their faces in their hands and walked away. None of us had ever seen anything so gratuitously horrible.

Taking infinite precautions, a section removed the cadavers. Two of them had been booby-trapped. We covered their bodies with debris, as we had neither the means nor the time to dig graves.

To all of us, the tactics of the partisans seemed more ignoble and senseless than anything else we'd seen. Wesreidau led a ceremony of final farewell to the eighteen massacred men. We removed our hats and caps and helmets, and stood bareheaded in the snow.

'Ich hatte einen Kameraden . . .

Our funeral song rang through the stone-age setting of Russian winter with the discordant sonorities of thousands of voices. There were no flags or fanfares – only profound consternation.

The spirit of revenge motivating the terrorists further destroyed the fragments of understanding so far spared by the war. Our men could not accept it. If they could still bear the torment of the trenches with heroic resolution they could not accept the treachery of the partisans.

Our column set out again. As we passed the centre blockhouse we saw the coarse placard thrust into the snowy mound. Across it, scrawled in charcoal, we read the word 'Revenge.'

We drove on for another hour. The snow, which deadened the noise of our vehicles, also intensified distant sounds. Suddenly we heard the crackle of automatic weapons. Wesreidau, together with our two other officers, ordered us to halt. Immediately, we heard the noise of firing more distinctly. Some five miles to the west, fighting was in progress. We were ordered forward on the double. The tank crews wanted to go on ahead and rush to the scene of combat, but our officers couldn't allow them to leave the column. We had to stay together, with our tank-tractors each pulling three Russian sleighs loaded with men and equipment. The half-tracks helped the trucks, which would never have been able to make it alone. I was riding on the third sleigh of one of these trains. Behind us was a large sidecar whose transmission was failing. The tanks were pulling with full power, to the great peril of their own mechanisms. The crackle of guns grew continuously louder. Suddenly, Wesreidau stopped the convoy and jumped down to check his maps. Everyone on the sleighs was ordered to follow him, and I found myself going into action once again. The Panzers detached themselves from their trains and drove toward the noise. We followed, running as fast as we could, waved forward by Wesreidau, who came with us in a large B.M.W. sidecar. A steiner with an 80-mm. mortar skidded past us in a cloud of whirling snow.

Gasping for breath, we ran along the track made by the tanks. They had pulled far ahead of us and entered into combat with the enemy some ten minutes before we reached the scene of fighting. We could hear their machine guns ripping into the air, sounding much louder than usual. The sidecar came back toward us and suddenly spun round.

'Spread out into the forest.'

We carried out the order, some of us remaining behind to pull out the sidecar, which was stuck in a drift, before running on through the trees, standing up as straight as the masts of ships. The virgin snow rasped and cracked in great sheets under our weight. We could no longer see the tanks, which seemed to be pursuing an enemy in flight.

We didn't meet any partisans ourselves. Twenty minutes later, a flare called us to the nearby blockhouse, which was like every other. It was supposed to guard the track, which in normal times was heavily used.

The post had been attacked by partisans – which, of course, we had to expect – probably the same band that had massacred the men we'd found earlier. Here, fortunately, there had been time for the defence to react. Of the twenty-two men holding the post, six had been wounded and two killed. Some twenty enemy dead or wounded lay on the trampled snow. There were also several guns: Russian and German and some American. A few wounded partisans were trying to crawl into the forest. No order could have stopped our men. They fired at the Russians and put an end to their suffering. Two shaggy prisoners had fallen into our hands. Their eyes rolled wildly like the eyes of trapped wolves, and they answered our questions with absurd, repetitive replies: 'We ... not ... Communists.' What did they take us for? Or did they really know nothing? That, of course, was possible. They looked like beasts being dragged to slaughter. No talk was possible, and our men were muttering for revenge.

Wesreidau looked at the partisans, and then at us. He tried a little longer to get something from the prisoners, but his efforts were unavailing. Finally, his patience exhausted, he raised his arm with feigned indifference. Our men grabbed the two prisoners and pushed them along in front of them. The human wolves looked back, snarling. But the sight of our guns made them lose their heads. They began to run, and ran until the first volley caught them and knocked them to the ground.

The post had been saved at the last possible moment. According to the men who'd been there, at least four hundred partisans had attacked them, and the fighting had lasted for over two hours. The men greeted us with bear hugs. They were overjoyed to hear that we had brought an evacuation order with us. For the moment, we seemed to be acting as the last broom of the Wehrmacht, making a clean sweep.

To crown the misery of the day, a hideous incident occurred within ten minutes of our departure from that place. The sidecar at the head of the column, preceding the first tank by some thirty to forty yards, drove back onto the track, moving through the snow with considerable difficulty. A tank followed it, rolling over the same ground. Suddenly an explosion shook the earth and reverberated through the air. Frozen snow showered down with a crystalline sound from the heavily laden branches all around us. The tank had been blown off its tracks and torn open from below. We could hear the roar of the flames as fat plumes of smoke rolled out from beneath the machine, spreading over the icy ground. The men on the sleighs which followed reacted immediately. One of the junior officers jumped onto the turret of the tank to try to free the frantic men inside, who were probably seriously wounded. Others ran to help, while the infantry spread out on either side of the road, to be ready for any eventuality. By now the tank was wrapped in thick black smoke, and we could do nothing to help the trapped men. We emptied three extinguishers onto the blackened metal, but the flames inside only increased in violence. The sleighs were hastily drawn back, as the tank's reservoir poured out forty gallons of flaming gasoline, which spread across the snow. In panic, the scorched landser yielded to the fire whose black plumes of smoke were climbing into the dark sky. In helpless anger, officers and men alike watched the immolation of three men. The smell of burned flesh mingled ignominiously with the smell of gas and oil. The two men in the lead sidecar had passed over the same spot a few seconds before the tank. Their tyres must have missed the detonator of the partisans' mine by only an inch or two. They also watched the hideous scene with cold sweat running down their spines.

The column abandoned the burning tank, whose flames had begun to make its ammunition explode. We also abandoned three heavy sleighs, and some of our matériel, which we burned. The men who had ridden on those sleighs found places on other vehicles. We all made a wide detour to avoid the exploding machine-gun bullets. We left behind the tomb of two men who had been killed without a chance to defend themselves, two men who had three years of fighting behind them and who deserved Valhalla.

We abandoned the territory to the Red waves that followed us. This was the final passage of the last European crusade – in the complete sense of the word.

The piercing cold was a continuous element we could never forget, even during moments of strong emotion, as in our recent clash with the partisans. A short time later, we rejoined the division in a town of a certain size and importance called Boporoeivska, if I remember correctly. Between the trenches and the barbed wire, the engineers and the Todt organization were busy mining the area. Other infantry regiments and an armoured unit equipped with Tigerpanzers had also reached this point. A dozen of these motionless monsters seemed to be grinning at us as they watched the passage of our battered equipment. The presence of the Tigers reassured everyone. They were like steel fortresses, and no Russian tank could equal them.

Several Wehrmacht civil servants had been billeted at Boporoeivska. These gentlemen were surprised and displeased to find themselves suddenly at the centre of a battlefield. They all seemed to be in an extremely bad humour, and their attitude toward us seemed tinged with a certain distrust. Perhaps their bureaucratic minds resented our fighting as we retreated. For them Russia meant this organized town where one could shelter from the cold and eat one's fill, provided one had established the proper connections with Supply. Perhaps there were also charming evenings with the charming Ukrainian women who seemed to abound in these parts. These ladies and girls seemed to be preparing for a hasty departure in the company of their gentlemen friends, to look for a distant and more tranquil spot. We, it seemed, would be given the honour of defending these bureaucratic love nests. This attitude infuriated us, and many brawls began, but were quickly stifled. In the end, we were too exhausted and hungry to bother with these people, and occupied the warm isbas we were given with the greatest satisfaction. In the isbas we found food and drink and the opportunity to wash. Our cabins were rarely equipped with candles or lamps, but the flames in the fireplaces, which we fed with every combustible substance we could find, brilliantly lit these fragments of paradise. Within a few hours of our arrival, several cubic yards of snow had been melted in each billet, and we were all stripped naked, scrubbing off our filth as best we could. We soaked our trousers, underwear, shirts, and tunics with feverish, almost panicky haste. Our opportunity would certainly be brief, and everyone wished to make the most of it. Someone had even found a box full of small cakes of toilet soap. These were mixed into the water of the largest tubs.

In turn, timed by a stop watch, we plunged into the warm, foaming bath: two minutes each and no overtime. We joked and larked as we hadn't done for months. The water spilled over the edge of the tub, and flooded the big room, where some thirty shadowy figures cavorted. We kept pouring water into the tubs, to keep the level up. The dim light prevented us from noticing that the foam which so delighted us had turned grey with filth. However, our lice died a scented death: Marie Rose.

When we had finished washing, we emptied the tubs into a hole we had dug inside the isba. There was no question of going outside. The thermometer registered twenty degrees below zero, and everyone was naked. When the water was gone, we broke up the tubs and burned them. The fire had a voracious appetite, which was difficult to satisfy. Hals was exultantly chewing a fragment of soap, laughing and shouting that he had to clean his innards too, as they were probably just as filthy and overrun with lice as his skin.

'Now the Popovs can come whenever they like,' he shouted. 'I feel like a new man.'

The door suddenly opened, letting in a blast of astonishing cold. Everyone howled in protest. Two soldiers stood on the threshold, their arms loaded with delicacies for the table. We gaped at this gift from heaven as the soldiers laid down their burden on a pile of damp overcoats: a string of spicy wurst, several loaves of gingerbread, several boxes of Norwegian sardines, a brick of smoked bacon. There were also eight or ten bottles – schnapps, cognac, Rhine wine – and cigars. The fellows kept right on emptying the huge pockets of their coats, and our shouts of astounded delight seemed to shake the flimsy walls.

'Wh ... where did you find it?' someone asked, almost sobbing with joy.

'Those goddamn bureaucrats were really living it up: Grandsk [our company cook] never saw anything like this. Those bastards were keeping it all here. They were ready to run off with it, too. This is just a small sample, but they're all as mad as hornets; said they'd report us for stealing personal possessions. Who the hell do they think they're fooling? They can take their goddamn report, and any time they like I'll tell them what they can do with it. To hell with them!'

Everyone plunged into that astonishing mound of delicacies. Hals's eyes were starting out of his head.

'Keep my share for a minute,' he said, pulling on his damp clothes. 'I've got to have a look for myself, and bring back some more. Those bastards think they're going to leave us to take care of the front while they clear out with all this delicatessen, for God's sake!'

Hals wrapped himself in a Soviet eiderdown and rushed out into the cold. Solma – a young fellow who was half Hungarian and had joined the regiment under more or less the same circumstances as I had – went with him. When they had gone, Pastor Pferham, aided by Obergefreiter Lensen, and Hoth, Lensen's number-two man at the Panzerfaust, divided up the food. We had to hack the bacon with our picks, because our bayonets were too blunt. Pferham, who must have left some of his religious convictions on the east bank of the Dnieper along with his virginity, was swearing like a pagan.

'To think that this damned thing which has already poked holes in plenty of guts should be stopped by a goddamned piece of bacon!'

'Borrow some dynamite from the Todt if you have to – but hurry up with it!'

No one was cheated; the amazing sense of comradeship and unity of the Wehrmacht held, and everyone received a fair share. The war had brought together men from many different regions and walks of life, who would probably have mistrusted each other under any other circumstances; but the circumstances of war united us in a symphony of heroism, in which each man felt himself to a certain extent responsible for all of his fellows. The bureaucratic attitude which had been preserved in this relatively peaceful atmosphere astonished rather than shocked us. We felt that it was perfectly legitimate to plunder these stockpiles of hoarded goods. The sense of order which was part of National Socialism was still very much alive among the troops who were fighting for it. Those who appropriated delicacies for themselves while combat troops were dying of hunger seemed to belong to another species. Pferham spoke of all this as he ate, comparing these officials to the bourgeoisie Hitler speaks of in *Mein Kampf*. Combat troops have immediate concerns. For men living the lives of hunted beasts, all leisurely conversation is a waste of time. We had to eat and drink what and when we could, and make love when we could, without taking any time for eloquence over the girl's hair or eyes. Every moment was precious; every hour might be our last.

Hals's and Solma's shares waited for them inside their helmets, which were turned upside down. We sang as we emptied the bottles. Our friends who'd gone out for more didn't come back, and later Hals cursed that impulse. He and Solma had been caught pinching some cognac from one of the bureaucrats – which meant six days of detention for both of them.

Stille Nacht . . . Heilige Nacht . . . Oh! Weihnacht!

Christmas night, 1943. The wind howled through the labyrinth of trenches north of Boporoeivska. Two companies occupied the positions prepared by the security division and the Todt organization, which had since withdrawn to the west, beyond the Bessarabian frontier. We had settled into these ice-coated molehills two days earlier. The front seemed solid, and we would almost certainly be fighting soon. The collapse of our southern front had forced this last retreat and regrouping along this line. The vast Soviet thrust was moving inexorably and slowly toward us, like a steamroller. We were well aware of this, and the continuous buildup of reinforcements in our sector led us to foresee a violent clash.

The country immediately around us was hilly and wooded. Tanks and mobile artillery waited in the frozen underbrush and terrible cold, which stripped the bark off the trees. The stocks of provisions in Boporoeivska had been repeatedly plundered; our commandant had tacitly consented to a few days of carousal, as if to compensate for the impending holocaust.

It was Christmas night. Despite our miserable circumstances, we were filled with emotion, like children who have been deprived of joy for a long time. Under our steel helmets and behind our silent faces moved a crowd of glittering memories. Some men talked of peace, others of childhoods which were still very close, trying to hide their feelings and hopeless, ludicrous dreams by hardening their voices. Wesreidau made his round of the trenches, talking to the men, but his words seemed only to be disturbing private reflections, and he soon withdrew into his own. He too undoubtedly had children and wished to be with them. Sometimes he stopped for a moment, and looked up at the sky, which had cleared. The frost glittered on his long coat like spangles on a Christmas tree.

For four days we had to endure nothing more severe than the cold. The sections in the line were relieved continually, and the unbearable nights were divided into two parts. Each day brought fresh cases of pneumonia. Frostbite had become commonplace. Twice, I was carried into an isba and brought back to consciousness and life from the brink of death. Our faces were badly cracked, particularly at the corners of the lips. Fortunately we had enough to eat. The cooks had been given special orders to prepare our food with as much fat as possible. Supplies arrived regularly, which enabled Grandsk to produce gluey soups, full of margarine.

These concoctions were nauseating but effective. Our cooks had learned something about cold-weather cooking from the ingredients of Russian soups. We also took saunas – a horse-doctor treatment which didn't coddle any weaklings. We moved straight from the hot steam into cold showers, a transition so violent that our hearts often threatened to stop beating. Like Grandsk's greasy soups, however, these shocks were effective, and we always felt better afterward.

'Make the most of it,' Grandsk told us. 'Eat up and enjoy it. In Germany, kids are going without dessert, so you can have this.'

Alas, Grandsk's words were too accurate. As Paula explained in a letter which reached me in only six days, rationing had become very strict. We were getting much closer to our own frontier, and every day the distance from home seemed smaller. Soon Germany at bay would no longer be able to send us even margarine.

One morning the feldwebels' whistles drove us from the overheated isba where we slept. A patrol of Soviet tanks was just over a mile from Boporoeivska. The cold as we ran outside was like a blow from the butcher's axe. Each man galloped to a precise point.

We had not yet reached our positions when the sound of heavy explosions shook the thin air to the west of us. Russian tanks, charging like maddened bulls, had driven onto our minefield. Now it was the turn of Russian tank crews to go up in smoke. Our observers were watching through their field glasses. Almost all the tanks were trying to withdraw the way they'd come. Our artillery remained silent, leaving the tanks to the mines. Firing might even set off these traps.

However, three Stalin tanks had managed to cross the minefield and were driving toward the town in a roar of chains and exhaust. With extraordinary courage, they took the fire of our thirty-seven anti-tank guns without slowing down, only to be hit by our camouflaged Tigers, with their terrible 88s. In a sequence as unreal as anything Hollywood could contrive, all three tanks were hit by the first salvo. One turned over and exploded. Another stopped dead like a boar hit behind the shoulder. The third, although hit, turned without stopping, exposing its flank to our anti-tank machine guns, which ripped off all its protruding guns. It continued in a circle broken by a series of banking turns, trying to execute a half turn. This dramatic attempt left us gasping with admiration. In his will to survive, the Russian driver headed straight for our minefield. A series of explosions ripped the tracks off his left side, and the tank slowly settled, like a vanquished beast. As the thick black smoke began to pour from its entrails, two dark figures climbed out. But our cold-stiffened fingers did not fire. Both Russians were holding their pistols, prepared to defend themselves. When they didn't hear any guns, they took a few steps toward our lines, then threw down their guns and raised their hands. A moment later, they were crossing our front line. The landser, who considered them heroes, grinned, and the Russians grinned back, their teeth gleaming very white, like Negroes' teeth, in their smoke-blackened faces. Our men took them to an isba and gave them some schnapps. Their attitude and performance seemed so far removed from those of the partisans that we felt no hate for them. Lensen watched them for a moment and said: 'If Wiener were here, he'd probably drink a toast with them.'

During the following night, we sent our patrols to re-lay the minefield. Our defensive fighting was relying increasingly on mines to take the place of weakened or missing lines. The next day there was a general reinforcement of the front. Two Rumanian regiments and a Hungarian battalion were sent to join us. We were told that we would also have the support of a squadron of fighter-bombers based somewhere near Vinnitsa.

'It seems we're getting ready for a big show,' Pferham observed. 'I don't like it.'

Obergefreiter Lensen took the opposite view, rejoicing in our increased strength. As he saw it, the Red tide must be stopped here. The idea that Prussia itself would soon fall into enemy hands never even crossed his mind. But then, that was true of all of us.

One night, the Russians sent a human wave of Mongols in a direct assault against our positions. Their function was to knock out the minefield, by crossing it. As the Russians preferred to economize on tanks, and as their human stockpile was enormous, they usually sent out men for jobs of this kind.

The Soviet attack failed, but Stalin hadn't been looking for success. The minefield exploded under the howling mob, and we sent out a curtain of yellow and white fire to obliterate anyone who had survived. The fragmented cadavers froze very quickly, sparing us the stench which would otherwise have polluted the air over a vast area.

The Russians had not even used any of their artillery to help the Mongols, which seemed to confirm our estimate of the situation. We sent out patrols to try to remine the field, but the

Russians were ready to fire on anything that moved. We were able to put down only a light sprinkling of mines, with regrettably heavy losses. It was clearly no longer possible to rely on mines to protect our front lines.

On another evening, when the cold had attained a dramatic intensity, the Russians attacked again. We were manning our positions in a temperature which had dropped to 45° below zero. Some men fainted as the cold struck them, paralysed before they even had a chance to scream. Survival seemed almost impossible. Our hands and faces were coated with engine grease, and when our worn gloves were pulled over this gluey mixture, every gesture became extremely difficult. Our tanks, whose engines would no longer start, swept the spaces in front of them with their long tubes, like elephants caught in a trap.

The muzhiks preparing to attack us were suffering in the same way, freezing where they stood before there was time for even one 'Ourrah pobieda.' The men on both sides, suffering a common martyrdom, were longing to call it quits. Metal broke with astonishing ease. The Soviet tanks were advancing blindly through the pale light of flares, which intensified the bluish glitter of the scene. These tanks were destroyed by the mines which lay parallel to our trenches some thirty yards from our front lines, or by our Tigers, which fired without moving. The Russian troops, with frozen hands and feet, faltered and withdrew in confusion in the face of the fire we kept steady, despite our tortured hands. Their officers, who had hoped to find us paralysed by cold and incapable of defence, were unconcerned about the condition of their own troops. They were ready to make any sacrifice, so long as our lines were attacked.

I managed to keep my hands from freezing by thrusting them, in their gloves, into two empty ammunition boxes, when the cartridges had run into the spandau. Our gunners, and everyone forced to use his hands, sooner or later turned up at the medical service with severe cases of freezing. There were a great many amputations.

The intense cold lasted for three weeks, during which the Russians restricted themselves to sending over music calculated to make us homesick, and speeches inviting us to surrender.

Toward the end of January, the cold lessened some
and became tolerable. At times during the day the thermo
meter rose as high as five degrees above zero. The nights were
still murderous, but with frequent shifts of duty we managed to
get through them. We knew that the Russian offensive would
soon resume. One night, or rather one morning, toward four or
five o'clock, blasts of the whistle sent us out once again to our
interception posts.

A mass of T-34 and Sherman tanks were moving forward in
a loud roar. An artillery bombardment had preceded them,
inflicting heavy damage on Boporoeivska, and provoking a
mass evacuation by the civilian population, which had been
waiting for the fighting in terrified apprehension. Our tanks –
about fifteen Tigers, ten Panthers, and a dozen Mark-2s and
-3s – had managed to start their engines, which had been
heated continuously the day before. At the beginning of the
offensive, two Mark-2s had been destroyed side by side in the
Russian bombardment. The front was once again threatening
to give way. We lay in our trenches, our eyes reduced to slits,
waiting for the hordes of Red infantry which would surely be
coming soon. For the moment our machine guns and Panzerfausts were quiet, leaving the way clear for our heavy artillery
and our tanks.

Adroitly camouflaged, the Tigers lay waiting, with their
engines idling. Almost every time a Russian tank came into
range, a sharp, strident burst set it on fire. The Russians were
moving toward us slowly, sure of themselves, firing at random.
Their tactic of demoralisation would have worked if there had
not been so many plumes of black smoke rising against the
pale February sky. Our 37s and Panzerfausts, designed to be
used at almost point-blank range, were scarcely called on. The
first wave of Soviet armour was consumed five hundred yards
from our first positions, nailed down by the concentrated fire
of our Tigers and Panthers and heavy anti-tank guns.

The Tiger was an astonishing fortress. Enemy fire seemed
to have almost no effect on its shell, which, at the front was five
and a half inches thick. Its only weakness was its relative
immobility.

A second Russian wave followed closely after the first, more
dense than the first, and accompanied by a swarm of infantry
which posed a serious threat.

We waited, dry-mouthed, our guns jammed against our shoulders and our grenades in easy reach. Our hearts were pounding.

Suddenly, like a miracle, thirty of our planes flew over. As promised, the squadron from Vinnitsa was attacking. This particular job was easy for them, and every bomb hit home.

A cry of 'Sieg Heil, der Luftwaffe,' rang so loudly from our trenches that the pilots might almost have heard it. We opened fire with everything we had, but the Russian offensive kept coming, despite overwhelming losses. Our tanks drove at the stricken enemy with an ardour worthy of 1941.

The noise became unbearable. The air was thick with bitter fumes and smoke, and the smells of gunpowder and burned gasoline. Our shouts mingled with the shouts of the Russians, who were reeling under the unexpected resistance.

We were able to watch the magnificent progress of our Tigers, pulverizing the enemy tanks before they were able to complete a half-turn. The Luftwaffe attacked again with rockets and 20-mm. cannons. The Russian rout was hidden by a thick curtain of luminous smoke.

The Russian artillery kept on firing at our lines, causing several deaths which we scarcely noticed. However, their guns were soon overrun by their own retreating troops, and fell silent.

A second wave of German planes, an undreamed-of extra luxury, completed the Russian debacle. We hugged each other in excitement, bursting with joy. For a year now, we had been retreating before an enemy whose numerical superiority was constantly increasing. Lensen was shouting like a man possessed by demons: 'I told you we'd do it! I told you we'd do it!'

Our achievement was mentioned in special bulletins. The front on the Rumanian border had held. After months of sustained attack and terrible cold German and Rumanian troops had once again pushed back the Russian offensive and destroyed quantities of enemy matériel.

The mass of broken, twisted metal strewn with corpses which lay in front of us was visible proof of what we'd done. Along a front of two hundred miles, the Red Army had launched sixteen attacks inside of a month. Taking into account the three weeks of inactivity during which all operations were impossible, these sixteen attacks had all occurred inside the space of one week. Five points had borne the brunt of the Russian effort, and at only one had the Russians come close to success. The front was broken to the south, but this thrust was cut off, and the Russian troops were either annihilated or taken prisoner.

In our sector all the lines had held, and we felt very proud. We had proved once again that with adequate materiel and a certain minimum preparation we could hold off an enemy of greatly superior size, whose frenzied efforts were never intelligently employed.

The veteran, Wiener, had often remarked on this Russian failing at difficult moments. At the sight of an enemy tank in flames, he would bare his teeth in a wide, wolfish grin.

'What a damned fool,' he would say, 'to let himself get caught like that. It's only their numbers that will get us someday.'

There were thirty Iron Crosses for the Gross Deutschland, and as many for the small tank regiment, which also earned the honour.

Chapter Fourteen

RETURN TO POLAND

The division had been routed several times, and had sustained serious losses. Units believed to be intact were often borrowed from us, and sent to bolster some faltering position. When they arrived they would be found short by about two-thirds of their strength. There was nothing to be done about it.

Our own group was enjoying a much-needed spell of relative calm. Our existence would have been almost idyllic except for the depressing and infuriating quality of barracks life. The exercises we were given, as if we were green troops in for basic training, brought us close to open revolt.

We had moved 250 miles, to a position in Poland, far from the front. Our camp was on the banks of the Dniester, some fifty miles from Lvov, in the foothills of the Carpathians. The river is quite narrow at this point, and its waters, when we arrived, were swift and tumultuous, running through a network of small islands loaded with snow and ice. On any wide stretch the river was frozen to a considerable depth, and the current ran beneath the ice, giving off a strange, muffled noise.

Our view was magnificent: a pale blue sky and a horizon marked by snow peaks, against which we could watch flights of eagles. For two months we enjoyed the agreeable change from the black and grey of a Ukrainian winter to the sportive landscape of eastern Galicia. Galician snows were also very heavy, and the cold was severe, but we slept in clean, heated barracks. Although an exaggerated sense of economy kept the heat at some fifty degrees or so, this at least enabled us to be fully alert when we were awake. Our camp was huge and organized with all the Prussian rigour of an army on the eve of battle. About 150 wooden buildings without floors had been built in blocks, carrying numbers and letters. Nearby, in the snow-covered woods, we could see a large stone building, which must have been part of the village beside the camp, and which housed our secretariat and principal officers. All our matériel had been repainted and overhauled. In these conditions of order and apparent abundance, none of us dreamed that Germany had reached the limit of its capacities. After the chaos of the front, the atmosphere of efficient organization, with its requirement that every move be registered in writing, made us feel like wild beasts suddenly caged.

The camp was built around a large central square for reviews and drills, in which young recruits were instructed in the art of manipulating arms, so useful in parades and so useless at the front.

The young recruits seemed to enjoy these exercises. Others, like Hals and me, were seeing ourselves as we had been a year and a half ago, back in Poland, where we had handled explosives for the first time. The memory of those days seemed at least ten years old – one ages quickly in wartime. Our world-weary attitude did not escape the attention of the young recruits, who responded by holding themselves even more stiffly, as if to show us that the war was now their affair.

This healthy enthusiasm of schoolboys suddenly transformed into soldiers was destined to weaken somewhat after a few nights in the mud and the shock of seeing a field hospital for the first time. We had been through all that. They would soon learn that war does not always create the same exaltation as the intoxicating explosion of the plaster grenades in the war games of training camp.

The Führer, who was now scraping the bottom of the barrel, had been forced to send his arrogant Polizei off to war. These elderly new recruits were having a hard time of it. The sight of policemen crawling through the mud on their bellies delighted us enough so that we almost forgot our sufferings. Police officers, whose competence in war was limited, handed over their men to officers of the Wehrmacht, who put them through the works. This spectacle, which gave us so much pleasure, was hard on the eager young recruits, directly exposed to the bad humour of those bastards who did everything they could to keep the younger men in a state of inferiority.

421

For us, life was also very far from perfect. Before settling into our new quarters, there had been a long and difficult journey. We had begun by tramping more than thirty miles on bad Russian roads, deeply rutted and coated with ice. Then we were loaded onto trucks, and driven as far as Mogilev, an oriental-looking town, where we boarded two trains, both in very bad condition, for the remainder of the journey, along the Bessarabian frontier, to Lvov, in Poland. From Lvov, trucks had brought us to the camp, where we had stumbled out, exhausted and filthy, under the suspicious gaze of polished, healthy officer-instructors.

We were allowed forty-eight hours to rest, before our clothes and equipment had to be in perfect order. At our first inspection, the condition of our uniforms shocked the inspectors, although we had brushed and beaten them as hard as we could. They had completely lost their original colour and appearance. Grey-green had become greenish piss yellow, decorated by tears and holes and reddish-brown burns. Our worn and crumpled boots had lost their black finish, and many were without heels or laces. We looked like a bunch of tramps, and the inspectors were ready to jump at the slightest sign of negligence. These evident traces of the battlefield struck them like slaps in the face, to which there was no answer. Those fops should, in fact, have been honouring us.

They knew it too, and the knowledge irritated them. They persisted in picking on details to try to save face. A short way off, sections of police and students in camouflage uniforms were marching to their daily sweat baths, singing gaily in the dry, cold air, which had brought out the colour in their cheeks.

> *Das schönste auf der Welt*
> *Ist mein Tirolerland. . . .*

However, instead of the Alps, the Carpathians witnessed their compulsory gaiety.

The instructors, intent on inspection, were insensible to the poetry of the scene. One of them stopped short in front of a gefreiter whose coat ended in a fringe as full of holes as a piece of Alençon lace. At last the stabsfeldwebel could unload a little rage in front of his sarcastic audience. Our heads turned slightly, scarcely noticeably, to the right, toward the fellow accused of negligence. We rolled our eyes as far as we could, trying to see who was getting it.

'Name and number!' shouted the stabs, stiffening his neck. Even if we couldn't see anything, we could hear it!

'Frösch, Herr Stabsfeldwebel,' the accused shouted, adding the number which each of us was supposed to know by heart.

Frösch ... The name stirred an echo in my memory: Frösch? And then the barracks the day after we crossed the Dnieper came back to me. Hot water, and a foolish-looking fellow of angelic good will. What was the stabs going to pin on him?

In the third row of men, some ten or twelve yards from me, Frösch was standing at attention, while abuse rained down on him. He was staring straight ahead, as required by convention. His gaunt, hollow face was partly hidden by his heavy steel helmet. Unfortunately his stupidity was obvious enough to give the stabs a sudden sense of confident superiority over this soldier, who had clearly seen a lot. Two large hands, red with chilblains, emerged from his ragged sleeves to press for warmth against the folds of filthy cloth. The coat no longer had any buttons. Frösch had fastened it at each buttonhole with a short piece of wire. With a touching sense of aesthetics, he had bent in the ends of each wire, as if to demonstrate his good intentions. Unfortunately, he had linked a lower buttonhole to a higher one, which produced an improper and all-too-visible crease. This anomaly leaped to the eye of the inspecting noncom, who couldn't let such a golden opportunity slip. However, in complete disregard of normal practice, the company officer intervened, reminding the stabsfeldwebel that our detachment had just survived an extremely difficult experience.

'Your supply report specifically stated that you possessed the necessary materials for keeping your clothes in good repair, Herr Leutnant, and specifically mentioned buttons.'

The lieutenant didn't know how to answer.

'In addition, Herr Leutnant, Gefreiter Frösch hasn't even bothered to line up the buttonholes correctly.'

There was a moment of charged silence. The lieutenant threw Frösch a look of despairing compassion. Couldn't he have spared himself all this and deprived the instructor of this ludicrous opening? But the facts were as they were, and the lieutenant, despite all his good will, couldn't alter them. He resumed his former position with an impassive air. A wave of irritation seemed to run through the company.

'Stillgestanden!' the feld shouted.

In a flood of gratuitous invective, Frösch was given twenty days' detention and a series of punitive fatigues. Without flinching, Frösch left his position to stand in the ranks of the guilty. He was the only one. The inspection was over. Quarter turn, left, left. Our companies went on to march around the camp. Frösch remained where he was, staring straight ahead. As the only man to be punished, he seemed a symbol of injustice, alone in his punishment as he had always been in life. He had found some comradeship in the Wehrmacht, but the exigencies of military life exacted a high price. Ten days later, when the rest of the unit drew new clothes, Frösch kept his rags. He had in truth become a symbol. He didn't know how to hate, and always wore his expression of touching stupidity and banal good will.

Later the veteran said of him: 'He's as humble as Diogenes. If he doesn't deserve victory, at least he deserves Paradise.'

Section forward! ... On the ground! ... On your feet! ... Run! ... Forward! ... On the ground! ... On your feet, facing me! ... The hard, frozen ground scraped our hands and knees, and the sharp twigs of the leafless scrub finished off our threadbare uniforms. They had put us through a series of exercises with concussion bombs. We, who had faced the fire of Russian Katushas, just laughed. Then we had made ourselves as flat as the Ukrainian soil. Now we lay propped on one elbow, half amused, half exasperated. Our attitude provoked torrents of abuse and a collective punishment for the whole company. We had to crawl along the entire perimeter of the camp. The ground, three or four inches beneath our eyes, soaked up the muttered curses of our progress. The instructor-noncoms were working hard, running along the carpet of soldiers.

A short way off, Wesreidau was watching this bad joke and arguing with the officers responsible for the camp. But he might as well have saved his breath. Orders from higher up had put an end to the coddling of troops just back from the front. We had to reinstate the rigidity of '40-'41, and wage war to the death.

We went on long marches, carrying all our gear. We tramped through villages in step, singing. These demonstrations were intended to impress the local population, who, in fact, greeted us as we went by – the boys waving and the girls smiling. The routine never let up. We even had to practise retreating in a series of backward leaps – a skill which might always come in handy.

Every fourth day, we were free from 5 to 10 P.M. We flooded into Nevotoretchy and Sueka, two villages near the camp, where the peasants often invited us into their houses and gave us something to drink, and sometimes even to eat. Our soldiers quickly amused themselves with the girls, who were not shy. These few hours of liberty, used to the utmost, made us forget the rest.

The following day we would return to the training routine. Despite the boredom, we cooperated, thinking that perhaps these were necessary measures. We were still inclined to believe in the validity of orders. Perhaps these exercises would help us bring the war to a quicker end.

At last we were issued new clothes. Some of the uniforms were quite different from the ones we'd always known, with blouses like those worn in the French army today, and trousers tucked into short, thick spats, looking like a grotesque parody of a golfing costume. This new design was for the most part distributed to new troops. The Gross Deutschland, as an élite division, kept the old design. We were even given new boots – a further sign of privilege.

However, the cloth of the uniforms was of very inferior quality, much more brittle than formerly. It reminded us of specially treated cardboard. The new boots were also markedly inferior, of rough, stiff, fourth-quality leather, which cracked at the ankle instead of forming the usual creases. The underclothes were the worst of all; they were made of a cloth which seemed to have substance only where it was doubled – at the hem and the seams. The new socks, which we appreciated immensely, also seemed curiously synthetic.

'If this is what we're getting,' Hals said, 'I'll keep my Russian socks.'

In fact, the new socks wore a great deal longer than the old ones. However, they were less warm. They were among the first to be made with nylon, which was still largely unknown.

We slapped a great deal of black polish from the store onto the boots, to make them lose their look of cardboard paste. We all felt better to be out of our stinking, tattered rags, and in new clothes, despite the synthetic fabrics. Our brightened appearance also had its effect on the local inhabitants, who decided that all must be well with the Wehrmacht.

Hals, in his fresh and dashing uniform, had fallen in love once more – this time with a pretty young Polish girl. With him, falling in love was compulsive. He really couldn't help himself, and lost a piece of his heart every time we stopped in a rest zone. This time, as always, he was ardently wooing a girl during our short periods of free time, and we all had to hear about it constantly.

'You're driving us all up the wall with your tart,' Lensen complained. 'Why can't you just kiss and run like everybody else?'

Lindberg grinned. He was remembering his last outing with Lensen, Pferham, and Solma. The four of them had trapped a Polish woman of about forty in a barn. She had yielded to their ardour, which had lasted the four hours remaining.

'Her husband came home while we were at it,' Solma remembered joyfully. 'He laughed with us, and said, "Mama too old for me now – for you!"' Later they'd all had a drink with the husband, who seemed perfectly content that they'd done him that service.

'She's nothing but a sow, your Polska,' Hals said. 'And you're just a bunch of pigs. No poetry at all . . .'

The barracks shook with our laughter. Pastor Pferham laughed too, because he couldn't do anything else, but all the same he was somewhat troubled. Our company's love life was doing far too well.

I myself didn't have any particular adventures. I had pawed one or two girls, but matters had never progressed any further than that. Of course, I was in love with Paula and wrote to her often. Above all, I longed for a leave, and lived on that hope. For the rest, strange bodies made me uneasy, almost sick. As soon as I saw naked flesh, I braced myself for a torrent of entrails remembering countless wartime scenes, with smoking, stinking corpses pouring out their vitals. All things considered, I preferred platonic love by mail. To me, Paula was in an entirely separate category from all these other women — something delicate and marvellous, which could not be eviscerated — or so I tried to think.

Then I was involved in an episode which gave everyone else a laugh at my expense.

We were on leave at Sueka. It was a beautiful day, with only a light trace of frost. We all felt like a spree, but were also extremely interested in food. Our rations were now so small that we were always hungry when we left the mess halls. The peasants would usually sell us something to eat in exchange for the paper currency which looked as though the Rentenbank was printing notes in excess of its reserves. We had, in fact, been given these notes as supplementary pay, in addition to the special tickets issued to occupation troops. Eggs were the easiest form of food to come by. At Sueka we divided the job. There were three of us: Hoth, Schlesser, and me. We had left Hals with his Polska at Nevotoretchy. Nevotoretchy was right beside the camp, and the soldiers had already stripped it of all extra food. We decided to go three miles farther, to Sueka, which was also on the Dniester, taking separate routes through the countryside to try our luck at the farmhouses whose location every man in the company had by heart.

I set off along a road which ran downhill between two walls of snow. I can see it still. At the bottom of the hill there was a frozen pond which pink-and-yellow ducks were tapping with their bills, apparently mystified by its solidity. I turned to the right. Ahead of me were two low columns twined round with what looked like lifeless Virginia creeper, and beyond them, an enormous pile of wood which almost hid the low, thatched house. To the left, with their backs to the river, was a group of squat, irregular buildings, made of rough wooden planks. The whole scene was inescapably rustic, but there was also a rudimentary sense of style, which was noticeable here even in the poorest, roughest setting.

I was walking toward the cottage when I saw a woman coming from one of the outbuildings. Her clothes might have belonged to a medieval peasant. We both smiled. She said something unintelligible.

'Guten Tag, Frau. Ei, bitte.' (I was sure she wouldn't understand French, but she might very well know the German for 'egg'.) 'Ei . . . ei, bitte.'

She came closer, still smiling and pleasant, speaking and making gestures I couldn't understand. I contented myself with returning her smile. She signalled that I should follow her, which I did. We walked over to a ladder, and she began to climb, signing me to hold it steady.

As she went up, laughing and talking, my eyes naturally followed her ascent toward a loft bulging with hay. My astonished gaze struck her rump, which was of very dubious charm, and a pair of enormous, meaty thighs. Her buttocks seemed to fill the view with a curious obstinacy. Her drawers had the texture of a loosely knit sweater. I stared at them as I might have stared at some medieval monument of the twelfth century. The Polska, who saw that I was watching, finally stopped by the false window of the loft, and waved at me to follow her. I felt awkward and uneasy. I had often watched a tank trying to outmanoeuvre a machine gun, but this type of manoeuvre was beyond me. I was used to going straight ahead, and climbed the ladder as if it were an assault wall which I had to scale under the eye of an officer. Then I was bent double in the piled-up hay, beside the Polska, whose thighs must have been a half yard round. She was laughing and clucking as if she herself were about to lay an egg. My gun caught on everything, and I felt once again as if I were crawling down a trench. The hay was full of chickens. The Polska chased them off and collected a few eggs. She turned back to me, still laughing. Her teeth were somewhat too widely spaced, but were dazzlingly white. She came toward me, holding out the warm eggs, which, in a manner of speaking, she had collected for me.

I felt her breath and the warmth of her body. As she thrust the eggs and her hands deep into the pockets of my tunic, her fingers pressed against my hips. My startled eyes rolled in my head, as I waited for the order to disengage. But the order didn't come, and the bold fingers of the enemy kneaded my flesh through the double folds of my pockets.

'For the love of God! Danke schön . . . Danke schön!' I wanted to make the quickest possible departure no matter what she thought of me.

She was now so close an embrace seemed inescapable. Her smile was one of certain anticipation, and her eyes were rolling feverishly.

Mein Gott! I braced myself for her cry of 'Ourrah pobieda.' There were two possible courses of action, as I saw it. I could withdraw in a hurry and risk cracking my skull at the bottom of the ladder, or counter-attack, rolling my adversary into the hay.

However, these calculations came too late. The woman, who must have weighed at least twenty pounds more than I did, suddenly enlaced me, adroitly pushing me to the left, so that I lost my balance. I found myself gesticulating in vain desperation beneath a massive enemy. One of her hands was already busy with the fly of my new synthetic trousers. The eggs in both pockets were broken, and my gun, which was slung behind my back, was no use to me.

If the Führer ever saw me like that, I'd be thrown out of the Gross Deutschland for good, shipped off to one of the Brandenburg disciplinary battalions. To complete my downfall, my ravisher, who was clearly more accustomed to manipulating an axe handle than the personal appendage in question, had grabbed me, and was making me jerk and shudder like an invalid with a severe case of hiccoughs. I might perhaps have been able to oblige her, if the Polska, in the height of her frenzy, hadn't suddenly flung up her petticoats over the obese folds of her stomach and thighs. This spectacle destroyed the minimal desire my predicament might have aroused in me, and the delicious memory of Paula offered a contrast which was too absurd. With a brusque twist of my body, I freed myself from this female in rut, who was exciting herself without any cooperation from me. Her somewhat porcine face, in which, a few moments before, I might have found a certain charm, now wore an expression of bovine ecstasy. I stood up and turned out my pockets, which were filled with liquid egg and broken shell. My companion regained some measure of self-control and tried to laugh, suddenly afraid that her audacity might provoke severe consequences. In a flash, I was at the bottom of the ladder, gesturing to the woman to bring me something to clean off my jacket. I myself was worried about the consequences the stains on my uniform might bring down on me. I tried to look furious, but an overpowering sense of inadequacy made me flush hotly instead

The Polska, half smiling, half uneasy, led me over to the house. We went through a door which opened outward, down a few steps, and then through a second door which opened inward.

The house was built into the ground to a depth of about two and a half feet. We came into a dark, low-ceilinged room with a single tiny window, whose yellowish panes admitted very little light. The building was divided by a heavy wooden gate – one side was for people, the other for animals. This explained the fetid smell which I noticed as soon as the door was open. A couple of pigs were being fattened just beyond the grate. The wide benches built against the grate and covered with straw ticks were obviously the beds. An old woman turned toward us as we came in. She smiled with the indifference of a sphinx. I doubt if the idea of 'a German' even existed for her. Two children were playing on a woodpile which stood in the middle of the room. The Polska brought me some water in a wooden dipper, like the ones used in Russia for measuring millet. I had to take off my tunic, and reveal the extent of my deprivation. The pullover my mother had sent me over a year and a half before no longer had any sleeves below the elbow, and the waistband had become a scant, lacelike fringe.

I was preparing to wash my tunic when the Polska took it from me. She rubbed the stains between a round stone and a stiff straw implement shaped like a large cork. With a graciousness which almost excused her excesses of a few minutes earlier, she returned my tunic, which was clean once more. I didn't dare smile lest I rekindle her amorous fury. However, all of that seemed to have been forgotten. These Polish peasants seemed curiously primitive, living wholly in the present, unburdened by any thoughts of the past or the future. I said goodbye, thrusting out my stiffened arm in a regulation salute.

While the old woman on the bench smiled – a smile which seemed to cross a gulf of several millennia – the younger one rummaged through a heap of cooking pots which stood on the table. She found an egg and held it out to me.

I accepted it, not knowing what expression to put on to

disguise my embarrassment. The egg recalled the loft of recent history. I could feel myself blushing as I went through my pockets for the correct change. However, the woman gestured to me that I need not pay. Still embarrassed, I withdrew in a flurry of 'danke schöns.'

I had already taken a few strides away from the house when the door behind me opened again. The woman stood there calling me, holding out the gun which I had left propped against the table. How humiliating! I recovered myself with another sequence of voluminous thanks, and feeling ridiculous, straightened my back and tried to look stern, to make up for what had happened. I knew that this episode was destined to lighten the evening hours of these people, and found it hard to forgive myself. What an idiot – to survive the battle of Belgorod, only to get my pants torn off by a fat Polish mama! I might be a proud member of a proud regiment, but all I had to show for it was a single egg, and an experience I wasn't going to disclose in a hurry for fear my friends would rip off my pants again, to make sure she hadn't stolen anything.

'Why didn't you tell us right away?' they asked me later. 'We would all have gone there, and all insisted on it. Reprisals, you know!'

Spring burst out with sudden brutality. On the Eastern Front, things were going from bad to worse, but our training continued in the spirit of an athletic team preparing for a competition. Even more extraordinary, our schedule of exercises was markedly reduced, and we were often given free half days. These were in fact necessary, to give us time to forage and keep adequately fed. Our official rations had been cut back again, and now amounted to a starvation diet. The two villages closest to the camp had almost nothing left to give us, and we had to go farther afield in search of the calories which were largely consumed by our comings and goings. We took up fishing in the Dniester. Unfortunately, we had neither the proper equipment nor any local knowledge. Three times, Herr Hauptmann Wesreidau went with us. As an officer, he had appropriated a certain number of explosive devices, which made the operation profitable. Some pools produced giant fish.

431

There was also an accident. Two fellows who went out to look for food disappeared. Their friends said they'd gone toward the mountains. Two days went by without any news of them. No one knew anything about them in the villages where we asked. It sounded like partisans. We sent out two search parties, which did, in fact, run into partisans, and suffered five stupid deaths without finding a trace of the missing men.

While the Red Army pushed into Poland toward our camp, which would soon be in the battle zone, we lay in the sun as much as we could, and waited for orders. Hals was daily more deeply in love, and spent as much time as he could with the girl he considered his fiancée. I often went with him, but never found a girl for myself. We had many pleasant times together, and Hals repeatedly told me that I must be due for a leave soon, and would surely see Paula. Sometimes, the two of them plainly wished to be alone, and I would take myself off.

The war seemed to have forgotten us in this enchanted place. But one morning our tranquillity and dreams of love came to an end. The camp hummed with activity, as companies packed up and prepared for action before our incredulous eyes. As motors hummed, the barracks were destroyed. Our amazement was complete.

'What's going on?'

'Los! Los! Schnell! We're clearing out!'

Before we had quite realized it, we were loaded onto dull grey-blue trucks, which bumped off to the north. In the beautiful fullness of germinating spring, the settled, organized camp went up in flames behind us. The convolutions of smoke rising into the pure, still air seemed like a sinister presage of things to come.

In the trucks, everyone was talking. What was happening? Why were they destroying the camp? Where was the front now anyway? Toward ten o'clock the Gross Deutschland column suddenly stopped, on a road dappled by the knobby shadows of branches loaded with thousands of buds bursting from the irresistible pressure of thousands of plump leaves still barely touched with green. The birds, as unprepared as we for what was coming, were singing, and swooping down low over the trucks. A sidecar from liaison delivered orders to the officers' Volkswagen. Then the noncoms told us to make a half turn.

Through the bursts of backfiring, we could hear the hum of a flight of planes. Then the whistles blew.

'Achtung! Enemy planes coming for us! Achtung!'

In a general rush, we jumped from the slowly moving trucks.

In fact, the Ilyushin fighter-bombers which had spotted us took their time. About fifteen of them were turning in the sky some four or five hundred yards above us. Some trucks had been precipitately abandoned, and were lying across the road. Our officers ran shouting at the drivers, who, caught between two fires, didn't know what to do. Finally, they jumped back into their machines, started them up again and crashed them into the bank at the last possible moment, as the flight of vultures swooped down on us.

First, there were bombs, which we watched fall until the first explosions. They looked like fat darts, with their long shafts, which allowed them to explode just above the ground. The planes had divided into two groups; the second unloaded at about the same spot as the first.

The shock was extraordinarily violent. Everything flew into the air and fell onto our heads. An overturned truck flew toward us, stopping some ten yards short of where we lay. The flames spread quickly in our direction, forcing us to move farther back. We no longer had any doubts about what was happening, and ran as far as we could from the road, which was attacked again with rockets and machine guns.

The running men, intent on getting away, hadn't noticed the second wave of planes and were cut down by the machine-gun fire, which passed over them like a pitiless reaper. Men were jolted off the ground as they ran, to fall back again in pieces, like puppets whose strings are broken.

When the enemy withdrew, eighteen of our machines were sending plumes of black smoke up into the sky. The attack had been so sudden and overwhelming that none of us quite grasped what had happened. We returned to the scene of the disaster with one eye on the sky; the enemy might only have pretended to leave, and might still be waiting to attack us again.

The road, still gluey from the recent thaw and the spring

rains, was strewn with debris and shattered bodies. The violence of the impact had smashed some of the victims wide open, scattering their entrails over distances of seven or eight yards. The peaceful roadway, which had been filled with the sounds of twittering birds only fifteen minutes before, looked defiled.

Within fifteen minutes our column, made up of thirty trucks transporting three companies, had lost twenty men and eighteen trucks. There were also three wounded men in critical condition.

We collected the remains of our dead, and dug graves. Among the victims were Hoth and Dunde, who had both received Iron Crosses for their bravery on the second Dnieper front. They were both friends with whom we had been laughing and joking barely twenty-four hours before. After the event, the tragic impact of what had happened crushed and overwhelmed us.

We piled onto the remaining trucks, which seemed to buckle under the extra weight. There were men on the runningboards, fenders, hoods, and bumpers. Budding twigs clung to these human swarms bumping forward at twenty-five miles per hour. Two of the trucks quickly died under the extra load, and the men they carried had to continue on foot.

They joined us six hours later, on the Rumanian frontier, as we were getting ready to join the carnage at Vinnitsa, between the central front, which had been broken, and the southern front, which still seemed to be holding. On the way, these men had been attacked by Russo-Polish partisans; however, they were fortunately able to turn the encounter to their own advantage. They had taken the partisans' horses, and a few more still left on neighbouring farms, and had joined us looking like an apparition of chivalric fantasy. The weather was warm and sunny – we were returning to Russia just after the period of melting ice. We requisitioned a few Rumanian trucks which had been left for civilian use, to replace the ones destroyed in the attack. These were old machines, bearing the names of private firms, which we didn't have time to paint out. Our section drove off in an English moving van which must have left the factory sometime around 1930.

Chapter Fifteen

RETURN TO THE UKRAINE

THE FINAL SPRING · THE DEATH OF HERR HAUPTMANN
WESREIDAU · EXODUS

After a rushed, jolting journey, we re-entered the Ukraine, where the ground had not yet entirely absorbed the spring runoff. There were long stretches of gluey mud which we were able to cross only with great difficulty. The weather was beautiful, even hot, and we often stripped to the waist.

On the road we received new orders. We were no longer to proceed to Vinnitsa. Instead, we were to re-establish communications between the rear and the front, which were continually harassed by partisans. We were ordered to annihilate these bands. Their attacks had grown increasingly virulent, and often paralysed the already uncertain flow of supplies. The Vinnitsa bridgehead had to be maintained as a starting point for new German offensives which would break up the wedge the Russians had driven into Poland before Lvov, and re-establish a connection with the North, which appeared to be holding.

Our detachments, together with other units, had been given the job of engaging the partisans in a contest of ambush, in which the advantage belonged to whichever side surprised the other. Once again, the division was broken up. The largest section was sent to fight north of Lvov and in the northern sector of White Russia. Other units like ours were scattered throughout the rear areas of the south and central sectors before rejoining the division a few weeks later. Our zone of operations extended through Bessarabia as far as the Russian frontier. As before, we were a strong mobile unit designed to move quickly to the support of particular points in imminent danger.

However, our mobility depended on the vehicles I have already described, which we gradually abandoned, continuing on horseback or on bicycles, whose tyres were often stuffed with grass. We requisitioned the horses, bicycles, and other vehicles from the thousands of refugees – Ukrainians, gypsies, Polish colonists and others who were fleeing the Red tide in a vast throng. Sometimes partisans infiltrated these crowds, posing as simple peasants who were also fleeing the Bolsheviks. Then, at a given moment, they would shoot some of our men in the back, sowing general confusion. These manoeuvres were supposed to crack our self-control, and provoke us to acts of reprisal, which would then turn the refugees against us. From their point of view, any means were justified.

Toward the end of May, we trapped a large band of rebels in a piece of wooded country. There were about four hundred heavily armed men. On our side, we had three companies to draw in the noose around the enemy.

The air was filled with woodland smells, and nothing seemed appropriate to the bloody events about to occur. The morning was splendid. Birds and small animals of every kind were running and fluttering through the branches, to get out of our way.

Wild animals, even ferocious ones, always flee armed men. This time the hunters were tracking far more dangerous game. The birds fearing and fleeing us could never have imagined that the masters of the world, who should have feared nothing, had created enemies of a size and ferocity which equalled their own. Human beings, rulers of the animal world, had created their own destruction. A process of natural selection, often very badly organized, periodically topples our crown.

We all felt extremely nervous. Despite the resignation which had once again taken hold of us, the moment of truth as always revealed who was afraid, who was a coward, and who still hoped to live. The soft leaves brushing against our heads weighted down with steel reminded us that life could be good – especially in such marvellous weather. For us, this was no baptism of fire, but almost a routine – a dangerous routine, in which medals for heroism were generally posthumous. We had already experienced most of its horrors, and had seen the upturned eyes of those who had won the medals. There was no longer much we could learn about that aspect of things. We deliberately maintained an attitude of morbid fatalism, which we punctuated with bursts of harsh, forced laughter, like machine-gun fire. Some of the very strong had even managed to persuade themselves that since no man is immortal, and everyone dies sooner or later, the hour of death was unimportant. Those men, the strong ones, walked along thinking of other things. Others – strong, but not that strong – lived to delay that final moment, watching through pupils as dark as the holes at the ends of their gunbarrels. The rest – which is to say the majority – were pouring with a cold sweat which ran down their bodies beneath their synthetic tunics, into their boots, and into the creases of their damp hands.

Those men were afraid, with an intense fear that reduced every conviction to nothing, and which no routine could soften. They were afraid before every operation, when time seemed to stand almost still. Even those who managed to stop thinking were still assailed by fear, as persistent as the daylight, which illuminates treetops one is still unaware of.

Contact with the enemy puts an end to this sort of fear. The opening shots raise the curtain on a drama which will fully occupy every sense. It is a pity that soldiers can think. When the first men have fallen, the tension slackens, and no one any longer pays attention to anything except the dry twigs crackling underfoot.

Feldwebel Sperlovski, who was leading our group, pointed to the signs of passage of a large number of men. The heavily trampled brush and the numerous empty gun emplacements indicated that we were approaching a large partisan camp. We had to watch carefully for mines – to watch each step, in addition to everything else. Sweat trickled down our temples, attracting clouds of belligerent flies. The brush under the trees and the low branches offered a thousand opportunities for concealed trip wires. Every yard required a desperate concentration. A plane passed over level with the treetops, and the throb of its engines made us all hold our breaths for fear the vibrations might be enough to set off the whole area. At last, there was a short blast on the whistle, and we all fell flat. A small fort of logs driven deep into the ground stood at the end of a vague foot path. At the far end of our group, fighting had already begun.

437

Sperlovski designated two men – Ballers and Prinz – to throw grenades at the fort. Prinz was one of the men in Lensen's Panzerfaust team. Today, however, the anti-tank group wasn't needed, so Prinz was just another Panzer-grenadier, panting as he crawled forward with his lethal burden. Ballers, more dead than alive, was crawling along the other side of the path, identically laden. We all watched, trembling with tension.

Who were Ballers and Prinz? Two men from anywhere. Were they good men or bad? Were they hateful? Was God with them, or had He condemned them? They were simply two men who had become our comrades in this group of madmen; men whose acquaintance we would probably have avoided in the ordinary circumstances of civilian life. Here, every step they took accelerated the beating of our hearts, and keyed up our pulse rate to equal theirs. Those two anonymous beings, both of them our men, were suddenly more important to every one of us than even our closest relatives – an egotistical transformation in which we all knew that we saw ourselves; had the circumstances fallen slightly differently, they would have been watching us. Motive seemed totally unimportant – if only they lived. They were already quite far from us, and perhaps very close to death, hidden from many of us by leaves. I could still see them. Prinz suddenly stood up and heaved his load toward the log fort. Then he plunged down again.

The entire woods felt the violence of the explosion. Its thunder echoed interminably under the trees. In the patches of sky visible through the branches we could see the birds shooting away from us like arrows. Prinz's bundle had fallen short, and had made a large crater crowned with broken branches some seven or eight metres from the partisan hideout.

'Scheisse,' muttered our sergeant.

'There's nobody there,' someone else said.

Then I saw Ballers running forward in turn. As he ran, I felt myself dying in his shoes. He too threw his packet of explosives, and then dived down as the trees all around us bent against a flash of light. The forest seemed to groan with the shock. This time there weren't any fleeing birds – only our mimetic uniforms, which confounded us with nature. Ballers had just stood up again. So had Prinz, a short distance ahead of him. Their figures were sharply outlined against the broken earth. Behind them, all that had formerly been visible of the fort had disappeared.

'This way, comrades,' shouted Ballers, proud of his exploit. 'There's nobody in there.'

We all stood up, prepared to join him. He was laughing nervously. A crisp detonation whistled through the leaves, followed by two more. Prinz was running toward us, but Ballers wasn't. He was walking hesitantly, stretching one hand toward us. Then he fell.

A short hour later, four hundred partisans were fighting like devils inside the circle we had drawn around them and were slowly tightening. Three companies almost at full strength — about eight or nine hundred men — were trying to knock out the circle of fire, which was produced by a variety of weapons of every calibre, and amounted to a serious destructive force. The partisan position was so well organized that any approach to it was almost suicidal.

During this hour, two of our men stepped on mines, and their shattered bodies were blown into the budding branches. We were under uninterrupted fire from a four-barrelled machine gun, and setting up a spandau was very risky. We tried to dig foxholes, but the earth was such a tangle of ineradicable roots that our position of attack was transformed into one of defence, which would be difficult to hold against an enemy breakout.

Only our light mortars, with their almost vertical fire, could touch the enemy position. Unfortunately, the partisans seemed able to absorb our fire without any apparent loss of strength. Two or three heavy howitzers — probably captured German equipment — were shooting at our encircling forces; the impact of the projectiles uprooted trees. The discharge of these guns was invisible, which made their destruction extremely difficult. Ten times we sent assault groups to attack the terrorist position. Each time, they were obliged to make a half turn, leaving some of their men screaming on the ground. Later we learned that Wesreidau had been moving heaven and earth to try to get some armoured and motorized support, but none was available in that area and we had to do without it. Everything that remained had been sent to the support of our crumbling front.

After an hour of waiting, and attempted assaults that came to nothing, our commander decided to risk everything once and for all. Leaving only a handful of isolated men in the ring around the fort, he shifted the rest of us, taking every precaution, so that the enemy would believe they were still surrounded by a strong force. In this way, he was able to mass five hundred men and send them all at once against the enemy's weakest point – a V-shaped trench held by forty men armed with rifles and one machine gun. At his order, five hundred men rushed the enemy position, attacking with grenade throwers. The enemy reeled under the force of this blow, and was unable to maintain an accurate fire.

Seven or eight of our men fell during this assault, but the manoeuvre was so magnificent that for the moment no one paid much attention to them. I was part of the second wave; two others followed us. When we reached the enemy position the job was already done. Some forty partisans had tried to resist, but our rain of grenades annihilated two-thirds of them. The remainder had died on the bayonets of the first Germans to reach the fortress. We followed hard on their heels. Another wave was right behind us. The underbrush rang with hideous screams, and smelled of powder and smoke and blood. I saw more partisans pouring from their log fort, and firing point blank at our men, who were exhilarated by the success of our action. In the general confusion, I opened fire along with everyone else. A tall Russian fired at me three times without hitting me, although I made no effort to dodge him. Then he rushed at me, shouting and waving his gun, holding the butt in the air. Two of our men joined me and fired at the Russian. He fell and tried to reload his gun, but we jumped him immediately, battering him with our butts. He died under our blows.

At the foot of the blockhouse, a desperate hand-to-hand struggle was in progress. Something exploded in the midst of the fighting, sending shattered fragments of German and partisan bodies flying through the air. Other men ran up to continue the fighting, surrounded by the dead and dying. Cries and curses mingled with the sharp crack of rifle fire. A moment later, we were in the thick of the fighting. One of the fellows with me had his arm broken by an exploding mine. Pressed against the wooden wall, men were fighting hand to hand with knives, shovels, feet, and stones. An obergefreiter had just hit a Russian in the face with his shovel, opening a hideous gash. The wounded man fell writhing to the ground. Kellerman was firing in short bursts at the partisans hidden behind the two howitzers which had given us so much trouble. Many Russians got away — at least half of them. Those who couldn't added to the numbers of the dead.

We collected all the stray guns and reserves of food, destroyed the howitzers, which we couldn't take with us, and buried seventy of our men. Then we left the place, carrying out the wounded on stretchers made of branches. In the evening we arrived at a kolkhoz, where we drank everything we could get hold of, trying to blot out the memory of a hideous day.

Spring in the Ukraine: endless days of almost unbroken light. A luminous darkness fell toward eleven at night, to yield to a pink dawn a few hours later. The weather was perfect: a warm, reviving wind, before the crushing heat of summer. Unfortunately, although the season made us dream of peace, the monster of war was finally able to emerge from the paralysis of winter and the thaw. The pale blue sky belonged to the Russians, whose air power had grown enormously. The Luftwaffe, whose numbers had been seriously reduced by the necessity of defending German cities and dealing with the increasing demands of the Western front, flew daily sorties which amounted to suicide flights against overwhelming enemy strength on the ground and in the air. Our few victories were the product of absolute heroism. The sky and the front belonged to the enemy. The rear areas were contested by two nearly equal opponents: the German army and the partisans. We continually sent out patrols. Almost every sortie produced a clash. Every hill and hedge and cottage held a mine, or hid an ambush. We had almost no vehicles of any kind, no gas, and no spare parts. We were also not receiving any fresh supplies. The odd, ill-assorted convoys still pressing through continuous air attacks were not destined for us but for the faltering, collapsing front. When they arrived in the forward zone, they were able to find the correct units only by accident. More often than not, their cargoes were absorbed by the hordes of starving men retreating under a deluge of fire.

We ourselves received at the greatest risk about a tenth of what we needed. We were obliged to live off the local inhabitants, who were very hard-pressed themselves and more than reluctant in their attitude toward us. The problem of food had become extremely serious. As it was spring, there were still very few fruits, and hunting was more dangerous for us than for the game.

A small hamlet sheltered what remained of our three companies. Between operations men slept almost naked on the ground. Those who sleep dine, says the proverb. For us, it was vitally important that this become the reality.

When planes came over, everyone took cover, and when they were gone, we laid our bony bodies out in the sun again. This helped to heal our winter louse bites. Half asleep, with our eyes half closed, we stared into the sky, apparently thinking of nothing. What was the use? We seemed to have broken completely with the past. Memories of peace floated up like fragments of books we might have read. The war had taught us to appreciate every minuscule good. Today, the sun took the place of our goulash and wurst and millet, and the mail which no longer came. We lay stretched on the Ukrainian soil, apparently calm and at peace. Tomorrow, perhaps, some food would arrive – and perhaps some gas, and some spare parts. Perhaps even some mail – a letter from Paula . . . But perhaps, too, there would only be ourselves and the earth and the sky and the sun. . . . What was the use of thinking about it?

One day, our radio crackled out an S.O.S. from a territorial post on the Rumanian frontier. It was surrounded by a band of partisans.

In the eyes of the Wehrmacht, we were still officially considered part of a motorized unit standing by, and therefore available. In consequence, we were always moving, and had to be ready to leave at a moment's notice for points anywhere within a radius of 150 miles. The post calling us was some 100 miles away, and had appealed to us because its officers had been told that in emergencies they could rely on our mobility. In fact, we had four trucks in bad condition, a small civilian van, a sidecar, and the C.O.'s steiner. Wesreidau tore his hair and cursed.

As quickly as possible, a hundred of us left to answer the S.O.S. We took along as many automatic weapons as we could to make up for our small number. Each truck carried two spandaus ready to fire. Above all else, we feared planes. We drove as quickly as we could along the terrible Russian roads, raising a thick cloud of dust. About 30 miles from our starting point, we hurtled through a village which could have belonged to prehistory. The inhabitants ran as fast as they could to get out of our way. We were bristling with weapons and black with dust, and we must have looked far from reassuring. As we left the village, a group of terrified residents scattered ahead of us. The steiner went through, and then the first truck, which crushed a dog. The second truck bumped a black pig, which ran out from nowhere and threw itself under the wheels.

I was in the third truck, and saw the whole sequence: the sudden braking ahead, the shrieking villagers running to the side of the road, the screaming pig, dragging itself through the dust. Five or six landser jumped off the truck to chase the pig, trying to kill it as it squealed in agony. Finally, they stabbed it with their bayonets. It was still kicking, spattering its executioners with blood, as they tied its feet with belts and ropes, and hung its 150 pounds from the tailgate of their truck.

Then we started off again, to catch up with the others, leaving the village in a squeal of gears. The pig too was soon covered with dust, which mingled with its streaming blood. We no longer objected to details like that; for those who survived, there would be fresh meat this evening. Sieg Heil!

We were now driving through a strange landscape of smooth black hills, almost like enormous boulders, scattered with a few stunted trees. Wherever the ground was broken, the soil was black and seemed as hard as stone. I wished that I knew something of geology; our route took us through this curious terrain for about fifteen miles.

We had just left that strange district when a group of planes was reported. One of our spotters confirmed that he had seen them through the treetops, slightly to our left. Our trucks pulled over to the side of the road, where they were screened by leaves. Wesreidau stared at the sky through his field glasses, but couldn't see anything. It seemed wise to wait for a few minutes. The landser in the third truck put the time to good account, slitting open the pig and getting rid of its guts with lightning speed. As the job wasn't quite finished when we started out again, they finished it on the back of the truck.

A few miles farther on, as we bumped through a chaotic landscape, two planes came over very low. We shouted at the drivers, who jammed on the brakes. There were no thick trees anywhere near us. As the planes passed directly overhead, we were all gripped by an insane, hopeless panic. Some men wet their pants. As the planes vanished into the distance, we lifted our heads and saw two ME-109Fs, which must have been the survivors of some squadron. No one thought of cheering the Luftwaffe; we had all been too afraid.

Toward four, we approached the zone of operations. Our trucks were following a winding track through mountainous country, driving very slowly for fear of ambush. Wesreidau's steiner was in the lead. Two observers, hunched on the hood, kept their eyes riveted on the dust along the way, and on the heights surrounding us. Nothing we could see was in any way reassuring. Suddenly, we were looking down into an open valley. We stopped, cutting off our engines, and immediately heard the distant sound of machine guns. Beyond all doubt, we had arrived. In the distance, through the heat haze, we could see what looked like a village. We kept the trucks a hundred yards apart, and maintained a moderate speed, as the men clung onto the outside of the railings. Once again our stomachs clenched at the approach of danger, and we wondered when we would begin to be adult men.

Naturally, the enemy knew we were coming. The first truck suddenly saw the commander's steiner driving backward at breakneck speed from a turn in the road. The vehicle was rolling down a slope when a sharp explosion burst on the track some ten yards ahead of it. Everyone plunged to the ground, and the trucks took whatever shelter they could. A second explosion tore a hole in the road, lifting a large cloud of dust. They were plastering us with shells from a 37-mm. gun. Then a burst of machine-gun fire riddled the first truck.

Luckily, everyone was already out. The driver must have watched in a cold sweat.

The enemy was hidden by the undulations of the country, and was very hard to see. Nonetheless, the men in the steiner knew they'd been lucky. It was miraculous that the 37-mm. gun hidden behind the trees to the right of the turning hadn't opened fire the moment the steiner appeared. The partisans had felled a tree across the road, right after the turn.

We set up two light mortars, and shelled the enemy gun, which soon fell silent.

'Probably amateurs,' Wesreidau remarked.

We deployed a dozen F.M.s, which made movement very difficult for the partisans firing from the mountainside. Our group slid through the brush and climbed the first rocky outcrops, while our mortars rained a hail of projectiles, more terrifying than destructive, onto any point that seemed to harbour opposition. We had just uncovered an enemy post – real Johnny-come-latelys giving Fritz a hard time in order to reap a reward from their grateful country.

'What bastards,' muttered Prinz to Smellens, 'coming to shoot at us just for the hell of it. We'll fix them.'

Our group attacked the partisans with grenade throwers. In that enclosed bowl of hills, the explosions made an overwhelming noise. Then someone raked the edges of the enemy ambush with a spandau, which we recognized by the sound of its fire. After two more grenades, the apprentice sharpshooters were ready to give up. A figure ran out, attempting a desperate flight. He was quickly cut down by the spandau.

'What a bastard!' Prinz shouted. 'It's horrible to shoot down idiots like that. Why can't they stay home and wait until the war ends, for the love of God! If I was in their shoes, no one could twist my arm – and you'd be the same, wouldn't you, Sajer?'

Home! The thought went to my head like a gulp of wine. Home, to wait for the war to end . . .

'Yes,' I said finally.

'And now we have to shoot them,' he said. 'It's disgusting.'

We could hear plaintive cries from the enemy entrenchment. To our left, spandaus and grenade throwers were destroying the tranquillity of the spring. Suddenly, one of the

Russian boys in an excess of zeal stood up, exposing half his body, and raked us with a burst of machine-gun fire. His loose, approximate fire wounded one of our men in the right hand, and then another, undoubtedly on the ricochet, in the calf. The Russian was shot down by our spandau, while our wounded man began to groan in a shaded corner.

'God damn it!' someone shouted. 'Will you stop this bullshit!'

Two figures climbed from the partisan position and, without any apparent hurry, began to run. Our F.M. sent them rolling in the dust too.

'Did you see that?' Smellens said to the gunner. 'You just got a girl.'

'A girl? Are you sure? If women are getting mixed up in this mess now, that's the last straw.'

A few minutes later we counted the bodies of the partisans: six young people about our age. Among them were two pretty girls, bathed in blood and covered with a swarm of blue flies.

We stared down at our victims, sickened by the sight. Why had they thrown themselves across the route of our misery? Their amateur barrier was quickly dismantled. We cleared the road, and marched to the village. The trucks followed slowly behind us.

Had the enemy been misinformed? Had they received exaggerated estimates of our minuscule capacity? Were they afraid? Whatever the reason, they abandoned their grip on the post which was almost theirs, and came out to meet us.

The sun was shining brightly on the narrow, dusty road. At the head of the column, our men were in contact with the enemy, who had taken refuge in the town cemetery. It was a typical Russian cemetery – blue and gold and white with no suggestion of sadness about it. The day was perfect, the spring of late June turning into summer. We could almost have been fighting for a lark. Each plume of smoke was immediately carried away by a gentle breeze. We would certainly have been satisfied by a light exchange of fire, but our commander saw things differently; we couldn't let the enemy think we were too weak to attack. So our grenade throwers and light mortars destroyed the blue cemetery. Two groups chased the partisans out, and occupied the cemetery gardens. The partisans had taken refuge in a nearby wooden building where the crops were stored. On the door, the enemy had just daubed the Marxist slogan: 'Workers of the World, Unite.'

This hasty scrawl, with dripping letters, gave a tearful impression of Marxist beliefs.

To dispose as quickly as possible of this flimsy, improvised fortress, we loaded the spandau with explosive incendiary bullets. The thatched roof caught on fire almost at once. The enemy, who were defending themselves with automatic weapons, did not spare their fire.

A salvo of mortar shells knocked the roof into the building, and the partisans had to abandon an untenable position. Our two groups ran toward the burning building to harass the Russians as they fled. An old bearded man was leaning against a pile of stones, shouting curses at us. His right hand rested on the head of a dead comrade who lay on the ground beside him. The old man was wounded himself, and his clothes were torn and burned. We walked past him at a distance of no more than three yards. The sight of our guns didn't silence him. He shook his fist at us, and cursed us. We all saw him through the smoke and sparks of the burning barn, but no one thought of shooting him. He showered maledictions at us until the collapse of the building buried him. A column of sparks rose into the azure sky. The first elements of our group were already in the village streets, firing on anything that moved.

The last of the partisans were running toward the mountains. For a moment, they were directly exposed to our fire, and we shot down twenty of them on the dusty road and among the junipers on the hillside.

The spandau, which had been fitted with a special magazine, took a horrible toll of the fleeing groups of partisans. Then we stopped firing, and the men from the German post came out and joined us. Many of them were wounded, and twelve were dead. We gave the wounded first aid, and drove the local residents from their huts. Fires were spreading everywhere, and had to be put out.

Men, women, and children joined us in fighting the flames. It took almost an hour to put the fires out. Then everyone, ourselves included, dragged the bodies of the dead to a central point. Women screamed and cried as they recognized a husband or son or lover. It looked as if most of the partisans had lived in this place.

Soon, however, the tears and sobs became threats and curses. We collected our own dead and wounded with the usual mute sentiment established by habit. The day was so beautiful it was hard to believe that any of this was really serious. Our eyes, disillusioned by so much accumulated fear and anxiety, no longer distinguished the tragedies of any particular moment.

Hals was staring at the magnificent mountain scenery, as he carried along a comrade whose tunic was blotched with brown stains. The birds had regained their sense of spring joy and were flying once again through the blue sky, which was faintly marked by smoke from the smouldering fires. For us, in the eastern armies, this joyousness of nature almost excused what had just happened. After the mud and the cold, we were like wild animals, overjoyed by the spring sun, and the knowledge that shelter for the night was no longer a serious problem.

We deplored what had just happened as a disturbance of the peace and quiet we so much appreciated.

The villagers were still caught in a crisis of tearful despair, and insults which were comprehensible simply by their tone shook our sense of well-being.

Someone threw a stone, which hit one of our wounded men in the face. Two landser spun around, brandishing their machine guns.

'Break it up, you pigs, or we'll drill you full of holes.'

But the shouted curses kept right on. We were ringed by faces, especially feminine faces, distorted by rage, spitting and cursing, and by shaking fists. Suddenly, six planes flying wing to wing appeared in that marvellous sky – six Soviet fighters, looking for one of our convoys. This sign heartened the Russians, who shouted, 'Ourrah Stalin,' and pointed at the planes, which blindly continued their search.

We could see such hatred on all these faces that we shivered, despite the fine spring day. We were all thinking of our tortured, mutilated comrades, murdered by men who were mixing themselves into a fight that had left them on the sidelines. We remembered once again the tragic deaths at the territorial posts all along our line of retreat during the winter: faces smashed open with axes, so that the gold teeth could be pulled out; the hideous agony of wounded men tied with their heads inside the gaping bellies of dead comrades; amputated genitals; Ellers' section, whom we had found tied up and naked, on a day when the temperature had dropped to thirty degrees below zero, with their feet thrust into a drinking trough which had frozen solid; and the faces of tortured men under the dark winter sky. . . .

With dry mouths, we listened to the mounting rage of these peasants, who were now paying a price they could have avoided for all time. If anyone had ordered us to fire, we would have obeyed without hesitation. I could see the gun shaking in the filthy, nervous hands of the man nearest me. A little way off, another of our men was no longer able to control the trembling of his face muscles. We had all stopped working, and our anger was rising like a storm.

A tall, slim figure strode between the two groups. We saw that it was Wesreidau, and that he was white with fury. He stopped five yards from the Russians, and threw them a look so terrible that silence fell at once. He had learned Russian during the long course of the campaign. He told the villagers to bury their dead with the same silence and respect he required of his troops. He said that the war would soon be over for them, and that they should wait for the end, keeping to the sidelines. He said that he had never imagined the war would bring him to shoot civilians, who had been misled into arming by false propaganda, and excused himself for what he had been forced to do. Then his voice became as hard as death. He said that he would not tolerate any further hostile manifestations; that he intended to return to camp with all his men still alive, and that the entire village would be held responsible if he did not.

Wesreidau's words had the effect of a soothing balm. Everything returned to a state of unexpected order. The dead were buried and sobs were stifled.

We found enough gas for our return in the stores of the outpost.

The men there entertained us with a few bottles they had put aside several months before. Then we returned to the road, leaving eight wounded men behind at the post, where the medical service would pick them up the next day. Six others failed to answer the roll call, and remained in the Ukrainian soil forever.

'Not so crowded this time,' someone said.

We acquiesced without speaking. Our eyes lingered on the village disappearing behind clouds of dust raised by the trucks. The beautiful spring light glowed all around our blackened, steel-capped faces, which seemed irrevocably cut off from the season. Our awareness of everything was similarly split. Our thoughts, like our eyes, couldn't settle on anything that seemed definite, or restful, and a sense of well-being had no place in the convoy.

The whirling dust hid the bursting spring. All we could see were the trucks, and the grotesque, dangling cadaver of the pig, covered with blood and flies.

The trucks lurched along the narrow mountain road, whose illogical course might have been traced by some wandering goat; obstacles like stone outcrops were included without modification, and natural, shaded ridges were avoided. Sometimes the track plunged into the bed of an unexpected stream, or through a temporary pond. At other times, we crossed deserts of dust, where the dryness seemed eternal. The trucks slowly pursued the twists and turns, carrying us along, penned between the rattling railings.

We seemed to be wandering endlessly toward new horizons on which we never had time to gaze, through an oversized, overintense spring which would not allow us to forget that we were at war. Our expressionless faces stared at the spring with the unhappiness of paupers staring into a shop window decorated for Christmas.

We too wanted the war to stop and dreamed of peace, like the seriously ill for whom the first sight of spring buds kindles a spark of life.

But the fighting didn't stop; there was never more than a semblance of peace, and always someone to fan the flames of war. These people – on both sides – perhaps had perfectly good reasons for what they did. On that day, one of them crossed the road as we climbed up the long slope. He had seen us coming, and quickly, perhaps inside of ten minutes, laid his trap, hiding it in one of the dozens of potholes that pitted the surface. Then he hid, perhaps waiting to see what happened. Perhaps he too saw the yellow flash that tore apart our lead car. As always, there was a loud noise and a great deal of smoke climbing in black plumes toward the desperately smiling sky. Six bloodstained men were slowly dying in the shadows of those plumes. The front of the steiner was gone. The rest of the machine was knocked over onto its side.

A few men pulled the victims from the flaming wreckage, while the rest assumed a defensive position. We laid Wesreidau and the five other occupants of the car against the bank of red earth. Two of them were already dead. Another had a leg torn open in several places by metal fragments; his thigh looked like a mille-feuille pastry. Wesreidau was covered with wounds, and his body seemed to be broken by multiple fractures. We did everything we could for him. The whole company thought of him as a friend. With everyone helping, we managed to bring him back to consciousness.

Unlike everyone else we had watched, our captain did not have a face twisted by the revulsion or agony of death. His swollen face even managed to smile. We thought we had saved him. In a very weak voice he spoke to us of our collective adventure, stressing our unity, which must hold in the face of everything to come. He pointed to one of his pockets, from which Feldwebel Sperlovski pulled an envelope, undoubtedly addressed to his family. After that, for nearly a minute, we watched our chief die. Our faces, used to such spectacles, remained impassive. But the silence was terrible.

We were able to save two of the men from the car, loading them carefully onto the vehicles which remained. Lieutenant Wollers took command, and organized a decent burial for our venerated leader. We walked past his grave one by one, saluting. We felt that we had just lost the man on whom the well-being of the whole company depended. We felt abandoned.

That night we returned to the isolated village where our comrades were anxiously waiting for our return. The announcement of our commander's death provoked stupefied consternation. We were all in danger of death, but the annihilation of Wesreidau seemed as impossible to us as life without their parents seems to small children.

We were prepared for every other death, but no one was ready to concede that fate for our leader.

Guard duty that night seemed more uncertain than before; our three companies seemed more vulnerable than ever. We all turned toward a source of strength which remained silent.

Who would our new leader be? On whom would the destiny of our group depend?

At the first light of dawn, after our radio message had reached headquarters, a DO-217 flew over, releasing a smoke signal. This told us that our three motorized companies should proceed quickly to a key position at the front, to the north of us.

We were ordered to destroy our base and most of the village. Nothing should be left which would aid or shelter the enemy. As we had no incendiary material, we limited ourselves to burning the thatched roofs of the cottages.

Then our motorized company left on foot, with our matériel loaded into the four ancient trucks we had left. The radio truck and sidecar preceded them. Every ten or fifteen miles, the trucks and sidecar stopped and waited for us. We would arrive at the front together or not at all.

Our orders made no sense. The officers issuing them seemed to be completely unaware of the actual condition of mobile units allegedly standing by. We were limited to doing the best we could.

Food was our most difficult problem. For a long time now, we had received no supplies, and our meals were produced by some kind of magic. We became hunters and trappers and nest robbers, and experimented with wild plants whose leaves looked like salad greens. After a long chase, we were sometimes able to catch an abandoned horse. But eight hundred men require substantial quantities of food, and every day we were faced with the same difficulties. Every day we called for help on the radio, and every day received the same reply: 'Supplies en route. Should have reached you.' The Army Postal Service seemed to have vanished too: no letters or packages – no news of any kind.

Despite the warm summer sun, which was now, in fact, somewhat too warm, the situation had become desperate.

Yesterday's pig had been grilled and boiled and devoured

the night before, along with a hundred and fifty quarts of hot water which we elevated to the status of 'pork bouillon.'

Today we were leaving for the front. Our eyes gleamed, like the eyes of famished wolves. Our stomachs were empty, our mess tins were empty, and the horizon was devoid of any hope. Murderous sentiments lurked behind our eyes, which glittered with hunger. Hunger produces a curious frame of mind. It is impossible to imagine dying of hunger. For a long time now, we had been used to living on very little. Our stomachs digested substances which would kill a comfortable bourgeois citizen in a few weeks. No one had any spare fat left – no bellies or double chins, and our long muscles stood out in relief, as though we'd been flayed. As our fast continued, our senses grew more acute. We looked like the bony animals with blazing eyes one might encounter in the desert. It would take days of marching and dust to extinguish that blaze. For the moment, despite the hollows in our bellies, everything still seemed possible. We would simply march until we found food. After all, Russia was not an empty desert. The immense prairie around us looked fertile, and we would surely come across a village we could ransack.

Sperlovski and Lensen checked the map. There were a great many villages in our sector; therefore, the situation wasn't too serious. The trouble was that our rectangle of paper represented an area as large as all of France. Between any two villages, there might be hundreds of absolutely empty miles. The smallest digression to reach one of the names on the map could mean several more days of marching.

'There's nothing really to worry about,' said Lensen, who didn't like to concede defeat. 'There are plenty of villages lost in the steppe which aren't marked on the map. And then there are the kolkhozes, too.'

We had been ordered to march north. There could be no more delay. In any case, there was nothing left to eat where we were. Our long file set out: 'Kompanie, marsch! marsch!'

Hour after hour, at two or three miles an hour, we tramped in growing desperation through the uncultivated prairie.

'Somebody could make money farming here,' remarked a Hannover country boy.

There were large fields of wheat near each village. Beyond these, over spaces as broad as a French department, there was nothing but wild grass and grey or red dust and thick forest, much of which was probably virgin. We had grown used to great distances. Above all, we thought of them as possible battlefields. Other reactions still lay in the future for those who returned to their native countries, with their suffocating densities and horizons which seemed close enough to touch, always marked by commonplace structures of public utility, stones arranged in some dubious style. These men, who had grown used to stretches of ground as vast as the sky, no longer knew how to sit on grass which always belonged to someone.

For us, at the moment, there was only limitless space, where our boots raised a cloud of multicoloured dust that settled on everything that disturbed it. We belonged to the earth far more than it belonged to us. Except for the war, we felt a vast, limitless pleasure in our surroundings, in a kind of plenitude for which, in later years, we would always feel nostalgia.

If only there had been something to eat!

After our eleven-o'clock break, our march began again. We had gulped down like a dose of medicine the cooked sprouts of young wheat which had been prepared two days earlier. As a last resort, we had some millet, cooked in water. The weather was very hot. Fortunately, our exceedingly light meals did not produce after-dinner somnolence.

We drank the warm water from our water bottles with a certain apprehension. Running streams were quite widely spaced, and water from ponds carried the risk of malaria, typhoid, and other diseases, like cholera. To keep up our spirits, we sang as we marched: 'Ein Heller und ein Batzen.' The words, like the tune, were carried into the emptiness by the light summer wind, losing all meaning – which no longer seemed strange to ears once accustomed to hearing them echo between the walls of flag-decked towns:

> *Der Heller ward zu Wasser*
> *Der Batzen ward zu Wein ...*

Not that we had any choice – there was no wine and the water had to be drunk sparingly and with caution.

Heidi, Heido, Heida! Heidi, Heido, Heida! Heidi – Heido – Heida! Ah, ah, ah, ah!

Kompanie, marsch, marsch. We marched, singing for no one but ourselves, and all of us already knew the tune.

Then it grew dark. Darkness fell very late on our bivouac and across the plain, on which it seemed we had hardly moved, on our dust-covered faces and aching muscles. We were already asleep on our feet. The silence seemed to have a special quality, as though it had come from the end of the world.

At daybreak, our march resumed. For hours the long row of hills on the horizon seemed to remain at the same distance from us. We were walking through a rocky plain where the highest rise in the ground was scarcely the height of a man. Small stands of trees, which reminded me of photographs of Africa, were scattered across the landscape. The trees were short and scrubby, curiously like the trees of high altitudes. The wind blew the red dust everywhere, as if we were tramping through a universe of powdered brick. For a long time now, we had given up marching in threes – the regulation order for marching troops – in favour of the system used by partisans. We were broken up into more or less compact groups, in which a man was ahead only until someone else caught up with him. Everyone was tired, and our pace was slackening.

We had given up all unnecessary conversations, keeping all our breath and strength to continue putting one foot in front of the other. How many thousands of steps did we still have to take? Our boots, the colour of the dusty universe, kept on across the rocky plain, which seemed to be leading us nowhere. The light wind filled our long, unkempt hair with dust; our position in relation to certain reference points on the horizon seemed unchanging; and the rhythm of our steps, the sounds of our progress, and the wind itself became overwhelmingly monotonous. From time to time we could hear a rumble from the great hollow of emptiness which filled our stomachs.

Just after the eleven-o'clock halt, during which we consumed the last of our millet, an incident disturbed the general monotony. Two twin-engined planes, which we had fortunately been able to see a long way off, appeared in the hot, blue sky. The horizon was so vast that anything which crossed it was visible for at least five minutes before it reached us. We scattered as usual, and assumed a position of anti-aircraft defence. Some of us were going to die.... The planes were either light bombers or reconnaissance planes – but unmistakably Russian.

The two planes flew over us at an altitude of about fifteen hundred feet. The snore of their engines pierced the gentle breeze and seemed to echo in the depths of our tense stomachs.

The two Popovs took our fire without sending down anything in return. They flew in a large circle, which we followed with anguished eyes. The second time around, they would surely let us have it.

However, their second swoop produced nothing but a swarm of white butterflies, flashing and fluttering against the blue of the sky.

As soon as the planes were gone, some of our men went out to pick up the leaflets. A fellow came over to me waving a dozen.

'Ivan doesn't seem to understand: if we can't eat, we can't crap. He's gone and sent us a lot of paper.'

We read the Communist tracts. 'German soldiers: You have been betrayed.... Surrender to our units, which will rehabilitate you.... You have lost the war.'

Then, to raise our morale, we were shown some bad photographs of anonymous ruins, which, it was claimed, were German cities flattened by bombs. Also, there were photographs of smiling German prisoners. Under each of these photographs was a short caption: 'Comrades: The temporary captivity which we are experiencing in no way resembles the lies we were led to believe. We have been agreeably surprised by the kindness of the camp officers. When we think of you, comrades, wading through the slime of the trenches to preserve the capitalist world, we cannot advise you strongly enough to lay down your arms.'

And so it went on.

One fellow, who had managed to escape from Tomvos, was shouting with rage. 'The bastards! For all I know, I'm the only survivor from that damned place.'

In disgust, he tore the leaflet to shreds, and scattered it into the wind.

We resumed our march. The leaflets were still circulating

from hand to hand, and their words and phrases 'the war is lost,' 'treason,' 'cities destroyed' echoed in our minds like a gloomy round.

Of course, it was Communist propaganda. All we had to do was talk to the fellow who'd escaped from Tomvos to understand that. But then anyone who'd been home on leave had seen the bombed German cities. And then there was our continuous and painful retreat, and our daily existence, with its total lack of transport, gas, food, mail, everything. Perhaps the war really was lost. But that couldn't be possible.

Here we were walking across the Russian plain. Was it still ours? Or was it simply witnessing our slow death?

But that, too, was impossible. We had to dismiss these black thoughts. We were simply living through a difficult period which was bound to pass.

Tomorrow, surely, we would get some supplies, and everything would once more make some kind of sense. We had to shake our heads and dispel our dark reveries. Today the sun was shining, and we had to press on.

We began to sing one of our marching songs with deliberate vehemence:

Auf der Heide blüht ein kleines Blümelein
Und das heisst Erika
Heiss von hunderttausend kleisen Bienlein
Wird umschwärmt Erika.

This was the second time Hals had shaken me awake. Despite the exhaustion which rapidly returned us to unconsciousness, it was annoying to be torn from such deep sleep.

'I'm telling you, I can hear guns,' he said.

I listened, but was aware of nothing except the pale, glittering night.

'Leave me alone, Hals, for the love of God. Don't wake me for anything. We'll be marching again tomorrow, and I'm so tired I could die.'

'I'm telling you that off and on we can hear guns. If you'll look around, you'll see that other fellows are standing up and listening too.'

I listened again, but still heard nothing except the gently blowing wind.

'Well, it's possible. But so what? This isn't the first time. Go back to sleep. You'll be better off.'

'I can't sleep on an empty stomach. I'm sick of this. I've got to find something to eat.'

'So that's why you wake me up?'

Someone walked over to us. It was Schlesser, who was on guard duty.

'Did you hear that, fellows? Guns.'

'That's what I was trying to tell this blockhead,' said Hals, nudging me.

Despite the sleep stagnating in me so that I was only half conscious, I felt obliged to listen to what my companion was saying.

'All we need here is a Soviet breakthrough,' Schlesser said.

'That would be the end of us,' said Hals, his voice suddenly hoarse.

'We can still fight, though,' said someone else who'd just come up.

'Fight!' said Hals, hideously objective. 'With what? Seven or eight hundred anaemic, half-starved men armed with light infantry weapons. You must be joking. It would be the end of us, I tell you. We haven't even got the strength to run.'

But the newcomer wasn't joking. His name was Kellerman. Although he was exactly twenty years old, he already had the lucidity of a much older man and an instant grasp of reality. This reality lifted the veil of fear, and exposed the anguish deeply inscribed on his face, whose hardened features seemed incompatible with his youth.

Then we all heard a distant rumble, carried to us on the wind.... We stared at each other. The noise stopped, began again, stopped again.

'Artillery,' said Schlesser.

The rest of us were silent.

I had heard the noise, like everyone else, but my exhaustion had produced the sensation of two simultaneous lives. Sleep and reality had become confused. I felt as though I were deeply asleep, dreaming of artillery fire, lost somewhere in time. My comrades went right on talking. I listened to them without really hearing what they were saying. Sergeant Sperlovski had joined us, and seemed to be making some deductions.

'It's still far off,' he said, 'but it's the front. We'll be arriving in a day, or a day and a half.'

'That would be an hour or two in a car,' Hals remarked.

Sperlovski looked at him. 'In a hurry? So sorry we're not motorized any more.'

'That's not what I meant,' Hals growled. 'I was thinking of Ivan, who must have gas and tanks. If he breaks through, he could be on top of us just like that.'

Sperlovski stalked off without another word. What business had he to be discouraged – a noncom in the Gross Deutschland?

'Let's go to sleep,' Kellerman said. 'There's nothing better to do.'

'It's a nice lookout,' I couldn't help saying. 'Here we are, like animals in a slaughterhouse, waiting for dawn, when the butchers will come.'

'Are we going to be killed with empty stomachs?' Hals roared.

Despite our hunger and fear, we managed to fall asleep again, and stayed asleep until daybreak – which arrived at what would be considered the middle of the night in any organized civilian life.

Here we had no bells or bugles, or even a whistle. The gentle commotion made by our group leaders was enough to drag us from the heavy sleep which, paradoxically, was very easily penetrated by sound and movement. According to the custom of troops approaching a combat zone, movement at night, or before full daylight, was preferred. The docile Wehrmacht, even in its death agony, clung to its professionalism and woke its soldiers at the customary hour, leading them in disciplined order to the field of glory.

The rules did not envisage that soldiers without food could avoid this or that trial, but stated that in all cases everything still possible should be accomplished with maximum efficiency. Time is measured out in equal quantities for the poor and the old and the underfed alike.

Our faded uniforms looked grey in the first faintly white light of day. Familiar silhouettes which had walked beside me for nearly two years now were advancing on either side of me in a rhythm that was also mine, and that has remained indelibly stamped on my memory. Whenever I think of those days, I can see again with absolute clarity details which are pointless in themselves: familiar profiles in a diffused light, the loose cloth of trousers improperly tucked into boots, belts loosened by their dangling load of heavy objects, and helmets hanging from one of our straps, always knocking against some other metallic object, with a dull sound I can still hear, without resonance, like a padded bell. And the smells, and the backs, hunched over in a thousand different ways, each one with its own expression, and its own arrangement of creases. The very anonymity of our uniforms created its own kind of individuality. No one uniform was precisely like any other, although no other uniform is so deliberately designed as the German to turn a man into a soldier, absolute and united with his fellows, and not just a civilian in special clothes. For the rest of the world, there are German soldiers with no distinction between them, but for us, the word 'Kamerad,' meaning one soldier just like any other, was exaggerated. Beyond the uniform and the formula, we were individuals.

That back over there, the same colour as thousands of others, is not just any back. It belongs to Schlesser, and over there, on the right, is Solma. Somewhat closer, that's Lensen, and his helmet. It's his helmet, unlike any other among the hundreds of thousands issued in the same series. Then there are Prinz and Hals and Lindberg and Kellerman and Frösch ... Frösch, whom I'd recognize in any crowd. Through our sameness, our individualism emerged, as it must have from all men stripped to essentials, since the beginning of time.

All our helmets were the same grey-green, covered with dust. But none stayed for long at a regulation angle, or moved in the same way, and all were distinctive and distinguishable. One thing above all remains more or less indescribable: the contagious anguish of soldiers stripped of everything, whom each step is carrying closer to an incomprehensible danger. There were also our resignation and our equally profound and violent desire to live.

Apart from these three sentiments in common, everything else was personal. But this was apparent only to us. To anyone else, all Huns were alike.

We saw them when we were still five hundred yards away. They were swarming around the three or four vehicles which had stopped to wait for us. There must have been at least ten thousand of them. Ten thousand men seems like nothing on the Ukrainian plain, but it is still a considerable number. Ten or twelve thousand soldiers in a pitiful state, storming our wretched trucks, rummaging through them again and again in search of some food or medicine. They had thrown themselves onto our battered machines as if they were revenging themselves for their abandonment. Then, as we arrived and they became aware of our miserable state, they collapsed into a torpor which was close to suicide.

Those wretched men, collected from several infantry regiments, were retreating after several days of fighting an implacable enemy who had toyed with them, decimating them as and when he chose. They were on foot, in rags, their faces livid after so much suffering, dragging along with them nauseatingly wounded men on litters made of branches, like the litters of the Sioux.

These men, numbed by too much disaster, were no longer fighting for any spiritual motive, but were more like wolves, terrified of starvation.

To oppose their sole and legitimate reason for living was to risk one's own life. These men, who no longer distinguished between enemies and friends, were ready to commit murder for less than a quarter of a meal. They were to demonstrate this a few days later, in a horrible phase of the confused flux of the war. These martyrs to hunger massacred two villages to carry off their supplies of food, but thirty of their men died of starvation anyway, near the Rumanian frontier.

Our shock at meeting combat troops in such a state was equal to theirs at finding us as we were.

'Where do you think you're going?' sneered a tall, emaciated lieutenant, swimming in a curious conglomerate uniform which was far too big for him.

He was talking to our lieutenant, who had led us since the death of Wesreidau. Our lieutenant pointed on the map to the position we were supposed to reach. He cited names, numbers, latitudes. The other listened, swaying stiffly, like a dead tree in the wind.

'What are you talking about? What sector? What hill? Are you dreaming? There's nothing left, nothing – do you hear me – but mass graves, which are blowing apart in the wind.'

The man talking like this still wore the 1935 commemorative National Socialist decoration pinned to his scorched tunic, which was marked by a thousand stains. He was tall and dark, and a heavy bundle of grenades hung from his belt.

'You can't be serious,' our lieutenant answered in a pleading tone. 'You've had a hard time, you're a little light in the head, and you're hungry. We too have been keeping ourselves alive by miracles.'

The other drew closer. His eyes were filled with such a hateful, disquieting light that we would gladly have killed him, as if he were a sick animal.

'Yes, I'm hungry,' he roared. 'Hungry in a way the saints could never have imagined. I'm hungry, and I'm sick, and I'm afraid, to such a point that I want to live to revenge myself for all mankind. I feel like devouring you, Leutnant. There were cases of cannibalism at Stalingrad, and soon there will be here, too.'

'You're crazy! If worse comes to worst, we can eat the grass, and there's all of occupied Russia, with plenty of reserves for the troops. For God's sake, pull yourself together. You keep going, and we'll cover your retreat.'

The other made a noise more like a hiccup than a laugh.

'You'll cover us, and we can take ourselves quietly away! Tell that to the men you see there. They've been fighting for five months, and have lost four-fifths of their comrades. They've been waiting for reinforcements, ammunition, vitamins, food, medicine, God knows what! They've hoped a thousand times, and survived a thousand times. You won't be able to tell them anything, Leutnant, but you can try. . . .'

We tried to shift some of the matériel from our decrepit vehicles – the last vestige of our motorization – onto our backs, to make room for some of the seriously wounded men among the retreating troops. They left first, driving past the rest of us, who were left to that extent less mobile than before on the great Ukrainian plain. We watched the trucks disappearing into the distance, envying the fate of the wounded, who might be going to escape the oppression of that immensity.

Then our motley collection of troops continued their retreat – a vain and empty march. We seemed to be tramping along a huge carpet on rollers, which unwound beneath our feet, leaving us always in the same place. How many hours, and days, and nights went by? I can no longer remember. Our groups spread out, and separated. Some stayed where they were, and slept. No order or threat was strong enough to move them. Others – small groups of men who were particularly strong, or who still had enough food to keep going – went on ahead. There were also many suicides. I remember two villages stripped of every scrap of food, and more than one massacre. Men were ready to commit murder for a quart of goat's milk, a few potatoes, a pound of millet. Starving wolves on the run don't have time to stop and talk.

There were still a few human beings left in the wolf pack: soldiers who died to save a can of sour milk – the last reserve of a pair of infants. Others died at the hands of their fellows for protesting against the savagery produced by famine, or were beaten to death because they were suspected of hiding food. Usually, these men were found to have nothing. There were a few exceptions: an Austrian had his head kicked in, and a few handfuls of crumbled vitamin biscuit were found at the bottom of his sack. He had probably collected them by shaking out the provision sacks of some commissariat which had ceased to exist several weeks before. Men died for very little – for the possibility of a day's food. When everything had been eaten, down to the last sprout in the meagre gardens, twelve thousand soldiers stared at the village, which had been abandoned by its terrified inhabitants.

Living corpses wandered here and there, staring at the tragic shreds of existence which remained to them. They stared at the scene of pillage, looking for some understanding of the past which might shed some light on the future. They stayed where they were until dusk. Then three or four armoured cars from the advancing Russian troops arrived, peppered with machine-gun fire the crowd of men, who didn't even try to escape, made a half-turn, and left. The desperate, ravening men scattered across the steppe.

Everyone fled, running for the west because the west drew them irresistibly, as the north attracts the needle of a compass. The steppe absorbed and obliterated them, leaving only small, scattered groups tramping toward the Rumanian frontier, which was very close, but still out of sight. I belonged to one such group. There were nine of us: Hals and me – inseparable as always – Sperlovski, Frösch, Prinz, an older fellow called Siemenleis, who must have been an incorruptible civil servant before the war, and three Hungarians, with whom all conversation was impossible. Were they volunteers, or had they been enrolled in circumstances similar to mine? No one knew. They looked at us with eyes full of hate, as if we were responsible for the misadventure of the Third Reich in which they had been involved. Yet they clung to us as if we were their last hope of ever returning to their distant firesides.

One day there was a line of trees, or a hedge of saplings, which I can still see, as in a drunken dream, and beyond it, the wide, very wide field which we planned to cross. We could see some buildings on the crest of a small hill, and had decided to search them for food.

Halfway across the field the sound of planes made us look up. Two Yabos were seeking some prey.

Seven of us melted into that enormous stretch of ground, and two ran – Frösch and myself.

Like hunted animals intent on self-preservation, each man thought only of himself, and no one shouted to us. The two Russian aviators spotted our wild gallop, and dived down at us. Although we had nothing left but our skins, we still represented the enemy to them, and had to be wiped out.

When the noise reached a certain pitch, we instinctively threw ourselves down on the thick grass. The bullets passed over our heads and landed far beyond us. When we lifted our heads, we could see the planes completing a graceful arabesque against the stormy blue and black summer sky. Gasping for breath, we ran desperately until the two vultures once again filled the air with overwhelming noise. The planes made two more passes after that, peppering the ground with bullets, each time twenty or thirty yards wide of the mark. Like a terrible joke, the planes roared down a fourth time at the trembling, sweating grasshoppers which were ourselves. Suddenly, as if by a miracle, we came to a ditch, and fell into it.

Without seeing them, we distinctly heard the roar of the Russian rockets, which turned both banks of our ditch into ridges of broken earth. Our friends were sure we were dead. The planes made one more pass, and flew off, undoubtedly

464

convinced that they had brought our wanderings to an end. When we walked out through the whirling dust, our companions greeted us with shouts of incredulous delight.

At the farm, which the inhabitants had abandoned some fifteen minutes before our arrival, we found a kettle full of steaming Jerusalem artichokes, which had undoubtedly been left to distract us. We went on our way, gorging on this unexpected windfall. Two days later, during which we twice collected potatoes from Russians at gun point, we ran into an interminable convoy retreating into Rumania, and were inescapably absorbed into it.

Then we experienced Rumania and its population, which seemed stunned by the sequence of events, by the route of their army, and by the painful disintegration of the Wehrmacht.

Civilian life was in a state of panic, with Rumanian and foreign partisans, daily overflights of foreign planes, raids for food and supplies, and Rumanian prostitutes who flocked around the troops in such numbers that it seemed as if most of the women in Rumania must be prostitutes.

We marched twenty, twenty-five, even thirty miles a day, pouring with sweat and stunned by disillusion. Our tortured feet were alternately bare in the dust of narrow, twisting roads, then back in our boots, and then naked and bleeding once more. Our hollow stomachs rumbled with hunger. There were raiding parties, re-formation of units, and a lunatic rabble, whose fringes and surface were skimmed by military police intent on discipline, and as always alert for the possibility of exemplary executions.

The landscape was profoundly romantic, but we had been transformed into ravening wolves, and thought of nothing but food.

A particular episode emerges from my memories of disorder — a tragic paroxysm which still seems to me a symbol of humanity gone mad.

We were in the mountains and had just been through a town called Reghin, which at that time was known as Arlau, or Erlau. We were tramping along, grey with dust and pouring with sweat. We had miraculously escaped incorporation into several scratch formations, and our interminable, wretched column was twisting through what seemed like an infinite chain of mountains. The column was broken up into groups of varying size, in which unkempt soldiers pushed along every kind of transport to move our basic necessities.

We requisitioned the most extraordinary vehicles. Anyone who found a bicycle grabbed it, even if it had no tyres, and went on ahead of the rest to skim off anything even remotely digestible. In this district of jagged peaks and crags, we were free of enemy aircraft, but the terrain was ideal for partisans, and there were many battles to the death between them and our men, who were now fighting simply to save their skins.

In this district, one group among many others of men in a motley conglomeration of clothes was struggling to reach the mother country. Behind our glittering eyes, deeply sunk into shadowy sockets, one belief sustained us. This was that, if we managed to survive, the mother country would receive us with tenderness, and try to help us forget the unimaginable trial which was nearly over. We thought that, once we reached home, the war would be over, and that in the worst imaginable case the army would be reorganized, so that no enemy would enter Germany itself. We held to this as the one final idea which would justify our sufferings and banish the solution of suicide which others had already accepted.

Yesterday's landser, members of élite units, Panzer-grenadiers who had confronted a thousand deaths to live for a chimera, clung to the idea that we had to live to be able to hope, and we had to hope passionately to be able to live as we were. We had to fight against daily ambush, and keep going no matter what, to get away from the Russians, who were hard on our heels. And we had to eat a certain minimum, which wasn't easy to do.

There were twelve in our group – many of them familiar companions: Schlesser, Frösch, Lieutenant Wollers, Lensen, Kellerman, and then Hals and me, kept together by a miracle of silent fraternity. Hals, who had grown startlingly thin, was forcing his large bony body along the narrow mountain road some four or five yards ahead of me. He often walked ahead of me, which gave me a certain sense of security, although his large body was seriously reduced. He was stripped to the waist, wearing a leather belt and a band of cartridges for the spandau across his chest. A Russian blouse, in anticipation of the cool evenings at this altitude, floated from the leather

466

pouch that held his few possessions along with four or five grenades. His heavy steel helmet seemed to be riveted to his head, and the lice in his filthy hair must have died for lack of light.

Many men had thrown away their heavy helmets, but Hals felt his was a last link with the German Army, and that during this terrible trial we should try to remain soldiers, rather than degenerate into tramps. I kept mine too, as a sign of solidarity, dangling from my belt.

Someone up ahead shouted for us to come and see. We looked down into a leafy ravine. A camouflaged truck bearing the inscription 'WH' had crashed to the bottom. Lensen was already running down to have a closer look.

'Watch out!' someone shouted. 'It might be a trap!'

Lieutenant Wollers had joined Lensen. We drew back, certain that the partisans had arranged a booby trap, and that we would see our two companions blown to pieces any minute. However, a reassuring shout floated up from the gulf.

'A windfall! Mein Gott, it's like a whole commissary!'

Within seconds we were all running toward the miracle.

'Look at that! Chocolate, cigarettes, wurst . . .'

'Good God! And here are three bottles, too!'

'Shut up,' shouted Schlesser, 'or you'll have the whole army down here! It's a miracle no one found this before.'

'So many delicious things,' said Frösch in an almost tender voice. 'Let's all grab everything we can. We can share it out later, on the road.'

Frösch and another fellow loaded themselves heavily, and climbed back to the road to keep watch. Thousands of men were wandering very close to us; we would try to take everything. We had almost completed the job when our two lookouts shouted: 'Achtung!'

We ran into the brush and heard the distant roar of a motorcycle. The engine slowed down and seemed to stop. We ran off through the thorny growth, clutching our precious cargoes. We were used to getting out of the way in a hurry and melting into the ground when an unfriendly eye might become too interested in our existence. We could hear some noncoms shouting, and supposed that our two companions had been caught by a military patrol, perhaps even by the military police.

'Those two sods were caught with bottles under their arms,' muttered Wollers.

'Let's get out of here as fast as we can,' said Lindberg, who had just run up.

'Someone's coming down,' whispered Lensen. 'An M.P. – I saw his badge.'

'Hell, let's get out of here.'

Everybody ran, scattering into the bushes as if Ivan himself were at his heels. We regrouped after five or six hundred yards, hiding behind a rocky outcrop.

'I've lost enough breath because of those bastards,' said Hals. 'If they want to chase us this far, I'll take care of them.'

'You're crazy,' said Lindberg. 'Don't talk like that. What are you trying to do to us?'

'Shut up!' Hals said. 'You'll never make it home anyway. Ivan's going to get you for sure. Why don't you think for a minute of Frösch and the other fellow who've been caught?'

'We might as well eat,' said Wollers. 'I've had enough of giving orders, and sweating, and shitting in my pants like a baby when I'm scared. So let's get started. If we're going to die for it, all the more reason to fill our bellies while we can.'

Like hungry beasts, we wolfed down the contents of the tins and the other provisions, masticating loudly.

'We'd better eat it all,' Lensen said. 'If we're caught with anything in our sacks that wasn't handed out, we'll be in trouble.'

'You're right. Let's eat it all. They won't slit us open to see what's inside, although it would be just like those bastards to check our shit.'

For an hour we gorged ourselves until we were almost sick. When it grew dark, we returned to the road by a devious route. Lensen stepped out of the brush first.

'Come on, the coast is clear.'

We went on for three or four hundred yards, passing once again the hole with its unexpected windfall which had allowed us to fill our famished stomachs for a moment. There was no one in sight. We went on for another two or three miles, and collapsed at the side of the road.

'I can't go any further,' said Schlesser. 'We're not used to eating any more, and this is what happens.'

'Why don't we go to sleep right here?' someone said. 'That will help our digestions.'

Toward two o'clock in the morning, a large group of German soldiers came by and woke us up.

'On your feet,' shouted an old feldwebel. 'Get going, or Ivan will be in Berlin before you.'

We resumed our trek. This bunch had collected several horse-drawn wagons, and for a while, we were able to ride. At daybreak, we arrived at a town built on the mountainside. Some men were splashing in an icy bathing place. Others were sleeping on the ground or on terrace walls. Farther on, still others had begun their march again, toward safety, the west, the mother country, waiting to receive them, whose true condition they couldn't begin to guess.

And then there was a tree, a majestic tree, whose branches seemed to be supporting the sky. Two sacks were dangling from those branches, two empty scarecrows swinging in the wind, suspended by two short lengths of rope. We walked under them, and saw the grey, bloodless faces of hanged men, and recognized our wretched friend Frösch and his companion.

'Don't worry, Frösch,' whispered Hals. 'We ate it all.'

Lindberg hid his face in his hands and wept. I managed with difficulty to read the message scribbled on the sign tied to Frösch's broken neck.

'I am a thief and a traitor to my country.'

A short way off, some ten policemen in regulation uniform were standing beside a sidecar and a Volkswagen. As we walked by them, our eyes met theirs.

469

PART FIVE

THE END
Autumn, 1944–Spring, 1945

Chapter Sixteen

FROM POLAND TO EAST PRUSSIA

THE VOLKSSTURM · THE INVASION

One September morning, we found ourselves in a farmyard somewhere in the south of Poland. The horror of our previous experiences had left us entirely without reaction, and we stared about us with the stunned eyes of someone who has been heavily drugged. A short way off an officer was shouting something at us – a speech or a report – which fell on deaf ears. We stared at the sky, to avoid thinking about the earth, which supported human life. Only an explosion, or perhaps a feld's whistle, could have dragged us from our lethargy.

However, in this district there was at least a semblance of order, and under cover of this last fragment of organization we were trying, as best we could, to recover our strength and some sense of morale.

The Russian thrust to the south was so strong that we had to consider Rumania enemy territory. We should soon be fighting in Hungary too, before Kekskemet, and then in Budapest.

The officer went on with his speech, to talk of a counter-offensive, of regaining control of events, regrouping our troops – even of victory, a word which no longer had any meaning for us. Although we couldn't conceive of the defeat which lay ahead, we understood that victory was not possible. We knew that we would still be obliged to make intense efforts defending some particular, organized positions, but we had no doubt that we could stop the enemy before the German frontier.

Despite our general unease and near-collapse and all our disillusion, we knew that we couldn't simply give up. The looming disaster was inconceivable to us. Even today, survivors of that experience find it difficult to accept all the

473

facts. But, despite our unshakable faith, we all felt temporarily unable to continue fighting; some time off, some rest, was absolutely essential. We were in a state of exhausted collapse, capable of nothing.

'General Friesener has re-established the Southern Front,' the officer was shouting. 'Our regiments will be re-formed and reinforced by substantial reserves. The enemy must not go any further. You will stop him.'

We were divided into groups, companies, and regiments, and loaded into trucks. It seemed there was still gas hereabouts. The Gross Deutschland units were sent north, which surprised us, as the rest of the division – or what was left of it – was fighting with Army Group Centre. Some units were already with Army Group North, and the two hard-pressed armies were eventually joined.

The trucks took us to a train which was waiting on a single track, sheltered by a pine forest. There was no station. We left in a long string of miscellaneous cars. My group was loaded onto an open platform like the one which had taken me out of Poland and into Russia so long ago. Today there was no need to fear any future in Russia: the Germans had been chased from that country. Today we were going north, slowly and carefully, as the track might be mined, or the sky full of bombs. The train took us to Lodz, where we saw many astonishing things.

We stayed in Lodz for about thirty hours. The front was very close, and like all towns near the fighting Lodz was full of troops. As in the south, men were being sorted out and regrouped. Thirty, forty, even fifty per cent of the names on the regimental lists had to be scratched off. In some cases, men already scratched off as dead or missing reappeared from the void.

The Gross Deutschland had a rallying point at Lodz – a former candy shop stripped of all its wares, the adjoining room for the concierge, and a long corridor. A large panel correctly painted black on white, and a stylized white helmet, the regimental emblem, hung over the door, which was still intact. Two sentries in correct uniform were stationed on either side of the door.

'Here we are,' Lensen said. 'Back at the Gross Deutschland.'

For an hour and a half we had been tramping through the city – from which nearly all the civilians had gone – looking for this place. Lieutenant Wollers presented the officer at the centre with his list of the men with him, including the numbers of their companies, regiments, and groups. There were about two hundred of us.

'Here is the list of men with me, Herr Hauptmann.'

'But you're bringing me a bunch of Russkis, Herr Leutnant,' the captain said, looking at our motley collection of clothes. Many of us were wearing padded Russian jackets.

'My apologies, Herr Hauptmann. We began to run short of uniforms.'

'Very short,' said the officer, smiling. 'I'm going to send you to the store, and you'll see if there's anything left. You'll have to be quick, because you won't be here long.'

In the next street, we found the divisional store, which was still much better stocked than the supply stores of ordinary divisions. Some of our men could be given quite a few of the things they needed. While we waited, we watched a crowd of men, part of a new Volkssturm battalion, swarm into a factory courtyard. When we looked more closely at these men recently called up by the Führer our eyes opened wide with surprise. They all belonged to the last class of reserves and seemed to be an even more extreme case than the Marie-Louise conscripts at the end of the Napoleonic era.

Some of these troops with Mausers on their shoulders must have been at least sixty or sixty-five, to judge by their curved spines, bowed legs, and abundant wrinkles. But the young boys were even more astonishing. For us, who had saved our eighteen-, nineteen-, and twenty-year-old lives through a thousand perils, the idea of youth meant childhood and not adolescence, which was still our phase of life, despite our disillusion. But now we were looking literally at children, marching beside these feeble old men. The oldest boys were about sixteen, but there were others who could not have been more than thirteen. They had been hastily dressed in worn uniforms cut for men, and were carrying guns which were often as big as they were. They looked both comic and horrifying, and their eyes were filled with unease, like the eyes of children at the reopening of school. Not one of them could have imagined the impossible ordeal which lay ahead.

Some of them were laughing and roughhousing, forgetting the military discipline which was inassimilable at their age, and to which they had been exposed for barely three weeks. We noticed some heart-wringing details about these children, who were beginning the first act of their tragedy. Several of them were carrying school satchels their mothers had packed with extra food and clothes, instead of schoolbooks. A few of the boys were trading the saccharine candies which the ration allotted to children under thirteen. The old men marching beside these young sprouts stared at them with incomprehension.

What would be done with these troops? Where were they expected to perform? There was no answer to these questions. Were the authorities going to try to stop the Red Army with them? The comparison seemed tragic and ludicrous. Would Total War devour these children? Was Germany heroic, or insane? Who would ever be able to judge this absolute sacrifice? We stood in profound silence, watching and listening to the final moments of this first adolescence. There was nothing else we could do.

Some hours later, we were driven to a new assembly area a few miles from the Vistula, in a town called Medau. There we found a large part of our full division, which had left us in the south long ago. Even our regiment was there, and its officers, with their familiar names. The auxiliary services of our autonomous unit had performed enormous feats of imagination to continue functioning. We were extremely surprised to find that the full Gross Deutschland Division was still quite strong – a discovery that raised our morale considerably. We needed to cling to some form of solidity to avoid recognition of the final tragedy which had engulfed us, and of our strictly limited choice between combat in the most desperate circumstances, captivity, or the end, once and for all. Here, on the banks of the Vistula, which could be considered the cradle of hostilities, we found companies restocked with young boys to fill the gaping holes the war had made in our élite division. We also found some familiar faces, including Wiener, the veteran, who seemed quite astonished that we were all still alive.

'We must really be indestructible,' he exclaimed. 'When I left you on the second Dnieper front, everything looked so black I really thought I'd never see any of you again.'

'Quite a few missing,' Wollers said.

'And quite a few still here. Mein Gott, Leutnant!'

We told Wiener that Wesreidau was dead, and Frösch. . . . He too had a list of names we could forget. No matter how intense the grief aroused by any particular name, the expressions on our worn faces never changed.

We pressed Wiener for news of Germany, of civilian life there and the situation of ordinary citizens. We all had reasons for concern and followed the movements of his lips, trying to grasp the implications of his inadequate words.

'I was in the Kansea military hospital in Poland,' he told us. 'I had lost so much blood and seemed so weak that for two horrible days they did almost nothing about me. I would never have guessed that life had so strong a grip on me. It would have been so easy – one last sigh, and then into the hole. But it didn't happen that way. I groaned and howled for ten days or so – especially the first two – and went through infection, transfusion, disinfection, reinfection, and here I am, back with you again, for another autumn of crap. Now I find the damp hard to take, too. I've got rheumatism, and that's fatal.'

As before, the veteran relieved his desperation by cracking jokes.

'But you must have had convalescent leave, didn't you?'

'Yes, Hals. I was in Germany. I went to Frankfurt, not am-Main, but am-Oder. I could have gone further if I'd wanted to, but there wasn't any particular reason. They put us up in a girl's high school – sad to say, without the girls. There wasn't enough to eat, but at least they let us alone. Have you noticed, by the way, that I'm missing an ear?' The veteran grinned sardonically.

When we looked, we saw that his right ear was gone, and that his skin where the ear should have been was a pale, shiny pink, which looked as though it might break at any minute. We had all noticed, without attaching any particular significance to it. So many men were missing one piece or another that we scarcely registered such things any more.

'Yes,' Prinz said. 'On that side, you look dead.'

The veteran grinned again. 'That's because you're so used to stiffs you're beginning to see them even where there aren't any.'

'Drop all the crap,' Solma shouted, 'and tell us about Germany.'

'Well ... yes.'

There was a moment of silence, which seemed to last forever.

'What's it like in Frankfurt?' asked Feldwebel Sperlovski, elbowing the rest of us aside. (He came from Frankfurt, and his family was probably still there.)

The veteran was no longer looking at us. He seemed to be staring into his own interior.

'The high school was on the east banks of the Oder, up on a hill. You could see a big piece of the town from there. It was all grey – the colour of dead trees – with walls sticking up here and there, all black from the smoke of fires. People were living down there, like landser in the trenches.'

As Sperlovski listened his face began to twitch, and his voice trembled as he spoke. 'But our fighters ... and flak ... wasn't there any defence?'

'Of course ... but so out of proportion ...'

'Don't worry too much, Sperlovski,' Wollers said. 'Your family was certainly evacuated to the country.'

'No,' Sperlovski shouted in a voice of despair. 'My wife wrote me that she had been conscripted and had to stay in town. No one has the right to leave his job.'

Wiener knew very well what effect his words must have on an audience starved for good news, but nothing seemed to distress him any more.

'It's total war,' he said, like an automaton. 'Nothing and no one will be spared, and German soldiers must be able to endure everything.'

Sperlovski walked away. He looked stunned. His eyes were glazed, and his steps faltered, as if he were drunk.

German soldiers would have to endure everything, in the world we had created. We were fitted only for that world, and were otherwise inadaptable. Lensen was as still as stone, and listened, stony-faced.

'Is it the same for all our towns?' Lindberg asked. He must have been thinking of his town, by Lake Constance.

'I don't know,' the veteran said. 'It's possible.'

'You certainly know how to raise morale,' said Hals in irritation.

'Do you want the truth, or a fairy story?'

I felt as though I were wandering through a landscape shrouded with fog and strewn with rubble. I knew that I could never manage to be disappointed again. Before mourning with the suffering world, I would somehow have to regain my balance. Of course I thought of Paula, but it was so long since I had heard anything from her that I wondered if I would even be capable of reading a letter if we should suddenly get mail. I was filling up with bad news like a barrel filling with water from a rainpipe. When the barrel is full to overflowing, all the torrents in the world are incapable of adding to its capacity.

We found ourselves in one of the rare trains still moving through that region, rolling toward East Prussia through the first frosts of our third winter of war – the fifth or sixth for some of the older men. We moved at night, with all our lights out, as Russian planes, which occupied our bases in Poland, were particularly active by day. We were moving toward Prussia, Lithuania, Lettonia, and the Courland front, to which the remnants of several German divisions were clinging.

Through the darkness and the thick fog we could see large masses of people moving on foot across the northern Polish landscape. At first, we thought we were watching infantry units on the march, but after several good looks we realized we were watching civilians – thousands of them – fleeing through the night and fog to escape the Red hordes who they sensed were very close behind them. We couldn't linger to watch those people, but could easily imagine their situation.

Then we crossed the Prussian frontier, into the home territory of Lensen and Smellens – two pure-bred Prussians, suddenly back on their native soil. Lensen stood up and leaned over the carriage door to get a closer look at his country. The rest of us didn't care so much: the landscape was scarcely distinguishable from that of Poland. Perhaps there were a few more lakes. Otherwise, as in Poland, there was forest.

'You really ought to see it when there's snow on the ground,' Lensen said. He was suddenly smiling again. 'This way, you can't really tell what it's like.'

As we remained silent and uninterested, he spoke up again. 'You're in Germany, for the love of God! Wake up! Think how long you've been dreaming of this.'

'East Germany,' Wiener said, 'practically the front. And then, I don't know if you realize it, but I have a compass, and I can tell you we're moving to the northeast, which is no good at all.'

Once again Lensen turned purple with anger.

'You're nothing but a bunch of milksops,' he said. 'It's your kind of defeatism that's brought us to this. The war is already lost inside your goddamned heads, but you've got to fight anyway, whether you want to or not.'

'Shut up!' shouted five or six voices. 'If they want us to win the war, let them treat us like normal soldiers.'

'You're just a bunch of whining puppies. The whole time I've known you, you've done nothing but whine. For you, the war has been lost since Voronezh.'

'For good reason,' Hals said.

'You'll fight, whatever the cost, and I'm the one who's telling you – because you have no choice. There's no other way out.'

The veteran stood up.

'Yes, Lensen, we'll fight – because we can't stand the idea of defeat any better than you can. And we have no choice. I don't, anyway. I'm part of a machine which operates a certain way, and only that way – and I've been part of it for too long.'

We stared at Wiener, somewhat taken aback. We had thought he would be able to adapt himself to any kind of life. And now here he was saying that he could live only for the cause which had already cost him so much.

Lensen went on grumbling, and we went on thinking confusedly about the glimpse of the future the veteran had given us. For me, from the vantage point of Prussia, France seemed remote and unimportant. The cause which Wiener spoke of was also my cause, and despite all the difficulties and disappointments I had endured, I still felt closely linked to it. I knew that the struggle was becoming more and more serious, and that we would soon be obliged to face appalling possibilities. I felt a strong sense of solidarity with my comrades, and I could think of my own death without too much flinching, as a soothing veil that would fall slowly over me and all my terrors of the past, present, and future. My head seemed to be filled with a milky fog, which was without joy, but which suddenly made everything easy. Did my comrades feel the same way? I couldn't be sure, but my resignation seemed general.

We rolled on for several hours at a reduced speed. Finally we stopped and walked through the grey, foggy morning to a camp of wooden huts, whose appearance recalled the robust military organization only recently lost. We were given an hour to rest, and the chance of a cup of hot water with a few grains of soya in it.

'And to think that some fellows volunteered for the food,' somebody muttered.

'There couldn't be too many volunteering these days,' another voice said. 'Very few are around for long enough even to dream of becoming an officer. There's hardly the time to make obergefreiter, before they're getting a posthumous stripe.'

A few were still around for a little longer than that.

Then a major, who was probably the camp commander, spoke to us.

'Proud soldiers of the Gross Deutschland,' he said. 'Your arrival in this sector fills us with joy. We know your reputation for courage in combat, which gives us a strong sense of support. Your comrades-in-arms in the infantry regiments fighting in the Polish forests near our frontiers feel as we do. Your arrival here reassures and comforts us, and also helps us in the extremely difficult task which has fallen on us: the defence of German and European liberty against the Bolsheviks, who would take it from us, employing the most extreme and bestial means. Today, more than ever before, our unity in combat must be total and deliberate. With the addition of your strength, we shall build a definitive rampart against the Soviet horde. Think of yourselves as the trailblazers of the European revolution, and feel proud that you have been chosen for this undertaking, however heavy it may be. I wish the greatest possible glory for you, and convey to you the congratulations of the Führer and of the High Command. Transportation and food have been specially placed at your disposal to help you in achieving

481

your aims. Bravo, soldiers, and courage. I know that so long as a single German soldier remains alive no Bolshevik will ever tread on German soil. Heil Hitler!'

We gaped at the elegant officer in stunned silence, trying to penetrate the veil of ignorance which hid our valour from us.

'Heil Hitler!' shouted a feld, who realized that the pre-scribed response to the major's remarks had not occurred.

'Heil Hitler!' we shouted heroically.

'Either I'm crazy,' Kellerman muttered, 'or he was expect-ing us to raise his morale.'

'Ssht,' said Prinz. 'We're getting another speech.'

This time, it was a hauptmann.

'It will be my privilege,' he said, 'to take two-thirds of the men in your regiment under my command, and lead them into battle.'

We all had known what was waiting for us, but that phrase made us swallow hard.

'The entire division will be operating in a sector to the north of us. It will be broken up into several fragments so that a series of widely scattered attacks can be made against the Russian thrust, which is extremely strong in this sector. I am expecting from you the utmost in courage and actions of distinction and glory. These are essential because we must stop the Russians here. No negligence or hesitation will be allowed. Three officers can constitute a court-martial at any time, and sanction any penalty. . . .'

(Poor Frösch! How many officers decided to hang you?)

'We shall be victorious here, or be covered with shame. No Bolshevik must ever, I repeat, ever, set foot on German soil. And now, my friends, I have some good news for you. There is mail for some of you, and citations, and promotions. But, before giving free reign to your joy, you must present yourselves at the store for fresh rations and ammunition. Dis-miss. Heil Hitler!'

We broke ranks without any clear idea of our situation.

'Things are looking up,' I said.

'A bastard who'd be glad to see us all killed,' muttered Hals.

We were standing in a long line in front of a large wooden building.

'So that's what we get instead of Wesreidau. Something tells me we'll be having a few eye openers, Prinz.'

'Impossible. We've already seen everything there is to see.'

'He's another one of these madmen,' said Hals.

'He's not. He's perfectly right,' said another voice behind us.

We turned around in surprise.

'He's right. It has to be here, or not at all. I can't explain why without taking too long . . . but he's right.'

More and more disconcerted, we stared at Wiener without saying a word, unable to grasp his attitude, which suddenly seemed so changed.

'I'll tell you why some other time,' Wiener said. 'For now, you're too thick to get it.'

Paula,

As I write, I'm looking at the letter I've longed for so much, and as I read your lines, I forget the icy ground, and the East, which is still so filled with menace.

Your letter, which is in my hand, seems like a miracle from heaven.

I don't expect anything more from the ordinary world, from which we seem entirely cut off. I read your lines as our comrade Smellens, who is lucky enough to believe in God, recites his prayers.

Nothing can help us any more, Paula. Prayers seem like vodka – they blunt the cold for a moment.

Happiness has become entirely relative, and can mean simply daybreak, because darkness makes us think of death.

I have been promoted to obergefreiter, and although the stripes are still in my left pocket, I already feel that much more important.

I think these extraordinary and difficult moments have made us into men.

I can hear a roar in the east, Paula, but maybe it's only the wind.

I look forward so much to reading another letter. . . .

For several days now, we had been fighting again as we retreated. The Bolsheviks must never set foot on German soil. However, three powerful Soviet armies had already crossed the German frontier at five or six points, penetrating to a depth of some thirty miles. These three armies had rolled over our defending troops, whose survivors were dragging with them through the autumn countryside the last weapons which supported their claim to be part of an army.

To my regret, I am unable to retrace in detail the chaos of those bitter moments. But I can outline the ends of my friends, like Prinz, Sperlovski, and Solma, and of Lensen, who, in spite of everything, was really a friend. And it is Lensen I wish to salute now, by describing the tragedy of his death, which I can still see clearly, through the memories of so many other deaths. Whatever Lensen may have thought of me at times, I am certain that for all of us, and for his country, he was a brave man, who would have sacrificed his life without hesitation to help the most insignificant fellow soldier. The manner of his death fully supports this view of him, and it is perhaps because of him that I am sitting here now, writing these lines.

Lensen could never have accepted life as it is lived today, with all the concessions the former troops of the Eastern Front are obliged to make. Like the order for which he died, he was irreversible. Men who have embraced one idea can live only by and for that idea. Beyond it, they have nothing but their memories.

Our attempt to save the Courland front failed, and the overpowering Russian thrust reached the Baltic at several points, which I can no longer locate with any precision. The Northern Front was cut in two – the far north, around the Bay of Riga, as far as Libau; and the sector to which we were sent, a continuously shrinking front to the west of Libau, in Prussia and Lithuania, clinging farther south to the Vistula, which was the scene of hideous carnage.

The division was split into several small groups which attempted to throw the enemy off balance by attacking simultaneously at many points. For the most part, these attacks were unsuccessful, and were hastily transformed into defensive actions. At that time, the division was precipitately attempting to regroup, in order to establish a defensive front some forty miles to the northwest. The bad roads, lack of fuel, mud, and faltering communications combined to slow down an operation which, under good conditions, wouldn't have lost us any time. In addition to our other difficulties, we had to contend with enemy aircraft, which had become increasingly active. Each overflight spread fresh disorder through our already weakened columns. When the order to regroup came through, our officers decided that the retreat should be spread out, and divided into small groups. This idea made sense in that we offered less of a target to planes. However, when an enemy armoured unit ran into two or three widely dispersed companies, our chances of survival were at best problematical. It was under these conditions, in a village of scattered houses, that an encounter took place which almost erased our group from the divisional list.

'I'm sure I've been here before,' said Lensen, who was shocked by the misery of the country. 'Everything looks so different now that I don't recognize any details, but I'm sure that over that way there are some villages I know. My own village is about sixty miles from here,' he gestured toward the southwest. 'Königsberg is over that way. I've been there several times, and once I went to Cranz, too. It was raining cats and dogs, but we went swimming anyway.'

He laughed, and we listened.

Despite the crushing retreat and numbing cold, Lensen seemed to have revived on his native soil. But he felt the anguished silence of this village, whose inhabitants had fled the day before, more intensely than the rest of us. Three hundred of us, exhausted by a march, which had begun at dawn, of twelve miles over waterlogged ground, were sitting doubled up for warmth, waiting for an uncertain eleven-o'clock distribution of food. Only Lensen was on his feet, pacing up and down the length of the stable wall, which the rest of us were leaning against, sheltering from the incessant rain. We heard his voice against a background of explosions which were more or less loud, more or less distant, coming from the southeast. We scarcely noticed the sounds of war any more. They had become so much the ordinary background of our lives that we no longer paid any attention to them unless they were inside a perimeter small enough to threaten immediate danger. Except for the noise to the east, everything was quiet. We were somewhat like people these days who cannot enjoy peace and quiet without a phonograph – who need noise before they can relax. Perhaps they are simply afraid of true silence. Unfortunately for us, we had no control over the volume of noise, and in fact would have been much happier without it.

Except for Lensen's harangue, nothing was happening. Some twenty-five yards from us, six men were preparing lunch. Somewhat further off, another group were seriously engaged in attending to personal needs. Others were resting, with their eyes half closed, or staring into space, dizzy with exhaustion. The melancholy autumn weather brushed our faces with its damp freshness. We had been through so much misery that we were unable to appreciate conditions which ordinarily would have moved us to pity.

Through our condition of near torpor, we were dimly aware of suffering and weeping. The wounded were groaning and dying. But none of that stopped anyone from sleeping whenever there was a chance.

The first part of our meal had been passed out: cellophane sausages stuffed with soybean purée – one for every two men. It goes without saying that these were cold. During the retreat the men in charge of supply, with a stirring display of professional conscience, had collected enough old and wrinkled potatoes to fill a sidecar. They were just handing them round to the men when four soldiers jumped over a wall. They were gasping for breath, and as they ran toward us they made large, sweeping gestures with their arms. One of them called to us without shouting too loud: 'Ivan!'

The sluggish mass of men stood up with a single movement. We knew that the next few minutes could face us with the most appalling danger. With the instinct of hunted beasts, we had already scattered – each man running to wherever he saw a possibility of the slightest protection. Those who were lucky enough to have already received their food wolfed it down hastily. Lieutenant Wollers had just joined us in a recess sheltered by a roof. His field radio, which he always kept near him, was already crackling out an alert. We waited in silence for about ten minutes, but nothing happened. The Russians could not have been very far off, as our sentries had announced them. But none of us knew whether we would be dealing with a section or a squad, a regiment or ten men. We hastily organized patrols. We had to find out whether we were going to fight or run as fast as we could.

The six fellows nearest Wollers were sent over toward the wall our two sentries had jumped. I was among them.

Two other groups of about the same size were sent in other directions. To describe my desperation and terror would be repetitive; it was the same as at Outcheni, Belgorod, the sheds where the partisans had hidden, and so on.

Like everyone else, I was resigned to the bad moments of our existence – to the sinking feeling which comes with being ripped from sleep to meet some disagreeable obligation. This was like that, only more so.

We moved along the other side of the stable against which we had been dozing a few moments before, and came out onto a rough piece of ground stacked with old timbers.

We were fully aware of our danger, and a heavy sense of desperation, which no longer accelerated the beating of our hearts, made us alternately hate death and long for it. My Mauser weighed down my hands like an object of no value, on which I could no longer count for anything. Formerly, as we marched through Polish and Russian villages, its weight of wood and metal had given me such a sense of confidence that I had felt almost invulnerable. Today the possibility of organizing any kind of effective defence with these weapons seemed entirely unlikely.

We crossed the waste ground and arrived at a cluster of buildings, where we separated into two groups of three men each, and continued to advance as carefully as if we were carrying explosives. We turned the corner of the building, and were able to see a much larger piece of the horizon, marked by a line of trees which had been almost entirely stripped of branches. Beyond the trees was a road, swarming with men. In the distance, we could see still more approaching.

'There must be at least three or four hundred of them,' whispered the man next to me. 'Look over there.'

We walked back past the building where we had been resting earlier. At its far end, a row of tar barrels stood out very black against the chalky soil. Beyond them was a small house. Our steps made a light crunching noise against the fine gravel. Still silent, we stepped into the space beyond the barrels. We took four steps and found ourselves face to face with four Russian soldiers on patrol, who were taking the same precautions and observing the same silence we were. For us, all process of thought froze.

Our gestures were without haste. The Russians opposite us were also moving very slowly, and watching us. It seemed as if, by some miracle, the same calm had been imposed on both sides. No one fired. With deliberate, calculated movements, both Russians and Germans withdrew to the shelter of the building. We stared at each other with enormous eyes.

'We've seen enough of them,' muttered Wiener. 'Half turn.'

We went back to our starting point, and Wiener made his report. We felt as if we'd been dreaming.

A quarter of an hour later, we had set up our defences in the northern part of the village and its approaches. According to our intelligence, we were involved with an infantry regiment of some two or three thousand men. There were three hundred of us, but we were not ordered to retreat.

Hours of agonized waiting went by. We were used to lengthy Russian preparations, but we also knew how steady their thrust would be. By the time the first contacts occurred, it was already growing dark. The first Russian assault units moved carefully up to the buildings under cover of dusk. The waves of Russian infantry no longer had the same dash as at Belgorod or on the Dnieper. Such astounding losses had been inflicted on those howling mobs throughout the reconquest of their territory that the Russian High Command had been obliged to conceive a somewhat less heroic tactic. Also, although they were fiercely determined to revenge themselves on us by trampling on German soil, they were fully expecting us to mount a desperate resistance. And they had come to count more heavily on the effectiveness of their tanks and aviation to reduce our smaller, underequipped units.

On our side, the magnificent lines of shouting soldiers were becoming increasingly rare, while the Bolsheviks were increasingly fighting in a 'European' style, using techniques more or less learned from us. This shift did not make our position any easier. Our group fired at a Russian patrol leaping toward us, but we saved our mortar for later; we were beginning to run out of shells.

This was only a small encounter, which seemed without importance to men accustomed to tornadoes of fire — a few fragments of brass hurtling through the dusk, breaking a shoulder, crushing a breastbone, or carrying off a life — nothing, in short, which even approximated the pitch of a real battle. Of course, if the same exchange should take place in Paris today, it would be considered sufficiently serious to empty a whole section of the city, and make all the headlines; each time has its own habits and style. . . .

Throughout that black and foggy night, the Russians continued to dig in beside our precarious positions. The thought that they might burst out at any minute was terrifying enough to make us sick. Perhaps this evening would be our last. Ivan would overrun us and put an end to this desperate chase which had lasted for nearly two years and covered thousands of miles marked with fear and blood. Probably tonight would be the night; we no longer knew what to hope for. But the night went by — a night of cold watchfulness broken by flares and distinguished by nothing in particular. The Russians, who seemed to be in no hurry, watched us, as we watched them.

I even managed to sleep, despite the watch we were supposed to keep unbroken. Several others did the same, and it was only the cold that kept us from having a real rest. Finally, dawn broke, and with it our tension increased. The air and ground shook. The rain, which usually muffles noise, seemed to have no effect on the heavy grinding of chains and the percussive exhaust of a large number of armoured vehicles. A column of tanks was driving toward the motionless village, where Russian infantry was already waiting, calm and resolute, for our deaths.

We knew that there were not enough of us for any kind of defence against tanks. We had no anti-tank guns, and the few Panzerfausts we had left would never be able to stop that mass of tanks, which we judged from the noise to be quite large. Our hair bristled with cold and fear as we organized our disengagement with the speed that had become familiar. Everyone was on foot except for the drivers of our two sidecars, which were used for liaison between the command group and ourselves. Ten soldiers were harnessed to each gun, as we couldn't let the Russians hear the sound of engines. The company withdrew in a silence worthy of Hollywood Indians, leaving just enough men to form three interception groups. Each of these was made up of ten men, with two Jägerpanzerfausts, and four covering riflemen.

My group included Smellens and a young boy who had been specially trained in handling a Panzerfaust. Lindberg, two other fellows, and I covered them. This proved to be the only time I was ever in command – a unique and tragic time during which I was responsible for five other men.

In the second group, I knew Lensen at the Panzerfaust. In the third group, no one.

Each anti-tank group had three Panzerfausts – heavy, cumbersome weapons which allowed us a total of eighteen chances. With maximum luck, if we hit home every time, we could hope to stop eighteen of the sixty to eighty tanks we knew were coming toward us.

We stiffened with terror as we grasped the desperate reality of our situation. Lieutenant Wollers told us that the enemy was slowing down, and that when five or six of their tanks were in flames their demoralization would increase. He said that we would rejoin the company within twenty-four hours. But nothing could distract us from the horrible mathematics of the situation. We knew too well that the implacable thrust of the war could not be stopped. Today, on this day accursed of all others, our turn would probably come.

The rest of the company moved silently past us, as we listened to the final recommendations of our superior. The rumble of tanks continued unbroken. I saw Hals going by beside the veteran, and ran out to grasp his hand. Lieutenant Wollers stopped talking when he noticed me. I produced a few obscenities for Hals and Wiener, inappropriate to the gravity of the moment, and briefly considered giving Hals something to send to my family later. But I couldn't find anything, and limited myself to a hoarse laugh. Hals couldn't think of anything to say to me, and Wiener dragged him off.

Wollers left us next, and our groups separated. I remained alone with my command, and with my doubtful friend, Lindberg, who had turned white and numb with fear. I – much too young for the job myself – had become a group leader, charged with dragging five other boys who had not yet attained their majorities into a horrible game of cops and robbers. I threw a quick glance at my subordinates. They were staring toward the south, where the noise was coming from. Lensen shouted, and waved toward a dip in the ground where there were four or five buildings – probably a farm. I and my group ran after Lensen. The third group looked for somewhere to hide along the road.

The wind was blowing in gusts, carrying the first half-formed flakes of the season. At that moment, the Russians began to pound the positions we had just left. The houses in the village about half a mile away were surrounded by geysers of black earth. Hastily, I sent my two jägers to a position among the large roots of some overturned trees. They began to dig frantically, trying to lower themselves a little deeper into the ground.

The rest of us looked for shelter nearby. I was with a young fellow whose name I forget but whose expression of determined tenacity remains ineffaceable. Lindberg and our sixth man ran into the house behind us. A hundred yards to our left, I could see Lensen and his assistant. The Russians were pounding the village into the ground. It was lucky we had left it when we did.

As we listened once again to the noise of tanks rolling through smoking ruins, we relived the sensation of waiting through the unbearably long minutes just before action begins. We tried hard to think, but the diabolic round of our past unwound through our memories – good and bad moments in a rush too fast for any of the relief tenderness can bring. For me, there was a mixture of childhood, the war, and Paula – and all the things I still had to do and should have done: the kind of debt which weighs on the heart, when time for settling has run out.

We were all torn between wanting to weep and run away, and to scream and run out to meet the danger. 'No Bolshevik will ever tread on German soil.' But they were there by thousands, crushing it with frenzy and jubilation – and there were eighteen of us to stop them: eighteen young men ready to cling to any miraculous superstition to go on hoping for a future as tormented as the present.

Then they appeared, ten of them at first, following the road guarded by our third group.

The third group watched them coming and did their duty. We helped them, inspired by almost unbearable emotion, played out by thousandths of a second.

The first tank was stopped some twenty yards from the two Panzerfausts in the third group. One of their projectiles burst on the tank's front apron scattering a shower of rivets and killing the monster and its occupants. The others were slowly manoeuvring, heavily attacking the incline of the bank, to make their way around the burning tank.

I couldn't stop myself from whispering. 'They're coming for us.'

But the tanks – three to be exact – climbed back to face up to the threat. They hoped to frighten the anti-tank crew, counting heavily on their terrifying appearance – a calculation which almost always worked. However, a second monster burst into flame. The tank behind it brushed past, opening up a passage. It reached the German position, and broke its occupants' nerve. We saw our comrades jump from their hole and run like madmen. They were trying to reach the woods, and began to climb the hill. The tank, which was following right behind them, drew so close it almost touched them, before knocking them to pieces with the machine guns on board. The rest of the defence suffered the same fate. In three or four minutes, the third group was knocked out. Ten or twelve tanks were roaring down the road the company had taken – on foot – an hour earlier. They were certainly too far for us to try to reach them with any prospect of success. Five more tanks appeared, following the dip of the valley, driving straight at the farm and at Lensen, who was just in front of it.

Lensen and his number-two man fired at the tanks, which were about twenty yards from them. They hit two, and the noise of the explosions flooded the valley with a wave of sound. A third tank passed the two wrecks and seemed to be heading directly for my group. Lensen's group fired a third time, missing the tank and nearly killing us. A building some five yards from our hole burst into flame. The explosion half buried us, and made us totally deaf for nearly a minute. The three tanks continued, pouring fire into the farm buildings. They must have thought our defence was centred there. Two more T-34s which had just appeared on the road left it, driving at Lensen's position. They were out of our range, but we fired at them anyway. Smellens fired at a tank some 150 yards away and just missed it. The shell touched the ground, bounced off it, and landed farther off without exploding. All we had done was to draw their attention to us. One of the tanks drove straight at us, using all its guns.

I could hear the shouts of my men. They were unable to fix their sights on the huge machine, which drove at the ruins of the house and skidded over them, probably in the belief that they were crushing us beneath their tracks. I could hear the grinding from my hole – a sound I shall never forget.

The monster stopped short and turned back toward its original route, along the road.

Lower down, the David and Goliath battle between Lensen's group and four more tanks, all firing with all their guns, continued. We heard the final crash of Lensen's Panzerfaust. The tank closest to them turned back on its tracks, bumping the tank behind it. We could hear horrible screams through the demented confusion of smoke and flame. A T-34 drove straight over the hole which sheltered Lensen and his companion. Then it reversed, and levelled the place. So Lensen died, on the soil of Prussia, where he had wished to die.

For us, the nightmare went on. If the tanks left us to continue their advance, we would be in terror of the infantry, which must be right behind them. In a state of indescribable fear, we looked about us. By 'we' I mean myself and my companion in our hole, and the two others, who remained as motionless as the roots that sheltered them.

What had happened to Lindberg and to the sixth man in my group? They had probably been crushed in the debris of the building knocked down by the tank. For the moment, that was the only possible conclusion. I also knew that the group on the road had been knocked out, and that Lensen had died a horrible death. Where were the rest of his men? Perhaps they too were lying under the rubble of the farm. Probabilities and possibilities poured through my head. It was most unlikely that any of us could remain unseen against that pale grey soil, where every protuberance was marked by a dark shadow. I thought of making a break for it, but quickly realized that every way out was in fact impossible. I might head for the pine woods to the left, but that meant at least three hundred yards entirely in the open. The Popovs would be sure to see me before I had gone even halfway. There was still a lot of smoke, but most of it was rising vertically and wouldn't hide anything.

Suddenly, in a spasm of egotism, I felt myself caught in a trap from which there was no escape. I was so sure of this that I ordered my companion to shoot me. He was feeling much as I was, and stared at me with anguish.

'No,' he said. 'I could never do that. But I wish you would kill me. Please kill me.'

Caught in our grotesque dilemma, we stared at each other, full of mistrust and rancour – each trying to hand over sole responsibility to the other.

'We're going to die here, you bastard,' I snarled. 'So shoot me. That's an order.'

'No. No, I can't,' he sobbed.

'You're afraid of being left alone, that's all.'

'Yes. And so are you.'

'But don't you see there's nothing else we can do?'

We could hear the sound of fighting. It was coming from the north – from behind us.

'Those bastards must have caught up with the company,' I said.

The noise continued. We stared at each other, motionless and silent. There was no more to say, because everything had already been said a long time ago.

Then my two forward men appeared, and a few moments later Lindberg, dragging along with him a fellow with a badly swollen face. We all squatted down, and then someone noticed some men whose moving figures blotted out the ruins of the farm. They were moving forward by cautious leaps, toward the woods, some 150 yards to the left.

'We should get over there too,' pleaded Lindberg. 'The Russians are nearly here.'

'That's easy enough to say,' I answered. 'But look at the open ground we'd have to cross. The Russians would see us right away.'

No one could argue with that. Everyone looked from the woods to the edge of the village to me. If only, at that moment, I had possessed the conviction and the decisiveness to impose on the others an idea of what to do, to take responsibility for the men entrusted to me. I remained as I was, incapable of dealing with either the circumstances or the men, who were looking to me for some sort of initiative. The damning appraisal Lensen had once made of me seemed crushingly true: I was unworthy of command, incapable of leading.

And it was here, a hundred yards from the site of Lensen's heroic death, that my incapacity manifested itself.

I remained where I was, overwhelmed by the thousand miseries of our situation, internally sobbing with despair.

I felt that my companions would make for themselves the decision I was unable to impose on them with any authority. Was I a simple coward? Wasn't I really as bad as Lindberg, whose all too obvious fear had so often disheartened us? I no longer wished for death, but simply cursed my existence, which had become a series of nightmares.

On that day, at a critical moment, I failed. I failed in everything I had hoped for, from others and from myself.

My head wobbled on my neck like the head of a drunk at the moment when his condition changes over from hilarity to despair. I was there, fully conscious, aware of everything, but paralysed by insurmountable panic. I shall never forgive myself for that instant, when reality touched the deepest recesses of my being.

Minutes went by, and my condition remained unchanged – minutes I should have been putting to good use. Fear nailed me where I was, in the midst of five other human beings who were all on the brink of madness. I was no longer trying to see where our danger might be coming from, but was turned inward, on myself. I found nothing but despair.

We could hear more tanks – the grinding of tracks and the roar of engines. I began to tremble uncontrollably, unable to tear myself from my obsession. The others were clinging to each other, their faces distorted with fear, ready to scream.

Lindberg stood up, in spite of himself. He wanted to see what was happening. He had lost his gun and was no longer thinking of defending himself. A wild thought had entered his stunned mind. He fell forward, across the edge of the hole, trembling convulsively, like me. He had just clenched his fists around two stick grenades. Death was stalking us, approaching with giant steps. This time, with a horrible shudder, I could feel its presence.

Once again, from all sides, we heard the firing of big guns. The explosions nearest us destroyed what was left of our lucidity. We were no longer in a state to understand anything, except that we could also hear the sound of a truck, quite nearby. Then we heard the barking of light machine guns. We stared at each other, without words. The sound of a voice speaking German fell on our incredulous ears. Behind the shattered building, beside a truck with a throbbing engine, some men were speaking German. We heard more tanks and automatic weapons, and stayed where we were, stiff with fear. A man leaned over our hole: a German officer. We observed his presence without really seeing him. Perhaps he thought we were dead. He went away again. But a few minutes later two Panzergrenadiers led us from that hole, and we followed meekly.

The anticipated German counter-attack had taken place, led by two S.S. armoured regiments, and had caught the Russians on the flank, inflicting heavy losses. We even took back the village for a few days, before continuing our retreat.

Chapter Seventeen

MEMEL

We moved back to the north, as a junction with the Courland front was no longer possible. What was left of the division gradually regrouped. The attempt to reunite the front had inflicted terrible losses. During this time, in a desperate lunge further to the south, the Russians reached the Baltic. Fighting of unequalled ferocity had taken place at many points through and around the swarms of terrified refugees, who made it very difficult for our troops to defend themselves.

The entire Prussian civilian population was fleeing toward the coast, in a tragic tide. We ourselves had two choices. We could turn south, opening a route through several advanced Soviet positions, or move back to the north, toward the newly established front at Memel. However, the divisional command quickly realized that we no longer had the means to move south, toward Königsberg, or even Elbing. Both towns were equally threatened, and the closest was some one hundred miles away. We would have to fight for every mile, with little chance of success and almost no possibility of picking up any food along this route of mass exodus.

So Memel was chosen: a short front which had been practically surrounded since the autumn. We would have to fight our way through, to make a passage for ourselves and for the flood of refugees moving with us, constantly slowing us down and often nearly paralysing us – a pitiful, imploring procession, dragging on foot through the bitter cold and the slush of the first snows. In spite of orders, we had to help, reassure, and support this chaotic wash of human beings. Everyone with an engine which would still run – even for an hour – carried a swarm of terrified children, trembling with cold and fear and God knows what else, while their families ran alongside, mixed in with the soldiers who were their last hope of protection.

We passed through towns and villages where the inhabitants had still been living a more or less normal life until four or five days earlier, although they had realized that their danger might become imminent at any time. Now, for the last two days, old men, women, and children had been desperately digging out the trenches, gun pits, and anti-tank ditches which were to stop the waves of enemy tanks. This pathetic and heroic effort before the infernal debacle which would sweep them into the flux of terrorized civilians was a preliminary shock for these virtuous civilians, who saw the front coming toward them in the form of exhausted, half-starved troops, tired of fighting and of living, who brushed aside human pawns without a qualm, as if they were pieces in a losing game of chess.

Every time a defence seemed possible, it was undertaken. The enemy at our heels were slaughtering the civilian population, who watched their approaching end in mute horror; the enemy had to be slowed down. The groups impressed into this effort accepted their fate in the ludicrous hope of putting out fires which were already raging. Their situation and sentiments were understood and their misery measured and valued by those who came to bid them farewell. These men had reached the point beyond which death seemed desirable, and still the war went on, like a blazing fire which no sentiment, however realized, could stop. Those who broke through and reached Memel would probably die at Memel. Death at Memel would seem a relief and release, and a more orderly end than death in a place which would never be distinguished by any military operation.

At this time and place, the absolute would be resolved by the absurd—unless, perhaps, they were already the same thing.

Finally, our division—which is to say, a third of it—broke through, and the command at Memel was able to include it in their strength. The division had broken through, and the fifteen hundred men it cost us simply represented another figure to swell the note of heroism. For those who had been in the fighting, besides the men who were killed, the losses included some twenty names which had to be scrubbed from the company lists, including Siemenleis and Wienke.

We might perhaps have fought our way into a trap. We even thought that perhaps the Russians had deliberately loosened their grip to let us through. We had brought along with us as many civilians as we could, but many others had stayed behind, and for them the game was nearly over. They had to dodge the tanks pursuing them, and multiple barrages of howitzers and quadruple machine guns, and Ivan's bayonets – all of which is very difficult for a mother with an infant at her breast and a small child hanging on to her skirts. But after all everyone is born to die.

We arrived in Memel with trucks pulled by men, and tanks serving as locomotives to trains of incredible length. We had reached the absolute limit of our capacities. Everything which still possessed a shred of human or mechanical life was moving, suppressing misery to a sense of gratitude that so much, at least, was still allowed them. Bombings stopped only those who were definitively dead. The rest – the merely wounded or dying – kept on, with burning eyes, pushing past the collapsing and the collapsed, whose bodies lay strewn along the road.

The town of Memel was still alive, in ruins beneath the flames, the smoke-darkened sky, the throb of Russian fighter-bombers, the heavy artillery, the terror, and the whirling snow.

Once again, I cannot find the words to describe what I saw. My impression is that all words and syllables were perfected to describe unimportant things. Words cannot describe the end of the war in Prussia. I was part of the exodus in France, fleeing the German troops which I later joined, and I saw mothers asking for milk at quiet farms. I also saw overturned cars, and was once even machine-gunned near Montargis. But my memories of all that are touched with only a small degree of anxiety, which is even somewhat intoxicating, like the memory of a trip on which one was not alone. Also, in France, the weather was beautiful. In Prussia, it was snowing and everything had been destroyed all around us. Refugees were dying by the thousands, and no one was able to help them. The Russians, when they were not fighting our troops, pushed the tide of civilians along in front of them, firing at them and driving tanks through the terrified mob. Anyone with a little imagination can try to conceive what I am talking about. Cruelty has never been more fully realized, nor can the word 'horror' ever adequately express what happened.

We had reached the Memel cul-de-sac, a half circle about fifteen miles across, backing onto the Baltic, whose cold, grey swells rolled in under a thick blanket of fog. We held this constantly shrinking space by some inexplicable miracle for most of the winter, harassed by continuous bombardment and permanent attack from the Russians, whose strength grew steadily as ours dwindled, overrun by thousands upon thousands of refugees. The extreme of misery to which these people were reduced can never be adequately described. They waited at Memel to be evacuated by sea, before the troops were taken off in mid-December.

The ruins of Memel could neither hold nor shelter the large segment of the Prussian population which had sought refuge there. This population, to which we could give only the most rudimentary help, paralysed our movements and our already precarious system of defence. Within the half circle we were defending, ringing with the thunder of explosions which covered every sort of shriek and scream, former élite troops, units of the Volkssturm, amputees re-engaged by the services organizing the defence of the town, women, children, infants, and invalids were crucified on the frozen earth beneath a ceiling of fog lit by the gleam of fires, or beneath the blizzards which emptied their snows over this semi-final act of the war. The food ration was so meagre that the occasional distributions which were supposed to feed five people for a day would not now be considered enough for a school child's lunch. Appeals for order and observation of the restrictions rang incessantly through the fog, which in part veiled the scene. Ships of every kind were leaving by day and by night, loaded with as many people as they could carry. Long files of refugees, whom the authorities tried vainly to register, moved toward the piers, creating targets for Russian pilots which were impossible to miss. The bombs opened hideous gaps in the screaming crowd, which died in fragments beneath these blows, but remained in line in hopes of getting on the next ship. These people were exhorted to patience, reminded of the rationing, and told to fast while they waited for deliverance. Old people killed themselves, and mothers of families, who would hand their children over to another woman, begging her to feed them with the ration card she herself was giving up. A gun taken from a dead soldier would accomplish these jobs. Heroism and despair were closely intertwined. The authorities tried to keep up the spirits of the crowd by speaking of the future, but at that time and place everything had lost its importance.

These martyrs often watched suicides without really trying to stop them. Some, in a surge of madness, shot themselves on the pile of bodies which civilian aides collected in each district. Capitulation would at least have put an end to this hideous nightmare. But Russia inspired such terror and had demonstrated such cruelty that no one even considered the idea. We had to hold, no matter what it cost us, until we were eventually evacuated by sea. We had to hold, or die. Or perhaps the High Command had another idea; perhaps they were planning to transform the stronghold at Memel into a bridgehead from which they would launch a counter-attack to split the Soviet thrust. This last speculation struck those of us holding the town as sheer fantasy. However, soldiers were still landing at Memel, as the civilians left. We could only suppose they had come to strengthen our position. The idea of a counter-attack seemed entirely unrealistic.

Here we fought with the stubbornness so much admired by the High Command, solely because we still hoped there might be some sort of launch left at the end to take us out after the last civilian had been evacuated. We had to hold on, even if despair had separated us from all other human conditions. At Memel, no one could stay out of the fighting; children and young girls dried their tears and helped the wounded, distributing food, resisting their desire to devour it, and suppressing horror and fear which were so fully justified. They performed tasks which their overburdened elders gave them, without argument or complaint. One either died or lived; no intermediate condition could be given any consideration. The children all felt this fact, without discussion or explanation. Those who survived this dramatic training would never be able to take the normal difficulties of normal life seriously. The German people really experienced the depth of things, and left me with an ineffable feeling of respect, which I can describe no further.

In the disorder of our advanced positions, civilians sometimes became directly involved in the fighting beside the soldiers; these civilians were often women. At the price of heavy sacrifice, the front held. By 'held' I mean that it did not crumble altogether. In fact, it was constantly yielding in one or several places, and constantly shrinking. The long anti-tank trenches we had dug beforehand played a large part in the consolidation of our defence. The Russians depended above all on their aviation and their heavy artillery – which they strengthened constantly – to knock us out.

Nonetheless, their attacks cost them heavily. The contraction of our front allowed us to concentrate our defence. Memel was ringed with innumerable carcasses of Russian tanks, and there were as many anti-tank gunners as there were ordinary soldiers. Carloads of mines were driven out by civilian volunteers and placed in front of our defences by the infantry in the course of small counter-attacks organized solely for this manoeuvre. We were defenceless only against aviation. Russian fighter-bombers flew over continually. To the northwest of our position the remains of several dismantled railway carriages underwent eight attacks in two days. What was left of our anti-aircraft defence was concentrated around the piers, where the peril was greatest. This target constituted a real danger to the Russian pilots, who preferred to attack the rest of the stronghold, where there was no serious resistance.

Thus, despite the hell of cold and fire and shortage, despite the names scratched daily from our lists, Memel, almost incredibly, held.

Then, one grey afternoon, some elements of our famous division were regrouped at a precise point. Ammunition for an offensive was handed out, and we were given two tins of food each, without regard to the contents. Some received a pound of apple sauce, others a pound of margarine. However, these variations seemed insignificant compared to the fact that the ghost of German military organization was still functioning during those days of grace on the fringes of a disintegrated city, which would still be known as Memel for a short time. Supplies, although obviously rationed to the limit, were still distributed before an offensive. Incredible as it may now seem, the vestigial remnants of the German Army in Memel were to attempt an offensive to the south, whose aim was to re-establish contact with the front at Cranz and

Königsberg. The officers who prepared the manoeuvre issued their directives to the disillusioned ears of combat veterans.

Hals and I were jolted from the void in which we had grown used to living. We were accustomed to the most astounding orders, but this time the fact that we were going to hurl ourselves into an assault with the incredibly slender means available to us made us tremble and reel with uncontrollable vertigo.

A few tanks which were still intact would support our progress. Matériel which belonged to the Courland soldiers, and even some from Germany, had been delivered. We were to proceed to a village some ten miles to the south, on the road which followed the coast, beside a large bay. The commanding officer of the operation chose a moment of appalling weather to launch his offensive. It was simultaneously snowing and raining. The atmospheric conditions were so disastrous that even the Russian artillery had practically stopped functioning. It was this circumstance which our leaders hoped to exploit on our last, lunatic expedition.

A dozen dirty-grey tanks went out to meet an inexorable fate. The black crosses painted on their grey sides, the colour of our misery, were scarcely visible. Inside the turrets, the 'Ride of the Valkyrie' was coming over the short-wave radios – a fitting accompaniment to suprême sacrifice. Decrepit trucks carrying field pieces and heavy machine guns followed close behind, replacing the full-track caissons of Panzergrenadiers of our prosperous days. A mass of infantry, mixed with the remnants of naval and aerial groups, ran along beside the motorized matériel. My group, in which, to my joy, I recognized the faces of Hals and Wiener, were clinging to the exposed chassis of an automobile which had been stripped of its skin.

With ludicrous ease, our point units surprised a camp of Russian armour lined up under the snow as if on parade. The Russians, staggered by this absolutely unforeseen blow, abandoned the camp, which we burned, using one of our special incendiary techniques. A supply of Soviet fuel allowed us to think of pushing our offensive even farther, and we went on, despite the gusts of wind which lashed our hands and cheeks. Several concentrations of Russian troops gave way before our surprise thrust.

However, the enemy was massed around Memel in depth, and as soon as they struck back, our thrust came to an end. We could hear the first Russian reaction, and knew that we would soon be inundated by a merciless rain of fire, and that the first Russian tanks were already rolling toward us.

As things were reaching a critical point for us, we heard artillery fire from the sea. The bad weather prevented us from seeing the ships just off shore, but their providential fire fell on the Red tide as it moved toward us. Two or three destroyers or torpedo boats had come especially to support us. Despite zero visibility, the coordinates supplied by our tanks in forward positions enabled the ships to fire with considerable precision, and the Russian thrust was more or less stopped. It was also possible that the Russians, who were further inland, misjudged the source of our fire, and supposed that we possessed more ground artillery than we actually did.

However, none of this made any real difference. The Russians possessed infinitely greater means than we did. Toward the end of the day, our meagre operation was attacked along a flank of some six miles. This was much more than we could take. Soon half our tanks were on fire. As foreseen, we had failed and were ordered to return to Memel – six miles back the way we'd come – which was far more difficult than the way out.

We abandoned the road we had followed for our last, epic attack – except for our motorized matériel, which separated as widely as possible when the Russians fired. In the darkness, striped with thousands of lights, breathless troops were running across the dunes from one hole to the next, valuing each step which brought them closer to Memel. As a crowning blow, the column had to cross a stretch of road we ourselves had mined that morning.

We tramped a mile lit by flares and streaked with white flashes. The road was narrow, but still more or less intact, except for a few shell holes.

The first vehicles drove full speed down that infernal space. The Russians had not yet had the time to adjust their aim, and their shells fell beyond us. However, their second round was more successful. Two trucks were hit dead on, and disintegrated. Two more, although they were mangled and torn, got through to less dangerous ground. The wreckage of the first two obstructed the road, and we were sent to clear it away. Ivan was now quite close, letting us have it with grenade launchers and peppering us with machine-gun fire. Despite our intense terror, we tried to keep on firing back as we climbed the slippery banks of flying gravel. The ditches where we might have found shelter had been mined; we were caught in a trap we had prepared ourselves. Several of our men fell, their arms flung outward and their eyes fixed for the last time on the dark, tormented sky. While we waited, our small band clung to the possibilities of survival. We waited beside the first two vehicles which had been wrecked and were obstructing the passage. All around us, Russian grenades were exploding, illuminating the darkness. A Russian quadruple machine gun was spraying the edge of the ditch, which was luckily somewhat higher than the road.

The Russian gun swept much of the wreckage from the road, jarring the shattered heaps further into disintegration with each salvo. Beside these fragments of metal, which had lost almost all their shape, lay two men in their ragged uniforms – men who, like us, had believed in a way out, and were now eternally at rest.

We would have to clear the road of the wreckage which still obstructed it, but anyone who stood up would probably be hit. Once again, Wiener, the veteran, emerged from our petrified group. On his knees under the flying bullets, he hurled a grenade at the first heap of metal and blew it from the road. The second wreck went up the same way. The third – a three-and-a-half-ton truck – required four grenades. Unfortunately, the wounded men inside the truck were blown up too – but that's war.

Toward midnight, at the height of the storm, two-thirds of our men were back in Memel. The command had become aware of our enterprise, and had provided covering fire. In a state of exhaustion, we arrived at the rear of our entrenched camp. Inventory of the missing was taken outside, among the ruins of a bathing establishment. Then, in the perpetual roar of noise from the front, we settled down and tried to sleep, even though the circumstances were so heavily against it that the attempt itself was an act of heroism.

The next day, toward eleven in the morning, when we had finished eating the rations distributed before the offensive, we were sent back to posts which had to be defended. In our dramatic situation, our rest periods could not be of any greater duration. Civilians continued to embark, despite all the risks this entailed.

Seas were running high, and all the buildings were covered with frost. Their human complement were waiting to leave from the jetty. Although the waves sprayed their bluish faces, there wasn't the slightest murmur of complaint.

Our troops continued to deny the Russians access to the town and its immediate surroundings. The possibility of evacuation by sea represented such a lifeline that a maximum effort was mounted to make it possible for us to hold on. Food, munitions, and medicines were sent in. On certain days our hammering from the Russians seemed to be diminishing, and despite the cold which grew daily more intense, life seemed easier. We didn't realize that the Soviet armies were concentrating their efforts farther south. Königsberg, Heiligenbeil, Elbing, and then Gotenhafen were increasingly threatened. The problem of refugees, as I learned later, was ten times greater in those places. The Russians abandoned Memel for the moment to cut further into Prussia, where they were met with desperate resistance. However, they swept it all aside. The three powerful Soviet armies which had entered German territory possessed means infinitely greater than those remaining to us. In addition to this, they were inspired by savage feelings of vengeance. The tortured population of Prussia were indelibly instructed in what this meant.

Elsewhere, scattered through the population, were Lithuanians, anti-communist Russians, Poles, and even English and Canadian prisoners, who shared our fate, even at Memel. The general terror of Russia superseded all national divisions and differences of opinion; it was a brute fact – simple and unassimilable. When no other course was possible, everyone fled – even the English and Canadian prisoners. The likelihood of being distinguished by the Russian assault units was too doubtful. Women of all ages were exposed to another form of outrage. The number of people evacuated by sea must have risen into the millions.

The veteran had carefully set up his F.M. in the ruins of a house whose walls rose no higher than three feet from the ground. From time to time he brushed the snow from the breech with the back of his hand, which had turned grey from repeated frostbite. Since our last attack to the south of the town, the veteran seemed to have regained his calm. The nervous excitement which affected all of us no longer seemed to touch him. He no longer took part in our desperate discussions, and seemed to have separated himself from all our sufferings. The war, the cold, and all the other horrors which plagued us no longer seemed to touch him. His manner was strange and we wondered about his frame of mind.

However, that morning, his F.M. had saved us from a Russian patrol which had become particularly interested in our group. Twenty Russian bodies lay stiffening in front of the Volkssturm truck which continued to function despite the fact that one of its back wheels was a thick log wedged against the chassis − another of the minor miracles of Memel. Then the Russians had sent a 50-mm. bullet under its hood, finishing off the two old men dressed as soldiers who sat in the cab. Hours later the damned thing was still blocking our view. The Russians had tried to use it as a shield to get close enough to wipe us out with grenades, but Wiener had riddled them with enough fire to finish them off too. Speed had been the critical factor, and Wiener had simply been the quickest. Now he sat in silence, wiping his gun as if it were a precious jewel. The rest of us − Hals, Lindberg, two others, and I − remained sitting in nervous agitation behind our cold, grey weapons, fully aware that they were no longer enough to guarantee our safety.

I had at my disposal three Panzerfausts, and the new P.M. which the Volkssturm had recently distributed − an extremely effective weapon which combined features of both the F.M. and the old P.M. I also had a small magnetic mine, which gave my stomach an extra turn. At Memel we each carried enough of an armoury to ensure a quick death − with all that load, there was no question of getting away quickly.

We were to hold our position for about two more weeks, fighting off more or less soft attacks every forty-eight hours. Our rear was no great distance from the front, which made it possible for us to rotate our rest periods at reasonably frequent intervals, and rest in a manner which was more or less refreshing. Not far from us, beside what was left of the street, was a signpost stating that we were five miles from the coast: the last five miles of our retreat from the Don – an almost incredible sweep of over a thousand miles, much of it on foot. As the veteran sometimes jokingly said to me: 'The same route your great-grandfather took with Napoleon, my boy. You might think of it as a family affair, if that's any consolation to you.'

Then, one evening, as we were returning to the damp and icy cellar we used as a dormitory during our rest periods, we noticed that the civilian population of Memel had almost disappeared. The last shipload of refugees must have left while we were at the front. We walked through the darkness of the town, which was more like an abandoned cemetery than a town, and returned to our cellar with something like joy in our hearts.

My companions sat huddled on their ragged pallets without talking, attacking whatever comestible Grandsk had been able to produce, without even noticing what it was. It didn't matter a damn; their attention was elsewhere. They were dreaming in the heavy silence, fixing their eyes, which burned with accumulated distress, on the dirty grey vault of our cellar. They were dreaming of the deliverance which must be near at hand, of the leaking hulk which would carry us out onto the sea against which we had been pressed for so long. They were dreaming, staring from their dark sockets with mad, transparent eyes, and it was understood that no one would speak. Their eyes, which had grown used to staring only at the war, had turned toward the possibility of an inner vision it was just possible to glimpse, with an intensity which I also felt in myself. They were dreaming, and so that the war wouldn't catch them at it, they tried to hide it, looking at no one and keeping their eyes fixed on some inner vision of hope.

I was the only one who saw them. I saw them because I had nothing else to see. I had already dreamed too much, and perhaps had lost that capacity. Too many of my dreams had been nightmares. Even if I had still been able to dream, I wouldn't have dared, because in the end, when one of the dreams came true, it was too painful.

So I no longer dreamed but watched the others, drinking

in some of their hope, and turning it for moments at a time into concrete images: worn boots on the slimy deck of a ship — boots, vomiting discoloured, empty uniforms. And then I would stop, because hope was so horrible. What forms did the hope of others take? It seemed that I no longer knew how to dream.

And yet I too still possessed this impatience, which we hid and cherished like a treasure which life had not yet stolen. I still had it too, and was hiding it inside myself. I felt it, and heard it, shrieking through my silence, shrieking so loudly that it overwhelmed me, like the noise of explosions. My balance was damaged by that sound, because I no longer dared lay claim to any particular hope or promise. I was afraid to ask too much, afraid that the least desire might seem like a demand.

I was still alive, and was afraid that somebody might notice. I had given everything else I had: my feelings, my anguish, my sorrow, my fear. I had also forgotten Paula, and, so that I wouldn't still seem too rich, I had forgotten that I was too young. I was not in very good health, but everything at Memel was hard. People with holes in their stomachs as big as fists were asked to be brave. Others, whose blood was pouring out onto the snow, fired at the war until their eyes grew glassy. I was lucky. In spite of my fits of coughing and my bloody phlegm, I still had a spark of life, which I kept hidden. One must no longer ask anything of anybody. Even if God heard our prayers, whatever we received would be consumed.

So I watched my companions as they dreamed. They too knew how dangerous dreams were in that place. Memel needed everything — dreams and hopes included. Men who still could hope fought better than those who couldn't. And we were all so tired of fighting.

From time to time one of us would emerge from torpor and scream. These screams were entirely involuntary: we couldn't stop them. They were produced by our exhaustion, by our organs, writhing with fatigue. Some laughed as they howled; others prayed. Men who could pray could hope, and for so many hope was dead — so they howled their prayers. In any case, it was too late. Even if their prayers had been heard, God would no longer have dared to appear. He had abused His mercy – as in the case of Smellens, who had died that morning. Smellens had wanted to die, but not until he had received some news of his little brother, whom he had only seen twice. With dry eyes, we had watched the road which should have brought us the post, but no news came. Smellens had hung on to life as long as he could; but here, in Memel, it was too late for the All-powerful.

During the following days the first military evacuations took place. First, the units which had been most sorely tried, with the gravely wounded given priority – except for the hopeless cases, who would be as well off dying in Memel as anywhere else. The silently impatient joy of the less seriously injured, who could go, helped them to forget their wounds, which were tortured by the cold. Gangrenous cases stopped thinking about the amputations which awaited them. It was as if a veil of confidence had drifted gently over the town. Except for the planes, which hammered at us continuously, life might also have become life again. Ships gutted by bombs blocked the approaches to the piers. Mutilated corpses floated in the debris. The Navy was performing a prodigious task. We would have been lost without it.

A barge packed with men had been bombed amidships by an adroit pilot who hit the bull's eye the first time. We were summoned from our rest period to deal with the mess. I shall omit the details, the memory of which still nauseates me. Our boots were red with blood. The human refuse which we threw off the front of the half-submerged wreck drew a throng of fish, and the smell of bodies torn open by gaping wounds is beyond expression, even though the water washing over the carnage diminished it somewhat.

The water in which we worked at first seemed warm in comparison to the air. After a short time, however, it began to seem like torture. Our gestures became slow and hesitant, and our hearts felt the wrenchings of pain which clouded our vision. We had to hang on. Two more ships were loading up with troops, and soon it would be our turn.

By mid-morning, the sky cleared. The pale sun attempting to shine over this scene of disaster filled us with unease. Any pleasure in the sun had long ago been killed for us. It invariably meant Russian planes.

Before we had finished our cleanup, the Russian fighter-bombers were overhead. This surprised no one. With good weather it could only be expected. Limping on our painful feet, we ran as fast as we could for whatever shelter we could find. All the true concrete shelters were used as first-aid hospitals, or shelters for the wounded. We had to huddle in the ruins, or in shell holes and bomb craters. We hid ourselves away in small clusters, and tried to concentrate on our imminent escape.

We could hear the anti-aircraft guns on all sides. Perhaps they would keep the planes away from the port itself. . . . But then we heard planes flying low overhead, making the icy air around us vibrate with their passage. We watched them, rubbing our fingertips, which were numb with cold, as they passed over the ruined town, and the men in rows, bowing beneath them like grasses in a wind. They passed over two ships which cast off their moorings to make less of a target. Five bombs fell simultaneously from the five planes gliding over the piers. Two fell in the water, where they burst, covering the waiting men with spray. A third scattered debris on the beach, while the last two opened a crater in front of a line of men who would not be leaving until much later. Bodies flew into the air. Some of the survivors gave way to despair, but those who still dared to hope supported them. There were no cries – except from a few wounded men, who howled without meaning to.

There were now some forty planes overhead, and others were coming up from behind the cliffs to the north. One of them exploded in the air; perhaps one of our guns had hit it. But there were no cries of triumph, as in the old days. Here there was only the noise of war; the men were silent.

The ships had drawn somewhat away from the piers, but the men waiting to embark remained in their places so they wouldn't lose them. The planes turned in the sky, probably looking for the most effective positions for letting go their bombs.

We watched, trembling with cold and despair. But no one questioned the sanity of the men who remained in line. We knew that, when our turn came, we would do the same thing. At that time and place, hope was worth everything – a fortune which there was no question of staking. Everyone there had invested everything their torments had spared them in the possibilities which those ships represented.

The planes came over again, and I hid my eyes so that I couldn't see. The rhythm was too horrible, and in the end I was only human, not God. I hadn't died on the Cross, and had no right to watch.

The days went by. Memel no longer existed, except on strategic maps. The front had shrunk, but a great many men had embarked. However, there were still thousands waiting their turn, shuttling between the positions they still had to hold and the semi-tombs where they slept their mutilated sleep. I still watched, through my dazed eyes, as these thousands wandered through the heights of tragedy, in a silence which, to my ears, drowned out all the noises of the earth. They had been stripped of their human condition, and I watched them in hideous loneliness, weeping internal tears as heavy as mercury.

How long were we there? For how many lifetimes? It is no longer possible to say, and the world will never know. I feel now as though I was born to experience that test. Memel had become the summit of my life, the ultimate peak, with only the infinite beyond it. We felt that after Memel nothing of us would remain, and that the life we would experience in the future would be like the crutches one offers to a cripple. Memel is the tomb of my life, the absolute. The silence which enveloped our groups had a miraculous quality, which allowed each of the living dead we had become to think about what would follow our misery. However foolish it may seem today, the thought that our wretchedness would be recognized later, even posthumously, was a comfort. Today, even this last concern has disappeared. Anything which might be said about our misery depends on a system of interpretation which is believed to be perfect. But the spectacle of Memel will not even be helped by the last judgment. It is growing dim and vanishing without ever having been seen.

We had left our cellar for a pillbox whose gun had been destroyed. I had stuffed my belongings into the space formerly occupied by the gun. Following my example, Hals, Schlesser, and another fellow had done the same. Wiener, Lindberg, Pferham, and seven or eight others occupied what was left of the turret itself. Our new lodging was less humid than the cellar, but that was not the reason for our transfer.

We had shifted because in our new quarters we were closer to the various points we might have to reach at maximum speed. Our defence perimeter had shrunk even further because once again the Russians had become interested in us. The German troops still holding the tiny Memel stronghold had to face the possibility of serious attacks which might prove decisive. As it was, we were often obliged to approach our positions with extreme caution. Our men, driven beyond desperation, sometimes surrendered to the Russians, who would then put on their captives' rags and wait for the relief.

Our wretched men had fallen into this trap several times. Even more often, in their exhaustion, they had failed to notice Ivan crawling toward them until it was too late. Then Ivan would replace them.

Wiener and two other fellows had almost fallen into one of these traps. The veteran had spotted it in time, and had exploded into the kind of rage we knew so well.

'He saved us,' stammered one of the men who'd been with him. 'He let them have all his grenades right in the face.' Both men talked in gasps, in an automatic nervous spasm. In fact, they both knew they were probably done for.

Wiener said nothing. He had recovered his silence, and lay prostrate against the bunker wall, which glittered with frost, while we looked at him. We had grown used to being saved by Wiener.

That evening, one of our men had tried to smoke a cigarette retrieved from a Russian cadaver. He had lit it and gone outside to relieve himself. Ivan had sharp eyes. He had spotted the glowing tip of the cigarette, and a 50-mm. shell had pierced the concrete, and burst in our comrade's back. He died without a sound.

'Ivan has come even closer,' muttered Pferham.

The next day, in a piercing cold, we went to our outermost position, which should have been in Russian hands for some time past. On our way, we passed the last tank remaining in that sector. It was an old M-2, which had already been on fire, and which bore the impact marks of many shells. Its own guns had been destroyed and replaced by others which weren't made for it. Each day it moved to a trench cut through the ruins of an alley, and held Ivan back whenever he tried to get through there.

The infantry in its neighbourhood had often rescued that old machine from contests that were too unequal, while the soldier gutter-rats infesting the ruins nearby held it in respect for the inestimable services it still performed.

Today, the tank's engine had broken down, and a team of ragged mechanics were labouring over it. We had huddled nearby to watch for a moment. One of the mechanics broke a tool and threw it on the ground in a rage. We heard the others talking. The machine was beyond repair. The men stood around, considering what to do with it. It had become a familiar part of our daily landscape.

Two planes had just flown over the ruins closest to us. All the tank crew took shelter beside the tank and stared up at the planes with feverish intensity. To our surprise, we found ourselves looking at two German reconnaissance planes. Where had they come from? They banked when they saw the tank, which no longer bore any insignia. For a moment we were all seized with a horrifying doubt: would the planes take us for Russians? We all stepped into the open and waved, with our arms spread wide, and the moment passed. The two planes flew over us very low, to the right. We could see the pilots. One of them even waved. They must have come from a German base – from Germany, where everything was still possible, perhaps.

Our grey faces followed their flight until they vanished. In imagination we followed them for longer still.

We were still faced with the problem of the tank. The passage of the two planes had given us a fresh stimulus. Everyone was standing around the machine. Someone suggested that we try to push it. Although it was a mad idea, we all took hold of the rough and icy metal. Shouting hoarsely, we tried to establish a rhythm. There were about thirty of us, hoping to synchronize our efforts. Our boots slipped and crunched against the icy ground, but the tank didn't move. Our emaciated bodies seemed to have lost their strength. The three crewmen swore at our impotence, but still the tank didn't move. After a hurried discussion, two of our men ran to the rear. We were about to follow them, when we heard the sound of an engine. There was also a truck left in Memel, which I hadn't known until that moment. However, it arrived, jolting and backfiring. Before it had quite reached

514

the tank the men had pressed pieces of wood against its radiator to protect it from the shock. Then it nudged up to the tank, shoving it from the rear. For a moment we thought it was going to stall too. Then, with a series of shoves, we managed to start the tank rolling, lifting it from behind, and letting it fall several times.

I stared at one of the slowly turning rollers. Its motion struck me as the essence of the miracle of Memel in miniature. The truck's engine roared, and our boots crunched against the solid ground. The tank rolled forward, and we continued on either side of it without losing our grip. My head was swimming from the effort, but I knew that something was happening in direct response to our will. Perhaps such knowledge is what constitutes joy. The heavy roller, studded with rivets, turned, and my eyes devoured it. It had also rolled across the infinity of the steppe, where part of my life had crumbled away, and it was turning now, just as I was still breathing. Joy is as simple as that. It would die, perhaps, within a short distance, as Hals or I might die, but until death came it would roll noisily down the slope. I felt very much akin to this huge metal object. In Memel, anything that moved was still alive. I was still alive. . . .

We returned twice more to the position. We would go again the next day, if we survived the night. However, that night Ivan was very much awake, raining death onto what was left of the town. The ground trembled continuously, and the sky was starred with flares. The light was as strong as broad daylight, reducing the luminous brilliance of the explosions. Our shelter cracked beneath the Russian blows, and as our lungs emptied of air, we sensed the presence of death. Wollers, our leader, tried to kill himself, but we pursued him outside and grabbed him by the belt. During the course of this rescue operation, one of the rescuers was killed.

Russian tanks had reached the hill to the south of our camp. Our soldiers who had been in the path of their advance had done their duty before they died. Then a heavy bombardment from the sea had struck the tanks as they slid over the dunes. Several tanks to the south of us went up in flames. The Russians were even forced to retreat a little, fighting as they went. The bombardment from the sea continued. Through the darkness and fog we could see the luminous discharges of the guns. With daylight, we were able to see the source of our help through heavy curtains of smoke. Two warships were standing close by the shore. One of them was the *Prinz Eugen*. The other was a ship of the same size. To the desperate defenders of Memel, they were a source of support we had never hoped for. The tanks respected their large guns, and kept their distance.

In the morning, we were supposed to return to the position described above. Overwhelmed by exhaustion, I had managed to sleep fitfully, like everyone else. Our sleep, under these circumstances, had its own peculiarities. We slept while we were wide awake, with our eyes open, like extinguished lamps. There was scarcely any difference between our faces and the faces of the dead. When I woke up, I wondered if I would still be able to move. My body felt like dead wood, and I no longer dared look at my arms, which were so emaciated they were like two sticks.

I felt an intense pain in my chest, as if another battle as fierce as the one outside were raging through my interior. Nonetheless, I had to wrench myself from my torpor. Everyone else looked as strange as I did. I stared at them all once again, as I stuffed my crumbling teeth with shreds of cotton torn from the hem of my coat. Their faces were as grey as the faces of the dead. One would have said they were dead – or else perhaps that nothing left in Memel was still alive, which seemed a distinct possibility.

We left. The Russians were firing haphazardly now, as if they were just passing the time – a bullet to the left, another to the right; after the night's bombardment, none of it seemed serious. As we drew closer to the front line, the chaos became indescribable. We had to climb through or over holes and protuberances of more than six yards. My head was spinning. I no longer had the strength of a child.

We could see the smoke hanging over the Russians' position as well. The Kriegsmarine must have scored several direct hits. On our way, we passed several fellows who were freezing behind their guns. They stared at us as if everything was our fault. We went on without a word. Manners, the weapon of the unmannerly, counted for nothing here. Everything was dead except courage, if that was still of any importance.

516

We had nearly reached our hole, with another 150 yards to go. I could see the earth heaped around it, and the empty munitions boxes, and the hole, where we would freeze for hours on end, and perhaps even die. What difference did it make where we were? It was just as cold in our bunker. . . . Anyway, to hell with it; I was still alive. . . .

But what was Wiener doing? He had stopped. I couldn't understand it – but it was all the same to me; I was so tired. But why was he firing? Wiener had set up his M.G. right on the ground, without even opening its front legs, and was sweeping the crest of our hole with short bursts of fire. Everyone else had instinctively found a hole. Hals was right beside me, but I couldn't look at him. He had grown old too quickly. He might have been fifty years old.

'We'll soon find out,' he muttered through clenched teeth.

The veteran threw a grenade which landed near our former position. What an extraordinary man Wiener was. If our own troops had been in the hole, they would have shouted.

The Popovs were quiet. If they had tried to fool us by shouting, we would have recognized that trick right away. But Wiener had obviously been right. They were firing at us now; that was their answer.

'Schweinhund!' shouted Wiener. 'Bastards!'

Wiener should have been a general, or even the Führer. We had more confidence in him than in anyone else. He was firing straight at those damned muzhiks. No one dared move – and to make matters even more disturbing, we could hear the noise of tanks coming toward us from behind the ridge of banked-up earth. We knew that there were one or two Russian tanks back there, which were now going to direct their fire at us.

Wiener had undoubtedly made the same calculations. He was sliding carefully backward, dragging his gun. To my left, one of our men had just been hit.

'Let's go back!' Hals shouted.

But moving back was just as dangerous as moving forward. Who could I think of to give myself more courage? My mother? Did I even have a mother? O Paula? But what good was my version of love in my universe? Of my own skin? My skin looked like Hals's, and I didn't have the courage to look at that any more. It's madness to have courage for nothing.... There was Wiener, our leader. He was worth dying for.

We had to abandon our friend Hans. His hip had been shattered, and under Russian fire we could do nothing for him. We said goodbye to him. He would know how to die, since he had known how to live at Memel. We didn't worry about it.

We reached a shell hole where we set up our two F.M.s ready to fire. As we had expected, the Russians were now plastering the area we had just left with fire from their tanks. The war machine was starting up again both to the north and to the south. The Russians were coming down into our trench. It was terrible to see them, and we felt half dead with fright. Wiener wasn't firing. He looked at us, and we looked at him, as if praying for advice. Reflected on his face, we could see the immensity of the disaster.

'Get out!' he shouted suddenly, his voice rising above the noise of the guns. 'Get out of here as quick as you can!'

We had already grabbed our things and plunged down into the bottom of the hole. We stopped for a moment, and stared at Wiener.

'Come on!' shouted Pferham.

'Shut up, pastor. You get out too.'

But Pferham had his duties, which kept him where he was.

'You go on, for the love of God. Clear out, and don't worry about me. I've had enough of fighting and retreating.'

'Wiener!'

'There'll be no room for me after the war, remember?'

The veteran had opened fire. He was firing like a madman at the Russians who were coming along the trench. Pferham called again, but the sound of the gun drowned out his voice. We ran back off that ground which was shifting and crumbling under our feet. The position was no longer tenable. Why didn't Wiener follow us?

Ten minutes later, we plunged down into our mortar and anti-tank positions. Five hundred yards to the east, we could see a thick cloud of smoke rising from the position we had just left. As the deluge of war poured over us, and the parapet of the gunpit trembled like the railings of a ship caught in a storm, we clung to our guns with trembling hands, as to our last salvation.

The fire from the ships made a critical difference to us. Without it we would have been overrun. The danger was so pressing that no one could leave his post. Through the sharp noise of the guns, we could hear the wounded groaning. Such a peak of tragedy was beyond understanding. Each of us felt alone, stripped of all feeling and all judgment. Perhaps there would not even be time for a few hours of rest before our deaths. The men waiting at the piers had gone back to points of defence. This was not altruism, but simple self-interest. They knew that if Memel fell, no one would leave. At a high pitch of fury, they drew on their last reserves of strength to keep watch, and prevent Ivan from destroying their calvary and their hope.

Memel still held — Memel, a small island of courage drawn from an infinity of anguish. But the boats didn't come. Had we been abandoned? Had this final reason for fighting vanished too? Was this the end?

However, the following night, a ship drew in to shore like a ghost. A crowd of dying men ran toward her, fighting among each other for places. No order could have held them back. In any case, the officers were in the same state as their men. Here, no one fought because a whistle blew. We fought because there was no other possibility.

It seemed that the ship had not come to pick up men, but food. We had enough food to hold out for another three months, but since we were to be withdrawn 'immediately,' these supplies should have been destroyed. However, to the south, there were hundreds of thousands of refugees who were dying of hunger and cold. The crowd which had collected near the shore heard the voice of the naval officer shouting through an amplifier. At first they couldn't understand these words, which seemed to be coming from another world, from a man whose floating mobility allowed him to see the worst from a distance. They vaguely grasped that from their misery they could still help other people farther to the south. A single word ran through their minds in an endless refrain: immediately ... immediately ... immediately. The boat loaded up with our supplies and took on a few wounded. Immediately ... The crowd stood motionless, wrapped in a silence as large as the night.

Our diminished group had been sent to the northern edge

of the stronghold, to a beach beside the sea, overhung by moderately high cliffs. We still held the clifftops, in bunkers which had been built facing the sea. However, the Russians had also reached the clifftops at several points, and even though they were not yet there in strength, they had sent out sharpshooters, who controlled the rocky beach along which we were crawling under their fire.

The German positions on these heights were fortified islands, surrounded by the enemy, and living on God knows what. There was no longer any question of the Gross Deutschland Division, or any other division. Everything which could still move in Memel was alive, and anything alive had to be used.

A ragged officer had brought us to this point, where he feared the Russians might break through our rear lines. Although the position was very dangerous, it was at least somewhat less dangerous than the official front. Tanks couldn't get through unless they reached the heights, which we still dominated and weakly defended. For shelter, we used the holes dug by civilian refugees who had waited here for deliverance by sea.

We were in almost constant contact with the Russians. Ivan moved along the length of the coast, peppering us from the cliffs. Sometimes he used mortars. The sandy soil was as churned up as if a harrow had been through it, and we were constantly digging out both the living and the dead. However, in this soft soil, the impact of missiles was usually dissipated. The Russians were just playing with us, but they gave us no respite. If our heads hadn't been empty, they would have burst with exasperation.

Although the cold was cruel, nature had also sent us fog, which was an ally. The Russians had infiltrated our lines, and were sometimes even killed from behind. They were afraid too and were hoping that support from their artillery and tanks would crush once and for all this cemetery where even the dead seemed to defy them. They infiltrated with great caution, and when they thought we could hear them, they shouted insults at us, telling us what they would do to our wives and mothers. They also said they were planning to remove parts of ourselves. Sometimes, too, they sang.

Hals and I listened, with our fingers on our triggers, because they often sang and shouted like that to distract us.

'Ai mayi drougii Germanski, kak sabatchi ch'olet! Ya tibai scajou spaciba ouyoudna mamenchka!'

Then they would count. 'Listen, German soldiers. You are going to die. Listen: raz, dva, tri . . .'

Then they would let off a volley, while we listened in silence, like antennae destined to pick up all the ignominies on earth.

During the night, two more boats came. At the risk of instant death, a crowd of ragged soldiers ran to board them. We were too far from the shore to get there in time. As the nausea rose in our throats, we stood powerless, trying to calculate our isolation. Every time a boatload withdrew, our defence was weakened to that degree. Nothing could stop Ivan now. As soon as the wave broke, we would run like rats. The long nightmare turned heavily in our minds, and we all trembled uncontrollably.

Hals had lifted his gun to his head. I must have stared at him with enough sorrow to stop him. He turned back onto his stomach, and crushed his face into the ground.

The next day, we were still covered with fog. The front was quiet. Were the Russians preparing something?

Hals and Schlesser had crawled toward the water, toward a smashed car which stood in the spray at the edge of the beach. I joined them, taking maximum precautions. Hals spoke in a half whisper.

'You help us, Sajer. We'll get those inner tubes. Three of them are still good.'

'To make floats?'

'Yes. A raft. But be careful. We don't have any tools, so we'll have to use bayonets. Do it like this – but be careful!'

I felt as if a shaft of light had pierced my mind. A raft. We might float for a long time, but this also might be our last chance. We had no tools, and we would have to get the tyres off the wheels without lifting them. Trembling with anxiety, we set about this desperate task. The inner tubes had to be full of air, otherwise they'd be no good to us. Pferham came over and joined us.

'You're crazy,' he said. 'Even if you get the tubes out,

521

they're sure to burst. After all, it's the tyre that holds the pressure in.'

It was true that we'd been half off our heads for quite a while now. We couldn't give up the idea of escape, and received Pferham's objectivity with ferocious scowls.

'Then let's take the whole wheel,' Hals said.

'I'm sure they won't float,' said Pferham.

'Shut up!' roared Hals. 'You stick to your God. Myself, I have more confidence in these tyres.'

Pferham said nothing more, and like the rest of us tried to free the nuts with the tip of his bayonet.

It took us at least two hours to complete the job. We also had to dig away the sand from under the right front tyre, as the wreck was lying on its side.

We could hear the sound of heavy mortars in Memel. The ground shook as far out as we were, and it seemed likely that the Russians had taken a big slice of what was left of the town. We no longer dared to think about what might be happening there, concentrating instead on the ridiculous work we had undertaken. Twice we were forced to give it up, and get back to our holes. The Russians were infiltrating all along our positions, crawling through the fog almost everywhere. Hals and I clung to each other in our refuge. For the seventh or eighth time, we had fired almost point blank on Asiatic-looking men, with Asiatic faces. Each time, our Volkssturm shook in our hands, and we trembled with fright.

By evening, the whole city looked like a volcano. Stalin's organs were howling without stopping, loosing a storm of random fire. Our shattered nerves no longer reacted. Everything was at once hazy and luminous. By now there were seven or eight of us fastening belts and boards onto the three tyres which would probably never float; seven or eight who would probably be killing each other within minutes, for it was clear that the raft would never hold all of us.

It was ready. Schlesser and Pferham pushed it toward the water. We followed, like wolves afraid of missing part of the feast.

'Wait a minute, I'll give it a try,' said Pferham.

We all took a step forward. Pferham looked at us. He

knew that if he went too far we would kill him. Our silhouettes wavered against the lights which were consuming Memel, and our eyes followed the movement of the raft as it pitched, half-submerged on the dark water which melted into the night and fog.

As Pferham tried to maintain a balance which every physical law made impossible, he must have prayed to the sadistic God who watched him sink. He didn't jump until the water had risen over his belt, as our safety foundered before our eyes.

The night passed slowly, lit by the huge fires. The beach, from which we stared with enormous eyes, shifted from pink to orange. A very young boy from one of the Volkssturm groups had succumbed to despair. His body remained wedged upright in the midst of our group, most of whom didn't even notice that he had died. Another suddenly stood up and walked off, as if hypnotized by the flames in the south, moving toward Memel in a state which was certainly not conscious. We watched him disappear into the brilliant, unreal half darkness.

The Russians could have taken us by surprise now, without any attempt on our part to intercept them. The horrified faces of the last soldiers in the armies of the East were fixed with fascination on the apocalypse of Memel. At daybreak, the fire over the ruins of the town had turned pale yellow, almost white. We were given no orders or co-ordinates, and remained where we were, motionless and almost senseless, lost in the hideous solitude.

Toward the middle of the day, Wollers, our leader, said that he was leaving for Memel. He didn't order us to follow him, but we did. Halfway there, we collapsed on the road. Our strength was gone, and the half mile we had been able to stumble was all we could manage.

Somewhere, a short distance to the east, they were still fighting. How was it possible that any of our men still survived? A heavy black cloud with a red base lay motionless across the whole horizon, and to the south, at the docks, there were other fires. Could anyone still be alive in that place? We lay where we were, prostrate and silent, with our eyes fixed on the enormity of the catastrophe. Hours passed. Our lives were running out, and our eyes had a strange fixity.

No one thought of opening the few cans we had left. We knew that any food would taste too bitter, with the taste of Memel.

Once again, darkness covered us, and our motionless group melted into the fog which lay like a winding sheet over Memel, and stagnated on the sea.

Another group of bent men walked slowly by some ten yards from us. They seemed somehow unreal. Were they German survivors still wandering through this little piece of the void which fate still allowed us? Were they Russians? Or were they, perhaps, a dream?

I don't know how long we stayed there. Perhaps for another day and night; no one can be exact about a nightmare. Also, it is a question of no great importance. Some things – like Memel – cannot be measured by any ordinary scale. I still need corroboration to believe that Memel really happened and is not the fantasy of a spell of madness. Describing it as I have done still makes me tremble with horror and suffer again, for even the memory is painful. The tomb of Memel, where no one has ever gone to meditate, will receive my recollections as a humble and discreet offering.

I make no appeals to humanity, and cry for no vengeance. Except for these lines I remain silent, because I have lost my power of discretion. I have also learned, in my solitude, that there is no power more unalterable than the power of forgiveness.

At some point, we became aware of sounds from the sea. Every sound from the sea could still mean life. We stood up and listened: the noise, which was scarcely audible, was muffled and heavy, like an idling engine. And then there was the sound of voices – at first, blurred and incomprehensible. We walked out into the water, scarcely aware of its touch. Through two bursts of thunder, we caught some words.

'Hier Windau! Hier Windau!'

They were asking about Windau, a city farther to the north. A boat with all its lights out was lost in the fog. The voice kept on calling. It was probably coming through a megaphone. We trembled, and shouted as loud as we could, with what was left of our strength: 'Windau!'

We had all run into the water, like madmen. The first shock revived us for a moment. We went on shouting, as the water reached our chests. Some men stumbled and fell, and then staggered to their feet again, still shouting. Soon the water was up to our chins. We thought we would pull off our clothes and swim. Then the vague outline of the boat emerged from the fog, and we shouted again. The boat scraped against the sand and stopped.

Half drowned, we went out to meet our salvation. Swimming, floating, sinking, and surfacing again, we reached the sides of the boat. We could just make out the men leaning over the side – sailors, who were throwing us lines and nets. They were asking us questions, but no one answered. We were all hanging on to anything that was thrown out to us, gasping and imploring. I thrust my fingers into a hole whose edge was encrusted with rivets. My fingers, half dead with cold, gripped like claws. Everyone was shoving and pushing for a rope or net.

The icy cold of the water began to break my will. Stiff with suffering, I kept my hold and fought against losing consciousness. An empty cigarette package floated from my pocket and lay on the water some inches from me. I stared at it to fix my wandering attention, and as I stared, my vision grew hazy.

Everything had become painless, and I scarcely felt the arms which were pulling me on board. They put me down on the deck, beside my exhausted companions. We were nothing but a shapeless, soaking mass, like a huge mound of wet sacking. Through my semi-consciousness, I realized they were passing around cups of boiling hot tea, which I swallowed down to the peril of my inner organs. My motionless gaze remained fixed on the flaming Prussian coast.

I no longer have any clear memory of what happened next. I don't really understand why we didn't die of exposure on the deck. Perhaps the sailors rubbed us to keep us warm. . . . I can only remember one thing clearly: the roar of the war coming from the land dominated all the sounds of the boat and of the sea.

Later, the boat arrived at Pillau, where we got off. On trembling legs, surrounded by a flood of refugees, we reached a first-aid station, where our physical condition was checked. A multitude of wounded men were sitting or lying all around us in huge open sheds. The little port seemed filled with a sense of feverish agitation and urgency. If the war had not yet arrived, it was nonetheless very close. We sensed its imminence, and could hear its thunder to the northeast.

Chapter Eighteen

CALVARY

PILLAU KAHLBERG · DANZIG · GOTENHAFEN
OUR LAST BATTLE

We stayed at Pillau for about three weeks. We had been declared unfit for service at the front, as we were all more or less wounded, and otherwise in a state which deserved treatment in a sanitarium.

Our liquefied brains were no longer able to grasp what was happening to us, or what was asked of us. However, although we were not in a condition to function under fire, this did not mean that we were exempted from service. The staggering flood of refugees which had poured into Pillau did not allow anyone who still had two arms and two legs to remain idle.

Along with others whose wounds were more serious than ours, we were absorbed by the first-aid organization which was trying to help the civilians waiting to leave, in the face of almost insuperable difficulties. All of these people had lived through a hideous exodus, and the horror of what they had seen was still impressed on their emaciated faces. There was also a swarm of wounded men, soldiers from Königsberg and Cranz, lying about wherever they could. This was often outdoors, in the intense January cold, which sometimes cut short their sufferings. Boats were still putting into Pillau, and leaving filled with people; three-quarters of each load was civilian, the rest, wounded soldiers.

This groaning crowd of men, clinging to a last hope of evacuation, was divided into two categories. The most severely wounded – those whose chances of survival were doubtful, who would at best be hideously mutilated – were not embarked. For them, everything was over. The rest, who might still have some hope of a decent life. were eligible for the boats, which, with any luck, would carry them to the

527

West, to that region we still imagined as a zone of relative quiet.

For every thousand persons embarked, some three thousand more arrived from the East, swelling the ranks of the mob which had turned to us for help.

If the fighting should reach us here, it would be the hell of Memel all over again, only worse. There were many more people here, and the numbers were continuously growing. People were coming in from the south, having crossed the Frisches Haff on anything that would float. They came from Heiligensbeil, Pomehrendorf, Elbing, and even from Preussisch Holland. They had been told that at Pillau they might be able to get on a boat.

We spoke to several of these wretched people. Almost everyone had lost one or two relatives on the way, and described in trembling voices scenes like the ones we had witnessed at Memel. We learned from them that the flight toward Danzig had been cut in two, and that the Russians had reached the Haff at several points. It sounded as if the horror of Memel was duplicated in almost every Prussian coastal town.

Swaying on our unsteady legs, we stared at the vast flood of human misery slowly washing toward the safety which had been promised. In spite of the most prodigious efforts it was clear that these people could not receive even a tenth of what they were expecting. If their prayers had been heard, heaven would have opened to succour their misery. But nothing happened, and misery subsided only for moments at a time, as on the tear-streaked face of a child who has collapsed into a passing sleep.

As winter closed in, the thermometer sank toward five degrees below zero, only aggravating the plight of the refugees and accelerating the death rate.

A crowd stretched as far as the eye could see, in front of a large building crammed with people. From the building a faint smell of the gruel cooking in large caldrons washed over the tightly compressed mass of people, who stood stamping their feet to keep from freezing. The thudding of their feet against the pavement sounded like a dull roll of muffled drums. The children were the most heart-wringing. Many were lost. When they tired of calling for their mothers, they collapsed into floods of tears which nothing and no one could console. These were the smallest ones, too young to grasp any explanations. Their faces, dabbed with tears which instantly froze, remain one of the most pathetic images of that time. We tried to gather them inside, near the caldrons, where they might feel some of the heat. We questioned them, hoping for some identifying information we could broadcast over loudspeakers, but they could only reply with tears and sobs.

Further on, a large metal cross, which stood on a slight elevation, glittered with frost. It looked like a huge sword, thrust into the breast of catastrophe. Another part of the crowd had collected here to listen to the prayers and encouragement of a priest.

The cold grew so intense that the Frisches Haff froze, creating new difficulties for the boats still coming into Pillau. The Frisches Haff froze, and despite the desperate consequences of such cold the fact was put to use. Hundreds of thousands, on forced marches across the ice, were able to reach the narrow strip of land at Nehrung, and Kahlberg, and finally, Danzig. People also left from the pocket at Heiligenbeil. They experienced every sort of hardship, including attacks from Soviet fighter-bombers, which tried to break the ice with strings of bombs, and often succeeded. Private cars and other vehicles of every kind frequently disappeared into crevasses covered over by thin films of ice.

However, nothing could hold back the flood of refugees, who were prepared to endure the most severe hardships. As the Russians grew increasingly active throughout the sector, large numbers of people left Pillau by this providential route. Russian planes were flying over Pillau every day, and it appeared that the defence of Königsberg had given way.

As the work at Pillau had become less intense, we planned to evacuate everyone who wasn't strictly essential. It was barely twelve miles from Königsberg to Pillau. The front at Cranz had also been shortened, and before long we too would probably be directly involved in the fighting. We were part of an inadequate reserve composed principally of fragments of broken or annihilated units, from which a certain standard of performance was still expected. No one knew any longer where the rest of the Gross Deutschland might be, but we still wore our divisional flashes on our worn and discoloured tunics, and there were still a few familiar names near me – principally, Lieutenant Wollers, with a dirty dressing on his right hand, which had lost two fingers; Pferham, our disillusioned pastor; Schlesser; Lindberg, who had survived his fear; and our cook, Grandsk, who had long ago exchanged his caldrons for an F.M.

There were also my friend Hals, whom I will never be able to forget, and I, who have consecrated the rest of my life to bearing witness. Then there were seven or eight others, whose names I never knew, who, with us, made up what was left of the Gross Deutschland Division in that area. Had our division been scratched off the list? Not yet, it seemed. An officer hailed us and ordered us to attention. Our eyes, which had already seen so much, studied this grey-faced hauptmann, who still clung to his sense of disciplinary strength.

This discipline, which had so often annoyed us in the past, touched us now like a soothing balm. Its demands were those made of living beings, of creatures still worthy of life. We analysed no further than that; for us, accustomed as we were to thinking only of the moment, this realisation was a kind of dividend. The captain spoke to us, and through his firm, official voice we caught the intense emotion of the crushing load which weighed on all of us: officers and troops, men, women, and children. The time of boasting and gratuitous bullying was so far behind us that no attitude incompatible with the gravity of the circumstances was possible. A man was speaking to us as men; no one could evade the situation.

However, this man still wore the vestiges of a military uniform, and was still trying to impose some semblance of order in a situation of cataclysm which had swept an entire nation into a devastating retreat. This man, who knew that everything was lost, was still trying to save the moment. He told us that we would have to withdraw; that we too would have to cross the ice of the Frisches Haff, and get to Danzig, where several sizable fragments of our division still remained. He tried to tell us, in a tone which was not peremptory, that there was still work for us to do as part of a particular organization which could be found where he had indicated. He was not trying to spare us a worse disaster when he gave us those orders; the worst was everywhere, and there was no escape. The hauptmann was already walking toward another group of men, saluting as he withdrew.

So we started to walk. A violent wind swept the snow from the mirrorlike expanse of ice. In the distance we could hear the gentle purr of the sea, behind us, the steady roar of war.

In the evening, we reached the Frische Nehrung, and the first anti-aircraft bunkers, which barely rose above the long grasses, bent over beneath their burden of snow. To crown my personal difficulties, I fell and injured my foot. It was forty miles across the Nehrung. I would have to make it anyway. For a long time now, I had known that fate was against me.

I found a broken broomstick to use as a crutch. So many people had suffered and died in this place that my minor discomfort seemed almost indecently trivial. We progressed very slowly. The hollow of a battered, overturned boat sheltered us for a few hours. We were not the only ones to use it; a group of shivering civilians were already inside, groaning as they tried to sleep. I buried my head against Hals's shoulder, hoping to pass out, despite our wretchedness.

We reached Kahlberg toward the middle of the next day. The small town was overflowing with starving refugees. People with the faces of madmen were wolfing down the flour which was the only food distributed to them. Cans of condensed milk were reserved for the children. Soldiers also had to stand in interminable lines, to receive, finally, two handfuls of flour apiece, and a cup of hot water infused with a minute portion of tea.

Our exhausting march resumed amid the pitiable swarms of faltering refugees. Twice we were attacked by Soviet planes, swooping low and scattering missiles which had been designed to destroy tanks. Each impact tore long, bloody furrows in the dense mass, and for a moment the wind was tinged with the warm smell of disembowelled bodies. Above all, I feared for the children, who could no longer understand anything about their situation. They didn't know that the planes were enemy aircraft, or how urgently they were faced with cold and hunger. Everything was a misery for them, and each step a trap. The sky could make them suffer, and the earth hurt them. Their hands and feet made them bite their lips with pain. They were lost in a state of constant fear, which was justified by a world of horror which never let them forget their pitiable weakness. They stared about them with unseeing eyes — at their swollen hands, which they wished were no longer attached to their bodies; at the people around them, who should no longer exist; and at the frozen grasses trembling in the wind, which they would never again enjoy as part of an innocent game.

I feared for these children, who were being punished before they had committed any crime, for whom the idea of existence would become synonymous with vengeance. I could do nothing but watch this tragic procession; even my life would be no help to them. I was not a redeeming Christ, and in any case I had discovered very good reasons for dying.

We reached Danzig three days after crossing the ice of the Frisches Haff. Everything was calm in the city, despite the tragic spectacle of hundreds of thousands of refugees. The war was to the south of us, so that we even escaped its noise, although frequent air raids struck at the heart of the crowded city. Danzig had become the terminal point of the Prussian exodus, and, although huge crowds were living day and night without shelter, there was nonetheless a substantial and organized effort to help them. It was still possible to leave for the West by rail, and the port was still open to maritime traffic. We waited down by the docks, in a dense mass of vagabonds.

Wollers went to a centre which should have been able to give us some information about reintegrating with our group. He waited for several hours under its flattened glass roof. I myself was in no hurry to move on, as the stiff folds of my boot pressed painfully against my swollen ankle.

A large ship had come into Neufahrwasser, and the crowd had flowed toward the pier. The ship had not yet cast off its mooring lines, and everyone would have to wait for several hours before they were loosed again, but in Danzig then time counted for nothing. Each aim was stubbornly pursued, even at the cost of maximum patience, endurance, and suffering.

As always, there were children, with their small faces twisted by emotion, staring and hating without comprehension, and without looking for any explanations. When sleep overwhelmed them, they slept where they were, without any release from trouble. I, immobilized by exhaustion and by my sense of solitude, tried to see no more than the seagulls did, as they flew overhead, seemingly part of another world.

For two days now, we had been waiting for some information, or some instructions, under the shattered glass structure of the station. A wind which made the inside as cold as the outdoors shook the metal frame, loosening and scattering the remaining glass fragments. We had to keep walking and waving our arms to avoid freezing on the spot. As it was very hard for me to walk, my comrades gave me a permanent place inside, while they took turns walking through the rubble of the port. Finally a piece of negative information reached us: there were no Gross Deutschland units in Danzig; perhaps they had moved on to Gotenhafen. Gotenhafen was several miles to the north, on the bay – only a short walk, if my foot would support me.

With the aid of Hals and my broomstick crutch, I managed to cross part of the town. On the way, Providence intervened to help us. Some civilians who had been watching us from their house came out to meet us, and took us back indoors. The house was warm, and it seemed as if the gates of Paradise had opened to receive us. There was already a crowd of people in the house – refugees from the East, including large numbers of silent children, who seemed to relish the wall bench on which they were sitting as if it were a marvellous toy.

There was water in the house, and our hosts offered us the opportunity to wash. Wollers knew that soldiers had no right to the privileges reserved for fleeing civilians. But his dressing was a mass of putrefaction, and his body was so exhausted he didn't know how to refuse. Even I was able to soak my swollen ankle in a basin of hot water. The owners of the house insisted that we rest there overnight and, in the evening, produced something for us to eat.

We spent the night in the warmth of the cellar. Unfortunately, we were so unused to being warm that we couldn't appreciate it as much as we should have. We shook uncontrollably for seconds at a time, as if some form of warning system were on continuous alert inside our heads. Our exhaustion, which we had been keeping more or less suppressed, broke out during this period of unaccustomed rest.

Lindberg trembled for minutes at a time. Hals felt so lost if he
fell asleep lying down that he spent the night propped against
the wall, whimpering. As for me, I was racked down the
length of my body with pains which seemed to rise and fall as
I breathed.

Were we no longer able to function like normal human
beings? This was certainly possible. However, one develop-
ment struck me as extremely favourable. The three hot
soakings I was able to give my foot put an end to the trouble
in record time. Perhaps, when our bodies have been deprived
of practically everything, they react favourably to the most
elementary care. Then, the most desperately wounded clung
to life after a glass of schnapps and a promise; today, a
simple cold can flatten a healthy man for several days. Then,
we were certainly not supermen, but men, in the most real
and complete sense in the world.

In the morning, we took leave of our benefactors, who told
us that their last reserves had been exhausted, and that they
were planning to leave Danzig and flee to the West while
there was still time.

With daybreak, which came late, the first fighter-bombers
appeared and attacked the port, and we said goodbye against
the roar of explosions and the barking of flak. We resumed
our march toward Gotenhafen, sharing the road with an
unbroken column of civilians, who were all moving west, as
Danzig could no longer be considered safe. Others were
moving north, following the coast to Hela, a port opposite
Gotenhafen, which was used almost as heavily as Danzig.

Gotenhafen, about a month before its destruction, was a
collection point for wounded men, who were then sent on to
villages and hamlets inland. Others passed through it, to
continue on the next lap of their miserable route, as always
on foot. Hela was the next stop, some thirty miles beyond
Gotenhafen.

We questioned the groups of soldiers we met along the
way. No one knew anything or had seen any trace of our
unit. Someone suggested the assembly centre, but when we
got there we hesitated to ask any questions of the harried
officials, who had been overtaken by the course of events. A
rumour was circulating through the throng of refugees: a
large ship had been sunk a few days earlier, almost certainly

after a torpedo attack. It had been crammed with refugees, relieved to be escaping to a region of greater security. It was easy to imagine the horror of the scene, in the black and icy night.

The news of this disaster had been officially withheld, but had nonetheless penetrated to the anxious mob, for whom the sea route was the last hope of escape. The ship in question was thought to be the *Wilhelm-Gustloff*.

We had still been unable to obtain any information about our unit. Finally, we were reincorporated in a defence battalion which, with civilian aid, was constructing a line of defence to the west of Zoppot.

We dug in, some twenty miles inland. I had no idea where the enemy was, but it seemed to me that the positions we were organizing faced the wrong way. The anti-tank and anti-aircraft guns pointed west and southwest — the only directions in which retreat was possible. I couldn't understand it — but that made no difference! It wasn't the first time, and others were undoubtedly thinking for us.

Aside from the problem of civilian refugees, overflowing from every farmhouse and outbuilding, life was much easier here. The Prussian farmers continued to function with order and discipline, despite the anxiety which visibly marked their faces. The future looked dark, and the miracle which yesterday might have saved them now seemed much less possible. Despite orders to avoid despair and panic, and despite an effort to continue life as usual in the rush of the exodus, these people were quietly and surreptitiously beginning to liquidate their stocks, rather than lose them to the enemy. Many cattle were slaughtered for food, which later proved to have been wisely done. A short time after that, cattle were collapsing and dying by the hundreds on the frozen soil.

Despite the hard work, and the endless watches and patrols, we regained some of our strength on a diet which was no longer tightly rationed. Meat had the greatest effect on our physical wretchedness, and we absorbed it, as the war absorbed everything, with maximum determination.

Grandsk had returned to his old job. With the help of civilian volunteers, he set up a huge kitchen in an open shed. Two trucks shuttled between Zoppot, Gotenhafen, and Danzig. Ammunition for the front was organized here, and transported in small loads. With the exception of a few air raids, life went on in a state of striking calm, which seemed incompatible with the gravity of the hour, toward the end of the war, in the beginning of 1945. Even the cold had lessened, and we no longer dared look at the sky, which brought us such indecent clemency. We spent long hours engaged in activities created by the necessities of the times, but which nonetheless seemed to us like a diversion.

Then one day toward the end of February an organization which we thought no longer existed invited us back to Gotenhafen. Our Gross Deutschland group had collected a few fragments which were to be embarked for the West. Everything seemed to be improving. We separated ourselves from the battalion which had utilized our service, and said goodbye to the comrades we had made. Grandsk left the kitchen he had organized so efficiently, with regret. This break, however, saved us from the horrible ordeal in which that battalion was practically destroyed. Heaven, which had so often overwhelmed us, spared us this time.

Russian tanks moved in from the west, and a storm of fire of unequalled violence broke over the positions we had so judiciously arranged. Our men took the first blow, but were soon swept aside. The Russians suffered frightful losses, but as we had learned, this made little difference to them.

From Gotenhafen, where we were waiting for orders, the roar of the war rang louder than ever. Russian infiltration had penetrated to within six miles of the city, and our retreating troops were engaged in fierce fighting. Through the rain of shells which cut them down, the fleeing civilians entrenched in the countryside moved back toward town. Large German battleships were firing from the sea at advanced Soviet positions. The ground trembled and shook, and any window panes still in place fell out.

We were trying to impose some sort of order on the swarm of terrified civilians who wished to embark for Hela. Retreating troops were also arriving in the city, which indicated that we could no longer count on our barrage. The town was gripped once again by frantic panic, and the civilians making their way to the port completed the paralysis of the order which had been maintained until then only with the greatest of difficulty. Although we all had evacuation papers, we were rounded up once again and sent to Zoppot to fill a gap in the line.

We left Gotenhafen, where despair had assumed a pitch of delirious intensity. With dry mouths and rage in our hearts, we climbed into the civilian cars which were to take us to our new Golgotha. Through the windows, which we kept shut against the cold, we watched the sky, where flights of fighter-bombers buzzed like enraged wasps.

At Brössel, we left our cars to plunge directly into the rubble. The town rang to the sounds of an exploding universe. The Russians were attacking everything that moved with rockets and bombs, and their planes came over so low we could almost see the grins on the pilots' faces. When they had gone, we moved back to our rickety cars, and started off again, through the flying dust. The road was strewn with rubble, and several times we had to dig our way through. We also had to skirt the enormous shell holes into which we otherwise would have disappeared entirely. Our journey ended when we were dumped, with our Panzerfaust, at the edge of a small village. We could hear the big guns some ten minutes to the south.

We ran toward a leafless hedge with a sidecar pulled up beside it. We thought we might receive some instructions, but we arrived too late: both occupants of the sidecar had been shot. The driver had collapsed over the handlebars, with his back reduced to a bloody pulp. The other man appeared to be asleep, but he too was dead. The bursts sounded closer each time. We had never imagined that the Russians were so close. Where were the rest of our men?

Then we caught sight of them. We climbed over a garden hedge, and came out onto a smooth piece of ground which sloped up to the horizon, some two hundred yards beyond and above us. Continuous trails of smoke marked the discharge of big guns and the impacts of their shells, and the grey sky was lit by flashes of white light.

We had to reach that high ground whatever the cost, and we all had our passports for the West in our pockets. I knew very well what kind of curse lay behind the closed faces of each of my companions.

As if the malevolence of the situation were drawing us on,

we completed our progress with a series of carplike leaps which were unknown to any system of physical training.

Three German half-tracks, which had been resuscitated from some unit, were pointing their D.C.A.s at some twenty motionless Soviet tanks, waiting on the brown-and-white ground. Soldiers crusted with mud crouched in shallow, hastily dug holes, pointing various anti-tank weapons at the monsters, which kept their distance. We had barely taken our places when a new salvo came over — first the bursts, and then a thick fog of smoke, rolling toward us, level with the ground. We could hear cries and moans from our positions. The half-tracks, which were more sheltered, were also firing, and all further speech was blotted out.

The Russian tanks, which still did not move, began to fire too. Some of them seemed to be paralysed, and the smoke leaking from their entrails mixed with smoke produced by our side, which a generous wind was blowing toward the enemy.

Then an inhuman order sent us forward: as the tanks were not rolling toward our Panzerfausts, we had to go out to meet them.

In a series of miraculous leaps we moved forward for several yards, through bursts of machine-gun fire which felled several of my companions.

Our fear reached grandiose proportions, and urine poured down our legs. Our fear was so great that we lost all thought of controlling ourselves. We drew still closer, tearing convulsively at our faces after each leap. The tanks were unaccompanied, and their myopia made their aim uncertain. One of them was burning, some sixty yards from a hole into which six of us had crowded. Then some of my comrades moved out. I stared after them with enormous eyes as they mocked their imminent deaths. Three tanks were moving toward us. If they rolled over the mound which protected us, the war would end for us in less than a minute.

I can still see those tanks, blotting out everything else. I can also see the metal plaque, and the nose of my first Panzerfaust, and my hand, stiff with fear, on the firing button. As they rolled toward us, the earth against which my body was pressed transmitted their vibrations, while my nerves, tightened to the breaking point, seemed to shrill with an ear-splitting whistle. Once again I understood that one could wear out one's life in a few seconds. I could see the reflected yellow lights on the front of the tank, and then everything disappeared in the flash of light which I had released, and which burned my face.

My brain seemed paralysed, and made of the same substance as my helmet. To the side, other flashes of light battered at my eyes, which jerked open convulsively wide, although there was nothing to see. Everything was simultaneously luminous and blurred. Then a second tank in the middle distance was outlined by a glow of flame. It had not been able to take the three projectiles we had lobbed toward it with a considerable degree of precision. Our fingers clutched feverishly at the launching tube, which jutted against the sky somewhat to the left of the burning tank. We could hear the noise of a third tank crossing a hillock just beyond our position. It had accelerated, and was no more than thirty yards from us, when I grabbed my last Panzerfaust. One of my comrades had already fired, and I was temporarily blinded. I stiffened my powers of vision and regained my sight to see a multitude of rollers caked with mud churning past in a dull roar of sound some five or six yards from us. An inhuman cry of terror rose from our helpless throats.

The tank withdrew into the noise of battle, and finally disappeared in a volcanic eruption which lifted it from the ground in a thick cloud of smoke. Our wildly staring eyes tried to fix on something solid, but could find nothing except smoke and flame. As there were no more tanks, our madness thrust us from our refuge, toward the fire whose brilliance tortured our eyes. The noise of the tanks was growing fainter. The Russians were backing away from the stubbornness which the devil seemed to have instilled in us. We collapsed onto the icy ground, whose touch seemed gentle to our exhausted bodies.

The first three attacking tanks had been destroyed. The others, from each of which we pulled a wounded man, had been stopped. The rest had no longer wished to expose themselves to our desperate resistance. They would undoubtedly reappear in greater numbers, with the support of planes or artillery, and our despairing frenzy would count for nothing.

We were still fighting, and, although the disproportion of our strength relative to the enemy's left us with no hope, our struggle was not in vain, because it allowed a host of civilians to escape.

During a sleepless night, other German troops joined us. We re-established our positions, and laid down a minefield, which a fresh delivery of supplies from Danzig made possible. The mines were a powerful support for our defence, but unfortunately they were effective only once, and the Russians would certainly give the ground a preliminary going-over with a heavy bombardment.

For three days, the Russians had been launching intensive attacks toward the bay, attempting to cut off Danzig from Gotenhafen. Pferham had been seriously wounded, and once again we had been forced to give up some ground. This time, we had the invaluable support of naval artillery. If the Russians had not been there with such vast quantities of men and matériel, they would probably have been obliged to withdraw.

The remainder of our forces was concentrated on a small piece of territory. The Russians were using planes against us, and it was above all their air power which overwhelmed us in the end. As we stared toward the horizon, we could see that the slightest projection had been eliminated. The territory, in which, even six months ago, life must have had a certain regularity and sweetness, was now experiencing an apocalypse. It was no longer possible to move during the day. The sky was constantly filled with Russian planes, which, despite the heavy opposition of our anti-aircraft defences, always returned in constantly increasing numbers. Our defences, moreover, were continuously weakening, as the evacuation of troops began.

We were among the first to return to Gotenhafen, where certain sections of the city were already the scene of fierce combat. Within a few days, the appearance of the town had entirely changed. There were ruins everywhere, and a strong smell of gas and burning filled the air. The wide street which led down to the docks no longer had any definition. The wreckage of the buildings which had once lined it was crumbled right across the roadbed, obstructing all passage.

Along with thousands of others, we were put to work

clearing away the rubble, so that trucks filled with civilians could get down to the harbour. Every five or ten minutes, planes came over, and we had to freeze where we were. The street was strafed and burned twenty or thirty times a day. Only our memories of Belgorod and Memel kept us from killing ourselves. We were no longer counting our dead and wounded: almost no one was entirely unhurt.

Heavily laden horses, which must have been spared by Supply, pulled a continuous train of sledges loaded with bodies wrapped in sacking or even paper. They had to be collected and buried with a speed which rivalled that of the Ilyushins' machine guns.

Exhausted people stood stunned and motionless on heaps of ruins, creating magnificent targets for Russian planes. As a finishing touch, the horizon to the west and southwest was reddish-black. House-to-house fighting had already begun in the outlying sections of the town, while thousands of civilians still waited down by the docks. From time to time, Russian shells reached as far as the embarkation area, and exploded there.

We were trying to snatch a short rest in a cellar, where a doctor was delivering a child. The cellar was vaulted and lit by a few hastily rigged lanterns. If the birth of a child is usually a joyful event, this particular birth only seemed to add to the general tragedy. The mother's screams no longer had any meaning in a world made of screams, and the wailing child seemed to regret the beginning of its life. Once again, there was streaming blood, like the blood in the streets, and on the earth, where we had known so much suffering, and where my appreciation of existence was continually spiralling down toward the abyss whose depths I occasionally glimpsed, defining life as a mixture of blood and suffering and groans of pain.

A short while later, after a last look at the newborn child, whose tiny cries sounded like a tinkle of delicate glass through the roar of war, we returned to the flaming street. For the child's sake, we hoped he would die before he turned twenty. Twenty is the age of ingratitude. It is too hard to be leaving life at the moment when one so much longs for it to flower.

We helped some old people, whom younger ones had left

to the mercy of the Soviets. In the darkness lit up by flames, we once again performed our duty. We supported and carried the old people down to the port, where a boat was waiting for them. Planes passed over, and in spite of the blazing fires which lined the street, they once again scattered their load of death.

They killed some fifteen of our number. We had tried to pull the victims down with us on our several rapid plunges to the ground, but the old people were unable to follow us. It didn't matter though – we saved a good many of them anyhow, finally hoisting them onto a trawler, after getting them through the thickly packed crowd. The boat had to slip its lines while loading, to escape an aerial attack.

As we moved away from the shore, Wollers ran back to the stern to see if the gangplank had really been drawn in. Then he came back to us, tramping through the refugees who crowded the deck. He looked at us as if he were about to speak. Then we all turned to stare at the flames.

'Do you still have your embarkation cards?' he asked suddenly.

We all pulled out our tattered, filthy cards.

'I would have lost my head first,' muttered Grandsk.

The water slid quietly by, less than a yard below us. The boat would probably sink if the weight of its human cargo shifted. No one moved so much as a finger. Once again, we had escaped from the Russians and their fury.

Chapter Nineteen

THE WEST

HELA · DENMARK · KIEL · THE ENGLISH PRISONER

Before daybreak, we arrived at Hela, without incident. We had passed several ghostly ships, navigating without lights, going back to Hela, or to Gotenhafen, and Danzig, where large numbers of civilians were still waiting for deliverance. Hela, which I had thought of as a large town, proved to be only a village, with a harbour of very secondary importance. Many ships were anchored off shore, and small boats were delivering a steady stream of passengers fleeing to the West.

We had scarcely set foot to the ground when the police, who were still functioning, made us step to one side. We stared at them with desperate unease. Was our good luck, which had brought us this far, going to melt like summer snow and send us back to Danzig, or Gotenhafen? The police turned their backs on us to direct the white-faced civilians. In any event, all of our papers were in order. But wasn't that the ship which was to take us further? And mightn't a counter-order arrive any moment? The minutes went slowly by, without giving us any glimpses into our future.

As it grew light, the cumulative exhaustion of many months seemed to crush our shoulders. We were now able to see the numerous grey outlines of ships, including many warships, riding at anchor on both sides of the peninsula. As we looked, the air-raid alarm sounded. Our eyes turned to the sky, as rumours began to circulate through the crowd.

'No panic!' shouted the police. 'Our anti-aircraft defences will hold them off!'

By now, we knew what that meant. All the shelters were filled with wounded, and each of us had to find what protection he could. If the bombs fell near the harbour, there would be an impressive carnage.

543

We moved toward an old hulk pulled up on the shore, whose tarred timbers might be able to ward off a few blows. We hadn't quite reached it when the massive crackle of an anti-aircraft barrage burst all around us, fired by our coastal defences or by one of the warships we had glimpsed earlier. This was my first experience of such a barrage. The falling fragments alone were capable of no small damage.

To the east, the sky was spattered with numberless black spots. The noise of firing was so loud that we couldn't hear the planes approaching. Finally we saw three of them, flying quite low, parallel to the shore, pursued by the black granules of exploding flak. We heard an explosion to the south, over the water; one of the planes must have been hit. The police had not been exaggerating – not one plane flew over Hela. We felt a wave of confidence and security; finally, the Russians had been stopped.

The police came and checked our cards.

'Be back here for embarkation on the — of March,' a noncom told us. 'While you're waiting, you can make yourselves useful north of town.'

We took ourselves off without any questions.

'What is the date today?' Hals asked.

'Wait a minute,' Wollers said. 'There's a calendar in my diary.' He looked through his pocket, but couldn't find it.

'In any case, we're not ahead of ourselves.'

'But we ought to know, all the same,' Hals persisted. 'I would like to know exactly how much longer we have to wait.'

We finally learned that it was Sunday, the 28th or 29th of March, and that we would have to wait for two days, as I remember: the last two days of the Ost Front, which had consumed so much of our lives.

We spent those two days in the throng of anxious refugees camping out on the narrow Hela peninsula.

There were two more attempted Russian air raids. The last victim I was to see was a dirty white horse.

A Russian plane had been hit, and was disintegrating above us. We all watched as the forward part of the plane, whose racing engine gave off a long howl, plunged toward the ground. The noise terrified the animal, which slipped its collar and galloped, whinnying, toward the spot where the roaring mass of metal would land. It must have taken about three steps before it was hit. Its flesh was scattered for over fifteen yards in all directions.

On the evening of April 1, during a spell of terrible weather, we boarded a large white ship, which must, at one time, have taken rich people on cruises. Despite the anxiety we all felt, despite the crowd, and the stretchers, and the wounded, with their rattling breath, my eyes gaped at all the magnificent and barely-faded details inside that elegant ship. I was reminded of the shop windows my father had always taken me to admire at Christmastime. But I didn't have the courage to rejoice; I knew that such feelings always end badly.

In the darkness, our boat pressed forward through the large hollow waves. A short while before, the sound and light which had filled the sky over the other shore of the Bay of Danzig had still reached us. Our comrades were still fighting and dying there. We scarcely dared think of the good fortune that had saved us – and that troubled us. For two days, our boat slid across the sea, toward the unbelievable West, which we had dreamed of for so long, where we could not imagine the war. We learned that our ship was the *Pretoria*, and although we were allowed only a small space on the bridge, lashed by wind and rain, the sweetness of the moment made us forget food and drink.

Of course, a torpedo could send us to the bottom at any minute, but we didn't think of that. We also had a battleship escort; everything was going very well.

We arrived in Denmark, where we saw things we had almost forgotten, like pastry shops, which we devoured with enormous eyes, forgetting our filthy faces ravaged by misery. We scarcely noticed the looks of mistrust fixed on us by the shopkeepers, who couldn't understand us. We had no money, and the wares on display were not free. For a moment, we even thought of our machine guns.

Hals could not resist temptation. He held out his big hands, which looked like dead wood, and begged for charity. The shopkeeper tried to pretend that he hadn't noticed, but Hals persisted. Finally, the baker put a stale cake into those filthy hands. Hals divided it into four pieces and we tasted a substance which had become unknown to us. We thanked the man, and tried to smile, but the rotting teeth in our grey faces must have produced an effect of grotesque grimace, and made the baker think we were mocking him. He turned on his heel, and disappeared into the back of his shop. He couldn't know how long it had been since we'd had the chance to laugh, and that we would need a little while to learn how again.

A less sumptuous boat took us on to Kiel, where we found a more familiar atmosphere, with no more bakeries and no more occasion to smile. In a setting of ruins, we were reincorporated, with alarmingly precipitate haste, into a scratch battalion. Hals asked if he might be given a leave to visit his home in Dortmund. An enlisted man of about fifty put a hand on his shoulder and told him that with a little courage and a little luck, if he managed to infiltrate the American and British lines, he might perhaps get there.

My friend's face reflected astonishment, stupefaction, and sadness.

'The American and British lines!'

In the West, which we had dreamed of and longed for so often, which we had finally reached, we were assaulted by the most overwhelming and terrible news. We were astounded. The West, the paradise we had been counting on in our icy holes at Memel, on the Dnieper, and on the Don; that chimerical paradise which should have taken us in and soothed our sufferings, the West, which had been our sole reason for surviving, was only a small country more or less thickly covered with buildings; a country where the silence was broken by the roar of planes, where terrified people crawled and ran. The West was also three dirty grey trucks carrying at high speed a reduced battalion of soldiers in grey toward another encounter with death; it was the place where my last illusions would crumble in conditions of inhuman grief.

The West was the other half of the vice tightening on our misery. Several armies were challenging our exhausted arms – several, among them the French Army. I cannot describe the emotions which this news produced in me. France, which in my thoughts had never abandoned me, 'la douce France,' had abused my naïveté. In the trenches of the steppe, I had loved France as much as any young man does as he talks revolution in the back room of a Paris café.

Most of my efforts had been for France, which I had made my comrades-in-arms appreciate and love. What could have happened, which had not been explained to us?

France had turned against me, when I was expecting her help. Perhaps I would have to fire at my French brothers — which I could no more do than I could fire at Hals or Lindberg.

What had happened? What had they kept from us? I no longer knew, or understood. My brain refused to take in any more, and the hope which the West had revived in all of us died in me.

We would have to fight again. Against whom and what? We knew that we no longer had any courage, and that nothing could lead us to hope any more. Despite Anglo-American cries of victory, there was no longer any opposition to the imposing matériel they had fabricated for nothing. No victory is possible over men who have died toward everything.

We had reached the banks of the Elbe, and were lying stretched out on the grass beside a small road which led to Lauenburg. British troops were in the sector, and we were supposed to try to react.

An older man was devouring the substance which fate still saw fit to deposit in our mess tins. Hals was a short way off, his eyes vacant, as he pondered imponderables. The older fellow did not seem too depressed. He muttered some barely audible words to me: 'With a little luck, the war should be over for us in a few days.'

What did he mean? I knew that when a war ended for soldiers on the side that lost it usually meant a small brownish hole in the head or the chest.

'I don't mean that,' the other said. 'We'll be prisoners — you'll see. That's not so grand either, but it's better than bombing and starvation. You'll see. These fellows aren't muzhiks. They're really not so bad.'

The night passed. It was mild, almost warm. We sat on the damp grass of the bank beside the road. Massive flights of planes growled invisibly through the starry sky. But nothing could interfere with our habit of half sleep, which we had perfected during three years of enforced watchfulness.

Toward three o'clock in the morning, we heard the roar of artillery somewhere to the north, and the sky was lit by flashes of light. The whole episode lasted for about forty-five minutes, during which our half sleep continued without interruption.

Daybreak came early, and a light spring sun rose over the horizon. A small battered car appeared on the road, bumping over the broken surface. The car was brown, and was occupied by three fellows whose uniforms were quite different from ours.

We watched as three brick-red faces beneath unusually large helmets drew closer to us. The owners of the faces appeared to be enjoying their morning outing.

It was my first encounter with Englishmen – the first three. To have fired at these cheerful individuals would have been a criminal act; however, some bastard in our group did fire – twice – at their heads. The car – a jeep – skidded into a panicky half turn which was slow enough to give us ample time to wipe them out.

The old man beside me roared with anger at the young fellow who had just done his duty, explaining that this ill-considered gesture risked bringing in motorized troops to attack us, against which we would have no defence. A startled hauptmann almost intervened, but saw that there was no point, and went back to stand beside his gunner.

An hour later, we heard the sound of several motors to the north of us: the old man's prediction was coming true. A reconnaissance plane flew over, directing the fire with considerable precision to the road beneath our bank. Clinging to the ground like treads, we crawled up the hollow of a small valley, thus escaping some fifty mortar shells, which would have inflicted heavy losses.

The English must have decided that further resistance would be limited to a few isolated shots, and sent four half-tracks after us. We watched with a certain anguish as they climbed over the bank. Two of our men stood up, with their hands raised. The Eastern Front had never seen anything like that. We wondered what would happen next. Would English machine guns cut them down? Would our leader shoot them himself, for giving up like that? But nothing happened. The old man, who was still beside me, took me by the arm, and whispered: 'Come on. Let's go.'

We stood up together. Others quickly followed us. Hals came over and stood by me without even thinking of raising his hands. We walked toward the victors with pounding hearts and dry mouths. This was the only time I was ever afraid of the Western Allies, and I had provoked the fear myself.

We were roughly jostled together, and shoved into place by English soldiers with vindictive faces. However, we had seen worse in our own army, particularly in training under Captain Fink. The roughness with which the English handled us seemed comparatively insignificant, and even marked by a certain kindness.

In this way, I laid down the arms and insignia of my second country, and the war ended for me and for my comrades.

To humiliate us, they made us stand in the sturdy trucks which brought the relief of their victory to our faltering ranks. The closed, flushed faces of the English continued to reflect their noncomprehension of the smiling remarks which emerged from our famished faces. Hals even received a slap in the face from an English noncom, without much of an idea of what had happened to him. He had simply been comparing our easy ride as prisoners to our forced marches in the East.

Then we met the other allies, tall men with plump, rosy cheeks, who behaved like hooligans, but hooligans who had been nicely brought up. Their bearing was casual, and seemed to be designed to give them the opportunity to roll their hips and shoulders. Their uniforms were made of soft cloth, like golfing clothes, and they moved their jaws continuously, like ruminating animals. They seemed neither happy nor unhappy, but indifferent to their victory, like men who are performing their duties in a state of partial consent, without any real enthusiasm for them.

From our filthy, mangy ranks, we watched them with curiosity. It seemed that we, in the ranks of the defeated, were happier than these children, for whom Paradise itself had no value. They seemed rich in everything but joy – a reassuring spectacle which reconciled us with humanity.

The Americans also humiliated us as much as they could – which seemed perfectly normal. They put us in a camp with only a few large tents, which could shelter barely a tenth of us. Even in prison, the Wehrmacht continued to organize itself. As at Kharkov, or on the Dnieper, at Memel, or at Pillau, or in the black depths of winter on the steppe, space in the tents was reserved for the sick and feeble.

In the centre of the camp, the Americans ripped open several large cases filled with canned food. They spread the cans onto the ground with a few kicks, and walked away, leaving the division and distribution up to us. Everyone received a share. The food was so delicious that we forgot about the driving rain, which had turned the ground into a sponge.

The packets of powdered orangeade and lemonade seemed the height of luxury, and collecting rainwater in the folds of our jackets to mix with them a gay, even joyous distraction. From their shelters, the Americans watched us and talked about us. They probably despised us for flinging ourselves so readily into such elementary concerns, and thought us cowards for accepting the circumstances of captivity – the distribution of food in the rain, for instance. Wasn't our condition as prisoners enough in itself to make us walk in silence, with that unbearable air which men have when their pride has been damaged? We were not in the least like the German troops in the documentaries our charming captors had probably been shown before leaving their homeland. We provided them with no reasons for anger; we were not the arrogant, irascible Boches, but simply underfed men standing in the rain, ready to eat unseasoned canned food; living dead, with anxiety stamped on our faces, leaning against any support, half asleep on our feet; sick and wounded, who didn't ask for treatment, but seemed content simply to sleep for long hours, undisturbed. It was clearly depressing for these crusading missionaries to find so much humility among the vanquished.

In due course, we were sent on to Mannheim, where we passed through a large processing centre.

Hals, Grandsk, Lindberg, and I had remained inseparable through all this, as in our worst moments. We understood only that the war had really ended for us, and had given no thought to the consequences of that fact. Everything was still too new, too much in the present. We knew that the worst was over, and that German ex-soldiers were organizing themselves to facilitate the task of the Allies, who had to count their prisoners and assign them to various jobs. Our men helping with this organization, often in rags, moved through the elegant ranks of the victors, attacking with them the same pressing necessities. Cigarettes were given to the prisoners, who had nothing to offer in return. Some even received chewing gum, which they chewed, laughing, and then swallowed by mistake. Orders were shouted in German, and ranks of men formed and broke up. Were they going to send us back to the line? That wouldn't be possible. A bastard noncom, carried away by the spirit of things, absent-mindedly shouted at a group of prisoners: 'Grab your weapons!'

He was answered by a howl of laughter.

This made the Americans angry, and they came outside to shout at us. This struck us as even funnier, but it was clear that we had to correct our attitude. The erring noncom, who suddenly realized his mistake, snapped to attention, expecting a reprimand. Three American officers protested in their language, hounding the delinquent, who was himself overcome with embarrassment.

A short while later, the prisoners were moving in long lines past a health inspection. Some were sent to a hospital, others to an endless series of offices from which a recruiting service would send them out to take part in the first efforts at cleaning up a country in ruins. Control and verification commissions then studied each case. These commissions often included representatives of several Allied armies: Canadians, English, French, and Belgian. My scraps of paper fell to a French officer, who looked up at me twice. Then he looked up again, and spoke, at first, in German.

'Is this the date and place of your birth?'

'Ja.'

'Well?'

'Yes,' I answered, in French this time. 'My father is French.' My French was now almost as bad as my German had been at Chemnitz.

The other looked at me with mistrust. After a moment he spoke again in French. 'Are you French, then?'

I didn't know what to say. For three years the Germans had persuaded me that I was German.

'I think so, Herr Major.'

'What do you mean – you think so?'

I felt embarrassed, and made no reply.

'What the hell are you doing with this bunch?'

I still didn't know what to say. 'I don't know, Herr Major.'

'Don't call me "Herr Major." I'm not "Herr Major." Call me "Mon Capitaine," and come with me.'

He stood up, and I had to follow him. From the ranks of dirty grey-green, I sensed Hals's eyes fixed on me. I waved to him, and called softly. 'Bleib hier, Hals. Ich komme wieder.'

'Who's that you're talking to?' the captain asked me, irritated.

'Das ist mein kamerad, Herr Kapitän.'

'Stop talking German, since you remember French. Come along this way.'

I followed him through a series of corridors, suddenly afraid that I wouldn't be able to find Hals again. Finally, we arrived at an office where four French soldiers were talking and laughing with a young woman, who spoke to them in English, I think.

The captain said he had brought along a doubtful case. They put me through an extended interrogation, to which my answers must have sounded far from convincing. My head was spinning, and everything I said seemed to ring false.

One of them – also an officer – called me a bastard and a traitor. As I remained apathetic and absent, they gave up on me, sending me off to a small room on the floor below. For a day and a night they left me there, thinking of my companions in wretchedness, and especially of Hals, who must have been wondering about me. I felt a sinister premonition that I wouldn't see him again, and a feverish restlessness kept me from sleeping.

The next morning, a lieutenant, who seemed in a very friendly mood, came to release me. I was taken back to the office of the day before and asked to sit down. This invitation was so unexpected that the words fell on my ears as if for the first time in my life.

Then the young lieutenant looked through my papers and spoke to me.

'Your story took us somewhat by surprise yesterday. Now we know that the Germans often forced young men with German fathers into their army. If that had been your case, we would have been obliged to keep you a prisoner for a while. However, with you it was the mother, and we cannot detain you. For your sake, I am glad,' he added gently.

'We have now liberated you, and this has been recorded on the papers I am handing back to you. You may return to your home, and resume your old life.'

'To my home!' He might just as well have been talking about the planet Mars.

'Yes, home.'

He paused for a moment, giving me an opportunity to speak, which I didn't take. I couldn't quite grasp what had happened, or find the proper words.

'Nevertheless, I would advise you to clear yourself by signing up for a term with the French Army, and in that way return to normal life in good order.'

My expression remained impenetrable. My thoughts above all were with Hals, and I only took in about half of what the amiable officer was saying. 'Do you agree?'

'Oui, mon Lieutenant,' I said, only partly aware of my own words.

'I congratulate you on your decision. Sign here.'

I signed my name, more interested by the French words than by their significance.

'You will be called up,' he said, closing my folder. 'Go home quickly and try to forget this adventure.'

I still didn't know what to say. Even the lieutenant seemed to be losing his patience. He stood up anyway, and walked me to the door.

'Do your parents know where you are?'

'I don't think so, Mon Lieutenant.'

'Didn't you write to them?'

'I did, Mon Lieutenant.'

'Well, then – you must have had answers from them, too. Don't the Boches have a post office?'

'Yes, Mon Lieutenant. They wrote to me too, but we haven't had any mail for almost a year now.'

He looked at me in surprise.

'The bastards,' he said. 'They wouldn't even send you your mail. Go along now. Get yourself home, and try to forget all this as fast as you can.'

EPILOGUE

RETURN

'Try to forget . . .'

In the train, rolling through the sunny French countryside, my head knocked against the wooden back of the seat. Other people, who seemed to belong to a different world, were laughing. I couldn't laugh and couldn't forget.

I had looked everywhere for Hals, but hadn't been able to find him. He filled my thoughts, and only my acquired ability to hide my feelings kept me from weeping. He was attached to me by all the terrible memories of the war, which still rang in my ears. He was my only friend in this hostile world, the man who had so often carried my load when my strength was failing. I would never be able to forget him, or the experiences we had shared, or our fellow soldiers, whose lives would always be linked to mine.

The train rolled on, carrying me minute by minute farther away from all that. If it had gone on like that for days, and carried me to the other side of the earth, it would still have made no difference. My memories would have remained at my side.

Then there was a station. My worn boots, which had tramped across Russia, scraped against the cement platform, and my disillusioned eyes took in the details of a place I knew well. Nothing had changed. The place seemed to be sleeping, although the unexpectedness of my arrival might very well have awakened it. Everything looked as it had; only I had changed, and I knew very well that I would not be able to fit myself in.

I stood for a while, staring at all the details, which seemed to me so small, walking slowly and hesitantly. Then I noticed that two station employees were glaring at me, clearly wishing me gone so they could go about their own business. I was the last person left on the platform. Everyone else had hurried away.

'Let's get going,' one of them said.

I went over to him with my papers.

'You'll have to show those to the stationmaster. This way.'

The stationmaster looked rapidly through my sheaf of documents, and clearly unable to make them out, rubber-stamped the lot.

'Mannheim,' he said. 'That's in Bochie, isn't it?'

'No sir,' I said. 'It's in Germany.'

He caught my atrocious accent, and looked at me doubtfully.

'For me, they're the same thing.'

I was still five miles from my house and from the end of my journey, and the place where it had all begun. It was a beautiful day, and I should have been impelled by joy to run the whole way, toward the incredible fact that drew closer with each step. However, my throat was knotted with anguish, and I could scarcely breathe. I felt my reason faltering, assailed by the incomprehensible emotion of seeing, touching and tasting the reality which surrounded me: the station I had just inspected with a fresh eye and my village, about to become visible in that damp, green hollow, and the imminent prospect of meeting my parents, which was so overwhelming I couldn't begin to think about it.

This reality suddenly seemed so huge that I felt afraid: the front of the house, edged by a vine, and cut by a door, which I had left three years earlier, and in the shadowy doorway an old man and an old woman. With my mind's eye, I composed features on those shadowy faces, corresponding to the features of my mother and father. Then, like forbidden pleasures suddenly exposed, the furtive image grew dim. I saw that my little brother was there too, and was amazed by how much he had grown.

A cold sweat suddenly began to pour down my emaciated body. The despair which had settled over me in the East was suddenly violated by a reality I had almost forgotten, which was about to impose itself on me once more, as if nothing had happened. The transition was too great, too brutal. I needed some sort of sieve, or filter. Hals and all the others, the war, and everything for which I had been obliged to live; all the names of all the men beside whom, my eyes huge with terror, I had watched death approach; and death itself, which could have overcome us at any moment; the names and faces of all the men without whom I would never have made these observations – all of these things were incompatible with what happened afterward. I could neither forget nor deny them, and my position became untenable.

My head was spinning like a boat with a broken rudder, as I walked slowly toward the encounter which I had so much longed for, and which I suddenly feared.

A plane flew over very low across the sunny countryside. Unable to stop myself, I plunged into the ditch on the other side of the road. The plane throbbed overhead for a moment, and then vanished, as suddenly as it had come. I pulled myself up by the trunk of an apple tree, without understanding what had just happened. I felt stunned. My blurred eyes watched the grass, which had been crushed by my weight, slowly straightening up again. It looked like badly combed hair. It was still yellow from the winter frosts and, like myself, was struggling to revive. This grass was not so tall, but otherwise reminded me of the grass on the steppe. It seemed familiar, and I let myself fall down again. The brilliance of the day rose over the points of the blades, forcing me to shut my eyes. The touch of the ground, silent witness of my emotion, reassured me. I managed to calm down, and fell asleep.

Only death is final. The hopes that Memel had been unable to destroy could not be destroyed by peace, either. When I woke, I set out again, to complete my journey. My sleep must have lasted for several hours; the sun was setting behind the hill, and I arrived at twilight – which was preferable to the glare of full day. I felt anxious enough about meeting my own family; I didn't want to meet anyone I used to know, who might not have forgotten me. So I arrived at the end of the day I had longed for so much, and started down the street as if I had just left it the day before. I tried to walk slowly, but each step seemed to resound like a parade step at Chemnitz. I passed two young men, who paid no attention to me. As I turned the corner, to the left, I saw my house. My heart was pounding so hard that my chest ached.

Someone appeared at the corner: a small old woman, whose shoulders were covered by a worn cloak. Even the cloak was familiar to me. My mother was carrying a small milk can. She was walking toward a neighbouring farm, which I knew well. She was also walking toward me. I thought I was going to fall. She was coming down the middle of the road, about two yards from the grassy verge along which I had been forcing my steps with the last of my strength.

Although my eyes were blurred by almost inconceivable emotion, I recognized her face.

My heart contracted so hard I thought I would faint.

My mother walked past me. I leaned against a wall to keep my balance. A bitter taste filled my mouth, as if it had filled with blood. I knew that within a few minutes she would come back the same way. I felt like running, but at the same time, couldn't move, and stood paralysed, letting the minutes trickle by.

After a few moments, as I had foreseen, she reappeared, going the other way, greyer and more shadowy in the deepening darkness.

She came closer and closer. I was afraid to move, afraid of frightening her. And then it was unbearable. I summoned up my courage and spoke.

'Maman.'

She stopped. I took several steps toward her, and then I saw that she was about to faint. The milk can fell to the ground, and I caught her in my trembling arms. She gave a long-drawn-out groan, and I was afraid someone would come.

Carrying my fainting mother, I hurried toward the doorway, in which a young man had just appeared. This young man was my brother. Suddenly alarmed, he called out. 'Papa! Someone's bringing Maman home! She's sick!'

Hours went by. I remained motionless and mute, surrounded by my family, who gazed at me as if they had forgotten that the earth was round. Over the fireplace I noticed a photograph of myself as a young man. Beside it stood a small vase which held a few faded flowers.

Time passed, leaving behind it a monumental silence. The tale was drawing to an end. It would take all of us – those who had waited, and I, who had hoped — a long measure of time to accept the evidence of our senses.

I also understood that my return could create complications for everyone, and that they too had needed courage to give up the habit of hope. The neighbourhood must not learn too quickly of my return, and for the time being our happiness would have to be kept secret. For the next few days, while I collapsed into an anaesthetising exhaustion, I could use the room of a sister, who had married during my absence.

In due course, I would enter the victorious French Army, which would make room in its ranks for a particle from the ranks of the vanquished. It was to prove an unexpected transfer for my unease, the filter I had been hoping for. Of course, I would be a damned Boche to whom a great kindness was being done. I would even be able to enjoy experiences which the others found tiresome. The discipline I was used to made it easy for me to be first, and I had to watch myself, so I didn't annoy the others. I would meet people who hated me, and others with generous hearts, who accepted the totality of my experience and offered me a glass of beer to help me forget.

My parents imposed an absolute silence; I would never be able to tell them the things which would have relieved me.

I listened attentively to the tales of the heroes on the other side — heroes to whose ranks I would never be admitted.

People who hated me would pursue me with vindictiveness, seeing in my past only cupidity and culpable error. Others might someday understand that men can love the same virtues on both sides of a conflict, and that pain is international.

The French Army, which I had entered for a three-year tour, finally kept me for only ten months. Despite my sense of well-being, I fell seriously ill and in the end was sent home.

However, before that, I took part in a huge parade in Paris, in '46. There was also a long silence of remembrance for the dead, to which I added these names:

Ernst Neubach, Lensen, Wiener, Wesreidau, Prinz, Solma, Hoth, Olensheim, Sperlovski, Smellens, Dunde, Kellerman, Freivitch, Ballers, Frösch, Woortenbeck, Siemenleis...

THE END

I refuse to add Paula to that list, and I shall never forget the names of Hals, or Lindberg, or Pferham, or Wollers. Their memory lives within me.

There is another man, whom I must forget. He was called Guy Sajer.